Monograph 13

COINS FROM THE EXCAVATIONS AT SARDIS

THEIR ARCHAEOLOGICAL AND ECONOMIC CONTEXTS

COINS FROM THE 1973 TO 2013 EXCAVATIONS

Archaeological Exploration of Sardis

Sponsored by
The Harvard Art Museums
Cornell University

Editors
Andrew Ramage
Nicholas D. Cahill

Monograph 13

COINS FROM THE EXCAVATIONS AT SARDIS

THEIR ARCHAEOLOGICAL AND ECONOMIC CONTEXTS

COINS FROM THE 1973 TO 2013 EXCAVATIONS

By Jane DeRose Evans

Archaeological Exploration of Sardis

Distributed by Harvard University Press
Cambridge, Massachusetts
London, England
2018

Volumes in This Series

Reports

1. *A Survey of Sardis and the Major Monuments outside the City Walls*, by George M. A. Hanfmann and Jane C. Waldbaum (1975)
2. *Sculpture from Sardis: The Finds through 1975*, by George M. A. Hanfmann and Nancy H. Ramage (1978)
3. *The Bath-Gymnasium Complex at Sardis*, by Fikret K. Yegül (1986)
4. *Love for Lydia: A Sardis Anniversary Volume Presented to Crawford H. Greenewalt, Jr.*, edited by Nicholas D. Cahill (2008)
5. *Lydian Architecture: Ashlar Masonry Structures at Sardis*, by Christopher Ratté (2011)
6. *Churches EA and E at Sardis*, by Hans Buchwald (2015)

Monographs

1. *Byzantine Coins*, by George E. Bates (1971)
2. *Ancient Literary Sources on Sardis*, by John G. Pedley (1972)
3. *Neue epichorische Schriftzeugnisse aus Sardis*, by Roberto Gusmani (1975)
4. *Byzantine and Turkish Sardis*, by Clive Foss (1976)
5. *Lydian Houses and Architectural Terracottas*, by Andrew Ramage (1978)
6. *Ancient and Byzantine Glass from Sardis*, by Axel von Saldern (1980), published jointly as a Corning Museum of Glass Monograph
7. *Greek, Roman, and Islamic Coins from Sardis*, by T. V. Buttrey, Ann Johnston, Kenneth M. MacKenzie, and Michael L. Bates (1981)
8. *Metalwork from Sardis: The Finds through 1974*, by Jane C. Waldbaum (1983)
9. *The Byzantine Shops at Sardis*, by J. Stephens Crawford (1990)
10. *The Corinthian, Attic, and Lakonian Pottery from Sardis*, by Judith Snyder Schaeffer, Nancy H. Ramage, and Crawford H. Greenewalt, Jr. (1997)
11. *King Croesus' Gold: Excavations at Sardis and the History of Gold Refining*, by Andrew Ramage and Paul Craddock (2000), in association with the British Museum Press
12. *The Hellenistic Pottery from Sardis: The Finds through 1994*, by Susan I. Rotroff and Andrew Oliver, Jr. (2003)
13. *Coins from the Excavations at Sardis: Their Archaeological and Economic Contexts*, by Jane DeRose Evans (2018)

Printed in the United States of America by Puritan Capital, Hollis, NH

Library of Congress Cataloging-in-Publication Data

Names: Evans, Jane DeRose, 1956- author.
Title: Coins from the excavations at Sardis : their archaeological and economic contexts : coins from the 1973 to 2013 excavations / By Jane DeRose Evans.
Description: Cambridge, Massachusetts : Harvard University Press, 2018. | Series: Archaeological Exploration of Sardis monographs ; no. 13. | Includes bibliographical references and index.
Identifiers: LCCN 2018005041 | ISBN 9780674987258 (hardcover : alk. paper)
Subjects: LCSH: Coins, Ancient—Turkey—Sardis (Extinct city) | Excavations (Archaeology)—Turkey—Sardis (Extinct city) | Sardis (Extinct city)—Economic conditions. | Coins, Greek—Turkey—Sardis (Extinct city) | Coins, Roman—Turkey—Sardis (Extinct city) | Coins, Byzantine—Turkey—Sardis (Extinct city) | Turkey—Antiquities.
Classification: LCC CJ619.S27 E93 2018 | DDC 737.4939/22—dc23
LC record available at https://lccn.loc.gov/2018005041

Contents

List of Tables and Figures

Tables

Figures (Plates 7–19)

Editors' Preface

Sardis, capital of the Lydian empire, is famous as the birthplace of coinage, its most important contribution to the world economy. In this monograph, Jane DeRose Evans presents the 8,000 or so coins dating from the Lydian through the late Roman eras found since 1973 at Sardis. Professor Evans builds on two earlier monographs on coins from the Harvard-Cornell Excavations: the very first Sardis Monograph, M1: *Byzantine Coins* by George E. Bates, which includes Byzantine coins found in 1958–1968, and M7: *Greek, Roman and Islamic Coins from Sardis* by Theodore Buttrey, Ann Johnston, Kenneth MacKenzie, and Michael Bates, which covers coins from the excavations through 1972, excluding those already published by George E. Bates.

With a few notable exceptions, the vast majority of coins from the Sardis excavations are not numismatic treasures, but ordinary small change lost by the city's inhabitants over the course of more than a millennium. Their real value lies in their archaeological contexts, and in the careful work that Jane Evans has done in identifying even the most minute, worn examples which might be passed over by other numismatists as illegible or simply unworthy of study. The coins come from a wide variety of contexts: hoards, burials, ritual contexts, destruction levels, and simple casual losses found in stratigraphically significant fills. The coins not only inform and sometimes date these contexts, but as she demonstrates, the contexts just as often inform and date the coins. Professor Evans thus comes to this study wearing two hats: as an experienced field archaeologist and excavation director with long experience dealing with the complexities of archaeological stratigraphy, and as a numismatist with deep familiarity with the coinage of Asia Minor, problems in ancient economics and trade, and related questions. Her two chapters, "Excavation Coins as Evidence of the Economy and Trade" and "Archaeological Contexts," reflect this twin focus of her study, while the catalog demonstrates the remarkable range and quantity of her material. She has pored over the publications, reports, fieldbooks, and other records from the excavation, worked closely with the excavators and with specialists on pottery, stratigraphy, and other aspects of the project, and so comes to consider not only the identifications and catalog of the coins, but also a host of more general questions about the circulation of coins in antiquity, and various non-economic behaviors such as ritual deposits, dedications, and funerary gifts.

It should be noted that the study of many of these contexts is ongoing. The author's definitive identifications of the coins are fundamental in further studies of the houses, public buildings, sanctuaries, streets, tombs, and other contexts, and her study in Chapter 2 is based on our best current, but still incomplete understanding of the complex stratigraphy, pottery, and history of the site. Further study will undoubtedly change that understanding; but this is the case with all our endeavors.

Special thanks are due to the many staff members who worked on these coins over the years. Clive Foss served as numismatist from 1973–1975. Among the student numismatists who offered preliminary identifications are Patricia Erhart (1979), Barbara Burrell (1980–1983), Robert A. McCall (1983), Katherine E. Welch (1984, 1986–1987), Barbara A. Baxter (1985), Mary Jane Rein (1988–1989), Richard T. Neer (1990–1991), Anne McClanan (1992), Jennifer

Trimble (1993), Catherine S. Alexander (1994, 2003), Christopher H. Roosevelt (1995–1998), Tumay Asena (1999), Corinne Crawford (2000–2001), Isabelle Pafford (2002), Patrick Crowley (2004–2006), and Andreya Mihaloew (2007). Jane Evans joined the expedition in 2008 and, as I remember, was in the depot looking at coins almost before she had unpacked.

That these unprepossessing (but sometimes overwhelmingly numerous) coins are legible at all is thanks to the meticulous care and patience of many conservators. Kent Severson offers a list of conservators from 1958–2008 in his article, "Understanding and Preserving the Material Culture of Sardis," in *Love for Lydia: A Sardis Anniversary Volume Presented to Crawford H. Greenewalt, Jr.* (2008). Since then, conservators Briana Feston, Astrid van Giffen, Jennifer Kim, Julia Sybalsky, Cybele Tom, Jill Hari, Hiroko Kariya, Catherine Williams, Brian Castriota, Jessica Walthew, Evelyn Mayberger, Harral DeBauche, Nuriye Arslaner, Emily Frank, Carolyn Riccardelli, Güler Sarıoğlu, Tony Sigel, Aybuke Sultan Koca, Chantal Stein, Lindsay Ocal, and Zeynep Arslan all helped make the coins both legible and stable.

Katherine Kiefer, who edited the Sardis Reports and Monographs series from 1996 until 2016, had a special interest in coins and particularly in the records and database. From 2008–2016 while we were converting our coin and other records to a single relational database, Kathy's intimate knowledge of the system, her sharp eye for inconsistencies, and her unfailing devotion to accuracy resolved innumerable difficulties with the coin database. Her assistant Sheila Nightingale contributed enormously to the endeavor as well.

Publications Data Manager Theresa Huntsman and Publications Coordinator Brianna Bricker have been key players in both the research and the production of this volume. Theresa's careful eye brought order to the frequently inconsistent recording of coins by so many hands. She also copyedited the volume and created the index. Brianna Bricker did page layout and further editing, proofreading, and checking. To all these talented archaeologists I offer my thanks. Maps were drawn by Tenninger Kellenbarger, Kaelin Jewell, and LauraLee Brott. Güzin Eren translated the abstract into Turkish. Production assistance was provided by Richard Denzer and his colleagues at Puritan Capital of Hollis, New Hampshire.

The Archaeological Exploration of Sardis was begun in 1958 by Professor George M. A. Hanfmann, of Harvard University, and directed by him until 1976. Professor Crawford H. Greenewalt, Jr., of the University of California-Berkeley, directed the expedition until 2008. Many of the coins were excavated under their careful leadership. A great many individuals and institutions have made the excavation, and this volume, possible through their administrative and financial support, and over the past half century, the Sardis Expedition has accumulated too many debts to list or repay. We are first and most profoundly grateful to the Republic of Turkey, to the Ministry of Culture and Tourism, and the General Directorate of Cultural Heritage and Museums for the privilege of working at the site. Many individuals in the Ministry and General Directorate have been instrumental in granting permissions and making excavation and research possible. In thanking the present Minister of Culture and Tourism, the Hon. Prof. Dr. Numan Kurtulmuş, as well as General Director Yalçın Kurt, we extend our gratitude to their predecessors as well. Special thanks are due to Melik Ayaz, Director of the Excavations Division of the General Directorate of Cultural Heritage and Museums, for his warm support.

The directors of the Archaeological and Ethnographic Museum in Manisa over the years have been continually supportive of research at Sardis, and we are very grateful to Lutfi Ekinci, Harun Güllü, Sevgi Soyaker, Müyesser Tosunbaş, Hasan Dedeoğlu, and Kubilây Nayır for their collegial generosity.

Martha Tedeschi, the Elizabeth and John Moors Cabot Director of the Harvard Art Museums, and the previous directors of the museum including Thomas Lentz and James Cuno, have provided the project with a welcoming and intellectually stimulating home and environment since its foundation. We are deeply grateful to Dr. Tedeschi for her continued interest in the Expedition.

Excavation, conservation, research, and publication at Sardis have been made possible by the financial support of the Harvard Art Museums and Cornell University, and by many generous individuals and foundations. Among these donors are Mr. and Mrs.

Max Barus, the Bollingen Foundation, the J. Stephens Crawford Trust, the Ruth Covo Family Foundation, the Ford Foundation, Mr. and Mrs. William Frederick, Dr. and Mrs. David Greenewalt and the David Greenewalt Charitable Trust, Dr. Richard Hamilton, the Institute for Aegean Prehistory, the J. M. Kaplan Fund, the John M. Kohler Foundation, Dr. Edwin H. Land and Mrs. Land, Mr. Thomas B. Lemann, the Loeb Classical Library Foundation of Harvard University, the Lucius N. Littauer Foundation, the Charles E. Merrill Trust, the Old Dominion Foundation, Mr. Donald I. Perry, the John and Emma Quint Memorial Fund, Mr. John J. Roche, the Billy Rose Foundation, the Rowland Foundation, Valerie Smallwood, the Susan G. Soderquist Trust, the Eleanor Ransom Swift Trust, Richard and Genevieve Tucker, the Vila B. Webber Charitable Trust, the estate of W. C. Burriss Young, and the Zemurray Foundation, as well as several anonymous donors and foundations. Research and publication have been supported by numerous grants from the U. S. Department of State and the National Endowment for the Humanities. Robert Neer and Ann Eldridge's generous donations allowed the Expedition to assemble an excellent numismatic library at the site, which greatly facilitated the research for this volume. The Supporters of Sardis have provided essential support, financial help, and friendly advice for the excavation, study, and publication of ancient Sardis. It is with great pleasure that we gratefully acknowledge their interest and encouragement.

Grids, Levels, Sectors,
Baskets, Lots, and Loci at Sardis

Since the first year of the expedition, excavations at Sardis have mostly been organized using a local grid based on a corner of the Roman Bath-Gymnasium building known as Building B, hence the B-Grid. That corner was given an arbitrary elevation of *100.00, indicated with an asterisk before the number. Other local grid systems include the Artemis Temple Grid, the Acropolis Grid, and various grids at Bin Tepe. The systems of grids and elevations are explained in previous Sardis publications.

Until 1980 contexts were primarily recorded in terms of the excavation sector and absolute coordinates and levels. In the early 1980s a new system of trenches, baskets, and lots was introduced. Baskets are units of excavation, which are both stratigraphic but also may be arbitrary, if it is not possible or desirable to excavate a complete stratigraphic unit at once. Baskets are combined into Lots at the end of the season, so establishing that season's stratigraphy in a particular trench. Recently we have added a third level of integration, the Locus, which combines lots excavated in different trenches and excavation seasons into larger stratigraphic units. Lack of space prevents us from including full stratigraphic information in the printed catalog of coins. However, the on-line database of these coins at http://www.sardisexpedition.org will have full contextual data available, as well as further photographs and other information.

The unpublished field reports, fieldbooks, and other notes to which Professor Evans refers in footnotes are located in the Sardis Office at the Harvard Art Museums.

Finally, the study of the Greek and Roman coins at Sardis has become synonymous with the names Buttrey and Johnston. Theodore V. Buttrey passed away in January 2018, leaving a legacy of scholarship on the coins and currency not only of Sardis, but throughout the world. Ann Johnston died some years earlier, in January 2010. It is with great sadness that we dedicate this volume to their memories.

Andrew Ramage
Associate Director
Archaeological Exploration of Sardis
Ithaca, New York

Nicholas Cahill
Director
Archaeological Exploration of Sardis
Madison, Wisconsin

Acknowledgments

My primary thanks are to Nick Cahill, who invited me to Sardis in the summer of 2008 to study the coins unearthed at Sardis since 2008. He has facilitated my work and provided helpful feedback on my manuscript at all points.

Much of the cooperative teamwork and congenial and stimulating discussion of all things Sardis is due to the leadership of Crawford H. Greenewalt, Jr. (Greenie), who remained as director emeritus at Sardis until his untimely death in 2012. I was fortunate to have known him in his element in the field, if only for a short time.

No less heartfelt thanks go to Marcus Rautman and Andrea Berlin, who shared their knowledge of pottery and helped me think through various deposits in this massive and complex site. Marcus was especially concerned to point me to interesting contexts and the small copper-alloy coin hoards, and I have leaned on his long familiarity with the site and his work on the deposits in MMS in order to sort out Late Roman and Byzantine Sardis. Although I owe Nick, Marcus, and Andrea many thanks for saving me from inaccuracies and unclear thought, any problems that remain are mine alone.

At least half of the joy of returning to the field every summer was a return to friends, all of whom were willing to tutor me in aspects of conservation, drawing, and making use of old records. Kathy Kiefer, who was occupied with the struggle of integrating the older coin records into the newer database, was a supportive sounding board with an eye for detail. Our draftsperson, Cathy Alexander, has eagle eyes and long experience handling Sardis materials, and tremendous stamina for long, talkative evening walks. Elizabeth Gombosi, Teoman Yalçinkaya, and Baha Yıldırım were excellent and expert companions at the tea and dinner tables. The young "Sardians" who provided me with assistance in the depot are too many to list individually, but Frances Gallart Marqués and Elizabeth DeRidder Raubolt bore the brunt of my questions and unstintingly gave help when needed. The conservators worked wonders on lumpy bits of bronze; our photographers quickly and reliably returned digital images to me. The Turkish commissioners were unfailingly helpful. Our wonderful house staff coddle the team in the most amazing ways.

Back in the States, I had help from Barbara Burrell—herself a "Sardian"—in the sections on the neokorate coins. Carmen Arnold-Biucchi helped me with puzzling identifications and invited me to speak at the Ilse and Leo Mildenberg Memorial Lecture (2013) on the coins from Sardis. I also thank audiences at the conferences of the International Numismatic Congress (Taormina, 2015), the American Institute of Archaeology (2012, 2017), the American Philological Association (now Society for Classical Studies, 2013), the American Schools of Oriental Research (2011, 2012, 2016), and the University of Pennsylvania (2013) for their questions and comments. Thomas M. Evans helped me greatly in my statistical exploration of the database, for which I am extremely grateful. A peer reviewer helped me sharpen my arguments. Brianna Bricker's sharp eye kept typos at bay. None are responsible for the errors that remain.

Only last in placement, but first in thought, are my thanks to my husband, for the time I was "in Sardis" both in body and in mind.

Summary

This book analyzes the coins from the Harvard-Cornell Sardis Excavations, from the years 1973 to 2013; the coins date from the Lydian period to the late Byzantine period, although Islamic coins will be published separately. An introduction in Chapter 1 outlines the methods of recording the coins, the overall aims of the book, and defines terms used in the book. Chapter 2 discusses the coins in terms of the economic structures of the city, region, and eastern Mediterranean. Beginning with an assessment of the value of excavation coins for the reconstruction of trade and economic processes, the chapter moves to a comparison of the Average Annual Coin Loss/1000 for cities in the eastern Mediterranean during the Roman Imperial period, which is checked by the Chi-Square Goodness of Fit test. The remainder of the chapter analyzes the excavation coins by chronological phases, starting with the earliest electrum coins from Lydia, and moving to the coins minted under Alexander III, Lysimachus, the Seleucid rulers, and the Attalid rulers. Within this discussion is an argument for the opening of the civic mint in the third century BC. Chronological discussion resumes with coins minted under the Roman emperors, including a consideration of the neokorate coins, through the coins of the fifth century AD, with an argument about the problem of recalled coinage, and the problem of fifth-century coin circulation and minting. In the discussion of the sixth and seventh centuries, the problem of urban decline is addressed, along with the problems of the evidence of excavation coins, in terms of circulation and economic activity. The lack of evidence for coins from the eighth through thirteenth centuries is noted.

Chapter 3 situates the coins within notable archaeological contexts. The chapter begins with a discussion of the types of deposits and the nature of the evidence of the coins. The precious metal coins of the Lydians (e.g., the "croeseids") are discussed in the few archaeological contexts of the excavation from which they came. Late fourth- to second-century BC deposits begin to show the length of time of circulation, and specific deposits (a small hoard in PN and in the Theater) are part of the analysis. The study of the following periods highlights the problem of finding Early and High Imperial contexts, but three specific contexts are evaluated: the votive deposit in Field 49; the votive deposit next to the "Wadi B" Temple; and coins used as grave gifts from the Hellenistic to the Late Roman period. The evaluation continues with the examination of identifying fourth-, fifth-, or sixth-century AD contexts, using a statistical method designed by the author (Mean Coin Date), to try and develop an idea of the length of time the coin remained in circulation in the Late Roman period. A brief discussion on coins used as amulets, and eight hoards of bronze coins follows.

The book includes appendices of the countermarks found on the coins; monograms found on the coins; a table of reverse descriptions; and formulas used in the statistical analysis. A full catalog of over 8,000 coins follows, with diameters, weights, die axes, excavation area, and analytical notes completing the description of types. Twenty-five figures, 44 tables, and six plates showing the excavation coins illustrate the arguments. A bibliography of works cited, a concordance between the field numbers and the catalog numbers, and indices of names and geographical places, as well as a general index complete the book.

Özet

Bu kitap, Harvard ve Cornell Üniversitelerinin 1973 ve 2013 yılları arasındaki kazılarında bulunmuş olan sikkeleri inceler. Sikkelerin tarihleri Lidya Devri'nden Geç Bizans Dönemi'ne kadar uzanır, ancak İslam Dönemi sikkeleri münferit olarak yayınlanacaktır. Giriş bölümü, sikkelerin belgelenme yöntemlerini ve kitabın genel amaçlarını ana hatlarıyla tanıtırken, kitapta geçen terimleri tanımlar. İkinci bölüm, kentin, bölgenin ve Doğu Akdeniz'in ekonomik yapısı çerçevesinde sikkeleri tartışır. Ticaretin ve ekonomik süreçlerin canlandırımı için kazı sikkelerinin önemini değerlendirerek başlayan bölüm, Ki-Kare Uyuşum Denencesi yöntemi ile test edilen Roma İmparatorluk Dönemi Doğu Akdeniz şehirlerinin Ortalama Yıllık Sikke Kaybı/1000 karşılaştırması ile devam eder. Bölümün geri kalan kısmı, Lidya'da üretilmiş en erken tarihli elektrum sikkelerden başlayarak, Büyük İskender, Lysimachus, Seleukos hükümdarları ve Attalos hükümdarları yönetiminde basılmış sikkelere uzanan maddi buluntuları zamandizimsel evrelere göre analiz eder. Bu tartışma dahilinde, kente ait sivil darphanenin MÖ 3. yüzyılda kurulduğu savı da yer alır. Kronolojik tartışma, Roma imparatorları yönetiminde basılan sikkelerle devam ederken, neokoros sikkelerinin değerlendirmesi, MS 5. yüzyıl sikkeleri ile bunların geri toplatılma sorunları ve MS 5. yüzyıldaki tedavül ve sikke basımı meseleleri de bu kapsamda sunulur. MS 6. ve 7. yüzyılların tartışmasında kentsel gerileme sorunuyla birlikte kazı sikkelerinin arkeolojik delil problemleri tedavül ve iktisadi faaliyetler açısından ele alınır. MS 8 ila 13. yüzyıllar arasında sikkelere dair delillerin yokluğu ayrıca belirtilir.

Üçüncü bölüm, sikkeleri önemli arkeolojik bağlamlarda değerlendirir. Bu bölüm, arkeolojik depozit tipleri ile sikkelere dair delillerin doğasını tartışmakla başlar. Lidyalıların değerli madenlerden üretilmiş sikkeleri (örneğin kroesidler), içinde keşfedildikleri az sayıdaki arkeolojik bağlamda tartışılır. MÖ geç 4 ila 2. yüzyıla ait tabakalar, tedavül sürelerinin uzunluklarına dair bilgi sağlarken, PN ve Tiyatro sektörlerindeki birer küçük define gibi belirli bırakıntılar analiz konusunu oluşturur. Takibindeki dönemlerin araştırması, Roma İmparatorluğu'nun özellikle erken ve yükselme dönemlerine ait kontekstleri bulma sorununun altını çizse bile, Alan 49'daki adak bırakıntısı, "Wadi B" Tapınağı'nın yakınındaki adak bırakıntısı ve Hellenistik Dönem'den Geç Roma Devri'ne kadar mezar hediyesi olarak defnedilmiş sikkeler olmak üzere özellikle üç kontekst ele alınmıştır. Değerlendirme, MS 4., 5. ve 6. yüzyıllara ait bağlamları tespit etmek üzere yapılan incelemeyle devam eder. Bu inceleme için Geç Roma Dönemi'nde sikkelerin tedavülde kalma süreleri hakkında fikir yürütebilmek adına kitabın yazarı tarafından geliştirilmiş istatistiksel yöntem (Ortalama Sikke Tarihi) uygulanmıştır. Bu bölümü ise tunç sikkelerden oluşan sekiz define ile nazarlık olarak kullanılmış sikkelerin tartışması takip eder.

Bu kitap, sikkelerin üzerinde yer alan darphane işaretlerini ve monogramları, sikkelerin arka yüz tasvirlerinin tablosunu ve istatistiksel analizde kullanılan formülleri kapsayan ekleri içerir. 8000'in üzerinde sikkenin tam kataloğu, sikkelerin çapları, ağırlıkları, kalıp yönleri ve kazı alanları ile tiplerinin tasvirini tamamlayan diğer analitik notlarla birlikte bu ekleri takip eder. Sikkeleri betimleyen 25 şekil, 44 tablo ve 6 levha ortaya atılan görüşleri görsel olarak destekler. Alıntıların kaynakçası, kazı ve katalog numaralarının bağlamlı dizini, kişi ve yer isimlerinin dizini ile genel dizin kitabı tamamlar.

Abbreviations

Abbreviations of Sectors (see Fig. 1.1 for map)

Ac	Acropolis
Ac-FT	Acropolis Flying Towers
AcN	Acropolis North
AcS	Acropolis South
AcT	Acropolis Top
TU	Acropolis Tunnels
AhT	Ahlatlı Tepecik
AT	Artemis Temple and Precinct
AT-Pac	Artemis Temple, Pactolus Bank
LA	Lydian Altar
Church M	Church M
For other AT features, see R1 fig. 59	
B	Bath-Gymnasium Complex
MC	Marble Court
Pa	Palaestra
For rooms BE, BSH, LNH, etc., see R3 fig. 7	
BK	Başlıoğlu Köy
Bldg A	Building A
Bldg C	Building C
Bldg D	Church D
BS	Byzantine Shops
For individual shops, see M9 fig. 4	
BT	Bin Tepe Cemetery
ByzFort	Byzantine Fortress
CG	Bath CG
CW	City Wall
CW6	Section at east of city
CW32	Section at west of city
SWG	Southwest Gate
For other CW sections, see R1 fig. 11	
EB	Eski Balıkhane
EH	Excavation House
E Road	East Road
F49	Field 49
F55	Field 55
F77	Field 77
HoB	House of Bronzes
MTE	Middle Terrace East
MTW	Middle Terrace West
UT	Upper Terrace
For other HoB features, see SPRT figs. 39, 186, 206	
KG	Kâgirlik Tepe
LAW	Late Antique Wall 31, near CW32
MD1/S	Mound 1/S
MD2	Mound 2
MMS	Monumental Mudbrick Structure
MMS/N	Monumental Mudbrick Structure North
MMS/S	Monumental Mudbrick Structure South
Nec	Necropolis
NEW	Northeast Wadi
PBr	Pactolus Bridge
PC	Pactolus Cliff
PIA	Pactolus Industrial Area
PN	Pactolus North
Church E	Church E
Church EA	Church EA
PT	Peacock Tomb
PW	Pactolus West
PyT	Pyramid Tomb
RT	Road Trench, south of B
MAS	Monumental Arch Structure
MRoad	Marble Road
Syn	Synagogue
ThSt	Theater-Stadium
Wadi B	Wadi B Temple and Precinct
W Road	West Road

Abbreviations of Sources

AA	*American Antiquity*
AJA	*American Journal of Archaeology*
AJN	*American Journal of Numismatics*
ANS	American Numismatic Society
ANSMN	*ANS Museum Notes*
ANSNNM	*ANS Numismatic Notes and Monographs*
AASOR	*Annual of the American Schools of Oriental Research*
BASOR	*Bulletin of the American Schools of Oriental Research*
BMC	British Museum Collection
BMC Caria	Head 1897
BMC Galatia	Wroth 1899
BMC Ionia	Head 1892
BMC Lycia	Hill 1897
BMC Lydia	Head 1901
BMC Mysia	Wroth 1892
BMC Phrygia	Head 1906
BMC Pontus	Wroth 1889
BMC Tauric Chersonese	Head and Gardner 1877
BMC Troas	Wroth 1894
BMC Vandals	Wroth 1966
BNJ	*British Numismatic Journal*
CCJ	*Cambridge Classical Journal*
CH	*Coin Hoards*
CQ	*Classical Quarterly*
DOC I	Bellinger 1965
DOC II	Grierson 1968a, 1968b
DOC III	Grierson 1973a, 1973b
DOP	*Dumbarton Oaks Papers*
GIC	Howgego 1985
HTR	*Harvard Theological Review*
HSCP	*Harvard Studies in Classical Philology*
INJ	*Israel Numismatic Journal*
INR	*Israel Numismatic Research*
JAN	*Journal of Archaeological Numismatics*
JAS	*Journal of Archaeological Science*
JÖB	*Jahrbuch der Österreichischen Byzantinistik*
JRA	*Journal of Roman Archaeology*
JRS	*Journal of Roman Studies*
LRBC	Carson, Hill, and Kent 1965
M1	Bates 1971
M7	Buttrey et al. 1981
M7 GR	Greek and Roman coins
M7 LR	Late Roman coins
M7 B	Byzantine coins
MIB	Hahn 1973
MIBE I	Hahn 2000
MIBE II	Hahn and Metlich 2009
NC	*Numismatic Chronicle*
OJA	*Oxford Journal of Archaeology*
QuadTic	*Numismatica e Antichità Classiche (Quaderni Ticinesi)*
RevBelgeNum	*Revue Belge de Numismatique*
RevNum	*Revue Numismatique*
RIC I^2	Sutherland 1984
RIC II	Mattingly and Sydenham 1968
RIC III	Mattingly and Sydenham 1930
RIC IV.1	Mattingly and Sydenham 1936
RIC IV.2	Mattingly, Sydenham, and Sutherland 1938
RIC IV.3	Mattingly, Sydenham, and Sutherland 1949
RIC V	Webb 1968
RIC VI	Sutherland 1967
RIC VII	Bruun 1966
RIC VIII	Kent 1981
RIC IX	Pearce 1951
RIC X	Kent 1994
RPC I	Burnett, Amandry, and Ripollés 2005
RPC II	Burnett, Amandry, and Carradice 1999
RPC III	Amandry and Burnett 2015
RPC IV	Heuchert and Howgego online
RPC VII.1	Spoerri Butcher 2006
RRC	Crawford 1974
SNG	*Schweizerische Numismatische Gesellschaft = Société Suisse de Numismatique*
SNG Ashmolean	*Sylloge Nummorum Graecorum: Great Britain V, The Ashmolean Collection, Oxford*
SNG Cop	*Sylloge Nummorum Graecorum: The Royal Collection of Coins and Medals, Danish Museum. Copenhagen*

SNG France	*Sylloge Nummorum Graecorum: France, Cabinet des Monnaies, Médailles et Antiques, Bibliothéque Nationale, Paris*
SNG Munich	*Sylloge Nummorum Graecorum: Deutschland, Munich Staatliche Münzsammlung*
SNG Tübingen	*Sylloge Nummorum Graecorum: Deutschland, Tübingen, Münzsammlung der Universität*
SNG Turk 1	Konuk 2002
SNG vAulock	*Sylloge Nummorum Graecorum: Deutschland, Sammlung von Aulock*
SNR	*Schweizerische numismatische rundschau = Revue suisse de numismatique*
WSM	Newell 1941

Chapter One

Introduction

The coins excavated at Sardis have been well served, as they have been carefully recorded and published. H. W. Bell's earliest efforts were some of the only artifacts from Howard Crosby Butler's excavation that received such treatment (1916). George E. Bates provided information about the Byzantine finds (1971); the Lydian, Hellenistic, Roman Provincial, Imperial, Late Roman, and a few Byzantine coins, along with some of the Islamic and modern coins, were published by the team of T. V. Buttrey, Ann Johnston, and Michael L. Bates, with Kenneth Mackenzie (1981).[1] Since August of 1972, the excavation coins were carefully cleaned, preliminarily identified by volunteer field readers, and placed into envelopes. Many of those envelopes, and the field records, were marked "necdem," short for "necessary details missing." Others were marked "needs further study." Thus, when I arrived in the summer of 2008, I found over 6,000 coins that were carefully noted in terms of findspots and usually satisfactorily placed within the correct chronological range, often thanks to the supervision and sharp eye of Andrew Ramage.

When coins are found in the field, the excavator assigns them a day number, draws the outline in his or her field notebook, and places the coin in an envelope detailing the year, trench, sector, month/day, and (by 1983) stratigraphic unit. At the end of the day, the excavator gives the coin to the registrar, who provides the coin a number, the first four digits of which announce the year it was found. Prior to my arrival, some coins, which were considered interesting for various reasons, were given a second number (thus, a coin could be 1980.0849 or C80.0039); if the coin was recovered outside of controlled excavation, it was given a "NoEx" number. This dual-numbering system has since been clarified: coins are now given a single coin number, and they are tracked with that number through conservation and photography. The process of cleaning and conserving the coins was essentially set up by Kent Severson; it should be noted that, because of careful lab procedures, very few disintegrate. Happily for me, even fewer are not assignable to a broad category, but they remain in chronological purgatory. Most of the coins remain in a secure facility on site, but some of the most legible or interesting coins are chosen annually to be housed in the Manisa Museum.

There is no need to review the history of the site, nor the history of the excavations, both of which are thoroughly covered in George Hanfmann's *Sardis from Prehistoric to Roman Times: Results of the*

1 Hereafter, cited as M7. Since I do not read Arabic, I have chosen to leave the Islamic coins out of the catalog; they will be published by Şule Pfeiffer Taş in a forthcoming article. Both the Islamic coins found since 1972 and those found earlier, but not published by Mackenzie in Buttrey et al. 1981, are available through individual records and corresponding photographs in the database. There were no Crusader coins found in the current excavations.

Archaeological Exploration of Sardis 1958–1975 (1983), Reports and Monographs on various aspects of the site, and preliminary reports in the *Bulletin of the American Schools of Oriental Research*, the *American Journal of Archaeology*, and *Kazı Sonuçları Toplantısı*. The coins in this monograph were largely unearthed when Crawford H. Greenewalt, Jr. was director, and work concentrated in sectors MMS, MMS/S, MMS/N, and ByzFort (Fig. 1.1). Under Cahill, excavations have concentrated on Field 49, the Theater, the Road Trench (across the road from MMS), and Field 55.

Cahill's development of an electronic database for the excavation has greatly facilitated my work. Not only does this allow us to track the coins more easily, but it also provides me with contextual information that is immediately helpful in my identification of the coins. After I make an identification of the coin, the excavators consult the same database to find out the information I have posted on "their" coins. The coins are assigned to "baskets," primarily a system of excavation units. After reading the pottery in the baskets, the excavator assigns the basket to a "lot," or stratigraphic unit, usually composed of one or more baskets. After the lots are entered into the database, I can tell at a glance what other coins were found in the lot and can reference useful information such as the type of pottery or other objects found in the same lot. Photographs of the coin (currently, not every coin is photographed, but the majority of legible coins are) are attached to the record, along with any drawings I have made of monograms. The database, digital images, and constant internet access allowed me to work in a manner that I suspect would have made the late Ted Buttrey and the late Ann Johnston envious; I remain in awe of the work they did in the publication of more than 15,000 coins in *Greek, Roman, and Islamic Coins from Sardis* (1981).

The second chapter discusses the coins within the larger Hellenistic, Roman, and Byzantine worlds. In it, I note parallels to other large urban centers in the eastern Mediterranean to help elucidate the use of copper-alloy coins within the monetized economy of Sardis. In the third chapter, I discuss the coins in their archaeological contexts. The discussions range from the perennial chronological problems to our understanding of how coins were used (and lost) in the city. I have returned several times to contexts from Hanfmann's excavations, when the subsequent study of materials from those years allowed me to say something about the contexts. I have not included the study I have made of coins from the Synagogue, as Andrew Seager is preparing a comprehensive volume on the building and its finds. My intent is twofold here: to give us an understanding of how the coins were used in non-economic contexts; and to explore the possibility of defining normal profiles for different chronological horizons, in order to help us gauge the number of years a coin may stay in circulation and to aid the archaeologist in reconstructing the chronology of the strata, especially the Late Roman layers. For the latter, I developed the use of a formula to ascertain the Mean Coin Date, based on a formula long used by archeologists of the modern era to determine the chronological horizons of their strata using the Mean Ceramic Date. The result is not a precise number, but an overall ratio that gives us some insight into fourth- and fifth-century AD deposits.[2]

I end here with a few words about the terms used in the book: Lydian and Persian (or Late Lydian) are used instead of Archaic and Classical, as they are more meaningful to Sardis. The Hellenistic phase is considered as beginning in the late fourth century and lasting until 31 BC. I chose the closing date since this is the opening of *Roman Provincial Coinage*,[3] although Rome had control of Sardis for over one hundred years by 31 BC. There are numerous Late Hellenistic issues produced through the first century BC.[4] Nevertheless, the numismatic watershed is the appearance of Octavian or Augustus on the obverses of coins, making this the divide between Hellenistic and Roman. In Sardis, the introduction of coins with the head of Augustus permanently changed the types, style, and (slightly later) metrology of the coins. The end of the Imperial period is conventionally placed when the reforms of the coins by Constantine similarly permanently changed the face of the coins and the users' interaction with them. The Imperial period is thus dated 31 BC to 324 AD. For the Late Roman period, I follow numismatic convention in dating the era between 324 and 498 AD, after which

2 All dates are AD, unless otherwise noted as BC.

3 Burnett, Amandry, and Ripollés 2005.

4 Burnett, Amandry, and Ripollés 2005, p. xiv.

we have another monumental numismatic reform. This can lead to some overlapping terminology in the field records only when other materials are discussed, such as pottery. In the database and in my catalog, the coins of Anastasius I begin the use of the term "Byzantine," even though for the first seven years of his reign, the mint only produced coins that would have fit quite comfortably in a Late Roman money purse.

Chapter Two
Excavation Coins as Evidence of the Economy and Trade

Numismatists studying Roman and Byzantine deposits have constructed most of the hypotheses of what excavation coins mean in terms of the reconstruction of the ancient society. However, scholars of the Hellenistic world, and to a lesser extent, the Lydian kingdom, have confronted the problem as well. Since the excavation coins are primarily copper-alloy coins, I focus my attention on them.

Most numismatists would agree with a recent assessment that excavation coins provide a way for us to understand the kinds of lower denominations in circulation, the level of monetization of a site (more transactions would lead to higher losses, as the coins changed hands more often), and economic ties to surrounding cities.[1] Richard Reece took pains to remind readers that the coins do not display the wealth of the people living on the site where they were excavated, nor the "condition of an economy" of the site.[2] Kevin Butcher objected to the use of excavation coins to analyze the ancient economy, noting that not all coins are tightly, or even well dated and the loss of the coins may be greatly impacted by local developments, such as the Sassanid sack of Zeugma. He is also uncomfortable calling each coin "lost" instead of "discarded"; perhaps the coins found on the site had been discarded as worthless since they could no longer be used in transactions.[3] However, as John Kroll pointed out for Hellenistic coins found in the Athenian Agora, some coins may have been discarded as useless for legal tender (and I would argue this may be the reason why certain coins are found in votive deposits). This is probably true for foreign coins—especially those similar in size and weight to local civic coinages—that appear to have been accepted in local circulation, and even hoarded together with local coins.[4] I will argue below that the bronze coins from the excavation allow us to say something about the local conditions of the period when they were discarded or lost. More information about the site and region can be obtained in the comparison of Sardis to regional and extra-regional sites in the East.

The number of coins found on a site is dependent on several factors, some of which we can no longer gauge more than very approximately. The size of the initial issue is of crucial importance. Although valiant efforts have been made to estimate the number of coins produced in an issue using die studies, these can only give us very rough estimates. In essence, the supply of the coins to the site is dependent both on the size of the issue and the means of distributing coins to the non-

1 e.g., Katsari, Lightfoot, and Özme 2012, p. 1.

2 Reece 2003, p. 143.

3 Butcher 2013, pp. 2–3.

4 Kroll 1993, pp. 168–70.

mint city.[5] A word of caution is in order; numismatists have largely backed away from estimating the size of the issue by mathematical models that use the number of dies known.[6] Further limiting this figure is the problem of doing die studies on corroded and worn Roman Provincial bronzes. In other words, we may only ever have a very approximate idea about the original size of issues from the coins found on an excavation and in museum collections.

Hopkins introduced the problem of the velocity of coin circulation.[7] Richard Duncan-Jones tried to assess the speed at which a coin changed hands by examining weight loss, concentrating on western coinages.[8] The problem is complex in a city like Sardis that minted its own bronzes. These coins would not have had to travel far, theoretically reducing wear on the coins, but they may have been exchanged often, as the city was highly monetized. The resulting wear on the coin can imply either a long period of circulation or a shorter period of circulation at a higher velocity. It is thought, for instance, that coins of the first century AD that are worn smooth show this wear because of long use; countermarks of the second and even third century on these coins would suggest this long period of circulation. The situation changed in the mid-third century, when Sardis no longer produced its own coins and was dependent on Imperial mints. The wear on the coin may only give us a clue as to how often it changed hands or remained in use, at least in gross terms.[9]

The difference between the time of issue and the time of loss may help us define how long it took coins to reach non-mint sites, especially after the municipal mints closed.[10] Anthony King used the minting date of the earliest and latest coin in the deposit to find the minimum period of circulation. His regression analysis suggests that the deposit should have eleven or more coins in it as the best predictor of the date of the deposit.[11] The numismatist must pay careful attention to deposits here, for if the coin is in a secondary deposit, then the calculation of minimum period of circulation can be skewed. However, taking into account the type of deposit in which the coin is found can lead to an understanding of the length of time coins were available to be used as legal tender (see especially Sections 3.5 and 3.6 on the Late Roman and Early Byzantine periods).

In order to get a closer look at how long coins remained in circulation, the numismatist must work carefully with the archaeologist and the pottery expert to assess the date of the stratum in which the coin was found.[12] Coins associated with pottery are often viewed as reliable indicators of the periods of circulation, in a manner similar to coins found together in a hoard.[13] As can be seen in the computation of the Average Annual Coin Loss per 1000 (e.g., Fig. 2.1; App. 4), almost all sites in the East report an increase in coins beginning around 250 and lasting until the mid-fifth century. This is a phenomenon that is well known across the Mediterranean, and is usually linked both to the loss of value of base-metal coins and to the higher rate of minting for coins of the mid-fourth to mid-fifth century.[14]

One variable that enters into the problem of the longevity of use of the coin is if the government recalled issues for reminting.[15] The problem is especially important in the Late Roman and Early Byzantine periods, and I address it specifically in Sections 2.5 to 2.7. Reminting continued to be a factor in Byzantine coinage, especially as copper grew scarce, although some of the difficulties of obtaining metal

5 Grierson 1966, p. v; Reece 2003, pp. 147–48.

6 Compare de Callataÿ 1995 and Buttrey 1993.

7 Hopkins 1980.

8 Duncan-Jones 1998, pp. 180–92; see a recent critique of Duncan-Jones's method in Hoyer 2013.

9 King 2013, pp. 30–31; Doyen (2011, p. 32) estimates the date of loss of a coin due to the wear shown on the coin, on a scale of 0–10. Unfortunately, this seemingly more precise method does not take into account post-depositional processes. For an unusually clear example of these processes, see Section 3.3.1. Doyen does caution the reader that his method cannot account for coins taken out of circulation for a time (e.g., in a hoard) and then re-circulated (pp. 32–33). More interesting is his example of coins circulating in bags (p. 34), leading him to the conclusion that wear is graphed in a Gaussian curve (p. 37).

10 Morrisson 2002, pp. 953–54.

11 King 2013, pp. 14, 16, 33.

12 For the problem in Late Roman deposits, see Butcher 1995, p. 308; Butcher 2001/2, pp. 96–100; also see Reece's pessimism on the number of sites that allow this kind of study (2003, p. 149).

13 cf. Wigg-Wolf 2009, pp. 109–10; Doyen 2011, p. 18.

14 See Butcher 1995, pp. 308–9.

15 Grierson 1966, p. vi.

to coin were solved by overstriking.[16] Paradoxically, it is overstriking that allows us to understand that coins up to 100 years old were available to the mint, but Philip Grierson warned that overstriking can distort our ideas about the distribution pattern of the original issue.[17]

As Douglas Newton pointed out, a common argument (which is rarely made, but which informs the publication of most excavation coins) is that "patterns in finds of accidentally lost coins mirror patterns in coins in circulation to a useful extent," as long as the numismatist accounts for the fact that low-value coins are most commonly lost due to the owner's presumed energy in retrieving a high-value coin.[18] He tested this argument by comparing coins lost in 2004 in the UK to known mint production and found "a strong relationship between the number of coins found and the numbers in circulation," with a very low standard deviation. Newton would thus see the excavation coins as reflecting ancient circulation. Nevertheless, in the end, he suggested that certain factors in antiquity might skew this strong correlation, including the problems of hoarding; degradation of the coin in the earth; and method of retrieval, especially true for tiny fifth-century coins.[19] Coins are only one of the pieces of evidence that we can use to reconstruct "everyday economic activity."[20]

While numismatists were content in the early twentieth century to simply list coins by mint and date of issue in excavation reports, John Casey developed the equation of dividing the coins not only by the length of reign (Average Annual Coin Loss), but dividing by 1,000 in order to more easily compare sites with few coins to sites with large numbers of coins (see App. 4).[21] Reece has especially advanced this approach, forming the periods for the western half of the empire. The intent of this equation is to get a basic understanding of the circulation pool from which the excavation coins are drawn.[22] I have pursued this approach and compared the Sardis cohort with other eastern Mediterranean sites.

In order to validate the numbers, I joined this equation with a Chi-Square Goodness of Fit test (as in Evans 2007; see App. 4). This test tells us whether the differences in the site totals are significant (and thus can be explained as something happening in the broad picture) or are not valid; the sample is an assortment of coins from sites but the collection has no larger meaning. If valid, the AACL/1000 results alert us to broad patterns of loss within cities. They cannot tell us when a particular coin is lost. Kenneth Harl suggested that the AACL/1000 test was particularly helpful in tracking periods of inflation, when more coins were lost and not recovered.[23] David Wigg-Wolf would eliminate coins from hoards and votive deposits from these calculations to provide a sharper picture.[24] I have decided to include the hoards in the AACL totals (very few coins come from votive deposits), though I tried to remain sensitive to the adjustments this might make in the statistical analyses (e.g., Section 3.5).[25] The problem is particularly accute for the fourth and fifth centuries, which I have analyzed with a new method, the Mean Coin Date, to try and determine the chronological composition of a fourth- or fifth-century deposit.

16 When an existing coin is used as a blank for a new coin type, the process is called overstriking. Traces of the earlier type can often be seen under the later impression.

17 Grierson 1966, p. vi.

18 Newton 2006, p. 215; cf. Reece 1984b, pp. 201–2.

19 Newton 2006, pp. 217, 220–21. Note that Newton did not distinguish between primary and secondary deposits; nor do other numismatists looking at overall patterns of loss in excavation coins. In a perfect world, numismatists would only compare primary deposits with other primary deposits, and our studies would be very small. Yet even when coins are found in secondary deposits, they must have once circulated in the city, which is why numismatists combine both kinds of deposits in their analyses.

20 Newton 2006, pp. 221–22.

21 Casey 1974.

22 Reece 1984a. Pottier (1983) introduced a much more complicated formula for a bronze hoard; since other numismatists have not used this formula, I have chosen to ignore it in order to make comparisons between Sardis and other sites. Another method of analysis to calculate the total value of the coins lost was initiated, then deemed "inconclusive" by Reece: see Reece 1975; 1984b, p. 200; cf. Doyen 2011, pp. 21–25, who also rejected the approach.

23 Harl 1996, p. 18.

24 Wigg-Wolf 2009, p. 111.

25 My reasoning is as follows: all but a very small hoard could be dated to the fifth century; only one of the hoards is sizable, and it closed in the fifth century; the fifth century is under-represented in the AACL calculations, since so many from this century were illegible; even so, given the large numbers of coins from the excavations, the largest hoard had little impact on the numbers.

We can never say that we are working with a random sample, since the number of coins on a particular site is only a small percentage of coins that came from the mint, and the number of coins found is only a small percentage of all coins that ever came to the city.[26] The coins may even be only a sample of the coins in the deposit. Thus, we actually have a sample of the coins that were lost, which is a sample of the coins that came to the city, and which is itself a sample of the coins in circulation.[27] The archaeological aims of the excavator ensure that the sample is not random, as the archaeologist does not randomly dig test pits across the city (and manages to find each phase of occupation in such pits), but sets up a hypothesis to be tested by digging. It is the Chi-Square Goodness of Fit analysis that allows us to say that the sample does mean something and is at least representative of the base-metal coins in circulation.

With all these caveats in place, the study of excavation coins can indeed tell us something about the site, and the region, beyond the contextual or use situations.[28] In order to view the site within the regional context, I have plotted the AACL/1000 and checked it with a Chi-Square Goodness of Fit test for large eastern cities comparable to Sardis, beginning with the region (Anatolia) and extending the study to Greece and ancient Palestine (Fig. 2.5). These areas were not very dependent on coins from western mints and are just now receiving this kind of numismatic attention, which has long been focused on western Europe. In exploring these other sites, I have attempted to set up a "normal" profile for the cities.[29] Deviations from the norm can thus be explored for significance, and while I am well aware of the limitations of older data and problems of publication of bodies of excavation coins, I think the experiment is worth doing.[30]

For the Imperial period, the graph shows that there are several "normal" cities within the profile: Sardis, Pergamum, Ephesus, Corinth, Butrint, and Caesarea Maritima (Fig. 2.2). Those not conforming to the overall pattern are Priene, Kenchreai, and Athens. In the normative profile, the high number of coins from the Augustan period drops through the Flavian period, rises again in the Antonine period, drops in the Severan, rises to a high in 238–284, and then drops in the Tetrarchic period.[31] Deviations from this profile will be discussed in the relevant sections below.

For the Late Roman and Early Byzantine periods (Fig. 2.3), the coins from the excavation at Kalenderhane Camii in Istanbul alone deviate from the "normal" profile. In eliminating this site from the profile (Fig. 2.4), we can see more easily the normative trends: a high point of finds from 324–364 (coins minted by the House of Constantine), which will surprise no numismatist, leading to a lesser number of coins for the rest of the fourth century. The numbers increase in the first half of the fifth century, leading to a drastic fall in the second half of the fifth century (there are variations in each of these periods at the different sites). Some sites show a recovery in the numbers for the reigns of Anastasius I through Phocas; the numbers plunge after this, leading to a low during the reign of Constans IV (after which Sardis has no real deposits, so I stopped assembling profiles). Again, deviations from this norm will be discussed in the sections below.[32] In order to test the results, I have performed a Chi-Square Goodness of Fit analysis; the results are that the AACL/1000 is valid.[33] For all the periods, the differences between the groups is significant: we are looking at a real pattern in the sample, not a random conglomeration of coins (see App. 4).

26 cf. Doyen 2011, pp. 14–15.

27 Grierson 1965, p. v.

28 See Reece 2003, pp. 146–47.

29 See Reece 2003, pp. 147–49, who has used this technique in the west.

30 As Howgego 1992, p. 4.

31 Although there are several places where the actual numbers of the cities overlap (e.g., 565–685 for Sardis and Priene), the actual numbers are much less useful as evidence than the trend of the numbers over time (e.g., the rise in value for the period).

32 For AACL/1000 calculations, I did not proportionally divide the "uncertain first to third century AD," "uncertain fourth," "uncertain fifth," "uncertain fourth–fifth century," or "uncertain Byzantine" coins, as it is clear that the totals for legible coins show a wide variety in the numbers lost within these time periods, and I chose not to mask these differences. I ignored the "uncertain 5th/6th" coins from the earlier excavation report (Buttrey et al. 1981), which does diminish the number of coins from the second half of the fifth century, I am sure.

33 For an explanation of the test and a program to run the test, see Preacher 2001.

2.1 The Lydian Period

Sardis was a prolific mint of electrum coins in the seventh and sixth centuries BC, in part because the rulers of the city invented electrum coinage and controlled most of the major electrum sources in Turkey. Numismatists are uncertain if the state held the monopoly on minting or if bankers and merchants were also allowed to strike coins.[34] The most widely accepted theory is that the coins were minted as a "practical convenience," especially for large-scale transactions by the state, such as payment of soldiers or collection of taxes.[35] Perhaps the soldier who died on the walls of Sardis with his fractional coin (no. **2.1**) is an indication of how coinage had penetrated into the life of citizens of the city.[36]

It is generally agreed that the electrum lion-head stater, weighing just over 14 g, and its fractions, were the first coins that can be definitely attributed to the mint in the Lydian royal city of Sardis. Alram argued that since there are a number of fractions associated with the stater (as here, coin nos. **1.1** and **1.2**), then the coins were in widespread use for many different types of transactions, even at this early date.[37] François de Callataÿ noted that even a guess of the number of dies known (although no complete die study exists of any electrum coinage), compared to the number of specimens known, as well as the range of denominations struck, suggests a "massive striking" which "implies levels of monetization not reached [again] until many centuries later."[38] Cahill suggested that these coins are a byproduct of "the rise of Lydian imperialism in the seventh [century] BC," especially given that the source of the metal for the coins may have come from northwest Anatolia, not the Pactolus River.[39]

The electrum coins maintained a very consistent weight and proportion of gold to silver in their alloy. The total percentage of gold in each coin approximates 54%.[40] Previous discussions on whether the gold is concentrated on the surface of the coin due to post-depositional processes have now been settled by SEM-EDS analysis of two electrum *trites* found on the Acropolis of Sardis (nos. **1.1** and **1.2**).[41] The enriched surface was intentional, not a product of the environment in which the coin remained hidden in ancient and modern times.

The date of the minting of both series has remained controversial, although the Sardis excavations show that Croesus minted both gold and silver coins. Some scholars argue for "high" dating of the initial striking, in the second quarter of the seventh century BC, based on the date of the Ephesus temple deposit; most argue for a "low" date of the last quarter of the seventh century BC.[42] Michael Kerschner and Koray Konuk prefer the mid-seventh century BC date as a *terminus ante quem*, based on their reassessment of the archaeological context of the Ephesus temple deposit.[43] Since the contexts of the earliest coins found at Sardis cannot add any evidence as to the chronology of the series, I have retained a measure of uncertainty in the catalog as to the date.

Scholars divide the "croeseid" coins into early and late groups, based on weight and stylistic considerations. The heavy standard consists of a stater that weighs about 10.71 g, which was issued in both gold and silver. Coin no. **2.1** is a fraction of the heavy stater; the style of the obverse (Naster's Massive, Carradice's Early, or Nimchuk's B type) has been called a "powerful and stocky form" with "large dimensions" in a "fine naturalistic manner."[44] The silver staters were produced longer than the half silver staters; as a result, the staters were more widely circulated and often appear more worn through longer use.[45] Silver staters such as the one found in a dump on the Acropolis (no. **3.1**) have been dated to ca. 560–525 BC, based on hoard evidence.[46]

No Persian sigloi or darics have yet been excavated at Sardis, leaving a long lacuna in the coin evidence.

34 Konuk 2012, p. 47; Wallace 1987, who argues strongly for the former; see also van Alfen et al., forthcoming.

35 Kraay 1976, p. 28; Price 1983, pp. 7–8; Wallace 1987, p. 386.

36 de Callataÿ 2013, p. 7.

37 Alram 2012, p. 62.

38 de Callataÿ 2013, p. 9.

39 Cahill 2013, p. 150; also Cahill et al., forthcoming.

40 Konuk 2012, pp. 44, 47; Walburg 1991, p. 12; Wallace 1987, pp. 386–87.

41 Cahill et al., forthcoming.

42 e.g., Price 1983, p. 4; Weidauer 1975, pp. 108–9; cf. Alram 2012, p. 62.

43 Kerschner and Konuk, forthcoming.

44 Naster 1965; Carradice 1987, pp. 74–75; Nimchuk 2000, p. 6.

45 Naster 1976, p. 131.

46 Nimchuk 2000, pp. 21–22; Wallace 2016 suggests a much earlier date for the beginning of Croesus's reign.

2.2 The Hellenistic Era: The Late Fourth to Early Third Century BC

By the late fourth and early third century BC, the numismatic picture of coin circulation in Sardis becomes clearer, if only because portraits of rulers on coins allow some discussion of the chronology of the period. The new era began when Sardis voluntarily submitted to Alexander the Great and was rewarded with a royal grant to build a temple to Zeus Olympios (Arr. *Anab.* 1.17.3–6).[47] Worship of Artemis must also have occurred in an important sanctuary in this period, even if the first evidence of building comes from later in the Hellenistic period.[48] Scholars used to consider temples as drains on the local economy that needed constant infusions of money, pointing to the need for upkeep or construction of sacred buildings and daily rituals. John Ma has suggested instead that sanctuaries contributed to the local economy by being taxed.[49] The temple also contributed to the marketplace (in terms of surplus offerings), held wealth in the form of votive offerings and land, and gathered fines or received legacies to offset some expenses.[50] Thus, two important sanctuaries in the city (the temple to Zeus has not yet been found; it is not known if it was ever built) contributed to the economy and growing monetization of the city.

Alexander authorized the mint at Sardis to reopen; from it came new denominations, weights, and types that were standardized across the entire region of Asia Minor, with a few exceptions.[51] However, Alexander's bronze issues cannot be clearly distinguished from the identical issues minted by his successors, which were also produced in Sardis. Martin Price argued that we should rely more on excavation coins than arguments about control marks in order to assign mints.[52] These coins of the late fourth and early third century BC are normally found in secondary or even tertiary contexts or are stray finds (see nos. 11–16). In several cases, the excavation coins suggest mints for previously unsettled coins (nos. 11, 14–18). These had either been given no attribution of mint or placed somewhere in western Asia Minor, as, for instance, a unit with the head of young Herakles r./rider galloping r., ΦΙ, but no accompanying symbol (no. **17**). Also probably from Sardis, though found in fewer numbers on the site, is the unit, no. 14 (and probably no. 15), with the head of young Herakles r./bow in case and club ΑΛΕΞΑΝΔΡΟΥ, and a cup. Along with this is a quarter unit, no. 16, with the same types as the unit.

Christopher Matthew suggested that the coin types show that the changing bosses of the shields on the obverses commemorate certain units of the Macedonian army (cf. no. 11). He thought that cities minted these in short bursts in order to commemorate the actions of the soldiers in recent battles. Hence, those minted in Sardis were minted for units who fought in the Battle of Granicus and are thus earlier than Price suggested; they were not struck for the use of the soldiers once they entered the city, but to make purchases in the local market.[53] Since we have no record of which units moved to Sardis after the battle, this is perhaps a circular argument, but Matthew's point about the brevity of minting might hold.

Price noted one example of the coin that is no. 18 here, head of young Herakles r./bow in case and club, ΒΑΣΙΛΕΩΣ, with a torch beneath. Since there are three more examples from the current excavations, it is likely again that the mint is Sardis. Price listed a number of these coins (and an associated series) with a countermark of a lion's head r. He seemed to favor J. G. Milne's suggestion that the countermark was stamped during Lysimachus' occupation of Ephesus, which would make the Sardis mint a strong contender for the series. Price dated the coins to 323–310 BC.[54]

It is clear that the number of bronze issues from the mints was always much smaller than the number of silver issues.[55] The denominations and weight standards of the coins are difficult to parse, given the variations in weight and diameter. Price suggested

47 For an overview of this period at Sardis, see Ratté 2008; Berlin and Kosmin, forthcoming.

48 Cahill and Greenewalt 2016, pp. 498–500.

49 Ma 1999, p. 134.

50 Dignas 2005; Chankowski 2011.

51 Mørkholm 1991, p. 50; Thompson 1983, p. 42. For a full discussion of the Hellenistic mint at Sardis, see Evans in Berlin and Kosmin, forthcoming.

52 Price 1991, p. 320, *contra* Thompson 1983.

53 Matthew 2009.

54 Price 1991, pp. 71, 343.

55 See Aperghis 2004, p. 217.

that we need to look at the weight, diameter, and type *in toto* in order to ascertain denomination.[56]

We know that Lysimachus held Sardis between 301 and 281 BC, and most probably struck tetradrachms and bronze coins here; he retained Alexander's types and struck on the Athenian standard.[57] The bronze coins are particularly problematic, but five examples of a unit with the reverse of a leaping lion and spearhead below would suggest that these were probably minted in Sardis.[58] Margaret Thompson believed that the mint closed in 287 when Lysimachus briefly lost control of the city.[59] It appears that bronze coinage in Asia Minor "virtually ceased" for a brief time after Lysimachus' reign and was only revived by the Seleucid kings.[60]

From the late fourth and early third century BC, the Ephesus mint supplied a number of coins found in the excavations, including the majority of coins from the small purse hoard discussed in Section 3.2.1 (nos. 34–37). Four more mints in Ionia each supplied a coin in the late fourth or early third century BC (Colophon, no. 33; Magnesia ad Maeandrum, no. 43; Erythrae, no. 41; Leucae, no. **42**); six came from nearby Cyme, nos. 30–32, a city with abundant issues in this era. Ionian mints dominated the circulation pool in Sardis; scholars have suggested that at this point, Sardis was politically dependent on Ephesus and may not have been an independent city.[61]

As bronze coins were rarely hoarded, we do not know how widely they circulated. It is generally thought that the circulation pool was quite local, and the mints represented in the excavations indicate trade routes.[62] For the coins coming into Sardis, it is clear that the strongest trade contacts were to the west in Ionia, and not cities farther east on the old Persian "royal road"; indeed, the mints represented can even be narrowed further, to the road that connected Sardis, Smyrna, and Pergamum (Fig. 2.6). Andrea Berlin's pottery analysis suggests that trade contacts—or at least numbers of imported pottery—were fairly low for this period, even if the Sardians were aware of and producing newer shapes.[63] Thus, the local nature of the coin supply and the pottery supply is in striking agreement.

2.2.1 Sardis as a Seleucid Mint: The Third and Second Centuries BC

When Seleucus I conquered Sardis in 282 BC, he retained the city as a capital and opened a royal mint in the city.[64] Since Sardis was the central point for several *oikonomiai* (akin to districts) and the city was the point of collection for taxes, the Seleucid kings appointed financial officers; the chief financial officer (whose title is unknown) lived and worked in Sardis. As in the time of the Lydian kingdom, Sardis' urban center was once more tied to the fortunes of the ruler, even if the ruler did not always live in the city.[65] It is likely that taxes, which up until this time had mostly been paid in kind, began to be paid in coin, leading to a deeper monetization of the economy in the city.[66]

Unlike the other diadochs, Seleucus did not put his portrait on his coins (at least not those from Sardis), although he did put his own name on the reverse. It is at this point that the king centralized economic control of the cities of his kingdom; it may be that he drove out the satrapal coin issues that had been minted in Sardis. However, it is likely that many of Seleucus' coins were never issued, as there were still large numbers of bronzes of Lysimachus, Pergamum, and Rhodes in circulation.[67] Coins of Lysimachus and of Pergamum were found in Sardis. We have a notice (Pseudo-Aristotle, *Oec.* 1345b)[68] that the setting of the weight standard and volume of minting was a

56 Price 1991, p. 39.

57 Mørkholm 1991, p. 81; see note for coins 8.1–2.

58 Evans in Berlin and Kosmin, forthcoming.

59 Thompson 1968, pp. 166, 173.

60 Houghton 2012, pp. 238–39.

61 See Hanfmann 1983, p. 113.

62 cf. Mørkholm 1984, p. 104; Çizmeli-Öğün and Marcellesi 2011, p. 297; Bransbourg 2011, pp. 97–98.

63 Berlin 2016, pp. 354–56; Berlin in Berlin and Kosmin, forthcoming.

64 For a history of Seleucid Sardis, see Kosmin in Berlin and Kosmin, forthcoming.

65 Ma 1999, pp. 135–36.

66 Aperghis 2004, pp. 29–32.

67 Golenko 1993, p. 87; Aperghis 2004, p. 233.

68 The source is of disputed date, but likely early in the Hellenistic period; Aperghis (2004, p. 135) prefers a date for this section of the *Oeconomia* of ca. 275 BC.

royal prerogative, at least in the case of gold and silver coins.[69] We are less certain whether bronze coins were minted at the behest of the local community, although the royal devices on them should show that Seleucus paid for the minting of these coins as well.[70] As can be seen in the excavation coins, Seleucus's Sardian bronze coins were not the only bronze coins circulating in Sardis, although examples from the furthest eastern mints are missing from the deposits. On the other hand, a small hoard from Gordion shows that Sardis coins were circulating farther east.[71] In order to simply give a broad suggestion on the pattern of exchange for the eras examined I will break down the mint of origin for the coins found on the site by the era of their minting. I understand that the coins of the third century BC could have been brought to the site at any point after their minting and we do not always have information on how soon the coin was lost after it arrived in Sardis.[72]

Brian Kritt suggested that bronze coins, unlike gold and silver coins, were struck to local standards.[73] The few surviving examples of the bronzes of Seleucus I in the excavation finds mean that Oliver Hoover is uncertain if the Medusa-bull coins are of the smallest or next-smallest denomination (nos. **69–70**).[74] Although the diameters diverge only slightly, the weights of the excavation coins vary from 1.83 to 2.45 g. Coins in collections, which have diameters from 14 to 16 mm, have a median weight between 2.5 and 2.99 g.[75] Variations in weight are known from other mints.[76]

We are uncertain how these coins were valued in relation to the many civic or municipal coinages circulating in western Asia Minor; it is possible that the types as well as the size helped the ancient user.[77] Hoards show that the coins from the royal mint could circulate widely, unlike the civic coins, which tended to remain within the city's orbit.[78] What is striking is the western orientation of the origin mints. Clearly, Sardian trade was focused on the Aegean coast, as coins from Ilium to Miletus are found in the excavations, with fewer coins from interior mints (Fig. 2.7).[79]

After the death of Seleucus I, the mint opened in earnest; however, the only coins from the excavations are coins of the smaller denomination minted under Antiochus I, and Hoover was uncertain if these were minted in Sardis or Smyrna (no. 72). Perhaps the number of examples found in the excavation, both in Johnston's catalog and here, would throw the balance to Sardis.

The Apollo/tripod coins from the reign of Antiochus II (261–246 BC) found in the excavation all came from the mint at Sardis. Otto Mørkholm called the series "very extensive," as such coins are found all over Asia Minor, into the Propontis.[80] Two denominations of Antiochus II were found in the excavations: denomination B or C and denomination D. The latter shows either a cithara or a tripod (this is the type also on the larger denomination). Coins

69 Aperghis 2004, p. 117.

70 Sherwin-White and Kuhrt 1993, pp. 22, 63.

71 *CH* IX, 490, Gordion hoard 9. See Çizmeli-Öğün and Marcellesi 2011; they did not break up the Hellenistic period into phases, but noted for Sardis more coins from outside the city in the excavation coins than in the rest of their sample (Ilium, Cyzicus, Assos, Pergamum, Colophon, Priene, Miletus, Aphrodisias, Caunos, Xanthos, Patara, and Side, most of which have small numbers of Hellenistic coins). They attributed the number of foreign mints to Sardis's role as a royal city from the Lydian period into the Hellenistic period, and its role as middleman between coastal and interior cities.

72 See discussion above, and Newton 2006.

73 In Houghton and Lorber 2002, II: 5; see also Mørkholm's (1991, p. 12) reluctance to give weight standards for bronze denominations, due to the loss of bronze in excavation coins complicating the picture. He did suggest three denominations weighing 1.5–2.5 g ("half"); 3.5–4.6 g ("unit"); and 6–8 g ("double") (p. 115). These weights only sporadically line up with the weights of bronzes recorded by Kritt in Houghton and Lorber 2002, II: 7–9. Kritt's theory is complicated by the apparent variation in weights across the Seleucid reigns, which do not clearly show any consistent weight standard across the Seleucid issues (see Fig. 2.12). The results lead to choices such as "denomination B or C" or "denomination C or D" in the Houghton and Lorber 2002 catalog. Perhaps we should rely, as Mørkholm suggested, on flan diameters. The smallest denomination would be 10–12 mm, the medium 14–17 mm, and the large 20–23 mm.

74 In Houghton and Lorber 2002, I: 16–17.

75 Houghton and Lorber, 2002, II: 7.

76 Aperghis 2004, p. 223.

77 Houghton 2012, p. 240.

78 See Golenko 1993, p. 81.

79 It is true that the cities of inner Anatolia are less monetized than the western cities, but if trade was occurring to a large degree with the East, we might expect Seleucid coins from farther eastern mints to appear in the Sardis deposits, since we know that they were minted in quantity.

80 Mørkholm 1991, p. 122; cf. Houghton and Lorber 2002, I: 184.

of denomination D are between 12 and 14 mm, and 1.50 to 3.41 g. The larger denomination is only slightly larger, with diameters from 15 to 17 mm and weights from 3.10 to 4.79 g; the reverses are exclusively tripods. Once again, a small pool of fairly local civic coinages reinforces the Seleucid finds: coins from the second half of the third century BC from the mint at Ephesus were found on the site (M7 GR 85).

Coins from more distant mints appear during the reign of Seleucus II (246–225 BC). The mint at Sardis is represented by denomination C coins (nos. 80, 81); Seleucia ad Tigrim produced a small (denomination D) bronze that could be recognized by its beveled edge (no. 83). And, for the first time since the Archaic period, a precious-metal coin appears in the finds (no. 82, a drachm). I suggested the mint as Antioch, although the control mark (see App. 2) is not found in Houghton and Lorber.[81] Unfortunately, the coin came from a later Roman dump and can tell us nothing about the context in which it was brought to Sardis and subsequently lost. Also from this time period comes a fine bronze of Ptolemy III or Ptolemy IV, minted in Alexandria (no. **65.1**), one of the two Hellenistic coins found on the site from this distant mint.[82]

Achaeus minted coins with his name on the reverse and the head of an archaistic Apollo on the obverse, mimicking his Seleucid king (Apollo was claimed as the father of Seleucus I; Justin 15.4).[83] By using this type, Achaeus might have been arguing that he was the legitimate Seleucid king or trying to bolster trust in the new issue, as the coin type was already familiar to users. However, he also referred to his new ally, Ptolemy IV, in the eagle reverse (nos. 84, **85**).[84] Two of these bronze coins were found at Sardis; one came from Hellenistic occupation layers in the "ByzFort" trenches that could be dated no closer than the third century BC. Both examples were countermarked with a horse head in a circular stamp, a product of the reopened mint under Antiochus III.

During his reign, bronze coins were issued in several series in five denominations; these are the most common Seleucid coins found in Sardis. Up to twelve of the coins found came from the mint at Sardis (nos. 86, **87**–90); three were from Antioch (nos. **91**–92). Hoover suggested that one small bronze in the Afyon Museum (Apollo/Apollo testing arrow, but denomination D) was minted in Sardis.[85] Since there were three such coins found in the excavations (no. 90), it is now very likely that the mint was correctly seen as Sardis.

Johnston identified thirteen coins as coming from the mint at Sardis under Antiochus Hierax.[86] These coins have been reassigned to Antiochus III.[87] Two coins, one from the earlier excavations (for which, see note in catalog, no. **79**) are from the smaller denomination, and carry the head of Tyche, turreted and veiled, with a reverse of a tripod and the name of Antiochus. Hoover was uncertain of the mint, but called it "probably" Sardis, and assigned it to Antiochus III.[88] That designation must be changed to "almost certainly" from Sardis, as one of these coins was excavated from the Hellenistic layers under the Synagogue and the other was turned in by a local resident.

The earliest coin from the mint at Rome found on the site dates to ca. 211–ca. 208 BC (no. 67); we can only speculate why it was brought east (a second coin from Rome, no. 66, cannot be dated this closely, only to the late third to first centuries BC). The coin comes from a large issue of bronzes struck during the Second Punic War, as the weight of bronze coins dropped very fast; they were overstruck, leading to a wide range of dates in the series. It was dated by the lack of any symbol in front of the prow, and the use of ROMA above. Closer to home, coins from Smyrna are dated between 240 and 190 BC (M7 GR 111; nos. 44–45); there are only a few for such a mint as close as Smyrna, testifying to the number of coins pouring from the Sardis mint under Antiochus III.

Hoover lists "notable provenances" for some of the bronze Seleucid coinages: coins from Sardis appear in Gordion (Hoards I and V), Cabyle, Gediz, Antioch,

81 Houghton and Lorber 2002, I: 255–57.

82 Also M7 GR 390.

83 See Ma 1999, pp. 57–58, 61.

84 The eagle "may reveal Ptolemaic influence," Mørkholm 1991, p. 126.

85 Houghton and Lorber 2002, no. 983(6).

86 M7 GR 376–378, based on Newell 1941, no. 1438; cf. Bell 1916, nos. 405–411.

87 Houghton and Lorber 2002, I: 375–76.

88 Houghton and Lorber 2002, I: 207.

Tarsus, Akko, Marisa, Susa, and Jebel Khalid.[89] Sardian bronze coins were countermarked in Priene, Miletus (?), Tralles, Ephesus, Colophon, Thyateira (or Mylasa), Pergamum (?), Phocaea (?), Chios (?), Olbia (?), and Cabyle. Thus, by the time of Antiochus III, at least, a broader circulation is found for Seleucid bronze coins of Sardis, encompassing Ionia, Mysia, Cilicia, the modern areas of Lebanon and Israel, and even farther east to Iran.

There are no longer any clear indications of the sack of Sardis after the revolt of Achaeus (which was described in Polybius 7.15–18). However, the economic repercussions of Antiochus' victory were severe. Ma argued that the city was fined, troops were billeted in the city, the city's gymnasium was appropriated for the soldiers' use, taxes were paid in coin, and the king made "requests" for "special contributions," also in coin. Antiochus later granted some relief for the city by providing grain, oil, and an exemption in taxes to help pay for the Laodicea festival. There is also notice of rebuilding projects in the city, so not all was bleak.[90] Excavations have revealed only glimpses of the Hellenistic city and cannot yet confirm what we know from the written sources.[91] The use of Sardis as a military garrison, which meant the arrival of goods to feed and equip the soldiers, testified to the economic importance of the city in the late third century BC, especially as a transit point on the road northwest to Mysia and west to Ephesus.[92] Berlin's study of the pottery shows that this period was (newly) characterized by imported pottery (Pergamum, Ionia, the southeast Aegean, Parthia, and Phoenicia) and wares such as wine and perfume vessels, suggesting the trade contacts (which are only hinted at in the coinage) and the prosperity of the city after it had recovered from the siege.[93]

Second-century BC coins show the heavy reliance the city had on coins from Pergamum (Fig. 2.8), as perhaps we can expect due to the changed political landscape, but the almost complete driving out of coins from any other mint is a little surprising. Interestingly, the trade of coins was not reciprocal, for Voegtli reported no Sardian coins from the Pergamene excavations.[94] Because of the new center of power, the traffic along the east-west trade road (which would have brought coins from Ephesus to Sardis) was diminished in comparison to the major movement northwest-southeast. And a new policy of selling grain locally, to convert it to cash in order to pay taxes, also changed the monetary picture in Sardis—for unlike the Seleucid rulers, the Attalid kings preferred to keep the state out of large grain purchases.[95]

For one second-century BC context, the pottery shows that there need be no long lag between the minting of a coin in Pergamum and the use of the coin in Sardis (no. 21.1, Athena/ivy leaf, dated 260–197 BC, found with latest datable material of 165 BC).[96] Note that Johnston preferred a more compact minting sequence for the Pergamene coins, as she thought that the importation of the Pergamene coins ended when the Sardis civic mint produced the Herakles/Apollo and Apollo/club coins, after 133 BC.[97] Since I argue that the date of the opening of the Sardis civic mint occurs in the third century BC, there is no longer any need to compress the Pergamene sequence.

In David MacDonald's study of the coins of Aphrodisias, he noted several patterns in Hellenistic cities: Aphrodisias was unusual because it had no mint until late in the era. Thus, most of the Hellenistic coins found in the city were from non-local sources, a situation found also in the excavations at Delos and Megalopolis. The second pattern is found at Sparta, Assos, and Priene, which provided coin for many of the surrounding cities. The third pattern is found at Sardis, which produced both regal and civic coins. Here, the local mint dominates the finds, and other coins trickled in from nearby cities. In this, Sardis was much like Athens, Antioch, and "to a lesser

89 Houghton and Lorber 2002, I: 186–89, 243–44.

90 Ma 1999, pp. 61–63, 110, 131, basing his arguments on Gauthier 1989; Thonemann 2013, p. 23.

91 See Stinson in Berlin and Kosmin, forthcoming.

92 Magie 1950, p. 42; Ma 1999, pp. 114–15.

93 Berlin, Final Hellenistic Pottery Report 2013, p. 13; Berlin in Berlin and Kosmin, forthcoming.

94 Voegtli et al. 1993.

95 Thonemann 2013, pp. 17–19.

96 Berlin 2016, p. 353.

97 Citing von Fritze 1910, pp. 475–84; Buttrey et al. 1981, p. 74.

extent" Pergamum and Tarsus.[98] With the evidence from the modern excavations, we can now say that the numismatic profile was indeed much like that of Athens, at least for the second century BC, which shows almost only locally-produced coins from the excavation.[99]

2.2.2 The Problem of the Opening of the Civic Mint for Bronze Coins at Sardis

According to the treaty formed after the Battle of Apamea, Sardis passed from Seleucid control to be ruled by the Pergamene kings until Attalus III willed the city to Rome in 133 BC. Pergamum remained an important source for bronze coins in the late second and first centuries BC (Figs. 2.8, 2.9). Other nearby cities provided smaller numbers, with only one coin from Ephesus from this era. Yet coins from farther afield—Bithynia, Adramyteum, and Alexandria Troas—also appear in small numbers. The same situation is seen in the coins reported from excavations at Pergamum, where excavators noted the majority of coins from foreign mints came from nearby: mostly Elaea, and other cities in the area controlled by Pergamum or the "Mysian-Lydian hinterland." However, a few coins also came from farther away, even Egypt, but the excavators still saw the cities of Atarneus, Gambreion, and Germe as dominated by Pergamene influence.[100]

A major problem in understanding Hellenistic Sardis is deciding when the civic mint opened.[101] Most numismatists peg the opening of the civic mint at Sardis to before 133 BC, following Barclay Head in *BMC Lydia*; he suggested that the issues should begin in 189 BC, when Sardis passed into the hands of the Attalid kings.[102] Mørkholm agreed in general, noting that municipal coinages as a whole arose after the Peace of Apamea.[103] Price—who concentrated on silver issues and not bronze coins—also supported a date in the 180s BC due to the presence of an "Alexander" tetradrachm in the Larisa Hoard, which he suggested closed in the 160s.[104] Johnston preferred to date the civic coins to after 133 BC; she thought the coins were produced only after there was neither another supply, nor any Attalid control of the mint—only nominal Roman control of the area.[105] Thus, scholars based their arguments on the date of the opening of the civic mint on the reason why coins were struck and the possibility of the need for royal permission to strike. To bolster these arguments, scholars turn to metrical, stylistic, and iconographic parallels, and archaeological or contextual information. I will examine each in turn, along with technical data about the making of the coin flans, and I suggest that we should consider a date in the third century BC.

The reason for a city to produce bronze coins is a matter that is still debated. The explanation for the creation of such coinage, the costs of which are borne by the city, varies, with explanations centering on market demands for coin in order to facilitate small-scale transactions, the ability to pay taxes, profit for the city, or civic pride. A secondary need may have been to provide soldiers with small change for local purchases. Although Lydia was home to the earliest coinage, the Macedonian conquest of Asia Minor and the resulting urbanization and need to develop infrastructure drove the demand for coin in the area.[106] As noted above, regal coins co-existed with civic coinages, struck at a wide variety of mints, leading to what Richard Ashton called an "exuberance of emissions" which peaked in the first century BC.[107]

From the earliest times, the precious-metal coins from the mint at Sardis carried the emblems of the ruler. The change in regimes was always marked by

98 MacDonald 1976, p. 44, who used only the information from the earliest publication of the coins of Sardis; these results were also noted by Çizmeli-Öğün and Marcellesi 2011, p. 313.

99 See Kroll 1993.

100 Voegtli et al. 1993, p. 6–7.

101 I am grateful for the chance to discuss the problems of Hellenistic Sardis with a group of scholars in the summers of 2014 and 2015, who were invited to Sardis by Nick Cahill: Andrea Berlin, Ruth Bielfeldt, Paul Kosmin, and John Ma. They provided stimulating insights and suggestions to further my arguments, as did the audience during the 2015 International Numismatic Congress in Taormina, Sicily and the Hellenistic Sardis group in fall 2016.

102 Head 1892b, p. xcviii.

103 Mørkholm 1984, p. 94; he did not specifically mention Sardis.

104 Price 1991, p. 321.

105 Buttrey et al. 1981, p. 79.

106 von Reden 2010, pp. 32–33; Meadows 2014, pp. 188–91.

107 For the reasons why bronze coins were invented, see e.g., Harvey 1989, pp. 80–85; Harl 1996, pp. 110–11; Meadows 2002, p. 126; Lightfoot 2002, p. 239; Reece 2003, p. 142; Matthew 2009; Bransbourg 2011, pp. 87, 97–98; Ashton 2012, p. 201.

the change in systems, weights, and types, beginning with the Persian rulers. The Persian satrapal coins themselves may have been slowly replaced, according to Susan Sherwin-White and Amélie Kuhrt:

> [as a] result of a deliberate centralising policy emphasising the chief authority of the king alone, who is the source of royal money, although it is a moot point whether Persian satraps were able to strike coins without royal authorisation. If so, the Seleucids abandoned an Achaemenid practice which had allowed satraps in western Asia Minor to mint in silver and bronze, usually to meet military expenditure.[108]

This argument reveals the authors' understanding of why bronze coins were minted by the Seleucids: to pay the army. Other scholars stress the need for coin to pay tribute or taxes.[109] Since Sardis was a royal capital from 282 to 189 BC, we would expect to find soldiers stationed here, although we are not certain that they were paid in bronze coin; nor is it certain that taxes were paid in low denominations. It is clear that inhabitants of the city were used to using bronze coin by the second century BC, but we cannot use an argument about why bronze coins were minted as an argument to decide when bronze civic coins were minted.

Most scholars also argue that permission to mint bronze coins was an integral part of the authority of the Seleucid kings.[110] Two crucial pieces of their argument come from 1 Maccabees 15:6, where Antiochus grants permission to Simon to mint coins (there is no evidence for such a coinage from Simon), and [Pseudo-Aristotle] *Oec.* 1345b, where the king is given absolute authority over the minting of coin, at least over gold and silver coins.[111] Yet since bronze coins were issued from "communities from Babylon to Sardis," it appears that the Seleucid king allowed the cities relative freedom to produce whatever bronze coins they needed, whenever they wished.[112] David Magie argued that cities had the freedom to strike at any time, because "this was primarily a practical concession to convenience, for their coins, which were of bronze and of low denominations, were evidently intended only for local circulation."[113] That is to say, civic coins were minted for local needs, and may have sprung from the desire of local aristocrats to dignify their city. It is not clear that they would need permission to strike an issue, especially if the city magistrates paid for the minting. The officials would have been able to impose fines or other penalties to raise money for the city, but any income would have to have been promptly dispersed—especially after 133 BC—for ambassadors, architects, religious festivals, or sacral officials. Most likely, city magistrates paid for their own expenses, and notices of benefactions become regular enough that it is probable that such gifts to the city came to be expected as part of the duties of the office, or even the means by which candidates were elected.[114]

However, the important question remains of how the city officials would decide when they would mint the coins. It is generally thought that the city must have been a *polis*, or have had autonomous status.[115] Yet Sviatoslav Dmitriev argued, "The minting of coins by a Greek city did not inevitably demonstrate that the city was autonomous"; the city could mint civic issues while ruled by a king.[116] In this, Dmitriev is following the argument of Thomas Martin, who effectively decoupled the issue of sovereignty and the right to coin, especially for bronze coins. Martin reasoned that the early diadochs (especially) only cared about obtaining gold and silver, which they would mint to pay their troops. They ignored bronze coins as "small change in purely local use," even if the cities were in need of small change at this point due to the level of monetization.[117] *Polis* or not, scholars are still uncertain if the city needed special permission of the Seleucid or Attalid overlord to strike a bronze coinage.

108 Sherwin-White and Kuhrt 1993, p. 23.

109 Aperghis 2004, p. 213.

110 e.g., Hoover 2004, pp. 486–87.

111 See Martin 1985, pp. 242–43; cf. Meadows 2001.

112 Sherwin-White and Kuhrt 1993, p. 63; cf. Aperghis 2004, pp. 119, 131, who preferred an earlier date for the closing of the satrapal mints.

113 Magie 1950, p. 136.

114 Dmitriev 2005, pp. 34–43.

115 Hence, the arguments over the date when the city became a polis: see Ma 1999, p. 250; Sherwin-White and Kuhrt 1993, pp. 182–83; Magie 1950, pp. 121–22.

116 Dmitriev 2005, pp. 65, 296; cf. Mørkholm 1984, p. 102.

117 Martin 1985, pp. 220–21.

The scholars who support the need for royal authority to coin suggest that the placing of the head of the ruler on the obverse changed the balance of the equation, so that by the time of the diadochs, minting became an exclusive royal prerogative, though these rulers could give permission for occasional "autonomous issues."[118] E.T. Newell argued for Antiochus III, who was willing to allow cities permission to make autonomous bronze coins.[119] While Martin conceded that such a coinage might have become a symbol of the sovereignty of the city, it is not at all clear that civic coinages carried the same symbolic function as coins with the head or name of the ruler.[120] Thus, he argued, we can dispense with the formula articulated by Henri Seyrig that only free cities could mint autonomous coins, as the kings wished to keep the profits from minting as their exclusive prerogative.[121] Nor did Mørkholm see a conflict between the minting of royal bronze coinage and the simultaneous minting of municipal bronzes; he stressed the profit to the Seleucid king from such a measure.[122] Fundamental to the discussion on sovereignty and civic coinages is an inscription from Sestus dated to the late second century BC, which names a certain Menas (*OGIS* 339). In it, Menas is honored for soothing city pride in the types placed on the coins and for overseeing the minting of bronze coin primarily to generate profit for the financially stricken city.[123]

While Martin emphasized the importance of profit to the local city in this inscription, Andrew Meadows suggested that the notice about the choice of coin type was "a reaction to the way in which civic coin types were beginning to slip out of the sphere of civic control" and into the hands of the men in charge of the minting. If so, then the choice of coin types by private citizens is a "curtailment of the normal prerogatives of a sovereign state."[124] Types of purely local interest, combined with local weight standards, should show "something more locally driven, at least at the level of execution." Meadows maintained that the king might issue a "limited grant of the right to issue bronze coin, with limited freedom to choose a reverse type."[125]

By the second century BC, cities were accustomed to receiving grants in order to strike civic coinages, especially as they developed civic institutions such as councils and assemblies.[126] Combined with "a reduction in flow in royal coinage" as Rome became more involved in the East, cities began to mint their own coins that carried neither a royal portrait, nor a legend noting the royal patron of the issue.[127] Richard Ashton agreed with Meadows that the situation was somewhat fluid up until the second century BC, but argued the opposite: the Seleucid monarchs, influenced by the Roman example of control over their subsidiary mints, began to impose such controls in the East in the second century BC.[128]

It is well known that although Seleucid precious-metal coins were minted to the Attic standard, bronze issues across Asia Minor varied widely in their weight standards due to local control of the minting.[129] If the same weight standard is found in neighboring cities, it is thought that those cities cooperated in order to facilitate trade. However, the city may have changed the weight of the coins to reflect new political or economic alliances.[130] The period of Attalid control seems especially to be a period when the kings allowed the local elites in the cities to make decisions unencumbered by much royal bureaucracy.[131]

Sardis minted at least nine different obverse and reverse pairs without the name of a king. I will concentrate on two series here, as they were by far the most numerous type-pairs to come from the mint: Herakles/Apollo (no. **52**) and Apollo/club (no. **55**). As noted above, Head preferred a date of 189–133 BC

118 e.g., Cox 1950, p. 47–48.

119 Newell 1941, pp. 398–99.

120 Martin 1985, p. 234.

121 See Martin 1985, pp. 235–38; cf. Seyrig 1986, pp. 19–22, 35–38, although he was only concerned with precious-metal coins.

122 Mørkholm 1984, pp. 101–2.

123 Martin 1985, pp. 238–40; Meadows 2001, p. 59.

124 Meadows 2001, p. 59.

125 Meadows 2001, p. 60.

126 Meadows admits that bronze coins are only dated by links to dates of supposed silver issues or by stylistic dating, making the dates of the coins problematic (2001, p. 60).

127 Meadows 2001, p. 62.

128 Ashton 2012, p. 192.

129 e.g., Aperghis 2004, p. 223.

130 von Reden 2010, pp. 65–68.

131 Thonemann 2013, pp. 12–13.

for the opening of the civic mint for bronze coins; he posited such a date because of a bronze coin (now discredited) carrying the legend ΑΘΕΝΑΣ ΝΙΚΗΦΟΡΟΥ ΣΑΡ, a supposed Sardian copy of a Pergamene issue. He also stated, contrary to most modern scholars, that coins with the full names of magistrates could be found among the earliest issues from the city.[132] Johnston argued that "there is no obvious overlap between the Pergamene coinage of the earlier part of the second century" and the Sardian bronze coins; there were no well-dated Lydian examples to use as stylistic and technical parallels; nor were there any archaeological contexts to draw upon to provide a date. Since there were, at her reckoning, more than sixty known monograms for the Apollo/club and over seventy names or monograms for the Herakles/Apollo coins, both series must have been struck over a number of years.[133] If the authorization came from the annual archon, then the issues may have been struck for almost a century—or even longer—for the Herakles/Apollo series, which also contains anonymous issues.

The coin blanks are thick, with the average mean of 15–17 mm for the diameter of the Herakles/Apollo and 13–15 mm for the Apollo/club series (Fig. 2.10). The coins that have magistrates' names on them comprise a smaller total than those with monograms; the differences in diameters between the groups were statistically insignificant, given the small number of examples. Since the chart only includes excavation coins, the weights vary more than the diameters;[134] the use of the name or the monogram on the Herakles/Apollo coin does not appear to influence the weight of the coin, which varies between 5 and 7 g (Fig. 2.11). Normally, the die axis is 12. A significant percentage of these coins have a club in an oval punch as a countermark on the obverse. They also can be recognized by touch as having a concave reverse, the product of a convex die.

132 *BMC Lydia*, p. xcviii; e.g., Thonemann 2016, p. 132.

133 Buttrey et al. 1981, p. 80.

134 As the coin gets worn the thickness suffers much more than the diameter, since people rub the surface of the coin or depositional forces such as water erode the faces of the coins much more than the thin edges.

Far fewer Apollo/club coins survive than Herakles/Apollo coins, both in the M7 catalog and the current excavations. It looks as if the Apollo/club was the smaller issue. The coins themselves are slightly smaller than the Herakles/Apollo coins, as the weight peaks range from 3 to 4.5 g; all of them have a magistrate's monogram, but none carry a full magistrate's name, nor are any countermarked. The die axes fall between 4 and 8, though there is more variation here than in the Herakles/Apollo group. Thus, given the change in weight, diameter, normative die axis, and the use of the convex die for only one of the series, it appears to me that these two groups of coins were minted at different times.

Weights for the bronze coins minted in Sardis for the Seleucids varied slightly by century (Fig. 2.12). It is possible that the Herakles/Apollo could act as a larger denomination of D/E for Antiochus II's coins (second series), but this denomination is already present in the same series (B/C). In short, there is no comfortable spot for the Herakles/Apollo coin in the Seleucid system. The Attalid weight standard appears to use the earlier Seleucid system, but the mint mostly struck a one-unit coin in the third to early second century BC, about 3.88 g, with smaller denominations of half and quarter units of ca. 2 and 1 g, respectively.[135] The Athena/ivy leaf coins from Pergamum present in the Sardis excavations function as a half unit (at Sardis, a mean of ca. 1.95 g); the Athena/serpent coin functions as a one-unit.[136]

The Apollo/club coins do appear to fall into denomination B/C (under Antiochus II) or C (under Seleucus II) or could even be tied to the Attalid one-unit coin. The Herakles/Apollo might parallel the Attalid two-unit (?) coin. Nevertheless, the result is not clear; the coins appear only to tell us that they were not obviously minted to conform to the weight of Seleucid royal bronze coins, nor to the bronze coins coming from the Pergamene mint. Mørkholm pointed out that since bronze coinages are token coinages, the weights of the coins do not have to remain within any particular precious-metal system, "economically

135 Westermark 1991, pp. 148–49, 152; but the excavation coins she lists fall below this theoretical weight.

136 At Sardis the mean is 3.15 g, while Westermark (1991, p. 152) found it to be averaging 3.97 g.

speaking, although they may have a psychological effect on the public using the coins."[137]

In terms of diameters, the results are similar. The Apollo/club falls into the range for "denomination C" for Antiochus I and Antiochus III and possibly the Attalid "unit"; the Herakles/Apollo finds fewer slots to fit into, perhaps "denomination B/C" for Antiochus II and "denomination C" for Seleucus II (Fig. 2.13). In other words, the Sardis coins function as do most bronze coins of the period, with changing weights and diameters making their relationships to any other bronze series minted unclear.

Stylistic analysis and iconographic study of the coins might help us understand a bit more about the milieu in which the coins were struck, although I would not want to base secure dating arguments on either argument. Johnston noted that "there are no apparent [stylistic] affinities between the coins of the handful of cities in the area" that were minting in the second and first centuries BC.[138] Nevertheless, we can perhaps make some headway with iconographic parallels. The Apollo on the Apollo/club coin is archaistic: Apollo's hair is rolled up alongside his head and is gathered into a large bun at the back of his head. Two long locks of hair trail down his neck. He is given a "Greek profile" with high cheekbones and a long neck. Although this head does not copy any particular Apollo on Seleucid coins, it is close in style to the archaistic heads found on bronze coins of Antiochus III from the mint at Sardis.[139] The type was revived for denarii minted for Cassius, with Servilius as his legate. These were minted in a traveling mint in Asia in 43–42 BC (*RRC* no. 505.3). As is common for Hellenistic coins, no legend is placed on the obverse.

The reverse shows the club of Herakles surrounded by a wreath, perhaps of celery or parsley, although it is commonly called oak. The leaves are spiky and not particularly oak-shaped.[140] The celery/parsley wreath was introduced to the Nemean Games by Herakles and was also a prize for the winners at the Isthmian Games (Pind. *Olympian* 13, *Isthmian* 2; Plut. *Quaest. Conv.* 5.3), although at least by the time of Augustus, it was also associated with Apollo.[141] On the coin, the legend "of the Sardians" is shoehorned into the area between the club and wreath; a magistrate's initials are almost always found at the break in the wreath.

There are only a few parallels for a club reverse: coins of Antiochus I from the mint at Ai Khanoum,[142] too far away to have an impact; and a coin from Antiochus III's mint at Tyre,[143] another unlikely source of inspiration. Clubs appear with a bowcase or caduceus on the reverses of fourth-century BC bronzes of Blaundus and other unspecified mints in western Asia Minor. Only four times does the club appear by itself in the type on bronze coins: the city of Tarsus minted such a reverse, though anepigraphic and with the same spiky-leaved wreath, for Antiochus IV. The obverse depicts a cornucopia.[144] A slightly better parallel shows the club surrounded by the name of the city on coins conventionally dated to the second or first century BC from Apollonis (Lydia); the obverses feature a Macedonian shield.[145] From Heraclea ad Latmum, a laurel wreath surrounds the club; the coins are dated to the early second century BC or later, and a second type combines the club in wreath with a bearded Herakles, lionskin knotted around his neck.[146] Finally, from Alinda (Caria) a coin depicts the head of Herakles, clad in his lionskin; on the reverse is a spiky-leaved (?) wreath enclosing both the name of the city and the club of Herakles capped by the lionskin.[147] It is conventionally dated to the second century BC due to the wreath; another issue from the same city has the head of a laureate male combined with a wreath and club on the reverse.[148] Thus, for the Apollo/club coin, the best iconographic and stylistic parallels come from coins conventionally dated to the second and first centuries BC.

137 Mørkholm 1984, p. 97.

138 Johnston 1983, p. 60.

139 Houghton and Lorber 2002, nos. 974–975; cf. nos. 976A–978.

140 Compare the oak wreath on a third-century BC coin from Smyrna, *BMC Ionia,* p. 237, no. 3, and the parsley wreath on *RPC* I, no. 1141.

141 See Mitchell 1990, p. 185.

142 Houghton and Lorber 2002, no. 445.

143 Houghton and Lorber 2002, no. 1082.

144 *SNG France* 2, Cilicie 1279.

145 *SNG Cop* 16.

146 *BMC Ionia*, p. 152, nos. 8–9, 11

147 *BMC Caria*, p. 10, no. 1, cf. nos. 3–7.

148 Imhoof-Blumer 1901, p. 106, nos. 2–3.

The second series depicts a head of a beardless Herakles; unlike the heads normally found on the Early Hellenistic coins, Herakles does not have his lionskin pulled up over his head, but leaves it knotted around his neck. Instead, he sports a laurel wreath. The die cutters emphasize his hulking physical presence, sometimes to the point of making him appear thuggish. The head is very different in style from the Seleucid Herakles, and very different from the other gods on the Sardis coins who retain their Hellenized profiles. As with the other series, there is no legend on the obverse. We do find the combination of lionskin scarf and somewhat brutal features in mid-third-century BC bronze coins minted by the city of Heraclea ad Latmum (as noted above, with a club in wreath reverse).[149] Occasionally, later rulers will show themselves with the lionskin knotted around their throats; these depictions also come from farther north and east than Sardis. But the combination is unusual. The coin type was revived briefly in Sardis during the reigns of Augustus (see note on coin **148.1**) and Tiberius.

The reverse matches Apollo with the Herakles obverse, the inverse of the Apollo obverse and Herakles-themed reverse of the first series. The nude Apollo stands frontally, but looking right. His left arm hangs in a relaxed manner by his side, while he bends his right arm at the elbow to hold a bird. The numismatic literature describes the bird as a raven or crow, the messenger of Apollo. However, the hawk is described as being Apollo's messenger, in the *Odyssey* (15.525) and in Aristophanes' *Birds* 516.[150]

On the best-preserved specimens, Apollo can be seen sporting the same archaizing hairstyle noted on the Herakles/Apollo coin. The legend "of the Sardians" is placed between Apollo's left arm and a filleted laurel wreath that encloses the reverse. Most of the coins carry a monogram of the moneyer's name beneath Apollo's outstretched hand; some carry instead the full name of the moneyer. I doubt that the coin reverse depicts a cult statue of Apollo in the city, but his pose—supporting the bird on his outstretched hand—is supposed to evoke the image of Zeus Lydios, also seen on coins from the mint at Sardis, who elevates an eagle (cf. no. **51**). Apollo was a familiar Seleucid type, although he is portrayed on Seleucid coins as leaning on a tripod or sitting on the omphalos. It is likely that the standing Apollo is a version of the Seleucid leaning Apollo, since the type is adapted for other city reverses.

Wreaths enclosing reverse types suddenly appear in Lydia on bronze coins conventionally dated to the second century BC. It is generally thought that wreaths appeared on coins due to the popularity of New Style Athenian tetradrachms, that is, after ca. 160 BC.[151] All the Lydian examples have the head of a deity on the obverse and no legend. All of the reverses have the attribute of a god enclosed, usually in a laurel wreath, with the name of the city on the reverse, and sometimes monograms of moneyers. Interesting tetradrachms of Aigai of the mid-second century BC depict a nude Zeus holding out an eagle, surrounded by an oak wreath,[152] a nice parallel for the Apollo type, even if Aeolis is a little distant to think of this coin as an inspiration for the Sardian bronze. A bronze type from Blaundus makes a stronger case, for, like the Sardis type, a god is surrounded by a wreath; in this case, it is Hermes holding a moneybag within an oak wreath.[153] The coin is dated to the second or first century BC. This is the second good parallel between the bronze coins of Blaundus and Sardis.

The combination of Herakles and Apollo would appear to refer to Sardis as a Seleucid city. The gods who appear regularly on the bronze coins of Pergamum are Asklepios and Athena, who had important sanctuaries in the city (Herakles, although the father of the founder of Pergamum, only appeared on some silver issues of the third century BC). If the coins date to the period of Pergamene control, the types do not

149 Bronze coins of Heraclea in Bithynia also show a young Herakles, with a laurel wreath and lionskin knotted around his neck on their obverses (*BMC Pontus*, p. 142, nos. 28–29), dated 338–306 BC.

150 Griffin 2004. I am grateful to Paul Kosmin for the suggestion of the hawk; he also noted that the bird may refer to Antiochus Hierax, although the use of the bird continues long after the death of Hierax.

151 Ashton 2012, p. 199. Frey-Kupper (2013) now has a series with a wreath around the reverse type, dated ca. 190 BC, from her meticulous work in Sicily; I thank her for our stimulating discussion on the problem of the civic mint at Sardis. I also appreciate the comments of Peter van Alfen and the students at the 2014 ANS Graduate Summer Program.

152 *BMC Troas*, p. 96, no. 9.

153 *BMC Lydia*, p. 44, nos. 20–23.

appear to refer to the Attalid rulers. However, there are also significant differences between the Seleucid and the Sardian Herakles. On the civic coinage, Herakles is specifically shown as a Lydian version of the god. He may then appear as the founder of the Lydian dynasty. Herodotus noted that Agron was a descendant of Herakles; he replaced the former line of the descendants of Atys as rulers of Sardis, due to an oracle (Hdt. I.7). Perhaps this genealogy is why Herakles is shown as having the lionskin knotted around his throat, so that one could recognize him as distinct from the lionskin helmeted type preferred under Alexander and his successors. This is the Lydian Herakles, specifically the Herakles associated with Sardis. The same impulse may be why Apollo is consistently linked to Herakles and shown on the reverse with a hawk. The combination may refer to the oracle that promoted the founding of a new ruling family; the hawk emphasized that oracle.[154]

One technical feature of the Herakles/Apollo coins may also help narrow down the century of minting. The reverse of the coins were made with convex dies, producing a reverse that can sometimes be identified by feel alone—one can easily fit the ball of one's thumb into the concave reverse. This type of die is not usual in Seleucid bronze coins (I have found no other mention of such dies used to produce civic coinages), but convex dies do appear, mostly in coinages to the south or far to the east of Sardis.[155] However, a bronze coin made with convex reverse dies was minted under Antiochus II (r. 261–246 BC), which may be when the technique became fashionable in Sardis.

Thus far, stylistic, iconographic, metrological, and technical arguments have given possibilities, and no good pointers to a date before or after 189 or 133 BC. The status of Sardis as a *polis* may have had no impact on the production of civic coinages, lessening the need to find a link between the autonomy of Sardis and the opening of the mint. Thus, we need not be uncomfortable in finding no good parallels in the weight standard of the Sardis civic coins to Seleucid or Pergamene bronze coins. On the other hand, the historical circumstances of the aftermath of the Peace of Apamea would seem to be an opportune time for a city to mint, as there was less central oversight of economic issues; this oversight became exponentially less after the area was ceded to the Romans. The iconography of the coins could speak to either the interest of Seleucid rulers or possibly a sense of pride in the indigenous founders of the Sardian city; they do not clearly speak to Pergamene control. However, there are good parallels certainly by the second century BC for some of the types. The technical production of the coins—especially the series made with convex reverse dies—finds parallels in Seleucid, and especially third-century BC mint practices.

An analysis of the archaeological contexts in which the coins were found can help resolve the issue. As noted in Section 3.2.1, a small purse was lost in a house fire in the late fourth or early third century BC, a date confirmed by the pottery found with the coins. There were no civic coins found in this purse. Additionally, a few tombs contained bronze coins of Alexander the Great and his successors, and the date of the pottery (when available) does not conflict with the late fourth- or early third-century BC date of the coins.[156] No civic coins are attested in tombs of this date.

Other archaeological contexts help us narrow the window of minting:

1. A small denomination coin, carrying types of Herakles and a kantharos, was found in a grave with a coin of Antiochus I; unfortunately, the coin came from Bell's reporting of early excavations, so a complete list of the Hellenistic pottery in the tomb did not survive (Grave S3).[157] If the association with the coin of Antiochus I stands, this would place the coin early in the sequence of the civic mint.
2. Shear recorded four intact burials with two coins, one illegible and the other the Herakles/kantharos Sardis civic coin. Rotroff and Oliver

154 Nollé (2005, p. 65) suggested that Herakles and Apollo are often linked in the East as protectors against animal plagues (perhaps still an issue for the Sardians raising their famous horses), locusts, or more generally as gods who fight as protectors of civilization.

155 Van Alfen also showed me two gold coins in the ANS collection that are said to be from Pergamum in the mid- to late 330s, also made with convex reverse dies; it is possible that this mint technique was favored in western Asia Minor for a period of time. I also note that Weisser et al. 2014, p. 657 identifies three otherwise illegible coins from the Priene excavations as Hellenistic due to their "characteristic" concave reverse.

156 Rotroff and Oliver 2003, pp. 15, 189, 206–8.

157 Bell 1916; see also Rotroff and Oliver 2003, p. 208.

dated the associated pottery to the first century BC.[158] Although the coin can only present a *terminus post quem* for the archaeologist, most of the graves appear to show some correlation between the closing date of the pottery and the coin included, hence my hesitation in assigning a date to this coin.

3. A large Tyche/Zeus Lydios coin comes from another grave (Bell 1916, Grave 61). It was the only coin recorded from the burial, which appears to have been a multiple burial, given the large number of lamps and unguentaria given as grave gifts. Rotroff and Oliver noted the presence of first-century BC material, though there was pottery from earlier centuries also present.[159] It is apparent that the practice of putting coins in graves waned considerably in the second half of the third and second centuries BC, leading to few datable contexts for Sardis civic coins in cemeteries.
4. Hellenistic strata were dug in sector ByzFort,[160] although the chronology of the strata was not always clearly separated from Early Imperial levels. It is worth noting that one Herakles/Apollo coin (no. 52.54) came from a level that appears to have had Hellenistic finds, but was dated by the coin. Three coins, one of Antiochus III (no. 86.1), one of Antiochus II (no. **75.1**) and a Dionysos/panther from the Sardis mint (no. 56.1) were all from a related Lot.
5. Berlin identified a Hellenistic dump in sector MMS/S, not associated with any architecture, but probably refuse from nearby houses.[161] She dated the pottery in the dump to the mid-third to mid-second centuries BC. Associated with the pottery were seven Hellenistic coins, four of which were legible: a coin of Antiochus III, minted at Sardis (no. 90.2) dating 213–203 BC (?); one from the mint at Pergamum (no. 23.5) dating between 215 and the early second century BC; and two Herakles/Apollo coins (nos. 52.114, 52.130). This context of the mid-third to mid-second century BC provides welcome reinforcement for the coins in ByzFort.
6. A civic coin was found in the upper Hellenistic fill of the Theater (no. **52.46**); noted above in Section 3.2.3, Berlin dated the pottery of that fill to 175–150 BC.[162] This coin, from the Herakles/Apollo series, had been worn and countermarked by the time it was deposited in the fill. The presence of the coin in a fill of this date now shows that the post-133 BC date of the opening of the civic mint can no longer hold: the civic issues can thus be dated to after the early third century and prior to 150 BC.
7. A Hellenistic fill from MD2 can be dated by the pottery to ca. 270/260–240/230 BC.[163] One coin was found under a plaster floor of a room remodeled in the Hellenistic period; it was a coin bearing the types Dionysos/forepart of lion (no. **53.1**). As suggested below, this is a small denomination that could have been paired with the Herakles/Apollo denomination. The fill shows that the civic mint opened in the third century BC.

The mint at Sardis was opened for the striking of bronze coins sometime between 300 and 280 BC, when Lysimachus had coins struck. It appears to have operated on a low level for Seleucid coinages, until Antiochus II ramped up production; this is when the first convex dies are recorded for Sardian coins. The Seleucid mint produced bronze coins for Seleucus II, until the revolt of Hierax. Hoover assigns no bronzes to the mint during the reign of Antiochus Hierax.[164] Indeed, there is a gap in the bronze coins until Achaeus strikes. Antiochus III resumed minting bronze coins during and after the siege of the city; these were the last royal issues to come from the mint at Sardis.[165] If the civic coins were struck after 189 BC, to replace the royal bronzes which had been supplied

158 Shear 1922, pp. 401–3; Rotroff and Oliver 2003, pp. 204–5.

159 Bell 1916; Rotroff and Oliver 2003, pp. 189–90.

160 ByzFort 85.11 Lots 2 and 3, "red gravel."

161 MMS/S 94.2 Lot 30; Berlin in Berlin and Kosmin, forthcoming.

162 Berlin 2016, p. 353.

163 Roosevelt, Final Field Report: MD2 96.1, p. 3; Berlin, Compiled Report 2015, p. 37.

164 Hoover in Houghton and Lorber 2002, I: 107–11, 320.

165 For the Sardis mint in the late fourth to early second centuries, see Evans in Berlin and Kosmin, forthcoming.

to the city by the Seleucid kings, this barely seems enough time to mint a coin, have it become worn, then countermarked, before being deposited by 175–150 BC (e.g., as coin no. **52.46**). There does not seem to be much reason to countermark the coin after 189 but before 150 BC.

Hence, I suggest that perhaps the Herakles/Apollo coins were minted during the "gap" in royal bronze issues, when the mint was actively striking silver, and when the technology of the convex die had been introduced—that is, between ca. 245 and 220 BC, at the moment when Seleucid power faltered, consumed by inter-dynastic rivalries and external conflict.[166] The striking of fiduciary bronze coins would have had the added benefit of making a healthy profit for the city at a time when taxes may not have been regularly paid. Coins of Antiochus II tend to have a die axis of 12 and are struck with straight-sided dies; the Herakles/Apollo coins also tend to 12 o'clock positions, but the Apollo/club coins do not. On the Herakles/Apollo coins, the Apollo reverse refers to the Antiochene Apollo, but he is portrayed in a Lydian manner. The Herakles type finds its closest parallel in mid-third-century BC coins from Heraclea; perhaps the types refer to the ancient Lydian ruling family in a time of political upheaval.[167] The date does not contradict the coins found in Hellenistic strata in MMS/S, MD2, and ByzFort. They would supplement the civic coins from other mints found in the excavations. It is possible that the coins continued to be struck through the early second century BC, when magistrates' names were spelled out in full.[168]

As argued above, the Apollo/club coins are a distinctly different series, likely minted at a different time than the Herakles/Apollo coins. Unfortunately, since there are significantly fewer numbers of these coins, none were found in Hellenistic strata to help us figure out when they were minted. It is only clear that the Sardians returned to the Apollo-Herakles type pair and lessened the weight and diameter of the flan. I would suggest that when the Apollo/club coins were minted, the Herakles/Apollo coins (and other earlier issues) still in circulation were countermarked with a stamp using the reverse type of the new coin. The stamp marked the new denomination.

Johnston noted that Hellenistic denominations were "almost always distinguished by size and certain types tended to be used consistently within a coinage for certain sizes."[169] In her earlier study, she suggested that "one would like the Herakles/Apollo to be the larger and the Apollo/club the smaller denomination, but both vary considerably in weight and fabric and no consistent distinction can be made."[170] In her later reconstruction, the Herakles/Apollo and the Apollo/club were two different denominations, of 4 (?) and 3, or 3 and 2 chalkoi; the Herakles/kantharos coin (which must have been a very small issue) provided the third division. This set is matched at some later period by Tyche/Zeus Lydios; Dionysos/horned panther; and Dionysos/forepart of lion, though there are also few of these coins surviving.[171] Johnston focused on these six type-pairs (Table 2.1).

Two type pairs were almost certainly minted around 189 BC, possibly until 133 BC. The larger denomination carries the head of Artemis, who is identified by the bow and quiver at her back; on the reverse is a standing Athena who extends her arm to hold a Nike. The magistrate's name is given in full. Only three examples have been found in the Sardis excavations, but with three different magistrates' names.[172] While Artemis is surely local, the Athena

166 See Ma 1999, pp. 43–50 for an assessment of the period; Ma (p. 47) suggested that the civic coins were minted after 226, when Sardis "escaped Seleukid authority . . . as [an] 'autonomous' city under the Attalids." Sherwin-White and Kuhrt (1993, pp. 182–83) had already suggested that there was a "brief period of independence from Seleucid rule in ca. 226–224, which is thought to be indicated . . . by the minting of independent silver coins." Note that Cox (1950, p. 47) proposed autonomous coins were produced in Antioch during the reign of Seleucus IV or even Antiochus III, when there was an intense need for small change.

167 Two control marks are paralleled on one silver coin and one bronze of Seleucus II and the Herakles/Apollo coin (no. **52.19**); cf. Houghton and Lorber 2002, nos. 654 (5), 655 (1); and M13 no. 55.6; cf. Houghton and Lorber 2002, no. 657 (1).

168 Johnston (Buttrey et al. 1981, pp. 80–81) provided comparanda of moneyers' names and names of local dignitaries in Sardis; several are dated to the first century BC. The Sestus inscription is a *terminus post quem* of when magistrates' names would appear on coins; thus it would appear that by the second century BC, magistrates are allowed to place their names on coins (see Ashton 2012, p. 202).

169 Johnston 2007, p. 3.

170 Buttrey et al. 1981, p. 80.

171 Johnston 2007, p. 3 n. 12.

172 M7 GR 243, 244; M13 no. 58.1.

Table 2.1 Comparison of suggested denominations, Hellenistic period, Sardis mint.

Johnston	Denomination	Suggested Chronology
Herakles/Apollo	large	Earlier: post 133 BC
Apollo/club	medium	Earlier: post 133 BC
Herakles/kantharos	small	Earlier: post 133 BC
Herakles/lion	large	Earlier?: post 133 BC
Tyche/Zeus Lydios	large	Later: post 133 BC
Dionysos/panther	medium	Later: post 133 BC
Dionysos/forepart of lion	small	Later: post 133 BC
Artemis/Athena	large	Uncertain or not mentioned
Dionysos/Demeter	medium	Uncertain or not mentioned
Evans	**Denomination**	**Suggested Chronology**
Tyche/Zeus Lydios	large	3rd century BC?
Herakles/Apollo	medium	245–220 BC into 2nd century BC
Dionysos/forepart of lion	small	3rd century BC
Artemis/Athena	large (Attalid 4-unit?)	189–133 BC
Dionysos/Demeter	medium (Attalid 2-unit?)	189–133 BC
Herakles/lion	large	2nd–1st century BC
Apollo/club	medium	2nd–1st century BC
Dionysos/panther	small	2nd–1st century BC
Herakles/kantharos	small	Highly uncertain, possibly early

must refer to the patron deity of the Attalids, and perhaps the establishment of the Panathenaic Games at Sardis.[173] The median weight of the coins is 7.98 g, equivalent to the 4 (?) unit of the Attalid system. The smaller denomination, which is likely to have been struck concurrently, depicts Dionysos and Demeter standing leaning on a long torch (no. 59). Only two examples were found in the current excavations; Johnston lists no coins of this type, and neither coin was found in a Hellenistic context. The weight, the median of which was 5.65 g, must be the Attalid 2 (?) unit. Dionysos appears on several Hellenistic and several more Imperial issues, most probably because of his protection of the rich agricultural lands around Sardis. Apollonius described the Sardians as being "special wards" of Demeter in the first century AD; she is likely here as another agricultural patron.[174] The large and small denomination coins have a style that is very different from the other eight issues from Sardis; they more closely resemble Pergamene die cutting. Thus, sometime between 189 and 133 BC the use of full magistrates' names is known on coin dies of Sardis.

A small issue (only known from two coins in the current as well as earlier Princeton excavations) has the head of Herakles helmeted in a lionskin and the reverse of a lion walking right, a fly over top, the legend ΣΑΡΔΙΑΝΩΝ arcing over all, and the magistrate's name ΜΕΝΕΜΑΧΟΣ in the exergue (no. 54). The style of the head is very different from any other Herakles on Sardian coins, as it is long and thin, with a large, upturned eye. The median weight of the issues is 7.2 g, which does fit comfortably within the Attic 4 (?) unit denomination, although neither the style nor the iconography compares favorably to Pergamene coins. The walking lion reverse became a favorite theme for Lydian coins of the third century AD, and there exists a late first century BC coin of Amyntas with a similar reverse, although the head of Herakles shows him as bearded, not helmeted, and carrying a club.[175] Johnston thought the Sardis coin was early, due to the "dumpy flan" of the example

173 Buttrey et al. 1981, p. 81.

174 Penella 1975, pp. 308–9; cf. Sappho frag. 96.

175 *BMC Galatia*, p. 3, no. 9.

she found;[176] the coin I identified was not nearly as dumpy. The inclusion of the full magistrate's name on the Sardian coin should place this issue in the second or first century BC. Both coins were countermarked with the same countermark, probably in Sardis (see App. 1). Neither coin was found in a Hellenistic context. The weight may place it as a double of the Apollo/club issue.

Johnston suggested that two issues were probably minted as a set, the Tyche/Zeus Lydios and the Dionysos/forepart of lion.[177] The Tyche/Zeus Lydios coin (no. **51**) would be the larger denomination, with a median of 7.15 g; the flans are large and fairly thin. The weight and style have no obvious parallels to Seleucid coins; the weight may perhaps place this coin in the Attalid 4 (?) unit denomination. The magistrate's name is only ever given as a monogram, some instances of which are shared with Dionysos/panther and Dionysos/forepart of lion. As Johnston noted, the types are typical of Sardis, in the depiction of the turreted and veiled Tyche and the Lydian Zeus. Two of these coins were countermarked with the club countermark (see App. 1), in Sardis in the late second or first century BC. For the smaller coin (no. **53**), the reverse depicting the forepart of lion recalls, as Johnston noted, the familiar coin types of Lysimachus and his successors.[178] Like the larger denomination, the flans are broad. Unlike the larger denomination, the ethnic runs in a straight line along the top of the reverse type. The median weight of these coins is 3.54 g, which may perhaps place this issue in the Attalid 1 (?) unit.

Another small denomination has a helmeted young Herakles on the obverse, paired with a high-stemmed kantharos on the reverse (no. **57**). While the kantharos can reflect Herakles' prodigious appetite for wine, it likely refers to Dionysos. The ethnic is broken into two parts, each one running alongside the drinking vessel; the moneyer's monogram is always present. There are no obvious iconographic or stylistic parallels to this coin. The median weight is 3.29 g, which again may possibly reflect an Attalid 1 (?) unit denomination. Because of their "dumpy" flans and some parallels between this coinage and the Apollo/club series, Johnston suggested this functioned as a "slightly smaller denomination that the Apollo/club."[179] It is unlikely to have functioned as such, since the median for the Apollo/club is 3.75 g. As noted above, the Herakles/kantharos coin was found in a tomb that contained a coin of Antiochus I, and another one was found in a tomb which was dated by the pottery to the mid-second to first century BC. The two tombs show a wide range of possible deposition dates for this coin type.

The Dionysos/panther issue is known in fifteen examples from the modern and current excavations, none of them in Hellenistic strata (no. **56**). The median weight is 4.7 g and not clearly part of any denomination, unless it is an Attalid half unit. Johnston noted that the weights fluctuated (she recorded a low of 3.83 g and a high of 6.16 g, which is not entirely dissimilar to other issues, see Fig. 2.11), and thus the coins may have been issued over a long period of time. She found monogram links with the Herakles/kantharos and the Tyche/Zeus Lydios issues. The result would be a set of three denominations. She also noted the presence of a horned panther breaking a spear in its mouth on a year 20 (114 BC) cistophorus carrying the name of Sardis.[180]

2.3 The Early Imperial Era: Augustus to the Second Century

In 27 BC, Augustus created Asia as a consular province, and although Sardis was identified as being in an area of influence, or *conventus*, there was no provincial capital. The Roman East remained relatively untouched by Imperial bronze (or silver) coinage, as the eastern cities had been producing small change for many years. Where once numismatists called the coins minted while the cities were under Roman authority "Greek Imperials," I will use the more preferred term, Roman Provincial coinage. Moreover, where the lack of emperors' portraits on the coins were considered a measure of autonomy for the city (hence, "pseudo-autonomous coins" for those without Imperial portraits), this no longer seems a valid distinction; it does not appear that the city needed permission from

176 Buttrey et al. 1981, p. 80.

177 Buttrey et al. 1981, p. 81.

178 Buttrey et al. 1981, p. 81.

179 Buttrey et al. 1981, p. 81.

180 Buttrey et al. 1981, p. 81.

the emperor to mint.[181] The production of a coinage may be more strongly linked to the desires of a local aristocrat to fund an issue, as part of the euergetism that developed in the cities in the Imperial period.[182] Hence, my catalog combines the coins featuring the head of the Imperial family with coins that depict a god or goddess on the obverse; I have placed these in chronological order.

Beyond the gesture that soothed city pride or announced the benefaction of a local noble, scholars are still uncertain as to why and when a city would produce an issue of bronze coins. Most scholars think that the pressure from the local markets, which needed small coin for daily transactions, is a sufficient explanation, just as in the Hellenistic period.[183] Harl argued that taxes were paid regionally in bronze coin, and the bankers converted the coin into silver denominations, returning the bronzes to "the exchange tables in markets hungry for small change"; he also saw the need for bronze coin to distribute during festivals, or when emperors visited.[184] Johnston suggested, at least for the later period, that bronze coins were minted for "non-economic reasons (as acts of euergetism by prominent citizens, to celebrate special events such as imperial visits or games or new civic titles)."[185] Although Constantina Katsari admitted that civic pride surfaced in legends boasting that a city was "first in Asia" or in the number of neokorate priesthoods owned by the city, she did not think this was the primary reason to coin. Instead, she emphasized the profit that a mint would make on the coins, especially when "the overvalued small denominations were exchanged for silver denarii."[186] Since there were no soldiers stationed in or near Sardis, we can remove the army as the consumer and possible producer of coin.[187] However, we are very much at a loss to suggest exact times when bronze coins were produced and how the city determined how large the issue would be.[188] These bronze issues can be (but at Sardis often are not) issued in conjunction with silver coins.

Augustan strata are not clearly distinguished yet at Sardis. It is thus hard to gauge the economic situation of the city, but we at least hear that a temple to Augustus was built during his reign (*IGR* 4.1756). Numismatically, the imposition of an Imperial government changed the city greatly, although there may have been a gap between the last years of the Hellenistic mint and the opening of the mint under Augustus, which Andrew Burnett, Michel Amandry, and Pere Pau Ripollès place around 10–1 BC.[189] The issues are small and intermittent, as are all the issues through the second century AD, and usually only two or three denominations are produced.[190] Two denominations are standard for the mint through the reign of Nero (one ca. 19 mm and the other ca. 15 mm); a third, large denomination was also briefly minted under Augustus.[191] Save for special issues such as the coins from "Asia" (CA coinage) of an uncertain mint, and coins from the Corinth mint, they do not fit with the Imperial bronze system; although some eastern bronze coins were reformed to do so, most coinages retained their earlier Hellenistic standards.[192] The coins that were minted on a Roman standard (from the "Asia" mint) will be discussed separately.

Augustan coins from the excavation are all from one denomination (1 assarion), 19–20 mm, and a little over 6 g; that is, the coins are broader than their Hellenistic counterparts and heavier than the Apollo/club coins, although they would fit comfortably in the Herakles/Apollo series (except one, see below). The new authority is announced by the presence of

181 Burnett 2011, pp. 2, 6, 8; Katsari 2011, pp. 225–26; Amandry 2012, pp. 394–99.

182 Harl 1996, p. 108; Dmitriev 2005, p. 305; Katsari 2011, p. 213.

183 See Mitchell 1993, p. 242; Mitchell and Katsari 2005, p. xxvi; Katsari 2011, p. 220; Burnett 2011, p. 2.

184 Harl 1997, pp. 24–25; cf. 1996, pp. 108, 240.

185 Johnston 2007, p. 242.

186 Katsari 2011, p. 214.

187 Economic historians of the Roman period still emphasize the importance of the army in terms of demand for bronze coins, but this cannot be a reason for the Sardis mint to coin bronzes; see Mitchell 1993, p. 255; Ziegler 1996, p. 121; Katsari 2005, pp. 261–62, 267. I will address this issue in the third-century coinages, in Section 2.4.

188 Katsari 2011, p. 225; Amandry 2012, pp. 395, 398.

189 Burnett, Amandry, and Ripollés 2005, p. 487.

190 Johnston 1983, p. 60.

191 Burnett, Amandry, and Ripollés 2005, p. 488.

192 Johnston 2007, p. 3; Spoerri Butcher 2009, pp. 223–24; Burnett 2011, p. 2.

the head of the emperor on the obverse, replacing the gods of the civic coins. As is argued below, Hellenistic coins continued to circulate for a long time; perhaps the city fathers minted the Early Imperial coins on a standard that would allow these coins to circulate in tandem with the Hellenistic coins.

There is one possible exception to the rule that an emperor's head is found on all obverses, a coin that is a revival of the Herakles/Apollo type. The current excavations unearthed a specimen with the name of Mousaios on the reverse (no. **148.1**). This magistrate is recorded as a *strategos* in 5 BC, when an envoy was sent to Augustus congratulating him on behalf of Gaius, who had just assumed the *toga virilis*.[193] His name appears on a coin minted for Augustus with a reverse of the Demoi of Pergamum and Sardis, which Burnett, Amandry, and Ripollès suggested was minted ca. 1 AD.[194] The Herakles/Apollo coin types reappear on a coin with the names of Opinas and Akiamos, a coin which is dated early in Tiberius' reign due to the simple city ethnic.[195] Although Mousaios could have served as *strategos* in 5 BC and later as a magistrate named on a coin from 14–17 AD, the Herakles/Apollo Mousaios coin should be dated to the Augustan period for several reasons: one is that the ethnic is found on the obverse (ΣΑΡΔΙΑΝΩΝ), replacing the single-word legend of Augustus's coins (ΣΕΒΑΣΤΟΥ). On the coins of Opinas and Akiamos, the ethnic moved to the reverse and both names were placed on the obverse. The relatively broad flan contrasts with the more compact Tiberian coin. And when magistrates appear on the coins of Augustus, they are singular; on the later coins they are paired. Mousaios makes better chronological sense in the Augustan period.[196]

Coins of the Early Imperial period were used for a long time; this phenomenon is not limited to Sardis.[197] As a result, many of the Imperial coins are too worn for identification. The Augustan-era coins that are found in Sardis do come from a variety of mints (possibly due to the intermittent striking of coin and lack of Late Hellenistic issues; Fig. 2.14). What is remarkable is that the pattern of mints resembles that of the first century BC, when coins from mints to the west and northwest far outnumber coins from Lydia. This map does not include two copies in bronze (probably once silvered) of a denarius minted in quantities, and imitated in many more, depicting Gaius and Lucius (no. 218), since scholars have not suggested a place for the mint. I also understand that since the Early Imperial coins were used for so long that this map does not give a snapshot of coins in circulation in Sardis during the reign of Augustus, but thought the exercise worth doing to see a selection of mints that were available to Sardians in the Imperial period.

Since bronze coins were minted on differing standards in various cities, we would expect only local or regional coins to appear in the excavations.[198] Johnston argued that local circulation was true of Anatolia, but not entirely true in Sardis in the first to third centuries, although she conceded that the largest number of mints represented in the excavation coins is found in the third century. The rough percentages of locally-minted coins she noted as being 50–80% in Troy, Priene, Ephesus, Aphrodisias, and Side, percentages which are confirmed by the few hoards we have of Roman Provincial coins. The remaining 20–50% are drawn from regional or extra-regional mints. This is in contrast to the Athenian Agora excavations, where 94% of the coins found were minted in Athens.[199] The current excavations in Sardis appear to confirm Johnston's argument.

Coins from "Asia," though the subject of specialized studies, are also from an uncertain mint, likely in the province of Asia (possibly at Ephesus).[200] These coins appear to have been minted on the Imperial standard and are thus given names of

193 Buckler and Robinson 1932, no. 8, pt. 1.

194 Burnett, Amandry, and Ripollès 2005, p. 487.

195 Burnett, Amandry, and Ripollès 2005, no. 2990 and p. 487.

196 It is not a Hellenistic issue, given the style of the head and the use of the ethnic on the obverse. The names that appear on the coins may not be magistrates, as Burnett points out. Without a designation they may only point out who was responsible for paying for the issue; eponymous magistrates; or simply a "wider mixture of people drawn from the city élites" (2011, p. 4). We know that Mousaios was a *strategos* in 5 BC, but we have no corresponding information about Opinas or Akiamos.

197 e.g., MacDonald 1976, p. 25.

198 Burnett 2011, p. 27.

199 Johnston 2007, pp. 5–6 and n. 22.

200 Burnett, Amandry, and Ripollès 2005, p. 380.

denominations of bronze coins in the west.[201] Katsari suggested that they were minted for payments to troops or "to cover for local deficiencies in the circulation of smaller denominations; but only in emergency cases."[202] Burnett, Amandry, and Ripollès proposed that the coinage was meant to "impose a unified currency on the Roman model on the communities of the eastern Empire," an effort that did not progress beyond these coins.[203] A number of these were identified both by Buttrey and in the current excavations (nos. **98**, 99). Many of them are halved, a phenomenon particular to Sardis.[204]

Disaster struck Sardis in 17 AD in the form of a devastating earthquake. Sardis was one of twelve cities in Asia that Tiberius favored with an Imperial decree to remit taxes for five years, along with a grant of ten million sesterces to restore buildings (Tac. *Ann.* 2.47). Great fills that were clean-up from the earthquake and rebuilding after the event are found in the terraces in Fields 49, 55, the Upper Terrace south of HoB, and on the site of the later Bath-Gymnasium Complex.[205] It appears that the city did not suffer another serious economic blow until well after the Imperial period.

Numismatically, the city responded with coins showing Tiberius raising the stricken Tyche (no. 152). In an inscription, Tiberius was called "founder of the city,"[206] and the coin legend is only slightly more subtle, renaming the city Caesarian Sardis.[207] Julio-Claudian coins tend to come from local mints more often than the Augustan coins (Fig. 2.15). The current and earlier excavations report coins mostly from Lydia. Coins of the Flavian era are even scarcer; no mints other than Sardis and Smyrna could be identified in Flavian coins from the current excavations, in part due to the wear on these coins, which must have been deposited long after the first century ended. Given the amount of money spent on infrastructure, one would expect coins from farther afield, but Katsari noticed the isolation of the circulation pool of Asia. She thought that the coins were traded mostly along the road systems.[208]

Post-earthquake Sardis was not lacking in building projects, in part due to the economic stimulus provided by Tiberius. Inscriptions record the completion of the aqueduct;[209] repairs were probably undertaken in the Theater and the Temple to Hera (?) (*SEG* 28.928). Hanfmann suggested that the stadium also dated to the later first century.[210] The monumental Wadi B Temple, which the excavators suggested was probably dated to the Julio-Claudian or Flavian period, seems more likely to be Julio-Claudian (see Section 3.3.2).[211] There are modest graves in HoB and areas farther from the city center, and an impressive chamber tomb as well.[212]

Barbara Levick suggested that the Flavian period was one of intense road building across the province, due to the milestones found along the old "royal road" and the north-south route between Smyrna and Adramyteum.[213] She also thought the province profited by the presence of legions in the northwest and on the Euphrates, necessitating the delivery of "food, drink, housing, clothing, armour and weapons," some of which may have passed through Sardis—this would have at least enriched the transporters and hospitality industry.[214] Magie argued for a period of moderate prosperity in Sardis in the Flavian period, due to an inscription noting a "modest gift" of grain to the city.[215]

Hanfmann suggested that rebuilding the city was slow, and the period after 55 AD was a period of recession, in large part due to the lack of Early

201 Burnett 2011, p. 9.

202 Katsari 2011, p. 59.

203 Burnett, Amandry, and Ripollés 2005, p. 371.

204 Buttrey et al. 1981, p. 92.

205 Cahill 2015, p. 419; Cahill 2014a, p. 125; cf. Hanfmann 1983, p. 141.

206 Hanfmann 1983, p. 144.

207 For such types in Asia Minor, see Delrieux 2012.

208 Katsari 2011, pp. 191–92.

209 See also Early Imperial waterworks at ByzFort: Greenewalt et al. 1990, pp. 155–59.

210 Hanfmann 1983, pp. 141–43; see also Yegül's reconstruction of the phasing of the Bath-Gymnasium Complex (1986, p. 5; 1987, pp. 47–49).

211 Ratté, Howe, and Foss 1986, pp. 67–68; Burrell 2004, 100–3; Greenewalt 2006, p. 176; Greenewalt 2007, pp. 743–44, Cahill 2015, pp. 421–22.

212 Greenewalt et al. 1990, pp. 161–64; for this phase in the city, see also Herrmann 1995; Rautman 2011, pp. 5–8.

213 See also Magie 1950, p. 570.

214 Levick 2004, p. 187.

215 Magie 1950, p. 586.

Imperial coins found on the site. He also noted signs of "class struggle and anti-Roman rebellion," famine, and general bad behavior in a letter to a local family by Plutarch and a letter to the Sardians by Apollonius of Tyana, if we can trust the latter.[216] Arjan Zuiderhoek suggested that the tension between the haves and have-nots was widespread throughout Asia, Bithynia, and Cilicia in both the first and second centuries.[217] Yet the letter to the church at Sardis in Revelation 3:1–6 (generally agreed to have been written in the late Flavian period) suggests no large-scale economic problems or civil unrest.

We know that Early Imperial coins are not common in eastern urban sites (see Fig. 2.2), reinforcing the argument that the number of excavation coins found in strata are not necessarily good indicators of economic prosperity or downturn. At Sardis, we may instead note the number of building projects occurring in the first half of the first century. Two of the largest were connected to the largest temples in Sardis: Cahill and Greenewalt suggested that the east end of the peristyle was begun in the Temple to Artemis.[218] When work was proceeding on that temple, the Wadi B Temple, which was probably largely funded by the city, was erected.[219] The cost associated with the building projects suggests that the Early Imperial period was not as bleak as Hanfmann proposed.

Second-century Sardis appears to have been a prosperous city: the Bath-Gymnasium Complex must have largely been completed, as a statue of Lucius Verus was erected in the halls; Hadrian visited the city twice; an inscription alludes to a temple to Hadrian; and the Artemis Temple was refurbished and probably housed the neokorate cult of Antoninus Pius.[220] A statue base may record a visit of Marcus Aurelius and Commodus to the city, possibly in 176.[221] As I argue in Section 3.3.2, a votive deposit shows that new attention was paid to the Wadi B Temple. In the second half of the century, the Chrysanthina Games were inaugurated.[222]

Johnston dated coins with the head of the Senate/Demeter from the Sardis mint to 80–96, since "several examples are stamped ΔOMITI on the reverse and one reverse die (*BMC* 73) was also used as the reverse for Nerva," but she noted that the die engraving is "unusually high" for the reign of Domitian.[223] The authors of *RPC* II must have disagreed, as the coin is not included in this volume, nor in the supplement (nor is it included in the online *RPC* for the Antonine period). The countermark is noted, but not pictured, in the *BMC Lydia* volume; it is noted on another British Museum specimen (and others) by Howgego.[224] Although Howgego entertained a Trajanic or later date for the countermark, suggesting that it perhaps refers to a proconsul named Domitianus (?), he recognized the argument for a Domitianic date of the mark. The style of the engraving is more often seen in Antonine coins in Sardis, especially the coins of Marcus Aurelius as Caesar (see nos. **178**, **184**). The die cutting shows the "Sardian mint style" at its best, with large, neatly-formed letters, a single figure or object in the reverse, with much empty space, using the broad flan completely.

One phenomenon of the second (and third) century is the use of dies shared within the *conventus*, a mint technique that was explored by Konrad Kraft and elucidated for the Sardis mint by Johnston.[225] Die-sharing tends to be of the obverse dies; while shared reverse dies are certainly known, they tend to be found in specialized issues, such as medallions. The obverse die sharing means that the reverses may depict images that are of specific interest to the city of minting. By the third century, shared reverse dies and shared dies for smaller issues became more common.[226] The first

216 Hanfmann 1983, pp. 142–45; cf. Dzielska 1986, pp. 38 n. 59, 54 n. 6.

217 Zuiderhoek 2009, pp. 66–67.

218 Cahill and Greenewalt 2016, p. 501.

219 As is normal for a neokorate temple: these temples are not erected with euergistic funds, but the city may have received some contributions from other cities in the conventus. See Cramme 2001, p. 56; Burrell 2004, pp. 3, 313; Heller 2006, pp. 180–82; Evans 2015, pp. 486–87.

220 Hanfmann 1983, p. 145; Cahill and Greenewalt 2016, pp. 502–4; for more honorary inscriptions of the second century, see Petzl, forthcoming.

221 Greenewalt et al. 1985, p. 79.

222 Hanfmann 1983, p. 129; see also honorific inscriptions from Sardis, Petzl, forthcoming.

223 Buttrey et al. 1981, p. 82.

224 Howgego 1985, p. 208.

225 Kraft 1972; Johnston 2007.

226 Kraft 1972, pp. 14–15.

shared obverse dies from Sardis come from the reign of Antoninus Pius, where Sardis shared with Daldis and Briula. Johnston also noted that she could discern one die engraver's hand from the 90s in Sardis, Hierapolis, Smyrna, Ancyra, and Tripolis, testifying to the problem of tracing die sharing—or perhaps just engravers or hubs. However, since there are no die links among these cities in the Flavian period, then it is the die engraver who moved, not the dies.[227]

Katsari warned that the workshop could supply cities 100–200 km away from the mint, and since the areas of shared dies overlaps, we "are unable to prove that the activities of the workshops affected the circulation of bronze coins."[228] The use of workshops may have little impact on the pool of circulation in the cities. Nor does the system of workshops mean that coins circulated more widely, especially as the cities that shared a workshop might not share weight standards. She thought that the Sardis mint was unusual in having greater numbers within the excavation coins that were produced in "distant mints"—over 500 km away—but their presence could be explained by traveling merchants, especially those carrying luxury goods.[229] While the mints of origin are fairly compact for the first half of the second century, the map does expand greatly in the second half of the century with coins from Rome, Alexandria, Corinth, and Anchialos, as well as distant mints in Anatolia such as Nicaea, Ancyra, and Pompeiopolis (compare Figs. 2.14, 2.15). This is the largest radius of any of the phases, from the Hellenistic period to the third century.

Coins from mints outside of Sardis present an interesting pattern in the first half of the second century as the number of coins minted outside of Sardis shows a great increase over the first-century coins (Fig. 2.16). Part of the reason why this was happening is because the number of coins produced at mints in Asia Minor increased, as did the number of cities minting. Along with second-century coins, first-century coins were still in circulation, as we can tell by the heavy wear on the latter. Many of the cities on the second-century map share dies in the third century with Sardis; almost all come from mints on the Sardis-Pergamum road and the southern route towards Laodicea. Rare coins come from mints outside of Lydia or Mysia.

It is only with the reign of Hadrian that western coins, in the shape of denarii, are more regularly found in the Sardis excavations.[230] It is not entirely surprising to begin to find second-century silver coins minted in Rome, as Trajan had reduced the fineness of the denarius. At the same time, the mint at Rome produced silver coins meant for circulation in cities in the East (e.g., Caesarea in Cappadocia); the eastern cities also used newly-minted or overstruck cistophori.[231] Thus, the East must have used a hodge-podge of silver coin in the second century. In Sardis, at least two bronze coins of this period were found in graves, either in the hand or mouth of the deceased. Otherwise, the coins were not found in contexts which would allow us to gauge how long they were in circulation before they were deposited. As a rule, they are less worn than first-century coins, suggesting that there are more bronze coins in circulation in the second century to supply local needs.[232]

Antonine coins, one of which was found in a sarcophagus (see Section 3.4.2) and eight which were found in the Wadi B Temple (Section 3.3.2), come from a much broader set of mints than the coins of the first half of the second century (Fig. 2.17). The mints are no longer mostly confined to the Sardis-to-Pergamum route. While Verus' journey took him south of Ephesus and the Sardis-Ancyra road (*Hist Aug. Verus* 6.9), there must have been shipments of material for the army throughout the province of Asia, leading to a wider variety of mints than in the previous half-century. However, the pattern of finds returns us to the overall pattern that Sardis saw in the second century BC, which was not found in the following centuries; that is, coins from the Aegean coast are absent and the NW-SE road seems to have suppied Sardis with its merchandise—or at least, its coins.[233]

227 Johnston 1983, pp. 60–61, 69; cf. Kraft 1972, pp. 60–62, though he found no die links.

228 Katsari 2011, p. 226.

229 Katsari 2011, pp. 226–30.

230 Although Buttrey et al. 1981, pp. 129–30 lists single coins from the Late Republic through Trajan.

231 Beckmann 2012, p. 406.

232 cf. Harl 1997, p. 225.

233 See a parallel situation—where Ephesus is largely missing from the coin record in the Imperial period—in Aphrodisias (MacDonald 1976, p. 40). No Sardis city coins are reported from the Ephesus excavations, nor are any described from Sagalassus finds.

The Early Imperial phase is largely missing from most other excavation catalogs in the East: cities with a normal profile (Butrint, Corinth, Pergamum, Ephesus, and Caesarea Maritima; see Fig. 2.2), to which we can add Sagalassus, Aphrodisias, Tarsus, and Zeugma, report few coins until the time of Hadrian (except the uncertain first to third century AD category). It could be that the lack of second-century coin is due to wear on the flan, making these coins unidentifiable; but in my experience, second-century coins show much less wear than first-century coins. The normal profile cities, except Corinth, show a small peak of coins that were minted in the reigns of Nerva, Trajan, and Hadrian, dropping slightly (except in the case of Butrint) during the Antonine period. Priene, Athens, and Kenchreai show very different patterns. There are two other correspondences among the cities that do not show up in the calculations: most of the cities pull coins only from mints in their adjacent areas; silver coins very rarely appear until the time of Trajan (after which they only remain rare).

2.4 The Third Century

The third century at Sardis saw a new level of civic activity. For instance, the Marble Court of the Bath-Gymnasium Complex was dedicated to Geta, Caracalla, and Julia Domna, and perhaps within the complex or nearby, statues were erected for the Imperial family and other dignitaries, through Severus Alexander.[234] Several other large building projects may have been completed in this century. Although Sardis supported Severus' rival Clodius Albinus, Elagabalus later funded the celebration of the Elagabalia Games. A statue base to a "world champion" boxer and pancratist shows the importance of games held here. The city could then compete with Ephesus in calling herself "the metropolis of Greece, Asia, and all Lydia," and home to three neokorate cults.[235] The municipal mint, like most other mints in Asia, produced great numbers of issues, often with types commemorating local gods and heroes.[236]

Nevertheless, information from the city falls silent in the second half of the third century, in part due to the lack of municipal coins, as mints all over the East closed. We do hear of destruction by Goths in Ephesus, Didyma, and Miletus, and Sassanian Persians raiding the eastern part of the province. No evidence has surfaced in Sardis for physical destruction by either party, but if the Roman city wall was built at this point, it may have been in response to perceived external threats. That Sardis remained an important hub of the province is seen as in Diocletian's promotion of the city to the capital of his new province of Lydia.[237]

Most scholars are ready to see the issues from the mints as reflective of the movement of the emperor and especially the army, but some scholars are ready to sever the connection. They point out that Imperial or military activities do not always align with the chronology of coins coming from the mint.[238] Thus, the proposed two trips that Caracalla made to Sardis cannot be deduced from new issues or types on the coins.[239] The reason why coin production increased in this century is still highly uncertain. Katsari suggested that provincial governors ordered the increase due to the lack of small change for the markets. The central authority would thus explain the use of centralized workshops.[240]

Along with a greater number of issues produced after 195 came the opportunity for more die sharing. Sardis is one of four large workshops Kraft isolated in Asia (with coins coming from, but the workshop not necessarily housed in, Sardis, Smyrna, Ephesus, and Pergamum).[241] During various reigns, coins from the mint at Sardis are linked by dies, die chains, or sometimes stylistic analysis to Acrasus, Ancyra, Apamea, Cilbiani Inferiores, Daldis, Dioshieron, Eumenia, Germe, Gordus Julia, Hadrianotherai, Hierapolis, Hypaepa, Laodicea, Maeonia, Magnesia ad

234 Greenewalt et al. 1985, p. 79; Yegül 1986, pp. 5–6, 12–13, 69, 146.

235 For municipal competition for these titles, see Heller 2006; Amandry 2012, p. 401.

236 Hanfmann 1983, p. 145; Evans in Berlin and Kosmin, forthcoming.

237 Hanfmann 1983, pp. 145–46: Rautman 2011, p. 8.

238 Scholars who connect the minting of coins primarily to the movement of the military and emperor: Johnston 1984, pp. 255–56; Katsari 2005, p. 267 (later modified), and Ziegler 1996. Arguing against this idea is Elton 2005, pp. 297–300; see also Katsari 2011, pp. 40, 217.

239 Hanfmann 1983, p. 145.

240 Katsari 2003; 2005, p. 267.

241 Kraft 1972, karte 1–7, 11.

Sipylum, Philadelphia, Saitta, Silandros, Stratonicea, Synaus, Tabala, Themisonium, Thyateira, and Tripolis.[242] It is not yet certain if the coins were minted in one location (or several), and then distributed to the cities, or if the dies and engravers traveled to the cities to mint, although Kraft favored the latter.[243] These workshops produced up to seven denominations, and probably used worn first- and second-century coins as flans.[244]

The workshop cities to some extent mirror the third-century coins found in the city (Fig. 2.18). The distribution of mints shows the impact of the workshop system, especially when compared to the map of the second half of the second century (Fig. 2.17). In the third century, the coins are from many more towns in Lydia, Ionia, Phrygia, and Caria; they are no longer just confined to the major transportation routes in and out of Sardis. Interestingly, coins from Ephesus are once again a large contingent, which had not been the case for many years. The map confirms Johnston's suggestion that workshop areas heavily affect circulation patterns: she predicted that the Sardis excavations would produce coins from Pisidia (Antioch) and Pamphylia (Attalia), with Bithynia and Pontus in a separate circulation pool.[245] A quick glance at all the distribution maps, from the Hellenistic period on, confirms local bronze circulation pools. The greatest number of mints represented at Sardis occurs in the first three quarters of the third century. Sardis never demonstrated a strong connection to Syria, nor did many coins come from western mints.[246]

Mints all over the East closed between 250 and 270; after this, only Imperial mints supplied small change. The local mints may have closed because bronze coins become too expensive to produce, due to increasing inflation that drove up the prices of goods.[247] Johnston argued that that the coins were not minted to provide small change since the issues were sporadic, but admitted that the large Severan issues could have been "intended to remedy a general shortage at the end of the second century." Many of the reverses refer to festivals or games, a city's status, homonoia agreements, new buildings, visits by the emperor, and benefactions to the city; they are markers of civic pride.[248]

By 270, billon coins replaced copper-alloy small change in all cities of the empire, and Sardis was no exception to this rule. It is not clear that radiate billon coins immediately drove out bronze coins, but they did circulate for a long time, as most are found in fourth- or fifth-century contexts (e.g., nos. 270.1, 276.2, 282.1, 288.1, 292.2, 292.7, 292.9, 292.10, 294.1, 295.1, 297.5, 297.6, 300.1, 300.3, 303.1, and see below, "barbarous radiates").

Johnston suggested that many coins were recalled and reminted ca. 200 and again ca. 260; at the same time, coin flans began to shrink.[249] The revaluation of older coins is clear from various countermarks of value that were placed on the coins. The most common of these countermarks is CAP B,[250] although no coins with this countermark were found in excavations since 1973. Sardis struck more denominations than it had in the second century, and like the other cities in Asia, the mint adjusted the module of the coins in the third century (see comments in catalog).

The first announcement of the second neokorate temple-warden granted to the city appeared on coins of the 190s, but the title did not become commonly used on coins until the early third century.[251] It was then that several varieties of issues were minted, including coins with reverses showing the multiple temples of the imperial cult with the legend CAPΔIANΩN ΔIC NЄΩKOPΩN (a reverse type seen in several cities at this time) or with reverses of Kore (?) or Zeus Lydios and the legend CAPΔIANΩN B NЄΩKOPΩN (M7 GR 260–1; no. **192**). The obverses bore the bust of

242 Johnston 1983, pp. 63–66; Spoerri Butcher 2006b, pp. 97–98, 103–4.

243 Kraft 1972, pp. 15–16, 92; Johnston 1983, p. 65; Johnston 2012, p. 459.

244 Johnston 1984, pp. 249–52.

245 Johnston 2007, p. 240.

246 *Contra* Katsari 2011, pp. 191–92, 196. See the study of the excavation coins of Athens and Corinth with the same upsurge in the Severan period, Kremydi and Iakovidou 2015.

247 Katsari 2003; 2005, p. 275; Johnston 2007, pp. 8, 242.

248 Johnston 2012, p. 455.

249 Johnston 2007, pp. 12, 15.

250 See Johnston 2007, pp. 20–21; cf. Buttrey et al. 1981, p. 73.

251 Evans 2015, pp. 487–88.

the Senate or Tyche, and so they are not as firmly dated as the coins carrying the obverse of Septimius Severus, Clodius Albinus, or Julia Domna. However, since all of the coins with Imperial portraits and the notice of Sardis's neokorate status are from the end of the second or beginning of the third century, it is very likely that the coins with Senate and Tyche also date to this period. They are also more stylistically comfortable in the third century, featuring squat heads and crowded and lengthier legends that are common to early third-century coins.

During the reign of Elagabalus (Burrell argued in June 221 or just afterwards)—after coins had already come from the mint with the second neokoros in the title—a third neokoros was added.[252] The magistrate's name, Hermophilos (as *archon*), appeared on coins with an obverse of Tyche and a reverse showing the rape of Persephone (e.g., *BMC Lydia* p. 249, no. 89). These announce Sardis as having only two neokorate temples and Hermophilos serving as *archon* for the first time: A APX, B NEΩKOPΩN. *Archontes* made up the governing body of each city (and the term probably includes *strategoi*);[253] this body was in charge of municipal finances, and thus it supervised the minting of coins, including paying for the issue.[254]

Hermophilos also appeared on coins that note the change in Sardis's neokorate status (e.g., Elagabalus bust r., with the reverse of an agonistic table with crowns; or two temples, as above with TPIC NEΩKOPΩN, ЄΠΙ ЄΡΜΟΦΙΛΟΥ AP A T B; *BMC Lydia,* p. 265, nos. 170–171). These occur when Hermophilos was serving as archon for the second time. Since *archontes* usually served for a year, Hermophilos's tenure in office must have occurred in 220/1 and 221/2.[255] Coins of Gordian III and Tranquillina from the mint at Saitta (*RPC* VII, nos. 234, 240, 241), which carry the name of Hermophilos on the reverse are die-linked to coins from Sardis. Hermophilos could not have served as *archon* for both of these cities, but Butcher suggested that the name could have been used simply as a chronological indicator of the year the coin was minted.[256]

Coins from the current excavations can help shed light on the problem of the award and withdrawal of the third neokorate. A rare coin has on the obverse a bust of Elagabalus with his normal titulature (AYT K M AYP· ANTΩNЄINOC) and on the reverse a revival of the Kore (?) type with a legend announcing three neokorate temples. Hermophilos is named as *archon* (no. **195.1**): ЄΠΙ ЄΡΜΟΦΙΛΟV APA[X]-CAPΔIANIΩN TP[IC NЄΩKOP]. A variation of this combination is known, in Paris (FG1284), but only noting two neokorates. The issue in Sardis must have come from the mint in 221/2, and is the basis for Burrell's argument for the date of the award of the neokorate.

After Elagabalus was assassinated, the awarding of a third neokorate temple-warden was withdrawn. But *when* it was withdrawn is a matter of conjecture. Burrell suggested "a period of indecision" on the part of the city, which was indicated by an inscription at Sardis.[257] This inscription, on a statue base of the *agoranomos* C. Asinius Neikomachos Frugianus, is much restored. However, the composer of the inscription only felt comfortable calling the city "many times neokoros."[258] According to Burrell, either the Sardians were squeamish about admitting the loss of a neokorate cult or "the correct title was still in adjudication." She preferred the latter, due to the coins that appeared from the mint with the bust of Severus Alexander and the legend of "two neokorate temple-wardens," with Asinius named as *archon*.[259] Heller saw this as a "passive resistance" to Roman power, a "temporary subterfuge to gloss over" the problem on the part of the local aristocracy.[260]

Coins of Julia Maesa consist of only two types, a bust of Julia combined with either Mên or Demeter, and the legend CAPΔIANΩN Γ NЄΩKOPΩN or CAPΔIANΩN TPIC NЄΩKOPΩN (M7 GR 307; no.

252 Burrell 2004, p. 110.

253 The problem of *archons* and *strategoi* is discussed in Bennett 2014, especially pp. 8–11, 23–27; the use of such eponyms begins in the Augustan period, peaking in the third century.

254 Magie 1950, p. 644; Mitchell 1993, p. 88; Katsari 2011, p. 211; Bennett 2014, p. 39.

255 Dmitriev 2005, p. 61.

256 Butcher 1988, p. 24.

257 Burrell 2004, p. 111.

258 Burrell 2004, p. 111, inscrip. 7.

259 Burrell 2004, p. 112, esp. coin type 8.

260 Heller 2006, p. 279, my translation.

196.1). The coins are conventionally dated to 218–222, but a coin from the Sardis excavations must show that the time of minting extended after Elagabalus's death. It has the normal obverse of Julia Maesa, with the reverse of Mên, but the reverse legend reads CAPΔIANΩN •B NEΩKOPΩ, in ex N, with the B clearly recut.[261]

The recutting shows two things: the neokorate status was important to the city, and the mint officials wanted to make the city's titles as precise as possible. But it also shows that the minting of Maesa's coins in Sardis must have extended into the reign of Severus Alexander. This is our earliest evidence of the withdrawal of the third neokorate status. Interestingly, this reuse of the die appears to have been short-lived, resulting in only a small issue; thus, the minting of coins for Julia Maesa did not extend significantly into the reign of Severus Alexander. Coins of the emperor do not show a change from third to second neokorate. The decision to revoke the third neokorate temple must have happened very quickly after the death of Elagabalus, and Sardis may not even have waited for official word from Rome about the revocation. We may then argue either that the composer of the statue base for Neikomachos Frugianus was caught in an extremely brief moment after Elagabalus's death or before the third neokorate temple was officially granted for Elagabalus. Or the stonecutter was not as sensitive to the number of awards of neokorates as we would wish him to be, just as the minters sometimes showed hesitations in announcing neokorate temples (although, admittedly, this is more of a first- or second-century phenomenon and is not the strongest possibility). In any case, the new coin shows how quickly the matter was resolved on the local level; the announcement of the third neokorate temple disappeared from Sardis's titles, at least until the middle of the third century, when coins of Valerian I again display the legend "tris neokoros."

Although the antoninianus (or radiate) was introduced by Caracalla, few of these coins appear in excavations, including at Sardis. It is not until Balbinus and Pupienus revived the coin and discontinued the denarius that antoniniani begin to appear regularly in any excavation; the higher rate of loss probably supports the idea that the coin was no longer a double denarius, but had dropped to a 1.5:1 exchange rate.[262] The decline in weight and fineness of the coins are in inverse proportion to numbers of antoniniani found on sites, especially after 253. Coins of Gallienus and Claudius II Gothicus with a "distinctive, 'local' style" and SPQR in the exergue come from an uncertain mint in Asia (no. 264.1; cf. **284.1**), though probably not Antioch.[263]

"Barbarous radiates" are known from all over the Mediterranean and occur in some number in Sardis as well.[264] They can be difficult to distinguish from badly-made official issues (which is why Buttrey did not distinguish the coins).[265] I tried to list those with nonsense inscriptions as barbarous radiates, but I will admit to there being great overlap between those coins given to official mints (nos. 296–303). Scholars agree that the barbarous radiates, probably minted in the West, filled the need for local bronze coins, which had not been struck since the middle of the century.[266] In Sardis, the barbarous radiates are represented by the flaming altar reverse, as well as standing goddesses and an eagle. Most hover at weights just above a gram, but can fall as low as half a gram. These coins are found especially in later contexts at Sardis (in hoards H1 and H7, both closed by 518, see Section 3.8; fifth century: 297.9, 300.1, 325.1; sixth century: 297.8).

The Average Annual Coin Loss/1000 for cities with a normal profile (Fig. 2.2) shows a rise in the Severan period compared to the Antonine in all cities except Butrint. From the Severan period, the AACL/1000 reaches its highest point in all normal cities and Priene, with large peaks; Caesarea Maritima shows a steady climb instead of a peak. After ca. 284, the cities show a drop in the numbers, but the totals are still generally above those of the Severan age. Clearly the centralization of mint production allowed more coins, not fewer, to reach the cities.

261 See Evans 2015.

262 See Katsari 2005, pp. 272–73; Bland 2012, pp. 515–16.

263 Bland 2012, p. 528.

264 M7 R 28ff; no. 241ff; cf. Katsari 2011, p. 156 chart 29; Bland 2012, pp. 519–20.

265 Buttrey et al. 1981, p. 135 n. 93.

266 Buttrey et al. 1981, p. 94; Bland 2012, pp. 526–27.

2.5 The Fourth Century

Almost every area of excavation in Sardis has Late Roman material, including areas of commercial and domestic use, and all the major buildings have Late Roman strata. Indeed, almost any square in Sardis would yield Late Roman remains, from the villas that appear alongside the Pactolus, to cemeteries that line the roads into Sardis.[267] The city appears to have been a bustling, densely-populated metropolis in this era.[268] Diocletian elevated the city to capital of the province; this change in status must have been reflected in outside money coming into the city. In Late Antiquity, the bishop of Sardis was an important member of the church hierarchy,[269] lending credence to the importance of the city. Widespread travel by pilgrims and church officials attending synods had a positive effect on the economies of the cities, as traveling bishops and their staffs spent money on food and lodging; secular leaders held assize meetings which also attracted foreigners to the city with the same needs.[270] Sardis was largely spared the damaging upheavals of accusations of heresy in the Christian church and efforts to root it out. At various times in the century Sardis was used as a military base;[271] Valens is recorded to have stayed in the city in 365.[272] In short, the fourth century was a time of prosperity, when public and private buildings were built, refurbished, or restored.[273]

The Bath-Gymnasium was still in use, and indeed, a fountain was relocated to function inside the frigidarium in the late third or early fourth century.[274] Seager suggested a mid-fourth century date for the conversion of a large room in the Complex into a synagogue.[275] The extensive city walls may date to the same period; in the mid- to late fourth century, tombs were constructed outside of this new urban boundary.[276] Bath CG appears to have been renovated, although by the following century it was probably abandoned because it was too far from the city center.[277] A monumental inscription naming Arcadius was attached to a still-unidentified structure.[278] Buildings and tombs were built around the Temple of Artemis, although the rapid excavation of this area in 1910–1914 and loss of most excavation records allows us to say little more.[279] More tombs are found along the Pactolus, and a large house (the "House of Bronzes") was erected across the road from the Bath-Gymnasium. The exception to this building and restoration was the Temple of Artemis; it appears that by the mid-fourth century, alluvial deposits covered the western end of the Temple. The sacred site shifted to the southeast corner of the Temple, as the small Church M was built on top of the alluvial deposits.[280] By the late fourth or early fifth century, the two columns *in antis* of the ancient temple were removed in a major reorganization of the eastern end, though the purpose of this reorganization is still unclear.[281] Buchwald proposed that Church EA was built around the mid-fourth century alongside the banks of the Pactolus, though this could not have been the major church of Sardis, given the importance of the bishopric.[282]

267 Marcus Rautman is preparing a monograph on the Late Roman houses; I thank him for his work with me in understanding the fourth through sixth century at Sardis. In keeping with numismatic tradition, I will consistently refer to the fourth and fifth centuries as "Late Roman" and not "Early Byzantine."

268 For a summary, see Hanfmann 1983, pp. 146–48, and more recently, Rautman 2011.

269 Foss 1976, pp. 4, 31–32; Rautman 2011, p. 8.

270 Kaçar 2005.

271 Foss 1976, p. 8.

272 Rautman 2011, p. 13.

273 Foss 1976, pp. 8, 35–47.

274 Yegül 1987, p. 47.

275 Seager 1974; Magness 2005 preferred a sixth-century date.

276 Hanfmann and Waldbaum 1975, pp. 35–52; Yegül 1987, p. 52; Rautman 2011, pp. 10–11.

277 Hanfmann and Waldbaum 1975, pp. 129–68; Rautman 2011, p. 11.

278 Rautman 2011, p. 13.

279 See Hanfmann and Waldbaum 1975, pp. 53–73.

280 Hanfmann and Waldbaum 1975, pp. 74–87; Hanfmann 1983, p. 195; Cahill and Greenewalt 2016, pp. 504–7.

281 Cahill and Greenewalt 2016, pp. 483–87.

282 Buchwald 2015, p. 9; cf. Foss 1976, pp. 34, 43–44; Scott 1987, p. 76.

2.5.1 Recalls, Primary Deposits, or Residuals? Fourth-Century Coins in Archaeological Contexts

All over the Mediterranean, Late Roman sites are characterized by the number of fourth-century copper-alloy coins, which seem to be strewn with abandon under floors, in drains, and in dumps; they were trodden underfoot, lost, or discarded throughout the century, but especially in the second half of the century. And the number of coins reported from sites continues to mount, even as numismatists struggle to identify the worn, clipped, badly-made, and badly-preserved coins from archaeological sites, leading to very high numbers of "illegible fourth- or fifth-century coins" in excavation reports.

There is no need here to list the many reforms of the coinages in the fourth century, as the coins in general become smaller and lose any silver once found in the alloy. In 318, the coins contained about 5% silver and weighed about 3 g; by the reign of Valentinian I, there was no silver in the alloy and the same denomination weighed about 2.5 g.[283] The alloy varied tremendously by mint and through time.[284] Even before the end of the century, very little tin was added to the copper; it was steadily replaced by lead.[285] Nevertheless, at each stage of the reduction of silver and size of the coins, numismatists have to decide if the government recalled the old coins while issuing new small change, or if they let the coins return to the mint by less-controlled means, in order to reuse the raw material to make new coins. Archaeologists need to be aware of the problem, for any recall would have an impact on the interpretation of the coins found in the strata, especially in the placing of a *terminus post quem*.[286]

The argument for recall rests on the assumption that the mint would recall earlier coins in order to extract what silver content was still available from the coin, and reissue the coins on the new, smaller, and less-fine standard. In general, the idea that when the mint issued new coins (usually, but not always, indicated by new types) on a smaller and less-fine module, the mint called in the old coins by making the old coins illegal.[287] Milne first promulgated this argument in 1914.[288] There are some numismatists who contend that the recalls were in force across the Mediterranean.[289] Thus, the argument concludes, fourth-century coins were no longer available for use by the mid-fifth century and should not be found in fifth-century deposits. Numismatists use as their primary evidence a provision gathered in the *Codex Theodosianus* (9.23.2) that speaks about Imperial recalls: "We command that only the *centenionalis nummus* shall be handled in public use, and that the coining of the *maior pecunia* shall be abolished. No person, therefore, shall dare to exchange the *decargyrus nummus* for another coin, and he shall know that the aforesaid money, which can be seized if found in public use, will be vindicated to the fisc."[290]

Among the problems of this provision are the date of this decree and the nature of the named coins.[291] For instance, Richard Abdy limited the recall to coins of Magnentius and Decentius, western usurpers.[292] Harl preferred to see the western emperor Honorius outlawing the use of "nummi other than two fractional pieces, a tiny coin on the AE4 module . . . and its possible double struck on an AE3 flan."[293] Roland Delmaire limited the recall to Gaul; J.P.C. Kent, more

283 Moorhead 2012, p. 614.

284 Moorhead 2012, pp. 614–15.

285 Kent 1994, pp. 20–22; Moorhead 2012, p. 615.

286 cf. Evans 2013b.

287 See Harl 1996, p. 172; cf. Callu 1980, pp. 96, 103.

288 Milne 1914, pp. 26–27.

289 See Callu 1980, pp. 99–103; Harl 1996, pp. 167, 169–70; Heinrichs (2007, pp. 87–89) suggested that the coins could still have been used very locally, but even intercity use of the coins would prove to undermine the mint system, and so could not be tolerated.

290 Trans. Pharr 1952, with original names for coins inserted. Harl (1996, p. 170) also suggested that *CTh* 9.23.1 was promulgated by Constantius II to outlaw the use of the *maiorinae*, *centenionalis*, old nummi, imitations, counterfeits, and coins of Magnentius. Other numismatists agree with Pharr, who translates the passage to comment only on the ban on melting coin to resell the metal or moving the coins to an area of scarcity (Delmaire 2003); I also agree that this law does not apply to recalls. The statute reads: "Quicumque vel conflare pecunias vel ad diversa vendendi causa transferre detegitur, sacrilegii sententiam subeat. . . ." Pharr translated as, "If any person should be detected in melting down money or in transporting it to different regions for the purpose of selling, he shall undergo the sentence for sacrilege. . . ."

291 See coin names in Melville-Jones 1990; Moorhead 2012, p. 616.

292 Abdy 2012, p. 596.

293 Harl 1996, p. 178.

generally the West.[294] Kent noted that the reform of 354 "left most of the older coinage still in circulation; we cannot be sure whether an original intention to demonetize was rescinded (or proved impossible to enforce), or whether the older coins were simply to be discounted or refused in official payments."[295] Given the law found in *CTh* 9.23.2, he argued that at the end of the fourth century the "eastern government may have prohibited the continued circulation of the AE2 (the *decargyrus nummus*), but it merely replaced one AE3 by another, and probably allowed its AE4 . . . to survive." Thus, the larger Salus Reipublicae AE4 coins circulated alongside the Concordia Aug/cross AE4 coins, without being recalled.[296]

A secondary decree, also found in the *Codex Theodosianus*, is even more problematic. In 371, Valens and Valentinian I decreed that the *aes dichoneutum* (literally, "twice-smelted") was to be delivered to the Imperial largesses (or not be delivered; the language is unclear), but it was to be withdrawn from use (*CTh* 11.21.1).[297] Harl defined the *aes dichoneutum* as a billon coin; Michael Hendy further defined the *aes* as the large coins of Julian II, Jovian, Valentinian I, and Valens, though he admitted that few of these were in circulation when the law was promulgated.[298] Given the uncertain nature of the coin that was or was not to be delivered, this is a very shaky base on which to make an argument for a widespread recall of coins.

Some numismatists prefer to use the term "demonetization," or a lack of official recognition of the coin.[299] The coin would not be allowed to be returned to the government for official payments, but could still be used for any other transaction. However, it is highly uncertain if copper-alloy coins were ever used for official transactions such as the payment of taxes; nor is it certain that they were provided as pay to soldiers, leading one to ask what the demonetization would have looked like. Arguing in favor of demonetization, Burnett noted that coin hoards have few coins minted between 300 and 350.[300] He further suggested that the removal of the coins by the mint served to shore up confidence in the new smaller and less-fine issues being produced.[301]

But fourth-century coins do still appear in fifth-century coin hoards and excavation strata in the East (see Sections 3.5, 3.6), causing Butcher to suggest that "obsolete coins may have remained in use . . . circulating unofficially within the private pay community."[302] Peter Guest noted that the "evidence for systematic recall . . . is patchy and in principle, therefore, bronze coinage could remain in use for many years." He referred especially to the coins of Valentinian I and Theodosius I, which circulated through the sixth century, citing the work of Butcher in the publication of the excavations of the Beirut souk.[303]

The unease Butcher and Guest felt with the recalling of coin may have rested on the expense the mint would incur in recalling, re-melting, and re-striking the coins—especially for the copper-alloy coins, which already circulated as a token coinage. Moreover, as more archaeological excavations publish their coins, the more it is clear that large numbers of fourth-century coins survived to be used in the late fourth and even the fifth century, at least in the eastern provinces. Yet, how do we know that the coins have survived to be used as coins (that is, are indigenous artifacts), and are not residual or infiltrated (cf. p. 50)? As suggested in Section 3.5, the few fourth-century contexts that we can isolate using the pottery show that there are a number of fourth-century contexts that are significantly earlier than the closing date given by the pottery. The Mean Coin Date calculations suggest this is normal for deposits.[304] The same information comes

294 Delmaire 2003; Kent 1994, p. 18.

295 Kent 1994, p. 18.

296 Kent 1994, p. 19.

297 Impp. Valentinianus et Valens aa. Modesto praefecto praetorio. Aes, quod dichoneutum vocatur, non modo deinceps largitionibus inferatur, verum de usu penitus et conversatione tollatur ac nemini publice hoc habere liceat. Et conflatores figurati aeris, adulteratores etiam monetae capitalis animadversio persequatur.

298 Harl 1996, p. 172; Hendy 1985, p. 473.

299 Burnett (1987, p. 137) suggests "perhaps removed," then p. 138 "demonetized"; Butcher 2001/2, p. 82; Guest 2012, p. 107.

300 Burnett 1987, p. 116.

301 Burnett 1987, pp. 131–32.

302 Butcher 2001/2, p. 82. Earlier, in finding a second-century coin in a fifth-century deposit, he noted that if the coin was still being used in the fifth century, "we should have to radically rethink our ideas about Roman monetary policies in the third, fourth, and fifth centuries" (Butcher 1995, p. 306).

303 Guest 2012, pp. 107, 110; cf. Butcher, 2001/2, pp. 97–114.

304 See below for the calculation of the Mean Coin Date, App. 4.

from hoards. There are no fourth-century hoards yet known from Sardis, and precious few from the Roman East. However, the hoard from Aphrodisias which closed at the end of the fourth century did contain coins from the early part of the century, which should suggest that fourth-century coins were used throughout the century.[305] One hoard from Sagalassus which contained only coins of the second half of the fourth century was found associated with pottery from the end of the fifth century.[306]

Fourth-century coins are found as important components of fifth-century strata in Sardis (see Section 3.5). About one-third of these are coins more than 16 mm in diameter, ranging up to 29 mm. Numismatists have amassed more examples fourth-century coins as integral parts of archaeological strata, such as at Jalame and Sepphoris.[307] The survival of fourth-century coins in excavation strata and hoards can show that there were no effective Imperial recalls of fourth-century coins in the East, and the archaeologist must carefully weigh the evidence of both the pottery and the coins before setting a chronological *terminus post quem* for the stratum.

2.5.2 AACL/1000 for Fourth- and Fifth-Century Coins at Sardis

The graph for the Average Annual Coin Loss/1000 shows less regularity among the sites than in previous periods (Figs. 2.3, 2.4). All of the comparison sites show a large rise in the number of coins dating from 324 to 364, from the previous Tetrarchic period. In the second half of the fourth century, a normal profile cannot be established, as four of the normal cities show a rise in the number of coins (with Sardis having the highest AACL/1000 of all), and four show declines. The same split appears in the first half of the fifth century: Sardis, like Ephesus, Priene, Caesarea Maritima, and Athens, show declines in the AACL/1000. Yet the decline is not necessarily linked to the lack of trade at these important commercial (and, for the most part, coastal) cities, as the AACL/1000 showed a slight rise in Corinth, Kenchreai, Constantinople, and Pergamum. By the second half of the fifth century, most of the cities show a decline, save Athens, Constantinople, and Caesarea Maritima.[308] The decline in the period of 450–498 is surely in part due to the number of "unidentified fifth-century" coins reported in large numbers in every modern excavation report, and is probably only an apparent decline, due to the difficulties of identifying these ill-made coins.

2.6 The Fifth Century and Coin Circulation

The composition of the circulation pool of fifth-century copper-alloy coins has become a matter of controversy due to Ze'ev Safrai's contention that the low number of these coins found on sites in Palestine pointed to a significantly stagnant economy in the fifth century.[309] Guest also found that the fifth century was a conspicuous trough between the fourth- and sixth-century peaks, even after he had adjusted for coins using the AACL/1000 equation, in the cities of Athens, Corinth, Nemea, Beirut, Caesarea Maritima, Jerusalem, and Sardis.[310] The scarcity of fifth-century coins was "conspicuous," beginning with the reign of Arcadius and reaching its nadir in the reign of Zeno.[311] Yet Guest is at pains to note that we "conflate coin production and coin use," when all the list of excavation coins tells us is when the coin was made, not when it was deposited.[312]

305 The hoard also contained a second-century BC coin and antoniniani; see discussion of hoard composition in Section 3.8; cf. Lauritsen 1984. The hoard from the "synagogue" in Caesarea Maritima was closed, according to Raphael and Bijovsky, in 361, although there are 11 coins from later time periods (up to 408–421). They suggested that these coins are intrusive, but the tailing off of the graph, rather than an abrupt end in 355–361, seems more in keeping with hoard behavior. This hoard also contained issues from the early fourth century (Raphael and Bijovsky 2014).

306 Stroobants and Poblome 2015, pp. 81–82, where they also noted a second hoard with only fourth-century coins in it, in an archaeological context that is dated to later than the closing of the hoard.

307 Bijovsky 2012, pp. 52–53, 83; Weiss 2005; cf. Reece 2003, p. 160.

308 To which we can add Sagalassus: although the coins excavated since 2004 have not been published, Stroobants and Poblome (2015, p. 78) noted that the number of coins on the site peak in the period 388–408, which is mirrored in the excavation results from Hierapolis, Perge, Side, and Amorium.

309 Safrai 1998.

310 Guest 2012. Butrint is the exception to the rule: Moorhead reported that "this analysis shows that . . . coin supply was the highest in the period 445–98 and that the greatest coin loss occurred in the second half of the fifth century and well into the sixth century" (Moorhead 2007, p. 291). He specifically noted the contrast to the picture of fifth-century Sardis (p. 292).

311 Guest 2012, p. 112; cf. Arslan 2003, p. 39.

312 Guest 2012, p. 117.

As pointed out by several scholars, most notably Gabriela Bijovsky, Safrai's thesis is in need of major modification, at least in terms of defining the fifth-century circulation pool.[313] Safrai did not take into account the numerous "illegibles" reported by every excavation, nor the problem of finding small fifth-century coins if sieving is not used. The lack of excavation coins may be due simply to the consequence of the size of the late fifth-century coin, the heavily-leaded alloy, and the shoddy production values, allowing many to escape the mint with types not struck or off center. The result is that many fifth-century coins are under-reported. In Sardis, Buttrey recorded 1716 illegible fifth-century coins (along with 1881 fourth- or fifth-century coins) and about 1450 legible fifth-century coins.[314] The current excavations have 1875 illegible fifth-century coins, compared to 1387 legible coins of the same century. I do not include in the totals the coins that disintegrated in cleaning, although more coins of the fifth century tend to disappear this way than coins of other centuries. Bijovsky has previously noted the problems of under-identification of fifth-century coins due to disintegration of the flan, as have other numismatists in their excavation reports.[315] The percentage of illegibles at Sardis is quite normal; Reece reported even more dismal statistics from Carthage, where of 3638 coins, 2796 disintegrated upon cleaning, leaving 397 illegible coins and only 413 which could be identified.[316]

As noted by Bijovsky, there does seem to have been an imperative need for small change that the government did not fully supply. In the fifth century, users started to press into service any small metal pieces, including coins from the Ostrogothic or Vandalic mints, blank flans (possibly mis-strikes, but possibly manufactured as such), snips from sheet metal, cast lead slugs, copies of various qualities, fourth-century coins, or, north of Palestine, clipped older coins and even coins dating to the Hellenistic and Imperial periods.[317] Adelson and Kustas suggested that the clipping of AE3s to the size of AE4s must have been official policy since "considerable amounts of AE3 [coins were] still in circulation."[318] The larger coins were thus "made to conform to their monetary system," in a sense becoming "retariffed" larger coins.[319] Cast copies are only recently being understood as a part of the circulation pool; these are best identified by the casting tangs which are still attached, which seem to be found mostly in the East.[320]

Part of the reason why so many older coins and other forms of coin were pressed into service was that the mint produced only a few AE2 issues (and rarer AE3 coins), leaving the tiny AE4 coins as the predominant product from the mint.[321] After 450, none of the larger bronzes is found at Sardis. It appears that the mint struck fewer coins than were needed on a local level, leaving the user to make up the difference—and this state of affairs lasted (at least) into the sixth century for the smallest denominations.[322]

Almost half of the fourth-century coins from the strata at the Triconch Palace in Butrint were "apparently lost in the fifth century," and a few of the second half of the century survived in the sixth-century levels.[323] Butcher recorded a number of fourth-century coins found in the fifth-century levels in the excavations of the souk in Beirut.[324] He had earlier published the finds from Nicopolis ad Istrum and had found that coins up to 200 years old were found in fifth-century deposits (that is, they are not residual coins).[325] Robert Knapp and John MacIsaac also reported a number of fourth-century coins from fifth-century strata.[326]

313 Bijovsky 2012; Moorhead 2012, p. 622.

314 Illegibles are called fifth/sixth century, since Buttrey placed the end of the minting of Anastasius I's nummi in 518 (see M7 R 1117; the totals of legible coins in his Table 8 was reduced, as his Valentinian I–Valentinian III group is composed partly of fourth-century coins).

315 See Bijovsky 2012, p. 153–56, citing earlier work; Moorhead 2007, p. 288.

316 Reece 1984a, p. 171.

317 Bijovsky 2012, pp. 76–77, 130–56; Moorhead 2012, pp. 622–24; Guest 2012, p. 118.

318 Adelson and Kustas 1960, p. 142.

319 Adelson and Kustas did note as well the presence of clipped AE4s in the hoard they were studying.

320 Kent 1994, p. lxxxvii; cf. Moorhead 2007, pp. 296–97.

321 Buttrey et al. 1981, p. 119; Kent 1994, pp. 90–92, 98, 105–8, 115, 119–21; Arslan 2003, p. 37.

322 Guest 2012, p. 120.

323 Moorhead 2007, pp. 292, 294.

324 Butcher 2001/2, pp. 98–100.

325 Butcher 1995, p. 305.

326 Knapp and MacIsaac 2005, p. 185.

Fourth-century coins were used in the fifth and into the sixth century in Carthage, until Vandalic coins finally supplied the populace with small change.[327] And now the deposits from Sardis can be added to the evidence. While third-century coins are a small portion of fifth-century deposits, fourth-century coins, and especially coins from the second half of the fourth century, are common in the same deposits. As Moorhead pointed out, "What is interesting is that it has taken archaeologists and site numismatists a long time to prove what hoard evidence had already told us"—that fourth-century coins were a vital part of the fifth-century monetized economy.[328]

Although the volume of the production of copper-alloy coins (and thus annual losses) may have been low, the remains show that Sardis was prosperous in the fifth century. Church EA was extended, and this may be the date of the villa built to the north of the church; Church M was inserted into the Sanctuary of Artemis around 400. Buildings and vaulted tombs surrounded the Temple of Artemis, which was no longer in use by the early fifth century. Housing was found in sector PC, along the banks of the Pactolus River. Simple houses flanking a five-meter-wide road have been excavated in the ByzFort sector; houses with light industrial installations may also date to the fifth century in MD2 and MD1/S. In Field 55 and MMS, fine residences filled the areas to either side of the streets; the House of Bronzes also had a fifth-century phase. The Bath-Gymnasium Complex was refurbished. The Byzantine Shops, which fronted along the Marble Road and backed into the Bath-Gymnasium Complex, were probably built around 400; the Synagogue was flourishing in the fifth century. The Marble Road was renovated in a major euergistic undertaking around 400, making the street about 20 meters wide and flanked by porticoes, with a piazza near the Shops. The Byzantine Shops speak eloquently of a thriving craft economy, while the houses and tombs show that mosaicists and painters would have found ready employment on the site; marble and pottery were still imported.[329]

327 Reece 1984a, p. 174.

328 Moorhead 2007, p. 294.

329 Foss 1976, pp. 41, 43–46; Hanfmann 1983, p. 195; Scott 1987, pp. 76–77; Yegül 1987, p. 51; Buchwald 2015, and see now especially Rautman 2011.

The nummi of Anastasius I appear far less often than Andrei Gândilă, in his study of excavation coins in the eastern provinces, expected to find, especially in western Anatolia, and particularly in Sardis. He thus posited the continuing use of the nummi of the fifth century in the following century, which is very likely.[330] Yet he was also unaware of Burrell's publication of the MMS/S hoard of nummi, which helps to fill the gap of the fifth-century corpus of coins excavated at Sardis.[331] Sardis, at least, did have access to the nummi of Anastasius I (see no. 1004, with 200 examples).

As noted (Figs. 2.3, 2.4), the AACL/1000 for the cities declines in the fifth century, sometimes dramatically.[332] Moorhead noted that mint supply for various sites differ—Butrint (and to a lesser extent, Corinth) obtained more coins from western mints than did Sardis—but coins did travel from western mints to Sardis, and eastern mints were represented in the west. The result is "a coherent economy in the mid- and eastern Mediterranean."[333]

2.7 The Byzantine Period: The Sixth through Thirteenth Centuries

2.7.1 The Sixth Century

The history of the sixth century in the East is punctuated by an earthquake in 528/9 (if we trust Malalas 18.35),[334] a famine brought on by an environmental catastrophe around 536,[335] and waves of a plague that began in 541/2.[336] Wars with Persia and a period of cold, dry winters may have contributed to losses in agricultural production and population. As a result, urban centers contracted, and spoliation of earlier monuments became the norm

330 Gândilă 2009, p. 167.

331 Burrell 2007.

332 The AACL/1000 for second half of the fifth century is artificially suppressed for Kenchreai, but Hohlfelder (1973) listed 257 coins as LR/EB, so there was no good way of subdividing the material.

333 Moorhead 2007, p. 295.

334 See Ambraseys 2009, pp. 189–92.

335 Koder 1996.

336 Almost everything about this plague is disputed, from the nature of the plague to the mortality effects it had on urban dwellers: see Horden 2005; cf. Whittow 1996, pp. 66–68; Sarris 2011, pp. 143, 158.

as buildings were repurposed.[337] The century was a transformative one across the Mediterranean, which Cécile Morrisson and Jean-Pierre Sodini labeled as an "urban withdrawal."[338]

The reassessment of the sixth century in Asia is reflected in studies about Sardis in this period. Building projects, imported pottery, and silver tableware led Mark Whittow to suggest that the sixth century was a period of prosperity.[339] Clive Foss was convinced that the urban core of Sardis was still economically sound in the sixth century.[340] The area around the Bath-Gymnasium Complex was still in use, and the large House of Bronzes was refurbished. The houses of MMS also show continued remodeling. Rautman's recent assessment of Late Antique Sardis upholds Foss's view.[341]

Jane Scott was more pessimistic, citing the change of the Bath-Gymnasium into a souk, piles of refuse in the colonnaded street in MMS, and the insertion of wells, suggesting the aqueduct was no longer functioning.[342] Morrisson and Sodini see Scott's assessment of Sardis as indicative of a larger trend, saying that after a bout of Justinianic building in the East, we see "the progressive degradation of the cities." Streets were overbuilt "shoddy and partitioned structures"; "baths and buildings of importance did service as habitations or workshops." Refuse piled up in public places, spolia were used for fills or left in heaps in the city, sewers and aqueducts were abandoned, city walls and houses left unrepaired, and burials were allowed inside city walls.[343]

Bronze coinage took on a new importance, if we are to understand that some troops began to be paid partly in bronze coins; additionally, they may have entered the marketplace as *charagma*, or change when the taxes were remitted in gold coin.[344] Yet by the sixth century, there is some evidence that earlier coins were being recycled for use,[345] even if the ancient texts and excavation finds suggest that there was a high level of monetization.[346] Scholars have suggested that the reformed coins of the Byzantine emperors reestablished the presence of small change for the markets on sites,[347] but it appears in the Roman East that the reformed coins did not drive out the Late Roman nummi. Certainly the hoard evidence, as Moorhead noted, points to the presence of fourth-century coins into the sixth century,[348] as do some deposits in Sardis.

The level of monetization is not seen in the number of sixth-century coins at Sardis, but in the continued use of fifth- and even fourth-century coins; while the fifth century had seen the use of coins one hundred years old, the following century continued the use of the same coins, now up to two hundred years old. In this way, the sixth century looks very different from the fourth and fifth centuries, in terms of the types of coins that make up the deposit, for more cities than just Sardis. All of the cities with normal profiles show a decline in the first quarter of the sixth century, except Caesarea Maritima (Fig. 2.4).[349] By the second quarter of the sixth century, all the cities except Caesarea Maritima and Corinth show a (slight) rebounding of the AACL/1000. This recovery continues through the last quarter of the sixth century, except at Ephesus and Kenchreai. The overall lack of sixth-century coins in Sardis may reflect the lack of coin supply; this lack, and not a weakening economy, is why sixth-century deposits consist mostly of fourth- and fifth-century coins.

The lack of sixth-century coins is surprising in light of the fact that all of the mints except Heraclea were reopened in the sixth century, although coins from mints other than Constantinople are rare at

337 Laiou and Morrisson 2007, pp. 38–39; Haldon et al. 2014.

338 Morrisson and Sodini 2002, p. 189; cf. Morrisson 2002, p. 955; Laiou and Morrisson 2007, p. 40. I will not attempt to give an exhaustive bibliography about the "demise" of, or the permanent changes that are visible in the city in the Early Byzantine period, a problem that has recently been discussed by various authors in Christie and Loseby 1996 and Brogiolo and Ward-Perkins 1999, among many others.

339 Whittow 1996, pp. 59–63.

340 Foss 1976, pp. 41–52; cf. Foss and Scott 2002, pp. 615–17.

341 Rautman 2011, esp. p. 24.

342 Scott 1987, pp. 77–80.

343 Morrisson and Sodini 2002, p. 189.

344 Hahn 2000, p. 8; cf. Lightfoot 2002, p. 239.

345 Morrisson and Sodini 2002, pp. 217–18.

346 Laiou and Morrisson 2007, p. 37.

347 Gândilă 2009, pp. 156–57.

348 Moorhead 2007, pp. 294–95.

349 Evans 2007, pp. 46–47; Sanders 2002, p. 648, at least until the middle of the century.

Table 2.2 Byzantine mint production and representation of the mints at Sardis, fifth through seventh centuries. (Note: Cherson is not listed, as production was small and sporadic; no coins from Cherson were found in the excavations; nor were any from the temporary mints of Alexandretta, Seleucia, nor Constantina in Cyprus.) The symbol "/" shows that the mint was open; "X" that the mint was open and coins from the mint were found in the excavations. Not all mints produced all denominations when the mint was open.

Issuer	Constantinople	Thessalonica	Nicomedia	Cyzicus	Antioch	Alexandria
Anastasius I	X	/	X		X (M7 B 45)	
Justin I	X	/	X (M1 72ff, M7 B 53)	/	X	/
Justinian I	X	X	X	X	X	/
Justin II	X	X	X	X	X	/
Tiberius II	X	X	X	/	X	
Maurice	X	X	X	X	X	/
Phocas	X	X	X	X	/	/
Revolt of the Heraclii						
Heraclius	X (sole mint after ca. 630)	X (M1 950–951)	X (interrupted 617/8–625/6, then closed 627)	X (interrupted 614/5–625/6)	/ (closed 610)	/

Sardis until the reign of Justinian I.[350] During the reign of Justin I at Sardis, most coins come from the mint at Constantinople; these are mostly pentanummia, with a portion coming from the mint at Nicomedia. Gândilă suggested that "local patterns of circulation" were the rule in Anatolia, so the picture may be different in other cities.[351]

In the eastern provinces, the number of coins that came from the mint early in the reign of Justinian I—up to 538—seems to drop, but the numbers recover after this date.[352] The picture is not as clear at Sardis, where about 25% of the coins from Justinian's reign come from the period 527–538, a somewhat smaller percentage than one would arrive at if one simply divided his reign into sections of equal length. Nummi were still minted during his reign, but this was the last wave of this type of coin that came from eastern mints. Gândilă's study tracked the growing importance of the pentanummia at Sardis, along with other sites in Anatolia and the Balkans, after the reform of 512.[353] Indeed, increasing numbers of these coins are found in the current excavations as well as in Bates 1971: about one-third of the coins from the reign of Justinian are pentanummia, in contrast to the much lower number of nummi (see nos. 1020, 1025, 1054, 1055). There is an increase in coins from the mint at Antioch as well, especially as this mint is not well represented in Sardis in any other period; the mint was increasingly important across Anatolia and the Balkans.[354] After the monetary reform in 550, the number of coins coming from the mints appears to continue to drop, except for decannumia, which pour from the mints at Constantinople, Nicomedia, and Cyzicus, possibly due to the great need for small coin after a period almost exclusively devoted to the production of folles.[355] For the period after 550 in Justinian's reign, Bates, Buttrey, and I recorded only ten folles (most from Constantinople) and nine half-folles, but 52 decannumia. Of the latter, 38% of these came from the mint at Constantinople; 17% from the mint at Nicomedia (two of which Bates classified as "barbarous"); and only 12% from the mint of Cyzicus. The folles, though the numbers are small, should reflect the increasing proportion of coin from the mints at Antioch, Nicomedia, and Cyzicus, especially in land-locked cities,[356] as happens minimally in Sardis. Yet the situation is reversed for the half-folles, where Constantinople is minimally represented (1), and Antioch and Thessalonica provide the coins for the site (each 4).

350 Hahn 2000, p. 5.

351 Gândilă 2009, p. 168.

352 Gândilă 2009, p. 168.

353 Gândilă 2009, pp. 169–70.

354 Gândilă 2009, p. 169.

355 Gândilă 2009, pp. 170–71.

356 Gândilă 2009, pp. 171–72.

The excavation coins are almost exclusively of the lighter standard for Justin II, and Vandalic and Ostrogothic nummi, as well as crude copies from an uncertain mint, supplemented smaller coins. Although the Vandalic and Ostrogothic nummi are not calculated in the AACL/1000,[357] Justin II's reign shows a peak for the average loss for any of the reigns of the Byzantine emperors in most of the cities. It has been suggested that the coinage flowing from the mints under Justin II reflects his "prodigal policy of expenditure," combined with the needs arising from epidemics and earthquakes.[358] Certainly, the coins in the Sardis excavations from Justin's reign far outnumber the longer-lived Justinian I: 278 are recorded from the period 565–578. Of these, almost half come from the mint at Constantinople; not quite 20% of the coins from the mint are half-folles, while slightly over half are pentanummia, a trait of several cities in Anatolia (Fig. 2.19).[359] The second-largest mint supplier to Sardis is Nicomedia, but only 10% of the coins represented in the sample are pentanummia. Pentanummia make up about 50% of the coins from the mint at Cyzicus. Only the half-folles from the mint at Thessalonica are represented, but the number of coins from this mint is a pattern seemingly unique to Sardis and coastal towns in western Anatolia.[360]

The varying weight standards of coins of Tiberius II and Justin II may have led to a revaluing of the coins in terms of the solidus; certainly, by the time of Phocas, the smallest denominations were rarely minted or stopped being minted.[361] Yet it does not appear that recalls were ever attempted, or if they were, they were very unenergetic or confined to cities with mints. Coins of Anastasius I are found in hoards that closed in the reign of Heraclius;[362] types of Heraclius are overstruck on coins of Justin I (e.g., M1 958). The coins of Tiberius II are not especially prominent on the site, nor are they common in Anatolia, except for the coastal town of Side, in part due to lack of output from the mints. Only five pentanummia and nine decanunmmia are present, in contrast to larger numbers of these coins from Anatolian sites.[363]

The mint totals decline again under Maurice, as does the AACL/1000; this is the first period that the practice of overstriking coins becomes prominent.[364] Yet of 183 coins featuring Maurice on the obverse, only three of them were overstruck; this number must be balanced with the knowledge that coins of Maurice disappeared under the types of Phocas and Heraclius, including coins that show evidence of having been twice overstruck.

By the 590s, the mints turned to reusing old flans for the coins, and overstruck coins become common.[365] Sometimes this is accompanied by trimming the older flans. During the reign of Heraclius, restriking revalued the coins (e.g., from a half-follis to a follis, no. 1208.1). This phenomenon is common across the eastern Mediterranean and should not be considered a *damnatio memoriae*, but a problem in the supply of copper for making new flans.[366] A few coins are pierced, which would mean that they were withdrawn from circulation (nos. 1048.1; 1182.1; M1 682, 1146, 1160); one of these is a huge follis of Justinian I, but it does not come from an excavated context, so we cannot tell when the user decided it was worth more as an amulet than a coin. Gândilă noted that pierced Justinianic heavy folles are not unusual in the Balkans and Anatolia, and he suggested that archaeological contexts show that the piercing occurred soon after the series was "withdrawn from circulation," as a reminder of the glory of this prosperous period.[367]

357 They were not included since the dates of their minting stretch out over two or more Byzantine emperors. There were few of them, and they would have only minimally impacted the totals.

358 Gândilă 2009, p. 178.

359 Gândilă 2009, p. 179.

360 Gândilă 2009, pp. 178–79, although the percentage is somewhat less than the coins reported by Bates 1971.

361 Grierson and May 1992, pp. 56–69; cf. Sarris 2011, p. 239.

362 Gândilă 2009, pp. 162, 172.

363 Gândilă, 2009, pp. 182–83.

364 Gândilă 2009, p. 183.

365 See nos. 1130.1; 1137.1; 1141.1; 1165.1; 1176.1; 1178.2; 1184.1, 4, 5, 9; 1186.1; 1195.1; 1203.1; 1204.1–5; 1206.1; 1207.1–2; 1208.2; 1211.1; 1212.1; 1214.1; 1218.1; 1220.1; 1221.1–2; 1223.1; 1227.1; 1233.2; 1235.1; 1238.1; 1242.1; 1243.1; 1245.4; 1250.1; 1252.2–3.

366 Gândilă 2009, pp. 173, 187.

367 Gândilă 2009, p. 177.

2.7.2 The Seventh Century

A reassessment of what happened to the eastern cities in the seventh century is ongoing, and the coin evidence from Sardis will have much to contribute. Some scholars argue that the century was one of economic and political collapse, where cities dissolved into much smaller towns oriented towards the agricultural fields surrounding them. The Persian or Arab invasions caused this collapse, with the resulting loss of a city-based market economy and of a monetized urban center. The century, then, was characterized by depopulation, a loss of land under cultivation, and a period of economic contraction that is partly demonstrated by the lack of coin in circulation.[368] Only ports, with access to cheaper transportation costs, had access to quantities of imported goods. The reduced economic resources contributed to the depopulation. Along with instability within the government (until Heraclius consolidated his power) and fighting on the eastern and southern borders came divisions within the Church.[369] All must have contributed to an economic downturn in the Byzantine Empire.

However, other scholars think this emphasis is misplaced: cities do shrink, but they survived as urban centers and retained their role as the center of a market economy, production of goods, and administration. These scholars argue that the city no longer looks like an imperial Roman city, but beginning in the sixth century, the city changed into something else—and would have done so, even without Arab or Persian invasions.[370]

Thus, some cities, such as Amorium or Euchaita, were preserved, although they do not look like the fourth- or fifth-century phase of the city. Earthquakes may have damaged Ephesus, Aphrodisias, Hieropolis, and Sardis; Laodicea may simply have been abandoned by the early seventh century; Anemurium continued to function until about 660.[371] Angeliki Laiou and Morrisson argued that the direct linkage between urban decay and Persian incursions is misplaced, especially as most of the evidence comes from Sardis, where some of the decline appears to pre-date 616. They suggested the decay comes from the loss of urban population, the decline in urban markets, and the decrease in long-distance trade, which is especially seen in the reduction of African Red Slip pottery found on sites.[372] Yet, overall, after mid-century, the material evidence suggests that the economy of Anatolia had stalled badly, leaving little trace of new building projects or imported goods. The once-heavily monetized economy may have been replaced with many transactions undertaken by barter or payment in kind.

The seventh century sees a dramatic change in the supply of coin, with the closing of several mints (Table 2.2); by ca. 630, only the mint of Constantinople produced coin on a permanent basis.[373] Smaller denominations were rarely minted even in Constantinople after this period, and so the coins of earlier reigns may have been pressed into service for a long time.[374] In the eastern Mediterranean, sites record a lack of seventh-century coins (Fig. 2.4).[375]

Foss argued that all urban culture came to a crashing end in Sardis in 616, when Persians may have invaded.[376] No ancient sources mention this incursion, and there is no evidence that the Persians stayed to rebuild. Yet Foss suggested that there was widespread destruction in the city based on burned levels in the Bath-Gymnasium Complex and the House of Bronzes and abandonment of many other sectors of the city.[377] He noted that "great numbers" of early coins "found in and below the level of destruction" dated between 498 and 616, none of them of a type issued later than 616.[378]

368 The debate about the economic conditions of the seventh century is long; to begin, see Harvey 1989, pp. 20–22, Harl 1996.

369 Whittow 1996, pp. 90–91; Haldon 1997, pp. 11–12.

370 Whittow 1996, pp. 94–95; 2003, pp. 407–16; Haldon 1997, pp. 93–95, 108; Brandes 1999; Zavagno 2009.

371 Williams 1977, p. 175; Trombley 1986; Cormack 1990; Haldon 1997, pp. 95, 103, 108; Morrisson and Sodini 2002, pp. 190–91; Morrisson 2002, p. 956; Schindel 2009, pp. 199–213; Arthur 2012, p. 279.

372 Laiou and Morrisson, 2007, pp. 40–41.

373 Laiou and Morrisson, 2007, p. 86.

374 Morrisson 2002, p. 913.

375 See Charanis 1972/3, pp. 177–80.

376 Foss 1975; cf. Foss and Scott 2002, pp. 615–17.

377 Hanfmann (1983, p. 161) did not mention burned levels in the Bath-Gymnasium Complex, nor are any burned levels noted for this period in the House of Bronzes. See the warning by Cormack (1990, p. 28) that Foss's theory has become too quickly canonical history.

378 Foss 1975, p. 20.

The excavator of the Byzantine Shops agreed with an early seventh-century destruction, but was unsure of the cause.[379] No material remains were found for the seventh or eighth centuries in sector PN, and a hoard that was stashed in the Temple of Artemis closed in the early seventh century.[380] In Field 55, a large building was destroyed and not rebuilt.[381] This is probably when the Temple of Artemis and the Bath-Gymnasium Complex were damaged. Rautman noted that public spaces were abandoned or at least "poorly maintained" in this century; houses were subdivided or transformed for non-domestic uses; and imported pottery is lacking. Yet some areas of the city (such as the Bath-Gymnasium Complex) do have material evidence pointing to continued habitation.[382] Certainly, the urban fabric of Sardis changed in the seventh century.

Gândilă argued that, with Phocas, we return to a high level of AACL/1000, mostly due to the folles that came from Constantinople. The rise in the AACL/1000 is also seen in Athens, Corinth, and Anatolian centers.[383] Coins from the period are suppressed in Butrint.[384] Gândilă noted that Antioch became an important supplier of coin to Anatolia—except for Sardis, where coins from Thessalonica (to which I now add Cyzicus) replaced the Antiochene coins from other sites.[385] He could not account for this substitution. Sardis is different as well in not being supplied with many coins of the smallest denominations, unlike other Anatolian cities.[386] I have found some half-folles, but only one pentanummium.

Under Heraclius, many coins were overstruck on earlier issues, as is normal in the East. Thus, Heraclius's AACL/1000 is kept somewhat artificially high, even as it marks a permanent downward trend in the graph. Gândilă noted that 20–40% of the early Byzantine finds at Sardis could be attributed to the reign of Heraclius: while the higher percentage is much too high, the coins of Heraclius do form a significant percentage of coins on the site of the period from 500–620.[387]

In the earlier excavations, coins of Constans II were found mainly in the Bath-Gymnasium Complex and the Acropolis.[388] Since Foss wrote, excavators have only retrieved unstratified coins of Constans II from MMS and ByzFort. Morrisson suggested that these coins "must be related to military expenditure and the cantonment of troops."[389] Foss associated the same coins with the road-builders who were housed in the Bath-Gymnasium Complex, since they were found in rooms that housed a large lime kiln.[390]

2.7.3 Late Seventh and Eighth Centuries

The absence of late seventh- and eighth-century coins is not just apparent in Sardis; Pergamum also reports a lack of coins in the eighth century and into the ninth.[391] The site of Side shows much the same pattern as Sardis, as very few of the excavation coins date from the sixth to the first half of the seventh; coins of Constans II appear as a slight blip, after which there are few coins until the tenth century. Ephesus shows the same abrupt decline, which led Foss to conclude that urban life ended here as well as in Sardis.[392] Hendy was unsure why the numbers of coins dropped in the excavations of the Kalenderhane Camii in Istanbul, but from Constantine IV to Theophilus, the number of coins per reign are usually two or three.[393] Few coins are found in excavations, hoards, as isolated finds, or in museum collections, so we cannot attribute the lack of coin to a withdrawal of earlier coin, Theophilus's monetary reforms, nor a "*damnatio memoriae* of iconoclastic coins."[394]

379 Crawford 1990, p. 2, esp. n. 11.

380 Bell 1916, pp. viii–ix; Foss 1976, pp. 53–54; Hanfmann 1983, p. 162; Scott 1987, pp. 79–80.

381 Evans in Berlin and Kosmin, forthcoming; see Cahill 2015, p. 156.

382 Rautman 2011, pp. 24–26.

383 Gândilă 2009, p. 187.

384 Moorhead 2007, p. 299.

385 Gândilă 2009, p. 185.

386 Gândilă 2009, p. 187.

387 Gândilă 2009, p. 189.

388 Foss 1975, p. 17.

389 Morrisson 2002, p. 956.

390 Foss 1975, pp. 21–22; 1976, p. 57; Foss and Scott 2002, pp. 617–18; Greenewalt, Johnston, and Buttrey 1973, p. 28.

391 Voegtli et al. 1993, pp. 9–10; cf. Foss 1975, p. 20.

392 Foss 1979, p. 103.

393 Hendy 2007, p. 175.

394 Morrisson 2002, p. 956; cf. Laiou and Morrisson 2007, pp. 86–89.

Lightfoot noted that the dearth of coins might in part be due to the lack of interest in Byzantine layers in excavations in Turkey, and the interest and availability for excavation for sites that were (largely) abandoned after ca. 650: Aezani, Ankara, Antalya, Izmir, Kayseri, Konya, Pessinus, and Sagalassus.[395] Or, the lack of coin can be due to a "reasonably active, even if very highly localized and at times and in places a very low level, market economy."[396] Haldon conceded that coins may not have played much of a role in the economy, as taxes may have been paid in kind or credited to one's account. Certainly, small change was no longer minted in any volume after 658, in part due to the closure of mints in this century, such as Antioch.[397] Yet the economy was still monetized, as can be seen by hoards, which often contain coins 50 years old or older at the time of deposition,[398] and by the sites of Athens, Magnesia ad Maeandrum, and Priene.[399]

Coins of the third quarter of the seventh and all of the eighth century are largely missing from Sardis. By the eighth century, the urban center consisted of houses on the Acropolis, a wall built of spolia from the ancient city along the edges of the Acropolis, and a road in the area of the Byzantine Shops.[400] Most of the late seventh- and eighth-century coins came to the current excavations from the fields outside of the excavation trenches, as unstratified finds. The coins that were excavated come from MMS, Road Trench, ByzFort, and areas in the former Bath-Gymnasium Complex (BS, BE, BSH). The latter are interpreted as belonging to the troops quartered here and the construction crews working on a cobbled road, only one section of which has been found.[401] There are also two interesting *fals* coins that were probably minted in cities under Muslim control, mimicking Byzantine types (nos. 1235.1, 1236.1).

395 Lightfoot 2002, pp. 230–33; 2007; cf. Whittow 1996, p. 94.

396 Haldon 2012, p. 100; cf. Lightfoot 2002, p. 235; Laiou and Morrisson 2007, pp. 41, 87.

397 Haldon 2012, pp. 108–9.

398 Haldon 2012, pp. 111–12.

399 Morrisson 2002, p. 957.

400 Foss 1976, pp. 56–58; Scott 1987, pp. 80–81; Foss and Scott 2002, pp. 617–18; Rautman 2011, p. 26.

401 Foss 1976, p. 57; Hanfmann 1983, p. 161; Foss and Scott 2002, p. 618.

2.7.4 The Ninth through Thirteenth Centuries

Few excavations across Asia Minor have attested ninth-century levels. While there is some evidence of recovery at Ephesus, overall, Sardis and Anatolia in general lagged far behind the cities in the Balkans.[402] The coin evidence remains sparse for this century in Sardis; remains of habitation do as well, with some settlements of people living around the partially-dismantled Temple of Artemis and around Church EA.[403] Foss described the city as a "typical medieval town with a fortress on the Acropolis" that participated in a revival of "trade and urban life."[404] The coins that were excavated come from MMS, but nothing is known about occupation levels during this period in this part of the city.

Numismatically, we know very little about the tenth and eleventh centuries at Sardis. Excavated coins come from sectors MMS and PN, but almost all of these coins were turned in to the excavation by local farmers, suggesting a scattering of residential sites around the area of old Sardis. These centuries are depressingly familiar to us—a litany of raids and physical remnants of ill-made walls—until 1098, when John Doukas captured the city, with a resulting 200 years of peace,[405] although Laiou and Morrisson saw an overall recovery in the East in the tenth century.[406] The eleventh century saw the introduction of billon *aspron trachy*. However, to save on labor, the size of the engraved dies shrank, and the thin coins end up with a cup shape (the incorrectly labeled "scyphate"). These must have circulated alongside the reduced-weight folles. Laiou and Morrisson suggested that the *trachea* outnumber folles on excavation sites, but this is not the case at Sardis.[407]

Coins of the twelfth century are only known to us from non-excavated finds; they consist of billon scyphate *trachea*, minted in Constantinople and Nicosia. The lack of twelfth-century coins is comparable to the

402 Harvey 1989, p. 21; Morrisson 2002, p. 960; Laiou and Morrisson 2007, p. 88; cf. Ivison 2012, p. 64.

403 Scott 1987, p. 82; Foss and Scott 2002, pp. 618–19.

404 Foss 1976, pp. 56, 66; cf. Foss and Scott 2002, p. 620.

405 Foss 1976, pp. 61, 66–72; Scott 1987, p. 82.

406 Laiou and Morrisson 2007, p. 89.

407 Laiou and Morrisson 2007, pp. 147–51.

excavations at Pergamum.[408] Yet the century was a period of some prosperity and an increase in population in the East, at least until a "major fiscal crisis" late in the century.[409] If this holds true in Sardis, then the urban agglomeration has not been discovered.

Buchwald has proposed that Church E belongs to the Lascarid period, probably in the second quarter of the thirteenth century, when "Sardis enjoy[ed] the safety and prosperity that make the construction of a new and well-built church likely."[410] He pointed out that the emperor John III Doukas Vatatzes lived in the area and paid for other churches nearby. This period of relative peace closed when the Turkish forces controlled the city at the very end of the century. Minting, even in Constantinople, was done only when individuals turned in metal to be made into coin, so coin circulation became regional.[411] The excavation coins from Sardis are mostly billon scyphate *trachea*, but one is a scyphate follis and one a copper tetarteron. Latin imitations are also present; most come from the mint at Constantinople, but the tetarteron was minted in Magnesia ad Sipylum. The coin of Manuel Doukas was the last coin of the Roman rulers found in the modern excavations. Between 1204 and 1453, Sardis was like the other cities in Asia Minor, in depending on a mixture of "national," feudal, and colonial coinages—from Latin imitations to Venetian and Ottoman issues.[412] Overall, the monetization of the city was at a low ebb, a situation not rectified until the modern period.

408 Voegtli et al. 1993, p. 9.

409 Laiou and Morrisson 2007, pp. 90–93, 160; cf. Harvey 1989, pp. 56–57.

410 Buchwald 2015, p. 99; cf. Scott 1987, p. 84; Foss and Scott 2002, p. 620.

411 Harvey 1989, p. 88; Laiou and Morrisson 2007, pp. 221–22.

412 Morrisson 2002, p. 961; Laiou and Morrisson 2007, p. 216; cf. Foss and Scott 2002, p. 621.

Chapter Three

Archaeological Contexts of Note

Situating excavation coins within the archaeological context of a site has only recently become a problem mulled by archaeologists and numismatists. Previous numismatic studies, especially of excavations in the eastern half of the Mediterranean, have tended to be composed of lists of the coins found on the site. Even the previous report of the excavation coins at Sardis contained only a few pages on specific contexts, and these pages were penned by George Hanfmann and Barbara Burrell—significantly, two archaeologists.[1] The numismatists noted that their interests "differed" from the archaeologists—who only needed a concrete date—but they did stress the need for archaeologists to use the coins as a *terminus post quem*, and the numismatists' desire to have undated coins dated by the archaeological context.[2]

As I have spent as many years digging as working with coins, I was able to bring archaeological and numismatic interests together. Hence, this chapter will discuss important contexts where coins can illuminate the history of the context, or the context can help illuminate the history of the coin. In some cases, I returned to some important contexts not fully explored in the previous report.

When publishing excavation coins, the numismatist has several factors to consider about the reasons why the coins are found within archaeological contexts. The size and material of the coin, the effort shown in antiquity to recover the dropped coin, the environment around the deposited coin, the modern methods of retrieval, and the conservation of the coin are all factors that contribute to the coins that are presented in the numismatic catalogue.[3] As the numismatist assesses these factors, she must work with the archaeologist to clarify the context (construction fill, a votive deposit, erosional wash, a hoard?). Close collaboration with the pottery specialists is most helpful.[4]

The first thing the numismatist must try to understand is whether the coins are coming from a primary or secondary (even tertiary) deposit. For urban sites, the common consensus is that once the people in the city became familiar with using coins, they dropped them in places where exchanges of goods or services and coins took place, thus allowing

1 Buttrey et al. 1981, pp. xx–xxiv. This pattern of moving from a list of coins to a short description of archaeological context is followed in Corinth (Edwards 1933 to MacIsaac 1987), has not yet been accomplished for Antioch (Cox 1950, with studies on the way by Alan Stahl), Pergamum (Regling 1913; Boehringer 1984); or Ephesus (Karweise 1986), among many others. For discussions on the importance of archaeological contexts and coins, see, e.g., Ellis 2017 and Evans 2013a.

2 Buttrey et al. 1981, p. xvii. See also Butcher 2016, p. 225: "However, since we know very little about the longevity of coins in circulation, their utility in [dating contexts] is rather more restricted than non-specialists might imagine."

3 Evans 2013a and, more briefly, Reece 1993.

4 See Butcher 2001/2, p. 29.

the archaeologist to find them many years later. In Pergamum, for example, the excavators did not find many Roman Provincial or Roman Imperial issues, except in their excavations of the Via Tecta sector, where they comprised about half of the excavated coins. It was suggested that the ill and pilgrims were responsible for these losses, as they would have used the route on the way to the Asklepion.[5] While Steven Ellis pointed out that the rate of this type of abandonment cannot be very high (at least until the Late Roman period) unless we are willing to see intentional placement of coins as a major contributor to the coin record, unintentional loss must still be the primary way that coins become "systemic," that is, no longer part of the economy, but part of the history of the strata found on the site.[6]

Primary deposits can tell us a great deal about the stratum: its function and a *terminus post quem* of when it was laid down are key. I explore the primary deposits in hoards,[7] including votive deposits. Due to the fact that Sardis remained intensely inhabited through the Late Roman period, intact Hellenistic and Roman deposits are few. Nor are there many destruction deposits, even though we know that Sardis endured at least one devastating earthquake. Since buildings were torn down, refurbished, and reinhabited, very few intact deposits were left in the city for archaeologists to study.

Secondary or tertiary contexts are much more common. The construction fills which were used to rebuild the city in the first century after the earthquake are secondary deposits of coins, along with such fills as that under the Roman road and portico mosaics in MMS, and under the mosaic in Rooms B and C in PN, and any deposit upon which a Hellenistic, Roman, or Byzantine structure is found. The deposits in MMS show a mixture of coins from the Hellenistic or Early Imperial period with fourth- and fifth-century coins, likely a moving of a fill (possibly for the second or third time) to another spot as houses were built and refurbished.

The result is that the coin can be classified as indigenous or non-indigenous.[8] Indigenous coins are those that are in use at the time when the deposit is formed. These are the coins that were in circulation when the user dropped or placed them in the stratum. Non-indigenous coins are of two types: residual and infiltrated. Residual coins are those which have been worked into a higher level from the stratigraphically-older deposits. Usually these residuals can be identified as being part of a secondary deposit—a trench for a water pipe, a pit, a rodent burrow, or any other modification of the original deposit. The field excavator identifies secondary deposits; coins from these deposits are scrutinized to determine whether they "fit" the chronological profile of the rest of the coins and the pottery in the deposit. Residual coins are not uncommon in urban settings, where repairs and refurbishments of buildings, water pipes, and roads are common.

Infiltrated coins are those that were minted after the deposit was laid down, but which have worked their way into the deposit, normally from above. Infiltrated coins are much more difficult to detect than residual coins, as the secondary nature of the deposit was not recorded (or obvious), yet the chronology of the coin does not "fit" with the pottery or the other coins in the stratum. The problem of labeling a coin "infiltrated" is acute, as we would very much like to know how long a coin remains in circulation; without knowing if it is infiltrated, we might suspect that the coin remained in circulation longer than it did. When an Early Imperial coin is worn to the point of being smooth, we can understand a long circulation period. When the coin is a fourth-century coin found in a stratum with fifth-century coins, then the decision to name it as an infiltrated coin and differentiate it from a circulating coin becomes difficult. At Sardis, this process has been eased in the recent excavations by the use of Lots (cf. p. 1), which helps me to make a determination if the coin is indigenous or non-indigenous.

Thus, the context of the coin is crucial. If the room has a floor that is easily swept, it is unlikely to

5 Voegtli et al. 1993, p. 7.

6 Ellis 2017, pp. 307–8; my thanks to Steven Ellis, who provided me with his paper while it was still in press. I also thank Phil Stinson for worrying with me about archaeological contexts as he prepared to publish his work at Aphrodisias.

7 A hoard is defined as two or more coins deliberately brought together by a user and then lost. Hoards can consist of votive deposits, purses (usually called circulation hoards), or savings hoards. In contrast, according to Grierson 1975, p. 124, there are cumulative finds, those "brought together by circumstance," such as water flowing through a drain or coins found in a dump.

8 See Gerrard 1993.

have "caught" many coins. However, the refuse from cleaning such floors may contain coins. Coins that were abandoned escaped notice by being dumped in the refuse, perhaps to be used in a tertiary deposit as a construction fill. Ellis notes the disturbing jibe against a nouveau riche man in Petronius' *Satyricon* 43, who "was always ready to pick a quadrans out of the dirt with his teeth"; clearly, coins were carried out with the trash.[9] Dirt floors might have captured coins more easily, since they may have been covered with mats, reeds or other organic materials, or the coins may have been pressed into the dirt. It can be difficult to separate coins that have landed on the dirt floor and those that are part of a fill used to rebuild the floor after long use. Coins from latrines or drains are also susceptible to being washed into a tertiary deposit, especially if they are small and light Late Roman issues. Similarly, the seasonal washes (especially in the Wadi B area) may have taken coins far from their secondary deposit; conversely, simply having a downward slope on a site may not have very much impact on small objects like coins.[10]

Why base-metal coins are found almost exclusively in non-votive strata is a question that needs to be answered. These may be accidental losses, or "deliberate discarding of unwanted or valueless coin."[11] The distinction between deliberate discarding and accidental loss may be impossible when the excavation is of a shop, market area, or a dump.[12] The copper-alloy coins may have been determined to be no longer useful and thus deliberately discarded, or of so little value that the ancient user did not find it worth his time to retrieve a coin that fell into the dirt, no matter what the context.[13]

One "truism" among non-archaeologists is that coins "percolate" up through layers, smudging our ideas of what was in circulation at the same time, or the date of the layer.[14] The agency involved in this movement is not named. Archaeologists who have tested the "trample" theory (the movement of coins within the stratum as the layer is used for walking) noted that coins might possibly move laterally, but half never moved, and none penetrated a cobbled surface. If there was any movement, it was subsidence, perhaps due to earthworm movement.[15] However, the archaeologist does need to be aware of other post-depositional forces, such as small animal burrowing or activity, tree roots disturbing the features, or later human agricultural activity.[16]

Other factors govern the body of excavated coins. Silver and gold coins are rarely lost; numismatists commonly cite the parable of the woman sweeping her house until she finds the silver coin she had lost to explain why we do not find precious-metal coins (Luke 15: 8–10). Although it is true that copper-alloy coins could mean a great deal to a person who could not afford to have silver coins in his or her possession (as seen in the parable of the "widow's mite" in Luke 21: 1–4), the fact that the coins may have been the same color as the earth on which they were dropped, coupled with their low(er) value, means that almost all of the coins found on a site that do not come from hoards are copper-alloy coins.

The methods of excavation will have an impact on the coins reported from that excavation, as can be seen especially in older excavations,[17] but the numismatist cannot wait for field methods to become consistent before publishing the excavation coins. One means of analysis that is used sporadically in the west, but rarely, if ever, in the east, is to estimate the volume of the earth from which the coins came. Some methods have a greater impact on the recovery of the coin, such as sieving. It is only when sieving is used that archaeologists can be reasonably certain of retaining the smallest coins, especially those of the fifth century.

The size of the coin becomes crucial in the Byzantine period, as folles are routinely at least 25 mm and over 10 g in weight, at least until the early seventh century. We would expect, then, that the ancient user abandoned folles less routinely; inversely, the modern user may recover them more routinely.

9 Ellis 2017, p. 316.

10 Rick 1976.

11 Butcher 1995, p. 308.

12 Reece 2003, pp. 150–51.

13 cf. Grierson 1966, p. xii.

14 e.g., Buttrey et al. 1981, p. xvii.

15 Adkins, Perry, and Evans 1989; also Nielsen 1991; Andrews 2006; cf. Canti 2003.

16 Schiffer 1996.

17 Grierson 1965, p. xi, specifically about Sardis.

Grierson suggested that we should discard arguments about the circulation pool based on the presence of folles, as only the smaller denominations could more truly reflect the pool; he based his arguments on data from Athens, Corinth, Antioch, Constantinople, and Sardis.[18] Gândilă observed that up to 80% of the Byzantine coins found in Balkan, Anatolian, and Near Eastern sites are either folles or half-folles. He noted that the sites reporting such high numbers of large coins also report the recovery of small fifth-century nummi, which means they are coming from excavations that practice similar (and thorough) recovery methods.[19] In Sardis, the half-folles and folles from the excavations are about 48% of the finds from the period 491–640.[20] Clearly, substantial numbers of small coins of the Byzantine period are being recovered in the Sardis excavations.

Legibility also has an impact on the interpretation of the body of excavated coins. For Hellenistic and Imperial coins, legibility is hampered by the length of time the coin was in use before being deposited. Numismatists are very familiar with Early Imperial coin flans worn to smoothed surfaces. Sometimes the alloy used by the mint, as is especially seen in Late Roman copper-alloy coins, exacerbates the problem. The percentage of illegible coins varies widely between sites and within a site: in Sardis, current conservation standards mean about 30% of Hellenistic coins are illegible (beyond knowing they are Hellenistic), and 45% of all the coins are illegible beyond mean groupings, e.g., first–second century or fourth–fifth century. I could not place a minute number of coins even in these broad categories. This compares to the 5% unidentifiable from the Pergamum excavations,[21] the 26% illegible coins from Sagalassus (where 56% are Late Roman),[22] and the 69% illegible rate reported for Butrint, where the huge majority of coins found dated to the Late Roman period.[23] When MacDonald reported on the Hellenistic to Diocletianic coins at Aphrodisias, he said 12% of the coins were illegible; he thought that most of the illegibles were of the Early Imperial period since they were the most worn.[24] Coins of the fifth century are often illegible due to poor strikes and high lead content; the latter leads to a higher rate of corrosion. Illegibility continues to hamper the interpretation of excavation coins into the Byzantine period. Christopher Lightfoot noted 25% of the total number of coins found in the excavations of Amorium are unidentified, beyond a general "Byzantine" category. These unidentified coins may be hiding a quantity of the poorly-manufactured coins made from the reigns of Heraclius to Theophilus. They thus have an impact on how we understand urbanization and the Arab conquests of the seventh century.[25]

One factor that certainly has an impact on the number of reported fifth-century coins is the number of illegible coins and coins that disintegrated during cleaning. Often these types of coins, along with unstratified coins, are removed from the site totals, although numismatists will now add "uncertain first to third" or "uncertain fourth or fifth century" categories.[26] For example, Hans Voegtli simply recorded 1065 "stratified" and 169 unexcavated coins from Pergamum; these are broken into very broad categories (antike, byzantinische, etc.), although Morrisson was more precise for Byzantine coins, listing all of them in an appendix.[27] The numismatists for Butrint did not appear to list unstratified coins, but did not clarify their methodology.[28]

Disintegrated or illegible coins, or sometimes even copies or imitations, are often elided in catalogues of excavation coins, especially in older publications, when they are ignored by the site numismatist. The differing standards in publication from the early twentieth century to the early twenty-first century can be quite stark, and we must use earlier information with

18 Grierson 1966, p. vi; Grierson 1986.

19 Gândilă 2009, p. 156.

20 This includes the Byzantine coins in Bates 1971, Buttrey et al. 1981, and the current excavations: 1783 coins, of which 856 are folles or half-folles.

21 Voegtli et al. 1993, p. 5.

22 Stroobants and Poblome 2015, p. 78.

23 Moorhead, Gjongecaj, and Abdy 2007, p. 78.

24 MacDonald 1976, p. 27.

25 Lightfoot 2002, p. 235.

26 In Sardian parlance, unexcavated coins are given the designation "NoEx." I have rejected some of the "NoEx" coins handed in to the excavation as problematic, since they appear to me to be modern fakes.

27 Voegtli et al. 1993, pp. 7, 9.

28 Moorhead, Gjongecaj, and Abdy 2007, pp. 78–79.

caution. Morrisson pointed this out for the excavation coins of Pergamum, where there were great disparities between the number of Byzantine coins reported in the 1904–1908 excavations and the more modern material.[29] The number (if any) lost in cleaning is not stated.[30] The early reports of the excavation coins at Corinth are a mirror of Pergamum. Katharine Edwards, who had a staggering total of over 15,000 coins from five years of excavations, did not record the illegibles or disintegrated coins, beyond "unstamped or illegible" coins.[31] When Joan Fisher reported a year's worth of excavation coins from Corinth, she noted 12 illegibles that were not included in the totals, 112 illegible fragments, and 44 disintegrated coins.[32] The problem of disintegrated coins is not mentioned in the earlier publication of the excavated coins at Sardis, although 1847 coins are listed as such in the coin record in the period covered by that catalogue. Since 1973, only 86 coins have disintegrated. It is perhaps because of the high percentage of disintegrated coins—very likely many were Late Roman nummi—that the Sardis excavations were cited as being unexpectedly light in fifth-century coins in previous publications. It is not because, as Grierson suggested, that the coins were "simply ignored" in the excavation.[33]

Grierson pointed out that chance or "stray finds are our best guide to the [broad] area over which the coins were used."[34] Other numismatists agree that chance finds are better representations of use at a site than hoards.[35] Excavation coins, on the other hand, are the "best guide to changes in the character and density of circulation from one period to another."[36] Indeed, there are coins that are only known from non-excavated contexts at Sardis, including all coins of the twelfth century. Our record of the numismatic history would be hindered if these coins were not taken into account (yet see Grierson's warning on putting too much reliance on these coins).[37] Wigg-Wolf argued that even a small sample could give a useful overview of the site, as long as fieldwalking or surveying are combined with other means of collecting the coins.[38]

As can be seen from the data from Sardis (Fig. 3.1), where most of the unstratified coins are turned in to the excavation by local landholders or excavators on walks, Wigg-Wolf's theory does show correspondence between the two methods of retrieving coins. The dip in the number of unexcavated Late Roman coins can be a measure of the difficulty of seeing smaller coins; and the corresponding slight rise in the unexcavated Byzantine coins can be due to the larger size of the flans. There are two caveats to relying too much on this data. Finer chronological divisions would make the correspondence less clear, and so Grierson's suggestion that excavated coins tell us more about the "character and density of circulation" is true in the smaller divisions of time. Secondly, the Hellenistic period and the first/second century are oddly suppressed in the excavated coins; this may be due to modern land use around the ancient city, where the larger coins are picked up as more interesting. It may also be due to the excavation efforts in areas of the city that were mostly rebuilt in the Late Roman period. In other words, the research projects do have an impact on site totals.

The rest of this chapter explores various contexts in the ancient city. The reader will note that only some of the problems deal with chronology of the coins, which can be the overriding interest that the archaeologist has in dealing with the coins. Nevertheless, the coins tell us much more about how they were used in the daily life of the inhabitants, in the city where western coinage was born.

3.1 Lydian Contexts

Due to the difficulty of locating and excavating deeply-buried Lydian levels, only a few Lydian coins have been found in the excavations since 1972. Nicholas Cahill and John Kroll have thoroughly published one important deposit, which has helped us to understand the chronology of the later Lydian coins.[39] A second context reveals little about chronology but opens

29 Voegtli et al. 1993, p. 10.
30 Voegtli et al. 1993, p. 5.
31 Edwards 1937, p. 255, cf. p. 249.
32 Fisher 1984, p. 250.
33 Grierson 1965, p. xi.
34 Grierson 1965, p. ii.
35 Wigg-Wolf 2009, p. 114.
36 Grierson 1965, p. iii.
37 Grierson 1965, pp. vi, xiii.
38 Wigg-Wolf 2009, p. 122.
39 Cahill and Kroll 2005.

up important issues concerning the metallurgical composition of the electrum coins and gives us insight into the use of the coins.[40]

Although two electrum *trites* (nos. **1.1** and **1.2**) and a silver stater (no. **3.1**) were found in an archaeological context, it was a robbed-out structure on Sardis' Acropolis; only the shadow of a rectangular foundation remained. The pit contained roof tiles, architectural terracottas, and pottery, along with the coins. The deposit contained pottery from the seventh to the mid-fifth century BC. Because of graffiti on two of the sherds, Cahill suggested that the structure was possibly a small sanctuary to Artemis, and the coins were originally a votive deposit, lost when the sanctuary was demolished and thus ending up in a secondary deposit.[41] He noted the parallel to the pot hoard found beneath the Temple to Artemis in Ephesus; the Gordion hoard, found in 1963,[42] was also associated with a building on the Citadel of that city. However, both hoards only contained electrum coins, unlike the mixture of electrum and silver found in the Sardis deposit.

Three (possibly four) coins were excavated in and under the debris of the monumental mudbrick city wall, which was partly demolished after the Persian sack of the city ca. 547 BC. Two coins were found beneath a surface in the recess of the wall. One was a gold 1/12th stater of the heavy standard (no. **2.1**), and one was a silver 1/12th stater (no. **4.1**). Since both were sealed by the destruction debris, these coins date no later than Croesus' reign.[43] A silver 1/24th was discovered near the head of a soldier whose body had been thrown off the wall and covered by wall debris (no. **5.1**).[44] These three coins confirm the scholars who argue for the high chronology of the heavy croeseids.[45]

Scholars agree that the silver fractions continued to be minted through the reign of Cyrus, with the style becoming "rude and clumsy."[46] A coin found in a later wall (no. 5.2) has a style that is not noticeably different from the coin found in the Persian destruction levels, so I have grouped it within the earlier time frame. It is assumed that Sardis was the primary mint for the coins.[47]

A silver stater (no. **3.1**) was found mixed with both Early and Late Lydian pottery, in a context that included pottery from the early sixth (?) to the second quarter of the fifth century BC. This is the same context as the two electrum coins.[48] Silver staters are known from a relatively large number of obverse dies, showing a heavy production of these coins.[49] A heavy hemihekaton found in the excavations of PN (M7 GR 133) attests to the long use of these coins, as it was associated with an Athenian black glaze sherd made between 470 and 450 BC.[50]

Coin no. **6.1**, minted in Miletus, is one of the many coins that were produced in this mint in the late sixth to early fifth century BC, that is, until the destruction of the city.[51] Their ubiquity means that they even appear to have been inserted into Samos's electrum hoards.[52] As the coin was turned into the excavation team, Cahill suggests that the context of the coin at Sardis is uncertain; hence it was given a NoEx designation.

3.2 Late Fourth-/Early Third- to Second-Century BC Deposits

3.2.1 PN Destruction Deposit

In 1965, part of a house was excavated in sector PN, the east side of the Pactolus River, a mixed industrial sector outside of the walls of the Lydian city; the later Hellenistic city was mostly found in areas to the east of PN. Although Johnston catalogued the coins of this

40 Cahill et al., forthcoming.

41 Cahill et al., forthcoming.

42 Bellinger 1968.

43 See Wallace 2016, who suggested an accession in the 580s BC, hence the range of dates given in the catalog.

44 The coin of Miletus, no. **6.1**, was turned in to the excavation during the summer when the soldier was being excavated, and was said to have been found in the debris. Cahill has asked me to designate the coin as NoEx due to these circumstances.

45 Cahill and Kroll 2005; also Velde in de Callataÿ 2013, p. 13; *contra* Carradice 1987.

46 Naster 1976, p. 131; see Robinson 1958, pp. 188–89; Price 1983, p. 8, no. 9; Carradice 1987, pp. 91–92; Alram 2012, p. 63.

47 Alram 2012, p. 63.

48 Cahill 2011, p. 360.

49 Walburg 1991, p. 14.

50 Bruce 2015; Hanfmann 1962, p. 22.

51 Konuk 2012, p. 55.

52 cf. Konuk 2005.

Table 3.1 Coins in the PN Domestic Unit XIX and XX Hoard.

Inventory No./ M7 No.	Johnston Identification on Envelope; in M7	Evans Identification	Date	Mint	Diam.	Wt.
C65.0145/ GR 399	"Small denomination of Alexander III?" [and successors]; Hellenistic illegible	Tyche/bee?	305–288 BC?	Ephesus?	12	1.12
C65.0147/GR 81	Tyche/bee	Now too corroded for identification	305–288 BC	Ephesus	10	1.04
C65.0148/ GR 399	~~Pergamum? Seleucid?~~ Alex III etc?; Hellenistic illegible	Herakles/horse and rider	Late 4th–early 3rd century BC	Macedon in M7, now given to Sardis?	19	6.00
C65.0611/GR 17	Herakles/club, bow in case, unit	Now too corroded for identification	Late 4th–early 3rd century BC	Macedon in M7, now given to Sardis?	20	4.87
C65.0613/GR 18	Herakles/club, bow in case, fraction	Now too corroded for identification	Late 4th–early 3rd century BC	Macedon in M7, now given to Sardis?	10	1.06
C65.0616/GR 81	Tyche/bee	Tyche/bee	305–288 BC	Ephesus	10	1.25
C65.0617/GR 81	Tyche/bee	Tyche/bee	305–288 BC	Ephesus	10	0.92
C65.0618/GR 81	Tyche/bee	Now too corroded for identification	305–288 BC	Ephesus	10	1.15
C65.0619/ GR 399?	Illegible	Possibly Tyche/bee	Possibly 305–288 BC	Possibly Ephesus	12	1.36

excavation, she did not fully explore the archaeological context. I re-examined the coins at the request of Andrea Berlin, who has published her reevaluation of the pottery in the deposit.[53]

The excavated portions of the house are called Domestic Units XIX, XX, and XXIX. The excavators noted that the pottery that was resting on the floors of XIX and XX was sealed by the collapse of a roof and the subsequent fall of roof tiles, mudbrick, and stones, which Hanfmann interpreted as the debris of the destruction of the city after Achaeus's revolt in 215–213 BC. Included in this deposit were nine bronze coins, probably from a small purse inside the house.[54] Rotroff and Oliver noted that the debris was "tentatively associated with the attack of Antiochus III on the basis of coins."[55] Berlin's re-examination of the pottery suggested a destruction date of the late fourth to early third century BC.[56] My re-examination of the coins confirmed that date, and suggested an important consideration for the date of the Herakles/Apollo Sardis civic coins.

Johnston carefully studied the nine coins, as could be seen by the revisions to the field readings that she wrote on the coin envelopes. While she ultimately classified three of the nine as "illegible Hellenistic," two were labeled "Alexander III [or successors]," and four as "Ephesos ca. 305–288 BC" (see Table 3.1).[57] Johnston argued that "dating by Seleucid coins [found above the destruction debris] confirms the correlation with the siege and punishment of Sardis in 213 BC."[58]

It can now be seen that the latest date of a coin in the small deposit is 305–288 BC, and all the coins agree with this late fourth to early third century BC date. The coins in Units XX and XIX thus close about two generations shy of Antiochus' siege. It could be that the destruction was a local incident, common

53 Berlin 2016.

54 Hanfmann noted "coins of Antiochus II" below the floor on which the debris rested, with coins in the destruction debris of Antiochus III or Antiochus IV (Johnston later identified the coins as one of Antiochus III and one of Antiochus Hierax). The coins of Ephesus were mentioned in context with the whole smashed pots on the floor (1965, p. 4 and Hanfmann et al. 1966, pp. 24–25). The coins of Ephesus were not mentioned when he later discussed the deposit (Hanfmann 1983, p. 110).

55 Rotroff and Oliver, 2003, p. 11.

56 Berlin 2016, p. 353.

57 One envelope in particular showed her thinking as "Pergamon? large helmeted head of Athena r., rev. very rotten," then "Seleucid?" was crossed out and replaced with "Alex III etc?," and as a consequence, she placed the coin in the illegible Hellenistic category. When the coin was re-cleaned, it could be read as a head of Herakles on the obverse, with (part of) a horse and rider on the reverse. I must note that Johnston was working when the Sardis depot had no electricity. I have the benefit of strong raking electronic light and microscopes.

58 Buttrey et al. 1981, p. xxi.

in houses with open fires; it cannot be due to the destruction after Antiochus III retook the city.

The third unit, XXIX, presented a less clear archaeological picture. The excavators recognized the floor level due to a burnt layer and sherds, although no restorable vessels were found. This floor was not sealed by a fallen roof, as was the deposit in XIX and XX, and it was further complicated by later building phases, especially a Roman mausoleum. Nevertheless, the deposit was also considered evidence of Antiochus' sack of the city.[59] Four coins were found in this deposit, or in association with it; one is a third-century AD coin of Maximian Herculius (C67.0031), clearly showing the contamination from later building in the area.

The three other coins were Hellenistic: C67.0039 was a nicely preserved Herakles/club and bow in case familiar from Units XIX and XX. The photograph and coin envelope identification of the second coin (C67.0032) identify it as a coin of Seleucus I (probably 282–281 BC). The third coin, labeled "Antiochus II or III" by Hanfmann, was given by Johnston (following Newell *WSM*) to Antiochus Hierax, coming from the Sardis mint and minted between 241 and 228 BC (C67.0034). The coin is now assigned to Antiochus III, from the mint at Sardis, dating to ca. 197 BC.[60] The die axis does conform to Houghton and Lorber's series. If the date of the last coin stands, the deposit is disassociated from the siege of Antiochus, which may already be arguable due to the lack of whole vessels on the floor or recovered in the immediate area. We can discard this little group of coins as not having a sealed context and thus unlikely to help us form a diachronic snapshot of late fourth- or third-century BC Sardis. Instead, it is a reminder that the Hellenistic domestic occupation of the area lasted beyond the early third century BC.

The group of coins found in Units XX and XIX may have been a little purse of circulating coins, lost in a fire in the house sometime at the end of the fourth or beginning of the third century BC. The dates of the coins are internally consistent, and the recovery of the coins along with restorable whole pots, as well as the sealing by the roof tiles, allows me to make such a judgment. Three of the coins—the unit and fractions with the types of Herakles/bow in case, Herakles/horse and rider, and Herakles/club types were probably minted in Sardis (see Section 2.2).

The coins from Ephesus are dated generally to the late fourth and early third century BC; the Ephesian series has not had the benefit of a numismatist's attention since Barclay Head arranged them for the British Museum catalogue in 1892. They may have been contemporary with the bronze coins minted for Alexander the Great and his successors, as their metrology would suggest that they also functioned as a fraction. Thus, the owner of the house may have had a purse of two units and seven fractions to spend, very likely all from the mint at Sardis or Ephesus. The circulation hoard shows us an interesting picture of what was available for smaller purchases at the end of the fourth and beginning of the third century BC: small bronze units or their fractions; coins from the Ephesus mint were circulating freely in Sardis as co-equal to the units; and fractions produced in the Sardis mint. Conversely, in the late fourth and early third centuries BC, it appears that the bronze Herakles/Apollo and Apollo/club coins from the Sardis civic mint were not yet in circulation.

3.2.2 Other Early Hellenistic Deposits

Given the few Hellenistic strata that have been excavated at Sardis, I will only be able to discuss Hellenistic coins in order to examine how long they may have been in circulation before being deposited. Unfortunately, this lack of intact Hellenistic strata hinders us from fully understanding the chronology of the late fourth- to third- century BC coins, some of which are still problematic in terms of the date of their striking. For instance, the Macedonian shield/Macedonian helmet bronzes are called either Lysimachean or dating to the period after Lysimachus' reign. Johnston (who preferred an early third-century BC date) identified 25 such coins (M7 GR 22–24); the archaeological contexts were not clearly Hellenistic for any of these coins. The current excavations have only recovered three of these coins, two of which were turned in to the excavation (NoEx) and one of which was from a secondary or tertiary (Late Roman) deposit. The many examples from sector HoB were from mixed fills: clearly there were Hellenistic buildings here, but the imposition of a Late Roman

59 Hanfmann, Mitten, and Ramage 1968, pp. 13–14.

60 Houghton and Lorber 2002, pp. 320, 375.

villa mixed the levels, especially in the laying of water pipes. Similarly, the other deposits in PN showed much mixing of material from Lydian to modern, due to intensive use of the area.

Third-century BC coins are found in a few third-century BC strata that have been recognized on the site. Hanfmann identified a phase in Building C (HoB) as being Hellenistic, due to three coins (C62.0178, a silver drachm of Alexander III; C62.0345, Alexander III or his successors; and C62.0238 of Antiochus III), with an amphora handle of the third century BC.[61] Berlin's study suggests that the Hellenistic layers are not necessarily distinguishable from the later Roman activity in the area; Building C itself, she suggests, dates to the fifth century BC.[62] Another Hellenistic building, in sector MMS, identified by the excavator to date to the fourth century BC due to the pottery, contained a coin that I identified as from the mint of Sardis during the reign of Antiochus II (no. 78.4). In the sarcophagus found at Hacı Oğlan (Tomb 61.3), the identified Hellenistic coin with the burial dated to the late fourth or third century BC (C61.0023), while the pottery was probably third century BC (see Section 2.5.1).[63]

One coin minted under Antiochus I (no. 72.4) comes from a Hellenistic-era deposit in Field 49; the coin may attest to a new area of residential building in the early third century BC, but the area remained in constant use for residences through the early first century AD. The coin appears in a context with late second- to first-century BC pottery.[64] The same span of dates is seen in a second coin of Antiochus that was excavated in the same residential area (no. 72.3), in a deposit that included a coin of Augustus (no. 98.1). According to pottery analyst Elizabeth DeRidder Raubolt, this deposit came from a destruction level dating to the early first century AD, but it is unclear if the coin was part of the fill that contained earlier materials. Coins of Antiochus I were also found with a coin of Seleucus II (no. 81.3). This deposit comes from the raising of the ground level in the second quarter to the middle of the first century AD, as terracing for the Wadi B Temple, where there is also Hellenistic pottery as a secondary deposit, along with first-century AD pottery.[65] It appears that the Hellenistic coins are in a secondary deposit, and do not show evidence that they were in use for 300 years.

Only one deposit might suggest a long period of circulation for Hellenistic coins. An Early Imperial context in sector MD2 yielded a coin of Antiochus III (no. 90.1), associated with a coin of Pergamum, under the magistrate Demophon between 4 and 10 AD (no. 106.1).[66] It was found on a plaster floor; the subfloor contained third-century BC pottery.

3.2.3 Theater Deposits

Sardis' Theater was excavated between 2006 and 2010 in order to understand the phasing of the site. The structure is argued to be the theater mentioned in Polybius (*Hist.* 7.15–18) during the dramatic recounting of Antiochus' siege of the city in 214 BC. Thus, before any excavations had taken place, scholars assumed that the building dated prior to the late third century BC;[67] after excavation, traces of the third-century BC structure remain elusive.[68] Excavators had to take into account massive construction and destruction fills, as well as intense modern agricultural usage of the area of the scaenae frons; the excavations encompassed a small part of the scaenae frons, part of the parados wall and retaining wall (which were reconfigured in the Roman period), and trenches within the seating area of the cavea. Much of the southern part of the cavea was built close to bedrock on shallow fills that contain few useful deposits of any period. Yet in the northwestern section of the cavea, deep fills were added over the remains of a Lydian house, destroyed in ca. 547 BC. Much of the fill was Hellenistic in origin, but the seats were robbed out or replaced, presumably beginning in the Imperial period, in order to expand the seating. The Hellenistic fill thus consisted largely of redeposited earlier material.[69] Almost all the coins found in the fill were minted in Sardis.

61 C62.0238 was mentioned, but not numbered, in Hanfmann 1963, p. 10; Rotroff and Oliver 2003, pp. 12–13.

62 Berlin, HoB Report 2015, pp. 4–5.

63 Rotroff and Oliver 2003, pp. 15–16.

64 Berlin, Compiled Report 2015, p. 48.

65 Cahill 2011, pp. 359–60.

66 Fieldbook MD2 96.1 I: 73.

67 e.g., Vann 1976, pp. 99–103.

68 Cahill 2010, pp. 63–64.

69 Greenewalt 2008, pp. 373–75; Cahill 2010, pp. 63–64; Cahill 2012, p. 212.

One coin minted in Pergamum, of contested date, was found in the fill (no. 21.1). The coin shows the helmeted head of Athena on the obverse and an ivy leaf with the name of Philetaerus on the reverse. It is worn. Hans von Fritze, who studied the series in 1910, suggested that these particular coins were only minted by Attalus I, and thus could be dated to 241–197 BC, a date broadened in *SNG Tübingen* to 260–170 BC.[70] Von Fritze's argument was that the flans became broader and flatter and a second curl pops out from under Athena's helmet in coins minted under Attalus II and Attalus III. Johnston dated the Athena/ivy leaf coins to the mid-second century BC, though she gave no reason why.[71] More recently, Ulla Westermark suggested that the date remain in the third century, specifically 260–230 BC.[72] It is now clear from the associated pottery (which has a *terminus post quem* of 175–150 BC) that the coin must have been struck before the mid-second century; the dates proposed by the German scholars are to be preferred.

The associated Sardis civic coin, the Herakles/Apollo denomination, had two countermarks on it, both found on the obverse (no. **52.46**). The underlying type was worn. The first countermark could not be read, but the second countermark was the club countermark used by the city in the first half of the second century BC (see App. 1).

There were more Hellenistic coins found in other Theater fills, which the excavators agreed were residual coins due to the Roman pottery in the same context. It is interesting that all of the Hellenistic coins come from Sardis (12 or 13) or Pergamum (1), and almost all of the Sardian coins come from the civic mint. There are a few comparisons that can be made within Sardis: the PN deposit noted above contained coins from Ephesus along with coins from the royal mint at Sardis (see above, Section 2.2.1). PN is particularly rich in coin from mints outside of Sardis, with third-century BC coins from Alexandria Troas, Colophon, Ilium?, Macedon, Miletus, Smyrna, Thrace, and coins from the civic and Seleucid mints at Sardis. Similarly, at HoB, where Hellenistic levels were present, but were difficult to distinguish from later levels, third-century BC coins from Aegae, Ephesus, Macedon, and Thrace were present, along with coins from the civic and Seleucid mints at Sardis. The coins from the Theater fills would represent the coins brought to the Theater in order to buy food or drink.[73] The coins could have been lost in the third-century BC Theater and brought into later levels when the seats were repositioned or replaced, or other elements of the Theater reconstructed or repaired. Alternatively, construction fills were brought in from an area outside the Theater, and thus the coins are in a tertiary deposit. The homogeneity of the coins argues against the latter solution, given other Hellenistic deposits in Sardis.

It is quite clear that the Theater was damaged and repaired in the Early Imperial period, very likely due to the earthquake of 17 AD; further repairs and construction are seen in the mortared rubble walls ringing the western half of the cavea.[74] Although there are no fills that can be dated exclusively to the Early Imperial period, perhaps seven coins from the fills came from the first century: Augustus (nos. 102.1, 104.1, 216.3); Nero (no. **157.2**); Vespasian (no. 220.4) and two first- to third-century unidentifiable coins (nos. 230.16, 230.80).

Continued use of the Theater can be seen in coins of the second and third centuries (nos. **109.1**, 116.1, 172.1, 303.2). Fourth-century coins may attest to performances continuing into this era; however, it should be remembered that fourth-century activity is found at the top of the hill as well, and so these coins may be relics of travel up and down the slope or secondary depositional forces. These coins range from the very beginning to the very end of the century (nos. 351.5, 353.6, 547.2, 560.21, 660.1, 679.2, 684.46, 699.1, 750.24, 790.2, 790.10, 836.12, 886.107). Small fifth-century copper-alloy coins were also found here. Several are illegible AE4 coins (nos. 1003.1805–11), but of the identifiable coins, the entire fifth century is represented (nos. 815.3, 944.2, 963.72, 963.123, 963.72, 987.30, 987.43, 1004.139). A few later coins were found as well; the last dates to the middle of the sixth

70 Von Fritze 1910, pp. 22–23; *SNG Tübingen* 4: nos. 2373–2375.

71 Buttrey et al. 1981, pp. 19, 74.

72 Westermark 1991, no. 8; cf. Chameroy 2012.

73 Plautus, *Poenulus* 5-10 pleads with the audience to remain in their seats instead of visiting the snack vendors.

74 Hanfmann 1983, p. 116; Cahill 2010, pp. 63–64.

Table 3.2 Coins from Hellenistic trash midden, MMS/S 94.2 Baskets 47–50 Lot 30.

Mint: Types	Date of Issue	Catalogue No.
Sardis: Herakles/Apollo	245/220–2nd century BC	52.114, 52.130
Pergamum: Athena/coiled serpent	215–175 BC	23.5
Sardis? For Antiochus III: Apollo/Apollo leaning on tripod	213–203 BC	90.2
Uncertain Seleucid	280–203 BC	93.4, 93.11
Uncertain Hellenistic	Late 4th–1st century BC	94.21

century, and are small enough to be considered coins lost in transactions in the cavea (nos. 1026.4, 1026.13, 1036.1). Perhaps the Theater saw its last performance or civic meeting only in the mid-sixth century.

One token was found in the excavations: it is lead, with an anchor and a Δ on the other face (**L4**); this may have been used as a theater ticket. A bronze tessera from Ephesus also comes from the theater; it dates to the first or second century. It is bifacial and has a bust of Artemis with a quiver behind her shoulder and a stag standing right, with the legend ЄΦЄCIΩN (no. 114.1). Some Ephesian tesserae have inscriptions testifying to their use as amulets to ward off diseases (known as "Ephesian letters"),[75] but it is more likely that this tessera was used as a theater ticket or a coin.

3.2.4 Second-Century BC Deposits

Except for the Pergamene coin found in the Theater deposit and those found in graves, most of the second-century coins of Pergamum are unstratified or found in Late Roman fills in HoB and Field 49. One primary deposit that included coins was a trash midden in MMS/S (Table 3.2), dated by its pottery to the mid-third to mid-second century BC (no. 23.5).[76] The coins are contemporary with the pottery.

One Pergamene second-century coin was found in a Late Hellenistic deposit (the date obtained by a lamp) in ByzFort (no. 24.2), accompanied by a second- to first-century BC coin from Smyrna (no. **48.1**).[77] A second Pergamene coin (no. 23.8) was found in a (late) Hellenistic ash layer, also in ByzFort.[78] One robber trench in Field 49 that may date to the second or first century BC contains a civic coin of Sardis (245/220–second century BC, no. **52.32**).[79] That is, the second-century BC deposits tend not to have many earlier coins in them, at least in the few deposits that excavations have allowed us to examine.

3.3 Early Imperial Contexts

Primary Augustan contexts are difficult to isolate at Sardis, very likely due in part to the cleanup of the earthquake of 17 AD, but there are a few primary deposits dating to the first or second century that include Augustan coins. We know from the wear on Early Imperial coins that these coins circulated for a long time before their deposition; it is unclear if we need to suggest that the coins circulated into the fourth century, even if those are the companion coins in the strata. It may be that the Augustan coins in Late Roman contexts are simply in a secondary context. For example, deposits from MMS that have Augustan and fourth-century coins may reflect the churning of the ground for the numerous roads, drains, and houses that were added to this area in the fourth and fifth centuries; that is, they are likely to be residual.

One primary deposit that contained an Augustan coin also contained a Hellenistic coin (see above). A plaster floor in a structure at MD2[80] had an occupation fill lying on top of it. In that fill or on the floor were found two coins: one coin from the Pergamene mint from the time of Augustus (no. 106.1) and one minted in Sardis (?) during the reign of Antiochus III (no. 90.1; very worn, see above). None of the pottery was Late

75 e.g., Head 1908.

76 Berlin, Compiled Report 2015, p. 36.

77 ByzFort 84.8 Basket 76, no Lot; Ratté, Final Field Report: SEBF 1984, p. 6).

78 ByzFort 84.5 Basket 13, no Lot; cf. Fieldbook SEBF 84 I: 67.

79 Field 49 09.1 Basket 61 Lot 60. See also Field 49 09.1 Basket 67 Lot 62, an occupation layer with a Sardis civic coin dating 245/220 to the second century BC (Herakles/Apollo no. 52.33) and an uncertain Hellenistic coin dating from the late fourth century to the first century BC (no. 94.70). The excavator thought that the fill dated to the Hellenistic era (Souza, Final Field Report: F49 09.1, p. 5), but thought the pottery needed more analysis.

80 MD2 96.1 Basket 13 Lot 41.

Table 3.3 Coins in soil layer within fill, ByzFort 91.17 Basket 19 Lot 47.

Mint: Types	Date of Issue	Catalogue No.
Uncertain: illegible (fragmentary)	Hellenistic	94.85
Uncertain: Head of Augustus r./worn smooth	27 BC–14 AD	216.2
Dioshieron: Head r. laur./head of Zeus	27 BC?–37 AD	136.1
Sardis: Herakles/Apollo, Opinas, Akiamos	14–27 AD	150.5
Termessus Minor: Head of Tiberius/galloping horse	17–37 AD	214.1
Sardis: Senate/Zeus Lydios, Mnaseas	65 AD	159.1
Sardis: Plotina/worn smooth	112–117 AD	172.3
Uncertain: worn smooth	1st–2nd century AD	230.9

Table 3.4 Coins from Field 49 09.1 Basket 45 Lot 49: earthquake cleanup.

Mint: Types	Date of Issue	Catalogue No.
Sardis, for Antiochus I: Athena/Nike	280–261 BC	72.3
Sardis, for Seleucus II: Athena/Apollo testing bow	246–241 BC	81.3
Uncertain Hellenistic	3rd–1st century BC	94.10, 94.83
"Asia": Augustus/inscription	27 BC–14 AD	98.1

Roman. It is possible that coin no. 66.1, a Republican *as* dating to 217–87 BC also originally came from this Early Roman layer, as the hard-packed earth floor from which this *as* came was said to have undulated and thus was difficult to follow in some spots.[81] Alternately, it could be residual, having been brought into the mix during the Late Roman remodeling in the house.[82]

An Augustan coin was part of the second-century votive deposit at the Wadi B Temple, placed by the Temple in the Antonine period (see below, Section 3.3.2). An Imperial secondary deposit is seen in a dump in the ByzFort sector.[83] It included a group of Augustan to Julio-Claudian coins with one early second-century coin; the last had one side worn smooth, suggesting either a long period of circulation before being deposited in the dump or exposure to severe secondary depositional forces (more likely the latter, since the obverse was legible).

A discrete soil layer within a fill in ByzFort contained one Hellenistic coin and seven first- to early second-century coins (Table 3.3).[84] The Hellenistic coin was worn, but so was the reverse of the coin of Plotina. Tentatively, then, we can suggest that Augustan and Julio-Claudian coins were available for use in the second century.

Most of the Julio-Claudian coins from the excavations come from the strata that were much disturbed in antiquity in MMS or ByzFort. One coin comes from a Hellenistic/Roman fill in MMS/S, where the latest pottery was dated to the first or second century (no. 154.2). In the same lot was an unidentifiable Hellenistic coin (no. 94.63) and several Hellenistic molded bowl fragments. Field 49 had a number of small fills that were dated to the Early Imperial period. Some of these contained coins of an Augustan or Julio-Claudian date, but many did not.

A fill in Field 49 was closely associated with the cleanup after the earthquake of 17 AD, due to the plaster fragments and other domestic detritus found in the layer. The Hellenistic coins here were found with Hellenistic pottery and probably Early Imperial sherds (Table 3.4). The deposit contained one coin

81 Pottery read by E. DeRidder Raubolt; Fieldbook MD2 96.1 I: 66–70.

82 The Roman *as* was given to Basket 12, Lot 40 "Late Roman Fill"; it also contained an illegible Roman Provincial coin (no. 230.89) and a late fourth-century AD coin (no. 765.1).

83 The layer that the coins were found in rested on top of the bedrock; there are no later coins found in this layer, but the pottery was not reported (Gürtekin, Final Field Report: SEBF 91.17, p. 6).

84 Gürtekin, Final Field Report: ByzFort 91.17, p. 6; the coins from this deposit were not cleaned until 1992.

Table 3.5 Coins from Early Roman fills in Field 49 (identified by pottery).

Trench/Lot No.	Mint: Type	Date or Era of Issue	Catalogue No.
09.1 Lot 56	1. Pergamum: Athena/serpent coiled 2. Sardis: Herakles/Apollo	215–175 BC 245/220–2nd century BC	23.4 52.113
09.1 Lot 62	1. Sardis: Herakles/Apollo 2. Uncertain Hellenistic	245/220–2nd century BC Late 4th–1st century BC	52.33 94.70
10.1 Lot 48	Sardis: Herakles/Apollo	245/220–2nd century BC	52.122
10.1 Lot 52	1. Uncertain Seleucid 2. Uncertain Hellenistic	280–187 BC Late 4th–1st century BC	93.37 94.19, 94.26, 94.44
10.1 Lot 56	Uncertain Seleucid	280–187 BC	93.16
10.2 Lot 4	Sardis: Herakles/Apollo	245/220–2nd century BC	52.49
11.1 Lot 88	Sardis: Herakles/galloping rider	Late 4th to 3rd century BC	17.2
11.1 Lot 90	Uncertain, worn smooth	1st–3rd century AD	230.43
11.1 Lot 91	Sardis: illegible/elephant l.	213–203 BC	88.2
11.1 Lot 93	Sardis: illegible/elephant l.	213–203 BC	88.1
11.1 Lot 104	Ephesus: bee/stag l.	305–288 BC	36.1
12.1 Lot 117	Uncertain Seleucid	280–187 BC	93.2
12.1 Lot 122	1. Sardis: Dionysos/panther 2. Ephesus	2nd–1st century BC 1st–3rd century AD (tessera)	56.4 **L1**
12.2 Lot 16	Alexandria: Alexander/eagle	246–205 BC	**65.1**
12.2 Lot 29	1. Sardis: Herakles/Apollo 2. Uncertain Hellenistic 3. Uncertain Roman Provincial	245/220–2nd century BC Late 4th–1st century BC 1st century AD	52.69 94.72 230.60
12.2 Lot 30	1. Ephesus: bee/stag r. 2. Uncertain Seleucid	202–133 BC 285–187 BC	**39.1** 93.36
12.2 Lot 34	Pergamum: Athena/coiled serpent	215–175 BC	23.10
13.1 Lot 113	Sardis: Augustus/illegible	10 BC–14 AD	149.2
13.2 Lot 139	Antioch: Antiochus III/Apollo	233–187 BC	**91.2**
13.2 Lot 140	1. Sardis: Apollo/Apollo with tripod 2. Uncertain Roman Provincial	213–203 BC 1st century AD	89.1 230.67

from the reign of Augustus.[85] Again, it is unclear if the Hellenistic coins were in circulation in the Augustan period, or if they are residual to the Early Imperial fill.

An undisturbed fill in the area (F49 09.1 Basket 48 Lot 56) contained two Hellenistic coins: one of Pergamum dated ca. 215–175 BC (no. 23.4), and one Sardis civic coin (no. 52.113), which I argued dates from 245/220 to the second century BC. In this case, there were no Roman coins; only the pottery provided the *terminus post quem* of the Early Roman period. Three deposits under floors then are composed primarily of Hellenistic coins, while the pottery in the deposit suggests that the deposit was not closed until the Early Imperial period; this may give us a suggestion that the coin pool in the Early Imperial period may have included a large number of Hellenistic coins.

A mixed fill in Field 49 12.2 Basket 19 Lot 34 was described as a fill underlying a floor within a residence; the latest pottery of this phase dated from the first century BC to the first half of the first century AD, although the fill included sherds from the Lydian and Hellenistic periods. The Lot contained one worn coin of Pergamum, which is dated ca. 215–175 BC (no. 23.10), but it is unclear if the coin was part of the circulation pool of the first century BC/AD or if it was residual.

The remaining fills in Field 49 were preliminarily identified as Early Roman by the pottery in the fill (Table 3.5); these are occupational fills associated

85 DeRidder Raubolt pers. comm. for all the Early Imperial deposits outlined here; Cahill, pers. comm.

with features in the trench. Of the 21 lots noted below, only five have Early Imperial coins in them; 20 have Hellenistic coins in them, and most of these Hellenistic coins date to the third or second century BC. This strongly suggests that Hellenistic coins, up to 200 years old, were widely in use in the first century AD.

Jeroen Poblome, who has written a series of articles studying the coin and pottery contexts in Sagalassus, found that the Early Imperial coins were also often part of a complex stratigraphic record, muddied by post-depositional events. He was not ready to make a comment on how long coins remained in use before being deposited, and indeed, suggested that coins are not good chronological markers for Imperial deposits; but he noted that "as a rule of thumb, a period of use up to a century should not be considered exceptional" for the coins.[86] For example, the strata dated by the pottery to 25 BC–50 AD had few coins, but the coins that were associated with these layers dated overwhelmingly to the Hellenistic period; some were minted 200 years before the pots were made.[87] Yet he admitted that there were some Late Roman coins in the same deposits ("infiltrated") and suggested that the complexity of the chronology may have been due to the amount of terracing that occurred in conjunction with building activity in the Imperial period.[88]

As noted above, the lack of Early Imperial coins is apparent in most of the comparison sites to Sardis. We would expect that the change in denominations and types would render older Hellenistic coins useless in the Imperial period. However, judging from the evidence of Early Imperial strata—which are dated by the pottery and not by the coins—up to two (or three?) hundred-year-old coins were still in circulation in Sardis (and probably most of Roman Asia) in the first century. This chronological disparity appears to be rectified in the second century, when Hellenistic coins seem to have finally dropped out of circulation.

3.3.1 The Votive Deposit in Field 49

An unusual group of well-preserved domestic artifacts was uncovered in Field 49, a monumental terrace that rises prominently above the Roman city. In addition to their importance as documentation of ritual activity practiced by Sardians during the first century AD, the deposits are evidence for the Roman revitalization of this area of the city as these excavations have revealed a rapid succession of occupational phases dating to the first century.[89]

Field 49 held at least moderately wealthy home(s) during the first century AD. Two ritual deposits were placed below the floor of a room located near the western edge of the terrace. One part of the deposit was found intact, buried just beneath the floor surface, which was laid over the remains of earlier foundations.[90] The other part had been shattered in antiquity, although all of the contents remained in place. The intact vessels of the deposit consisted of a pair of identical, locally-made bowls, one of which was flipped over and placed on top of the other. Inside the bowl was found a complete eggshell, pierced by a small hole in order to empty its contents; one bronze nail; one long bronze needle; two badly-corroded iron implements that appear to feature decoration, one of which was stuck to a small white pebble; and a coin, giving a *terminus post quem* of 65 AD to the entire deposit (no. **157.1**).

The second part of the deposit was found at the same level as the first, about a meter to the north. Here, a thin-walled mug was nestled between two slightly upturned stones on the southern face of an earlier drain. It was covered by an Eastern Sigillata B dish acting as a lid. Although the vessels were crushed in antiquity, the same implements as the other deposit were found clearly associated with the two vessels, including an eggshell, a bronze pin, a bronze needle, and iron implements. A second coin dating between 54 and 59 was found during sieving of the associated earth and was also likely placed inside of the mug (no. **124.1**).

The former coin was minted in Sardis during the reign of Nero, as can be seen by both the portrait and

86 Poblome 2008, pp. 194, 198; cf. Poblome 1995; Stroobants and Poblome 2015.

87 Poblome 2008, pp. 195–96; see also Travaglini and Camilleri 2010, p. 8, who find the same for Hierapolis levels.

88 Poblome 2008, pp. 198, 202.

89 DeRidder Raubolt provided me with information about the pottery in the deposit.

90 See Cahill 2014b and 2015.

the surviving portions of the legend. This is a copper-alloy coin of the smaller of two denominations minted under Nero. The reverse depicts Zeus as he is commonly shown in Lydia, standing looking left, with a long tunic and himation, and holding a staff under his left arm. In his outstretched right hand he holds an eagle. The legend reads ΕΠΙ(meleia) ΤΙ(berius) MNASEOU CΑΡΔ[ΙΑΝΩΝ]: "from the mint at Sardis, under the care of [the magistrate] Tiberius Mnaseas." The detail on Zeus is flattened, but the details of the head of Nero, even in the higher sections, appear to be intact under the corrosion; additionally, the "C" in CΑΡΔΙΑΝΩΝ is fading. Thus, the flattening of the details is due to the use of an older die; the coin came almost directly from the mint into the bowl. Tiberius Claudius Mnaseus was a magistrate who minted several coin types for the city; Burnett, Amandry, and Ripollès argued that stylistically, Mnaseus' issues can be placed between 63 and 68.[91] The deposit can date no earlier than this coin, and I argue that it was probably assembled close to that date.

The obverse of the latter coin has the head of the Senate and traces of the legend ΘΕΟΝ CΥΝΚΛΗΤΟΝ (Holy Senate), with Z-MY dimly visible beside the head. Thus, the coin was minted in Smyrna, and Burnett, Amandry, and Ripollès gave it a date of 54–59 due to the magistrate (who should be) named on the reverse, Aulos Gessios Philopatris, combined with the head of the younger Nero found on other coins of Gessios.[92] On this coin, the Roma reverse was hammered completely flat—there was neither trace of the legend nor the figure—and engraved with a beautiful little roaring lion standing on a ground line.[93] This was no amateur attempt at carving the figure, as can be seen in the impression of the reverse, but it was done by a practiced hand who supplied a figure he apparently could not find on a coin reverse. This coin shows clear indicaations of wear, which may be primarily the result of the condition of the vessel with which it was associated: unlike the Nero coin above, it was exposed to post-depositional processes after the mug shattered. The wear could also have occurred as the reverse was hammered.

Thus, we have two local copper-alloy coins in the deposit, one chosen because of the reverse of Zeus Lydios. Since the depositor could not find an appropriate reverse of the female goddess he wanted to honor, he chose a comparable coin that had a lion, the animal of the goddess Cybele, engraved on the reverse.[94] On the reverses we have paired in the deposit the Father of the gods and the Mother of the gods (or Mother of the mountains), whose powers encompass both the storms and the land. Perhaps they were paired here in a plea for protection from further destructive earthquakes.[95]

The ritual deposits are nearly identical to several small finds uncovered during the early twentieth-century excavations of the site around the Temple of Artemis. Like the Field 49 deposit, ceramic vessels were found placed at the bases of walls, though usually outside of buildings; several were placed behind the row of stele bases on the north side of the "Lydian Building" (Lydian Altar). Butler described the deposits as:

> more than a dozen ovoid cups . . . These were found at the base of walls, and usually outside of buildings; several of them behind the row of stele-bases on the north side of the Lydian Building. Each cup contained a coin, the shell of an egg, and a small bronze instrument . . . apparently consisting of twisted wire . . . seven are still perfectly preserved, and in one the egg-shell is whole but for a small hole in one end.[96]

Bell noted that all of the coins were bronze and most were illegible, although due to the size of the flans,

91 Burnett, Amandry, and Ripollés 2005, p. 488.

92 Burnett, Amandry, and Ripollés 2005, p. 418.

93 I am not sure we should set much weight on the obliteration of the Roma reverse, in part because the head of the Sacred Senate—which is the Senate in Rome—was left intact, as was the head of Nero. It is thus difficult for me to see the repurposing of the coin reverse as an anti-Roman statement; the depositor needed an image that referred to Cybele, and there was no coin available to fulfill this need.

94 I know of only one denarius and one copper-alloy coin that were flattened on one side and engraved, though with inscriptions, not figural work: see Bonner 1950.

95 Copper-alloy coins are fairly common as votive objects. A peculiarly apt parallel comes from another site I helped excavate, Javols (Languedoc-Rousillon). Beneath a large stone possibly serving as a statue base, we found a life-size bronze hand, a pig skull, a pitcher, a roof tile, and a second-century AD copper-alloy coin (Evans, Ferdière, and Marot 2009, p. 266). It was clear that the deposit was made when the statue was dismantled; the ancient inhabitant buried this hoard to turn away any misgivings the goddess may have had by the destruction of her statue.

96 Butler 1922, pp. 127–28.

Table 3.6 Coins from the terrace fill for the Wadi B Temple.

Mint: Types	Date of Issue	Catalogue No.
Sardis: Herakles/Apollo	245/220–2nd century BC	52.66, 52.73, 52.86, 52.120
Sardis: Tyche/Zeus Lydios	245/220–2nd century BC	51.1
Tralles: Zeus/eagle	100–27 BC	62.1
Uncertain Seleucid/Hellenistic	Late 4th–1st century BC	93.3, 93.19, 93.32, 93.34, 94.40, 94.84

he suggested that most came from Roman Provincial mints. He also noted that the pottery dated to the Imperial period.[97] Another example of this type of deposit is seen in one grave, which contained two cups, one serving as a lid for the other (see below, AhT Grave 67.15). Inside was a coin carrying on the obverse the head of the Senate and on the reverse a hexastyle temple (C67.0838, M7 GR 255), the coin dating to the end of the first or beginning of the second century. There were no other recorded finds from the grave deposit.

The votive deposit in the house shows that the depositor carefully selected and manipulated coins for it, probably around 65 AD. The deposit was likely made in order to protect the new structure and those who lived there from malevolent forces, including further destructive earthquakes. The fairly short time span to which the Field 49 ritual deposits, those found around the Artemis Temple, and that in one grave belong may suggest that the proliferation of this local form of ritual activity was in response to particular historical and social circumstances during the rebuilding of the city in the first (and second ?) centuries.

3.3.2 The Wadi B Temple

The large plateau at the northern edge of two ridges (ByzFort and Field 49) was named Field 55. In order to make the plateau larger in antiquity, a massive temenos wall was built to hold the terrace that held the huge Early Imperial temple dubbed the "Wadi B Temple."[98] The Temple dates to the Julio-Claudian period, hence the fills should represent secondary deposition of Early Imperial coins, much like the earthquake repair fill in Field 49. Only a portion of this terrace has been excavated, and results remain preliminary.[99] The coins identified from this fill are all Hellenistic (Table 3.6); much of the pottery is also Hellenistic, but the latest dated examples do come from the Early Imperial period. Again, this may be an indication that the city relied heavily on earlier Hellenistic coins during the last part of the first century BC and the early first century AD. Overall, it looks like Early Imperial terrace fills from Sagalassus, which show the same disjunction between the dates of the pottery and the dates of the coins found with it.

The resulting Temple was the second-largest known temple in the city, constructed in the center of the Roman city. Since a fragment of an inscription mentioning the Senate was found on an architrave

97 I am a little confused as to the identity of the coins found in these deposits. After describing the deposit, Bell wrote, "These cups were for the most part (cf. nos. 208, 228) found in the same general part of the excavations, to the west of the north side of the temple." Bell's note 5 here records "No. 242 was found in quite a different part of the excavations." The fact that only three of the coins proved to be legible makes it difficult to generalize about them; but in every case they were of a copper-alloy; none, so far as could be determined, were from the Roman Imperial mints; the cups and bowls containing them seem all to have been made in Imperial times, though coin no. 242 dates from before 133 BC (Bell 1916, p. ix). Possibly the coin found in the cup was of the type seen in Bell's no. 242 (Apollo/club), but was not legible enough to get a separate number? Coin 208 is another Late Hellenistic coin, from Smyrna (Tyche/Aphrodite Stratonikis, with the magistrate Apollonios, now dated to 75–50 BC; Milne 1928, no. 362); coin 228 is from Germe with the head of Trajan and the reverse is the head of Apollo. Coins 208 and 228 have two very different coordinates, different levels, and were found about two months apart; coin 242 has a third date of discovery, different coordinates, and a different level. However, there are four coins that are given the same coordinates, levels, and date of discovery: 208, 213, 101, and 257. Bell listed coin 213 as Nero/Nike l., from Smyrna, providing an interesting parallel to the discovery in Field 49. Coin 101 dates to the time of Philip V (Herakles in a lionskin helmet/youth on horseback). And coin 257 is a Late Hellenistic coin from the mint at Sardis: Herakles in a lionskin helmet/lion walking, another interesting parallel to the Field 49 votive deposit, if it was found in a cup. It is noteworthy that the pottery is called Imperial in date, but some of the coins in the cups may date to the Hellenistic period, perhaps another confirmation of how prevalent these older coins were in the Imperial marketplace.

98 Greenewalt 2004, p. 482; 2006, p. 176; 2007, pp. 743–44; Cahill 2015, pp. 421–22.

99 The terrace fill was dug in 2002 and 2004 (Greenewalt 2006, p. 176). For the Julio-Claudian date of the Temple, Stinson and Yıldırım, pers. comm.; information about the lots that formed the terrace fill; Cahill, pers. comm.

Table 3.7 First- and second-century coins found in the excavations of the Wadi B Temple.

Catalogue No.	Obverse Type/Reverse Type	Mint	Context
230.98	Livia?/Julia?	Pergamum? (cataloged as uncertain mint, 1st century AD)	Trench II "a group of four coins (so far) all found together, between .59 and .63 below top of column base right up against the west side of the plinth" (Fieldbook SE Wadi B 81 I: 43)
100.1	Smoothed [Hadrian]/octastyle temple	Bithynia	As above
180.1	Faustina Major/hexastyle temple	Sardis	As above
126.1	Antoninus Pius/Cybele enthroned	Smyrna	As above
151.5	Germanicus/Athena standing	Sardis	"0.46 m north of central paving block, 0.55 m below top of column base" (information from coin envelope)
161.1	Augustus?/illegible	Sardis?	"Trench VII Lot 30, directly in front of N stylobate" (information from coin envelope)
222.1	Faustina Major/illegible	Uncertain	"Trench VII Lot 24 deposits cut by streambed" (Fieldbook Wadi B IB 82 I: 82)
Coin No. 1982.0178	Not a coin? Or a coin beaten flat (to 38 mm) so no images are apparent?		"Trench VII, cutting back W scarp" (Fieldbook Wadi B IB 82 I: 148, no. 2)
178.3	Marcus Aurelius as Caesar/winged caduceus	Sardis	Trench XII Lot 71 "on top of Lot 73," with brick, mortar, architectural fragments (Fieldbook Wadi B IB 82 I: 165–66. This was the only coin found in the lot.)
178.2, 178.5	Marcus Aurelius as Caesar/winged caduceus	Sardis	Trench XII Lot 73 "gravel in SW corner" (Fieldbook Wadi B IB 82 I: 173; these were the only coins found in the gravel)
178.1	Marcus Aurelius as Caesar/winged caduceus	Sardis	Cleaning scarp, Trench XII, probably from bottom of trench (1982) (information from coin envelope)
177.1	Marcus Aurelius and Caesar/ inscription in wreath	Sardis	Trench XII Lot 67 reddish, muddy, with mortar and Late Roman coins (Fieldbook Wadi B IB 82 I: 156–57)

associated with the Temple, it was suggested that the Temple was built in response to the bestowal of a neokorate priesthood to the city. Ratté, Howe, and Foss suggested a Vespasianic date for the neokorate award, due to coins that were issued from the mint with a tetrastyle temple on the reverse; these coins do not use the word "neokoros" in the legend.[100] They cited similar reverses on coins of Miletus, which also were missing the word, although the city may have had a neokorate temple to Caligula.[101] Johnston had earlier dismissed the likelihood that the coins of Sardis reflected a neokorate cult under Vespasian, since temple types are not always connected to actual buildings.[102] According to the coins, Sardis obtained a second neokorate, probably sometime in the second century; the earliest coin mentioning Sardis' second neokorate dates to the end of this century.[103] Thus, it is likely that the first neokorate was awarded in the first century; as with all other cities in Roman Asia, the cult was not noted in coin legends.

The original excavators suggested the Temple was destroyed in the second century, to lie in ruin for the remainder of antiquity. They based their arguments on the coins found in destruction debris overlying the Temple—none later than the second century—since there was no datable pottery in the layer. Above this layer were a series of deposits laden with fourth-century coins and fourth- or early fifth-century pottery. When I re-examined the contexts (see Table 3.7), I found that the Antonine coins were almost all found in Lots that had neither Late Roman pottery,

100 As noted in Section 2.3, at present, it is not possible to determine the date of these coins.

101 Ratté, Howe, and Foss 1986, p. 66.

102 Buttrey et al. 1981, p. 12; in the debate whether temples on coins represent actual buildings, I think that the skeptics have a stronger argument than the positivists, e.g., see Burnett 1999; Drew-Bear 1974. Burrell and Hanfmann dated the award of the neokorate to the Hadrianic period: Burrell 2004, pp. 100, 102; Hanfmann 1983, p. 145. Johnston (1983, p. 60) suggested Antoninus Pius.

103 Evans 2015, p. 487.

nor later coins in them. I thus reinterpreted the coins not as showing the destruction date of the Temple, but rather as a renewal of the purpose of the building in the second century. Antonine coins are not commonly found at Sardis. Of the 71 (possibly 72) Antonine coins known from the entire site from the excavation years 1958–2013, eight of them were found in the Wadi B Temple deposits. Four of the coins were found together. The coins are interesting in that they are all large copper-alloy coins, mostly of a size that is too large to lose easily and not be retrieved by the owner. This is especially true of the largest coin, which has a diameter of 34 mm and weighs almost 23 g. Only one of the four came from the mint at Sardis (no. 180.1); one was from Bithynia (no. **100.1**); one from Smyrna (no. 126.1); and one perhaps from Pergamum (no. 230.98). Thus, it does not appear that this is a random collection, but a selection of coins, one from a mint rarely attested at Sardis.

The owner of the coin from Bithynia rubbed off Hadrian's head, inscription, and border of the obverse. Only under raking light is the outline of the top of the head clear. Yet there are no obvious scratches on this coin, so the owner carefully smoothed the obverse to make it appear one-sided, or to focus attention on the octastyle temple reverse, since the Temple at Wadi B was also octastyle. Uniface coins are known, though they are not pictured in dealers' catalogues, nor are they collected by museums; they remain rare.[104]

The temple reverse on the coin from Bithynia is matched by the coin from the Sardis mint, which also bears a temple on the reverse (this one minted for Faustina), albeit a hexastyle temple. The third reverse shows Cybele, and the last may depict two women of the Augustan house. The selection seems deliberate, and it can be compared to the choice of reverse types from votive deposits at Bath,[105] or in the votive deposit in Field 49 (see above).

Also found around the foundations were two Julio-Claudian coins minted at Sardis, one depicting Germanicus and Athena (nos. 151.5, 161.1), and a flattened metal disk that may once have been a coin (1982.0178). The most common type of Antonine coin found in deposits around the Temple are those that have the head of the young Marcus Aurelius on the obverse and a winged caduceus on the reverse, from the mint at Sardis. One of those coins was bent and cut with a chisel, perhaps a way of making the coin useless to anyone but the gods (no. **178.1**); we are past the age when coins were commonly halved to provide smaller denominations.[106] The same could be said about the coin from Bithynia, where the head of the emperor was smoothed away, making the coin appear to be a one-sided medallion, effectively "killing" it as well as the chiseling did. Such behavior is not uncommon with votive objects. Philip Kiernan reported that "bent, scratched and otherwise mutilated coins are common on French sites" and less common in Britain, but still present. He saw this especially happening in the second century, usually on coins minted earlier.[107] Wigg-Wolf defines numismatic votive deposits as containing coins that are defaced and/or are gathered in one spot in a sacred area, and here, I think, we have both characteristics.[108] In Corinth, coins in tombs are defaced with scratches (not as neatly obliterated as the Bithynian coin here, but the intent must be the same) or cut into roughly square shapes.[109] Scratched, burned, and pierced coins are also found in some graves in Nempont-Saint-Firmin (France).[110] These are likely to have been defaced for the same reason (to provide a suitable votive deposit), rendering the coins unusable in the physical world.

Thus, the placement, size, iconography, and dates of the coins argue that we are looking at (the remains of?) a votive deposit, not simply a marker of destruction. Given the size, iconography, wear, and the "killing" of one coin, as well as the special attention paid to the coin of Bithynia, I would suggest that the coins found in the trench were votive offerings. Coins are a normal part of votive gifts. Although temple inventories normally pay attention to gold and silver

104 William Metcalf (pers. comm.) noted that the temple shown on the coin may also have been a neokorate temple in Nicomedia. One example comes from a tomb in Nempont-Saint-Firmin (France), although it dates to the fourth century; see Duchemin 2012, fig. 11.

105 Clay 1989.

106 See note on coin no. 98.6.

107 Kiernan 2001, pp. 18, 27, 29.

108 Wigg-Wolf 2005, pp. 371–72.

109 Mary E.H. Walbank, pers. comm.; for the final publication on the tombs, see Slane 2017.

110 Duchemin 2012, pp. 160–72.

coins, we know from other archaeological examples that copper-alloy coins were often given to the gods.[111] Grierson classified these finds as "abandoned hoards," hoards that were never intended to be retrieved and are votive in nature.[112] They may have functioned as something like foundation deposits and may have been placed in sacred pits or *thesauri* beside the temple. This is especially apparent in the four coins found grouped 60 cm below the plinth (and thus next to the foundation), the coin found 55 cm below the column base, and the coin found in front of the stylobate ("foundation for the columns" in fieldnotes).

3.4 Grave Gifts

Graves of all types have been found around Sardis, from built tombs to pithos burials, from sarcophagi to cist graves.[113] Many of these were looted (beginning in antiquity), reused, or disturbed before archaeologists could excavate them. While this is not the place to study burial practices, there is one burial practice that can be examined in this volume, and that is burials with a coin included in the grave goods. A huge number of graves did not contain coins—sometimes that is a symptom of the era.[114] It is clear that the placing of one coin with the deceased, most often near the head, is a ritual that was introduced in the Early Imperial period in Sardis, and it represents the introduction of a new manner of burial, especially when Sardis had strong ties to the Imperial government, in the period just after the earthquake of 17.

3.4.1 Hellenistic Burials

Some Hellenistic burials in Sardis contain coins, usually with other grave goods, including pottery. The few in which we can compare the minting date of the coin to the *terminus post quem* of the pottery shows us that the coins chosen for the burials are contemporary with the pottery.[115] However, Butler Grave 407, with two coins in it, provides a glimpse into how long coins could remain in circulation before being deposited in a grave. The burial contained a coin of Antiochus I and one of Pergamum dated to the late third or early second century BC. Thus, the Pergamene coin is found with a Seleucid coin, which was minted at least 50 years prior to the former. Rotroff and Oliver dated the pottery in the grave to ca. 150 to before the

111 Coins in contexts with cults or statues: coins were deposited in the temple in the Grove of Feronia at least during the Republican period (Livy XXVI.11); Lucian notes the offering of bronze coins to a cult statue (*Philopseudes* 20); Juvenal *Sat.* X.114–7 describes schoolboys offering bronze coins to "thrifty" Minerva; Suetonius *Aug.* 57.1 notes the annual rite of throwing a bronze coin into a well to ask for the health of Augustus; in Abu Mina (Egypt), an alabaster krater was excavated from under the altar which was placed over the grave of St. Menas, with coins ranging from the first century to the early fifth (Noeske 2000, p. 16).

"Thesauri" are known from physical remains and inscriptions as receptacles for votive coins throughout Italy. Copper-alloy coins are mentioned specifically, as temple personnel could retrieve these coins to pay for sacrifices or other temple upkeep. Some of these deposits are of single coins; some have large groups of coin, possibly contained in purses or pouches and sometimes hung from trees or buildings, or placed in boxes or pots. Crawford's study is limited to Italy and focuses on Republican practices (Crawford 2003). One thesaurus in Corinth, a hollowed-out stone, contained a lamp, stones, and 11 coins dating from the second to the first centuries BC. The coins only came from mints outside of Corinth (Edwards 1937, p. 247; Melfi 2014). Thesauri (Opferstöcke) become common in temples in Germany in the late first and second century AD. Pits along the north site of the temple at Bastendorff, newly renovated in stone in the second century, contained copper-alloy coins, including defaced coins (Wigg-Wolf 2005, pp. 378–79).

Copper-alloy and some silver coins were scattered in the sanctuary of Demeter and Persephone in Cyrene (Buttrey and McPhee 1998, pp. 1–2). Large deposits of antoniniani were excavated at Castellberg and Martberg, both Gallo-Roman temple sites of the Imperial period. "Irregular" coins were preferred at both sites, with reverses of Pax, Consecratio (flaming altar), and Consecratio (eagle), the highly-preferred reverse types (Kacynski and Nüsse 2009, pp. 96–100).

Copper-alloy coins are also used in foundation deposits: two such deposits were reported from the Sanctuary of Sol Indiges (Torvaianica, near Rome). One consisted of just one copper-alloy coin in the leveling layer; the other had five copper-alloy coins and a cup placed in a creamware jar. The deposits are dated to the Republican period (Jaia and Molinari 2011). Three copper-alloy coins were found in the "foundation for the foot of a libation-table in Lerna Square," Corinth. They dated to the third and second centuries BC (Edwards 1937, p. 247).

112 Grierson 1975, pp. 135–36.

113 For an overview of the cemeteries around Sardis, see McClanan in Buchwald 2015, pp. 153–54.

114 "Charon's obol" as thought to be a normal part of burials: Cormack 2004, pp. 116–17; *contra* Toynbee 1971, p. 49. Parallels in Roman Asia include Mytilene (Archontidou 2004, p. 72), Hierapolis (Travaglini and Camilleri 2010, pp. 12–13), and Pessinus (Thoen 2003, pp. 60–61); cf. Roman Palestine (Bijovsky 2015), Roman Corinth (Slane and Walbank 2006, p. 379), and Kenchreai (Rife et al. 2007, p. 160).

115 The Hellenistic burials with coins can contain jewelry, and normally contain multiple vases. Most have only one or two bronze coins; four have drachms: Bell 1916, nos. S3, S4, SW4, 25, 50, 60, 61, 143, 220, 302, 314, 352, 407, 421, 433, 435, 819, and 836; Shear 1922, no. ΘA; Hanfmann 1983, p. 123, but *sic* material of coin at Hacı Oğlan, Tomb 61.3 (both coins bronze); see Rotroff and Oliver 2003, pp. 189–208.

end of the first century BC (they give no indication of any earlier material in the grave, nor of any missing information).[116] If the grave group is that late, then the coins were still available 50–100 years after they were minted, and the grave shows again why coins must only be used as a *terminus post quem*. Overall, it appears that the fashion for including precious metal or even bronze coins with the grave goods had largely passed by the second century BC.

Butler Grave 61 had a Hellenistic coin from the mint at Sardis, with the types of Tyche and Zeus Lydios (for the reverse, see below), found in a large assemblage of goods, including numerous lamps and unguentaria. Rotroff and Oliver dated the pottery to the first century BC, but noted that the group contains "earlier material."[117] I have suggested an early date for this issue, given that one of these coins carries a countermark likely to have been placed on Sardian coins in the second century BC (Section 2.2.2). The coin was either residual from the earlier Hellenistic phase of the grave, or was still in circulation in the first century BC.

3.4.2 Early to High Imperial Burials

The ritual of including a coin in some burials was revived in the early first century AD (Table 3.8). Judging by the pottery, most coins have a mint date approximating the time of burial (18 were found with coins that matched the date of the pottery: Butler Graves 55, 520; PN Graves 61.24, 63.2, and 63.5; HoB Grave O; PC Zone A Burial A; AhT Graves 67.15, 67.16, 67.18, 67.19, 67.26, 67.28, 67.32, 67.37, 67.39, 67.41, and 68.9). These range in date from the very early first century to the late second century. Grave 55 has an interesting combination of coins, a third- to second-century BC Sardis civic coin and a Julio-Claudian issue, also from Sardis. Rotroff and Oliver dated the pottery to the early first century AD; there was no earlier pottery in this grave.[118] As can be suggested by the few Early Imperial contexts that we have, third- to first-century BC coins seem to be in circulation in the first century AD (see above); thus, the coin is not residual and appears to have been plucked from circulation to be placed into a grave two to three hundred years after its minting.

Apparently, incorporating a coin into the grave goods was an important part of the burial ritual for many, with care taken to select a proper reverse type. Eight graves contained a coin with a reverse of Zeus Lydios; five of these have a Senate obverse and were minted in 65 (*RPC* I: 3008). Perhaps significantly, they were found in a cemetery with other unidentifiable Julio-Claudian coins (AhT Graves 67.16, 67.23, 67.32, 67.35, and 67.37), and this particular reverse was found in Butler Tumulus 1alpha[119] and the votive deposit in Field 49. Two of the burials contained the Augustan version of the reverse (PN Grave 67.4 and AhT Grave 67.19), and once the Hellenistic version of Zeus Lydios was placed in a grave (Butler Grave 61). Clearly, the local god of storms was thought to be efficacious in watching over the dead.[120] It is hard not to see some special event that prompted the use of this particular reverse in the graves and a domestic votive deposit.

A generation later, it appears that the favored reverse is a temple: ten such graves from all over Sardis contain coins with this reverse (Butler Grave 520; AhT Graves 67.13, 67.15, 67.33, 67.39, and 68.9; PN Grave 61.24; HoB Grave O and HoB Grave 80.4; and the "Tomb of the Lintel").[121] The coins were minted between 1 and 120 AD, with the vast majority minted in the Flavian period. The widespread use of coins with the types of the Senate and a tetrastyle temple show that it was not just a single family with a predilection for the coin type.

It appears that the placing of a coin in the burial continued in the early Antonine period, ending abruptly with coins of Marcus Aurelius as Caesar (Butler Graves

116 Rotroff and Oliver 2003, pp. 196–97.

117 Rotroff and Oliver 2003, pp. 189–90.

118 Rotroff and Oliver 2003, pp. 187–89.

119 As reported in Bell 1916, no. 226, there dated to the Flavian period; found in this phase of the cemetery but not in a surviving grave were two more examples of the type: C67.0488, and C67.0659.

120 The use of specific coin types in burials has been attested elsewhere in the Roman world. In a cemetery in Avenches, dating from the second half of the first to the early third century, depositors chose coins with the reverses of Salus, Felicitas, Pax, or Roma (Koenig 1999, pp. 456–58).

121 Two more Early Imperial coins were not associated with particular graves in the AhT cemetery, but they must belong to the same phase of use in the cemetery, and perhaps once did belong to graves: C67.0037, a copper-alloy coin from Pergamum with Demos and Silvanus on the obverse and a tetrastyle temple on the reverse, dated 4 AD or later (*RPC* I: 2364); and C67.0635, a Flavian issue from Sardis, Athena/tetrastyle temple (*RPC* II: 1306), wrongly identified in the coin register, but identified as such by Johnston on the coin envelope.

S6, 423; HoB Grave 80.1; PN 63.2; cf. PC Zone A Burial A). The winged caduceus was a preferred reverse type, at least in Grave 423, where it appears on four coins (see also Butler Grave S6). Perhaps significantly, this was also the preferred type for the Antonine coins found associated with the Wadi B Temple. It appears that the custom of burying a body with a coin ended in the late second century at Sardis.

3.4.3 Late Roman Burials

Many examples of fourth-century and later tombs have been excavated, especially around Churches E and EA and on the Acropolis,[122] yet very few of these burials included coins (Table 3.9). Two burials, PN 62W and PN 63.1, contained single coins; the former had no other grave goods.[123] PN Grave 63.1 was a rich burial, comprising of more than one adult, and containing glass dating to the Late Roman period and a figurine dated to the third or fourth century. The excavator and Hanfmann rejected the coin as part of the grave gifts, but it dates to the end of the fourth century and was recorded to have been found near a skull; it could thus have been part of the assemblage. One grave held four coins, which make their inclusion somewhat more likely to be deliberate: PN Grave 67.1 (cf. PN Grave 67.5). Overall, the practice of placing coins in graves was not at all a common part of the burial ritual in the fourth and fifth centuries.[124]

Two tombs stand out as significantly different from this very conservative picture of the fourth and fifth centuries: the HoB Mausoleum, containing four cist graves, and the Peacock Tomb at PN. The area that was later overbuilt by the "House of Bronzes" was originally a cemetery, probably dating from the first century BC (?) to the early second century AD. The HoB Mausoleum (a small built tomb common in Sardis and elsewhere) was found under the House of Bronzes, and thus may have been part of the earlier cemetery. It appears that the cemetery was not used in the third century, allowing the tombs and graves to fall into disrepair. The "House of Bronzes" was built over top of the Mausoleum after it was razed.[125]

The remains of the tomb show that it was tightly packed with four cist graves, all with their cover slabs still in place when excavated. Goods in several of the graves may show that the burials were made in the second century. However, third- through fifth-century coins and Late Roman or Early Byzantine lamps are found in all the cists (one is missing a lamp); these show the later use, probably at the end of the fifth century. I will argue that it is at this time that the graves were reopened, (perhaps prior to a construction phase in HoB?), the coins were scattered in the cists, a lamp was placed in the cist, the cist was reclosed, and the tomb was dismantled; the living had allowed the dead to remain at ease in their graves.

I will begin with the cist found closest to the entrance (see Fig. 3.2). Grave 80.3 probably held multiple burials. It contained a coin of the late second or third century, which possibly belonged to the second-century phase of the use of the tomb. I would suggest that the bone inlay, glass bead and bronze ring also date to this phase, as these types of grave goods do not seem altogether typical for fifth-century graves. Among the fill were 81 coins from the second half of the third century to the early fifth century; these coins are typical of the fifth-century circulation hoards (including clipped coins) found in Sardis (see Fig. 3.5). The coins appear to have been scattered across the grave, not stored in a perishable container. The number of coins found in this cist is surprising, rivaling the hoards for size. Also placed in the cist at this time was a Late Roman lamp.[126]

Grave 80.2, which the excavator considered "relatively untouched," contained fragments of two individuals and an intact ceramic unguentarium dated to the Early Imperial period. Marcus Rautman confirmed the date of the unguentarium to the late first or early second century. Other rich objects were included in this burial—items more typical of a second-century burial than a fifth-century one.

122 Hanfmann 1983, p. 204.

123 See also Late Roman coins included in later burials in Field 49; since this area was occupied in the Late Roman period, the coins must be residual in the graves.

124 Contrast a fourth-century cemetery in Nempont-Saint-Firmin (France), where 35 of 83 burials included coins, four with more than one coin; some of the coins were ritually defaced. Although not rare, this is a high percentage of graves to include coins as grave gifts (Duchemin 2012, Table 1).

125 Foss 1976, pp. 43–44; Hanfmann, Mitten, and Ramage 1968, pp. 10–11.

126 Rautman, Roman Pottery Final Report 2013, p. 3.

Table 3.8 Imperial tomb groups containing coins (not listed are coins of uncertain date, due to illegible types, since they offer no insight into the chronological nor iconographical uses of the coin in the burial).

Tomb No.	Mint: Type: Coin No.	Coin *Terminus Post Quem*	Pottery *Terminus Post Quem*	Reference
Butler 520	Pergamum: Pergamum crowns Sardis/Augustus in temple	ca. 1 AD?	Lamps and pottery dated from Hellenistic to early 1st century AD	Bell 1916, no. 164; Rotroff and Oliver 2003, p. 198 (coin slightly redated in both)
PN Grave 63.5	Sardis?: probably Augustus/ illegible: C63.0181	14 AD[i]	Lamp dated 1st century BC to 1st century AD	Hanfmann 1964, p. 23
PN Grave 67.4	Sardis: Augustus/Zeus Lydios: C67.0698	10 BC–14 AD	Augustan; possible intrusion in Late Roman grave	Ramage, Final Field Report: PN 1967, Appendix, p. 2; Fieldbook PN 67 III: 153
Butler 55	1. Sardis: Herakles/Apollo 2. Sardis: Tiberius and Sardis/Livia	1. 245/220–2nd century BC 2. 17–37 AD	Lamps, pottery dated to early 1st century AD	Bell 1916, no. 250, 279; Rotroff and Oliver 2003, pp. 187–89 (earlier coin redated)
AhT Grave 67.23	Sardis: Senate/Zeus Lydios: C67.0828	ca. 65 AD	No other objects; cemetery *terminus post quem* is 1st–early 2nd century AD	Mitten, Final Field Report: AhT 1967, p. 19; Fieldbook AhT IV: 51; coin redated
AhT Grave 67.16	Sardis: Senate/Zeus Lydios: C67.0829	ca. 65 AD	1st century AD	Mitten, Final Field Report: AhT 1967, p. 15; Fieldbook AhT 67 IV: 52–53; coin redated
AhT Grave 67.35	Sardis: Senate/Zeus Lydios: C67.0833	ca. 65 AD	No other objects; cemetery *terminus post quem* is 1st–early 2nd century AD	Mitten, Final Field Report: AhT 1967, pp. 22–23; Fieldbook AhT 67 IV: 81
AhT Grave 67.37	Sardis?: probably Senate/ Zeus Lydios:[ii] C67.0832	ca. 65 AD	1st century AD	Fieldbook AhT 67 IV: 92–93
AhT Grave 67.32	1. Uncertain, worn smooth on both faces: C67.0803 2. Sardis: Senate/Zeus Lydios: C67.0804	1. 1st–2nd century AD 2. 54–68 AD	Glass and pottery dated 1st–2nd century AD; figurine to Flavian period	Mitten, Final Field Report: AhT 1967, p. 21; Fieldbook AhT 67 IV: 17–18; von Salten 1980, nos. 112–114; Gallart Marqués 2015
AhT Grave 67.19	1. Uncertain Julio-Claudian: C67.0830 2. Probably Sardis: Augustus/Zeus Lydios:[iii] C67.0831	By 68 AD	1st century AD	Fieldbook AhT 67 IV: 64–65 (coins reattributed)
AhT Grave 67.26	Uncertain Julio-Claudian: C67.0801	By 68 AD	1st–early 2nd century AD	Mitten, Final Field Report: AhT 1967, p. 19; Fieldbook AhT IV: 41, 128–29; coin date broadened
AhT Grave 67.28	Uncertain Julio-Claudian: C67.0681	By 68 AD	1st–early 2nd century AD	Mitten, Final Field Report: AhT 1967, p. 20; Fieldbook AhT 67 III: 5
AhT Grave 67.18	Uncertain Julio-Claudian: C67.0932	By 68 AD	1st–early 2nd century AD	Mitten, Final Field Report: AhT 1967, p. 16; Fieldbooks AhT IV: 130; V: 159
AhT Grave 68.9	Sardis: Athena/tetrastyle temple: C68.0286	70–73 AD	1st–early 2nd century AD	Mitten, Final Field Report: AhT 1968, pp. 12–13; Fieldbook AhT 68 III: 65
AhT Grave 67.15	Sardis: Senate/hexastyle temple: C67.0838	Late 1st–early 2nd century AD	1st–early 2nd century AD	Mitten, Final Field Report: AhT 1967, p. 15; Fieldbook AhT 67 IV: 14–15; coin redated. Note: two cups arranged as in votive deposit in Field 49 (see above), coin near skull, but not in cups

AhT Grave 67.13	Sardis: Senate/hexastyle temple: C67.0841	Late 1st–early 2nd century AD	No other objects; cemetery *terminus post quem* is 1st–early 2nd century AD	Mitten, Final Field Report: AhT 1967, p. 14; Fieldbook AhT 67 IV: 120–21; coin redated
AhT Grave 67.33	Probably Sardis: illegible/ hexastyle temple: C67.0777	Late 1st–early 2nd century AD	No other objects; cemetery *terminus post quem* is 1st–early 2nd century AD	Mitten, Final Field Report: AhT 1967, p. 21; Fieldbook AhT 67 IV: 9
PN Grave 61.24	Sardis: Senate/hexastyle temple: C61.0430	Late 1st–early 2nd century AD	Earrings dated 1st–2nd century AD	Beneath Peacock Tomb. Hansen, Final Field Report: PN 1961, p. 30; Fieldbook PN 61 III: 96; Hanfmann 1962, p. 32 (coin not mentioned)
HoB Grave O	1. Sardis: Senate/tetrastyle temple: C59.0348 2. Sardis: Tyche/Kore: C59.0401 3. Illegible: C60.0221	1. Flavian (reattributed) 2. 200–220 AD 3. 1st–2nd century AD	1st–2nd century AD	Fieldbook HoB 59 V: 24–26; Hanfmann 1960, p. 28 (grave reused, only mentioned one coin); note that fieldbook records the number of only one coin, but mentions 2 coins found in grave; coin envelopes list 3 coins found in grave
AhT Grave 67.39	Nacrasa: Trajan/temple: C67.0056	98–117 AD	1st–early 2nd century AD	Mitten, Final Field Report: AhT 1967, p. 23; Fieldbook AhT 67 IV: 88–89
Butler 423	1. Sardis: Sabina/Hermos 2. Sardis: Aurelius/winged caduceus (4 coins) 3. Uncertain number of illegible coins	1. 117–138 AD 2. 140–161 AD 3. Uncertain	No pottery *terminus post quem* suggested	Bell 1916, nos. 288, 293–296; Rotroff and Oliver 2003, p. 206
PC Tomb D	1. Sardis: Herakles/ Omphale: C60.0215 2. Uncertain: C60.0214 coins found "stuck together"	1. 90–100 AD 2. 1st–2nd century AD	Lamps dated Hellenistic to first half of 2nd century AD	Del Chiaro, Final Report: PC 1960, p. 1; Fieldbook PC 60 II: 15–18; Hanfmann 1961 does not mention coins
AhT Grave 67.41	Uncertain: C67.0834 coin worn smooth, countermarked with YN*Γ, in crescent stamp, which AJ (M7, p. 73) dated to 1st–2nd century AD	1st–2nd century AD	1st–early 2nd century AD	Mitten, Final Field Report: AhT 1967, p. 24; Fieldbook AhT 67 IV: 75
Butler S6	Sardis: Aurelius/winged caduceus	140–161 AD	Pottery not given a *terminus post quem*	Bell 1916, no. 297; Rotroff and Oliver 2003, pp. 202–3
HoB Grave 80.1	Sardis: Dionysos/torch: M13 184.4	140–161 AD	Late 1st or early 2nd century AD	Fieldbook HoB 80 II: 5, 10
PN Grave 63.2	Sardis: Aurelius/inscription in wreath: C63.0148	140–161 AD	Pottery not given a *terminus post quem*	Robertson, Final Field Report: PN Graves 1963, p. 3, who rejected coin as part of burial; Fieldbook PN 63 III: 45; Hanfmann 1964, p. 23 accepted coin as part of grave goods
PC Zone A, Burial (Tomb) A	Uncertain: bust of emperor or empress/bust or Tyche, turreted: C60.0035	2nd century AD	Lamp dated second half of 1st–2nd century AD	Fieldbook PC 60 I: 22; Hanfmann 1961, p. 18
Tomb of the Lintel	1. Sardis: Athena/tetrastyle temple (*RPC* II: 1305): C59.0276 2. Illegible: C59.0277[iv]	1. 70–73 AD 2. 2nd–3rd century AD?	Lamps dated 2nd century BC–1st century AD	Hanfmann 1960, p. 18; Rotroff and Oliver 2003, pp. 13–14

i *Coin envelope reads "perhaps Tiberius?," then in Johnston's red pen, "or Augustus." Hanfmann (1964, p. 23) reported the coin as "perhaps Julio-Claudian." I prefer Johnston's identification.*

ii *I agree with Andrew Ramage's field reading; coin now illegible.*

iii *Johnston's red pen on the coin envelope noted the identification as "probably"; types not visible today.*

iv *Field notes cite the Hellenistic date of coins and the coin register records a date of third century AD for both; Johnston wrote "2nd–3rd" on the envelope. The field reading did suggest the Athena/tetrastyle temple, and the EΠI in the exergue confirms this reading for C59.0276. The field reading suggested a bust of Tyche for C59.0277; there might be some turrets on the edge and a galley stem on the reverse, possibly a coin of Phocaea? Johnston wrote "1st–3rd" on the envelope, then later crossed out "1st."*

Table 3.9 Late Roman and Byzantine grave gifts of coins (for coin reverse types see App. 3).

Tomb No.	Emperor or Reverse Type: Coin No.	Coin *Terminus Post Quem*	Pottery or Object *Terminus Post Quem*
PN Grave 67.1[i]	1. Constans: C67.0175 (M7 R 467) 2. Constantius II: C67.0174 (M7 R 329) 3. Illegible (2 coins)	1. 341–346 AD 2. 351–354 AD 3. Not stated, probably Late Roman	Late Roman lamps
PN Grave 67.5[ii]	1. Probus: C67.0054 (M7 R 103) 2. Virtus Exerciti 2: C67.0779 (M7 R 1059) 3. Gloria Romanorum 21: C67.0780 (M7 R 923) 4. Uncertain (3 coins)	1. 276–282 AD 2. 395–408 AD 3. 402–408 AD 4.Hellenistic (field reading; residual?)	No other objects
HoB Mausoleum Grave 80.2[iii]	1. Pergamum: Asklepios/staff: M13 25.9 2. Claudius II (2 coins): M13 290.2, 294.5 3. Uncertain: Iovi Conservatori: M13 387.4 4. Uncertain: barbarous radiate (2 coins): M13 297.4, 300.2 5. VNMR: M13 423.12 6. Fel Temp Reparatio FH3: M13 557.14 7. Illegible: M13 1001.45 8. Arcadius: M13 809.6 9. Salus Reipublicae: M13 869.5 10. Gloria Romanorum 3 emperors: M13 940.25 11. Cross in Wreath: M13 963.111 12. Illegible (2 coins): M13 1003.192, 1003.193	1. 133–27 BC 2. 270 AD 3. 250–325 AD 4. After 270 AD 5. 341–346 AD 6. 346–361 AD 7. 4th century AD 8. 383–408 AD 9. 388–395 AD 10. 406–408 AD 11. 425–435 AD 12. 5th century AD	Late Roman bottle, fragment of Late Roman/Early Byzantine lamp with stamped cross relief
HoB Mausoleum Grave 80.4[iv]	1. Sardis: Apollo/club: M13 55.25 2. Sardis: Athena/tetrastyle temple: M13 **163.2** 3. Uncertain follis (2 coins): M13 387.1, 387.2 4. Vot Mult: M13 503.3 5. Fel Temp Reparatio FH (3 coins): M13 530.2, 557.15, 559.24 6. Salus Reipublicae (2 coins): M13 770.1, 800.13 7. Virtus Exerciti 2: M13 876.2 8. Gloria Romanorum 3 emperors: M13 940.36 9. Cross in Wreath: M13 963.65 10. Illegible: M13 1003.198	1. 2nd–1st century BC 2. 70–73 AD 3. 3rd–early 4th century AD 4. 347–348 AD 5. 346–361 AD 6. 388–392 AD 7. 395–401 AD 8. 406–408 AD 9. 425–435 AD 10. 5th century AD	No datable objects
HoB Mausoleum Grave 80.3[v]	1. Attalea: Dionysos/Pan: M13 135.1 2. Rome: Gallienus/Provi Aug: M13 251.1 3. Rome: Constantine I/Soli Invicto Comiti: M13 370.2 4. Gloria Exercitus 2 standards (2 coins): M13 471.1, 489.1 5. Gloria Exercitus 1 standard (6 coins): M13 458.1, 491.2, 511.2, 513.2, 583.1, 597.19 6. VNMR (6 coins): M13 413.1, 415.1, 418.5, 418.6, 423.1, 423.5 7. Ivst Ven Mem: M13 417.1 8. Victoriae dd Auggq nn (3 coins): M13 495.1, 495.2, 495.3 9. Vot Mult (23 coins): M13 475.3–5, 479.2, 484.5, 486.3, 488.5, 488.10, 488.11, 488.17, 500.1, 503.1, 503.4, 506.2, 507.1, 580.1, 587.1, 589.3, 595.6, 595.12, 595.16, 595.24, 595.28 10. Fel Temp Reparatio emperor and captives: M13 538.1 11. Fel Temp Reparatio FH (5 coins): M13 525.1, **540.1**, 556.1, 557.25, 604.5 12. Spes Reipublice (2 coins): M13 537.1, 545.6 13. Securitas Reipublicae: M13 637.5 14. Gloria Romanorum 8 (2 coins): M13 616.1, 680.6 15. Salus Reipublicae (3 coins): M13 703.2, 750.6, 886.23 16. Virtus Exerciti 2 (5 coins): M13 778.1, 803.13, 885.13, 885.48, 885.81 17. Illegible (8 coins): M13 606.16, 1001.46–52 18. Concordia Augg Cp Victoriola: M13 939.12 19. Concordia Auggg cross: M13 944.4 20. Gloria Romanorum 3 emperors (2 coins): M13 915.4, 940.21	1. 180–300 AD 2. 260–268 AD 3. 314–315 AD 4. 330–335 AD 5. 336–340 AD 6. 341–346 AD 7. 342–347 AD 8. 347–361 AD 9. 347–348 AD 10. 348–350 AD 11. 346–361 AD 12. 355–361 AD 13. 364–375 AD 14. 364–388 AD 15. 383–395 AD 16. 395–408 AD 17. 4th century AD 18. 401–403 AD 19. 404–406 AD 20. 406–408 AD	Late Roman/Early Byzantine lamp

	21. Gloria Romanorum 2 emperors (2 coins): M13 843.1, 859.2 22. Victoria Augg: M13 946.7 23. Marcian monogram: M13 969.55 24. Illegible (3 coins): M13 1003.194, 1003.195, 1003.196	21. 408–423 AD 22. 425–435 AD 23. 450–457 AD 24. 5th century AD	
HoB Mausoleum Grave 80.5[vi]	1. Lion standing l.: M13 984.23 2. Illegible: M13 1003.197	1. 457–474 AD 2. 5th century AD	Early Byzantine lamp
PN Tomb 61.14, Peacock Tomb[vii]	16 or "some 20" coins, of which 5 are identified in the record 1. Salus Reipublicae: C61.0344 2. Gloria Romanorum, 2 or 3 emperors: C61.0345 3. Anastasius I pentanummium: C61.0166 4. Phocas half-follis: C61.0164 5. Constans II: C61.0165 6. Illegible or disintegrated, uncertain number	 1. 393–395 AD 2. 402–423 AD 3. 498–518 AD 4. 605–606 AD 5. 653–654 AD	Final report suggested 5th-century date for tomb, by coin finds; Hanfmann's date due to stylistic parallels to paintings in 4th century AD

i *Fieldbook PN 67 I: 53; Ramage, Final Field Report: PN 1967, Appendix, p. 1.*
ii *Fieldbook PN 67 V: 10; Ramage, Final Field Report: PN 1967, Appendix, p. 2 added coin of Probus and three Hellenistic; Hanfmann, Mitten, and Ramage 1968, p. 11 called the grave fourth or fifth century.*
iii *Referred to as Grave 2 in fieldnotes. Fieldbook HoB 80 II: 57ff; Mitten, Final Field Report: HoB 1980, pp. 9, 23, 25; Greenewalt et al. 1983, p. 19.*
iv *Referred to as Grave 3 in fieldnotes. Fieldbook HoB 80 II: 77ff; Mitten, Final Field Report: HoB 1980, pp. 10, 25.*
v *Referred to as Grave 1 in fieldnotes. Fieldbook HoB 80 II: 67ff; Mitten, Final Field Report: HoB 1980, pp. 9–10, 25.*
vi *Referred to as Grave 4 in fieldnotes. Fieldbook HoB 80 II: 92ff; Mitten, Final Field Report: HoB 1980, pp. 10, 25; Greenewalt et al. 1983, p. 19.*
vii *Fieldbook PN 61 I: 88ff; Hansen, Final Field Report: PN 1961, p. 30; Hanfmann 1962, pp. 32–33 (coins not detailed).*

Along with the finds was a Hellenistic coin. This coin could have been residual even during the second-century AD burial phase, but it is not impossible that it was still in circulation, and it was chosen for its appropriate imagery of Asklepios (no. 25.9). During the fifth century, 14 more coins were introduced into the cist, the latest datable the Cross in Wreath reverse type (425–435). The deposit again looks very much like the fifth-century hoards found in Sardis, with a mixture of fourth- and fifth-century coins. Probably also associated with the burials were a coin of Licinius II (no. 362.1) and an uncertain fourth- to fifth-century coin (no. 1002.81), although they were not recorded as found specifically in a grave. A Late Roman lamp was included in this cist.[127]

The cist with the fewest number of goods in it was Grave 80.5. No early coins came from the grave. Only two fifth-century coins were found in the cist, the latest datable to 457–474, which may date the renovation. Three Late Roman lamps accompanied the coins.

Finally, Grave 80.4 had a Hellenistic coin and a coin from the second half of the first century AD, the latter with the preferred reverse (of that time) of a temple. In the fifth century, 12 coins were introduced. They range from the late third to the fifth century, ending with the Cross in Wreath reverse (425–435). Only a fragment of a lamp was recorded from this cist.

The HoB Mausoleum may have seen two phases of use before it was abandoned. The original burials may have belonged to the first or early second century AD, when coins were deposited in the graves (see Grave 80.4); other goods may have been retrieved when the grave was reused, but the coins escaped notice. It is possible that the Hellenistic/Early Imperial coins in 80.4 and 80.2 were residual, as the area was outside the city wall and could have been used as a dump (possibly even a cemetery) in the second or first century BC; there is evidence for an earlier dump here.

The cists were re-entered in the third quarter of the fifth century. Two different scenarios could explain the coins in the graves in the HoB Mausoleum. One possibility is that the derelict cemetery was discovered when the "House of Bronzes" started being built. The builders could have reused the tomb for their own fifth-century burials, perhaps as their "family" mausoleum. The old burials were pushed aside and new bodies put in, and coins were scattered across the bodies (in a fashion that is, admittedly, unusual in the fifth century; it is possible, though unlikely, that the scatter could be due to the intrusion of water into

127 Rautman, Roman Pottery Final Report 2013, p. 3.

the cist graves).[128] On the other hand, it is possible that the tomb was rediscovered in the fifth century as houses were rebuilt and expanded in this area; the discoverers venerated it as family monument. As the area was reconfigured for living quarters, the builders may have piously included coins and lamps as votive deposits to the newly-disturbed dead. Hanfmann noted that a smaller, painted tomb at the House of Bronzes was built in the fourth century, and "was carefully preserved under a Christian residence of the sixth century," possibly because the house builders perceived the tomb as a Christian tomb.[129] It is possible that we have a similar scenario with the HoB Mausoleum. Nevertheless, once the graves were resealed in the third quarter of the fifth century, they were left alone, and probably forgotten by the end of the century.

The Peacock Tomb in PN was excavated in 1961. The area was used as a cemetery from about 350 to the close of the fourteenth century, in and around the churches built in this sector.[130] The painted chamber tomb was built over first- or second-century graves, and the painting style is reminiscent of other fourth-century tombs in Sardis.[131] "Some 20 coins" noted by the excavator were ultimately reduced to five legible entries (I assume; an unrecorded number disintegrated). The excavator, Donald Hansen, described the coins as being found in the northwest corner of the tomb, along with a "tiny ring?" and earring. The primary burial was identified as a male, and it was found in the center of the tomb. Hanfmann associated the earliest coin in the group with the primary burial, at the end of the fourth century; the excavator preferred a date for the group in the fifth century, due to the presence of one coin dated to the first quarter of the fifth century. Yet one coin from the group dated to the early sixth century, one to the early seventh, and one to the mid-seventh century.

Clearly the group was not part of a grave gift in the fourth century, even if the inhumation dates to that period. It is likely, given the placement in the corner of the tomb, that the coins were contained in a bag or other perishable container. Foss suggested that the tomb was repeatedly visited, and visitors dropped votive coins, "for centuries."[132] The placement of one coin about every 50 years for a period of 150 years seems a little odd; this practice would also not explain the earring. Given the type of deposits that date to the mid-seventh century (see Section 3.6), it is much more likely that the bag of coins came from the mid-seventh century, as the family "cleaned up" a tomb constructed in the fourth century for reuse in the seventh century. If the painted decorations were perceived as belonging to a Christian tomb, we may even be able to see this as an offering to the perceived saintly original occupant.

3.5 Late Roman Contexts: The Fourth and Fifth Centuries[133]

The major areas of excavation of Late Roman material in Sardis include the area of the Synagogue[134] and Byzantine Shops; MMS, MMS/S, and MMS/N (houses, colonnaded street); and Field 49 (houses). However, almost any square in Sardis would yield Late Roman remains, from the villas that appear alongside the Pactolus, to cemeteries that lined the roads into Sardis (the latest uncovered in 2012). I will focus on the Late Roman deposits of MMS.[135]

The problem with identifying Late Roman contexts is that the pottery from this period is often dated in full centuries, not generations, and there is an overall lack of closely-dated fine wares in primary contexts to use as a benchmark. Hence, the coins date the deposits; the pottery expert uses the closing date of the deposit to narrow down the typology of the pottery in order

128 "Shear's Tomb" in Corinth provides a parallel. This was a tomb built in the second century, with burials placed in the tomb into the fifth or sixth century. Coins minted between the first and fourth centuries were found with the burials, but no fifth-century coins—and especially no large scattering of coins—were found in the latest burials (Walbank and Walbank 2015).

129 Hanfmann 1983, p. 208, no. 5.

130 Hanfmann 1983, p. 206.

131 Hanfmann 1983, p. 208, no. 7.

132 Foss 1976, p. 47.

133 In keeping with numismatic terminology, I will refer to the fourth and fifth centuries as Late Roman, not Early Byzantine, which is the preferred label for pottery specialists. For a fuller description of the reverse types, see App. 3.

134 Andrew Seager is preparing the final publication of the Synagogue; I am writing the section on the coin finds.

135 Marcus Rautman presented me with these contexts, and I thank him for his collaboration, but it should be stressed that the pottery from these deposits is still under study as Rautman prepares the final publication of the houses of Sardis.

to find fourth-, fifth-, or sixth-century forms. What can be noted by isolating the following contexts is to show the coins that were in circulation at the same time, and to reinforce the point that the latest coin only gives a *terminus post quem* to the deposit.

However, the problem of residual coins and the length of circulation is especially acute in the Late Roman period, as many small copper-alloy coins are found in the Late Roman strata of any city. I have adapted a formula used for finding the Mean Ceramic Date (MCD) of historical pottery to try to find a profile of a fourth-, early, middle, or late fifth-century deposit (see App. 4).

3.5.1 Fourth-Century Contexts

Deposit 1 (Table 3.10a)[136]

The *terminus post quem* from the coins is the middle of the fourth century. The stratum was dated to the mid- to late fourth century due to pottery and coins.[137] The presence of a late third-century coin in this deposit is not surprising in a fourth-century context. Three of the four deposits contained coins of the late third century, as did several fifth-century deposits, including HoB Graves 80.2, 80.3, and 80.4, and PN Grave 67.5, and one hoard closed in the fifth century (H8, see below). It appears that late third-century coins were part of the circulation pool in the fourth century and into the fifth century.

Deposit 2 (Table 3.10b)[138]

The absence of first half of the fourth-century coins is interesting, but not disturbing, given the few coins that were found in this deposit. The use of third-century coins in fourth-century contexts has already been noted above; the size and weight of this coin (15 mm, 1.6 g) would allow it to circulate comfortably in the fourth century.

Deposit 3 (Table 3.10c)[139]

Rautman dated these Lots to mid- to late fourth century by the pottery; the coins show a mixture of dates, with one late fourth-century issue.[140] The Hellenistic issues could be residual, as residual Hellenistic pottery appeared in other deposits in MMS.[141] The third-century coins are more likely to reflect fourth-century circulation, especially given their size. The *terminus post quem* from the coins is the very end of the fourth century, but this *terminus* is reflected in one coin, which is at least 30 years older than the next two coins in the deposit.

Deposit 4 (Table 3.10d)[142]

One coin (no. 230.24, first to third century) was rejected as residual, since it was 25 mm and 7.82 g. Although the Imperial layers have not been isolated in MMS/N, the area was likely occupied in the Imperial period, since it was within the city limits.[143] The Roman Provincial coins from this occupation may have been reintegrated into the strata in the building activities in the fourth century; yet two of them could have circulated into the fourth century, since their module is close to fourth-century coins. Rautman noted the fourth-century context of the imported pottery and used the deposit to help clarify the picture of locally-produced fourth-century pottery.[144] He has more recently suggested that "the pottery runs through the mid/late fourth century, with little or any that must date after 400."[145] If the resulting group of coins reflects the normal circulation pattern of fourth-century coins, the result is a heavy reliance on coins of the end of the third century. There are fewer coins of the first half of the fourth century surviving, with a rise in numbers of issues of Valentinian I, Valens, Valentinian II, and Theodosius I that are reflected in the overall numbers of fourth-century coins in Sardis. However, we would expect more coins, especially

136 For an overview of the Late Roman Townhouse, see Rautman 1995b. Although I am aware that King's research (2013, pp. 14, 16, 33) suggested that 11 or more coins were needed for an analysis, Rautman has only been able to isolate a few fourth-century deposits; I thank him for providing me with these contexts. The evidence of these small deposits should be used with caution.

137 Greenewalt and Rautman 2000, p. 645.

138 Rautman 1995b, p. 57.

139 Rautman 1995b, p. 56.

140 Rautman, Roman Pottery Final Report 2011, pp. 1, 5.

141 Rautman, Roman Pottery Final Report 2011, p. 7.

142 Greenewalt, Ratté, and Rautman 1995, pp. 3–7.

143 Cahill, pers. comm.

144 Greenewalt, Ratté, and Rautman 1995, p. 7.

145 Rautman, pers. comm.

Table 3.10a 4th c. Deposit 1: Room 7 of the Late Roman Townhouse, packing beneath sloping tile floor (MMS-II 93.1 Lots 13, 14 and MMS-II 96.1 Lots 18, 22), 7 coins.

Issuer or Issue	Date	Catalogue No.
Claudius II, posthumous	270 AD and later	294.1
Licinius I	318–320 AD	348.1
Constantine II	320 AD	**384.1**
Licinius II	321–324 AD	360.3
Constantius II	337–348 AD	474.1, 488.14
Fel Temp Reparatio phoenix globe	348–351 AD	594.1

Table 3.10b 4th c. Deposit 2: Room 6 of the Late Roman Townhouse, under tile floor (MMS-I 82.B Lots 22, 29; MMS-I 85.1 Lot 18), 6 coins.

Issuer or Issue	Date	Catalogue No.
Sardis	212–217 AD	193.1
Constantius II	348–361 AD	533.4, 533.5, 559.6
Gloria Romanorum 8	364–388 AD	680.2
Illegible	4th century AD	1001.71

Table 3.10c 4th c. Deposit 3: Room (Corridor) 4 of the Late Roman Townhouse (MMS-I 90.1 Lots 104, 113, 114, 115), 6 coins.

Issuer or Issue	Date	Catalogue No.
Alexander III and successors	336–227 BC	14.1
Seleucus II	246–241 BC	80.3
Philip II	244–249 AD	**210.1**
Gallienus	260–268 AD	248.1
Licinius I	321–324 AD	351.6
House of Constantine	324–361 AD	606.2, 3
Virtus Exerciti 2	395–401 AD	885.5

those dating after 341, as the overall numbers from Sardis show a substantial number of recovered coins from this period (Fig. 2.4). The *terminus post quem* for the coins is the end of the fourth century, although the *terminus* is defined by only two coins.

Since three of the four deposits outlined here have fewer than 11 coins in them, conclusions about fourth-century deposits must be made with caution. The coin *termini post quem* for the deposits ranges from not very reflective of the pottery *termini* to closely aligned. Perhaps the size of the sample in Deposit 4 (drain latrine context in MMS/N) allows us to have some confidence that the coin *terminus* and the pottery *terminus* should be closely aligned in fourth-century deposits. All of the deposits include third-century coins, which can now be seen as part of the body of circulating coin in the fourth century. It is also interesting that the largest deposit contains a substantial number of coins from the first half of the fourth century, even though the deposit was closed by the end of the century. It thus appears unlikely that there was a substantial, or thorough, recall of early fourth-century coins as the module decreased (see above, Section 2.5.1).

A calculation of the Mean Coin Date for Deposit 4 (the only one with enough coins for a reasonable calculation) is suggestive of the broad range of coins that are still being used as legal tender—that is, are indigenous to the deposits. The calculation provided an MCD of 332, with 49% of the coins in the deposit falling before that date.[146] The deposits do not appear to tail off as hoards do, with coins from within the 25 years of the date of closure of the deposit being abundant and the 25 years prior normally of the same level (admittedly,

146 The calculation of the MCD without the second-century and third- to early fourth-century coin produced a marginally different number (339), with 51% of the coins falling before that date.

Table 3.10d 4th c. Deposit 4: Closure of drain and latrine complex under the lower mosaic of the south portico of MMS/N plaza (MMS/N 90.1 Lots 46–48, 51 and MMS/N 91.1 Lots 59, 72, unlotted), 37 coins.

Issuer or Issue	Date	Catalogue No.
Roman Provincial	2nd century AD	137.1 (19 mm, 4.40 g)
Antoninianus or follis	3rd or early 4th century AD	387.11 (21 mm, 4.71 g)
Claudius II Gothicus, barbarous radiate	270–300 AD	297.5
Galerius Maximian	293–305 AD	335.1, 339.1
Diocletian	295–296 AD	327.2, 327.4
Maximian Herculius	295–299 AD	331.3
Constantius Chlorus	295–296 AD	340.2
Crispus	317–326 AD	383.1
Constantine I	317–320 AD	375.1
Licinius I	318–324 AD	347.1, 349.1, 349.3, 353.4
Constantine I	306–320 AD	368.1, 374.1, 379.1
Constantine I, posthumous	337–346 AD	414.2, 422.1
Constantine II	337–340 AD	454.2
Constans	337–340 AD	498.1, 511.1
Constantius II	347–361 AD	488.13, 560.16, 560.42
Julian II	355–361 AD	570.2
Securitas Reipublicae	364–375 AD	676.1, 684.32, 684.77
Gloria Romanorum 8	364–388 AD	680.7
Theodosius I	378–395 AD	753.1
Illegible	4th century AD	1001.132
Illegible	4th or 5th century AD	1002.212, 1002.396, 1002.397, 1002.433

the graph shows only fifth-century hoards, since there are no fourth-century hoards from the modern excavations in Sardis). In hoards, the earlier issues show a substantial drop-off commensurate with their age, a result different from the deposits noted here.[147] Instead, the numbers show a small group of coins comes from the latest phase of the deposit. Some deposits only show their age with one coin or even no coins that coincide with the pottery *terminus*. Almost all of the deposits appear to show a heavy reliance on issues dating 20, 30, or 50 years earlier than the latest-dated coin.

3.5.2 Fifth-Century Contexts

I will begin by looking at deposits found under the lower mosaics of the south portico of MMS/N Road and Plaza; this is the mosaic with inscription noting the prefecture of Flavius Archelaus. I stress that this list does not necessarily date the mosaics, but only discusses the coins found under the mosaics and attempts to find a normal profile for the fifth-century strata.[148]

Deposit 1 (Table 3.11a)[149]

It appears that there are three coins (Marcian, no. 967.2; and Leo I, nos. 973.2 and 986.10) that are intrusive in this context, as the mortar did not entirely seal the layer, but stopped short of the back of the stylobate.[150] The coins may have worked their way into this crack from the bedding of the upper mosaic of the south portico of the MMS/N Plaza (see Table

147 Coins of the second half of the fourth century were gathered into a small hoard found near the Artemis Temple by Bell (1916, p. viii); the hoard closed around 400. As recorded by Bell, this hoard has the normal profile of a hoard (see below).

148 I am indebted to Rautman for providing me with the list of Lots and Baskets that make up this deposit.

149 Greenewalt, Sterud, and Belknap 1982, p. 17, where fifth-century coins are noted on top of the mosaic, helping to date it. However, there are discrepancies among the fieldbook, the final report, and the published version, so the coins cannot provide a reliable *terminus ante quem* for the deposit. For the coins in the metaling, see Harward, Final Field Report: MMS/N 78.1, p. 11. For 79.1, Rautman, pers. comm. For 90.1, this deposit was not sieved (Umholtz, Final Field Report: MMS/N 90.1, p. 3); for locus numbers, see Rautman, Revised Coin List Report 1995. For 91.1, Fieldbook MMS/N 91.1 I: 81–89.

150 Fieldbook MMS/N 91.1 I: 129–33.

Table 3.11a 5th c. Deposit 1: Bedding of the lower mosaic of the south portico of MMS/N plaza (MMS/N 78.1, not lotted; MMS/N 79.1, not lotted; MMS/N 90.1, Lots 13, 45; MMS/N 91.1 (Lots 13, 45, 71), 58 coins.

Issuer or Issue	Date	Catalogue No.
Illegible	1st to 3rd century AD	230.22
Illegible	3rd century AD	387.24
Gallienus	253–260 AD	242.1
Claudius II Gothicus, posthumous	270 AD and later	292.1
Diocletian	295–296 AD	327.1
Maximian Herculius	295–298 AD	331.4
Galerius Maximian	302–303 AD	334.1
Licinius I	313–324 AD	350.3, 351.4
Crispus	317–320 AD	382.1
Licinius II	321–324 AD	353.1, 5, 361.2
Constantine I	327–335 AD	395.1, 398.3
Urbs Roma	330–336 AD	431.1
Constans	337–340 AD	505.1
Constantine I, posthumous	341–346 AD	421.4, 422.2, 423.4
Constantius II	330–348 AD	480.1, 483.2, 484.2, 484.3, 486.1, 487.1, 488.1, 488.7, 488.8, 524.1, 530.1, 559.23
Julian II	355–361 AD	569.1
House of Constantine	324–361 AD	595.29, 606.42
Valentinian I	364–367 AD	610.1
Securitas Reipublicae	364–383 AD	679.7, 684.48, 684.73
Victory l.	364–435 AD	887.34
Theodosius I	378–383 AD	733.1
Vot Mult	383 AD	825.4
Honorius, Arcadius	395–401 AD	772.1, 792.6, 796.7, 832.3, 836.9, 851.1, 855.5, 855.6, 885.9, 885.47
Theodosius II, Eudoxia	401–408 AD	811.1, 913.2, 915.3
Gloria Romanorum 3 emperors	400–408 AD	940.9
Gloria Romanorum 2 emperors	408–423 AD	942.19
Illegible	4th or 5th century AD	1001.140, 1002.278, 1002.451, 1002.452, 1002.453, 1003.1305

3.12b). The mosaic was dated in preliminary reports to the second half of the fourth or beginning of the fifth century, due to the coin evidence.[151] Only one coin in the deposit extends this *terminus* to ca. 425, a pattern we will find repeated in other fifth-century deposits. Also fairly typically, the number of fourth-century coins is approximately equal to the number of fifth-century coins; the deposit also includes coins that predate the 354 reform, as well as coins of the late third century. The period between 364 and 388 is something of an anomaly here, as the number of coins from this period is less than previous and later periods.

Deposit 2 (Table 3.11b)[152]

It is possible that so many coins were in this installation due to its function as a water basin, with water piped in. Note that the presence of mortar greatly magnified

151 Greenewalt, Ratté, and Rautman 1995, p. 7; Greenewalt 1991, p. 458.

152 Rautman 1995b, p. 59; Greenewalt, Rautman, and Cahill 1988, pp. 57–59.

Table 3.11b 5th c. Deposit 2: Late Roman Townhouse, Room 10 hydraulic feature (MMS-I 85.1 Lots 51 and 57), 97 coins.

Issuer or Issue	Date	Catalogue No.
Securitas Reipublicae	364–367 AD	684.84
Victory l.	364–435 AD	887.36
Theodosius I or II	379–450 AD	927.10
Salus Reipublicae	383–395 AD	886.137
Arcadius, Honorius	395–401 AD	870.9, 885.76
Cross in Wreath	425–435 AD	922.7, 963.44, 963.182
Marcian	450–457 AD	969.61, 969.81, 969.90
Leo I	457–474 AD	977.3, 984.11, 984.30, 985.27, 985.39, 988.1, 987.50, 987.51
Zeno	476–491 AD	995.14, 997.65, 997.69
Uncertain monogram	450–498 AD	999.35, 999.47, 999.76, 999.93, 999.123, 999.137, 999.181, 999.229, 999.259
Illegible	4th century AD	1001.72, 1001.73
Illegible	4th or 5th century AD	1002.131–148
Illegible	5th century AD	1003.385–428, 1003.440

Table 3.11c 5th c. Deposit 3: Late Roman Townhouse, Room 3, sealed beneath tile floor (MMS-I 85.1 Lot 82, with MMS-I 83 Basket 49, not lotted), 37 coins.

Issuer or Issue	Date	Catalogue No.
Julian II	355–361 AD	575.4
Victory l.	364–435 AD	887.30
Cross in Wreath	425–435 AD	963.93
Leo I	457–474 AD	975.8
Illegible	4th century AD	1001.75
Illegible	4th or 5th century AD	1002.152
Illegible	5th century AD	1003.432, 1003.438
Hoard 6, 29 coins	Latest identifiable: 457–474 AD	Evans 2013b

the corrosion of these coins, making a high percentage illegible (two disintegrated in cleaning). The *terminus post quem* from the coins is the end of the fifth century. The deposit lacks coins of the first half of the fourth century. However, there are coins of the later fourth century present in the deposit.

Deposit 3 (Table 3.11c)[153]

The datable coins in both the matrix and the hoard range from the middle of the fourth to the third quarter of the fifth century, a wide range for a small sample. The *terminus post quem* from the coins is the end of the fifth century, a date obtained by both the coins in the matrix and in the hoard.

Deposit 4 (Table 3.11d)[154]

This small deposit is compact, with datable coins only from the fifth century (one residual coin from the first or second century was discarded, no. 230.80); the end of the fifth century is thus the *terminus post quem*.

Deposit 5 (Table 3.11e)[155]

Coins from the first half of the fourth century are missing, as is seen in other deposits. Although the *terminus post quem* for the coins is the very end of the fifth century, more coins in the deposit can be dated to the third quarter than to the last quarter of the century; only two coins give the *terminus*.

153 Rautman 1995b, p. 61; Greenewalt, Rautman, and Cahill 1998, p. 61.

154 Greenewalt, Ratté, and Rautman 1995, p. 7.

155 Rautman 1995b, p. 59.

Table 3.11d 5th c. Deposit 4: House west of the Late Roman Townhouse, floor (MMS-III 93.1 Lot 5), 7 coins.

Issuer or Issue	Date	Catalogue No.
Marcian	450–457 AD	969.53
Anastasius I	491–498 AD	1004.146
Uncertain monogram	450–498 AD	999.290
Imitation	5th century AD	1115.1
Illegible	4th or 5th century AD	1002.259, 1002.261
Illegible	5th century AD	1003.903

Table 3.11e 5th c. Deposit 5: Late Roman Townhouse, Room 23, packing for floor (MMS-II 91.1 Lot 159), 34 coins.

Issuer or Issue	Date	Catalogue No.
Constantius II	355–361 AD	560.53
Theodosius I	383–395 AD	738.2
Arcadius	383–408 AD	809.11
Cross in Wreath	425–435 AD	963.188, 189
Marcian	450–457 AD	969.20
Leo I	457–474 AD	987.32
Anastasius I	491–498 AD	1004.47
Uncertain monogram	450–498 AD	999.213, 999.253
Illegible	4th or 5th century AD	1002.216, 1002.217
Illegible	5th century AD	1003.582–603

Deposit 6 (Table 3.11f)[156]

The late third-century coin may be a residual coin as well, as there was activity in tombs in this area at this time, yet third-century coins appear to be part of the circulation pool in the fifth century, as noted above. There is a gap in the coins until the middle of the fourth century, not an uncommon pattern for the fifth century. Only a few coins date the *terminus post quem* of the mosaic to 425–450, but this can be seen as an expected coin behavior, as in several of the deposits listed above. More coins date to the last quarter of the fourth century than the quarter century of the *terminus post quem*. The deposit has a peak in the first quarter of the fifth century.

The coins look like an intentional scatter: that is, there are more coins per square meter than are found in other fills, suggesting that the coins were intentionally introduced into the bedding. Thus, with the evidence from PN, the lower and upper mosaics of the south portico of the MMS/N Plaza (see also below, Section 3.6), and the Synagogue, we can perhaps postulate that there was some effort to throw coins in the bedding matrix of mosaics.

Deposit 7 (Table 3.11g)[157]

The *terminus post quem* is provided by one coin of the total, from the third quarter of the fifth century. The presence of a third-century coin in a fifth-century context is no longer surprising, nor is the fact that the deposit is dated by only one coin.

Deposit 8 (Table 3.11h)[158]

Note that I rejected four coins as being residual, as they are large and are found at the transition to another Lot (possibly the insertion of a pipe): Sardis, 245/220–second century BC (no. 52.59); Seleucid, third or second century BC (no. 93.27); uncertain

156 Buttrey cataloged the coins (and I did not recheck the identifications): Buttrey et al. 1981, p. xxii. Rautman suggested this deposit to me as an appropriate fifth-century deposit; he is working on the final publication of the villa and the results should be considered preliminary.

157 Greenewalt and Rautman 2000, p. 671.

158 Greenewalt, Ratté, and Rautman 1994, p. 26; cf. Evans 2013b.

Table 3.11f 5th c. Deposit 6: Mosaic bedding from the Late Roman domestic complex in PN (excavated in 1960 and 1961), 53 coins. The mosaics of Rooms B and C are not clearly distinguished, so they are combined in this entry.

Issuer or Issue	Date	Catalogue No.
Maximian Herculius	295–296 AD	C61.0204
Constantius II	351–361 AD	C61.0144, 200, 261, 266–268, 273
Valens, Valentinian I	364–375 AD	C61.0197, 260, 262, 263
Valentinian II	378–383 AD	C61.0298.1
Theodosius I	383 AD	C61.0199
Salus Reipublicae	383–395 AD	C61.0156, C61.0278; M13 298.2
Arcadius	395–408 AD	C61.0145–50, 152, 153, 201, 277; M13 298.3
Concordia Aug cross	395–408 AD	C61.0154
Concordia Augg Cp	402–408 AD	C61.0274; M13 298.4
Gloria Romanorum 3 emperors	402–408 AD	C60.0102
Gloria Romanorum 2 emperors shield or globe	408–423 AD	C61.0151, 275; M13 298.5
Theodosius II	425–450 AD	C61.0264, 276
Victoria Aug(gg)	410–455 AD	C61.0155
Illegible	4th or 5th century AD	C61.0298.6–10, 603, 610, 622, 624, 626, 629, 631, 632
Illegible	5th century AD	C61.0607, 623

Table 3.11g 5th c. Deposit 7: Late Roman building complex, under floor (MD2 96.1 Lot 16), 8 coins.

Issuer or Issue	Date	Catalogue No.
Otacilia Severa	244–245 AD	239.1
Valentinian II, Arcadius, Honorius	383–395 AD	709.12, 800.20, 835.2
Arcadius, Honorius	395–401 AD	783.7, 847.3
Leo I	457–474 AD	987.37
Illegible	5th century AD	1003.213

Table 3.11h 5th c. Deposit 8: Roman building, floor with Hoard 4 underneath (ByzFort 91.17 Lot 52), 94 coins.

Issuer or Issue	Date	Catalogue No.
Claudius II Gothicus	253–270 AD	288.1
Diocletian	284–305 AD	329.65
Constantius II	346-361 AD	549.1
Securitas Reipublicae	364–375 AD	684.27, 684.60, 684.95
Vot Mult	383 AD	956.2
Concordia Aug(gg) or Cross in Wreath	404–435 AD	963.129
Leo I	457–474 AD	988.6
Uncertain monogram	450–498 AD	999.228
Illegible	4th century AD	1001.195
Illegible	4th or 5th century AD	1002.46–48
Illegible	5th century AD	1003.91–98
Victory l., Vandalic	5th or 6th century AD	1107.2
Hoard 4, 71 coins	Latest datable, 474–491 AD	Evans 2013b

Hellenistic (no. 94.30); and Pergamum (no. 105.1).[159] The coins in the matrix reflect the coins in the hoard, with some late third-century coins added to the mix, a not unusual addition to fifth-century coinage.

The Mean Coin Date (MCD) for the deposits with more than seven coins fell between 346 and 443: the earliest was in the bedding of the lower mosaic of the south portico of the MMS/N Plaza, a deposit which appears to have closed in the early fifth century. About half of the coins in the deposit (48%) were minted before the MCD; these numbers are close to those of the fourth-century drain/latrine complex in MMS/N, which is not entirely surprising, since that complex closed in the late fourth century. Of interest is the MCD for the stratum under the mosaics in the villa at PN, which had a *terminus post quem* of the mid-fifth century: it was 394, with 32% of the coins in the deposit minted prior to the MCD. None of the other fifth-century deposits had such high numbers of coins minted prior to the MCD (see Fig. 3.3).[160]

The deposit with a mid-fifth century *terminus*, MMS Late Roman Townhouse Room 3, had an MCD that was closer to the *terminus* of the deposit, 428, with 24% of the coins in the deposit minted before that date. By the end of the fifth century, the deposits could have low MCDs (the hydraulic feature in the MMS Late Roman Townhouse, Room 10, which was calculated at 439 and the Roman Building in ByzFort, which had an MCD of 423). However, the Late Roman Townhouse in MMS, Room 23, had an MCD of 443. All of these end-of-the-fifth-century deposits had low numbers of coins minted before the MCD: 11%, 12%, and 15%, respectively.

It thus appears that in deposits that were spread under mosaics, depositors used third-century coins—which were still available—but they had fewer coins from the first half of the fourth century available. The other deposits, especially those of the mid- to late fifth century, show this lack more starkly. The mid-fifth-century deposit still has a number of fourth-century coins, but the end of the fifth century shows that they are much less common in the circulation pool. The MCD calculation of the fifth-century deposits, then, shows that the indigenous coins normally are composed of a percentage of coins that were minted 50 or more years before the calculated mean. This profile is like the larger fourth-century deposit, and it fits closely with the argument that was made by Gabriela Bijovsky and others—that the fifth century uses earlier coins as legal tender.

3.6 Byzantine Contexts: The Sixth through Early Seventh Centuries

Most Byzantine contexts were isolated within the residential quarter of MMS; Rautman provided me with specific information about these contexts. Isolating these deposits gives us a glimpse into the circulating coin pool in the sixth and seventh centuries. Deposits that can be isolated to the eighth through twelfth centuries are missing from Sardis.

Deposit 1 (Table 3.12a)[161]

Although it appears that the *terminus post quem* from the coins for this deposit is ca. 475, and it looks very much like a fifth-century deposit, a deposit sealed underneath this floor contained a coin of Justin I (no. 1014.3).

Deposit 2 (Table 3.12b)

Rautman suggested that the well was regularly cleaned, given the absence of sediment in the bottom; it was filled with architectural debris. The well was opened in the early fifth century, closing in the early seventh century (or possibly later), based on his reading of the pottery.[162] Yet the *terminus post quem* for the closure of the well in the numismatic profile is the first quarter of the sixth century. I am not certain if the Roman Provincial coin is residual or infiltrated (the weight and diameter could well circulate in the fourth to mid-fifth century), but there were fourth-century, as well as fifth-century coins in this deposit,

159 Fieldbook ByzFort 91.17 I: 128–32.

160 Deposit 1, the mortar bedding for the lower mosaic of the south portico in MMS/N Plaza, had an MCD of 374, with 46% of the coins in the deposit minted before the mean. The Late Roman Townhouse hydraulic feature (Deposit 2) had a MCD of 449, with 43% of the coins minted prior to this date. Deposit 6, under a mosaic in PN, had an MCD of 390, with 39% of the coins minted prior to the mean. Many fewer were minted after the median. Deposit 3 (Late Roman Townhouse Room 3 floor) and Deposit 9 (ByzFort) had MCDs of 437 and 444, respectively, with 72% and 23% of coins falling below their MCDs. Deposits 4, 5, 7, and 8 were too small to run the calculations.

161 Greenewalt, Rautman, and Cahill 1988, p. 57.

162 Rautman 1995a, p. 40 "Courtyard Well."

Table 3.12a 6/7th c. Deposit 1: Late Roman Townhouse, Room 3, under plaster bedding for floor (MMS-I 85.1 Lot 42), 6 coins.

Issuer or Issue	Date	Catalogue No.
Urbs Roma	330–336 AD	436.1
Restitutor Reip	364–365 AD	614.6
Leo I	457–474 AD	985.3
Illegible	4th or 5th century AD	1002.153
Illegible	5th century AD	1003.373, 1003.439

Table 3.12b 6/7th c. Deposit 2: MMS-II 85.1 well, 12 coins.

Issuer or Issue	Date	Catalogue No.
Roman Provincial	1st to 3rd century AD	230.66 (19 mm, 2.96 g)
Illegible	4th century AD	1001.83
Illegible	4th or 5th century AD	1002.181–183
Illegible	5th century AD	1003.491–493, 500–501
Decanummium	498–607 AD	1199.4
Justin I	518–527 AD	1010.3

even if they were not legible. It appears that sixth- and seventh-century deposits at Sardis cannot be primarily dated by coins, as the coins of the sixth and seventh centuries can be missing entirely from a deposit.

Deposit 3 (Table 3.12c)[163]

The Hellenistic coin is probably infiltrated into this layer, as there is ample evidence of Hellenistic coins under the Synagogue and Byzantine Shops, and the weight is not within the bounds of normal fourth- or fifth-century coins. I have left this coin out of the MCD calculations, as I did for the Roman denarius and Roman Provincial coin (also too heavy to circulate easily in this era).

The coins from under the upper mosaic of the south portico of the MMS/N plaza show a pattern consistent with other mosaic floors in Sardis: there were a number of coins under the mosaic, with coins ranging from the fourth to the sixth century, and with about 20% of the coins dating to the fourth century (see Fig. 3.4). This deposit is a little unusual in that a few coins from the first half of the fourth century are present. As in the other deposits, the highest percentage of coins comes from periods at least 25 years before the youngest coin in the deposit. The *terminus post quem* from the identifiable coins is around 580–600, although only a small number of coins (from one year of excavation) provide the *terminus*.

The Mean Coin Date for the date when the coins came from the mints for this entire deposit is very low (416), which underscores how few coins give the coin *terminus post quem*. Fully 70% of the coins in the deposit fall below the MCD (Fig. 3.3). The fourth- and fifth-century coins cannot have been residual or infiltrated; they must reflect circulating coins of the sixth century. The MCD underlines the lack of new coins coming into Sardis in the sixth century, necessitating the use of the older coins.

163 Rautman has prepared a preliminary list of coins from this context; I am grateful for his help. For 78.1, Harward, Final Field Report: MMS/N 78.1, p. 11. For 80.1, Fieldbook MMS/N 80.1 II: 23–24, 27, 57, 59. For 90.1, Rautman, Revised Coin List Report 1995. For 91.1, Fieldbook MMS/N 91.1 I: 67–73. For 92.1, Fieldbook MMS/N 92.1 I: 5; McIntosh, Final Field Report: MMS/N 92.1, pp. 9–10. For 96.1, Prieto, Final Field Report: MMS/N 96.1, pp. 17, 22–23. It should be noted that the latest coins come from 92.1 Lot 72 Basket 43, which Rautman preliminarily suggested was not an intrusion into the deposit. Even without this Basket, the *terminus post quem* would be a coin of Tiberius II, minted in 578, and the MCD would be lowered by only a few years.

Table 3.12c 6/7th c. Deposit 3: Bedding of the upper mosaic of the south portico of MMS/N plaza (MMS/N 78.1 not lotted; MMS/N 79.1 not lotted; MMS/N 80.1 not lotted; MMS/N 90.1 Lots 6, 8, 41; MMS/N 91.1 Lot 42; MMS/N 92.1 Lots 70, 71, 72; MMS/N 96.1 Lots 194–202), 678 coins. It appears that all or most of the deposits were sieved; a number disintegrated upon cleaning.

Issuer or Issue	Date	Catalogue No.
Sardis civic coin	245/220–2nd century BC	52.57 (17 mm, 6.30 g)
Lucius Verus, denarius	165–166 AD	233.1
Roman Provincial	2nd–3rd century AD	142.1 (15 mm, 2.02 g); 230.116 (frag'y)
Illegible antoninianus	3rd–early 4th century AD	387.10, 387.18
Victorinus	269 AD	304.1
Licinius I	313 AD	345.1
Constantine I	311–328 AD	376.1, 389.2, 581.2
Providentiae Augg	324–328 AD	401.1, 409.1
Helena?	324–340 AD	428.1
Providentiae Caess	325–326 AD	447.1
Urbs Roma	330–337 AD	432.1
House of Constantine	324–361 AD	606.36, 606.39, 606.43, 606.46
Victory on prow	330–336 AD	439.1, 441.2
Gloria Exercitus 1 or 2 standards	330–340 AD	408.1, 437.2, 485.1, 448.1, 460.1, 505.3, 597.4, 597.9, 597.12, 597.17, 597.21, 598.1
Constantine I, posthumous	341–346 AD	421.5
Victory l.	342–347 AD	599.2
Fel Temp Reparatio FH	346–361 AD	526.2, 527.4, 555.1, 557.20, 557.28, 558.8, 558.12, 559.8, 559.18, 559.35, 562.1, 604.10
Vot Mult or Victoriae dd Auggq nn or VNMR	347–348 AD	418.7, 493.1, 503.2, 587.3, 589.1, 595.7, 595.13, 595.30
Spes Reipublice	355–361 AD	534.1, 546.1, 560.8, 560.13, 560.14, 560.19, 560.24, 560.27, 560.31, 560.41, 560.45, 560.47, 560.51, 560.52, 571.1, 575.3, 575.6, 605.8
Securitas Reipublicae or Restitutor Reip	364–367 AD	612.1, 614.1, 618.1, 619.2, 621.1, 684.29, 684.34, 684.36, 684.68, 684.78, 684.80, 684.81, 684.82, 684.86, 684.94, 684.96, 684.98
Securitas Reipublicae	364–383 AD	622.3, 622.5, 622.8, 679.6
Gloria Romanorum 8	364–375 AD	642.3, 682.3, 685.20, 685.54
Valentinian I or II	364–392 AD	761.4
Victory l.	364–435 AD	887.25, 887.27, 887.41
Concordia Auggg or Virtus Romanorum	378–383 AD	655.1, **711.1**, 726.2, 763.2, 763.5, 763.6, 763.8
Victoria Augg(g) 2 Victories	378–435 AD	958.1, 958.3
Theodosius I or II	379–450 AD	927.1, 927.6, 927.7
Vot Mult	383 AD	665.1, 696.1, 713.1, 754.1, 825.14
Salus Reipublicae	383–395 AD	703.1, 722.3, 722.4, 750.14, 787.1, 800.1, 878.1, 886.6, 886.26, 886.40, 886.43, 886.63, 886.72, 886.79, 886.82, 886.86, 886.87, 886.114, 886.121, 886.131, 886.140, 886.146
Arcadius, Honorius	383–408 AD	808.1, 809.1, 809.3, 857.1, 870.5
Vot Mult	383–435 AD	956.5
Gloria Romanorum 18 or emperor horseback	392–395 AD	723.3, 731.2, 854.2, 889.3
Urbs Roma Felix	394–395 AD	829.1, 829.2

Virtus Exerciti 2	395–401 AD	778.19, 778.27, 783.6, 803.27, 803.31, 847.14, 847.15, 855.6, 855.26, 880.3, 885.1, 885.11, 885.39, 885.50, 885.54, 885.71, 885.73
Victoria Augg Victory l.	395–435 AD	959.1
Arcadius, Theodosius II	401–406 AD	791.2, 791.4, 799.1, 811.3, 913.1, 939.19
Concordia Aug(gg) cross	404–406 AD	944.7, 944.8
Gloria Romanorum 3 emperors or Concordia Auggg cross	406–408 AD	793.1, 797.1, 852.1, 940.4, 940.12
Gloria Romanorum 2 emperors	408–423 AD	859.1, 859.6, 860.1, 892.2, 916.1, 917.1, 934.1, 941.2, 941.23, 942.5, 942.10, 942.11, 942.15, 943.5
Victoria Augg	410–423 AD	830.2, 830.3
Concordia Aug	423–425 AD	896.2, 928.1
Cross in Wreath or Victoria Augg or Vrtvs Romanorvm or Concordia Aug Victory or Salus Reipublicae	425–435 AD	903.2, 909.1, 922.15, 922.28, 946.6, 946.8, 949.1, 954.1, 960.1, 963.3, 963.4, 963.9, 963.14, 963.17, 963.20, 963.40, 963.41, 963.47, 963.51, 963.55, 963.60, 963.73, 963.75, 963.86, 963.87, 963.99, 963.103, 963.105, 963.107, 963.117, 963.122, 963.136, 963.146, 963.150, 963.156, 963.162, 963.180, 963.184, 963.191, 963.192, 963.195
Vt XX V	435 AD	900.1, 924.7, 924.8
ConcordiaAgv	437 AD?	901.1
Theodosius II, Valentinian III	425–450 AD	**911.1**
Marcian	450–457 AD	964.2, 967.1 968.1 969.5, 969.7, 969.18, 969.26, 969.27, 969.49, 969.54, 969.57, 969.68, 969.72, 969.75, 969. 89
Leo I	457–474 AD	974.7 975.1, 975.2, 976.1, 976.5, 976.7, 976.9, 983.1, 984.4, 984.8, 985.4, 985.10, 985.14, 985.36, 985.37, 986.15, 986.19, 986.31, 987.15, 987.17, 987.44, 987.48, 988.5
Zeno	474–491 AD	997.2, 997.5
Uncertain monogram	450–498 AD	999.5, 999.30, 999.54, 999.101, 999.102, 999.119, 999.127, 999.149, 999.175, 999.189, 999.212, 999.243, 999.256, 999.263, 999.291, 999.307
Anastasius I	491–498 AD	1004.9, 1004.48, 1004.99, 1004.145
Vandalic?	518–526 AD?	1121.1
Vandalic? Copy?	450–550? AD	1108.1, 1111.1, 1113.1
Illegible	4th century AD	1001.111, 1001.12, 1001.120–129, 1001.131, 1001.133–136, 1001.138, 1001.139, 1001.141, 1001.142, 1001.143, 1001.145, 1001.146, 1001.149
Illegible	4th or 5th century AD	1002.288–320, 1002.327, 1002.328, 1002.356–371, 1002.373, 1002.376–383, 1002.388–395, 1002.403–421, 1002.423–432, 1002.435, 1002.436, 1002.443, 1002.444, 1002.445, 1002.468–474, 1002.476–504, 1002.506–509, 1002.545
Illegible	5th century AD	1003.117, 1003.118, 1003.912, 1003.913, 1002.915, 1002.984–1034, 1002.1045, 1002.1046, 1048, 1071, 1085–1089, 1096, 1113–1115, 1138, 1169, 1171–1179, 1181–1205, 1211–1216, 1252–1253, 1256–1268, 1270, 1272–1289, 1298–1299, 1334–1335, 1337, 1340–1374, 1436–1446
Anastasius I–Justin II, half-follis	498–578 AD	1103.1
Anastasius I–Heraclius, follis	498–640 AD	1224.1
Justinian I, decanummium	559/560 AD	1036.2
Justin II, follis	566/567 AD	1084.1
Tiberius II, decannumium	578 AD	1126.1
Tiberius II or Maurice, half-follis	578–602 AD	1178.1
Maurice, follis	582–602 AD	1176.1
Maurice, half-follis	588/589 AD	1146.1
Maurice, follis	590/591 AD	1164.1

Table 3.12d 6/7th c. Deposit 4: Tile fall on top of the upper mosaic of the south portico of MMS/N plaza (the collapse of the portico) (MMS/N 78.1 not lotted; MMS/N 89.1 Lots 10 and 11; MMS/N 90.1 Lot 11; MMS/N 92.1 Lots 62, 63; MMS/N 94.1 Lots 5, 61), 205 coins.

Issuer or Issue	Date	Catalogue No.
Antiochus II	261–246 BC	78.1
Pergamum	133–27 BC	28.1
Roman Provincial	1st century AD	230.112
Gallienus	253–268 AD	262.1
Claudius II Gothicus	268–270 AD	271.2, 280.1
Barbarous radiate	270–300 AD	297.9
Constantius Chlorus	295–299 AD	341.4
Licinius I	314–324 AD	344.1, 351.1
Gloria Exercitus 1or 2 standards	330–340 AD	398.2, 398.7, 453.66, 465.1, 478.3, 480.3, 597.3
Vot Mult	347–348 AD	479.1, 488.2, 584.1, 587.5, 593.1, 595.19, 595.27
Fel Temp Reparatio FH	348–361 AD	527.6, 544.1, 557.10, 557.24, 557.29, 559.19, 567.2, 602.11, 603.1
Spes Reipublice	355–361 AD	560.9, 560.30, 575.8, 605.3, 605.10
House of Constantine	324–363 AD	606.7
Securitas Reipublicae or Gloria Romanorum 8	364–367 AD	673.1, 676.2, 684.47, 684.61, 684.66, 684.100, 685.51
Valens	364–375 AD	643.3
Concordia Auggg Roma	378–383 AD	716.1, 763.1
Victory l.	364–435 AD	887.18, 887.29, 887.42, 887.50
Victoria Auggg 2 Victories	383–388 AD	690.1
Vot Mult	383 AD	661.1, 706.3, 720.1
Salus Reipublicae	383–392 AD	742.1, 750.2, 750.7, 767.1, 794.4, 798.1, 800.7, 813.2, 862.5
Gloria Romanorum 18 or emperor on horseback	392–395 AD	801.1, 879.1
Virtus Exerciti 2	395–401 AD	778.2, 778.4, 803.17, 803.21, 832.1, 885.49, 885.72
Arcadius, Honorius	401–408 AD	930.2, 939.14
Gloria Romanorum 3 emperors or Concordia Aug cross	406–408 AD	805.1, 841.3, 940.12, 940.43, 944.1
Gloria Romanorum 2 emperors	408–423 AD	918.1, 941.5, 941.16, 942.3, 942.8, 942.17, 943.4, 943.6
Cross in Wreath	425–435 AD	922.12, 922.22, 963.8, 963.15, 963.19, 963.29, 963.49, 963.126, 963.174
Marcian	450–457 AD	967.4, 968.1, 969.18, 969.49, 969.50, 969.57, 969.69, 969.92
Leo I	457–474 AD	984.19, 985.13, 985.17
Zeno	474–491 AD	995.2, 995.17, 997.55, 997.68
Uncertain monogram	450–498 AD	970.2, 999.37, 999.59, 999.62, 999.80, 999.124, 999.174, 999.182, 999.187, 999.257, 999.284
Illegible	4th century AD	1001.118, 1001.19
Illegible	4th or 5th century AD	1002.341–354, 384–387, 398–399, 461–466
Illegible	5th century AD	1003.942–943, 945, 1156–1164, 1166, 1217–1223, 1241–1242, 1319–1321, 1325, 1395–1397, 1870
Anastasius I, nummus	491–498 AD	1004.115, 1004.128
Anastasius I, half-follis	498–512 AD	1005.2

Anastasius I, pentanummium	512–518 AD	1007.1, 1007.2, 1007.3, 1007.4
Justin I–Justinian I, pentanummium	518–538 AD	1063.1
Justinian I–Justin II?, pentanummium	538–578 AD?	1050.1
Justinian I, follis	539/540 AD	**1021.2**
Justinian I, follis	546/547 AD	1029.1
Justinian I, decanummium	556/557 AD	1033.1
Justin II, pentanummium	565–578 AD	1073.2, 1073.16
Justin II, half-follis	566/567 AD	1074.2
Justin II, half-follis	568/569 AD	1077.1
Justin II, follis	569/570 AD	1085.1
Justin II, half-follis	571/572 AD	1068.1
Justin II, half-follis	574/575 AD	1082.1
Justin II, follis, half-follis	575/576 AD	1070.1, 1071.2, 1083.2
Tiberius II, half-follis	579–582 AD	1134.1
Maurice, half-follis	582/583 AD	1159.1
Maurice, follis	584/585 AD	1141.1
Maurice, decanummium	582–602 AD	1157.1
Phocas, follis	602/603 AD	1181.2
Phocas, half-follis	603–610 AD	1184.2, 1184.10

Deposit 4 (Table 3.12d)[164]

It is possible that the Hellenistic, Roman, and Roman Provincial coins are a secondary deposit (i.e., washing in from nearby soils), but in this area, the Hellenistic and Roman layers are deeply buried, due to the construction phases and long period of inhabitation in the fourth through sixth centuries. It is more likely that they have infiltrated from the lower levels. The coins are not included in the calculations for the MCD. The latest coins from the tile fall are coins of Phocas, found only in the first season of excavation of this deposit.

As in circulation hoards, the peak of the dates fall in the quarter-century before the deposit closed, as happens here. However, it is interesting that the largest number of legible coins in this deposit comes from the second half of the fourth century, with plentiful numbers from the previous 50 years as well the first quarter of the fifth century (Fig. 3.4). A somewhat similar profile is seen in the deposits under the upper mosaic of the south portico of MMS/N and all the deposits dated to the fifth century.

The MCD for the tile fall deposit is 424, again a low figure for a deposit that closed in the early seventh century. In this case, 41% of the coins in the deposit are earlier than the MCD (which is in keeping with fourth- and early to mid-fifth-century deposits); only 2% of the coins give the coin *terminus post quem* (Fig. 3.3). These calculations reinforce the argument that fourth- and fifth-century coins were an important part of sixth- and early seventh-century coin circulation.

The overall profile for both the tile fall and the upper mosaic bedding of the south portico of MMS/N follows the same trend as the AACL/1000, with a higher peak for the upper mosaic in fifth-century coins (compare Figs. 2.3, 2.4). Since the numbers for the AACL, upper mosaic, and tile fall are similar, it thus appears that the lack of coin supply drastically affects the circulation pool of the city. Fewer coins are lost, or not recovered, from the sixth and early seventh centuries, even given the increasing size of the individual coin. It is very likely that individuals were lacking in small change and had to be content with old issues (see above, Section 2.7). The difference between

164 Rautman is preparing the final report on the area; the following is a preliminary list of coins from the deposit. Since the current monograph examines coins only up to and including the 2013 season, I will be publishing in the future a deposit of coins in Field 55, also from the seventh or eighth century. For 78.1, Harward, Final Field Report: MMS/N 78.1, p. 10; cf. MMS/N 78.1 II: 79, 87 for coins not included in the final report, but found in the tile fall. For 89.1, Rautman, Final Field Report: MMS/N 89.1, pp. 24–25. For 90.1, Rautman, Revised MMS/N 1990 Coin List Report 1995, p. 1–2. For 92.1, Fieldbook MMS/N 92.1 I: 4. For 94.1, Chabot, Final Field Report: MMS/N 94.1, p. 36; Fieldbook MMS/N 94.1 I: 2.

the two large deposits is significant, as is shown in an analysis of Chi-Square Goodness of Fit test of the two. This statistical analysis tests the differences between the measured results and the theoretically-expected result. The results show that there was no difference in proportion between the two groups of coins. Thus, the finding that the tile fall is only eight years "older," on average, than the upper mosaic bedding, is shown by the p-value to be to be a strongly significant comparison (see App. 4.3).[165]

A similar result was reported for the early sixth-century levels at Carthage by Reece, in Beirut by Butcher, Butrint by Moorhead, and in mid-sixth-century levels in Sagalassus.[166] Butcher and Moorhead had argued that large Byzantine bronze coins circulated alongside nummi, at least in the eastern provinces in the first half of the sixth century. Their evidence came from both excavation levels and hoard evidence. These results should be cautionary to archaeologists who use the coins in dating the strata. Even when sixth- or early seventh-century coins are present, they form a very small percentage of the total number of recovered coins. That is, the coins do not consistently show the true *terminus post quem* of the sixth and early seventh centuries.

The loss of mints along with a disinterest by the government in producing the smaller denominations may reflect the reasons why there are so few sixth- and seventh-century coins in sixth- and seventh-century deposits. Clearly, the Sardians had to press into service coins that were 200 or even 300 years old, at least when they were transacting monetary exchanges. More interesting is the problem of defining when the monetary economy was severely disrupted. While natural disasters and/or invasions may have contributed to the lack of excavation coins, this phenomenon began in the sixth century and would continue for the rest of Byzantine Sardis.

3.7 Coins Used as Amulets

Another interesting use of coins in a magico-religious context is their reuse as amulets. Several of the coins recorded in the current excavations were pierced for hanging or attachment. Most were pierced so that the head of the emperor was hung upright: Gordian III (no. 202.1, the reverse of Tyche would be upside down); Maximian Herculius (no. 332.1, the reverse is illegible); uncertain emperor of the early fifth century (no. 942.7, neither side upright if hung); Phocas (no. 1182.1, emperor's face upright); lead token, with a quadruped walking (**L13**). One coin was pierced, but neither Salonina nor the figure of Tyche on the reverse would have been shown upright (no. 120.1); two were pierced for attachment through the middle of the coins (nos. 264.1, 986.8), possibly to show the Fortuna or the emperor dragging a captive on the reverse (coins of Gallienus and Leo). A coin of Galerius Maximian, was pierced around 2 o'clock, so neither the head of the emperor nor the Genius would be shown upright (no. 336.1). No orientation could be discerned for a coin of Theodosius (no. 752.1), nor a coin from the House of Constantine (no. 582.1), nor an Augustan coin (no. 218.2), nor two fourth- or fifth-century coins with a victory type (nos. 887.17, 887.56). One Hellenistic coin, worn smooth and countermarked, was pierced to hang at some point in its life (no. 94.82).

A huge follis of Justinian I was pierced twice for attachment (no. 1048.1). It is clear that the use of a coin as an amulet was popular, at least in Late Antiquity, for John Chrysostom inveighed against wearing "bronze coins of Alexander of Macedon" as amuletic bracelets and anklets (*ad illuminandos catechesis* II.5, PG 49:240).[167] A post-reform follis of Justinian, engraved by the user with a cross followed by the words K(υρι)E (or Χριστε) ΒΟΗΘΙ ΤΟΝ

165 I examined the data in two ways: one calculating the difference between groups that had more than counts of five: the distribution of the coins was no different in the upper mosaic and the tile fall, as the chi-squared value was 42, with the degrees of freedom 36, and the p-value of 0.2 (the probability that the comparison could have been more extreme than in the samples; since it is more than .05, the results are significant). If the groups are examined the same way, except all the values between 499 and 624 AD (to cut down on the number of cells with values less than five), the result is similar, with a chi-squared value of 56, degrees of freedom 49, and the p-value remains the same. There are no detectable differences between the groups. My thanks to Thomas M. Evans for the statistical work.

166 Reece 1984a, pp. 172–73; Butcher 2001/2, p. 102; Moorhead 2007, pp. 297–98; Poblome 1995. See also the Tel Malot hoard (Israel): although only about half of the approximately 26,000 coins have been identified, ca. 1% of the coins were minted prior to the fourth century; 9% came from the fourth century; 90% were minted in the fifth century, and so far, only one coin dates the closing of the hoard in the sixth century. The jug in which the hoard was concealed is dated to the first half of the sixth century (Kindler 2000).

167 cf. Maguire 1997, p. 1040.

ΦΟΡΙΝΤΑ, "Lord help the wearer" is illustrated by Mary Margaret Fulghum; the phrase is common on lead seals (cf. **L17–19**).[168] Fulghum suggested that the NIKH in the exergue may have prompted the use of this coin as an amulet.[169] The Sardis coin, minted in Cyzicus, fails to have this association. More probably, in my mind, the coin was chosen for the horse and rider on the emperor's shield (as Fulghum), which was equated with Alexander the Great, the Holy Rider, or perhaps a militant saint or the emperor.[170]

Pierced coins were placed in graves through the Early Byzantine period.[171] No pierced coins have been found in graves in Sardis. Even in the twelfth century, the teacher of rhetoric Michael Italikos sent a coin to the emperor bearing "Constantine the Great," "Helena" and "Christ" as "an imperial *nomisma* invested with an ineffable force" that would work against "all evils," but especially diseases. It was not just the images that were powerful, but also the fact that the images were impressed on a coin made them potent: "there is an ineffable power peculiar to this object . . . that has perhaps been injected into it by the instruments of the metalworkers."[172]

Only a few contexts of these pierced coins are known.[173] The coin of Gordian III came from a possible occupation layer in a house, dated by a lamp to the Late Roman period (fifth century?). However, the coin may have been part of a fill that was used to level the floor of the room, and although it is worn, it may not have been in use for 300 years before deposition. The coin of Maximian Herculius came from a dump, as did the coin of the House of Constantine and one of the victory coins (no. 887.56). The Hellenistic coin may have come from a Roman-era wall (later destroyed), which would make sense, given its worn types. The coin of Galerius was found in a sixth-century context in a fill beneath a floor; the early fifth-century coin was from a context that included an early seventh-century coin (a not-uncommon association; see Section 3.8). The Phocas coin came from a fill that contained Hellenistic and Late Roman coins. Deposits closer in date to the minting of the coin include the coin of the first half of the fourth century, from Late Roman fill around graves in HoB; the coin of Leo I, found in a fill from the fifth century; and one of the victory coins (no. 887.17), from another fifth-century fill. Russell cites an instance of a second-century coin found on a seventh-century floor in Anemurium, and he notes that first-century coins were used in fourth-century necklaces.[174] The contexts of the pierced coins at Sardis may not be defined as clearly as at Anemurium, but it is clear that from the first century AD to the twelfth century, coins were used to ward against evil that threatened the Sardians.

3.8 Hoards

Eight hoards were discovered in the recent excavations; seven of these were deposited in the fifth century and consist of small copper-alloy coins.[175] These contribute to our understanding of the circulation of coin in the fifth century. Six of the Late Roman hoards have been previously published,[176] and details of those hoards will not be repeated here; also of note are the hoards in Graves 80.2, 80.3, 80.4, and 80.5 in the HoB Mausoleum, which all closed in the mid to late fifth century (see above, Section 3.4.3).

H1 Third-century hoard in MMS-II 85.1

This small accrual of coins was found in the debris of a roof collapse in the "Late Roman Townhouse" in MMS (Table 3.13). The excavator identified the accumulation as a "savings hoard."[177] Because of the circumstances

168 A version of this blessing was found on an ampulla in MMS/S (P95.046; see Greenewalt and Rautman 1998, p. 486), though it is not, as Fulghum wrote, "an inscription . . . from the entrance of a late Roman house at Sardis" (2001, p. 141).

169 Fulghum 2001, p. 147.

170 cf. Fulghum 2001, p. 147.

171 Russell 1995, p. 48 n. 37, noting that they were found only in tombs, not the settlement, in Beth Yerath.

172 Maguire 1997, p. 1044 (quoting Michael Italikos).

173 NoEx or surface coins: **L13** (seal), Augustan-era coin (no. 28.2), Salonina (no. 120.1), Gallienus (no. 264.1), and Theodosius (no. 752.1).

174 Russell 1995, pp. 47–48.

175 Only one fourth-century hoard has been recorded at Sardis (Bell 1916, p. viii). Hoard D, an early sixth-century (?) hoard in PN, was recognized as a hoard stashed in an industrial sector of Unit Q; there may have been some contamination. About 120 minimi/nummi were found, but 69 were reported to have disintegrated upon cleaning. Buttrey dated the legible remainders from 375–392 to 518–527; he preferred to see this as an accumulation, not a hoard (Buttrey et al. 1981, p. xxii; cf. Burrell 2007, p. 240). I did not graph this hoard, since so few coins survived for review.

176 Evans 2013b.

177 Rautman, Final Field Report: MMS-II 85.1, p. 9.

Table 3.13 Hoard 1: Late Roman Townhouse, Room 10, Lot 25.

Date of Issue	Mint	Catalogue No.
190–75 BC	Smyrna	48.2 (15 mm, 3.3g)
260–268 AD	Rome	253.1
260–268 AD	Rome	245.1
260–268 AD	Rome	250.1
260–268 AD	Rome	252.1
270–300 AD?	Uncertain	294.10
270–275 AD	Ticinum	315.2

of its secondary deposition, any container was destroyed, and the coins were scattered. It is likely that the hoard consisted of seven coins, including a Hellenistic coin (of a size that would circulate in the third century), a coin of Severina, and a posthumous issue of Claudius II Gothicus. Six of the coins are antoniniani, four of them minted under Gallienus. The hoard seems to have closed before the reforms of Diocletian; it is likely to have been a circulation hoard since the antoniniani were all minted with a few years of each other. It is unclear how this hoard ended up in a Late Roman house.

H2 MMS/S 1982 [178]

The hoard was buried in a cloth bag near a door on the MMS Road (unnumbered room). Consisting of 695 coins, the small copper-alloy issues ranged in date from the first century BC to ca. 518 AD, with the vast majority of the coins dating to the second half of the fifth century. Since the value of the hoard was low, in Grierson's terms, this is an "accidental loss" hoard, small change accumulated from circulating coins;[179] there is no known emergency in Sardis at the very beginning of the sixth century that would account for this hoard. It contributes to our understanding of circulating coin in the fifth century, the body of which was made of newly-struck issues, worn older (sometimes much older) coins, slugs or unstamped flans, and largely lead blanks. Also included in this hoard were nine Vandalic coins, an unusual group of coins for Sardis, dating to the reign of Thrasamund. As Burrell pointed out, the hoard sheds light on the monetary reforms of Anastasius I and his endeavor to restore the place of copper-alloy coins within the monetary system.[180]

The pattern of coin loss (Fig. 3.5) shows a long taper on the curve for earlier coins, including some from the early fourth century (coins of the first century BC and first century AD were left out of the data, as the length of the tail would have skewed the graph into illegibility). This long "tail" is normal, as coins of earlier periods are not as common in the coin pool, due to loss from circulation, or sometimes due to reminting.[181] The bulk of the coins should come from the period just before the coin hoard was deposited, since these coins were still very much in circulation, as occurs in most of the hoards in this graph. We would expect only a few coins of the latest period, especially the monograms of Anastasius I, if the hoard closed during his reign, as they had more recently entered the circulation pool and would not have penetrated to the non-mint cities as deeply as the coins of previous rulers. Indeed, the nummi hoarded here were all produced in the first seven years of Anastasius I's reign, yet they comprise the bulk of the coins from the period. Once the reformed folles of Anastasius I were introduced, the nummi were driven out of circulation, to be hoarded or even discarded. However, as can be seen in the deposits, these nummi circulated long into the sixth century. Although the number of coins seems impressive (and endless to the numismatist who must record them), 695 nummi was worth comparatively little, perhaps "a few days' wages."[182]

178 Previously published in Burrell 2007 and Burrell 2008 and mentioned in Greenewalt, Rautman, and Meriç 1986, p. 10; Greenewalt et al. 1985, p. 76.

179 Grierson 1975, p. 131.

180 Burrell 2007, pp. 253–54.

181 cf. Moorhead 2012, p. 622.

182 Burrell 2007, p. 235.

H3 Long North Hall (Bath-Gym Complex) 1968 [183]

The hoard consists of only 12 coins, placed in a small jug and abandoned in an unfinished room of the Bath-Gymnasium Complex at the close of the fifth century. It is an "accidental loss hoard" as well. The coins were published in the earlier catalogue, but Buttrey did not discuss the coins individually or as a hoard.[184] The hoard closed slightly earlier than Hoard 2, probably during the reign of Zeno, or by 491; the earliest coins in the hoard dated to 335–341. Like Hoard 2, it contained coins that are sometimes conjectured to have been recalled by the fourth-century Imperial mint (see Section 2.5.1). Figure 3.4 shows this long taper, as in Hoard 2, but the percentage of coins from the closing quarter-century (475–498) is equal to the previous quarter-century (450–474). The number of coins in this hoard is very small, and it cannot be used to provide a pattern for the other hoards.

H4 Byzantine Fortress 1991[185]

The hoard consists of 71 coins which were placed in a pilgrim flask and hidden under a tile floor in a domestic quarter in an area near the center of the ancient city. Like Hoard 3, it is closed with a coin carrying a monogram of Zeno (474–491); but the composition should mean that it was a savings hoard. There are a number of illegible fifth-century coins in the hoard, but no evidence of clipped coins. There are no coins predating 383–392; however, as Hoard 2, the peak in the percentage of coins comes in the period before the closing of the hoard.

H5 MMS-III 1986[186]

Found not far away from Hoard 2, this hoard consisted of 83 coins, also originally in a cloth bag, hidden in a garbage dump, and an accidental loss hoard. The hoard closed with issues of Leo I (457–474), with the earliest coin dating to ca. 351–361. Clipped coins were present in this hoard, with illegible flans (some possibly unstamped), and some heavily-leaded flans, again testifying to the varied nature of coins in use at the end of the fifth century. The coins stop abruptly with the reign of Leo I, forming a loss peak in this quarter of the fifth century; they are thus unlike the pattern of Hoards 2, 4, 6, and 8. They form a regular descent into the mid-fourth century, a pattern we can see is normal for fifth-century hoards (see Fig. 3.5).

H6 MMS-I 1983[187]

This hoard was found in the same residential quarter as Hoards 2 and 4, in Room 3 of the Late Roman Townhouse. It consisted of 29 coins. Found under a tile floor, it was perhaps unintentionally concealed as the house was renovated; no traces of a container were found, as is typical for an accidental loss hoard.[188] Two of the coins were clipped, and the earliest coin dated to 364–388. Like Hoard 5, it contained heavily-leaded flans and flans without apparent types; as with Hoard 5, it closed in the reign of Leo I. It appears (see Fig. 3.5) to follow the rules of coin loss for hoards, as the period of Leo's reign forms only a secondary peak in the year of issue in the hoard, with a long tailing off to the third quarter of the fourth century.

H7 MMS-I 1985[189]

There were only ten coins in this small hoard, which was kept in a textile bag in the corner of Room 3 in the Late Roman Townhouse. The hoard was forgotten, and a mortar floor covered the area where it was concealed; it, too, is an accidental loss hoard. Like Hoards 5 and 6, the last identifiable issue came from Leo's reign, 457–474; more than half of the coins were unidentifiable beyond the century of minting, leading to a hoard pattern (Fig. 3.5) that is difficult to use as a pattern for other hoards.

H8 Field 49 11.1 Lot 107

This hoard (Table 3.14), not previously published, was discovered in a residential area of the Late Roman period. The context of this hoard was a deep fill in a chamber with no entry, underneath a stone bench; the fill contained a large number of lamps, which showed signs of use. The lamps may suggest that this chamber

183 Published in full in Evans 2013b.

184 Buttrey et al. 1981.

185 Published in full in Evans 2013b; mentioned in Burrell 2008, p. 166; Greenewalt, Ratté, and Rautman 1995, pp. 24, 35, no. 15.

186 Published in full in Evans 2013b; mentioned in Burrell 2008, p. 166; Greenewalt et al. 1990, p. 140.

187 Published in full in Evans 2013b.

188 Grierson 1975, p. 131.

189 Published in full in Evans 2013b.

Table 3.14 Hoard 8: Field 49 11.1 Lot 107 (note: two disintegrated in cleaning).

Date of Issue	Reverse Type (see App. 3); Mint (if known)	Catalogue No.
270 AD and later	Bust r. rad./flaming altar, variable legend; one from Rome or Mediolanum	292.7, 297.6
324–330 AD	Helena/standing figure, clipped into oval shape	426.1
337–340 AD	Constantine II/Virtus Augusti; Rome, clipped	445.1
347–348 AD	House of Constantine/Vot Mult; Nicomedia, clipped into oval shape	587.2
348–361 AD	Constantius II/Fel Temp Reparatio FH	559.28
355–361 AD	Constantius II/Spes Reipublicae; Cyzicus (1)	545.4, 560.48
364–375 AD	Uncertain/Gloria Romanorum 8, possibly clipped	685.47
364–375 AD	Uncertain/Securitas Reipublicae	684.56
364–435 AD	Uncertain/Victory l.	887.20
378–450 AD	Theodosius I or II/illegible	927.3
378–383 AD	Gratian/Vot XV Mult XX; Nicomedia	656.1
383–395 AD	Uncertain/Salus Reipublicae	886.4, 886.9, 886.21, 886.34, 886.38, 886.52, 886.83, 886.84, 886.117
388–395 AD	Arcadius/Salus Reipublicae	800.9
392–423 AD	Honorius/illegible, clipped	863.5
395–401 AD	Honorius/Virtus Exerciti 2	855.28
395–401 AD	Uncertain/Virtus Exerciti 2	885.28, 886.37, 886.64
400–450 AD?	Bust r. pd [...]VSPFAVG/SAB(?)LICAE; Constantinople?	872.1
425–455 AD	Valentinian III/Victoria Augg; Rome	946.2
425–435 AD	Theodosius II/Cross in Wreath; Constantinople	898.4, 922.4
425–435 AD	Uncertain/Cross in Wreath; Constantinople (1)	961.3, 963.45, 963.66, 963.157
450–457 AD	Marcian/monogram	969.13, 969.31, 969.40, 969.41, 969.47
457–474 AD	Leo I/emperor and captive	986.2, 986.3
457–474 AD	Leo I/empress b/E	987.2
476–491 AD	Zeno/monogram; Cyzicus (2)	995.11, 995.22, 997.59
450–500 AD	Uncertain monogram	999.11, 999.52, 999.66, 999.87, 999.107, 999.122, 999.140, 999.244
4th century AD	Illegible; assigned by module	1001.191, 1001.192, 1001.193
4th or 5th century AD	Illegible	1002.53–65
5th century AD	Illegible; assigned by module	1003.104–149, 151–154

was entered via a ladder or steps, with no exterior exit. This hoard was found spread shallowly in a 3–4 cm horizontal layer, but no signs of its container were found; it must also have been an accidental loss.[190]

The coins must have been in a box or bag, and possibly unintentionally dumped into the fill, for the closing date of the hoard is contemporary with the latest pottery in the deposit.[191] The coins in the hoard thus comprise a picture of the coins in circulation at the end of the fifth century. Since the soil around the coins contained a great deal of mortar, many of the coins were illegible and could only be dated to the fourth to fifth century or just the fifth century (the date of the latter is due to the size of the coins, which were about 10 mm and weighed less than 1 g). The hoard consisted of 123 coins, all small copper-alloy coins, and closed with coins stamped with the monogram of Zeno (see Fig. 3.5). It follows the regular pattern of a long "tail" leading to a peak in the 50 years before the closing of the hoard.

190 Cahill 2014a, p. 126; cf. Fieldbook F49 11.1 II: 59–74.

191 Rautman and DeRidder Raubolt, pers. comm.

The closing date of the hoard is harder to assess, given the number of fifth-century illegible coins: the hoard probably closed in the reign of Zeno, certainly by 498. Coins that were over 200 years old were included in the hoard; judging by the few mints that could be discerned, eastern mints predominated, but occasional coins from western mints were present. One copy was included, but no Vandalic coins were detected.

The hoard was unique for Sardis in containing billon antoniniani issued after the death of Claudius II; yet deposits of the fourth and fifth centuries contain these coins (see above). They appear to be Imperial issues, but even when they came from the mint, they were quite small and weighed less than two grams. Many coins of this type were clipped in antiquity, though it does not appear that these particular coins were. They would have been among the larger coins of this hoard. Seven other coins do appear to have been clipped; as one would expect, the earlier coins are clipped, as well as the larger end-of-the-fourth-century coins. Clipped coins are found in hoards and excavations in Asia Minor but not further south.[192]

Coins from almost every decade of the fourth century are found in the hoard, and would have been saved as legal tender. The coins span several reforms of the Late Roman coinage, and the case for recalling fourth-century coins gets that much weaker. Figure 3.5 shows a peak in the date when the coins were issued at 450–474, with a slight dropping off in the next period (475–498), the period when the hoard closed, and a long taper back to the beginning of the coins of Constantine, ca. 324–346.

Conclusions about the Late Roman Hoards at Sardis

As I noted in my publication on Hoards 2 through 6, parallels to the hoards in Sardis are difficult to make, since publication of hoards of small copper-alloy coins lags far behind the interest in gold hoards.[193] However, the patterns noted in the composition of the hoards were already apparent to Kent by 1994. In his discussion of fourth- and fifth-century hoards, he noted that third-century radiates could be present in western hoards, along with Gloria Exercitus, Fel Temp Reparatio FH, and Spes Reipublicae reverses. Gloria Exercitus and Salus Reipublicae reverses were most commonly found in hoards, of all the reverses minted in the second half of the fourth century. Kent also observed that coins from western mints, such as Honorius's Urbs Roma Felix, Gloria Romanorum (of both varieties), and Victoria Augg were present in eastern hoards; he noted that copies or counterfeits (which can be difficult to distinguish from the technically-poor strikes coming out of Imperial mints) are common in hoards.[194]

In hoards in the eastern Mediterranean that close in the late fifth century (Table 3.15), we find a variety of Hellenistic to Roman Provincial coins included in pots or bags as legal tender (Kish, Qaw el-Kebir, Abu Mina, "Lebanon" 1988, Tel Malot, Corinth 1930, and Volo, to which add Sardis H2). We can no longer consider these as intrusions or "keepsake" coins,[195] but as normal component parts of fifth-century circulation, which pressed every available official-looking piece of copper-alloy coinage into use.[196] This might be surprising considering the number of small coins pouring from the official mints, but clearly demand outstripped supply, as blanks, lead slugs, and crude copies accompanied these early coins. These early inclusions come from almost every province and are not just evidence that monetary supply to one province lagged.

If fourth-century coins had been subjected to recalls, demonetization, or decrees that rendered them worthless or illegal we would expect to see them in very few hoards. Yet, from Egypt to Palestine to Syria to Greece, coins of Constantine and his sons are included in hoards. If the hoard was a votive hoard, one could argue that the depositor gave the coins to the deity, as they were unusable in the physical world. However, the circulation hoards from Kish, Kellia, Hawara (nos. 1–4), Qaw el-Kebir, Egypt (nos. 3 and 4), Hama, "Beirut," "Lebanon" 1988, Haft-tapeh, Taburabat, and Corinth, as well as Sardis H2, H3, H6, and H8, all contain coins from the first half of the fourth century.

As noted above, we would expect to see the bulk of coins coming from the period just before the closing of the hoard (and not from the period of closure). This is certainly true of five of the hoards of Sardis. There are some differences among the provinces. For

192 Burrell 2007, p. 239; Bijovsky 2012, p. 59.

193 Evans 2013b.

194 Kent 1994, pp. lxxxvi–lxxxvii.

195 As, e.g., Hohlfelder 1973, p. 91, no. 6.

196 See Bijovsky 2012, pp. 458–60; Butcher 2001/2, p. 281.

instance, we are now able to see a pattern in fifth-century coinage in Sardis that is different from the fifth-century circulation in Palestine. Hoards from Palestine do not include clipped coins as do the hoards in Sardis, but the hoards farther south include imitation Axumite and Vandalic coins as well as coins from Alexandria. In Egypt and Syria/Lebanon, we also see imitation Axumite coins, along with coins from Rome, at least during the reign of Valentinian III. Imitation Axumite coins are rare to non-existent north of Palestine; coins from the mint at Alexandria are scarce. Vandalic coins, which make a sizable component of Palestinian hoards, are not very common at all at Sardis. Some coins of Valentinian III from the mint at Rome were found in the excavations, but they were not found in the hoards in Sardis. Local imitations are much more prevalent in Egypt and Syria than in Sardis.

Table 3.15 Comparative hoards of copper-alloy coins closed in mid- to late fifth or early sixth century from the eastern Mediterranean.

Hoard Location	Date of earliest coin–latest issue	No. of Coins	Mints Represented, when legible	Details
Kish, Iraq[i]	Greek–ca. 440 AD?	169	Includes Sassanian	1 "Greek," Cyzicus, Antioch
Kellia, Egypt[ii]	ca. 270 to 450–457 AD	ca. 200	Cyzicus, Nicomedia	In monastery or hermitages; the bulk of the coins date to the reigns of Theodosius I, Arcadius, and Honorius; few mints recorded; 3 imitations (2 barbarous radiates, 1 Fel Temp FH type)
Hawara 1, Egypt 1892[iii]	306–336 to 474–491 AD	866	Local imitations, uncertain eastern, Axum	Only 49 coins identified
Hawara 2, Egypt 1938[iv]	324–336 to 474–491 AD	43	Constantinople, uncertain eastern, local imitations	
Hawara 3, Egypt 1938[v]	324–336 to 474–491 AD	892	Rome (Valentinian III), Aquileia, Constantinople, Antioch, uncertain eastern	Only 4 coins of Zeno reported, but 58 of Leo I; includes imitations? of Gloria Romanorum 8; 9 lead blanks
Hawara 4, Egypt 1938[vi]	324–346 to 518 AD	348	Rome (Valentinian III), Vandalic coin, Constantinople, uncertain eastern, local imitations	Imitation Victory l.
Hawara 6, Egypt 1938[vii]	383–395 to 518 AD	ca. 1300	Vandalic, uncertain eastern, local imitation	Only 9 coins identified; imitation of Victory l.
Qaw el-Kebir, Egypt[viii]	4th century BC to 474–491 AD	2747	Arelate, Rome, Ticinum, uncertain western, Siscia, Constantinople, Nicomedia, Cyzicus, Thessalonica, Antioch, Alexandria, uncertain eastern, Axum, local imitations	Includes 1 coin each from the 4th century BC (Neandria); 2nd century BC (Side); 3 coins from the 2nd to 1st century BC (Uncertain Seleucid, Judaea, Alexandria); 3 from the 2nd century AD (Alexandria); 4 from the 3rd century AD (1 from Rome); most of the coins span the entire 4th and 5th centuries
Egypt 2[ix]	324–ca. 480 AD	43	Includes Antioch	Includes Constantinian imitation; 14 uncertain
Egypt 3[x]	324–ca. 480 AD	ca. 943	Not published	ca. 500 uncertain
Egypt 4[xi]	324–ca. 480 AD	339	Not published	167 uncertain
Abu Mina, Egypt[xii]	1st–2nd century AD coin; antoninianus of Gallienus; then continuous from ca. 324–498 AD	ca. 8600	Alexandria	Found in pilgrim flask in a crypt under the altar of a church as a votive deposit. Includes "many good imitations"
Northern Syria 1976[xiii]	335–337 to 474–491 AD	2430	Rome (Valentinian III, Majorian, Libius Severus), Mediolanum (Odavacar), Thessalonica, Heraclea, Constantinople, Nicomedia, Cyzicus, Siscia, Antioch, Alexandria, uncertain eastern	Includes over 300 coins of Zeno and 36 "forgeries" (local imitations)

Hama, Syria[xiv]	ca. 320–ca. 470 AD	904	Eastern mints only: Aquileia, Thessalonica, Constantinople, Nicomedia, Cyzicus, Antioch	815 uncertain
"Beirut," Lebanon[xv]	ca. 320–ca. 490 AD	2377	Rome (Valentinian III, Libius Severus), Siscia, Thessalonica, Heraclea, Constantinople, Cyzicus, Nicomedia, Antioch, Alexandria	Almost half from uncertain mint
"Lebanon" 1988[xvi]	Greek–ca. 490 AD (continuous from ca. 320 AD)	9530	Includes Constantinople, Nicomedia, Cyzicus, Antioch, uncertain western mint for Valentinian III, Libius Severus	Includes 18 Greek and three 3rd-century, copies of Theodosius II monograms, "late Victories," 874 fragments, 237 barbarous, 4381 uncertain
Beirut Souks Hoard 4, Lebanon[xvii]	457–474 AD (all coins of Leo I)	8	Uncertain eastern	2 cast blanks, 2 illegible
Beirut Souks Hoard 5, Lebanon[xviii]	348–498 AD	32	1 Rome?, all others illegible	21 illegible
Tel Malot, Israel[xix]	4th century BC to 540 AD?	ca. 26,000		Not fully processed or published; found in a Gaza jar; included Persian, Hellenistic, Hasmonaean, Nabataean, Roman Provincial, Roman Imperial coins; note that hoard included over 5,700 5th-century coins, and only one 527–565 AD (Justinian I). This coin matches the date of the jar, but Bijovsky urges caution in making it the closing date.
Ashkelon,[xx] Semadar Hotel, Hoard A, Israel	341–491 AD	35	Rome?, Siscia, Nicomedia, Constantinople	In cloth bag; foundation deposit for private dwelling?
Caesarea Maritima baths (Insula W2S3), Israel[xxi]	350–457 AD	106	Not published	In fill of pit, mostly 4th-century coins
Haft-tapeh, Israel[xxii]	ca. 320–ca. 476 AD	86	2 Cyzicus	49 uncertain
Taburabat, Turkey[xxiii]	ca. 320–457 AD	3381	Rome (Urbs Roma Felix), Siscia, Thessalonica, Heraclea, Constantinople, Nicomedia, Cyzicus, Antioch, Alexandria	1 Victory l. imitation?; 3333 uncertain
Turkey I[xxiv]	ca. 330–ca. 465 AD	83	Not published	18 uncertain
Corinth III, Greece[xxv]	324–498 AD	169	Not published	114 uncertain
Corinth 1930 near "Justinian's" Wall[xxvi]	Classical?–498 AD	742	Not published	336 legible; 1 clipped coin from Messane ("old Greek"); 1 imperial aes, quartered; 1 Claudius II; 1 Constans, 1 Valens, 21 Theodosius I, 1 Honorius, 7 Arcadius, 28 Theodosius II, 15 Marcian, 32 Leo, 38 Zeno; 40 Victory dragging captive or Victory with wreath, emperor standing, camp-gate; 148 Anastasius I; 1 Baduila considered intrusive
Volo, Greece[xxvii]	Greek–ca. 480 AD	2231	Rome, Thessalonica, Constantinople, Nicomedia, Cyzicus, Antioch	1 Philip II; 13 Constantinian (1 Divus Constantine, the rest Fel Temp Reparatio or Spes Reipublice); 1 Constantius Gallus; 1167 illegible and "disregarded," all 187 AE3s clipped; 62 barbarous, including some from west
"Yale" Hoard (Balkans?)[xxviii]	ca. 320–ca. 480 AD	928	Rome, Thessalonica, Heraclea, Constantinople, Nicomedia, Cyzicus, Antioch, Alexandria	173 AE3, all clipped; 338 AE4 clipped; 84 barbarous AE4; 413 illegible

i	*Kent 1994, p. cxlvi.*
ii	*Noeske 2000, pp. 222–27.*
iii	*Noeske 2000, pp. 291–93.*
iv	*Noeske 2000, pp. 337–39.*
v	*Noeske 2000, pp. 337–39.*
vi	*Noeske 2000, pp. 343–44.*
vii	*Noeske 2000, pp. 343–44.*
viii	*Noeske 2000, pp. 365–82.*
ix	*Kent 1994, p. cxxxviii.*
x	*Kent 1994, p. cxxxviii.*
xi	*Kent 1994, pp. cxxxviii–cxxxix.*
xii	*Noeske 2000, pp. 16–57.*
xiii	*Noeske 2000, pp. 508–16.*
xiv	*Kent 1994, p. cxliii.*
xv	*Kent 1994, p. cxxxi.*
xvi	*Kent 1994, p. cxlviii.*
xvii	*Butcher 2001/2, p. 281.*
xviii	*Butcher 2001/2, pp. 281–83.*
xix	*Kindler 2000; Bijovsky 2011, p. 83; Bijovsky 2012, p. 74.*
xx	*Bijovsky 2004.*
xxi	*Preliminary report only available, Bijovsky 2011, p. 97.*
xxii	*Kent 1994, p. cxliii.*
xxiii	*Kent 1994, p. clx.*
xxiv	*Kent 1994, p. clxiii.*
xxv	*Kent 1994, p. cxxxvi.*
xxvi	*Edwards 1937, pp. 248–49.*
xxvii	*Adelson and Kustas 1962.*
xxviii	*Adelson and Kustas 1960.*

APPENDICES

Appendix 1
Countermarks

The excavation coins from the Hellenistic through the Roman Imperial period can carry countermarks. It has been suggested that these small stamps are used to revalue the denomination of the coin, to reassure the user of the value of the coin (sometimes due to wear), or to mark an assurance of continued validity even if the coin is from another city or a disgraced ruler. The countermark may imply that the coin had passed through the mint at a moment of payment of taxes, or perhaps payment of wages or donatives.[1] However, no ancient author mentions the process of countermarking; we are thus never entirely sure why particular coins were marked, if they were recalled to be marked, or if the mint profited by the countermarking.[2]

Lydian "Banker's Marks"

Countermarks, or banker's marks, have been found on electrum coins that had been minted in Sardis in a hoard at Gordion.[3] It has been suggested that these early countermarks, which can number more than ten on one coin, were stamps given by particular bankers or moneylenders to show that the coin was of the correct weight and or alloy.[4] No countermarks were stamped into the Lydian coins found in the excavations at Sardis.

Hellenistic City Countermarks

The common owl countermark was placed on coins of Pergamum by the Pergamene mint. The type, which is found in both of its forms (with wings folded and wings outstretched), is found in a variety of sizes, suggesting either a series or a long period of countermarking.[5] The countermark of the owl with wings outstretched, found on coin no. 24.2, obscures the entire reverse.[6] The underlying coins can only then be roughly dated to 281–133 BC, but the countermark may date to the second century BC, when the owl type was introduced in the Pergamene mint. By countermarking the coin this way, the coin was "turned into" a coin with the types Athena/owl with wings outspread;[7] this was perhaps a way of revaluing the coins since the coin with the types Athena/owl with wings outspread are slightly smaller than the Athena/countermark coins. A larger countermark accomplishes the same thing on coin no. **24.1**, though the owl has its wings folded. The result is close to, but does not exactly imitate, coins of Pergamum with an owl in an olive wreath or sitting on a thunderbolt;[8] it was probably placed on the reverses in the second or first centuries BC. The same date for the smaller countermark of an owl with wings folded can be surmised (nos. 25.1, 25.2). This countermark is found on larger coins of the Asklepios/staff or Asklepios type. The largest coin (Athena/trophy) carries the smallest countermark, though it retains the owl with wings folded (no. 27.4).

The most common countermark on the excavation coins is the knobby club countermark, found chiefly on the Herakles/Apollo civic bronzes minted in the third to second centuries BC (nos. 52.33–**46**, 100–104) and the slightly larger coin showing Tyche/Zeus Lydios (nos. **51.2**, 51.5). The club is placed in an oval punch; the countermark is never found directly over the face of the deity on the obverse. It is occasionally combined with a second countermark, which should suggest that these other countermarks were also placed on the

1 Buttrey et al. 1981, p. 72.

2 Howgego 1985, p. 2

3 Bellinger 1968.

4 Konuk 2012, p. 47.

5 Buttrey et al. 1981, p. 20, nos. 39, 49 noted the presence of owl countermarks on coins of Pergamum, but on different series than are presented here.

6 For a parallel, see *SNG France* 5: 1695.

7 *BMC Mysia*, p. 132, nos. 190–204.

8 *BMC Mysia*, p. 131, nos. 183–188.

Table App. 1.1 Countermarks on Hellenistic coins.

Countermark	Obv. or Rev.	Date and Mint of Coin	Date and Mint of Countermark	Reference	Cat. No.
Owl with wings outstretched, facing, 8–10 mm circle	R	281–133 BC Pergamum	Possibly 2nd–1st century BC Pergamum	cf. *SNG France* 5:1695	**24.1** 24.2
Owl with wings folded, r., head facing, 7–8 mm circle	R	133–27 BC or 197–159 BC Pergamum	Possibly 2nd–1st century BC Pergamum		25.1 25.2
Owl with wings folded, r., head facing, 5 mm circle	R	133–27 BC or 159–133 BC Pergamum	Possibly 2nd–1st century BC Pergamum		27.4
Knobby club, 3 by 5–7 mm oval	O	240/220–2nd century BC Sardis	2nd century BC? Sardis	cf. M7 GR 208, 216, 233	**51.2**, 5; 52.33–**46**, 100–104; 94.6
Male head?, 4 by 4 mm square	O	240/220–2nd century BC Sardis	Uncertain		52.41, **52.46** (second countermark), 52.99 (second countermark)
 6 mm circle	O	2nd–1st century BC Sardis	Uncertain Sardis?	As M7 GR 182, but the l. side is cut off	54.1
[…]TVS in 5 by 6 rectangle	Uncertain	3rd–1st century BC uncertain	Uncertain		94.82
Unbearded male bust r., dr. between VΛ-VP (2x)	Uncertain	1st century BC–1st century AD uncertain	Uncertain		95.9

coin at the Sardis mint, as it is unlikely that the coin would be minted in Sardis, countermarked in Sardis, move to a second city to be countermarked, and then return to a deposit in Sardis (nos. 52.46, 52.99). The club countermark was likely placed on the Herakles/Apollo coin when the new, slightly smaller Apollo/club coin was minted in the second century BC, to show viewers that both coins were of the same value. Since we do not have any archaeological contexts that date the Apollo/club coins with any specificity, I can only suggest that the change in coinage may have occurred in 189 or 133 BC.

Two more countermarks were found on coins excavated in Sardis and produced by the Sardis mint. One is a male head in a square; it is only found on Herakles/Apollo coins (once without the club countermark, nos. 52.41, **52.46**, 52.99). It is likely that this was also placed on the coin by the Sardis mint, perhaps when the club countermark was being used. The second is a monogram found on a Herakles/lion coin (no. 54.1), which I suggested was coined in the second or first century BC. It is possible that this is an Early Imperial countermark.

The last two countermarks in Table App. 1.1, […]TVS and male bust between letters, may have been added to the coins in the Imperial period, as it is very likely that Hellenistic coins were still available and in circulation. The coins on which they are placed are today unrecognizable, and so we do not know where or when the countermarks were made.

Seleucid Countermarks

The elephant head countermark is found on a smaller denomination minted in in the third century BC in Sardis or Smyrna. Hoover suggested that the mark was military in origin and "may have been applied at Smyrna," as this mint had produced a coin with an elephant reverse.[9] He later expanded his argument to note that the elephant type was "tentatively attributed" by Newell to Smyrna;[10] it referred to Antiochus' victory over the Galatians "who had targeted Smyrna," a victory that was partially achieved by using elephants. Thus, Hoover believed

9 Houghton and Lorber 2002, I: 121–22.

10 *WSM* 1495.

Table App. 1.2 Countermarks on Seleucid coins.

Countermark	Obv. or Rev.	Date and Mint of Coin	Date and Mint of Countermark	Reference	Cat. No.
Elephant head in 4 mm circle	R	280–261 BC Sardis or Smyrna	2nd century BC? Sardis?	Houghton and Lorber 2002, II: 51 no. 25	72.2
Horse-head, 5–6 mm circle	R	220–214 BC Sardis	ca. 213 BC Sardis	Mørkholm 1991, p. 126; Houghton and Lorber 2002, II: 65; cf. M7 GR 373, 380	84.1 **85.1**

the countermark was produced with payment to the army in mind.[11]

A horse-head countermark is normally placed on the reverses of Achaeus' Apollo/eagle bronzes. Mørkholm suggested that they were placed on the coins in Sardis as Achaeus wanted to "increase their nominal value" when the city was under siege.[12] Achaeus only minted in Sardis, and his tetradrachms do carry the horse head as a symbol within the type of striding Athena. In this, he used a symbol common on Seleucid coins since the time of the founder of the dynasty. While Hoover was willing to entertain Mørkholm's suggestion, he also proposed that Antiochus III countermarked the coins when he retook the city. Antiochus, who may have already struck small bronzes as *sitarchia* to pay for his troops in the camp (see Section 2.2.1), needed small change in the city immediately after the siege. It is preferable to think that he used the already-minted coins of Achaeus as a stopgap measure until his own mint could restart production of bronze coins. As Hoover points out, the overstriking of small bronzes of Antioch show that the Sardis mint was under pressure to produce coins.[13]

Roman Imperial Countermarks

Although Roman Provincial coins were certainly countermarked in the first and second centuries, it appears that the most intensive countermarking was done in the third century. Usually a mint countermarked coins of its own production, or at least those circulating within the city, but occasionally, inactive mints countermarked circulating coins.[14] As Johnston pointed out, coins from outside the city comprised 25–50% of Imperial coins reported from excavations; these were available for countermarking when the need arose.[15]

There are no countermarks known from Sardis excavation coins of legionary detachments, nor of the Roman governor, other likely sources of countermarks. The latter, though reported in museum collections or in trade, was not found on any excavated coins in Sardis.[16]

Although it appears that there are local reasons for countermarking—by looking at the table, one might suggest that heavily-worn coins could be countermarked for continued use—there are also broader reasons for countermarking coins, such as the commemoration of an imperial visit, a victory, change in title, or the death of a (disgraced) emperor.[17] Sometimes countermarks clearly revalue coins, especially when they are Greek letters showing the new value. But the reasons for countermarking are not always clear.

The clearest reason for countermarking is seen in the CAP Γ and CAP Δ countermarks, which are used to revalue the coin or confirm a worn coin's value. This practice occured when the Roman systems of denominations were introduced, but they are most common in the third century.[18] Christopher Howgego suggested that the CAP B, CAP Γ, and CAP Δ countermarks were put on foreign coins (i.e., not from the Sardis mint, unless they were completely worn) and were used by the Sardis mint soon after 260 AD, after the mint was shut. The numbers show the 2-, 3-, or 4-assaria value of the coins. Johnston

11 Houghton and Lorber 2002, II: 51

12 Mørkholm 1991, p. 126.

13 Houghton and Lorber 2002, II: 65.

14 Howgego 1985, p. 3; Johnston 2007, p. 6.

15 Johnston 2007, pp. 5–6.

16 cf. Howgego 1985, no. 533.

17 Howgego 1985, pp. 5–6.

18 Howgego 1985, p. 9.

Table App. 1.3 Countermarks on Roman Provincial coins.

Countermark	Obv. or Rev.	Date and Mint of Coin	Date and Mint of Countermark	Reference	Cat. No.
Aphrodite Anaitis?, 6 mm oval	O	139–161 AD Anchialos, Thrace	ca. 200?	*GIC* no. 233?	**97.1**
, 5 mm circle	O	29–18 BC "Asia"		*RPC* not, *GIC* not	98.7
Illegible, circle	Uncertain	29–18 BC "Asia"			98.9
Julia Domna bust in beaded border, 10 mm circle	O (over face)	145–161 AD Sardis	ca. 200? Sardis?	*GIC* not	**172.2**
Illegible, in uncertain shape	O	140–160 AD Sardis	Sardis?		**184.3**
Male advancing l. (Marsyas?), 5 × 7 rounded rectangle	O	161–169 AD Pompeiopolis (Soli)	Late Antonine/Severan? Uncertain city of origin		215.1
Tyche? Standing, facing r., 7 × 4 mm rectangle	O	27 BC–AD 68 Uncertain mint	Uncertain date Uncertain city of origin	*GIC* not	**219.2**
CAP •Γ•, 8 mm circle, with second smaller circle of illegible type	O	68–96 AD Uncertain mint; Sardis?	250s (Johnston 2007, p. 20) or soon after 260 (*GIC*) Sardis	*GIC* no. 560, M7 GR 398	**220.1**
CAP •Δ•, 13 mm circle	O	117–138 AD Uncertain mint	ca. 260 (Johnston 2007, p. 20) or soon after 260 (*GIC*) Sardis	*GIC* no. 561	228.1
, 9 mm circle	O	200–250 AD Ephesus?	Uncertain date Uncertain city of origin	*GIC* not	**229.1**
Illegible, 5 × 5 square	O (over face)	161–175 AD Sardis			223.1
1. Jug and knife?, 3 × 7 mm rectangle 2. Nike l. in rectangle punch 3. Object, 5 mm circle 4. Lyre, 5 × 7 oval 5. Note that opposite side has crescent-shaped countermarks (no types?)	Uncertain	1st to 3rd century AD Uncertain mint	Uncertain date(s) Uncertain city or cities of origin (no. 4 from Mytilene?)	2. cf. *GIC* no. 264 4. *GIC* no. 421?	230.46
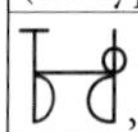, 8 mm circle	Uncertain	1st to 3rd century AD Uncertain mint		M7, p. 72 no. e	230.41
Emperor head r., 6 mm circle	Uncertain	1st to 3rd century AD Uncertain mint		cf. *GIC* no. 53ff	230.36
Illegible, 5 × 7 rectangle	O	1st to 3rd century AD Uncertain mint			230.81
Illegible (letters?) in 2 × 8 mm rectangle	R	1st to 3rd century AD Uncertain mint			230.17
Illegible, oval	O	80–100 AD? Sardis			**169.1**
Illegible, 6–8 mm circle	Uncertain	1st to 3rd century AD Uncertain mint			230.3 230.52
Illegible, 2 × 5 mm rectangle	Uncertain	1st to 3rd century AD Uncertain mint			230.43
Illegible, 4 × 10 mm rectangle	Uncertain	1st to 3rd century AD Uncertain mint			230.6
(twice, once faintly and almost off flan) laur. bust of [young beardless male] r., to l. VA?, to r. CVPΔ in circle 28 mm	Uncertain	1st century BC to 1st century AD Uncertain mint	Johnston in M7, p. 72 suggested ca. 255 Sardis	Johnston 2007, p. 95 cited as having 2 countermarks, one CAP Δ and one *GIC* 36 (Smyrna "probably with Γ on reverse")	95.9

dated the first two to a "slightly earlier" period, but as Howgego points out, she did not have access to a later coin bearing one of these marks.[19] However, the countermarks do show the number of coins circulating in Sardis in the third century that were not from the Sardis mint, though the coins predominantly came from the Ephesus mint.[20]

In Johnston's study of value marks added through countermarks, she confirmed that the CAP B, CAP Γ, and CAP Δ countermarks were added to very worn coins or "foreign" coins circulating in Sardis, most of them from the province of Asia.[21] The CAP Γ marks, she reiterated, were struck in 255–260, as "modules were shrinking and face values were being raised in Pamphylia and Cilicia."[22] Although the module was not changing in Sardis at this point, she argued that "foreign" coins which were "especially ambiguous in local terms—on account of their types or size or degree of wear," were chosen by the mint for countermarking.[23] I suggest that the mint for coin no. **220.1**, with a CAP Γ countermark was Sardis, but the reverse was worn completely smooth. Due to the traces of the bust on the obverse, I also suggest that the coin dates to the Flavian period; this shows how long coins remained in circulation. Its size (28 mm and 8.42 g) places it within the module for a 3-assaria coin in the 250s,[24] which is what the mark of Γ confirms.

Some of the CAP Δ countermarks can be seen to have a dash (thus, CAP Δ-), which Howgego read as 4½.[25] Johnston preferred to read this as only signifying that the letter was not part of the word "Sardineion," but that the letter referred to the numerical value of four. She noted that the coin that Howgego called later than 260 was "erroneously attributed to Gordian III," but it should be given to Gallienus, restoring her theory on the date of the countermark.[26] Two coins from the excavation have this countermark, one of them known to her (no. 95.9). This coin also carries a countermark probably applied at Smyrna.[27] It is too worn for identification of the types or mint; its module (29 mm, 9.51 g) would appear to place it in the 3-assaria denomination in the 250s for Sardis,[28] but the mark shows perhaps that the mint was revaluing the coin at 4-assaria, which may argue for the later date. It is likely that the 3-assaria mark used by Smyrna was an earlier revaluation, and the Sardian mint officials used the CAP Δ mark, at least in this case, to revalue the coin.

The second coin to carry the CAP Δ countermark, unknown to Johnston, is a coin from an uncertain mint, dating to the Hadrianic period (no. 228.1). This coin, at 35 mm and 20.32 g, clearly falls into—or actually exceeds—the 4-assaria module for the 250s and perhaps shows the reluctance of the mint to re-melt the old coins if the mint could more easily substitute a countermark.

Howgego's number 36, as noted above, is found on one coin from Sardis (no. 95.9). This was another countermark, probably by the city of Smyrna, used on worn flans to revalue the coins in the third century. Usually this countermark is combined with an obverse countermark with the letters CVMP and a male head r.; Johnston suggested Elagabalus or Severus Alexander. She concluded that the mark must have been used between 218 and 235, marking large flans as 3-assaria.[29] As was noted above, the earlier date of this countermark allows us to see a change in the valuation of flans from ca. 235 to 260, as the value changed from 3- to 4-assaria in these two closely-related cities.

19 Buttrey et al. 1981, p. 72; Howgego 1985, pp. 10, 43, 214–16.

20 Buttrey et al. 1981, p. 72; Howgego, 1985, pp. 43–44.

21 See Howgego 1985, Map 12; Johnston 2007, pp. 15, 20, 95.

22 Johnston 2007, p. 95 and p. 21, Table 2.

23 Johnston 2007, p. 95.

24 See Johnston 2007, Tables 2 and 4b.

25 Howgego 1985, p. 216.

26 Johnston 2007, p. 95.

27 Howgego 1985, no. 36, see below.

28 See Johnston 2007, Table 2.

29 Johnston 2007, p. 96.

Appendix 2
Monograms and Control Marks

I cannot claim to have made an exhaustive search for the monograms, but have consulted the *SNG* online database (smaller collections in the UK), the British Museum catalogs, *SNG Cop*, *SNG vAulock*, *SNG Tübingen*, *SNG Munich*, *SNG France* (Mysia), Weber Collection, Fitzwilliam Collection, Hunterian Collection, and the online images for the American Numismatic Society, Boston Museum of Fine Arts, Princeton University, Harvard University Art Museums, and Yale University.

Table App. 2.1 Monograms on Hellenistic Coins.

Monogram	Cat. No.	Reference
	9.1	Lysimachus, Thrace. Athena/forepart of lion. Monograms are common on this series. cf. *BMC Tauric Chersonese*, p. 195, no. 1? (on a different bronze denomination of Lysimachus).
	9.3	As above. No published parallel for this monogram?
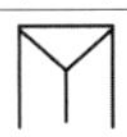	9.6	As above. No published parallel for this monogram?
	10.1	Demetrius II, Macedon. Macedonian shield, monogram as boss/Macedonian helmet: always found on this series.
	**19.1**	Bithynia, for Papirius Carbo. Dionysos/thyrsus. No published parallel for this monogram?
	23.1	Attalus II, Pergamum. Athena/coiled serpent. No published parallel for this monogram?
	23.2	As above. As M7 GR 37.
	23.3	As above. As *SNG Tübingen* 4, monogram 35, but on Asklepios/snake around omphalos.
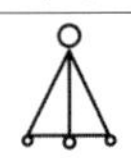	**26.1**, 26.2	Pergamum. Asklepios/snake around omphalos. No monogram noted in catalogs, but found in trade.
	28.1	Pergamum. Athena/owl on palm branch, under r. wing; monogram under l. wing obscure. No published parallel for this monogram?
	28.2	Pergamum. Athena/owl facing. As *BMC Mysia*, p. 133, no. 204.
	30.1	Cyme. Forepart of horse/cup. Monograms are common on this series. No published parallel for this monogram?
	44.1	Smyrna. Cybele/tripod. Milne 1923, no. 34 suggested this monogram was for a magistrate named Pyrrhos.
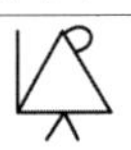	52.1	Sardis. Herakles/Apollo. Monograms are common for this series; in 1981, Johnston knew of more than 70 monograms or names (M7, p. 80).
	**52.2**	As above. Same as 52.7?
	52.3	As above. Bell 1916, no. 245.

	52.4	As above. As *SNG Ashmolean* V, monogram 25.
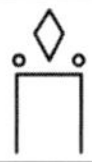	52.5	As above.
	52.6	As above. Probably as Bell 1916, no. 240.
	52.7	As above.
	52.8	As above.
	52.9	As above. As *SNG Cop*, monogram 28.
	**52.10**, 52.11 52.12	As above. cf. *SNG Munich*, monogram 33.
	52.13	As above.
	**52.15**	As above.
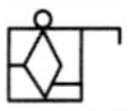	52.16	As above. cf. Fitzwilliam, McClean Collection, no. 8709, for Apollo/club.
	**52.17**, **52.18**	As above.
	**52.19**	As above.
	52.20	As above.
	52.21	As above.
CΩ	52.22, 52.23 52.24, 52.25	As above. As M7 GR 212; *BMC Lydia*, p. 239, no. 22. This is, by far, the most common monogram found on these coins. It may show either a very large issue, or more than one moneyer using these letters.
	52.26	As above. As M7 GR 214.
T (obscure)	52.27	As above. Entire monogram not legible.
 ΗΡΑΙΟΣ	**52.32**	As above. As *BMC Lydia*, p. 240, no. 36; compare Bell 1916, no. 250; M13, no. 52.29
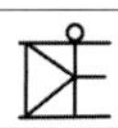	**53.1**	Sardis. Dionysos/forepart of lion. As *BMC Lydia*, p. 241, no. 47; M7 GR 241; Bell 1916, no. 261.
	55.1	Sardis. Apollo/club. Monograms are almost always found on this series (see M7, p. 80, where Johnston knew of "over sixty").
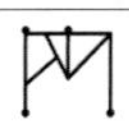	**55.2**	As above.
	55.3	As above. As M7 GR 195.
	55.4	As above.
	55.5	As above, see *SNG Ashmolean* V, monogram 11.

	55.6	As above. As *BMC Lydia*, p. 238, no. 12.
	**55.7**	As above. As *SNG Tübingen*, monogram 18.
	55.8	As above.
	55.9 52.14	As above. As *BMC Lydia*, p. 239, no. 21; Boston MFA 65.795. Also: Sardis Herakles/Apollo.
	55.10	As above. As *SNG Ashmolean* V, monogram 16.
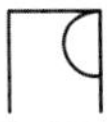	55.11	As above.
	55.12	As above. As *BMC Lydia*, p. 239, no. 30.
	**55.14**	As above.
	56.1	Sardis. Dionysos/panther. As *BMC Lydia*, p. 241, no. 42; Bell 1916, no. 258.
	**57.1**	Sardis. Herakles/kantharos. As *BMC Lydia*, p. 241, no. 46.

Table App. 2.2 Seleucid Control Marks.

Monogram	Cat. No.	Reference
First between hind legs, second below belly 	71.1	Seleucus I, Sardis. Medusa/bull butting r. As Houghton and Lorber 2002, no. 151(2)b.
To l. A, above M, to r. ΔI	**73.1**	Antiochus II, Sardis. Apollo/tripod. As Houghton and Lorber 2002, no. 520(3), which does not record the M.
Outer l. Σ, outer r. ΔI, below, anchor r.	74.1	As above. As Houghton and Lorber 2002, no. 522(2).
Outer l., with anchor r. below 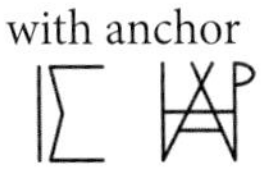	**75.1**	As above. As Houghton and Lorber 2002, no. 523(a).
Below anchor, to r. 	78.3	Antiochus II, Sardis. Apollo/cithara. As Houghton and Lorber 2002, no. 528(3).
Outer l. Σ	**79.2**	Antiochus II, Sardis. Tyche/tripod. Not previously published.
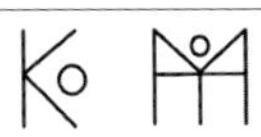	81.1	Seleucus II, Sardis. Athena/Apollo. As Houghton and Lorber 2002, no. 660(5), but outer r. illegible.
Below arrow (outer l.) 	82.1	Seleucus II, Antioch? Athena/Apollo. Houghton and Lorber 2002 does not list this control mark.
Outer r.  outer l. is off flan	84.1	Achaeus, Sardis. Apollo/eagle. Houghton and Lorber 2002 does not list this control mark, although cf. no. 955(2).
To r. ΔI	**85.1**	As above. Houghton and Lorber 2002, no. 956.
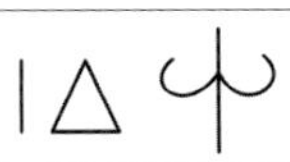	**87.1**	Antiochus III, Sardis. Apollo/elephant l. As Houghton and Lorber 2002, no. 981(1).
	87.2	As above. As Houghton and Lorber 2002, no. 981(2).

Table App. 2.3 Late Roman Monograms.

Monogram	Cat. No.	Reference
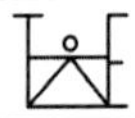	**911.1**	Theodosius II, *RIC* X type 5.
	968.2, 969.1–5	Marcian, *RIC* X type 1.
	965.1–2, 966.1–5, 967.1–2, 968.3–4, 969.6–26	Marcian, *RIC* X type 2.
	967.6	Marcian, *RIC* X type 2, variant.
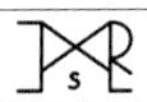	967.3	Marcian, *RIC* X type 3.
	967.4–5	Marcian, *RIC* X type 4.
	966.6, 969.27–30	Marcian, *RIC* X type 5.
	968.1	Marcian, *RIC* X type 7.
	964.1	Marcian, *LRBC* type 9.
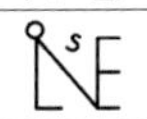	976.1–5, 985.1–39	Leo I, *RIC* X type 1.
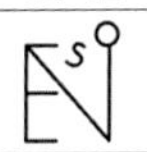	973.1–2, 976.6	Leo I, *RIC* X type 4.
	985.42	Leo I, *RIC* X type 5.
	982.1–3	Leo I, *RIC* X type 6.
	989.1	Libius Severus, *RIC* X type 1.
	990.1–2	Odavacar, *RIC* X type 1.
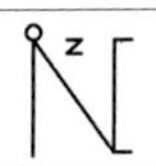	994.1–3, 997.1–54	Zeno, *RIC* X type 1.
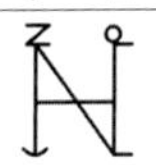	995.1–2	Zeno, *RIC* X type 4.
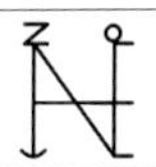	997.55–58	Zeno, *RIC* X type 5.
	996.1–5	Zeno, *RIC* X type 10.
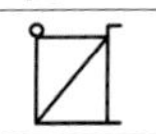	995.3–7	Zeno, *RIC* X type 13.
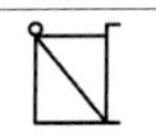	995.8–21	Zeno, *RIC* X type 14.
	991.1	Basiliscus and Marcus, *RIC* X type 1.
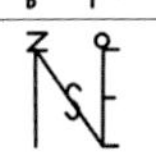	992.1–7	Zenonis, *RIC* X type 1.
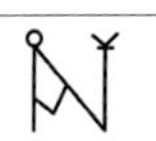	1004.1–200	Anastasius I (variations not given separate types).

Table App. 2.4 Lead Seals.

Monogram	Cat. No.	Description
	**L13**	Hatching shows area obscured by piercing: flip side is quadruped Byzantine: 450–700?

Appendix 3
Reverse Descriptions of Late Roman Bronzes

Modified from Carson, Hill, and Kent 1965, *LRBC.*

Table App. 3.1a Reverse types, 324–348 AD.

Reverse Type	Description
Gloria Exercitus emperor standing	Emperor standing l., head r., holding spear in r. and leaning on shield
Gloria Exercitus 1 standard	Two soldiers standing, each holding a spear and leaning on shield; between them, one standard
Gloria Exercitus 2 standards	Two soldiers standing, each holding a spear and leaning on shield; between them, two standards
Ivst Ven Mem	Aequitas standing l. holding balance and transverse scepter; paired with an obverse of veiled head r. DVCONSTANTINVSPTAVG
Libertas Pvblica	Victory on galley, holding wreath in either hand
Pax Publica	Pax standing l. holding branch and transverse spear; paired with an obverse of bust of Helena diademed; r. FLIVLHELENAEAVG
Providentiae Augg	Camp-gate with two towers, star above
Providentiae Caess	As above
Quadriga	Emperor in quadriga ascending r., above, hand of God, no legend; paired with an obverse of veiled head r. DVCONSTANTINVSPTAVG
Securitas Reipublice	Securitas standing l. holding branch; paired with obverse of bust of Helena r. FL HELENA AVGVSTA
Victoriae dd Auggq nn	Two Victories standing face to face, each with a wreath
Victory on prow	Victory l. holding transverse scepter and shield, on prow; paired with obverse of helmeted head of Constantinopolis l., scepter over shoulder CONSTANTINOPOLIS
Virtus Augusti	Emperor standing looking r., holding inverted spear in r. and resting l. hand on grounded shield
VN MR	Emperor standing r., veiled; paired with an obverse of veiled head r. DVCONSTANTINVSPTAVG
Vot Mult	Vot /XX /Mult /XXX in wreath
Vot XXX	Vot/XXX in wreath, DNCONSTANTINIMAXAVG around
Wolf and twins	Wolf, beneath twins, above, two stars; paired with an obverse of the helmeted head of Roma l. VRBSROMA

Table App. 3.1b Reverse types, 324–364 AD.

Reverse Type	Description
Fel Temp Reparatio emperor and captives	Emperor in armor moving l., holding labarum in r. and shield in l.; in front are two kneeling captives
Fel Temp Reparatio FH3	Virtus with shield on l. arm spearing fallen horseman, who raises l. arm
Fel Temp Reparatio FH4	Virtus with shield on l. arm spearing fallen horseman, who clutches horse's neck
Fel Temp Reparatio galley	Emperor stands on galley l., holding phoenix on globe in r. and labarum in l.; galley is steered by Victory seated l.
Fel Temp Reparatio hut	Virtus moving r., head turned l., holds spear in l. and leads prisoner from hut beneath tree
Fel Temp Reparatio phoenix globe	Phoenix to r. on globe
Spes Reipublice	Virtus standing l., holds globe in r. and spear in l.

Table App. 3.1c Reverse types, 364–450 AD.

Reverse Type	Description
Concordia Agu	Two nimbate emperors facing, each with spear; between them they hold a long cross
Concordia Aug or Auggg cross	Latin cross surrounded by legend
Concordia Aug empress	Empress enthroned facing, star in l. field
Concordia Aug Victory	Victory facing, holding wreath in each hand
Concordia Aug Victory l.	Victory striding l., holding wreath and palm
Concordia Auggg Cp or Concordia Augg Cp	Constantinopolis enthroned facing, helmeted head r., holds scepter in r. and globe in l., prow by r. foot
Concordia Augg Cp Victoriola	As above, but holds Victoriola instead of globe
Concordia Auggg Roma	Roma enthroned facing, helmeted head l., holds globe in r. and spear in l., one leg bared
Concordia Auggg Roma 2	As above, but globe in l. and spear in r.
Glor orvis terrar	Emperor standing facing, holds labarum in r. and globus cruciger (sic *LRBC*) in l.; star in l. field
Gloria Novi Saeculi	Emperor standing facing, head r., holds labarum in r. and rests l. on shield
Gloria Reipublice camp-gate	Camp-gate with two towers
Gloria Romanorum 8	Emperor dragging captive r.; holds labarum in l. hand (no cloak)
Gloria Romanorum 18	Emperor standing facing, with globe in r. and labarum in l.
Gloria Romanorum emperor galley	Emperor standing facing on galley, head l., raises r. hand; Victory at helm
Gloria Romanorum emperor horseback	Emperor on horseback r., raising r. hand
Gloria Romanorum empress	Empress enthroned facing, crowned by hand of God; paired with bust of empress r., pd., crowned by Hand of God
Gloria Romanorum three emperors	Three facing emperors with spears in hand and resting hand on shield; middle emperor is smaller than the other two
Gloria Romanorum two emperors globe	Two facing emperors with spears in hand and holding between them a globe
Gloria Romanorum two emperors shield	Two facing emperors with spears, resting hands on shields
Reparatio Fel Temp	Emperor facing, head r., holds spear in r. and resting l. on shield
Restitutor Reip	Emperor facing, head r., holds standard in l. hand and Victoriola in r.
Restitutor Reipublicae	As above
Salus Reipublicae	Victory moving l., holds palm in r. and dragging captive with l.
Salus Reipublicae empress	Empress standing frontally, hands crossed on chest
Salus Reipublicae Victory seated	Victory seated r., writing on shield resting on small column
Salus Reipublicae Victory shield	Victory seated r. on cuirass, pointing to shield inscribed with chi-rho supported by small column; paired with bust of empress r., pd., crowned by hand of God
Salus Reipublice	Victory moving l., holds trophy in r. and dragging captive with l.; chi-rho in l. field
Securitas Reipublicae	Victory rushing l. holds wreath in r. and palm over l. shoulder
Spes Romanorum camp-gate	Camp-gate with two towers, star above
Urbs Roma	Roma seated l. holds spear in r. and Victoriola in l., cuirass by feet
Urbs Roma Felix	Emperor standing facing, holds labarum in r. and Victoriola in l.
Victoria Aug emperor	Emperor standing facing, holds globe in r. and spear in l.

Victoria Augg or Victoria Auggg	Victory striding l., holds wreath in r. and palm in l.
Victoria Augg captive	Victory striding l., holds trophy and drags captive
Victoria Augg emperor	Emperor standing facing, head l., holds Victoriola in r. and standard in l.
Victoria Augg 2 Victories or Victoria Auggg 2 Victories	Two Victories face to face, each elevating a wreath
Virtus Exerciti	Emperor moves r. holds standard in r. and globe in l., spurning captive with foot
Virtus Exerciti 2	Emperor facing, head r., holds spear in r. and places l. on shield; to r., Victory crowns him and holds palm in l.
Vot V	Inscription in two lines in wreath
Vot X Mult XX	Inscription in four lines in wreath
Vot XV Mult XX	Inscription in four lines in wreath
Vot XX Mult XXX	Inscription in four lines in wreath
Vot XXXX	Inscription in two lines in wreath
VT XXX V	Inscription in three lines in wreath

Table App. 3.1d Reverse types, 450–498 AD.

Reverse Type	Description
Emperor and captive	No legend. Emperor standing facing, head l., holds in r. a long cross and places l. on head of kneeling captive
Empress b/E	Empress standing facing, holds globus cruciger and transverse scepter b/E
Emperor cross and globe	Emperor standing facing, holds long cross in r. and globe in l. ZENO
Two enthroned emperors	Two nimbate emperors enthroned facing, between them a cross
Victoria Augg	Victory striding l., holds wreath in r. and palm in l.

Appendix 4
Statistical Analysis Formulas

Annual Average Coin Loss per Thousand

The AACL/1000 calculation has been used since the 1970s to try and provide a rough average of coins per reign found on excavations; by multiplying by 1000, sites that have fewer coins can be compared to sites with larger numbers of coins (although see the caveat for the Chi-Square Goodness of Fit test) or shorter periods with longer periods. The equation is:

$$\frac{\text{Total of coins in reign}}{\text{Years of reign}} \times \frac{1000}{\text{Total number of coins found on site}} = \text{AACL/1000}$$

Table App. 4.1 Periodization for AACL/1000 calculations.

Period No.	Name of Period	Years in Period
1	Augustan, 27 BC–AD 14	41
2	Julio-Claudian, 14–68 AD	54
3	Flavian, 69–96 AD	27
4	Nerva–Hadrianic, 96–138 AD	42
5	Antonine, 138–192 AD	54
6	Severan, 193–238 AD	45
7	third century, 239–284 AD	45
8	Tetrarchic, 285–324 AD	39
9	Constantine–Julian II, 324–364 AD	44
10	Jovian–Valentinian II, 364–392 AD	28
11	Theodosius I–Theodosius II, 392–450 AD	58
12	Marcian–pre-reform of Anastasius I, 450–498 AD	48
13	Post-reform Anastasius I–Justin I, 498–527 AD	29
14	Justinian I, 527–565 AD	38
15	Justin II–Maurice, 565–602 AD	37
16	Phocas–Heraclius, 602–641 AD	39
17	Constans II–Constantine IV, 641–685 AD	44

Comparative cities, sample size, and sources:

Amorium: n = 728, Katsari et al. 2012, but the sample of identified coins was so small that I eliminated this city from the calculations, as the sample would not have been valid in the Chi-square Goodness of Fit test.

Aphrodisias: n = 246, MacDonald 1976, through Tetrarchic only; the sample would also have been invalid in the Chi-square Goodness of Fit test, and so was not used.

Assos: n = 270, Bell 1902, an uncertain number of which were purchased, not excavated. No coins of the fifth century were published; the sample would have been invalid in the Chi-square Goodness of Fit test.

Athens: n = 76,049, Thompson 1954; Kroll 1993, Kroll noted that at least 4,000 were discarded as unidentifiable before he saw the coins.

Butrint: n = 2,000, Moorhead, Gjongecaj, and Abdy 2007, almost all from post-300 AD to the fifth and possibly the early sixth century (see Moorhead 2007, p. 287); there are no coins from the fifth century in the Chi-square Goodness of Fit test, since the numismatists could not identify the half-century from which the coins came, hence I had to eliminate them from the test. The raw data are found in Moorhead, Gjongecaj, and Abdy 2007 and Guest et al. 2004; these are interpreted in Moorhead 2007.

Caesarea Maritima: n = 8048, Evans 2007.

Corinth: n = 51,652, Harris (1941, p. 155) noted that over 50,000 coins had been found at Corinth by that date, 43,000 of which she had charted, but in large chronological spans, so I could not use all her data. Also note that since the numismatists did not often separate the pre-reform from post-reform Anastasian issues, the number for period 13 may be a little high (see also Edwards 1933; 1937; Harris 1941; Fisher 1984; Zervos 1986; MacIsaac 1987; Sanders 2002). N.B.: I did not comb each year's excavation reports in *Hesperia*; references to these may be found in Kremydi and Iakovidou 2015 (whose divisions were too broad for use in this study).

Ephesus: n = 3198, Vetters 1979; 1980; 1983; Karweise 1986; Schindel 2009.

Hierapolis: n = 402, Travaglini and Camillieri 2010, the sample would not have been valid under the Chi-square Goodness of Fit test, since so few coins were identifiable.

Kalenderhane Camii, Istanbul: n = 441, Hendy 2007, Late Roman and Byzantine only.

Kenchreai: n = 574, Hohlfelder 1978.

Pergamum: n = 3,480, Regling 1913; Voegtli 1984; Boehringer 1984; Voegtli et al. 1993.

Priene: n = 1,460, Regling 1927, but note no coins from the second half of the fifth century were reported.

Sagalassus: n = 428, Scheers 1993a; 1993b; 1995; Scheers et al. 1997; Scheers 2000. Larger totals are reported in Poblome 1995 and in Stroobants and Poblome 2015, but most coins are unpublished at this point; since the total was small, I eliminated this site from the calculations.

Sardis: n = 23,000, M1, M7, and this volume, all from database.

Side: n = 127, Atlan 1976, but the sample was so small that I eliminated this city from the calculations.

Tarsus: n = 380, Cox 1950, but the identifiable coins were so small that this site was eliminated from the calculations.

Zeugma: Frascone 2013; Butcher 2013. I did not use these coins in the calculations, since the third-century sack of the city preserved far larger numbers of these coins than in other cities of the eastern Mediterranean, tremendously skewing the "normal" profile for the AACL/1000 of eastern cities.

Chi-Square Goodness of Fit Test

The Chi-Square Goodness of Fit test is used to determine whether the sample data (in this case, the coins from the excavation) are consistent with a hypothesized distribution (if the sample reflects a standard number of coins from each period, which must substitute for the number of coins coming from the mint, a number that we will never know). The Chi-Square Goodness of Fit test can be used when the sample is a simple random sample, but if the expected frequency is below 1 or if the expected frequency is less than 5 in more than 20% of the cells, then the test is inappropriate. The equation for the Chi-Square Goodness of Fit test is:

$$\chi^2 = \sum_{i=1}^{r} \sum_{j=1}^{k} \frac{(O_{ij} - E_{ij})^2}{E_{ij}}$$

O_{ij} is the observed value of cases categorized in row *i* of column *j*. E_{ij} is the number of cases expected in H_0 (the null hypothesis) to be categorized in row *i* of column *j*. The double sum (two sigmas) indicates that the sum is to be calculated over all the *r* rows and the *k* columns (i.e., over all the cells). The E_{ij} is the expected frequency for each cell, which is calculated by multiplying the marginal row and the marginal column total common to a cell, and then dividing that product by the grand total. The O_{ij} is the observed frequency. The p-value, or calculated probability, is the probability of finding the observed results, when H_0 of the study is true. Generally, a p-value of less than 5% is thought to reflect the probability that the results are observable and thus valid.

Table App. 4.2a Chi-Square Goodness of Fit test results for "normal" cities, periods 1–8.

Period No.	Sardis	Pergamum	Ephesus	Priene	Athens	Corinth	Kenchreai	Butrint	Caesarea Maritima	Σ_j
1	96	63	31	14	2008	219	18	7	48	2504
2	95	16	14	10	122	486	38	4	102	887
3	49	3	10	28	41	137	10	1	21	300
4	82	69	32	47	1717	120	10	7	44	2128
5	68	50	34	9	3999	284	9	13	6	4472
6	135	46	77	26	186	319	12	4	30	835
7	384	168	133	100	1915	326	35	20	52	3133
8	241	101	25	12	417	181	22	8	53	1060
Σ_i	1150	516	356	246	10405	2072	154	64	356	15319

The Chi-Square value is 5692.824, with 56 degrees of freedom and a p-value of 0, which means the differences between the groups is significant.

Table App. 4.2b Chi-Square Goodness of Fit test results for "normal" cities, periods 9–17.

Period No.	Sardis	Pergamum	Ephesus	Priene	Athens	Corinth	Kenchreai	Butrint	Caesarea Maritima	Σ_j
9	2267	184	239	177	4992	2224	99	4	379	10565
10	2157	48	193	69	3385	994	57	1	428	7332
11	1982	114	262	114	2166	2336	116	15	268	7373
12	992	5	149	0	837	269	27	13	289	2581
13	152	10	15	3	80	484	39	135	195	1113
14	308	26	105	21	276	134	48	18	106	1042
15	444	47	65	27	217	535	30	84	96	1545
16	340	25	6	21	280	165	2	51	101	991
17	107	125	0	9	847	55	2	120	11	1276
Σ_i	8749	584	1034	441	13080	7196	420	441	1873	33818

The Chi-Square value is 7363.87, with 64 degrees of freedom; the p-value is 0, which again means the differences between the groups is significant.

Mean Coin Date

The calculation is: $\mathrm{MCD} = \dfrac{\sum x_i f_i}{n}$

where the result is expressed as mean coin date (MCD); *x* is the mean date of manufacture, *f* the frequency within the deposit and *n* the sample size.

The equation is adapted from Gerrard 1993. I thank Thomas M. Evans, who helped me with the statistical analysis.

CATALOGUE OF THE COINS

1973–2013

Lydian through Roman Coins (Seventh Century BC–330 AD)

All coins are bronze, unless specifically noted. Within mints, unless stated, dates are as above. An empty slot in the denominations column means that no denomination has been assigned to the coin. The specific entries list the die axis (when relevant), mintmark (when relevant), diameter, weight, and sector. H1–H8 designates that the coin belongs to one of the hoards discussed in Section 3.6. **Bold** numbers indicate the coin is included in the plates. Numbers in references refer to coin numbers, not page numbers. Standard abbreviations include:

C/m	control mark	i.d.	identification	off.	officina
cm.	countermark	laur.	laureate	o/s	overstruck
cuir.	wearing cuirass	lig.	ligatured	pd.	pearl-diademed
ex.	exergue	mg.	monogram	rd.	rosette-diademed
gl. cr.	globus cruciger	M/m	mintmark	var.	variant
helm.	helmeted	n.s.	not seen by the author		

Lydian Royal Coinage

Alyattes?

Sardis

ca. 630–580/560 BC? EL trite (Lydo-Ionian standard)

obv. Head of roaring lion r. with "nose wart" of multiple rays

rev. Double punch incuse

SNG Turk 1: 1013; Weidauer 1975 type XVI; SNG vAulock 8: 2868–2870; Cahill et al., forthcoming

1.1 12 × 9 4.70 (5 rays) Ac-FT

1.2 13 × 11 4.75 (5 rays) Ac-FT

Weidauer (1975) used lion heads on East Greek pottery to date coins by style and notes on pp. 103–4 that her type XVI must have been a larger series than the few surviving pieces would suggest, due to the few die links among the specimens known. Recent research dates the coins by the pottery from the Artemision at Ephesus; see Kerschner and Konuk, forthcoming. There are no die links between the Sardis coins and those illustrated by Weidauer. Trites of the same type are found in the Gordion 1963 Hoard, which Bellinger (1968, pp. 12–13) dated to 625–610. See a new reconstruction of the date of Alyattes's coinage in Wallace 2016. For metallurgical analysis, see Cahill et al., forthcoming; both were found with no. **3.1** in a dump on the Acropolis.

Croesus

561–547 BC Au 1/12th stater (heavy Croesid standard)

Forepart of roaring lion r. confronting bull head l.

Square incuse

SNG Munich 23: 9

2.1 7 × 6 0.89 MMS

Konuk 2012, pp. 49–50; Naster's (1965) Massive Style; Carradice's (1987) Early Style; Nimchuck's (2000) Type B; somewhat worn or struck with worn die, details obscured. This coin was found in a recess of the Lydian fortification, beneath debris from the Persian sack of the city, see Cahill and Kroll 2005; analysis of the date of the sack of Sardis in Wallace 2016.

AR stater

Forepart of roaring lion r. confronting bull head l.
Double punch incuse
SNG vAulock 8: 2873–2874; SNG Turk 1: 1018; Cahill et al., forthcoming

3.1 21 × 15 10.25 Ac-FT

Naster's (1965) Forceful/Nervous Style; Carradice's (1987) Early Style; Nimchuk's (2000) Type A; slightly worn. Found with two electrum trites in dump on the Acropolis.

AR 1/12th stater

Forepart of roaring lion r. confronting head of bull l.
Double punch incuse
SNG vAulock 8: 2880; SNG Turk 1: 1020

4.1 9 0.72 MMS

Cahill and Kroll 2005, also from the early part of Croesus's reign. Naster's (1965) Massive style; Carradice's (1987) Early Style; Nimchuk's (2000) Type B; somewhat worn. Found with no. **2.1**, in a recess of the Lydian fortification, associated with debris from the Persian sack of the city. See Cahill and Kroll 2005; Wallace 2016.

AR 1/24th stater

Forepart of roaring lion r. confronting head of bull l.
Single punch incuse
Carradice 1987, pl. 10.5; SNG Turk 1: 1022

5.1	6	0.35	MMS
5.2	6	0.22	MMS/S

Naster's (1975) Massive Style; Carradice's (1987) Early Style; Nimchuk's (2000) Type B. No. **5.1** is misnumbered in Cahill and Kroll 2005; associated with a skull of a soldier killed in the Persian sack of the city. Coin shows some wear. 5.2 is from a much later archaeological context and is worn; coin not seen by me, and assigned here because of module (pictures unhelpful).

Miletus AR hemihekaton

Late sixth–early fifth century BC (Milesian standard)
Forepart of lion l., head of roaring lion r.
Star-flower in incuse, one side indented
SNG vAulock 6: 2082; SNG Turk 1: 468–476; M7 GR 104

6.1 10 × 8 1.08 NoEx

For circumstances of discovery, see Cahill and Kroll 2005.

Hellenistic Coins

Lysimachus

Thrace

306–281 BC larger denomination

Head of Athena in Phrygian helmet r.
Trophy ΒΑΣΙΛΕΩΣ-ΛΥΣΙΜΑΧΟΥ
SNG Cop: 1164–1167

7.1	12	23	7.87	AT-Pac
7.2	2	20	7.06	AT-Pac

Possibly Sardis

306–ca. 280 BC? unit

Head of Athena in crested helmet, r.
Lion leaping r., spearhead below
ΒΑΣΙΛΕΩΣ-ΛΥΣΙΜΑΧΟΥ, illeg. mg.
SNG Cop. 1149–1157; Mørkholm 1991: 183; M7 GR 2

8.1	5	21	5.43	NoEx
8.2	4	20	4.51	NoEx

Note that Mørkholm (1991, p. 82) thought that the chronology and the mints of this denomination and the following "have not yet been worked out." For suggestion of mint, see Evans, forthcoming.

Probably Sardis

306–ca. 280 BC? half unit

Head of Athena in crested helmet r.
Forepart of lion r., spearhead below
ΒΑΣΙΛΕΩΣ–ΛΥΣΙΜΑΧΟΥ
M7 GR 3–6

9.1	12	16	2.70	MMS/S, mg. App. 2
9.2	6	15	2.33	AT, mg. illeg.
9.3	6	14	2.54	NoEx, mg. App. 2
9.4	6	14	2.33	NoEx, mg. illeg.
9.5	3	14	1.94	LAW, mg. illeg.
9.6	12	14	frag'y	NoEx, mg. App. 2

For suggestion of mint, see Evans, forthcoming.

Demetrius II

Uncertain Mint, Macedon

239–229 BC unit

Macedonian shield, mg. as boss, App. 2
Macedonian helmet ΒΑ-ΣΙ
SNG Cop: 1224; Mørkholm 1991: 435

10.1	3	16	4.54	HoB

Macedonian Kings

Probably Sardis

Late fourth century BC?/297–294? half unit

Macedonian shield, Gorgoneion as boss

Macedonian helmet B-A, caduceus below l.

Price 1991: 3158; Mørkholm 1991: 73; M7 GR 22

11.1	7	16	3.59	NoEx
11.2	5	16	3.30	MMS/S
11.3	1	15	3.28	NoEx

For suggestion of mint, see Evans, forthcoming.

Note that Price (1991) suggested a mint in Salamis and a date of 323–315 BC; Mørkholm (1991, p. 60) suggested Miletus, minted by Cassander's sons in 297–294. The one known context for this coin is Late Roman.

Miletus?

317–300 BC half unit

Macedonian shield with thunderbolt as boss

Macedonian helmet B-A

Price 1991: 397; SNG Cop: 1119–1121

12.1	3	17	2.10	MMS/S

Ashton (1998, p. 45) suggested Miletus as the mint, due to provenance of the coins and die axis.

Uncertain Mint

Uncertain date half unit

Macedonian shield, boss missing or illeg.

Macedonian helmet, all other symbols illeg. B-A

M7 GR 24

13.1	—	16	4.78	F49
13.2	—	16	4.26	NoEx

Alexander III or his Successors

Probably Sardis

336–323 BC? unit

Head of young Herakles in lionskin helmet r.

Bow in case/club ΑΛΕΞΑΝΔΡΟΥ, below, cup

Price 1991: 325; M7 GR 11

14.1	10	19	6.64	MMS

Field notes suggest cup not certain, now completely corroded. Price (1991) noted that three examples were found from the Sardis excavations, but M7 lists only one; cf. Ashton 1998, p. 45, agreeing with mint. Price assigned the coin to an unspecified mint.

Head of young Herakles in lionskin helmet r.

Bow in case/club ΑΛΕΞΑΝΔΡΟΥ symbol illeg.

M7 GR 17

15.1	6	19	5.05	NoEx
15.2	12	15	4.88	NoEx

Head of young Herakles in lionskin helmet r. quarter

Bow in case/club, no symbol

Price 1991: 267; M7 GR 18

16.1	7	11	1.57	NoEx

For suggestion of mint, see Evans, forthcoming. Price (1991) assigned the coin to an unspecified mint.

Philip III

Probably Sardis

323–317 BC unit

Head of young Herakles in lionskin helmet r.

Rider galloping r. ΦΙ, no symbol

Price 1991, p. 126, no. P2; M7 GR 20–21

17.1	7	19	6.02	ByzFort
17.2	6	19	3.68	F49
17.3	12	18	5.42	MMS

Price (1991, p. 117) noted that eleven [nine are listed in M7] other examples of this coin were found in the Sardis excavations, calling the mint in western Asia Minor "virtually certain"; cf. Ashton 1998, p. 45. For the suggestion of mint, see Evans, forthcoming.

Philip III or Antigonus I

Probably Sardis

323–310 BC unit

Head of young Herakles in lionskin helmet r.

Bow in case/club, ΒΑΣΙΛΕΩΣ, beneath, torch

Price 1991: 2800

18.1	3	20	6.23	ByzFort
18.2	3	20	5.94	NoEx
18.3	—	20	5.20	MMS/S

Price (1991) suggested a mint in western Asia Minor. For the suggestion of mint, see Evans, forthcoming.

BITHYNIA, Nicomedia

61–57 BC

Head of Dionysos ivy wreath r. ΝΙΚΑΙЄΩΝ [Β]ΚΣ, mg. below chin, App. 2

Thyrsus tied with fillet [ЄΠΙΓΑΙΟΥ-]ΠΑΠΙΡΙΟΥ-ΚΑΡΒΩΝΟ[Σ]

Recueil 1910, p. 398, nos. 8–9 (sic Apollo); Stumpf 1991: 102–3

19.1	12	20	4.07	F49

For date, see Stumpf 1991 pp. 67–68.

MYSIA, Pergamum

270/260–230/225 BC half unit?

Helm. head of Athena r.

Two stars, above patera?

SNG Cop: 325

20.1	—	13	1.24	ByzFort

I.d. based on style of head, module. For date, Westermark 1991, p. 4.

260–197 BC half unit

Helm. head of Athena r.

Ivy leaf ΦΙΛΕ-ΤΑΙΡΟΥ

Westermark 1991: 8; M7 GR 32

21.1	12	13	2.02	ThSt
21.2	—	13	2.43	MMS, i.d. prob.

For the date of this coin, see Section 3.2.2.

ca. 250–230/220 BC half unit

Head of Apollo r.

Thyrsus ΦΙΛΕ-ΤΑΙΡΟΥ

Westermark 1991, p. 17

22.1	12	11	1.61	NoEx

Attalus II

ca. 215–early second century BC? unit

Helm. head of Athena r.

Coiled serpent ΦΙΛΕΤΑΙΡΟΥ, mg.

Westermark 1991: 14; M7 GR 34–40

23.1	12	17	4.00	F55, mg. App. 2
23.2	12	17	3.75	AT-Pac, mg. App. 2
23.3	12	13	1.72	ByzFort, mg. App. 2
23.4	—	16	4.70	F49, mg. illeg.
23.5	3	16	3.63	MMS/S, mg. illeg.
23.6	12	15	5.30	MMS/S, mg. illeg.
23.7	—	15	3.49	MMS/S, mg. illeg.
23.8	8	15	3.53	ByzFort, mg. illeg.
23.9	12	15	2.52	MD2, mg. illeg.
23.10	6	14	4.02	F49, mg. illeg.
23.11	12	14	3.78	AT, mg. illeg.
23.12	12	13	2.70	MMS/N, mg. illeg.

Note that Mørkholm (1991, p. 129) suggested that coins with the name of Philetaerus should primarily date to the third century, though he does not exclude a minting date in the early second century. See also Westermark 1991, p. 152 for the date given above; Chameroy (2012, p. 141) agrees with this date. Two of these coins came from lots that were dated to the first century BC to the first half of the first century AD; others came from Late Roman or unstratified contexts.

ca. 215–175 BC? unit?

Helm. head of Athena r.

Unc. rev., ΦΙΛΕΤΑΙΡΟΥ

cf. SNG France 2: 1695

24.1	—	14	3.41	HoB

Table App. 1.1, obliterates rev. type

24.2	—	14	2.49	ByzFort

Table App. 1.1, obliterates rev. type

Westermark (1991) only lists Athena/coiled serpent with an owl countermark; these coins are likely to have had such a reverse.

ca. 197–159 or ca. 133–27 BC

Head of Asklepios r., magistrate's name illeg.

Staff of Asklepios ΑΣΚΛΗΠΙΟΥ-ΣΩΤΗΡΟΣ

BMC Mysia, p. 128, nos. 150–157; M7 GR 43–46

25.1	12	16 × 19	4.45	NoEx, cm. App. 1
25.2	12	17	3.80	NoEx, cm. App. 1
25.3	5	16	3.56	NoEx
25.4	10	16	3.29	AT-Pac
25.5	12	15	3.50	NoEx
25.6	12	15	3.36	NoEx
25.7	10	15	3.25	MMS/N
25.8	3	14	3.55	MMS/N
25.9	12	14	3.17	HoB
25.10	12	14	3.15	NoEx
25.11	—	16	3.16	MMS/S

Johnston, in M7, followed von Fritze (1910, pp. 22–24) in seeing that these coins were no longer minted after the creation of the province of Asia. When findspot is known, contexts are Late Roman.

ca. 197–159 or ca. 133–27 BC

Head of Asklepios r.

Snake coiled around omphalos ΑΣΚΛΗΠΙΟΥ- ΣΩΤΗΡΟΣ mg. App. 2

BMC Mysia, p. 128, no. 158 var.; M7 GR 47–50 var.

26.1	12	22	6.96	MMS/S
26.2	11	22	6.69	MMS/S

For dating, see note on no. 25; also only known from Late Roman contexts.

ca. 159–133 BC
Helm. head of Athena r.
Trophy ΑΘΗΝΑΣ-ΝΙΚΗΦΟΡΟΥ, mg. indistinguishable
BMC Mysia, p. 130, nos. 172–182; M7 GR 56

27.1	2	22	5.91	AT-Pac
27.2	12	20	7.08	NoEx
27.3	6	18	5.37	NoEx
27.4	—	18	4.46	F49, cm. App. 1 rev. type obscure
27.5	—	19	7.28	NoEx, rev. type obscure

For dating, see note on no. 25; when from excavated contexts, they include Late Roman material. See Westermark 1995, series 5.

ca. 159–133 BC
Head of Athena in crested helmet with star r.
Owl on palm, wings outspread ΑΘΗΝΑΣ- ΝΙΚΗΦΟΡΟΥ
BMC Mysia, p. 132, nos. 190–204; M7 GR 52–54

28.1	6	17	2.70	MMS/N, mg. App. 2
28.2	12	15	3.13	NoEx, mg. App. 2
28.3	6	21	3.62	MMS/S, details illeg.
28.4	6	16	1.63	Syn, same

Schultz (1997, p. 19) believed that the bronze issues minted in the sanctuaries of Athena Nikephoros and Asklepios are not well sorted, nor can they be dated; he suggested that the Hellenistic coins that feature Athena and Asklepios cannot be distinguished from Roman-era issues of similar iconography. Von Fritz 1910 and Johnston in M7 dated them to ca. 159–133 BC. Coins 28.1, 28.3–4 come from Late Roman contexts; coin 28.2 was NoEx. See Westermark 1995, series 2.

Second century BC
Head of Athena in crested helmet r.
Uncertain reverse

29.1	—	19	4.02	NoEx

AEOLIS, Cyme
320–250 BC
Forepart of horse r. ΚΥ
One-handled vase, mg. in l. field
BMC Troas, p. 108, nos. 40–52; M7 GR 70

30.1	10	15	4.06	ByzFort, mg. App. 2
30.2	12	19	5.17	Ac-FT, mg. illeg.

Eagle standing r.
One-handled vase ΚΥ, mg. illeg.
BMC Troas, p. 107, nos. 27–39; M7 GR 69

31.1	6	16	3.42	NoEx

Illeg. obv.
One-handled vase ΚΥ

32.1	—	18	4.90	MMS

IONIA, Colophon
330–285 BC dichalkon
Head of Apollo r.
Forepart of horse galloping r. ΚΟΛ [magistrate name illeg.]
BMC Ionia, p. 38, nos. 20–26; M7 GR 77

33.1	12	14	1.93	AT

Date after Milne 1941.

Ephesus
390–380 or 305–288 BC
Tyche head, turreted l.
Bee ΕΦ
BMC Ionia, p. 55, nos. 68–70; M7 GR 81

34.1	6	10	1.19	NoEx
34.2	12	10	1.04	NoEx
34.3	12	10	0.90	NoEx

Earlier date in SNG Turk 1: 193.

387–295 BC
Bee ΕΦ
Forepart of stag kneeling r., head turned back
SNG Cop: 244

35.1	6	12	1.40	AT

305–288 BC
Bee ΕΦ
Stag kneeling l. head turned back; Magistrate's name illeg.
BMC Ionia, p. 54, nos. 63–67; M7 GR 80

36.1	—	12	2.65	F49

Illeg.
Forepart of kneeling stag (head not turned back), both legs folded and drawn up [...]ΝΤΙΑ?
cf. BMC Ionia, p. 54, no. 58, magistrate named Antialkidas

37.1	6	17	2.24	MMS/N

280–258 BC
Bee with straight wings
Stag standing r. ΑΠΟΛΛΟΔΩΡΟΣ
BMC Ionia, p. 57, nos. 80–81

38.1	12	15	3.60	MMS

202–133 BC
Bee with straight wings
Stag standing r., quiver above ΕΡΜΟΤΡΕ[ΦΕΣ] down on r.
Imhoof-Blumer 1901, p. 51, no. 22

39.1	12	16	3.81	F49

Fourth to third century BC
Bee
Illeg.

40.1	—	11	1.40	MMS

Erythrae
387–300 BC
Head of young Herakles in lionskin helmet r.
Club and bow in case ΕΡΥ [...]ΟΥ
BMC Ionia, p. 124, nos. 66–81

41.1	6	11	1.24	NoEx

Leucae
350–300 BC
Helm. head of Athena ¾ facing
Lion r. looking back ΛΕΥ
BMC Ionia, p. 157, no. 7

42.1	1	9	1.21	MMS/N

Magnesia ad Maeandrum
350–190 BC, poss. 350–320 BC
Horseman r. with couched spear
Humped bull butting l. ΜΑΓΝ-ΛΥΚΟΜΗΔΗΣ-ΑΡΙΣΤ
BMC Ionia, p. 161, no. 27

43.1	4	16	2.16	NoEx

Note that the magistrate's name ΛΥΚΟΜΗΔ is found on a tetradrachm, which Konuk, in SNG Turk 1: 409, dated to 350–320 BC.

Smyrna
240–230 BC — larger
Turreted head of Cybele r.
Tripod SMYPNA, mg. App. 2, grain of wheat
Milne 1923: Type F, no. 34 (period V)

44.1	12	18	3.74	NoEx

240–190 BC — smaller
Turreted head of Tyche r.
Palm tree ΣΜΥΡ[...?], magistrate name illeg.
Milne 1923: Type G

45.1	12	13	0.92	ByzFort

75–50 BC — larger
Turreted head of Cybele r.
Statue of Aphrodite Stratonikis ΖΜΥΡΝΑΙΩΝ-Δ-ΜΗΤΡΟΔΩΡΟΣ
BMC Ionia, p. 240, no. 27; Milne 1928: Type M

46.1	6	18	5.19	NoEx

Dated by Milne.

Laur. head of Apollo r.
Homer seated on rock ΖΜΥΡΝΑΙΩΝ
Milne 1928: Type J, magistrate's name illeg.

47.1	11	22	13.86	MMS/S

Head of Apollo r. — smaller
Hand in caestus, palm ΖΜΥΡΝΑΙΩΝ, magistrate's name
BMC Ionia, p. 242, nos. 47–60

48.1	11	13	3.21	ByzFort

ΑΘΗΝΑΓΟΡΑΣ; BMC Ionia no. 47; Milne 1928: 390

48.2	12	15	3.30	MMS, H1

ΙΑΤΡΟΔΩΡΟΣ; BMC Ionia no. 52; Milne 1928: 403
Dated by Milne.

LYDIA, Caystriani peoples
Second or first century BC
Head of Dionysos r.
Bucranium-lyre ΚΑΥCΤΡ-ΙΑ-ΝΩΝ, mg.
BMC Lydia, p. 61, nos. 6–9

49.1	1	14	2.90	MMS/S, mg. ΔΚ
49.2	12	13	2.37	NoEx, mg. off flan

Philadelphia
Second century BC
Bust of Artemis r.
Apollo Musagetes standing r. ΦΙΛΑΔΕΛΦΕΩΝ-ΕΡΜΙΠΠΟΣ-ΑΡΧΙΕΡΕΥΣ
BMC Lydia, p. 188, nos. 13–15

50.1	12	17	5.38	NoEx

Sardis
ca. 245/220–second century BC — large
Turreted veiled bust of Tyche r.
Zeus Lydios ΣΑΡΔΙΑΝΩΝ, illeg. mg.
BMC Lydia, p. 242, nos. 49–52; M7 GR 231, 233–234

51.1	12	24	9.86	F55
51.2	12	23	10.49	ThSt, cm. App. 1
51.3	12	22	7.41	ByzFort
51.4	—	20	5.99	AT
51.5	12	20	5.70	MMS, cm. App. 1

Head of young Herakles r. medium
Nude Apollo holding hawk ΣΑΡΔΙΑΝΩΝ, mg. at l.
BMC Lydia, p. 239, nos. 22–36; M7 GR 199–227
Tends to have a thick flan, reverse is concave

52.1	12	14	6.88	CW6, mg. App. 2
52.2	12	15	5.25	ThSt, mg. App. 2
52.3	12	15	5.28	NoEx, mg. App. 2
52.4	12	15	5.45	NoEx, mg. App. 2
52.5	12	15	5.90	ThSt, mg. App. 2
52.6	12	15	6.26	NoEx, mg. App. 2
52.7	11	16	4.90	MMS, mg. App. 2
52.8	12	16	4.92	NoEx, mg. App. 2
52.9	6	16	6.30	MMS/S, mg. App. 2
52.10	11	16	6.18	ThSt, mg. App. 2
52.11	1	16	6.68	MMS, mg. App. 2
52.12	6	15	6.66	NoEx, mg. App. 2
52.13	12	16	6.76	NoEx, mg. App. 2
52.14	12	16	7.54	ThSt, mg. App. 2
52.15	1	17	4.90	MMS, mg. App. 2
52.16	1	17	5.20	NoEx, mg. App. 2
52.17	1	17	5.89	ThSt, mg. App. 2
52.18	1	17	5.24	HoB, mg. App. 2
52.19	6	17	6.30	F49, mg. App. 2
52.20	12	17	7.62	MMS/S, mg. App. 2
52.21	12	18	5.97	ByzFort, mg. App. 2
52.22	1	17	frag'y	MMS/S, mg. App. 2
52.23	1	16	6.64	MMS/S, mg. App. 2
52.24	12	15	4.30	MD2, mg. App. 2
52.25	12	15	5.01	NoEx, mg. App. 2
52.26	12	16	5.56	MMS/S, mg. App. 2
52.27	12	15	6.14	MMS/S, mg. App. 2
52.28	12	17	6.70	NoEx

ΔΗ-ΜΟΦΩΝ ΘΗ-ΒΑΔΟΥ
As BMC Lydia, p. 239, no. 35; Bell 1916: 248

52.29	1	16	6.32	MMS/S

[…]ΟΣ
As Bell 1916: 250?

52.30	—	16	5.25	NoEx

[…]ΟΛ ΛΩ[…]

52.31	6	16	5.38	F49

Σ[…]

52.32	12	17	7.07	F49, mg. App. 2

Monogram illeg., cm. of club in oval on obv.

52.33	—	18	5.89	F49
52.34	—	17	6.70	NoEx
52.35	12	17	6.18	MMS/S
52.36	—	17	6.11	F55
52.37	12	16	5.80	MD2
52.38	—	16	5.42	LAW
52.39	—	16	5.07	MMS
52.40	—	16	4.83	MMS
52.41	—	16	4.52	NoEx, cm. App. 1
52.42	11	15	6.20	MMS
52.43	2	15	5.14	NoEx
52.44	—	15	4.93	ByzFort
52.45	—	15	4.84	NoEx
52.46	12	15	5.14	ThSt

Two cm., Table App. 1.1 and Section 3.2.2

Monogram illeg., no countermarks

52.47	—	19	4.50	MMS
52.48	3	18	7.35	NoEx
52.49	12	18	6.99	F49
52.50	12	18	6.50	F55
52.51	—	18	4.77	MMS
52.52	12	18	4.13	MMS
52.53	—	17	7.21	F49
52.54	1	17	6.97	ByzFort
52.55	1	17	6.70	MMS
52.56	1	17	6.50	NoEx
52.57	—	17	6.30	MMS/N
52.58	—	17	6.20	MMS
52.59	12	17	6.70	ByzFort
52.60	—	17	6.07	MMS/S
52.61	—	17	5.76	MMS
52.62	2	17	5.76	MMS/N
52.63	2	17	5.52	MMS
52.64	—	17	5.15	NoEx
52.65	—	17	4.90	MMS/S
52.66	12	17	4.45	F55
52.67	—	17	4.30	MMS
52.68	1	17	4.20	HoB
52.69	6	17	3.90	F49
52.70	4	16	7.53	F49
52.71	12	16	6.40	MMS/S
52.72	—	16	6.32	NoEx
52.73	12	16	6.30	F55
52.74	12	16	6.07	ThSt
52.75	—	16	5.85	MMS

52.76	12	16	5.60	NoEx
52.77	6	16	5.58	NoEx
52.78	—	16	5.50	MMS
52.79	12	16	5.45	MMS
52.80	12	16	5.44	NoEx
52.81	12	16	5.30	F55
52.82	7	16	5.12	AT-LA
52.83	1	16	5.10	MMS/S
52.84	6	16	4.70	MMS/S
52.85	2	16	4.65	MMS/S
52.86	—	16	4.37	F55
52.87	—	16	3.70	MMS/N
52.88	—	16	3.70	MMS
52.89	12	15	6.68	ThSt
52.90	12	15	6.06	MMS
52.91	1	15	5.96	F49
52.92	12	15	5.81	HoB
52.93	—	15	5.67	MMS/S
52.94	—	15	5.65	MMS
52.95	1	15	5.30	NoEx
52.96	2	15	5.02	MMS/S
52.97	4	15	3.08	NoEx
52.98	—	14	3.22	MMS

Prob. Herakles/Apollo, due to concave rev. and module, but all illeg.

52.99	16	3.80	MMS, two cm. App. 1
52.100	16	4.27	NoEx, cm. App. 1
52.101	16	5.70	NoEx, cm. App. 1
52.102	17	5.03	MMS/S, cm. App. 1
52.103	17	5.95	MMS/N, cm. App. 1
52.104	21	6.30	MMS/S, cm. App. 1
52.105	19	7.10	MMS
52.106	18	6.60	MMS/N
52.107	18	6.20	MMS
52.108	18	6.10	MMS
52.109	18	5.80	MMS
52.110	18	5.57	MMS/S
52.111	18	4.80	F49
52.112	18	4.35	MD1/S
52.113	17	6.70	F49
52.114	17	4.13	MMS/S
52.115	16	8.61	ThSt
52.116	16	6.80	MMS
52.117	16	6.41	MMS
52.118	16	5.74	Wadi B
52.119	16	5.50	MMS
52.120	16	5.38	F55
52.121	17	3.10	MMS
52.122	17	3.38	F49
52.123	16	4.12	MMS/S
52.124	16	4.00	NoEx
52.125	16	3.20	MMS
52.126	15	6.64	MMS/S
52.127	15	6.07	NoEx
52.128	15	4.96	F55
52.129	15	3.90	MMS
52.130	15	2.57	MMS/S
52.131	11	6.46	MMS

small

Head of young Dionysos r.
Forepart of lion r. ΣΑΡΔΙΑΝΩΝ, mg.
BMC Lydia, p. 241, nos. 47–48; M7 GR 238–242

53.1	11	16	4.39	MD2, mg. App. 2
53.2	—	18	2.39	MMS, mg. off flan

Second–first century BC large

Head of young Herakles in lionskin helmet r.
Lion r., insect above ΣΑΡΔΙΑΝΩΝ, in ex. MENE-ΜΑΧΟΣ
BMC Lydia, p. 240, no. 37; M7 GR 182

54.1	2	18	5.60	MMS/S, cm. App. 1

Head of Apollo r. medium

Club in wreath, mg. below, ΣΑΡΔΙ-ΑΝΩΝ
BMC Lydia p. 238, nos. 10–21; M7 GR 183–198
Dies much smaller than flans; thick flans

55.1	9	13	3.12	NoEx, mg. App. 2
55.2	1	13	3.20	MMS/S, mg. App. 2
55.3	8	13	4.12	ByzFort, mg. App. 2
55.4	3	13	4.57	CW6, mg. App. 2
55.5	6	14	3.06	NoEx, mg. App. 2
55.6	6	14	3.49	NoEx, mg. App. 2
55.7	12	14	4.10	MMS/N, mg. App. 2
55.8	4	14	4.18	PA, mg. App. 2
55.9	12	14	4.59	HoB, mg. App. 2
55.10	12	15	3.55	MMS/S, mg. App. 2
55.11	4	15	4.80	PN/E, mg. App. 2
55.12	6	16	2.87	NoEx, mg. App. 2
55.13	3	16	2.79	NoEx, No mg., as M7 GR 197
55.14	4	17	3.96	MMS/S, mg. App. 2

Illeg. monogram

55.15	9	19	2.84	MMS
55.16	6	18	5.71	F55
55.17	6	17	4.50	MMS/S
55.18	—	16	3.20	MMS
55.19	7	15	5.11	NoEx
55.20	12	15	4.07	MMS/S
55.21	6	15	4.04	NoEx
55.22	6	15	3.84	NoEx
55.23	5	15	3.83	MMS
55.24	—	15	3.72	MMS/S
55.25	6	15	3.66	HoB
55.26	1	15	2.86	NoEx
55.27	6	14	5.51	NoEx
55.28	—	14	4.76	MMS/N
55.29	—	14	4.18	ByzFort
55.30	6	14	3.90	NoEx
55.31	5	13	4.01	NoEx

Head of young Dionysos r. small
Horned panther with broken spear l.
ΣΑΡΔΙ-ΑΝΩΝ, monograms
BMC Lydia, p. 241, nos. 40–44; M7 GR 235–37

56.1	12	18	3.33	ByzFort, mg. App. 2
56.2	12	17	3.61	MMS/S, mgs. illeg.
56.3	12	18	5.20	MMS/S, same
56.4	12	18	7.00	F49, i.d. prob., no mg. leg.

Third–first century BC small
Head of young Herakles in lionskin helmet r.
Kantharos ΣΑΡΔΙ-ΑΝΩΝ to r. and l., below mgs.
BMC Lydia, p. 241, nos. 45–46 (sic bearded); M7 GR 228–230

57.1	12	14	3.00	NoEx, mg. App. 2
57.2	12	16	3.08	PA, mg. illeg.

189–133 BC Attalid 4-unit
Bust of Artemis r.
Athena standing ΣΑΡΔΙΑΝΩΝ-ΑΛΚΑΙΟΣ-ΑΛΚΑΙΟΥ
BMC Lydia, p. 243, no. 57

58.1	12	21	7.46	MMS/S

Head of young Dionysos r. Attalid 2-unit
Demeter in chiton leaning with l. on torch ΣΑΡΔΙΑΝΩΝ
BMC Lydia, p. 243, nos. 60–61

59.1	7	19	4.47	MMS, illeg. name
59.2	6	20	6.83	MMS

In l. field, vertical: ΘΕΟ-[. . .]Τ?Ι?[...]; else name not published?

Thyateira
Third to early second century BC
Head of Apollo r.
Double axe ΘΥΑΤΕΙ-ΡΗΝ-ΩΝ
BMC Lydia, p. 292, no. 4

60.1	11	15	4.33	MMS/S

Tralles
Second–first century BC
Zeus standing holding Nike, in wreath
Bull walking r. ΤΡΑΛΛΙ-ΑΝΩΝ
BMC Lydia, p. 336, nos. 61–62

61.1	6	15	5.00	MMS

First century BC
Head of Zeus r.
Eagle on thunderbolt; ΤΡΑΛΛΙΑΝΩΝ,
illeg. magistrate's name
BMC Lydia, p. 336, no. 69

62.1	6	21	8.93	F55

PHRYGIA, Apamea
133–48 BC
Turreted head of Artemis r.
Marsyas advancing r. on meander pattern, playing flutes
ΑΠΑΜΕΩΝ, illeg. magistrate's name
BMC Phrygia, p. 80, no. 62

63.1	—	17	3.40	MMS/S

LYCIA, Phellus
First century BC unit
Head of Apollo r.
Bow and quiver in incuse square ΛΥΚΙ-ΦΕ
Troxell 1982: 72

64.1	12	10	1.18	MMS/S, H2

Ptolemy III

EGYPT, Alexandria
247/6–221/20 BC
Head of Alexander in elephant-skin helmet r.,
centering hole
Eagle, wings closed, standing on thunderbolt, cornucopiae
on shoulder, head turned back ΠΤΟΛΕΜΑΙΟΥ
ΒΑΣΙΛΕΩΣ, between legs Ε
Svoronos 1908: 976

65.1	12	24	8.02	F49

Unknown Ruler

ITALY, Rome

217–87 BC as, uncial standard

Janiform heads of Dioscuri

Prow of ship ROMA

66.1 3 30 22.28 MD2

ca. 211–208 BC quadrans

Head of young Herakles r., three dots

Prow r., three dots ROMA

RRC: 56.5

67.1 9 20 6.32 MMS/S

This was a highly-varied series, with weights ranging from ca. 4–12 g. Crawford 1974 gives a date of "after 211 BC," but the series was not likely struck much after, as the word "Roma" shifts to the bottom of the flan after that date.

Uncertain Mint

Second or first century?

Diademed head r. (Apollo, Artemis, or Tyche?)

Stag (or horse) springing l. [?]XA-I-O[I or N or M?]

68.1 6 15 3.16 F49

Seleucid Coinage

Seleucus I

Sardis

282–281 BC denomination C or D

Winged head of Medusa r.

Humped bull butting r. ΒΑΣΙΛΕΩΣ in ex. ΣΕΛΕΥΚΟΥ

ΣΙ between legs, C/m as Houghton and Lorber 2002: 6 (1)

Houghton and Lorber 2002: 6; M7 GR 354

69.1 11 14 2.29 MMS/S

69.2 12 14 1.83 HoB

282–281 BC? denomination C or D

Winged head of Medusa r.

Humped bull butting l. ΒΑΣΙΛΕΩΣ in ex. ΣΕΛΕΥΚΟΥ; no C/m visible

Houghton and Lorber 2002: 6 var.

70.1 3 14 2.45 NoEx

The type is listed in Houghton and Lorber 2002 as above, with straight edge, "delicate style and low relief," but the butting bull left, no controls, is given to Antioch Denomination B (18–19 mm), Houghton and Lorber 2002: 24.

Seleucia ad Tigrim

285–280 BC denomination A

Winged head of Medusa r.

Bull butting r. ΒΑΣΙΛΕΩΣ in ex. ΣΕΛΕΥΚΟΥ

Houghton and Lorber 2002: 151

71.1 11 23 9.98 F49

Concave rev., App. 2 for C/m

Antiochus I

Sardis or perhaps Smyrna

280–261 BC denomination C or D

Bust of Athena facing

Nike l. with wreath and palm ΒΑΣΙΛΕΩΣ- ΑΝΤΙΟΧΟΥ, C/m illeg.

Houghton and Lorber 2002: 315; M7 GR 358; Bell 1911: 368–376

72.1 12 13 1.97 MMS/S

72.2 1 13 2.53 ThSt, cm. App. 1

72.3 12 14 1.92 F49

72.4 11 15 2.65 F49

72.5 9 17 2.57 NoEx

Since nine of these coins (including four in M7 GR 357–358) have been found in the Sardis excavations, Sardis should be preferred as the mint.

Antiochus II

Sardis

261–246 BC denomination B or C, first series

Head of Apollo r.

Tripod, anchor below ΒΑΣΙΛΕΩΣ-ΑΝΤΙΟΧΟΥ

Houghton and Lorber 2002: 520 var.

73.1 7 17 3.33 ByzFort, C/m App. 2

Head of Apollo r. denomination B or C, second series

Tripod, anchor below ΒΑΣΙΛΕΩΣ-ΑΝΤΙΟΧΟΥ

Houghton and Lorber 2002: 522; M7 GR 360

74.1 1 16 4.48 MMS/N, C/m App. 2

Head of Apollo r. denomination C, third series

Tripod, anchor below ΒΑΣΙΛΕΩΣ-ΑΝΤΙΟΧΟΥ

Houghton and Lorber 2002: 523; M7 GR 382

75.1 12 17 4.79 ByzFort, C/m App. 2

Head of Apollo r. denomination B or C

Tripod, anchor below ΒΑΣΙΛΕΩΣ-ΑΝΤΙΟΧΟΥ

Houghton and Lorber 2002: 526–527

76.1 6 13 2.39 NoEx, C/m illeg.

Head of Apollo r. denomination B or C
Tripod, anchor below ΒΑΣΙΛΕΩΣ-ΑΝΤΙΟΧΟΥ
Houghton and Lorber 2002: 522–527

77.1	12	15	3.10	MMS/S, C/m illeg.

Head of Apollo r. denomination D
Cithara, anchor below ΒΑΣΙΛΕΩΣ-ΑΝΤΙΟΧΟΥ
Houghton and Lorber 2002: 528; M7 GR 369

78.1	7	12	2.80	MMS/N, C/m illeg.
78.2	6	14	3.11	NoEx, C/m illeg.
78.3	12	14	2.12	CW6, C/m App. 2
78.4	—	12	1.70	MMS, C/m illeg., i.d. prob.

Turreted and veiled head of Tyche r. denomination D
Tripod ΒΑΣΙΛΕΩΣ-ΑΝΤΙΟΧΟΥ
Houghton and Lorber 2002: 585

79.1	12	12	3.40	NoEx
79.2	1	12	1.50	E Road, C/m App. 2

These two coins share an obverse die, and likely a reverse die; both have a concave reverse. No. **79.2** is listed in records as M7 GR 368, which is incorrect. It appears that the coin was not included in M7, and so it is included here. The obverse shows a small head with feminine features, and a long vertical bar at the rear of the head showing the beginning of a turreted crown. On both coins the name of the king is legible. **79.1** has a thick flan. The control mark is not given in Houghton and Lorber 2002.

Seleucus II

Sardis
246–241 BC denomination C
Head of young Herakles in lionskin helmet r.
Apollo seated on omphalos l. ΒΑΣΙΛΕΩΣ- ΣΕΛΕΥΚΟΥ
Houghton and Lorber 2002: 657, C/m illeg.

80.1	12	14	2.22	MMS/S
80.2	—	17	3.10	MMS/N, concave rev.
80.3	6	17	4.58	MMS, concave rev.
80.4	10	17	4.85	MMS/S

Hoover (in Houghton and Lorber 2002, p. 241) suggested the coins were minted in the city before the revolt of Hierax. He does not mention a concave reverse.

denomination C
Head of Athena in crested Attic helmet r.
Apollo standing with bow ΒΑΣΙΛΕΩΣ-ΣΕΛΕΥΚΟΥ
Houghton and Lorber 2002: 660; M7 GR 372, 374

81.1	12	17	3.58	NoEx, C/m App. 2
81.2	5	17	2.40	F55, C/m illeg.
81.3	—	17	4.94	F49, C/m illeg.

Antioch on the Orontes?
244–226 BC AR drachm
Head of Athena in crested Attic helmet r.
Apollo standing resting on bow, holding arrow ΒΑΣΙΛΕΩΣ-ΣΕΛΕΥΚΟΥ
cf. Houghton and Lorber 2002: 691, not listed with this C/m

82.1	12	17	3.70	MMS, C/m App. 2

Seleucia ad Tigrim
246–226 BC denomination D
Three-quarter head of Athena l.
Nike standing l. ΒΑΣΙΛΕΩΣ-ΣΕΛΕΥΚΟΥ
Houghton and Lorber 2002: 769

83.1	12	15	2.60	NoEx, C/m illeg.

Beveled edge

Achaeus

Sardis
220–214 BC denomination B
Head of Apollo r.
Eagle with palm ΒΑΣΙΛΕΩΣ-ΑΧΑΙΟΥ
cf. Houghton and Lorber 2002: 691, not listed with this C/m

84.1	6	20	4.30	NoEx

cm. App. 1; C/m App. 2

Head of Apollo r. denomination C
Eagle with wreath ΒΑΣΙΛΕΩΣ-ΑΧΑΙΟΥ
Houghton and Lorber 2002: 956; M7 GR 380

85.1	12	16	2.95	ByzFort

cm. App. 1; C/m App. 2

Antiochus III

Sardis denomination D,
213–203 BC? series 1 horizontal legend
Head of Apollo r.
Elephant l. ΒΑΣΙΛΕΩΣ-ΑΝΤΙΟΧΟΥ, no C/m
Houghton and Lorber 2002: 979 (1); M7 GR 381

86.1	—	12	1.68	ByzFort
86.2	12	12	1.71	AT
86.3	—	12	2.01	AT-Pac

Date suggested by Hoover in Houghton and Lorber 2002, p. 355.

denomination D, series 1 vertical legend

Head of Apollo r.

Elephant l. ΒΑΣΙΛΕΩΣ-ΑΝΤΙΟΧΟΥ

Houghton and Lorber 2002: 981

87.1	12	13	1.91	ThSt, C/m App. 2
87.2	12	11	1.40	NoEx, C/m App. 2

Illeg. denomination D

Elephant l.

88.1	—	12	1.87	F49
88.2	—	12	1.88	F49, concave rev.
88.3	—	14	1.96	MMS

213–203 BC? denomination C, series 2

Head of Apollo r.

Apollo leaning on tripod testing arrow ΒΑΣΙΛΕΩΣ-ΑΝΤΙΟΧΟΥ

Houghton and Lorber 2002: 983

89.1	1	16	3.81	F49

Hoover reassigned this coin from Hierax to Antiochus III.

Sardis? denomination D? series 2

Head of Apollo r.

Apollo leaning on tripod ΒΑΣΙΛΕΩΣ-ΑΝΤΙΟΧΟΥ, no C/m

cf. Houghton and Lorber 2002: 983 (6)

90.1	6	10	1.61	MD2
90.2	12	10	1.77	MMS/S
90.3	—	10	1.39	MMS/S, i.d. prob.

Hoover noted another possible example of this denomination in the Afyon Museum.

Antioch on the Orontes

233–211/10 BC denomination C

Laur. head of Antiochus as Apollo r.

Apollo on omphalos ΒΑΣΙΛΕΩΣ-ΑΝΤΙΟΧΟΥ

Houghton and Lorber 2002: 1049

91.1	12	12	3.15	NoEx
91.2	12	12	2.60	F49

C/m illeg. or off flan; given to mint due to obv.

211/10–209/8 BC denomination A, series 2

Laur. head of Antiochus as Apollo r.

Apollo seated on omphalos ΒΑΣΙΛΕΩΣ-ΑΝΤΙΟΧΟΥ

Houghton and Lorber 2002: 1054

92.1	12	22	12.80	F49, no C/m visible

Uncertain Seleucid Ruler

Uncertain Mint

286–187 BC

M7 GR 400; corrosion can be quite granular

93.1	11	1.00	MMS
93.2	11	1.47	F49
93.3	11	1.48	F55
93.4	11	1.60	MMS/S
93.5	11	1.60	F49
93.6	11	1.65	Tomb 07.2
93.7	12	0.52	F55
93.8	12	1.10	MMS
93.9	12	1.43	MMS/S
93.10	12	1.54	MMS/S
93.11	12	1.62	MMS/S
93.12	12	1.76	MMS
93.13	12	1.78	NoEx
93.14	12	1.87	MMS/S
93.15	12	1.96	MMS/S
93.16	12	1.99	F49
93.17	12	2.10	MMS/S
93.18	13	frag'y	MMS
93.19	13	1.36	F55
93.20	13	2.17	MMS/S
93.21	14	2.55	Wadi B
93.22	14	2.20	MMS
93.23	14	2.24	F55
93.24	14	2.41	MMS/S
93.25	14	2.72	MMS/S
93.26	14	3.00	MMS
93.27	14	3.10	ByzFort
93.28	15	3.16	F49
93.29	15	1.69	ByzFort
93.30	15	1.69	F49
93.31	15	1.80	MMS
93.32	15	2.26	F55
93.33	15	2.96	PA
93.34	16	3.52	F55
93.35	16	2.40	MD2
93.36	16	2.44	F49
93.37	17	3.21	F49
93.38	17	3.40	MMS
93.39	18	4.80	MMS
93.40	18	2.30	MMS
93.41	18	3.88	Wadi B
93.42	18	4.67	MMS
93.43	19	4.47	MMS

Uncertain Hellenistic

350–27 BCE

M7 GR 399; corrosion often shows in layers on side of flan

94.1	10	0.73	MMS/S, head/goat r.?, H2
94.2	10	1.20	MMS
94.3	10	2.85	MMS
94.4	11	0.84	MMS/S
94.5	11	1.74	MMS
94.6	12	0.84	MMS/N, cm. App. 1
94.7	12	0.95	F49
94.8	12	2.28	NoEx
94.9	12	3.48	NoEx
94.10	13	1.80	F49
94.11	13	1.93	MMS
94.12	13	2.24	CW6
94.13	13	2.86	MMS
94.14	13	2.95	MMS/S
94.15	14	1.60	MMS
94.16	14	1.80	MMS
94.17	14	2.19	AT
94.18	14	2.20	MMS
94.19	14	2.26	F49
94.20	14	2.40	MMS
94.21	15	2.20	MMS/S
94.22	15	2.20	MMS
94.23	15	2.30	MMS
94.24	15	2.98	ByzFort
94.25	15	3.39	MMS/S
94.26	15	5.25	F49
94.27	16	3.05	F55
94.28	16	3.36	F55
94.29	16	3.37	MMS/S
94.30	16	3.40	ByzFort
94.31	16	3.42	MMS/S
94.32	16	3.49	MMS/S
94.33	16	3.70	MMS
94.34	16	3.80	MMS
94.35	16	3.85	F55
94.36	16	3.86	MMS/S
94.37	16	3.98	NoEx
94.38	16	4.40	MMS
94.39	16	4.60	MMS/N
94.40	16	4.63	F55
94.41	16	5.49	NoEx
94.42	17	2.07	MMS
94.43	17	2.47	F49
94.44	17	2.68	F49
94.45	17	3.20	MMS
94.46	17	3.64	MMS
94.47	17	4.41	MMS/S
94.48	17	4.49	MMS/S
94.49	17	4.60	MMS
94.50	17	5.20	MMS
94.51	17	5.20	MMS
94.52	17	6.51	NoEx
94.53	17	frag'y	AT
94.54	18	2.76	F49
94.55	18	3.32	ByzFort
94.56	18	3.34	MMS
94.57	18	3.90	MMS
Prob. second or first century BC			
Head of Zeus or Herakles r. laur. […]Θ[…], rev. illeg.			
94.58	18	4.07	ByzFort
94.59	18	5.09	MMS/S
94.60	18	5.25	MMS/S
94.61	18	6.27	MMS
94.62	18	6.34	MMS/S
94.63	18	frag'y	MMS/S
94.64	19	4.20	MMS
94.65	19	4.37	MMS/S
94.66	19	4.40	NoEx
94.67	19	4.80	PA
94.68	19	4.80	MMS
94.69	19	5.53	NoEx
94.70	19	5.73	F49
94.71	19	5.95	F49
94.72	19	7.42	F49
94.73	19	9.39	MMS/N
94.74	20	3.64	NoEx
94.75	20	5.37	MMS/N
94.76	20	5.76	F49
94.77	20	6.30	MMS
94.78	20	6.93	MMS
94.79	20	8.23	MMS/S
94.80	21	3.32	MMS/S
94.81	21	4.11	MMS/S
94.82	22	4.08	MMS/S, cm. App. 1, pierced
94.83	23	8.33	F49
94.84	24	9.08	F55
94.85	—	frag'y	ByzFort
94.86	—	frag'y	MMS/N

Uncertain Hellenistic to Roman Provincial
First century BC–first century AD
M7 GR 401

95.1	15	2.69	MMS
95.2	18	3.90	MMS
95.3	18	4.97	MMS
95.4	19	2.67	MMS
95.5	19	5.90	MMS/S
95.6	20	4.70	MMS
95.7	22	3.86	MMS/S
95.8	22	6.80	MMS
95.9	29	9.51	MMS/N, cms. App. 1

Roman Provincial

Note: the catalog does not give proper breaks in the legends (as these can vary within a series) nor direction of legends, as per examples in RPC.

ACHAEA
Corinth
1–2 AD Augustus as
Head r. bare AVGVSTVS CORINT (lig.)
P AEBVT SP F C IVLIO HERA IIVIR QVI ITER (lig.) in wreath
RPC I: 1138

96.1	6	21	5.70	MMS/S

THRACE
Anchialos
139–161 AD Marcus Aurelius
Bust r. dr. [...]PHΛIOCOY[...] (not visible on this coin)
Statue group of Hermes and baby Dionysos
ANXIA.... (not visible on this coin)
RPC IV: temp. no. 4518; Lacroix 1949: 298; Schwartz 1893

97.1	6	28	13.30	NoEx, cm. App. 1

Only one other example of this coin is known. This reverse type is otherwise only known in Pautalia, for Caracalla.

"ASIA"
ca. 25 BC Augustus as, class 2
Head r. bare CAESAR
AVGVSTVS in laurel wreath
RPC I: 2235; M7 R 3

98.1	—	24	11.25	F49
98.2	12	25	9.83	NoEx
98.3	—	26	9.70	MMS
98.4	1	26	11.13	MMS
98.5	7	30	10.40	MMS
98.6	—	24	4.32	MMS, halved

Halved coins of these types are only common from excavations at Sardis.

98.7	—	28	6.49	HoB, cm. App. 1, halved
98.8	12	26	4.71	NoEx, halved
98.9	—	23	3.54	PA, halved, rev. type uncertain but likely; cm. (also halved) App. 1

ca. 27–25 BC as, uncertain class
Head r. bare
Inscription in wreath

99.1	9	20	11.49	MMS
99.2	—	20	12.49	NoEx

BITHYNIA
Nicomedia?
117–138 AD Hadrian
[Head of emperor r. laur.]
Octastyle temple, pellet between center columns; in pediment, emperor with spear sacrificing over an altar, and in each corner, pellet KOINON in ex. BЄIΘYNIAC
RPC III: 1013

100 .1		34	22.77	Wadi B

This coin is unique since, in antiquity, the obverse was almost entirely obliterated to make essentially a one-sided medallion. See discussion, Section 3.3.2.

MYSIA
Parium
181–192 AD Commodus
Bust r. laur. IMP CAIA COMMOD
Founder plowing behind team of oxen CGIHP
BMC Mysia p. 105, no. 101 (sic obv. inscrip.)

101.1	12	16	2.17	HoB

Pergamum
10–2 BC Augustus 1 assarion?
Bust r. laur. ΣEBAΣTON
Hexastyle temple on podium XAPINOC ΓPAMMATEYΩN
RPC I: 2358

102.1	12	19	4.77	ThSt
102.2	1	21	5.20	MMS

half assarion?
Bust of Livia r. dr. ΛΙΒΙΑΝ ΗΡΑΝ ΧΑΡΙΝΟΣ
Bust of Julia r. dr. ΙΟΥΛΙΑΝ ΑΦΡΟΔΙΤΗΝ
RPC I: 2359

103.1	1	17	3.60	NoEx
103.2	—	18	3.77	MMS/S
103.3	12	18	3.55	MMS/S

1 AD? 1 assarion?
Demos of Pergamum crowning Demos of Sardis
ΠЄΡΓΑΜΗΝΩΝ ΚΑΙ ΣΑΡΔΙΑΝΩΝ
Distyle temple with cult statue of Augustus
CЄΒΑCΤΟΝ ΚЄΦΑΛΙΩΝ ΓΡΑΜΜΑΤЄΥΩΝ
RPC I: 2362; M7 GR 62

104.1	12	20	5.57	ThSt
104.2	12	22	5.45	MMS

1–4 AD
Head r. bare (Gaius), legend illeg.
Head r. bare (Lucius), legend illeg.
Prob. RPC I: 2363, 2365

105.1		16	3.80	ByzFort

4–10 AD 1 assarion?
Male figure crowning togate figure
ΣΙΛΒΑΝΟΝ ΠΕΡΓΑΜΗΝΟΙ
Tetrastyle temple with statue of emperor
ΣΕΒΑΣΤΟΝ ΔΕΜΟΦΩΝ
RPC I: 2364; M7 GR 61

106.1	11	20	4.29	MD2
106.2	1	20	5.90	NoEx

80–150 AD Domitian to Hadrian
Bust of Athena r. in Corinthian helmet ΠЄΡΓΑΜΗΝΩΝ
Nude figure crowning self CTP I ΠΩΛΛΙΩΝΟC
BMC Mysia, p. 136, nos. 227–229

107.1	12	15	1.79	MMS
107.2	—	15	1.94	NoEx

Latter coin n.s., but described in fieldnotes.

Bust of Athena with crested helmet, no legend
Telesphoros standing in hooded garment; ΠΕΡΓΑΜΗΝΩΝ
BMC Mysia, p. 137, no. 232; M7 GR 58

108.1	7	13	1.94	ByzFort

AEOLIS
Elaea
161–169 AD Lucius Verus
Head r. bare ΛΟΥΚΙΟC ΚΑΙCΑΡ
Kalathos with poppy-heads and ears of wheat ΕΛΑΙΤΩΝ
BMC Troas, p. 130, no. 46; M7 GR 72

109.1	11	15	2.67	ThSt

Temnus
222–249 AD
Bust of Senate bare r. ΙΕΡΑ CVΝΚΛΗΤΟΣ
Two Nemeses plucking chitons and turning towards one another CT AV ΝΕΙΚΟCΤΡΑΤΟV, in ex. ΤΗΜΝ
BMC Troas, p. 144, no. 16

110.1	5	25	6.60	NoEx

IONIA
Ephesus
ca. 25–20 BC Augustus AR cistophorus
Head r. bare IMP CAESAR
Garlanded altar with two hinds AVGVSTVS
RPC I: 2215

111.1	1	16	10.07	ByzFort

First or second century AD
Head r. bare (prob. an emperor)
Stag standing l.

112.1	6	18	3.96	NoEx

Illeg., or no type
Deer or stag standing l., looking back

113.1	—	15	2.73	NoEx

Prob. a tessera

Bust of Artemis r., quiver behind shoulder, no legend
Stag standing r. ΕΦΕ-CΙΩΝ

114.1	6	16	2.33	ThSt

Prob. a tessera

161–180 AD Marcus Aurelius
Bust r. laur. cuir. ΑΥ ΚΑΙ ΜΑΥ ΑΝΤΩΝΕΙΝΟC
Cult statues of Artemis Ephesia and Sardian Kore
ΕΦΕCΙΩΝ ΚΑΙ CΑΡΔΙΑΝΩΝ ΟΜΟΝΙΑ (all except final word retrograde)
BMC Ionia, p. 112, no. 416; RPC IV: temp. no. 9709; M7 GR 90

115.1	6	32	22.84	EH

Alliance coin of Ephesus and Sardis.

198–217 AD CARACALLA 1½ assaria
Bust r. laur. ΑΥΤΚ ΜΑΥΡ ΑΝΤΩΝΕΙΝΟC
Artemis subduing stag ΤΡΙC ΝΕΩΚΟΡΩΝ ΕΦΕCΙΩΝ
BMC Ionia, p. 86, no. 277
116.1 6 22 5.35 ThSt
Johnston 2007, p. 84 for denomination

198–250 AD
Bust r. bare dr.?
Artemis r. drawing arrow from quiver, legend illeg.
117.1 6 24 5.29 MD1/S

Bust r. laur. dr. [...]A[...]OC
Artemis r. drawing bow or pulling arrow from quiver?, at feet, hunting dog [...ΝΕΩΚ]ΟΡΩΝ
118.1 7 20 4.73 NoEx
Johnston 2007, p. 84 for denomination

Metropolis
198–211 AD CARACALLA
Bust r. laur. [...]ΩΝΕΙ[...]
Emperor standing holding spear ΜΗΤΡΟΠΟΛΕΙΤΩΝ
BMC Ionia, p. 176, no. 7
119.1 6 20 3.07 NoEx

253–268 AD SALONINA
Bust r. dr., behind crescent CΑΛΩΝ ΧΡVCΟΓΟΝΗ CΕΒΑ
Tyche standing with armed emperor ΜΗΤΡΟΠΛΕΙΤΩΝ ΤΩΝ ΕΝ ΙΩΝΙΑ
BMC Ionia, p. 181, no. 34
120.1 6 23 4.93 NoEx
Pierced for suspension (neither bust nor Tyche upright)

Phocaea
244–249 AD
Bust of Tyche r., turreted ΦΩΚΕΑ
Galley with caps of Dioscuri ΦΩΚΑΙΩΝ
BMC Ionia, p. 219, nos. 118–121; M7 GR 109
121.1 6 17 3.70 MMS
121.2 5 19 3.54 MMS/S

Smyrna
37–38 AD CALIGULA 1½ assaria
Head r., laur. ΓΑΙΟΝ ΚΑΙCΑΡΑ ΓΕΡΜΑΝΙΚΟΝ ΕΠΙ ΑΟΥΙΟΛΑ
Head of Germanicus confronting bust of Agrippina ΓΕΡΜΑΝΙΚΟΝ ΑΓΡΙΠΠΕΙΝΑΝ ΣΜΥΡΝΑΙΩΝ ΜΗΝΟΦΑΝΗC
RPC I: 2471; Klose 1987: XXIX
122.1 6 21 5.65 MMS/S
RPC I (p. 418) and Klose and Johnston (2007, table 74) agree on the denomination; this denomination typically has two portraits on the obverse. One example in Istanbul is recorded from the 1913 Sardis excavations (6848).

54–59 AD NERO 1 assarion
Head r. laur. of Nero confronting bust of Agrippina ΝΕΡΩΝΑ ΣΕΒΑΣΤΟΝ ΑΓΡΙΠΠΙΝΑΝ ΣΕΒΑΣΤΗΝ
Winged Nemesis advancing r. holding caduceus, snake at foot, uncertain legend
RPC I: 2478–2479; Klose 1987: XXXIII
123.1 6 18 4.08 MMS/S edges chiseled off
Denomination according to RPC I (p. 418) and Johnston (2007, table 74); Klose preferred 1½ assaria.

Bust of Senate r. ΘΕΟΝ CΥΝΚΛΗΤΟΝ ΖΜΥ
Reverse flattened and obscured by graffito of lion
RPC I: 2481; Klose 1987: II
124.1 — 17 4.53 F49
Denomination suggested by RPC I, p. 418; Klose preferred a half. See discussion of this coin in Section 3.3.1.

77–78 AD TITUS 1 assarion
Head r. laur. ΤΙΤΟC ΑΥΤΟΚΡΑΤΩΡ ΚΑΙCΑΡ
Herakles standing holding kantharos, club and lionskin ΙΤΑΛΙΚΩ ΑΝΘΥ ΙΟΥΛΙΑC ΑΓΡΩΝ ΖΜΥΡ
RPC II: 1007; M7 GR 120; Klose 1987: XXXVI
125.1 12 22 4.22 NoEx
Klose called this a 2-assaria coin; RPC II (p. 24) and Johnston (2007, table 74), 1 assarion.

138–141 AD ANTONINUS PIUS 4 assaria
Head r. laur. [...]ΑΙΛΙΟC ΑΝΤΩΝΕΙΝΟC
Cybele enthroned l. with tympanum and patera, lion at feet ΕΠΙ C ΡΟΥΦΕΙΝΗC ΦΟΥCΚΟΥ ΘΥ, in ex. CΜΥΡ
Klose 1987: XLVII series D; RPC IV: temp. no. 234
126.1 6 28 13.85 Wadi B

First or second century AD
Head of Dionysos? r. with low bun and one lock trailing down neck, wreathed?; behind head, l. to r. vertically, Α?ΜΕΩΝ
Amphora with upright handles, to r. ΝΜΥΡ and to l. top down ΙΑΝΩΝ, vertically
127.1 12 24 7.57 F49
Not previously published?; N is sic for Z. The diam. and wt. conform to the 1½ or 2 assaria of Smyrna in the first century AD.

175–200 AD 1 assarion
Bust of Tyche r. turreted CMYPN[...]
Winged Nemesis l. CMYPNAIΩN
Klose 1987: VII series A Group a
128.1 7 18 2.50 MMS
Denomination agreed upon by Johnston (2007, table 75) and Klose (1987).

198–202 AD CARACALLA 3 assaria
Bust r. laur. cuir. AVT K M AVP ANTΩNЄINOC
Victory crowning emperor, who holds scepter and patera over flaming altar ЄΠI CTP K POYΦINAI, in ex. CMYP
Klose 1987: LIX series A Group a
129.1 12 29 10.85 MMS
Denomination suggested by Johnston (2007, table 4b); Klose (1987) preferred 4 assaria.

241–244 AD TRANQUILLINA 1½ assaria
Bust r. dr. ΦOVP TPANKYΛΛЄINA C
Herakles standing with kantharos and club CMYPNAIΩN Γ NЄΩKOPΩN
Klose 1987: LXXI Series B; RPC VII.1: 315; M7 GR 122
130.1 6 22 3.42 MMS
130.2 6 22 4.00 NoEx
Denomination suggested by Johnston (2007, table 4b); Klose (1987) preferred 2 assaria: RPC VII.1, p. 83 as next-to-smallest denomination, without valuing in assaria.

Teos
Third century AD
Turreted bust of young Dionysos r., thyrsus over shoulder TЄΩC
Dionysos facing, pouring from kantharos, holding thyrsus CTP AVP ЄPMOΓЄNOVTHIΩN
BMC Ionia, p. 318, no. 65
131.1 6 22 5.21 F49

CARIA
Antiochia ad Maeandrum
238–268 AD
Bust of young Senate r. IЄPA CYN KΛHTOC
Tyche standing with cornucopiae and rudder ANTIOXЄΩN
BMC Caria, p. 17, no. 19
132.1 6 23 5.55 MMS/N

LYDIA
Acrasus
193–211 AD SEPTIMIUS SEVERUS
Head r. laur. AY KA Λ C CЄOYHPOC
Asklepios resting on serpent-staff AKPACIΩTΩN
BMC Lydia, p. 13, no. 22
133.1 7 20 3.72 MMS/N

Apollonis
69–125 AD
Bust of young Senate r. ΘЄON CYNKΛHTON
Bust of Apollo? r. AΠΠOΛΛΩ-ͶIΔЄ[ΩN]
RPC II: 952
134.1 12 17 3.30 EH

Attalea
Late second to third century AD
Head of Dionysos r. wreathed in ivy, no legend
Pan advancing l. with pedum and grapes ATTAΛЄATΩN
BMC Lydia, p. 26, nos. 3–4; M7 GR 135
135.1 6 16 2.05 HoB

Dioshieron
27 BC–AD 37 PROBABLY TIBERIUS
Head r. laur. ΣEBAΣTOΣ
Head of Zeus r. laur. ΔIOΣIEPITΩN
RPC I: 2558
136.1 6 19 2.31 ByzFort

100–200 AD
Turreted bust of Tyche r. ΠOΛIC
River god reclining ΔIOCIЄ, in ex. PЄITΩN
RPC IV: temp. no. 1434
137.1 12 19 4.40 MMS/N

Gordus Julia
193–250 AD
Bust of mature Herakles r., no legend
Telesphoros facing IOYΛIЄ ΓOPΔHNΩN
BMC Lydia, p. 92, no. 16
138.1 12 14 1.42 NoEx

Hyrcanis
50–100 AD?
Head of Senate r. laur. IЄPACYN KΛHTOC
Recumbent river god looking l., with cap? and horizontal reed YPKANΩN [EΠI M?], in ex. BЄTTIO in mirror image
Imhoof-Blumer 1923: 314 var.

139.1 12 18 3.62 NoEx

Imhoof-Blumer (1923) records the type with the legend in the l. field ΠΙΔΑCOC and nothing in exergue; Imhoof-Blumer 1895, p. 235, no. 3 lists a coin of Hyrcanis with an obverse of Trajan and the name of Bettios on the reverse. My thanks to Carmen Arnold-Biucchi for tracking down Bettios.

Mostene

50–54 AD Claudius

Jugate head and bust of Claudius and Agrippina r.

ΤΙ ΚΛΑΥΔΙΟΝ ΚΑΙCΑΡΑ ΘЄΑΝ ΑΓΡΙΠΠΙΝΑΝ

Rider on horse carrying labrys

ЄΠΙ ΠЄΔΑΝΙΟΥ ΚΑΙCΑΡЄΩΝ ΜΟCΤΗΝΩΝ

RPC I: 2461; M7 GR 166

140.1 12 20 5.91 MMS/S

Stumpf (1991, no. 203) dates this 49/50 or 50/1 AD.

Nacrasa

Second century AD

Bust of young Senate r. ΘЄΟΝ CΥΝΚΛΗΤΟΝ

Tyche head r. turreted ΝΑΚΡΑCЄΙΤΩΝ

BMC Lydia, p. 166, no. 10

141.1 6 18 2.60 NoEx

161–180 AD

Head of mature Herakles r. bare ЄΠΙ ΜΙΛΩΝΟC

Stag walking r. ΝΑΚΡΑCЄИΩ

BMC Lydia, p. 167, no. 13; RPC IV temp. no. 1356

142.1 12 15 2.05 MMS/N

Saitta

193–211 AD Julia Domna

Bust r. no diadem ΙΟΥΛΙΑ CЄΒΑC

Tyche standing l. holding rudder in r. and cornucopiae in l. CΑΙΤΤΗΝΩΝ

ANS no. 1998.18.67

143.1 12 17 2.58 EH

200–250 AD Severan

Bust of Tyche r. turreted CΑΙΤΤΑΙ

Herakles with club over shoulder drags Cerberus r. CΑΙΤΤΗΝΩΝ

SNG vAulock 8: 3090, same dies

144.1 6 18 3.50 MMS/N

Sardis

10 BC–AD 14 Augustus 1 assarion

Head r., bare ΣΕΒΑΣΤΟΥ

Zeus Lydios standing. ΣΑΡΔΙΑΝΩΝ ΔΙΟΔΩΡΟΣ ΕΡΜΟΦΙΛΟΥ

RPC I: 2986; M7 GR 267

145.1	12	21	8.45	NoEx
145.2	12	20	4.66	MMS/N
145.3	12	20	2.61	MMS
145.4	12	19	8.89	ByzFort
145.5	12	19	5.48	NoEx
145.6	11	19	4.20	MMS
145.7	12	19	4.00	MMS/S
145.8	12	18	4.16	NoEx
145.9	12	18	3.70	MMS
145.10	10	18	2.99	LAW

Rev. legends of nos. 147.2 and 147.7 clearly end in -ΟΥ. For denomination, for the Augustan through Flavian period, see note under type 152.

Head r., bare ΣΕΒΑΣΤΟΥ

ΣΑΡΔΙΑΝΩΝ ΔΑΜΑΣ in wreath

RPC I: 2987; M7 GR 268

146.1	—	21	6.26	F55
146.2	—	19	6.20	MMS/S

Head r., bare ΣΕΒΑΣΤΟΥ

Demoi of Pergamum and Sardis ΣΑΡΔΙΑΝΩΝ ΚΑΙ ΠΕΡΓΑΜΗΝΩΝ ΜΟΥΣΑΙΟΣ

RPC I: 2988; M7 GR 269

147.1	12	19	6.36	MMS/S
147.2	12	18	6.28	F49
147.3	5	18	3.54	NoEx

Last coin n.s.; fieldnotes record type but not the legend. Mousaios is recorded as strategos in Sardis in 5 BC, (Buckler and Robinson 1932, no. 8, pt. 1). RPC I, p. 487 suggested that the portrait on this coin is similar to that on coins minted by the magistrates Damas and Diodoros, and "a similar issue from Pergamon (2362), dating to about AD 1."

10 BC–AD 14? 1 assarion

Head of young Herakles r. ΣΑΡΔΙΑΝΩΝ to r.

Apollo with hawk, in wreath, to r. ΜΟΥΣΑΙΟΣ

148.1 1 17 5.46 MMS/S

Concave reverse. This coin is given to the reign of Augustus due to the placement of the city name on the obverse, the style of the head of Herakles (Johnston's "'later' generous proportions." Buttrey et al. 1981, p. 80), and the relatively broad flan. The magistrate's name is not attested on Hellenistic issues of Herakles/Apollo.

Probably Sardis mint
Head r., bare, illeg. legend
Worn smooth or illeg.

149.1	—	23	8.36	NoEx
149.2	—	21	6.15	F49
149.3	—	18	5.10	NoEx

14–37 AD Tiberius
Head of young Herakles r. ΟΠΙΝΑΣ ΑΚΑΜΟΣ
Apollo with hawk, in wreath ΣΑΡΔΙΑΝΩΝ
RPC I: 2990; M7 GR 245

150.1	—	17	4.35	AT-Pac
150.2	12	16	6.20	NoEx
150.3	12	16	5.35	MD2
150.4	12	15	5.91	LAW
150.5	12	17	4.20	ByzFort

14–37 AD
Head l., bare ΓΕΡΜΑΝΙΚΟΣ ΚΑΙΣΑΡ
Athena standing ΣΑΡΔΙΑΝΩΝ ΜΝΑΣΕΑΣ
RPC I: 2993; M7 GR 273

151.1	1	19	3.65	MMS
151.2	6	18	3.18	MMS/S
151.3	11	17	3.88	MMS/S
151.4	1	16	3.82	ByzFort
151.5	2	16	3.45	Wadi B
151.6	1	15	4.20	NoEx
151.7	1	14	3.11	NoEx

17–37 AD 1 assarion
Togate figure of Tiberius raising Tyche of Sardis ΣΕΒΑΣΤΟΣ ΚΑΙΣΑΡΕΩΝ
Livia seated ΣΕΒΑΣΤΗ ΙΟΥΛΙΟΣ ΚΛΕΩΝ ΚΑΙ ΜΕΜΝΩΝ
RPC I: 2991; M7 GR 270

152.1	11	17	3.69	MMS/S

Denomination suggested in RPC II, p. 199.

17–19 AD half assarion
Head r., bare ΓΕΡΜΑΝΙΚΟΣ ΚΑΙΣΑΡΕΩΝ
Head r., bare ΔΡΟΥΣΟΣ ΣΑΡΔΙΑΝΩΝ
RPC I: 2992; M7 GR 272

153.1	12	17	2.46	NoEx
153.2	12	17	2.40	NoEx
153.3	12	16	2.62	MMS

Denomination suggested in RPC II, p. 199.

28–29 AD 2 assaria
Drusus and Germanicus seated ΔΡΟΥΣΟΣ ΚΑΙ ΓΕΡΜΑΝΙΚΟΣ ΚΑΙΣΑΡΕΣ ΝΕΟΙ ΘΕΟΙ ΦΙΛΑΔΕΛΦΟΙ, restruck legend
Oak and laurel wreath enclosing ΚΟΙΝΟΥ ΑΣΙΑΣ around flan: ΓΑΙΩ ΑΣΙΝΝΙΩ ΠΟΛΛΙΩΝΙ ΑΝΘΥΠΑΠΩ, restruck
RPC I: 2995; M7 GR 274

154.1	12	28	14.29	NoEx
154.2	—	28	13.49	MMS/S
154.3	—	27	12.87	MMS
154.4	10	21	13.26	NoEx

The mint is given to Sardis by RPC I, p. 487, over the objections of others, including Johnston (2007, p. 245 n. 392), based on the provenance of the coins. These four examples solidify the argument in RPC. For the denomination, see RPC I, p. 488; Johnston 2007, table 74; RPC II, p. 199.

45–54 AD Claudius half assarion
Head l. bare ΤΙ ΚΛΑΥΔΙΟΣ ΚΑΙΣΑΡ
Head of mature Herakles l. ΣΑΡΔΙΑΝΩΝ
RPC I: 2996; M7 GR 275

155.1	12	16	3.20	HoB

Second specimen not in M7 though identified by Johnston.
Denomination suggested in RPC II, p. 199.

60 AD Nero 1 assarion
Head r. laur. ΝΕΡΩΝ ΚΑΙΣΑΡ
Dionysos standing with panther ΕΠΙ ΜΙΝΔΙΟΥ ΣΑΡΔΙΑΝΩΝ; ΣΤΡΑ ΤΟ Β (lig.)
RPC I: 2997

156.1	12	18	5.48	MD2
156.2	12	17	4.99	LAW
156.3	12	16	5.01	LAW

Denomination suggested in RPC II, p. 199.

65 AD
Head r. laur. ΝΕΡΩΝ ΚΑΙϹΑΡ
Zeus Lydios ΕΠΙ ΤΙ ΚΛ ΜΝΑϹЄΟΥ ϹΑΡΔΙΑΝΩΝ,
RPC I: 3007; M7 GR 276

157.1	12	18	4.14	F49

See discussion of this coin in Section 3.3.1.

157.2	1	17	7.40	ThSt

See discussion of this coin in Section 3.2.2.
Denomination suggested in RPC II, p. 199.

65 AD
Bust of young Senate r. ΘЄΟΝ CΥΝΚΛΗΤΟΝ
Zeus Lydios standing ЄΠΙ ΤΙ ΜΝΑCЄΟΥ CΑΡΔΙΑΝΩΝ
RPC I: 3008; M7 GR 246

158.1	6	19	3.60	ByzFort
158.2	6	18	4.92	MMS/S
158.3	6	18	3.50	NoEx

Denomination suggested in RPC II, p. 199.

half assarion
Head of mature Herakles r. ΕΠΙ ΤΙ ΜΝΑCΕΟΥ CΑΡΔΙΑΝΩΝ
Nike l. with wreath and palm CЄΒΑCΤΗ
RPC I: 3010

159.1	6	16	3.66	ByzFort

Denomination suggested in RPC II, p. 199.

10 BC–AD 65 Augustan or Julio-Claudian 1 assarion
Bust r. bare
Zeus Lydios standing, illeg. inscription

160.1	2	18	3.50	NoEx

Denomination suggested in RPC II, p. 199.

Bust r. bare half assarion
Illeg.

161.1	—	16	3.16	Wadi B

Denomination suggested in RPC II, p. 199.

70–73 AD Flavian 1 assarion
Helm. head of Athena/Roma r. ЄΠΙ ΤΙ ΚΛΑΥ ΦΙΛΙΝΟΥ CΤΡΑ
Tetrastyle temple with seven stars in pediment CΑΡΔΙΑΝΩΝ ΜΑΡΚЄΛΛΟΥ, to l. ΤΟ (lig.), to r. Β, in ex. ЄΠΙ

162.1	1	18	5.34	ByzFort

RPC II: 1305; M7 GR 247
Denomination suggested in RPC II, p. 199.

As above, but head of Athena/Roma l.
As above, but nothing in pediment
RPC II: 1306; M7 GR 248

163.1	1	22	4.42	MMS, o/s?
163.2	6	20	4.10	HoB

RPC I (p. 488, "Exclusions" no. 4) noted that Imhoof-Blumer (1890, p. 198, no. 616) misread the overstriking sequence of the coin; RPC authors dated the coin to the Flavian, not Neronian period. The denomination is given as 1½ assaria (RPC I, p. 488; Johnston 2007, table 74) or 1 assarion (RPC II, p. 199). Note the stylistic similarity to coins of Ilium.

75 AD 1 assarion
Bust of young Dionysos r. ЄΠΙ ΦΛ ЄΙCΙΓΟΝΟΥ
Zeus Lydios standing CΑΡΔΙΑΝΩΝ CΤΡΑ (lig.)
RPC II: 1316

164.1	12	20	5.76	F55

Denomination suggested by RPC II, p. 199.

half assarion
Laur. head of young Herakles r. with lionskin CΑΡΔΙΑΝΩΝ
Herakles standing l. with club and lionskin CΑΡΔΙΑΝΩΝ, in wreath
RPC II: 1310 var. (no wreath noted); M7 GR 250

165.1	8	15	2.82	NoEx

Denomination from Johnston 2007, table 74; RPC II, p. 199.

70–80 AD? 1 assarion
Bust of young Senate r. ΙЄΡΑ CΥΝΚΛΗΤΟC
Tetrastyle temple CΑΡΔΙΑΝΩΝ
RPC II: 1309; M7 GR 254

166.1	7	18	2.77	MMS/S (leaded bronze)
166.2	2	18	3.92	F49 (disc in pediment)

RPC II suggested a Vespasianic date, while Johnston (in M7, p. 82) favored 100–120, in part due to the style of the coin and in part to the direction of the legend, which runs clockwise. Coins minted under Vespasian have obverses with counterclockwise legends. Johnston also noted a broken-crossbar A, which is found on coins of Marciana and Plotina; thus, she thought the temple on the reverse was Sardis's first neokorate temple, probably to Hadrian. The authors of RPC noted uncertainty about the coin. They thought the style fitted better in the Vespasianic period, while the legend was more typical of second century issues. Coin no. 166.1 was residual in a Late Roman context. Coin no. 166.2 was found on a packed earth floor beneath fall from a roof collapse; the pottery associated with the fall cannot distinguish between the termini of 80 and 120. Denomination suggested in RPC II, p. 199.

79–81 AD Titus
Bust r. laur. cuir. ΤΙΤΟ...ΟΡΟΣ
Emperor sacrificing at altar ΕΠΙ Τ ΦΛ ЄΙCΙΓΟΝΟΥ
RPC II suppl. 2: 1315a

167.1	7	23	10.43	NoEx

Johnston (2007, table 74) saw this as a 2-assaria coin; the diameter and weight do not fit comfortably into the table of denominations in RPC II, p. 199, but RPC II: 1304, also minted under Titus at Hierapolis, does appear to be the same denomination as this coin.

81–96 AD Domitian

Minerva seated l., resting l. hand on shield and holding Victory

Head r. laur. ΔΟΜΙΤΙΑΝΟϹ ΚΑΙϹΑΡ ϹЄΒΑϹΤΟϹ ΓЄΡΜΑΝΙΚΟϹ in r. ЄΠΙ Τ ΦΛ ΜЄΤΡΟΔΩΡΟΥ ϹΤ ΤΟ Β ϹΑΡΔΙΑΝΩΝ

RPC II: 1320; M7 GR 279

168.1	1	33	13.75	MMS/N

RPC II, p. 199 preferred a 3-assaria coin; Johnston (2007, table 74), 4-assaria.

80–100 AD?

Bust of young Senate r. dr. ΙЄΡΑ ϹΥΝ ΚΛΗΤΟϹ

Demeter standing ϹΑΡΔΙΑΝΩΝ

BMC Lydia, p. 246, no. 73; M7 GR 251

169.1	12	28	7.86	AT-Pac, cm. App. 1
169.2	12	27	9.98	ByzFort
169.3	—	27	9.88	AT

RPC II, p. 199 prefers a 2-assaria coin, Johnston (2007, table 74), 3-assaria. See note about dating the coin, Section 2.3.

End of the first–beginning of the second century AD?

Bust of young Senate r. dr. ΙЄΡΑ ϹΥΝ ΚΛΗΤΟϹ

Hexastyle temple ϹΑΡΔΙΑΝΩΝ

RPC III: 2410; M7 GR 252 or 255

170.1	7	20	2.48	NoEx, n.s.
170.2	11	19	3.01	MMS/N
170.3	12	18	3.58	CW6
170.4	1	15	3.08	NoEx

(same dies as above and M7 GR 252)

No coin comes from a datable context. Johnston's earlier group (252) has clockwise legends, the letter form A and a reverse legend in two parts. Her later group (255) can have a clockwise or a counterclockwise broken legend on the obverse, with broken crossbar As. The reverse can have the legend broken in two or three places, with a broken crossbar A. When I returned to her series, I only found one coin with a clear broken crossbar A. However, the coins in her 252 series had temples with a disk in the pediment and acroteria. The coins she grouped in the other series (255), when the details could be ascertained, had either acroteria or disks, but not both. When As were visible, they appeared to be formed without the broken crossbar, save one. Hence, I have combined the two series that Johnston separated, as they appear to be part of a large issue, and the die cutters appear to have introduced variants on the initial design. The authors of RPC III reached the same conclusion, calling the coin Trajanic/Hadrianic.

112 AD Marciana 1 assarion

Bust r. dr. ΜΑΡΚΙΑ ϹЄΒΑϹΤΗ

Pelops galloping r. ϹΑΡΔΙΑΝΩΝ ΠЄΛΟΨ

RPC III: 2398; M7 GR 283

171.1	6	19	2.72	ByzFort

112 AD Plotina 1 assarion

Bust r. ΠΛΩΤЄΙΝΑ ϹЄΒΑϹΤΗ

Pelops galloping r. ϹΑΡΔΙΑΝΩΝ

RPC III: 2397; M7 GR 284

172.1	7	21	5.01	ThSt
172.2	—	20	2.30	BS-W15, cm. App. 1 Rev. worn smooth, prob. i.d.
172.3	—	20	3.10	ByzFort Rev. worn smooth, prob. i.d.

112 AD Marciana or Plotina 1 assarion

Bust r.

Pelops galloping r., legend illeg.

173.1	12	19	3.85	EH

98–117 AD Trajanic half assarion

Bust of young Dionysos r. wreathed in ivy ϹΑΡΔΙΑΝΩΝ

Thyrsus bound with taenia, in r. field bee or fly

ϹΤΡ ΛΟ ΙΟ ΛΙΒΩΝΙΑΝΟV

RPC III: 2393; M7 GR 256

174.1	8	17	2.21	NoEx
174.2	12	15	2.80	F49
174.3	6	15	2.37	NoEx
174.4	—	15	2.10	NoEx

117–138 AD Sabina 2 assaria

Bust of Sabina r. ϹΑΒЄΙΝΑ ϹЄΒΑϹΤΗ

Recumbant river god holding cornucopiae ϹΑΡΔΙΑΝΩΝ, in ex. ЄΡΜΟϹ

RPC III: 2405; M7 GR 287

175.1	12	24	7.51	NoEx

100–140 AD half assarion

Head of young Herakles r. lionskin knotted at neck

Bow in case, club, insect ϹΑΡΔΙΑΝΩΝ

SNG Cop: 510; RPC III not; M7 GR 257

176.1	6	17	2.20	EH
176.2	6	16	2.52	MMS/S

140–161 AD Marcus Aurelius as Caesar 1 assarion?
Bust r. bare Μ ΑVΡΗΛΙΟC ΚΑΙCΑΡ VΠ
Legend in wreath CΑΡ/ΔΙΑΝ/ΩΝ ЄΠ/Ι ΔΑΡΙΟV
BMC Lydia, p. 258, no. 141; M7 GR 290

177.1	12	22	2.97	Wadi B

Bust r. bare Μ ΑΥΡΗΛΙΟC ΚΑΙCΑΡ ΥΠΑ 1 assarion?
Winged caduceus ЄΠΙ ΝЄΙΚΟΜΑΧΟΥ CΑΡΔΙΑΝΩΝ
BMC Lydia, p. 258, nos. 143–144; M7 GR 292

178.1	6	23	3.32	Wadi B, bent and cut
178.2	6	22	3.20	Wadi B
178.3	6	22	3.12	Wadi B

See discussion of the Wadi B coins in Section 3.3.2.

178.4	6	21	3.06	ByzFort
178.5	6	21	2.82	Wadi B
178.6	6	20	3.29	HoB
178.7	6	20	3.00	NoEx
178.8	6	19	2.60	MMS

These coins show the Sardis mint style nicely: dies are slightly small for the flan, which is large and thin. The engravers tend to leave negative space, the legends have large letters pushed to the edge of the die, and often the reverses simply read CΑΡΔΙΑΝΩΝ. The style begins in the late Flavian period (see BMC Lydia, p. 246, no. 73, for which see Section 2.3) and can be seen in one traveling engraver who made dies for a variety of cities, including Sardis, Smyrna, Hierapolis, Ancyra, and Tripolis (Johnston 1983, p. 60). By the third century, the style is rarer, as legends become longer and more elements are placed on the reverses.

180–193 AD Commodus 1 assarion
Bust r. bare Μ ΑVΡ ΚΟΜΜΟΔΟC ΚΑ
Cult statue of Kore of Sardis enthroned between wheat ear and poppy CΑΡΔΙΑΝΩΝ
BMC Lydia, p. 259, no. 145

179.1	12	21	4.68	NoEx

139–144 AD Faustina Major 4 assaria
Bust r. dr. ΘЄΑ ΦΑΥCΤЄΙΝΑ
Hexastyle temple with cult statue within
ЄΠΙ ΚΛ ΦΡΟΝΤΩΝΟC ΑCΙΑΡΧ CΤΡΑΤΗΓΟ Α CΑΡΔΙΑΝΩΝ
RPC IV: 1426; M7 GR 289

180.1	6	35	35.35	Wadi B
180.2	6	35	21.48	F55
180.3	6	33	20.32	NoEx

For a discussion on the meaning of Asiarch, see Kampmann 1997, p. 88.

138–169 AD half assarion
Bust r. dr. ΦΑΥCΤ(Є)ΙΝΑ CЄΒΑCΤΗ
Aphrodite standing l. with apple CΑΡΔΙΑΝΩΝ
RPC IV: temp. no. 1427; M7 GR 288

181.1	6	19	4.90	NoEx

138–190 AD Antonine half assarion
Head of mature Herakles l.
Omphale walking r. CΑΡΔΙΑΝΩΝ
BMC Lydia, p. 247, nos. 79–80; M7 GR 253

182.1	6	22	3.64	EH
182.2	—	22	3.52	NoEx
182.3	—	21	3.64	MMS/N
182.4	6	19	4.95	NoEx
182.5	6	18	3.75	NoEx

Head of young Herakles r. laur. half assarion
Herakles standing with club and lionskin CΑΡΔΙΑΝΩΝ
BMC Lydia p. 247, no. 81; M7 GR 249

183.1	6	19	5.03	MD1/S
183.2	—	18	4.27	MMS/N

Johnston, in M7, dated this issue to ca. 75, due to the counterclockwise legends, found on coins of Nero and Vespasian, but noted the lettering and style are uncharacteristic of Neronian coins of Sardis.

140–160 AD 1 assarion
Head of young Dionysos r. ЄΠΙ ΔΑΙΡΟΥ
Torch CΑΡΔΙΑΝΩΝ
SNG vAulock: 3139; M7 GR 259

184.1	12	21	2.50	MMS/N

Same die as 184.3 and M7 C61.0059

184.2	12	21	2.32	NoEx
184.3	12	20	1.92	NoEx, cm. App. 1
184.4	12	19	2.31	HoB

The magistrate's name is also on coins of Antoninus Pius and Marcus Aurelius (BMC Lydia, p. 257, no. 138; p. 258, nos. 141–144) and the style of the engraving looks much like the latter (especially with isolated cult implements). The winged caduceus reverse of Aurelius with a different magistrate's name is surely by same die engraver. He makes small dies for the flan, beautifully proportioned busts (with heads tilted slightly up), leaving much room between the head and beaded border (with dots so small it almost looks like a line border) and a great deal of space between sparse letters on legends. Flans are thin.

117–180 AD HADRIANIC OR ANTONINE 2 assaria
Bust of Zeus Lydios l. ΣЄΥC ΛΥΔΙΟC
Roma seated holding Nike ΘΕΑ ΡΩΜΗ
BMC Lydia, p. 246, no. 77; RPC III, IV not
185.1 — 27 6.72 NoEx

197–213 AD JULIA DOMNA 1 assarion?
Bust r. dr. ΙΟΥΛΙΑ CЄΒΑCΤΗ
Zeus Lydios CΑΡΔΙΑΝΩΝ Β ΝЄΩΚΟΡΩΝ
BMC Lydia, p. 261, no. 157
186.1 6 20 2.64 Wadi B
Denominations for ca. 200–260 follow Johnston (2007, pp. 21–23). Spoerri Butcher (2009, pp. 223–24) disagrees with this approach.

1 assarion
Cult statue of Kore of Sardis between ear of wheat and poppy CΑΡΔΙΑΝΩΝ Β ΝЄΩΚΟΡΩΝ
BMC Lydia, p. 260, no. 149; M7 GR 293
187.1 6 19 3.65 RT

uncertain denomination
Bust l. as Tyche, wearing kalathos and holding cornucopiae ΙΟVΛΙΑ CЄΒΑCΤΗ
Prize crown with palm on inscribed base ЄΠΙ Γ ΚΛ ΜΙΘΡΟV ΑΡΧ Α CΑΡΔΙΑΝΩΝ Β ΝЄΩΚΟΡΩΝ; on base, ΧΡVCΑΝΘΙΝΑ
BMC Lydia, p. 260, no. 150; M7 GR 294
188.1 7 23 14.53 MMS
This coin does not fit Johnston's denominations.

200–217 AD 1½ assaria
Bust r. dr. ΙΟΥΛΙΑ CЄΒΑCΤΗ
Eagle with Ganymede CΑΡΔΙΑΝΩΝ Β ΝЄΩΚΟΡΩΝ
BMC Lydia, p. 261, nos. 155–156
189.1 12 23 4.65 MMS/N

Bust r. dr. illeg. legend
Worn smooth
190.1 — 22 5.67 ByzFort
Mint prob., not certain.

212–217 AD CARACALLA 2 assaria
Head r. rad. ΑVΤ ΚΑΙ ΜΑVΡ ΑΝΤΩΝЄΙΝΟC
Tyche standing with cornucopiae and rudder CΑΡΔΙΑΝΩΝ Β ΝЄΩΚΟΡΩΝ
BMC Lydia, p. 263, no. 162; M7 GR 299
191.1 6 26 7.98 MMS/N

200–220 AD SEVERAN 1 assarion
Bust of Tyche r., turreted CΑΡΔΙC
Cult statue of Kore CΑΡΔΙΑΝΩΝ Β ΝЄΩΚΟΡΩΝ
BMC Lydia, p. 249, nos. 90–91; M7 GR 261
192.1 6 22 4.48 CW32
192.2 12 20 4.47 MMS/S
192.3 — — — NoEx
The style of carving the die (including the strong beaded border and use of negative space) and thinness of flan are traits which are seen in late first- and second-century coins of Sardis.

212–217 AD half assarion
Bust of Zeus r. laur. ΣЄVCΛV ΔΙΟC
Young Herakles standing with club and lionskin CΑΡΔΙΑΝΩΝ•
BMC Lydia, p. 248, nos. 85–86; M7 GR 262
193.1 6 15 1.60 MMS

218–222 AD ELAGABALUS 2 assaria
Bust r. rad. dr. cuir. ΑVΚ ΜΑ ΑΝΤΩΝЄΙΝΟC
Athena Nikephoros CΑΡΔΙΑΝΩΝ Β ΝЄΩΚΟΡΩΝ
M7 GR 302
194.1 7 24 6.01 MD1/S
BMC Lydia, p. 262, no. 161 lists only for Caracalla; Johnston (1982) more carefully differentiates between Caracalla and Elagabalus.

3 assaria
Bust r. laur. cuir. palud. ΑVΤ Κ Μ ΑVΡ• ΑΝΤΩΝЄΙΝΟC
Cult statue of Kore of Sardis, surrounded by wheat ear, bucranium, poppy and wreath, ЄΠΙ ЄΡΜΟΦΙΛΟV ΑΡΑ[Χ]-CΑΡΔΙΑΝΙΩΝ ΤΡ[IC ΝЄΩΚΟΡ]
Paris FG 1284, var. reverse legend; Evans 2015
195.1 7 30 10.38 NoEx
Obverse die same as Paris coin; see Section 2.4.

218–222 AD JULIA MAESA 2 assaria
Bust r. dr. ΙΟΥΛΙΑ ΜΑΙCΑ CЄ
Mên standing CΑΡΔΙΑΝΩΝ ΤΡΙC ΝЄΩΚΟΡΩΝ
BMC Lydia, p. 266, no. 174
196.1 7 28 4.08 MMS/S

Bust r. dr. on crescent ΙΟΥΛΙΑ ΜΑΙCΑ ΑV
Mên standing CΑΡΔΙΑΝΩΝ-•Β ΝΕΩΚΟΡΩ, in ex. Ν
(Β begins after scepter, recut legend)
Evans 2015
197.1 6 23 6.14 F49

222–235 AD SEVERUS ALEXANDER 1 assarion
Bust r. laur. cuir. AVT K M AVP CЄ AΛЄΞANΔPOC
Tyche holding cornucopiae, wheat ear, poppy, rudder ЄΠ CTP ΔAMIANOV CAPΔIANΩN B NЄΩKOPΩN
BMC Lydia, p. 266, no. 176; M7 GR 308
198.1 6 21 4.15 NoEx

235–238 AD MAXIMINUS THRAX 2 assaria
Bust r. laur. dr. cuir. AYT K Γ I OVH MAΞIMЄINOC
Athena with olive branch, spear and shield
CAPΔIANΩN B NЄΩKOPΩN
BMC Lydia, p. 268, no. 180
199.1 6 25 7.54 NoEx

238–244 AD GORDIAN III 2 assaria
Bust r. laur. cuir. AYT K M ANT ΓOPΔIANOC
Wreath enclosing bucranium and torch
EΠI POVΦЄINOV CAPΔIANΩN B NЄΩKOP
RPC VII.1: 233; M7 GR 310
200.1 — 24 7.86 ByzFort

Zeus Lydios holding eagle and scepter 2 assaria
CAPΔIANΩN B NЄΩKOPΩN
RPC VII.1: 237
201.1 11 24 5.08 NoEx

Tyche standing with cornucopiae and rudder
CAPΔIANΩN B NЄΩKOPΩN
RPC VII.1: 239
202.1 6 24 6.06 F49
Pierced for suspension (head of emperor upright)
202.2 7 24 5.44 NoEx

238–244 AD TRANQUILLINA 1½ assaria
Bust r. dr. ΦOVP TPANKVΛΛЄINA CA
Mên with pinecone and scepter CAPΔIANΩN B NЄΩKOPΩN
RPC VII.1: 243
203.1 1 23 4.96 MMS
203.2 10 21 4.10 NoEx

244–249 AD PHILIP II AS CAESAR 1 assarion
Bust r. dr. M IOVΛ ΦIΛIΠΠOC
Zeus Lydios, Dionysos, or Tyche standing CAPΔIANΩN B NЄΩKOPΩN
204.1 5 21 4.06 NoEx
204.2 6 21 3.26 NoEx
204.3 2 17 2.29 MMS/N, clipped

Tabala
193–217 AD JULIA DOMNA
Bust r. dr. IOYΛIA CЄBACTH
Cybele enthroned, at feet, lion TABAΛЄΩN
BMC Lydia, p. 290, no. 11
205.1 7 21 3.84 MMS/S

Thyateira
138–192 AD
Head of mature Herakles r. laur., no legend
Eagle with head turned back ΘYATAEIPHNΩN
RPC IV: temp. no. 3188
206.1 12 16 2.68 MMS

218–222 AD ELAGABALUS
Bust r. laur. AVTKMA ANTΩNЄINOC
Rome Nikephoros seated l. with shield and spear ΘVATЄIPHNΩN
BMC Lydia, p. 313, no. 114
207.1 6 26 7.64 NoEx

222–256 AD SEVERUS ALEXANDER AND LATER
Bust of Tyche r. turreted dr. ΘYATЄIPA
Homonoia standing ΘYATЄIPHNΩN
BMC Lydia, p. 301, no. 56
208.1 6 19 2.60 NoEx

Tralles
253–260 AD VALERIAN I
Head r. laur. cuir. AYT K ΠO ΛIKINIOC BAΛЄPIANOC
Tyche standing ЄΠI ΓP (both lig.)
KΛ MЄNIΠΠOY TPAΛΛIA in ex. NΩN
Mionnet 1809: 1121
209.1 6 28 9.70 MMS

PHRYGIA
Appia
244–249 AD PHILIP II
Bust r. dr. M IOVΛ ΦIΛIΠΠOC AV
Tyche standing l. with rudder and cornucopiae
ЄΠ ANTЄPΩTOC AP AΠΠIANΩN
Not previously published?, cf. BMC Phrygia, p.108, no. 9 for the name of the magistrate during the reign of Philip.
210.1 7 21 5.54 MMS

Peltae

193–213 AD CARACALLA

Head of youthful Caracalla, r. rad. M AY ANTϢNЄINOC

Tyche standing with rudder and cornucopiae ΠЄΛΤΗΝΩΝ CTP TATAPIΩNOC

BMC Phrygia, p. 351, no. 26, slight var. in rev. legend

211.1	6	22	4.49	Wadi B

PISIDIA

Termessus Major

238–268 AD

Head of Zeus r. laur. TEPMHCCEΩN

Solymus seated l. on throne AVTONOMΩ, in ex. N

BMC Lycia, p. 274, no. 48

212.1	11	29	13.75	MMS

PHRYGIA?

Prymnessus?

Second or third century AD

Bust of Senate r. laur. [Θ]EONC – [YNKΛ]TON

Cybele enthroned with two lions at feet

Π-VHN-HCO[...]C

213.1	12	21	5.07	MMS/N, lathe hole in rev.

LYCIA

Termessus Minor?

17–37 AD TIBERIUS

Bare head of Tiberius r.

Galloping horse r. [...]-O[I]

RPC I: 3360, i.d. poss.

214.1	—	18	4.50	ByzFort

CILICIA

Pompeiopolis (Soli)

161–169 AD MARCUS AURELIUS AS AUGUSTUS

Bust of Aurelius confronting bust of Verus [...]ANT[...]

Worn smooth

cf. RPC IV: temp. no. 9736, which approximates style of heads, size and weight

215.1	—	33	24.05	MMS/N, cm. App. 1

Uncertain Mint

27 BC–AD 14 AUGUSTUS

Head r. bare

worn smooth

216.1	—	27	11.18	MMS
216.2	—	23	6.30	ByzFort
216.3	—	20	4.25	ThSt
216.4	—	10	1.18	MMS/S, H2

Head r. SC, obscure rev., tessera

216.5	—	20 × 25	4.40	NoEx, wreath on rev.?

1 BC–AD 10

Two standing figures

Temple with statue of emperor

Either RPC I: 2362 or 2364

217.1	12	19	4.42	NoEx

Coin n.s., prob. Sardis mint

2 BC–AD 14

Bust r., laur. CΛESΛR ΛVGVSTVS DIVI F PΛTER PΛTRIΛE

Gaius and Lucius standing, between shield and spear, lituus and simpulum; ΛVGVSTI F COS DESIG PRINC IVVENT, in ex. CLCΛESΛRES

218.1	3	19	3.28	MMS
218.2	2	19	3.03	NoEx, pierced for attachment

After RIC 1^2, p. 56, no. 210; on p. 55 n. 205ff. Sutherland notes that unbarred As are normal for the entire series and "imitations are of widespread provenance." May be later imitation of Augustan type from Lugdunum mint (nice style). Plated, traces of silver on both sides.

27 BC–AD 68 AUGUSTAN TO JULIO-CLAUDIAN

Male head r. (bare?)

Worn smooth

219.1	—	20	4.91	MMS
219.2	—	18	3.78	MD1/S, cm. App. 1
219.3	—	18	2.95	MMS/S

68–96 AD FLAVIAN

Bust r. laur., illeg. inscription

Worn smooth

220.1	—	28	8.42	CW32, cm. App. 1
220.2	—	26	10.17	MMS
220.3	—	19	4.66	EH
220.4	—	16	3.24	ThSt, prob. Sardis mint

50–80 AD

Bust of young Senate r., illeg. legend

Worn smooth

221.1	—	20	4.06	NoEx, prob. Sardis mint

141–161 AD FAUSTINA MAJOR
Bust r., illeg. legend
Illeg. rev.
Poss. BMC Lydia, p. 258, no. 139, prob. Sardis mint

222.1	—	30	13.73	Wadi B

161–175 AD FAUSTINA MINOR
Bust r.
Worn smooth

223.1	—	25	7.95	ByzFort, cm. App. 1

First to third century AD
Bust r. dr. of Senate?, illeg. legend
Zeus Lydios, clockwise up l. side [...]T[...]

224.1	6	18	2.24	F55

Bust of young male r., (not an emperor) bare, illeg. legend
Type off flan, [...]TINY| (staff or exergual line?)

225.1	—	17	3.95	NoEx

75–100 AD
Bust of young male r.
Wreath containing SC

226.1	6	11	0.75	MMS/S, H2

Second century AD
Head r.
Standing divinity l., illeg. legend

227.1	6	28	14.23	MMS/N

117–138 AD HADRIAN
Head r. laur., legend illeg.
Worn smooth

228.1	—	35	20.32	MD1/S, cm. App. 1

Ephesus?
212–235 AD CARACALLA TO SEVERUS ALEXANDER
Bust r. laur., illeg. legend
Tetrastyle temple with patera in pediment, cult statue inside, obscure legend below steps

229.1	6	30	12.67	NoEx, cm. App. 1

Uncertain Mint
Uncertain first to third century

230.1		35	19.00	EH
230.2		33	19.94	CW32, sestertius?
230.3		32	10.47	MMS, cm. App. 1
230.4		31	14.51	CW32
230.5		30	6.03	MMS
230.6		29	10.59	F49, cm. App. 1
230.7		29	8.89	ByzFort
230.8		28	10.84	NoEx
230.9		28	8.30	ByzFort
230.10		28	7.61	MMS/S
230.11		28	7.35	MMS/S
230.12		28	7.20	BS-E14
230.13		28	6.98	MMS/S
230.14		27	16.78	MMS/S
230.15		27	7.89	MMS/N
230.16		27	7.43	ThSt
230.17		27	6.40	F49, cm. App. 1
230.18		27	5.49	ByzFort
230.19		27	frag'y	MMS
230.20		26	10.10	ByzFort
230.21		26	halved	MMS, prob. first century AD
230.22		26	frag'y	MMS/N
230.23		25	8.64	MMS/N
230.24		25	7.82	MMS/N
230.25		25	6.45	MMS
230.26		25	frag'y	MMS, chisel cuts on both faces for attempted halving
230.27		24	8.43	ByzFort
230.28		24	7.60	NoEx
230.29		24	6.84	NoEx
230.30		24	5.67	MMS
230.31		23	8.33	F49, head r., prob. first century AD
230.32		23	7.42	NoEx
230.33		23	6.90	NoEx
230.34		23	6.86	F49
230.35		23	5.21	F49
230.36		23	4.01	NoEx, cm. App. 1
230.37		23	frag'y	MMS/S
230.38		22	6.92	MMS/S
230.39		22	5.22	MMS/N
230.40		21	13.27	MMS
230.41		21	4.95	MMS/N, cm. App. 1
230.42		20	6.00	AT-Pac
230.43		20	5.93	F49, cm. App. 1
230.44		20	5.80	MMS
230.45		20	5.10	F55
230.46		20	5.10	MMS, four cm., App. 1
230.47		20	4.99	MMS

230.48	20	4.21	MMS, worn smooth
230.49	20	3.89	MMS/N, head r., prob. first century AD
230.50	20	3.28	PA
230.51	20	frag'y	RT
230.52	19	6.77	MMS/S, cm. App. 1
230.53	19	4.90	MMS/S, head r., prob. first century AD
230.54	19	4.61	ByzFort
230.55	19	4.50	F55
230.56	19	4.38	ByzFort
230.57	19	4.21	MMS
230.58	19	4.17	MMS
230.59	19	4.14	Wadi B
230.60	19	4.02	F49, head r., prob. first century AD
230.61	19	3.50	F49
230.62	19	3.43	MMS
230.63	19	3.40	MMS
230.64	19	3.18	NoEx
230.65	19	3.14	MMS/S
230.66	19	2.96	MMS, halved, prob. first century AD
230.67	19	2.36	F49, first century AD context
230.68	19	frag'y	AT-Pac
230.69	18	6.10	NoEx
230.70	18	4.42	NoEx
230.71	18	4.07	NoEx
230.72	18	3.92	ByzFort
230.73	18	3.90	MMS
230.74	18	3.87	F55
230.75	18	3.82	NoEx
230.76	18	3.71	ByzFort
230.77	18	3.70	NoEx
230.78	18	3.61	HoB
230.79	18	3.50	MMS
230.80	18	3.50	MMS
230.81	18	3.46	ThSt, cm. App. 1
230.82	18	3.19	MMS/S
230.83	18	2.79	NoEx
230.84	18	2.56	F49
230.85	18	2.35	ByzFort
230.86	17	5.42	MMS/S
230.87	17	4.92	MMS/S
230.88	17	4.86	Tomb 07.1
230.89	17	4.81	MD2

230.90	17	4.18	MD2
230.91	17	3.61	MMS/S
230.92	17	3.50	NoEx
230.93	17	3.22	MMS/S
230.94	17	2.93	ByzFort
230.95	17	2.86	Wadi B
230.96	17	2.60	MMS
230.97	17	2.48	MMS
230.98	17	2.12	Wadi B, female head r., first century AD
230.99	17	1.45	Wadi B
230.100	16	2.98	MMS
230.101	16	1.70	MMS/S
230.102	15	7.27	ByzFort
230.103	15	3.75	MMS/S
230.104	15	3.70	ByzFort
230.105	15	2.95	MMS
230.106	15	2.60	MMS/N
230.107	15	2.42	ByzFort
230.108	14	5.81	ByzFort
230.109	14	2.82	ByzFort
230.110	14	2.80	ByzFort
230.111	13	6.24	NoEx
230.112	13	5.18	MMS/N
230.113	13	4.50	ByzFort
230.114	—	frag'y	ByzFort
230.115	—	frag'y	MMS
230.116	—	frag'y	MMS/N
230.117	—	frag'y	MMS/N
230.118	—	frag'y	MMS/S

Roman Imperial

Hadrian

Rome
119–122 AD AR denarius
Bust. r. laur. no drape IMPCAESARTRAIAN-HADRIANVSAVG
Concordia seated l. with patera PMTRPCOSIII
RIC II, p. 350, no. 82
231.1 17 2.64 Tomb 07.1

Faustina Minor

Rome
161–180 AD AR denarius
Bust r. dr. FAVSTINA-AVGVSTA
Diana standing holding torch DIANA-LUCIF
RIC III, p. 268, no. 674
232.1 18 — MMS/N

Lucius Verus

Rome
165–166 AD AR denarius
Head r. laur. no drape LVERVSAVGARM-PARTHMAX
Pax standing l. with cornucopiae and olive branch PAX-AVGTRPVICOSII
RIC III, p. 258, no. 555; M7 R 15
233.1 20 2.90 MMS/N

Commodus

Rome
191/2 AD AR denarius
Head r. laur. LAELAVRELCO-MMAVGPFEL
Mars leaning on shield and holding spear MARTI-VLTORIAVG
RIC III, p. 396, no. 257
234.1 18 1.37 NoEx

Caracalla

Rome
211–217 AD Bi. antoninianus
Bust r. rad. ANTONINVSPIVSAVGGERM
Venus standing with scepter and Victoriola, leaning on shield VENVSVICTRIX
RIC IV.1, p. 259, no. 311d
235.1 23 4.98 HoB
Banker's marks (lines of dots) on obv. and rev.

Severus Alexander

Rome
231–235 AD AR denarius
Bust r. laur. IMPALEXANDERPIVSAVG
Jupiter with fulmen and eagle IOVIPRO-PVGNATORI
RIC IV.2, p. 88, no. 238
236.1 20 2.63 MMS

232 AD
As above
Sol standing with raised hand and globe PMTRPX-I-COSIIIPP
RIC IV.2, p. 79, no. 112
237.1 20 2.55 MMS/S

Philip I

Rome
244–247 AD Bi. antoninianus
Bust r. rad. IMPMIVLPHILIPPVSAVG
Annona with cornucopiae, prow behind ANNONAAVGG
RIC IV.3, p. 72, no. 29
238.1 24 4.26 MMS/S

Otacilia Severa

Rome
244–246 AD Bi. antoninianus
Bust r. diademed, on crescent MARCIAOTACILSEVERAAVG
Pietas raises r. hand and holds incense box, child to l. PIETASAVG
RIC IV.3, p. 83, no. 122b
239.1 21 2.86 MD2

Valerian I

Rome
254 AD as
Bust r. laur. IMPCPLICVALERIANVSAVG
Jupiter holding fulmen and scepter IOVI CONS-ERVATORISC
RIC V.1, p. 53, no. 194
240.1 21 6.13 MMS

Gallienus

Rome
260–268 AD antoninianus
Head r. rad. IMPGALLIENVSAVG
Pax holding transverse scepter and olive branch PAXAE-TERNAAVG N|
RIC V.1, p. 153, no. 252
241.1 19 2.70 NoEx

253–260 AD
Head r. rad. GALLIENVSAVG
Providentia with globe and transverse scepter
PROVIDAVG, no M/m
Besly and Bland 1983: 1017
242.1 19 2.49 MMS/N

260–268 AD
Bust r. rad. GALLIENVSAVG
Abundantia standing r. pouring out cornucopiae
ABVNDANTIAAVG B|pellet (or die break?)
RIC V.1, p. 144, no. 157, poss. var., M7 R 33
243.1 18 1.60 NoEx

Head r. rad. GALLIENVSAVG
Aequitas standing holding scales and cornucopiae
AEQVITASAVG
RIC V.1, p. 144, no. 159; M7 R 34
244.1 19 2.12 MMS/N
In r. field Є, not noted in RIC (poss. Antioch?)
244.2 20 1.82 MD2 No M/m
244.3 22 2.47 NoEx If M/m, obscure

As above
Centaur standing l. holding globe and rudder
APOLLINICONSAVG, in ex. N
RIC V.1, p. 145, no. 164 (sic), M7 R 37
245.1 19 2.71 MMS, H1

As above
Emperor standing with spear and patera, to r. kneeling suppliant CONSERVATPIETAT, in ex. XII
RIC V.1, p. 145, no. 171a; M7 R 39
246.1 18 2.07 MMS/S

As above
Doe standing l. with head turned back
DIANAECONSAVG, symbol in ex. unc.
RIC V.1, p. 145, no. 176
247.1 18 1.56 F49

As above
Antelope l. DIANAECONSAVG, in ex. Γ
RIC V.1, p. 146, no. 180; M7 R 41
248.1 22 2.26 MMS

As above
Jupiter standing, fulmen in r. hand IOVI PROPVGNAT XI|
RIC V.1, p. 149, no. 214 (sic)
249.1 20 2.11 MMS/S
249.2 19 broken MMS/S

As above
Hippocamp r. NEPTVNOCONSAVG, in ex. N
RIC V.1, p. 152, no. 245; M7 R 48
250.1 21 3.67 MMS, H1

As above
Providentia standing holding baton and cornucopiae, at foot, globe PROVIAVG |N
RIC V.1, p. 154, no. 267
251.1 19 2.27 HoB

As above
Securitas seated holding scepter SECVRITORBIS, in ex. VI
RIC V.1, p. 155, no. 278
252.1 23 3.27 MMS, H1

As above
Standing female with purse and cornucopiae
VBERITASAVG |Є
Besly and Bland 1983: 1200; M7 R 53
253.1 19 1.66 MMS, H1

Bust r. rad. cuir. IMPGALLIENVSAVG
Victory standing with wreath and palm VICTORIAAVG
RIC V.1, p. 157, no. 298
254.1 19 2.50 NoEx

Bust r. rad. dr. GALLIENVSAVG
Soldier standing with shield and spear VIRTVSAVG |VI
RIC V.1, p. 159, no. 325
255.1 22 4.15 NoEx

As above
Standing female holding scales (Aequitas?)AVG
256.1 22 3.19 MMS/N

253–268 AD
Bust r. rad.?, illeg. legend
Figure standing l., raising r. hand, transverse scepter in l.
Pax Aeterna Aug?
257.1 19 1.80 ByzFort

Mediolanum?
260–268 AD
Bust r. rad. cuir. dr. IMPGALLIENVSAVG
Jupiter standing with scepter and fulmen IOVISTATORI
no M/m
RIC V.1, p. 173, no. 488 var.
258.1 20 3.04 MMS/S
Variant in obv. legend; Antioch mint?

Head r. rad. GALLIENVSAVG
Pax running l. with olive branch and transverse scepter
PAXAVG |S
Besly and Bland 1983: no. 1661
259.1 20 2.87 MMS

As above
Pietas standing by altar, hands raised PIETASAVG P|
RIC V.1, p. 175, no. 507
260.1 21 2.74 NoEx

Bust r. rad. dr. cuir. GALLIENVSAVG
Victory walking l. VICTORIAAVG T|
RIC V.1, p. 176, no. 523; M7 R 59
261.1 21 3.82 NoEx

Siscia
260–268 AD
Head r. rad. GALLIENVSAVG
Fortuna holding rudder on globe and cornucopiae
FORTVNAREDVX |ς
RIC V.1, p. 181, no. 572; M7 R 61
262.1 19 2.05 MMS/N

As above
Panther walking l. LIBEROPCONSAVG, in ex. B
RIC V.1, p. 181, no. 574
263.1 21 3.01 CW32

"Asia"
260–268 AD
As above
Fortuna standing with rudder and cornucopiae
FORTVNAREDVX, in ex. SPQR
RIC V.1, p. 187, no. 637
264.1 12 3.87 NoEx, pierced middle

Probably "Asia"
260–268 AD
Bust r. rad. legend missing
Roma seated l. holding Victory and spear
ROMAEAETERN
265.1 — — BE-A, quartered

Uncertain Mint
260–268 AD
Head r. rad., illeg. legend
Standing figure ORIENSAVG
266.1 18 1.80 F49

Head r. rad. GALLIENVSAVG
Female figure standing, raising r. hand, illeg. legend
267.1 17 1.75 NoEx

253–268 AD
Bust r. laur. dr. cuir.? IMPGALLIENVSAVG
Illeg.
M7 R 65
268.1 20 4.15 MMS/S

Salonina

Siscia
259–268 AD antoninianus
Bust r. on crescent SALONINAAVG
Fortuna standing with cornucopiae and rudder,
FORTVNARED
RIC V.1, p. 199, no. 74
269.1 19 3.54 ByzFort, no M/m

Claudius II Gothicus

Rome
268–270 AD antoninianus
Bust r. rad. cuir. IMPCCLAVDIVSAVG
Standing goddess with ears of wheat and cornucopiae
ANNONAAVG
RIC V.1, p. 213, no. 18
270.1 21 2.20 MMS/N

As above
Felicitas holding caduceus and cornucopiae FELICITASAVG
RIC V.1, p. 214, no. 32 (sic)
271.1 18 2.62 NoEx
271.2 18 2.60 MMS/N
271.3 18 2.02 NoEx

Bust r. rad. cuir. IMPCLAVDIVSAVG
Felicitas holding caduceus and cornucopiae
FELICITASAVG |B
RIC V.1, p. 214, no. 33 (sic)

272.1	18	2.82	CW32

Bust r. rad. cuir. IMPCCLAVDIVSAVG
Fides holding two standards FIDESEXERCI, no M/m
RIC V.1, p. 214, no. 34

273.1	20	2.95	CW32
273.2	19	3.00	F49

Bust r. rad. cuir. IMPCLAVDIVSAVG
Fortuna holding cornucopiae and rudder FORTVNARED
RIC V.1, p. 214, no. 40

274.1	19	3.35	NoEx

Bust r. rad. cuir. IMP(C)CLAVDIVSAVG
Jupiter with fulmen and scepter IOVIVICTORI |N
RIC V.1, p. 215, no. 54 or 55

275.1	17	2.31	MMS/N

Bust r. rad. cuir. IMP(C)CLAVDIVSAVG
Libertas standing holding pileus and scepter LIBERTAVG
RIC V.1, p. 216, nos. 62–63 (sic); M7 R 80

276.1	13	0.75	MMS/S, clipped
276.2	17	1.90	MMS/S

Bust r. rad. cuir. IMPCCLAVDIVSAVG
Jupiter standing holding scepter and fulmen IOVISTATORI
RIC V.1, p. 215, no. 52

277.1	18	2.17	NoEx

Bust r. rad. cuir. IMPCLAVDIVSAVG
Pax with olive branch and transverse scepter
PAX AVGVSTI
RIC V.1, p. 217, no. 81 var. (no M/m)

278.1	19	2.80	RT

As above
Securitas leaning on small column with scepter
SECVRITAVG |XI
RIC V.1, p. 218, no. 100

279.1	22 × 16	2.22	NoEx
279.2	21	3.40	MMS/N

Bust r. rad. cuir. [IMPC?]CLAVDIVSAVG
Fortuna with cornucopiae and rudder, illeg. legend

280.1	19	2.20	MMS/N

Siscia
268–270 AD
Bust r. rad. cuir. IMPCLAVDIVSAVG
Laetitia standing holding wreath and cornucopiae
LAETITAAVG
RIC V.1, p. 226, no. 181; M7 R 85

281.1	18	2.06	MMS/N

Cyzicus
268–270 AD
Bust r. rad. cuir. IMPCLAVDIVSPFAVG
Trophy between two seated captives VICTORIAEGOTHIC, no M/m
RIC V.1, p. 233, no. 252 var.; M7 R 89

282.1	18	3.14	ByzFort
282.2	22	3.31	MMS/N

268–270 AD
Bust r. rad. cuir., legend illeg.
Illeg., in ex. SPQR

283.1	25	2.47	MMS

Smyrna
268 AD
Bust r. rad. IMPCMAVRCLAVDIVSAVG
Wolf and twins r. PMTRPOPP in ex. SPQR
Gysen 1999, p. 38; Klose 1987, not

284.1	21	4.07	MMS/S

Uncertain Mint, probably Rome
268–270 AD
Bust r. rad. IMPCLAVDIVSAVG
Standing female with cornucopiae [...]AVG (Aequitas?)
Prob. RIC V.1, p. 212, no. 14; M7 R 74

285.1	15	1.40	MMS/N

Uncertain Mint
268–270 AD
Bust r. rad. [...]CLAVDIVS
Felicitas with long caduceus and cornucopiae
FELICITTEMP

286.1	20	3.44	F49

Not in RIC, but similar found in Minster Hoard (Bland

1988), although with IMPCLAVDIVSAVG. There is no AVG or IMP after the name, though there is room for it.

253–270 AD
Bust r. rad. illeg. legend
Goddess with transverse scepter, illeg. legend

287.1	17	1.57	MMS

Bust r. rad. IMPCLAVDIVSAVG
Goddess with patera and scepter [...]G

288.1	6	frag'y	ByzFort

Bust r. rad, illeg. legend
Standing female figure, illeg. legend

289.1	15	0.87	NoEx
289.2	15	1.04	HoB
289.3	18	2.40	MMS

Bust. r. rad. IMPCLAVDIVSAVG
Female standing l. with scepter in l. and branch? in r. [...]AVG

290.1	16	1.61	MMS, clipped?
290.2	16	1.28	HoB

Bust r. rad. [IMP]CLAVD[IVSAVG]
No type?

291.1	19	frag'y	MMS

Posthumous Claudius II Gothicus

Mediolanum or Rome
270 AD and later antoninianus
Bust r. rad. DIVOCLAVDIO
Flaming altar CONSECRATIO
RIC V.1, p. 233, nos. 259–262; M7 R 93

292.1	21	2.88	MMS
292.2	18	1.45	Wadi B
292.3	17	2.09	NoEx
292.4	16	0.92	MMS/S
292.5	16	1.84	NoEx
292.6	15	1.80	RT
292.7	15	1.66	F49, H8
292.8	15	1.29	MMS/S, clipped
292.9	17	2.41	MMS
292.10	17	2.26	MMS/N
292.11	16	1.53	MMS/N
292.12	15	1.65	MMS/N
292.13	15	1.40	MMS/S

Cyzicus
270 AD and later
As above
Funeral pyre CONSECRATIO
RIC V.1, p. 234, no. 267

293.1	22	3.17	NoEx

All Mints
As above
Eagle CONSECRATIO
RIC V.1, p. 234, no. 266; M7 R 94

294.1	22	2.60	MMS
294.2	18	2.01	Tomb 07.1
294.3	17	2.46	HoB
294.4	17	2.02	Tomb 07.1
294.5	16	1.19	HoB
294.6	15	2.90	MMS/S
294.7	15	1.95	MMS/S, H2
294.8	15	1.40	MMS/S
294.9	15	1.40	NoEx
294.10	15	1.19	MMS, H1
294.11	14	1.93	AT, clipped
294.12	13	0.95	NoEx, clipped

Uncertain Mint
As above
Uncertain rev., Fortuna Redux?

295.1	14	1.11	F49

Uncertain Mints: Barbarous Radiates
Bust r. rad., nonsense legend
Aequitas holding scales and cornucopiae, nonsense legend

296.1	13	1.46	MMS

Bust r. rad. DIVOCLAVDIO or version of
Flaming altar CONSECRATIO or version of

297.1	17	1.48	ByzFort
297.2	14	1.66	MMS
297.3	14	1.39	MD2
297.4	14	0.87	HoB
297.5	13	1.10	MMS/N
297.6	12	1.10	F49, H8
297.7	12	0.74	NoEx
297.8	12	0.70	MMS/N
297.9	11	0.44	MMS/N
297.10	11	0.43	F49
297.11	—	frag'y	Tomb 07.1

Bust r. rad. DIVO CLAVDIO, or version of
Eagle standing, head turned back CONSECRATIO or version of
298.1 12 1.13 NoEx

As above
Eagle with outspread wings, CONSECRATIO or version of
299.1 16 1.33 HoB, no legend on rev.

Bust r. rad.
Standing goddess holding scepter?, no legend or nonsense legend, crude style
300.1 15 1.30 MMS/N
300.2 15 1.02 HoB
300.3 13 0.66 F49
300.4 13 0.63 HoB

Bust r. rad.
Standing figure with cornucopiae?
301.1 13 0.90 ByzFort

Bust r. rad., nonsense legend
Figure standing facing in military dress, holding scepter in r. and unc. in l. _|*, no legend
302.1 12 0.50 F55

Bust. r. rad. illeg. or nonsense legend
Figure moving l. IIII
303.1 15 0.80 MMS/N
303.2 14 1.00 ThSt

Victorinus

Cologne
269 AD antoninianus
Bust r. rad. dr. IMPCVICTORINVSPFAVG (RIC has bust l.)
Pax holding olive branch and transverse scepter PAXAVG V|*
RIC V.2, p. 397, no. 118 var.
304.1 22 3.20 MMS/N

Quintillus

Rome
270 AD antoninianus
Bust r. rad. IMPCMAVRCLQVINTILLVSAVG
Aeternitas rad. raises r. hand and holds globe in l. AETERNITAVG _|N
RIC V.1, p. 240, no. 7
305.1 20 2.80 NoEx

270 AD
As above
Fortuna holding cornucopiae and rudder FORTVNAREDVX _|Z
RIC V.1, p. 241, no. 20
306.1 21 1.84 NoEx

Tetricus I

Trier
271–274 AD antoninianus
Bust r. rad. IMPCTETRICVSAV(G)
Aequitas holding scales and cornucopiae AEQVITAS AVG
RIC V.2, p. 406, no. 52
307.1 16 1.41 NoEx

Bust r. rad. IMPTETRICVSPFAVG
Pax standing sacrificing at altar, nothing in l. hand PAXAG
RIC V.2, p. 409, no. 109 var.
308.1 15 0.89 NoEx
Pax without perfume box; rev. legend

Bust r. rad IMP[...]
Laetitia? Holding wreath? and scepter/baton [...]ITE(?)
309.1 14 1.54 Wadi B

Tetricus II

Trier
273–274 AD antoninianus
Bust r. rad. CPE(S)TETRICVSCAES
Spes holding up r. hand and holding dress with l. SPESPVBLICA
RIC V.2, p. 424, no. 272
310 .1 18 2.65 NoEx

Aurelian

Rome
273–274 AD denarius
Bust r. laur. IMP[C]AVRELIANVSAVG
Victory l. with wreath and palm, captive by feet VICTORIAAVG, in ex. A
RIC V.1, p. 273, nos. 72–73
311.1 18 2.10 ByzFort
Note redating of Greenewalt et al. 1990, p. 155 n. 32

275 AD antoninianus
Bust r. rad. IMPCLDOMAVRELIANVSAVG
Fortuna holding rudder and cornucopiae FORTVNAREDVX
RIC V.1, p. 269, no. 29
312.1 17 2.40 NoEx

Cyzicus

270–275 AD antoninianus

Bust r. rad. IMPAVRELIANVSAVG

Genius holding patera and cornucopiae, to r. standard GENIVS EXERCITI

RIC V.1, p. 304, no. 345

313.1	20	3.23	PA
313.2	19	3.65	RT

Uncertain Mint

270–275 AD

Bust r. rad. IMPCDOMAVRELIANVSAVG

Obscure

314.1	18	3.19	MMS/S

Severina

Ticinum

270–275 AD antoninianus

Bust r. diadem, on crescent SEVERINAAVG

Concordia holding two ensigns CONCORDIAEMILITVM

RIC V.1, p. 316, no. 8

315.1	22	4.00	MMS/N, in ex. QXXT
315.2	24	3.10	MMS, H1, in ex. SXXT

Tacitus

Rome

275–276 AD antoninianus

Bust r. rad. IMPCMCLTACITVSAVG

Laetitia holding wreath and rudder LAETITIAEFVND, ex. miss.

RIC V.1, p. 335, no. 89

316.1	17	1.90	MMS

Probus

Rome

276–282 AD antoninianus

Bust r. rad. IMPPROBVSAVG

Roma seated in a hexastyle temple ROMAE AETER, in ex. R wreath Γ

RIC V.2, p. 37, no. 185

317.1	23	3.28	MMS/S

Siscia

276–282 AD

Bust l. rad. IMPCMAVRPROBVSPFAVG

Pax holding olive branch and scepter PAXAVG, in ex. XXIP

RIC V.2, p. 92, no. 704

318.1	22	3.30	MMS

Carinus

Antioch

282–283 AD antoninianus

Bust r. rad. IMPCMAVRCARINVSNOBC

Jupiter handing Victoriola to emperor VIRTVSAVGGG, between Δ, in ex. XXI

RIC V.2, p. 164, no. 208 var.

319.1	23	3.87	NoEx

RIC does not list this off. for Antioch, but similar found in trade.

Uncertain Mint

283–285 AD

Bust r. rad. dr. MCARINVSAVG

Aequitas standing with cornucopiae and scales AEQVITASAVG VI|VI , nothing in ex.

RIC not

320.1	22	2.79	HoB

Uncertain Ruler

Uncertain Mint

250–300 AD antoninianus

Bust r. rad.

Standing goddess with scepter

321.1	19	3.36	MMS/N

Bust r. rad.?

Standing figure with cornucopiae

322.1	24	3.44	NoEx

Bust r. rad.

Standing goddess with scepter

323.1	19	1.54	MMS/S

Bust r. rad.

Illeg.

M7 R 1113

324.1	14	1.43	MMS
324.2	14	1.07	Wadi B

Bust r. rad. CA[…]

Sol holding whip […]IV[…] S|

325.1	17	2.13	Tomb 07.1

Illeg.

326.1	20	frag'y	CW32

Diocletian

Heraclea

295–296 AD fraction

Bust r. rad. IMPCCVALDIOCLETIANVSPFAVG

Jupiter handing emperor Victoriola, M/m between

CONCORDIA MILITVM

RIC VI, p. 531, no. 13; M7 R 108

327.1	HA	22	3.10	MMS/N
327.2	HB	23	2.40	MMS/N
327.3	HB	21	1.70	MMS/S
327.4	HΔ	22	2.90	MMS/N
327.5	HΔ	21	3.58	F49
327.6	HЄ	21	3.36	MMS/N
327.7	HЄ	20	3.15	MMS
327.8	HЄ	20	2.95	NoEx

Cyzicus

295–299 AD

Bust r. rad. IMPCCDIOCLETIANVSPFAVG

Jupiter handing emperor Victoriola, M/m between

CONCORDIA MILITVM

RIC VI, p. 581, no. 16a; M7 R 109

328.1	KA	21	2.77	HoB
328.2	KΓ	21	2.64	NoEx
328.3	KΓ	22	2.80	MMS/N

Uncertain Mint fraction?

Bust r. rad. […]IO[…]

Illeg. rev.

329.1		18	3.50	ByzFort

Maximian Herculius

Heraclea

295–298 AD fraction

Bust r. rad. cuir. IMPCMAVALMAXIMIANVSPFAVG

Jupiter handing Victoriola to emperor, M/m between

CONCORDIA MILITVM

RIC VI, p. 531, nos. 14, 22; M7 R 113

330.1	HΔ	21	2.71	AT-Pac
330.2	HЄ	22	3.47	HoB

Cyzicus

295–299 AD

Bust r. rad. cuir. (dr.) IMPCMAMAXIMIANVSPFAVG

Jupiter handing Victory to emperor, M/m between

CONCORDIA MILITVM

RIC VI, p. 581, nos. 15b, 16b; M7 R 115, 116

331.1	KA	22	2.62	MMS
331.2	KB	22	3.26	HoB
331.3	KB	22	2.40	MMS/N
331.4	KΔ	23	2.67	MMS/N
331.5	KΔ	21	2.20	NoEx
331.6	KΔ	20	3.20	RT
331.7	KЄ	22	3.30	MMS/N
331.8	KЄ?	20	2.48	MMS

Uncertain Mint

291–310 AD

Bust r. rad. IMPCMAMAXIMIANVSPFAVG

Illeg.

332.1		19	1.61	MMS

Pierced for suspension, so emperor's head is upright

295–299 AD

Bust r. rad. IMPCM[…]ANVSPFAVG

Jupiter handing Victoriola to emperor

CONCORDIA MILITVM, all M/m missing

333.1		19	1.91	MMS

Galerius Maximian

Thessalonica

302–303 AD follis

Bust r. laur. GALVALMAXIMIANVSNOBCAES

Genius with cornucopiae and patera

GENIO POPVLI ROMANI, in r. field Γ, in ex. • TS •

RIC VI, p. 513, no. 26

334.1		28	9.38	MMS/N

Heraclea

293–305 AD fraction

Bust r. rad. GALVALMAXIMIANVSNOBCAES

Jupiter hands Victoriola to emperor, M/m between

CONCORDIA MILITVM

RIC VI, p. 531, no. 16; M7 R 121

335.1	HA	21	2.32	MMS/N
335.2	HΓ	22	3.64	NoEx

305–307 AD follis

Bust r. laur. IMPCGALVALMAXIMIANVSPFAVG

Genius with patera and cornucopiae

GENIO POPVLI ROMANI, in ex. HTB

RIC VI, p. 533, no. 24b or 30

336.1		27	6.78	MMS, pierced for suspension

309–310 AD follis
As above
Genius standing GENIO IMPERATORIS, in ex. HTB
RIC VI, p. 535, no. 41

337.1	23	7.09	AT

Cyzicus
295–299 AD light fraction
Bust r. rad. GALVALMAXIMIANVSNOBCAES
Jupiter hands Victoriola to emperor, KA between
CONCORDIA MILITVM
RIC VI, p. 581, no. 18b; M7 R 122

338.1	23	2.98	MMS
338.2	22	2.38	MMS/S
338.3	22	2.54	HoB

295–299 AD fraction
Bust r. rad. dr. cuir. GALVALMAXIMIANVSNOBCAES
Jupiter hands Victoriola to emperor
CONCORDIA MILITVM, KA between
RIC VI, p. 581, no. 19b; M7 R 123

339.1	22	2.50	MMS/N

Constantius Chlorus

Heraclea
295–296 AD fraction
Bust r. rad. FLVALCONSTANTIVSNOBCAES
Jupiter hands Victoriola to emperor, M/m between
CONCORDIA MILITVM
RIC VI, p. 531, no. 15

340.1	HB	21	3.23	MMS/S
340.2	HЄ	22	4.49	MMS/N

Cyzicus
295–299 AD light fraction
As above
Jupiter hands Victoriola to emperor, KB between
CONCORDIA MILITVM
RIC VI, p. 581, no. 18a; M7 R 126

341.1	24	3.68	MMS
341.2	22	3.33	Wadi B
341.3	21	3.08	NoEx
341.4	20	2.90	MMS/N

Maximinus Daia

Trier
312–313 AD follis
Bust r. laur. MAXIMINVSPFAVG
Mars standing with spear MARS CONSERVATORI, in ex. PT
RIC VI, p. 298, no. 123a

342.1	23	4.23	MMS

Antioch
311–312 AD follis
Bust r. laur. IMPCGALVALMAXINVSPFAVG
Genius standing GENIO AVGVSTI *|Γ, in ex. ANT
RIC VI, p. 642, no. 162b

343.1	21	4.44	AT

Licinius I

Rome
314–315 fraction
Bust r. laur. DNLICINIVSPFAVG
Sol standing with globe SOLI INVICTO COMITI RX|F
RIC VII, p. 299, no. 30

344.1	21	3.10	MMS/N
344.2	20	2.24	MMS

Siscia
313 AD follis
Bust r. rad. IMPLICLICINIVSPFAVG
Jupiter standing with Victoriola and scepter, at l. eagle IOVI CONSERVATORI _|Δ, in ex. SIS
RIC VI, p. 484, no. 230a

345.1	20	3.23	MMS/N

Heraclea
313 AD follis
Bust r. laur. IMPCLVALLICINLICINIVSPFAVG
Jupiter standing with Victoriola and scepter, at l. eagle IOVI CONSERVATORI _|Γ, in ex. SMHT
RIC VI, p. 541, no. 73

346.1	21	2.70	MMS

318–320 AD follis
Bust l. laur. cuir. with globe, scepter, mappa
IMPLICINIVSAVG
Camp-gate, three towers PROVIDENTIAE AVGG _|Δ, in ex. MHTB
RIC VII, p. 544, no. 16 note

347.1	23	3.82	MMS/N

318–320 AD follis
Bust r. laur. dr. with globe, scepter, mappa
IMPLICINIVSAVG
Camp-gate, three towers PROVIDENTIAE AVGG _|Δ,
in ex. SMHΓ
RIC VII, p. 547, no. 49 (sic)

348.1		20	2.40	MMS

RIC VII wrongly describes as bust l.

321–324 AD follis
Bust r. rad. cuir. IMPCVALLICINLICINIVSPFAVG
Jupiter standing with Victoriola and scepter to l. eagle, to r. captive IOVI CONSERVATORI in r. field X/IIΓ, in ex., M/m
RIC VII, p. 548, no. 52; M7 R 141

349.1	SMHA	20	3.54	MMS/N
349.2	SMHB	20	3.30	NoEx
349.3	unc.	19	3.03	MMS/N

Nicomedia
313–317 AD follis
Bust r. laur. IMPCVALLICINLICINIVSPFAVG
Jupiter standing with Victoriola and scepter, to l. eagle IOVI CONSERVATORI, in r. field off. letter, in ex. SMN
RIC VII, p. 601, no. 13; M7 R 142

350.1	A	20	2.42	F55
350.2	Γ	21	2.31	MMS
350.3	Є	20	3.95	MMS/N

321–324 AD follis
As above
Jupiter standing with Victoriola and scepter, to l. eagle, to r. captive, IOVI CONSERVATORI, in r. field X/IIΓ, in ex. SMN with officina letter
RIC VII, p. 607, no. 44; M7 R 145

351.1	A	19	2.00	MMS/N
351.2	A	20	3.50	MMS/S
351.3	A'	17	2.98	NoEx
351.4	B	23	3.25	MMS/N
351.5	B	19	2.80	ThSt
351.6	Γ	20	2.90	MMS
351.7	Γ	20	2.69	MMS
351.8	Δ	19	3.51	Tomb 07.1

Cyzicus
313–315 AD follis
Brockage
Jupiter standing with Victoriola and scepter IOVI CONSERVATORI to l. eagle _|Δ, in ex. SMK
RIC VII, p. 643, nos. 3–4; M7 R 146

352.1		20	2.91	Church EA

321–324 AD follis
Bust r. rad. IMPCVALLICINLICINIVSPFAVG
Jupiter standing, eagle and one captive
IOVI CONSERVATORI in r. field X/IIΓ,
in ex. SMN with off.
RIC VII, p. 645, no. 15; M7 R 147

353.1	A	29	3.05	MMS/N
353.2	A	20	2.30	PA
353.3	A	19	3.09	MD1/S
353.4	A	19	2.00	MMS/N
353.5	B	20	2.47	MMS/N
353.6	B	19	3.65	ThSt
353.7	Δ	20	1.31	NoEx
353.8	A or Δ	20	2.67	MMS/S

Antioch
317–320 AD follis
Bust l. laur. IMPLICINIVSAVG
Jupiter standing, to l. captive IOVI CONSERVATORI _|S,
in ex. SMANT
RIC VII, p. 680, no. 27

354.1		19	2.63	NoEx

Uncertain Mint
308–324 AD follis
Bust r. laur. IMPCVALLICINLICINIVSPFAVG
Sol standing SOLI INVICTO COMITI

355.1		25	2.90	MMS

Bust r. laur. DNLICINIVSPFAVG
Jupiter standing with Victoriola, to l. eagle IOVI CONSERVATORI

356.1		20	3.43	NoEx

Bust r. laur. IMPCLICINIVSPFAVG
Jupiter standing with Victoriola, to l. eagle to r. captive IOVI CONSERVATORI, in r. field X/IIΓ

357.1		20	1.59	F55

Bust r. laur. cuir. IMPLICI-NIVSPFAVG
Jupiter standing with fulmen
IOVI CONSERVATORI, in r. field obscure mark

358.1		17	2.20	MMS/S

Bust l. laur. cuir. IMP[...]LICINIVS[...]
Camp-gate PROVIDENTIAE[....]

359.1		19	2.08	NoEx

LICINIUS II

Heraclea
321–324 AD fraction
Bust l. helm. cuir. spear, shield DNVALLICINIVSNOBC
Jupiter standing holding Victoriola and scepter, to l. eagle, to r. captive IOVI CONSERVATORI, in r. field X/IIΓ, in ex. SMH and officina number
RIC VII, p. 548, no. 54

360.1	A	20	3.07	MMS/N
360.2	A	18	3.00	MMS/N
360.3	B	19	2.57	MMS

Nicomedia
321–324 AD follis
As above
Jupiter standing with eagle and one captive
IOVI CONSERVATORI, in r. field X/IIΓ, in ex. SMNA
RIC VII, p. 608, no. 49; M7 R 154

361.1		28	2.21	MMS/S
361.2		21	3.50	MMS/N

Cyzicus
317–320 AD follis
Bust l. laur. with globe or scepter, mappa (large bust)
DNVALLICINLICINIVSNOBC
Jupiter standing with Victoriola IOVI CONSERVATORI CAESS <u>wreath|B</u>, in ex. SMK
RIC VII, p. 644, no. 11; M7 R 157

362.1		20	3.60	HoB

Antioch
321–323 AD follis
Bust r. helm., cuir., spear, shield
DNVALLICINLICINIVSNOBC
Jupiter standing, eagle and one captive
IOVI CONSERVATORI, in r. field X/IIΓ, in ex. SMANTA
RIC VII, p. 682, no. 36

363.1		21	2.61	MMS/S

CONSTANTINE I

Londinium
321 AD follis
Bust r. laur. cuir. with eagle-tipped scepter
CONSTANTINVSAVG
Altar with inscription VOT/IS/XX
BEATA TRA *** NQVILLITAS <u>P|A</u>, in ex. PLON
RIC VII, p. 110, no. 205

364.1		19	3.20	HoB

Arelate
322–323 AD
Bust r. laur. CONSTANTINVSAVG
VOT/XX in wreath DN CONSTANTINI MAX AVG, in ex. P*AR
RIC VII, p. 261, no. 252

365.1		20	3.20	MMS/S

Ticinum
319–320 AD
Bust r. helm. CONSTANTINVSAVG
Standard inscribed VOT/XX between two captives
VIRTVS EXERCIT, in ex. PT
RIC VII, p. 376, no. 114

366.1		20	2.70	MMS

Trier
315–316 AD
Bust r. laur. CONSTANTINVSPFAVG
Sol standing with globe SOLI INVICTO COMITI <u>B|S</u>
RIC VII, p. 170, no. 76

367.1		19	2.81	AT-Pac

Rome
313–319 AD
Bust r. laur. IMPCONSTANTINVSPFAVG
Sol standing with globe SOLI INVICTO COMITI <u>R|F</u>, in ex. R*P
RIC VII, p. 298, no. 18

368.1		23	3.41	MMS/N

313 AD
As above
Sol standing with globe SOLI INVICTO COMITI <u>R|F</u>, in ex. R*S
RIC VII, p. 298, no. 19

369.1		19	2.80	NoEx

314–315 AD
As above
Sol standing with globe SOLI INVICTO COMITI in l. field R/X, in ex. M/m, in r. field F
RIC VII, p. 299, no. 27

370.1	RP	21	2.23	MMS
370.2	RQ	19	2.17	HoB

314–315 AD
Bust r. laur. cuir. IMPCONSTANTINVSPFAVG
Sol standing with globe SOLI INVICTO COMITI _|F, in ex. RT
RIC VII, p. 299, no. 28 or 34

371.1		20	2.18	MMS

Siscia
313–315 AD
Bust r. laur. IMPCONSTANTINVSPFAVG
Jupiter standing with Victoriola and scepter, at l. eagle
IOVI CONSERVATORI _|A, in ex. SIS
RIC VII, p. 423, no. 5 or 7

372.1		21	frag'y	NoEx

315–316 AD
As above
Jupiter standing holding Victoriola and scepter, to l. eagle
IOVI CONSERVATORI _|Δ, in ex. •SIS•
RIC VII, p. 424, no. 15

373.1		21	3.40	MMS/N

318 AD
Bust r. helm. laur. IMPCONSTANTINVSPFAVG
Two Victories supporting shield inscribed VOT PR over altar decorated with *, VICTORIAE LAETAE PRINC PERP, in ex. ASIS*
RIC VII, p. 431, no. 47

374.1		18	1.89	MMS/N

Heraclea
317–320 AD
Bust l. laur., holding mappa and scepter IMPCONSTANTINVSAVG
Camp-gate, three towers PROVIDENTIAE AVGGG, in ex. [.]H[..]
RIC VII, p. 544, no. 16 or 38

375.1		20	3.20	MMS/N

Nicomedia
311–313 AD
Bust r. laur. IMPCFLVALCONSTANTINVSPFAVG
Jupiter standing with Victoriola and scepter, to l. eagle
IOVI CONSERVATORI _|B, in ex. SMN
RIC VI, p. 566, no. 69c

376.1		22	2.26	MMS/N

Cyzicus
317–320 AD follis
Bust l. helm. laur. with scepter IMPCONSTANTINVSAVG
Jupiter standing with Victoriola and scepter
IOVI CONSERVATORI AVGG wreath|Δ, in ex. SMK
RIC VII, p. 644, no. 8

377.1		20	3.40	Wadi B

329–330 AD
Bust r. laur. CONSTANTINVSAVG
Camp-gate with two towers, star above
PROVIDENTIAE AVGG, in ex. SMK, officina number
RIC VII, p. 652, no. 59; M7 R 193

378.1	Γ	19	3.26	AT
378.2	S	19	2.71	MMS

Uncertain Mint
306–320 AD
Bust r. helm. cuir. IMPCONSTANTINVSPFAVG
Two Victories supporting shield inscribed VOTPR on altar of uncertain decoration

379.1		18	1.80	MMS/N

316–320 AD
Illeg. […]VALC[…]
Jupiter standing with Victoriola and scepter and eagle
IOVI CONSERVATORI

380.1		20	frag'y	MMS

Crispus

Arelate
321 AD follis
Bust r. laur. CRISPVSNOBCAES
VOT/V in laurel wreath CAESARVM NOSTRORVM, in ex. A crescent Q
RIC VII, p. 260, no. 235

381.1		19	3.20	MMS/S

Cyzicus
317–320 AD follis
Bust l. laur. DNFLIVLCRISPVSNOBCAESS
Jupiter standing with Victoriola and scepter
IOVI CONSERVATORI CAESS wreath|A, in ex. SMK
RIC VII, p. 644, no. 10

382.1	17	3.23	MMS/N

Uncertain Mint
317–326 AD
Bust r. laur. CRISPVSNOBCAES
Emperor standing in military gear
PRINCIPI IVVENNTVTIS

383.1	18	3.30	MMS/N

Constantine II

Lugdunum
320 AD
Bust r. laur. cuir., seen from back
CONSTANTINVSIVNNOBC (no breaks)
Two Victories facing each other holding shield inscribed VOT/PR, over altar VICTORIAE LAETAE PRINC PERP, in ex. P two bound captives L
RIC VII, p. 128, no. 90 var.

384.1	20	1.90	MMS

Variant in obverse legend; in RIC VII, p. 127 n. 77 the author suggests that the previous recording of the legend from Finland (Imajoki Collection) is in error, but now can be seen it is not.

Uncertain Emperor
(Licinius or House of Constantine)

Cyzicus
308–330 AD
Bust l. laur. cuir., illeg. legend
Camp-gate PROVIDENTIAE…. in ex. SMKA

385.1	23	frag'y	ByzFort

Uncertain Mint
308–330 AD
Bust r.
Camp-gate

386.1	18	2.30	NoEx

200–330 AD unc. antoninianus or follis

387.1	18	2.02	NoEx
Bust r./IOVI CONSERVATORI			
387.2	20	4.01	MMS/S
Bust r./IOVI CONSERVATORI			
387.3	20	4.40	MMS/S
Illeg./IOVI CONSERVATORI			
387.4	23	4.56	HoB
Bust r./IOVI CONSERVATORI			
387.5	15	1.68	MMS
Bust r./Jupiter standing with Victoriola			
387.6	20	2.40	Wadi B
IMP[…] /[SOLI INVICTO COM]ITI			
387.7	23	3.81	EH
387.8	23	3.32	MMS/N
387.9	22	3.26	HoB
387.10	22	frag'y	MMS
387.11	21	4.71	MMS/N
387.12	21	4.03	MMS
387.13	21	3.91	MMS
387.14	21	3.69	NoEx
387.15	21	3.31	MMS/S
387.16	20	3.65	MMS/N
387.17	20	2.45	HoB
387.18	20	frag'y	MMS/N
387.19	19	3.63	F49
387.20	19	3.63	Church EA
387.21	19	3.00	MMS/S
387.22	19	2.56	MMS/N
387.23	17	frag'y	MMS/N
387.24	—	frag'y	F55

Late Roman Coins (324–491)

Unless stated, coins are copper alloy and obverses show an emperor bust r. pearl-diademed, cuirassed, draped. The specific entries list the mintmark (when relevant), diameter, weight, and sector. For fuller description of reverse types, see Table of Reverse Descriptions, Appendix 3. For monogram types, see Table App. 1.1. Note that all officinae Es are rendered on coins as Є.

324–348 AD, ALL FOLLES

Constantine I

Heraclea

336–337 AD
RIC VII, p. 561, no. 150
Bust laur. CONSTANTINVSMAXAVG
Gloria Exercitus 1 standard

388.1	SMHΓ	15	1.64	F49

325–326 AD
RIC VII, p. 550, no. 69
Head laur. CONSTANTINVSAVG
Vot XXX

389.1	SMHA	18	1.63	F49, unc. obv.
389.2	SMHB	18	1.88	MMS/N

Constantinople

327–328 AD
RIC VII, p. 572, no. 16
Head laur. CONSTANTINVSMAXAVG
Gloria Exercitus emperor standing, in l. field off. letter, CONSΓ

390.1		19	1.48	F55
390.2		16	frag'y	MMS/S
390.3		14	1.20	NoEx
390.4		14	frag'y	MMS/N

330–333 AD
RIC VII, p. 579, no. 59; M7 R 177
CONSTANTINVSMAXAVG
Gloria Exercitus 2 standards

391.1	CONSH	18	1.92	MMS/S

333–335 AD
RIC VII, p. 581, no. 73; M7 R 178
As above

392.1	CONSH•	18	2.10	MMS/N

330–335 AD
As above, but uncertain M/m

393.1	CONS[..]	18	1.48	MMS/N
393.2	CONS[..]	15	1.20	MMS/S

336–337 AD
RIC VII, p. 589, no. 137; M7 R 180
Bust rd. CONSTANTINVSMAXAVG
Gloria Exercitus 1 standard

394.1	CONSA	16	1.10	MMS/S
394.2	CONS[.]	16	1.36	Tomb 07.1

Constantinople?

327–328 AD
RIC VII, pp. 572–73, nos. 18, 25
Bust r. pd., illeg. legend
Libertas Pvblica?

395.1	—	16	1.72	MMS/N
395.2	—	15	1.40	NoEx

Nicomedia

324–325 AD
RIC VII, p. 615, no. 90; M7 R 185
Head laur. CONSTANTINVSAVG
Providentiae Augg

396.1	SMNA	17	1.96	MD2
396.2	SMNA	21	3.28	F55

328–329 AD
RIC VII, p. 625, nos. 153, 155; M7 R 188
Head pd. or rd. CONSTANTINVSAVG
Providentiae Augg

397.1	SMNA	—	—	NoEx
397.2	SMNA or Δ	17	2.68	NoEx

330–335 AD
RIC VII, p. 633, no. 188; M7 R 189
Bust rd. CONSTANTINVSMAXAVG
Gloria Exercitus 2 standards

398.1	SMNA	19	2.54	MMS/N
398.2	SMNA	17	2.30	MMS/N
398.3	SMNA	17	2.38	MMS/N
398.4	SMNA	19	2.58	NoEx
398.5	SMNB	17	2.11	NoEx
398.6	SMNΓ	19	1.90	NoEx
398.7	SMNE	18	2.40	MMS/N

336–337 AD
RIC VII, p. 635, no. 199; M7 R 190
As above
Gloria Exercitus 1 standard

399.1	SMNB	16	1.44	PA
399.2	SMNB	16	1.35	MMS
399.3	SMN[.]	15	1.59	MD1/S

337–340 AD
RIC VIII, p. 471, no. 7
Head laur. rd. DNCONSTANTINVSPFAVG
Gloria Exercitus 1 standard

400.1	SMNA	18	2.30	RT

Cyzicus
324–325 AD
RIC VII, p. 647, no. 24
Head laur. CONSTANTINVSAVG
Providentiae Augg

401.1	SMKA	20	3.30	MMS/N
401.2	SMKB	20	2.94	HoB
401.3	SMKΔ	21	2.70	MMS/N
401.4	SMKΔ	21	3.40	NoEx

329–330 AD
RIC VII, p. 652, no. 59; M7 R 193
Bust laur. CONSTANTINVSMAXAVG
Providentiae Augg

402.1	SMK[.]	18	3.30	NoEx

330–333 AD
RIC VII, p. 655, no. 77; M7 R 194
As above
Gloria Exercitus 2 standards

403.1	SMK[.]	17	2.18	NoEx

336–337 AD
RIC VII, p. 659, no. 122
Bust laur. rd. CONSTANTINVSMAXAVG
Gloria Exercitus 1 standard

404.1	SMKA	17	1.41	AT
404.2	SMK[.]	16	1.36	MMS

Antioch
325–326 AD
RIC VII, p. 688, no. 63
Head laur. CONSTANTINVSAVG
Providentiae Augg

405.1	SMANTΓ	19	3.70	MMS/S

335 AD
RIC VII, p. 693, no. 86; M7 R 199
Bust rd. CONSTANTINVSMAXAVG
Gloria Exercitus 2 standards

406.1	SMANA	18	2.30	NoEx

335–337 AD
RIC VII, p. 697, no. 108; M7 R 200
As above
Gloria Exercitus 1 standard

407.1	SMANB	14	1.79	Tomb 07.1
407.2	SMAN[.]	15	1.65	Wadi B

Alexandria
337–340 AD
RIC VIII, p. 539, no. 13
Bust laur. CONSTANTINVSMAXAVG
Gloria Exercitus 1 standard

408.1	SMALA	15	1.87	MMS/N

Uncertain Mint
324–329 AD
Head laur. CONSTANTINVSAVG
Providentiae Augg

409.1		18	2.41	MMS/N

330–335 AD
M7 R 205
Bust rd. CONSTANTINVSMAXAVG
Gloria Exercitus 2 standards

410.1		18	2.20	NoEx

Constantine I, Posthumous

Constantinople
337–340 AD
RIC VIII, p. 450, no. 39; M7 R 211
Quadriga

411.1	CONS[.]	16	1.11	ByzFort
411.2	CONS[.]	15	1.17	MMS/S

342 AD
RIC VIII, p. 452, no. 62; M7 R 212
Ivst Ven Mem

412.1	CON[..]	14	1.23	MMS/S

347–348 AD
RIC VIII, p. 453, no. 68; M7 R 213
VN MR

413.1	CONSΓ	15	1.20	HoB
413.2	CONS[.]	19	1.60	MMS

Nicomedia
337–340 AD
RIC VIII, p. 472, no. 18; M7 R 214
Quadriga

414.1	SMNA	16	1.30	F49
414.2	SMNA	16	1.80	MMS/N

347–348 AD
RIC VIII, p. 474, nos. 48, 57; M7 R 216, 218
VN MR

415.1	SMNB	15	2.03	HoB
415.2	SMNΘ•	15	1.28	MMS/N
415.3	SMN[.]	15	1.30	PN/E
415.4	SMN[.]	14	1.40	MMS/S, H2

Cyzicus
337–340 AD
RIC VIII, p. 490, no. 4ff; M7 R 219–221
Quadriga

416.1	SMK[.]	15	1.57	NoEx

342–347 AD
RIC VIII, p. 491, no. 35
Ivst Ven Mem

417.1	SMKA	16	1.62	HoB

347–348 AD
RIC VIII, p. 493, no. 46; M7 R 222
VN MR

418.1	SMKA	14	1.08	MMS/N
418.2	SMKB	15	1.19	NoEx
418.3	SMKE	15	1.57	NoEx
418.4	SMKH	14	1.57	NoEx
418.5	SMK[.]	16	1.21	HoB
418.6	SMK[.]	15	1.81	HoB, clipped
418.7	SMK[.]	14	1.31	MMS/N

Alexandria
347–348 AD
RIC VIII, p. 541, no. 41
VN MR

419.1	SMALΓ*	15	1.10	HoB

Antioch or Alexandria
341–346 AD
VN MR

420.1	SMA[...]	17	1.74	F55

Uncertain Eastern Mint
337–340 AD
M7 R 231
Quadriga

421.1		17	1.13	MMS
421.2		15	1.97	MMS
421.3		14	1.97	MMS
421.4		14	1.45	MMS/N
421.5		—	frag'y	MMS/N

337–347 AD
M7 R 232
Ivst Ven Mem

422.1		19	2.40	MMS/N
422.2		13	0.85	MMS/N

347–348 AD
M7 R 233
VN MR

423.1		17	1.38	HoB
423.2		16	1.29	Wadi B
423.3		15	1.67	MMS/N
423.4		15	1.54	MMS/N
423.5		15	1.52	HoB
423.6		15	1.46	NoEx
423.7		15	1.32	Wadi B
423.8		15	0.95	MMS
423.9		15	0.95	MMS/N
423.10		14	1.66	F55
423.11		12	0.93	F49, clipped?
423.12		—	frag'y	HoB

Helena

Constantinople
330 AD
RIC VIII, p. 449, no. 34, M7 R 236
Pax Publica

424.1	CONS[E]	15	1.39	NoEx

Alexandria
325–326 AD
RIC VII, p. 709, no. 38
Securitas Reipublice

425.1	SMAL[.]	19	2.98	Syn

Uncertain Mint
324–330 AD
Standing goddess

426.1		11	0.97	F49, clipped, H8

330–340 AD
Pax Publica

427.1		13	1.29	Tomb 07.1
427.2		12	0.63	MMS/N, clipped

324–340 AD
Uncertain rev.

428.1		16	2.15	MMS/N

Urbs Roma

Thessalonica
330–333 AD
RIC VII, p. 524, no. 187
Wolf and twins

429.1	SMTSE	18	2.20	MMS/N

Heraclea
333–336 AD
RIC VII, p. 560, no. 143; M7 R 239
As above

430.1	SMHE*	18	2.02	MMS

330–337 AD
RIC VII, p. 557, no. 114, M7 R 239–242
As above

431.1	SMH[.]	19	1.80	MMS/N

336–337 AD
RIC VII, p. 561, no. 156; M7 R 243
Gloria Exercitus 1 standard

432.1	SMHA	15	1.71	MMS/N
432.2	SMHB	18	1.58	ByzFort

Constantinople
330–333 AD
RIC VII, p. 579, no. 62
Wolf and twins

433.1	CONS[.]	18	2.75	Wadi B

337–340 AD
RIC VIII, p. 450, no. 46
Gloria Exercitus 1 standard

434.1	CONSE	13	1.18	ByzFort

Alexandria
337–340 AD
RIC VIII, p. 539, no. 16
Wolf and twins

435.1	SMALA[•?]	17	2.08	ByzFort

RIC VIII, p. 540, no. 24, with dot after officina letter; note mentions unpublished Sardis excavations.

Uncertain Mint
330–340 AD
As above

436.1		19	2.09	MMS
436.2		18	2.25	MMS/N
436.3		18	1.30	MMS/S
436.4		15	1.29	HoB

336–340 AD
Gloria Exercitus 1 standard

437.1		14	1.20	MMS/N
437.2		—	frag'y	MMS/N

Ancient copy of Urbs Roma/wolf and twins

438.1		13	0.98	MMS/N

Constantinopolis

Heraclea
330–333 AD
RIC VII, p. 557, no. 115
Victory on prow

439.1	SMHA	20	1.87	MMS/N

Constantinople
330–333 AD
RIC VII, p. 579, no. 63; M7 R 257
As above

440.1	CONSIA	18	2.42	MMS/N
440.2	CONSZ	18	2.20	MMS/S
440.3	CONSZ	17	2.16	NoEx
440.4	CONS[.]	17	2.10	MMS/N

Nicomedia
330–335 AD
RIC VII, p. 634, no. 196
As above

441.1	SMNA	18	2.22	MMS/S, H2
441.2	SMNΔ	18	2.22	MMS/N

Cyzicus
332–335 AD
RIC VII, p. 657, no. 108
As above

442.1	SMKA	17	1.90	NoEx
442.2	SMKΓ	19	2.29	NoEx

Uncertain Mint
330–340 AD
M7 R 263
As above

443.1		19	2.42	MMS
443.2		15	1.10	MMS/N
443.3		9x11	frag'y	MMS/S, H2

Crispus

Cyzicus
324–325 AD
RIC VII, p. 647, no. 25
Bust laur. l. FLIVLCRISPVSNOBCAES
Providentiae Caess, SMKB
444.1 19 3.63 F49

Constantine II

Rome
337–340 AD
RIC VIII, p. 249, no. 4
Bust laur. and rd. VICCONSTANTINVSAVG
Virtus Augusti
445.1 14 1.70 F49, clipped, H8
445.2 12 1.35 MMS/S, H2, i.d. poss.

Thessalonica
330–333 AD
RIC VII, p. 524, no. 184; M7 R 272
Bust laur. CONSTANTINVSIVNNOBC
Gloria Exercitus 2 standards, SMTSB
446.1 18 2.10 MMS

Heraclea
325–326 AD
RIC VII, p. 551, no. 77
Bust laur. CONSTANTINVSIVNNOBC
Providentiae Caess, SMHΓ
447.1 17 3.66 MMS/N

337–340 AD
RIC VIII, p. 431, no. 15
Bust laur. CONSTANTINVSAVG
Gloria Exercitus 1 standard, SMHA
448.1 15 1.47 MMS/N

Constantinople
327 AD
RIC VII, p. 572, no. 20
Bust laur. CONSTANTINVSIVNNOBC
Providentiae Caess Γ|_, CONS
449.1 20 3.05 MMS

330–333 AD
RIC VII, p. 579, no. 60; M7 R 279
As above
Gloria Exercitus 2 standards
450.1 CONSΘ 17 1.95 NoEx
450.2 CONSΘ 21 2.75 ByzFort

333–335 AD
RIC VII, p. 582, no. 81
As above, •CONSTΓ•
451.1 19 1.90 MMS/S

336–337 AD
RIC VII, p. 589, no. 138
Bust laur. CONSTANTINVSIVNNOBC
Gloria Exercitus 1 standard
452.1 CONSA 15 1.22 MD1/S
452.2 CONSB 17 1.80 MMS/N

336–337 AD
RIC VII, p. 590, no. 150
As above
Gloria Exercitus• 1 standard
453.1 — 17 1.31 F49
This is the only mint where the combination of the obverse legend, bust and reverse legend is found.

337–340 AD
RIC VIII, p. 449, no. 24
Head rd. DNCONSTANTINVSPFAVG
Gloria Exercitus 1 standard
454.1 CONSA 17 1.21 NoEx
454.2 CONSA 15 1.30 MMS/N
454.3 CONSA 14 1.90 NoEx
454.4 CONSA 14 1.25 MMS/N
454.5 CONSΘ 18 1.31 MMS

Nicomedia
325–326 AD
RIC VII, p. 621, no. 127
Bust laur. CONSTANTINVSIVNNOBC
Providentiae Caes•, MNΓ
455.1 20 3.70 NoEx

330–335 AD
RIC VII, p. 633, no. 189; M7 R 284
As above
Gloria Exercitus 2 standards, SMN[.]
456.1 18 2.53 ByzFort

336–337 AD
RIC VII, p. 635, no. 200
As above
Gloria Exercitus 1 standard, SMNA
457.1 16 1.84 MMS/N

337–340 AD
RIC VIII, p. 471, no. 7
Head laur. rd. DNCONSTANTINVSPFAVG
Gloria Exercitus 1 standard, SMNB
458.1 15 1.35 HoB

Cyzicus
325–326 AD
RIC VII, p. 649, no. 37
Bust l. CONSTANTINVSIVNNOBC
Providentiae Caess, SMKB•

459.1		17	2.17	MMS/S, H2

Note change to Burrell 2007, no. 6.

332–335 AD
RIC VII, p. 656, no. 97
Bust laur. CONSTANTINVSIVNNOBC
Gloria Exercitus 2 standards

460.1	•SMKA	18	2.20	MMS/N
460.2	•SMKΔ	18	1.89	NoEx

332–335 AD
RIC VII, p. 656, no. 98
Bust pd., otherwise as above

461.1	•SMKA	19	2.32	MMS

336–337 AD
RIC VII, p. 659, no. 123; M7 R 290
Bust laur., otherwise as above
Gloria Exercitus 1 standard

462.1	SMKA	16	1.00	BS-W13
462.2	SMKΓ	16	1.15	NoEx

Antioch
330–335 AD
RIC VII, p. 693, no. 87; M7 R 292
Bust laur. CONSTANTINVSIVNNOBC
Gloria Exercitus 2 standards

463.1	SMANA	19	2.30	MMS/N

335–337 AD
RIC VII, p. 697, no. 109; M7 R 293
As above
Gloria Exercitus 1 standard

464.1	SMANS	16	1.20	BE-E
464.2	SMANS	14	1.38	MMS
464.3	SMAN[.]	17	2.16	F49

Uncertain Mint
330–335 AD
As above
Gloria Exercitus 2 standards

465.1		18	2.00	MMS/N

Constantius II

Siscia
324–325 AD
RIC VII, p. 446, no. 186
Bust laur. l. FLIVLCONSTANTIVSNOBC
Providentiae Caess

466.1	[.]SIS	19	2.88	MMS/N

330–333 AD
RIC VII, p. 453, no. 221
Bust laur. FLIVLCONSTANTIVSNOBC
Gloria Exercitus 2 standards

467.1	ASIS	18	2.2	MMS/N

Thessalonica
330–333 AD
RIC VII, p. 524, no. 185
As above

468.1	SMTSA	18	1.66	NoEx

335–340 AD
RIC VIII, p. 407, no. 56
Bust laur. rd. CONSTANTIVSPFAVG
Gloria Exercitus 1 standard, SMTSB

469.1		18	1.65	RT

347–348 AD
RIC VIII, p. 411, no. 99; M7 R 320
As above
Victoriae dd Auggq nn, SMTSA

470.1		16	1.53	Wadi B

Heraclea
330–333 AD
RIC VII, p. 558, no. 118
Bust laur. FLIVLCONSTANTIVSNOBC
Gloria Exercitus 2 standards, •SMHΓ

471.1		17	1.56	HoB

Constantinople
333–335 AD
RIC VII, p. 581, no. 75
As above, CONSI

472.1		20	2.26	MMS/S

336–337 AD
RIC VII, p. 589, no. 139
As above
Gloria Exercitus 1 standard, CONSS

473.1		15	1.46	MMS/S

337–340 AD
RIC VIII, p. 449, no. 27; M7 R 334
Head rd. DNCONSTANTIVSPFAVG
Gloria Exercitus 1 standard

474.1	CONSA	16	1.20	MMS
474.2	CONSΓ	14	1.16	NoEx
474.3	CONSΘ	16	1.82	MMS/N
474.4	CONS[.]	17	1.37	MMS

347–348 AD
RIC VIII, p. 453, no. 69; M7 R 335–336
As above
Vot Mult

475.1	CONS[.]	18	1.80	NoEx
475.2	CONS[.]	17	1.15	Wadi B
475.3	CONS[.]	16	1.81	HoB
475.4	CONS[.]	15	1.68	HoB
475.5	CONS[.]	15	1.26	HoB

Nicomedia
330–335 AD
RIC VII, p. 633, no. 191; M7 R 304
Bust laur. FLIVLCONSTANTIVSNOBC
Gloria Exercitus 2 standards

476.1	SMN[.]	19	1.93	F49

336–337 AD
RIC VII, p. 635, no. 201
As above
Gloria Exercitus 1 standard

477.1	SMNA	16	1.75	MMS/N

337–340 AD
RIC VIII, p. 471, nos. 10–11; M7 R 355
Head rd. or laur. rd. DNCONSTANTIVSPFAVG
Gloria Exercitus 1 standard

478.1	SMNΓ	15	0.98	PA
478.2	SMNΓ	14	1.48	MMS
478.3	SMNΔ	17	1.10	MMS/N

347–348 AD
RIC VIII, p. 474, nos. 49–50; M7 R 356, 358
Head pd. or rd. DNCONSTANTIVSPFAVG
Vot Mult

479.1	SMNA	14	1.44	MMS/N
479.2	SMNA	13	1.32	HoB, clipped
479.3	SMN[..]	15	1.35	MMS/N

Cyzicus
330–335 AD
RIC VII, p. 654, nos. 69, 84, 113; M7 R 306
Bust laur. FLIVLCONSTANTIVSNOBC
Gloria Exercitus 2 standards

480.1	SMKA•	18	2.34	MMS/N
480.2	SMKΓ	19	3.00	PN/E
480.3	*SMKS	18	2.15	MMS/N

330–348 AD
RIC VII, p. 655, no. 85
As above, but not dr.
Gloria Exercitus 2 standards

481.1	SMKB	19	2.25	F49

336–337 AD
RIC VII, p. 659, no. 126; M7 R 308
Bust laur. FLIVLCONSTANTIVSNOBC
Gloria Exercitus 1 standard

482.1	SMKB	17	1.47	MMS/N
482.2	SMK[.]	16	1.26	AT

337–339 AD
RIC VIII, p. 490, nos. 16, 32; M7 R 365
Head laur. DNCONSTANTIVSPFAVG
Gloria Exercitus 1 standard

483.1	SMKΓ	16	1.47	F49
483.2	SMKΔ◡	18	1.09	MMS/N
483.3	SMK[.]	14	1.56	ByzFort

347–348 AD
RIC VIII, p. 493, nos. 48, 49; M7 R 369
Head pd. or rd. DNCONSTANTIVSPFAVG
Vot Mult

484.1	SMKA	16	1.27	MMS/N
484.2	SMKA	15	1.42	MMS/N
484.3	SMKA	15	1.67	MMS/N
484.4	SMKΓ	15	1.18	MMS
484.5	SMK[.]	14	1.66	HoB

Antioch
335 AD
RIC VII, p. 693, no. 88
Bust laur. cuir. FLIVLCONSTANTIVSNOBC
Gloria Exercitus 2 standards

485.1	SMANH	18	2.7	MMS/N

347–348 AD
RIC VIII, p. 521, nos. 113, 118; M7 R 392, 393
Head pd. DNCONSTANTIVSPFAVG
Vot Mult

486.1	SMANA	15	1.06	MMS/N
486.2	SMANA	14	1.63	NoEx
486.3	SMANB	16	1.28	HoB
486.4	SMANE	16	0.74	MMS
486.5	SMANE	13	1.36	MMS
486.6	ANT[.]	15	1.52	MMS/S

Alexandria
347–348 AD
RIC VIII, p. 541, nos. 33, 36; M7 R 402
As above
Vot Mult

487.1	SMALA	17	1.27	MMS/N
487.2	SMALΓ•	15	1.20	MMS/N

Uncertain Eastern Mint
347–348 AD
M7 R 408
Head pd. or rd. DNCONSTANTIVSPFAVG
Vot Mult

488.1	16	1.88	MMS/N
488.2	16	1.40	MMS/N
488.3	16	1.29	MMS
488.4	16	1.19	MMS/N
488.5	15	1.67	HoB
488.6	15	1.56	MMS/N
488.7	15	1.41	MMS/N
488.8	15	1.37	MMS/N
488.9	15	1.22	HoB
488.10	15	1.08	HoB
488.11	14	1.83	HoB
488.12	14	1.81	MMS
488.13	14	1.59	MMS/N
488.14	14	1.45	MMS
488.15	14	1.04	NoEx, clipped?
488.16	14	0.90	NoEx
488.17	13	1.29	HoB, clipped?
488.18	13	1.22	Wadi B, clipped
488.19	12	0.95	MMS, clipped

Uncertain Mint
330–348 AD
Head laur. FLIVLCONSTANTIVSNOBC
Gloria Exercitus 2 standards

489.1	17	2.17	HoB

335–337 AD
As above
Gloria Exercitus 1 standard

490.1	16	1.03	Wadi B
490.2	15	1.50	MMS/N

337–341 AD
DNCONSTANTIVSPFAVG
Gloria Exercitus 1 standard

491.1	17	0.90	HoB
491.2	16	1.05	HoB

341–348 AD
CONSTANTIVSPFAVG
Victoriae dd Auggq nn

492.1	14	1.15	MMS/S, H2

Constans

Lugdunum
347–348 AD
RIC VIII, p. 180, no. 47
Bust laur. rd. CONSTANSPFAVG
Victoriae dd Auggq nn, between S/T

493.1	PLG	14	1.55	MMS/N

Thessalonica
335–336 AD
RIC VII, p. 526, no. 201
Bust laur. CONSTANSNOBCAES
Gloria Exercitus 2 standards

494.1	SMTS[.]	19	2.4	RT

347–348 AD
RIC VIII, p. 411, nos. 100, 105; M7 R 431
Bust laur. rd. CONSTANSPFAVG
Victoriae dd Auggq nn

495.1	SMTS[.]	17	1.68	HoB
495.2	btw, leaf SMTS[.]	15	1.61	HoB
495.3	btw, dot SMTS[.]	15	1.38	HoB, var. found in trade

Heraclea
337–340 AD
RIC VIII, p. 431, no. 25; M7 R 432
Bust laur. l. CONSTANSAVG
Gloria Exercitus 1 standard

496.1	SMHB	15	1.36	MMS
496.2	SMH[.]	16	1.26	NoEx

347–348 AD
RIC VIII, p. 433, no. 47
Head rd. DNCONSTANSPFAVG
Vot Mult

497.1	SMHΓ	14	1.21	Tomb 07.1

Constantinople
ca. 330 AD
RIC VIII, p. 450, no. 45; M7 R 440
Head rd. DNCONSTANSPFAVG
Gloria Exercitus 1 standard

498.1	CONSΔ	15	0.90	MMS/N

ca. 330 AD
RIC VIII, p. 449, no. 29; M7 R 441
As above, but GLORIA EXERCITVS•

499.1	CONSI	16	1.70	Wadi B

347–348 AD
RIC VIII, p. 453, no. 70; M7 R 442
As above
Vot Mult

500.1	CONS[.]	15	1.42	HoB

Nicomedia
337–340 AD
RIC VIII, p. 471, nos. 14, 15; M7 R 446, 447
Head laur. pd. or rd. DNCONSTANSPFAVG
Gloria Exercitus 1 standard

501.1	SMNA	15	1.74	MMS
501.2	SMNB	15	1.77	MMS/S

348–351 AD AE2
RIC VIII, p. 476, no. 72
Bust l. pd. cuir. dr., globe in r. hand
DNCONSTANSPFAVG
Fel Temp Reparatio hut *|, SMNA

502.1		20	3.60	NoEx

347–348 AD
RIC VIII, p. 475, nos. 58, 58A; M7 R 448, 449
Head laur. rd. or rd. DNCONSTANSPFAVG
Vot Mult

503.1.	SMNA•	14	1.10	HoB
503.2	SMNA•	14	1.74	MMS/N
503.3	SMNB•	13	1.56	HoB, clipped
503.4	SMNE•	15	1.49	HoB
503.5	SMN[.]•	16	1.43	MMS

Cyzicus
331–334 AD
RIC VII, p. 655, no. 87
Bust laur. FLIVLCONSTANSNOBC
Gloria Exercitus 2 standards

504.1	SMKB	18	3.08	MMS

337–340 AD
RIC VIII, p. 490, no. 18; M7 R 450
Head laur. DNCONSTANSPFAVG
Gloria Exercitus 1 standard

505.1	SMKA	16	1.61	MMS/N
505.2	SMKΓ	16	1.76	F49
505.3	SMKΔ	16	1.30	MMS/N

347–348 AD
RIC VIII, p. 494, nos. 51, 52; M7 R 456
Head pd. or rd. DNCONSTANSPFAVG
Vot Mult

506.1	SMKA	16	1.28	MMS
506.2	SMKE	15	1.34	HoB

Antioch
347–348 AD
RIC VIII, p. 521, no. 116; M7 R 459
Head pd. DNCONSTANSPFAVG
Vot XV Mult XX, SMAN[.]

507.1		16	1.35	HoB
507.2		13	1.48	MMS/S, H2

Alexandria
348–350 AD AE2
RIC VIII, p. 542, no. 60
Bust l. pd., cuir., globe DNCONSTANSPFAVG
Fel Temp Reparatio Hut, ALEA

508.1		21	4.23	MMS

Uncertain Eastern Mint
347–348 AD
M7 R 467
Head pd. DNCONSTANSPFAVG
Vot Mult

509.1	[...]I	14	1.12	NoEx

Uncertain Mint
335–341 AD
Bust l. laur. FLCONSTANSNOBCAES
Gloria Exercitus 1 standard

510.1		14	1.61	MMS

337–348 AD
M7 R 464
Head laur. rd. DNCONSTANSPFAVG
Gloria Exercitus 1 standard

511.1		15	1.70	MMS/N
511.2		15	1.63	HoB
511.3		14	1.65	MMS

347–348 AD
M7 R 466
Bust laur. CONSTANSPFAVG
Victoriae dd Auggq nn

512.1		16	1.40	Wadi B

Dalmatius

Cyzicus
336–337 AD
RIC VII, p. 659, no. 132
Bust laur. FLIVLDELMATIVSNOBC
Gloria Exercitus 1 standard

513.1	SMKA	15	1.38	NoEx
513.2	SMKΓ	16	1.18	HoB

Uncertain Mint
336–337 AD
As above

514.1		16	1.72	MMS

348–364 AD

Constantius II

Rome
348–350 AD AE2
RIC VIII, p. 259, no. 148
Behind head A DNCONSTANTIVSPFAVG
Fel Temp Reparatio galley A|

515.1	RP	23	5.57	NoEx

Aquileia

348–350 AD AE3
RIC VIII, p. 323, no. 94
DNCONSTANTIVSPFAVG
Fel Temp Reparatio FH3

516.1	AQ[..]	17	1.16	Tomb 07.1

Thessalonica

350–355 AD AE2
RIC VIII, p. 419, no. 180
Behind head Δ DNCONSTANTIVSPFAVG
Fel Temp Reparatio FH3

517.1	TSA	21	2.93	MMS/N

350–355 AD AE3
RIC VIII, p. 419, no. 192
DNCONSTANTIVSPFAVG
Fel Temp Reparatio FH3

518.1	SMTS[.]	18	2.61	MMS/S

355–361 AD AE4
RIC VIII, p. 422, no. 213; M7 R 324
As above
Spes Reipublice

519.1	SMTS[.]	17	0.93	MMS/N

Heraclea

348–351 AD AE2
RIC VIII, p. 434, no. 65
As above
Fel Temp Reparatio FH4

520.1	SMHE	19	3.21	MMS/N

351–355 AD AE3
RIC VIII, p. 436, no. 90; M7 R 329
As above
Fel Temp Reparatio FH3

521.1	SMHΔ	17	2.16	HoB
521.2	SMH[.]	17	3.40	MMS/S

355–361 AD AE3
RIC VIII, p. 437, no. 93; M7 R 330
As above, but on rev. M|

522.1	SMHA	16	1.66	NoEx

Constantinople

348–351 AD AE2
RIC VIII, p. 454, no. 87
Bust with globe l. DNCONSTANTIVSPFAVG
Fel Temp Reparatio emperor and captives Γ|

523.1	CONSΘ*	19	4.27	MMS

351–355 AD AE2
RIC VIII, p. 457, no. 108
Behind head Δ DNCONSTANTIVSPFAVG
Fel Temp Reparatio FH3 Γ•|

524.1	CONS[.]	18	1.79	MMS/N

351–355 AD AE2
RIC VIII, p. 457, no. 112
As above, but FH4

525.1	B•| CON[.]	16	1.70	HoB
525.2	Γ•| CON[.]	19	4.10	MMS

351–355 AD AE2
RIC VIII, p. 457, no. 116; M7 R 341
DNCONSTANTIVSPFAVG
Fel Temp Reparatio FH4 •S•|*

526.1	CONS[.]	19	3.21	NoEx
526.2	CONS[.]	18	2.48	MMS/N

351–355 AD AE3
RIC VIII, p. 458, no. 118; M7 R 342
As above
Fel Temp Reparatio FH3

527.1	CONSA	17	2.69	NoEx
527.2	CONSΘ	20	1.74	Wadi B
527.3	CONSIA	18	1.94	NoEx
527.4	CONS[.]	17	2.39	MMS/N
527.5	CONS[.]	17	2.34	MD2
527.6	CONS[.]	17	2.10	MMS/N
527.7	CONS[.]	16	1.70	MMS
527.8	CON[..]	16	1.67	NoEx
527.9	CONS[.]	13	0.97	NoEx

351–355 AD AE3
RIC VIII, p. 458, no. 119
As above
Fel Temp Reparatio FH4

528.1	CONSB	16	1.90	NoEx
528.2	CON[.]	19	1.93	Wadi B

351–355 AD AE3
RIC VIII, p. 458, no. 121; M7 R 344
As above
Fel Temp Reparatio FH3, on rev. •|

529.1	CONSA	19	2.05	MMS

355–361 AD AE3
RIC VIII, p. 460, no. 137; M7 R 345
As above, but on rev. •M•|

530.1	CONSA	15	1.76	MMS/N
530.2	CONSE	16	2.52	HoB
530.3	CON[..]	18	2.71	NoEx

355–361 AD AE3
RIC VIII, p. 460, no. 139
DNCONSTANTIVSPFAVG
Fel Temp Reparatio FH4 •M•|

531.1	CONS[.]	17	2.02	NoEx
531.2	CON[..]	—	frag'y	MMS

348–361 AD AE3
M7 R 349
As above
Fel Temp Reparatio, FH3 or FH4

532.1	CONSΘ	16	2.35	NoEx
532.2	CON[.]	18	1.40	NoEx
532.3	CONS[.]	14	1.29	MD2

355–361 AD AE4
RIC VIII, p. 461, nos. 149, 151; M7 R 350
As above
Spes Reipublice

533.1	CONSA branch	16	1.99	MMS
533.2	CONSΓ branch	15	1.44	Tomb 07.1
533.3	CONS[.] branch	15	2.44	NoEx
533.4	CON[..]	18	1.80	MMS
533.5	CON[..]	15	1.70	MMS

355–361 AD AE4
RIC VIII, p. 461, no. 153; M7 R 351
As above, but C|

534.1	CONSA	10	1.55	MMS/N
534.2	CONS[.]	13	1.08	MMS/N

Nicomedia
348–351 AD AE3
RIC VIII, p. 476, no. 73
As above
Fel Temp Reparatio phoenix globe

535.1	SMNA	17	1.40	RT

351–361 AD AE3
RIC VIII, p. 479, nos. 96, 104; M7 R 361
As above
Fel Temp Reparatio FH3

536.1	SMNB	15	2.04	NoEx
536.2	SMN[.]	15	2.21	CW6

351–355 AD AE4
RIC VIII, p. 482, no. 112; M7 R 364
As above
Spes Reipublice

537.1	SMN[.]	17	1.95	HoB

Cyzicus
348–350 AD AE2
RIC VIII, p. 496, no. 84; M7 R 373
Bust l. with globe DNCONSTANTIVSPFAVG
Fel Temp Reparatio emperor and captives *|

538.1	SMKE	22	3.90	HoB

348–350 AD AE3
RIC VIII, p. 496, nos. 89, 90 var.
DNCONSTANTIVSPFAVG
Fel Temp Reparatio phoenix globe

539.1	|* SMKA	17	2.11	CW32
539.2	SMKA	18	2.62	MMS/S

Note that although RIC VIII, p. 496 n. 90 cites Sardis excavations (unpublished) for officina Δ, I read as A, and in-trade example with A.

351–354 AD AE2
RIC VIII, p. 497, nos. 95–96; M7 R 377
As above
Fel Temp Reparatio FH3 Γ|

540.1	•SMKS	23	5.56	HoB

351–354 AD AE2
RIC VIII, p. 498, no. 102; M7 R 380
As above, but on rev. •S•|

541.1	SMKB	20	4.95	MMS

351–361 AD AE3
RIC VIII, p. 498, nos. 104, 110; M7 R 381
As above, nothing in field

542.1	SMKA	17	2.72	MMS/N
542.2	SMKA	15	2.48	NoEx
542.3	SMKΓ	20	3.74	MMS
542.4	SMKΓ	17	2.39	MD2
542.5	SMKE	17	1.90	NoEx
542.6	SMKE	16	2.35	ByzFort
542.7	SMKE	16	1.30	MMS/S
542.8	SMK[.]	17	1.90	BS-E17

355–361 AD AE3
RIC VIII, p. 499, no. 115; M7 R 384
As above
Fel Temp Reparatio FH3 •M•|

543.1	SMKA	19	2.57	F55

351–354 AD AE2
RIC VIII, p. 497, no. 92; M7 R 376
As above
Fel Temp Reparatio FH3 Γ|

544.1	SMKA	21	4.13	MMS/N

355–361 AD AE4
RIC VIII, p. 499, no. 117; M7 R 385
As above
Spes Reipublice

545.1	SMKA	18	2.12	MMS/N
545.2	SMKA	16	1.73	MMS
545.3	SMKA	16	1.71	MMS

545.4	SMKA	16	1.70	F49, H8
545.5	SMKB	15	2.04	MMS
545.6	SMKE	16	2.05	HoB
545.7	SMK[.]	11	1.98	MMS/N

355–361 AD AE4
RIC VIII, p. 499, no. 119
As above, but on rev. Γ|

546.1	SMKA	14	1.57	MMS/N
546.2	SMKΔ	15	1.96	MMS/S

Antioch

350–355 AD AE2
RIC VIII, p. 523, no. 138; M7 R 396
Behind bust Δ DNCONSTANTIVSPFAVG
Fel Temp Reparatio FH3

547.1	ANA	15	2.76	MMS/N
547.2	ANA	12	1.05	ThSt, clipped

350–361 AD AE3
RIC VIII, p. 524, nos. 143, 155, 188; M7 R 397
DNCONSTANTIVSPFAVG
Fel Temp Reparatio FH4

548.1	ANA	16	1.95	MMS/N

346–361 AD AE3
As above
Fel Temp Reparatio FH, uncertain variety

549.1	ANT[.]	18	1.70	ByzFort

Alexandria

347–348 AD AE2
RIC VIII, p. 541, no. 44
As above
Fel Temp Reparatio FH4

550.1	ALEB	14	0.98	HoB, double struck

351–355 AD AE3
RIC VIII, p. 544, nos. 80, 82; M7 R 403
As above, but FH3

551.1	ALEA	16	2.35	Wadi B

355–361 AD AE4
RIC VIII, p. 545, no. 87; M7 R 405
As above
Spes Reipublice

552.1	ALEA	13	1.68	MMS/N

Uncertain Mint

348–351 AD AE3
As above
Fel Temp Reparatio phoenix globe *|

553.1	18	2.40	PN/E

350–355 AD AE2
M7 R 411
Behind bust Δ DNCONSTANTIVSPFAVG
Fel Temp Reparatio FH3

554.1	22	3.39	MMS
554.2	21	3.91	NoEx

351–355 AD AE2
M7 R 555
As above
Fel Temp Reparatio FH4

555.1	20	3.30	MMS/N

348–355 AD AE2
M7 R 412
DNCONSTANTIVSPFAVG
Fel Temp Reparatio FH, uncertain variety

556.1	20	5.17	HoB
556.2	20	3.30	MMS/S

348–361 AD AE2/3
M7 R 411, 413
As above
Fel Temp Reparatio FH3

557.1	20	4.49	MMS
557.2	19	1.89	MMS
557.3	18	2.93	MMS
557.4	18	2.57	F55
557.5	18	2.50	BS-W13
557.6	18	2.43	MMS/S
557.7	18	2.35	MMS/N
557.8	18	1.98	F55
557.9	18	1.85	MMS
557.10	17	3.27	MMS/N
557.11	17	2.37	NoEx
557.12	17	2.31	MMS/S
557.13	17	2.26	NoEx
557.14	17	2.25	HoB
557.15	17	2.23	HoB
557.16	17	2.20	NoEx
557.17	17	2.04	Wadi B
557.18	17	1.71	Wadi B
557.19	17	1.47	F55
557.20	17	1.17	MMS/N
557.21	16	2.55	MD2
557.22	16	2.36	EH
557.23	16	2.26	MMS
557.24	16	2.10	MMS/N
557.25	16	1.81	HoB
557.26	16	1.37	NoEx
557.27	16	1.20	MMS/N
557.28	15	2.24	MMS/N
557.29	15	1.34	MMS/N
557.30	15	1.28	NoEx
557.31	14	2.04	MMS/S

557.32	14	1.63	MMS/S
557.33	14	1.42	MMS
557.34	14	1.15	MMS/N
557.35	13	1.49	Wadi B
557.36	13	0.91	MMS/S
557.37	12	1.10	MMS/N

351–361 AD AE3
M7 R 414
As above, but FH4

558.1	18	2.04	HoB
558.2	17	1.71	ByzFort
558.3	16	1.90	MD2
558.4	16	1.67	NoEx
558.5	16	1.63	ByzFort
558.6	15	2.41	MMS/N
558.7	15	1.73	NoEx
558.8	15	1.60	MMS/N
558.9	15	1.28	MMS, H5
558.10	15	1.07	NoEx
558.11	14	2.67	MMS
558.12	13	1.16	MMS/N
558.13	11	0.61	AT-Pac, clipped

348–361 AD AE3
M7 R 412
As above, but FH uncertain variety

559.1	19	3.77	NoEx
559.2	18	1.87	Wadi B
559.3	18	1.63	NoEx
559.4	18	1.43	MMS
559.5	18	1.16	ByzFort
559.6	17	2.24	MMS
559.7	17	2.15	NoEx
559.8	17	2.10	MMS/N
559.9	17	2.05	F55
559.10	17	1.80	NoEx
559.11	17	1.72	MMS/S
559.12	17	1.55	Wadi B
559.13	16	2.21	NoEx
559.14	16	1.90	MMS/N
559.15	16	1.78	MD1/S
559.16	16	1.65	Wadi B
559.17	16	1.64	F49
559.18	16	1.28	MMS/N
559.19	15	2.40	MMS/N
559.20	15	1.83	MMS
559.21	15	1.60	E Road
559.22	15	1.37	F55
559.23	15	1.29	MMS/N
559.24	15	0.94	HoB
559.25	15	0.83	MMS/S
559.26	14	2.03	Wadi B
559.27	14	1.58	NoEx
559.28	14	1.59	F49, H8
559.29	14	1.39	NoEx
559.30	14	1.06	MMS/S, clipped
559.31	12	1.69	MMS/N, clipped
559.32	12	1.42	Tomb 07.1, clipped?
559.33	12	frag'y	MMS
559.34	—	frag'y	MMS/N
559.35	—	frag'y	MMS/N
559.36	—	frag'y	ByzFort

355–361 AD AE4
M7 R 415
As above
Spes Reipublice

560.1	18	1.08	MMS/N
560.2	17	1.27	MMS
560.3	17	1.16	Wadi B
560.4	16	2.30	MMS/N
560.5	16	2.05	NoEx
560.6	16	2.01	Wadi B
560.7	16	1.87	ByzFort
560.8	16	1.80	MMS/N
560.9	16	1.70	MMS/N
560.10	16	1.68	MMS
560.11	16	1.60	NoEx
560.12	16	1.55	HoB
560.13	16	1.48	MMS/N
560.14	16	1.47	MMS/N
560.15	16	1.33	EH
560.16	16	1.14	MMS/N
560.17	15	2.29	NoEx
560.18	15	2.17	Syn
560.19	15	2.00	MMS/N
560.20	15	1.93	MMS
560.21	15	1.84	ThSt
560.22	15	1.79	MMS/N
560.23	15	1.75	F49
560.24	15	1.70	MMS/N
560.25	15	1.70	MMS/N
560.26	15	1.70	CW6
560.27	15	1.59	MMS/N
560.28	15	1.52	MMS/S
560.29	15	1.39	F49
560.30	15	1.21	MMS/N
560.31	15	1.20	MMS/N
560.32	15	1.00	MMS/N
560.33	15	frag'y	MMS/N
560.34	14	1.59	MMS/N
560.35	14	1.52	NoEx
560.36	14	1.49	MMS
560.37	14	1.46	MMS
560.38	14	1.37	HoB

560.39	14	1.23	MMS/S, H2
560.40	14	1.20	MMS
560.41	14	1.17	MMS/N
560.42	14	1.08	MMS/N
560.43	14	1.02	MMS
560.44	14	0.90	F49
560.45	14	frag'y	MMS/N
560.46	13	1.00	MMS/N
560.47	13	frag'y	MMS/N
560.48	13	0.69	F49, H8
560.49	12	1.23	MMS/S
560.50	12	1.21	NoEx
560.51	8	0.90	MMS/N, clipped
560.52	—	frag'y	MMS/N
560.53	—	frag'y	MMS
560.54	—	frag'y	HoB
560.55	9	frag'y	MMS/S, clipped, H2

337–361 AD AE3
M7 R 416
As above
Uncertain rev.

561.1	15	1.37	MMS/N
561.2	12	1.75	MMS

Constantius Gallus

Constantinople
351–355 AD AE3
RIC VIII, p. 458, no. 122
Bust bare DNFLCLCONSTANTIVSNOBCAES
Fel Temp Reparatio FH3 •|

562.1	CONSS	17	2.53	MMS/N

Nicomedia
351–355 AD AE3
RIC VIII, p. 479, no. 90; M7 R 481
As above, but Δ behind head, no • on rev.

563.1	SMNA	15	2.62	NoEx

Antioch
350–355 AD AE2
RIC VIII, p. 524, no. 149
Bust bare DNCONSTANTIVSNOBCAES
Fel Temp Reparatio FH3 S|

564.1	ANH	18	4.85	HoB

Uncertain Mint
350–355 AD AE3
M7 R 489
Bust bare DNFLCLCONSTANTIVSNOBCAES
Fel Temp Reparatio FH, uncertain variety

565.1	19	2.44	NoEx

Julian II

Constantinople
355–361 AD AE3
RIC VIII, p. 460, no. 138; M7 R 494
Bust bare DNCLIVLIANVSNOBCAES
Fel Temp Reparatio FH3 •M•|

566.1	CONSE	16	1.86	NoEx
566.2	CON[..]	16	2.74	F49

RIC VIII, p. 460, no. 140
As above, but FH4

567.1	CONSΓ	16	2.44	HoB
567.2	CONS[.]	16	2.80	MMS/N

Nicomedia
355–361 AD AE4
RIC VIII, p. 482, no. 113; M7 R 499
As above
Spes Reipublice

568.1	SMN[.]	16	1.95	MMS/S

Cyzicus
355–361 AD AE3
RIC VIII, p. 499, no. 112; M7 R 500
Bust bare DNFLCLIVLIANVSNOBCS
Fel Temp Reparatio FH3

569.1	SMKΔ	17	1.32	MMS/N

RIC VIII, p. 499, no. 118; M7 R 502
As above
Spes Reipublice

570.1	SMK[.]	18	2.23	MMS/S
570.2	SMK[.]	16	2.30	MMS/N

Antioch
355–361 AD AE4
RIC VIII, p. 528, no. 194
Bust pd. DNIVLIANVSNOBCAES
Spes Reipublice

571.1	ANΓI	15	1.90	MMS/N

Uncertain Mint
355–361 AD AE3
M7 R 506
Bust bare DNFLCLIVLIANVSNOBCS
Fel Temp Reparatio FH3 •M•|

572.1	17	1.77	NoEx
572.2	16	1.88	HoB
572.3	15	1.47	HoB

355–361 AD AE3
M7 R 507
Bust bare DNCLIVLIANVSNOBCAES
Fel Temp Reparatio FH4

573.1	18	2.21	MMS

351–361 AD AE3
M7 R 508
[…]IVL[…]
Fel Temp Reparatio FH, uncertain variety

574.1	15	1.88	NoEx

355–361 AD AE4
M7 R 509
DNCLIVLIANVSNOBCAES
Spes Reipublice

575.1	16	1.64	NoEx
575.2	16	0.84	NoEx
575.3	15	2.30	MMS/N
575.4	15	2.21	MMS
575.5	15	1.72	MD2
575.6	15	1.29	MMS/N
575.7	14	1.97	MMS/S
575.8	14	1.60	MMS/N
575.9	13	2.10	MMS

360–363 AD AE3
DNFLCLIVLIANVSPFAVG
Vot X Mult XX

576.1	13	0.78	NoEx

House of Constantine

Trier
347–348 AD follis
Victoriae dd Auggq nn, between M, in ex. TRP

577.1	15	1.02	HoB

Rome
337–340 AD follis
Head laur. and rd. […]ON[…]
Virtus Augusti, in ex. R*P

578.1	13	2.11	Wadi B

347–348 AD follis
Victoriae dd Auggq nn

579.1	R branch P	15	1.40	HoB

Heraclea
347–348 AD follis
M7 R 530
Vot Mult

580.1	SMH[.]	15	1.73	HoB
580.2	SMH[.]	14	0.78	Wadi B

Constantinople
327–328 AD follis
Head r.
Gloria Exercitus emperor standing, off. letter obscure/missing

581.1	CON	17	1.94	NoEx
581.2	CON	17	frag'y	MMS/N

330–335 AD follis
M7 R 531
Bust rd. or laur.
Gloria Exercitus 2 standards

582.1	CONSA	18	1.87	HoB
582.2	CON[..]	18	2.09	MMS
582.3	CONS[.]	16	1.17	NoEx

336–337 AD follis
M7 R 532
Bust r., uncertain diadem
Gloria Exercitus 1 standard

583.1	CONSA	16	1.18	HoB
583.2	CONSΓ	15	1.13	HoB
583.3	CONSΘ	15	1.70	HoB
583.4	CON[..]	15	2.70	MMS/N
583.5	CON[..]	15	2.02	NoEx
583.6	CON[..]	15	0.99	F49
583.7	CON[..]	14	1.28	MMS
583.8	CO[…]	—	frag'y	NoEx

347–348 AD follis
M7 R 533
Head rd./pd.
Vot Mult

584.1	CON[..]	16	1.50	MMS/N
584.2	CONS[.]	13	1.69	MMS, clipped

Nicomedia
330–335 AD follis
Gloria Exercitus 2 standards

585.1	SMNA	18	1.99	PA

336–337 AD follis
M7 R 535
As above, but 1 standard

586.1	SMNA	15	0.70	MMS/S
586.2	SMN[.]	15	1.61	HoB

347–348 AD follis
M7 R 536
Vot Mult

587.1	SMNB	15	1.72	HoB
587.2	SMNB	15	1.60	F49, H8
587.3	SMNB	15	1.16	MMS/N
587.4	SMNΓ	14	1.02	MMS/S
587.5	SMN[.]	15	1.30	MMS/N
587.6	SMN[.]	15	1.69	HoB
587.7	SMN[.]	14	frag'y	MMS/N

Cyzicus
336–337 AD follis
M7 R 538
Gloria Exercitus 1 standard

588.1	SMKA	14	1.03	PA
588.2	SMKE	15	2.14	NoEx, clipped

347–348 AD follis
M7 R 539
Vot Mult

589.1	SMKA	14	1.84	MMS/N
589.2	SMKA	13	1.41	F49
589.3	SMKE	16	1.72	HoB

348–350 AD AE3
M7 R 540
Fel Temp Reparatio phoenix globe

590.1	SMKΓ	17	2.03	HoB

Antioch
347–348 AD follis
Vot Mult

591.1	SMAN[.]	15	1.25	HoB

Alexandria
337–340 AD follis
Gloria Exercitus 1 standard

592.1	SMALA	16	1.40	MMS/S

347–348 AD follis
Vot Mult

593.1	AL[..]	16	0.84	MMS/N

Uncertain Eastern Mint
348–351 AD AE3
M7 R 554
Fel Temp Reparatio phoenix globe

594.1	18	1.90	MMS

347–348 AD follis
M7 R 550
Vot Mult

595.1	16	2.64	MMS/N
595.2	16	1.70	Wadi B
595.3	16	1.35	LAW
595.4	16	1.35	MMS
595.5	16	1.28	Wadi B
595.6	16	1.20	HoB
595.7	15	2.25	MMS/N
595.8	15	1.80	MMS/N
595.9	15	0.96	Wadi B
595.10	15	0.87	MMS, H6
595.11	14	1.80	Wadi B
595.12	14	1.53	HoB
595.13	14	1.43	MMS/N
595.14	14	1.41	MMS/N
595.15	14	1.36	MMS/N
595.16	14	frag'y	HoB
595.17	14	frag'y	NoEx
595.18	14	frag'y	NoEx
595.19	14	frag'y	MMS/N
595.20	13	2.34	MMS/N
595.21	13	1.76	NoEx
595.22	13	1.50	MMS/N
595.23	13	1.46	EH
595.24	13	1.38	HoB
595.25	13	1.25	RT
595.26	13	0.66	Church EA
595.27	12	1.71	MMS/N
595.28	12	1.37	HoB
595.29	—	frag'y	MMS/N
595.30	—	frag'y	MMS/N

Uncertain Mint
330–348 AD follis
M7 R 546
Gloria Exercitus 2 standards

596.1	18	2.20	MMS/N
596.2	17	2.11	MMS

336–340 AD follis
M7 R 548
Gloria Exercitus 1 standard

597.1	17	1.27	NoEx
597.2	16	1.55	HoB
597.3	16	1.38	MMS/N
597.4	16	1.09	MMS/N
597.5	16	1.01	Tomb 07.1
597.6	15	1.80	MMS/N
597.7	15	1.51	MMS
597.8	15	1.50	MMS/N
597.9	15	1.33	MMS/N
597.10	15	1.13	NoEx
597.11	15	0.83	Tomb 07.1
597.12	14	1.96	MMS/N
597.13	14	1.15	NoEx
597.14	14	1.10	MMS/N
597.15	14	0.90	MMS/N
597.16	14	frag'y	MMS
597.17	13	1.38	MMS/N
597.18	13	1.20	ByzFort
597.19	13	0.47	HoB
597.20	12	1.70	MMS/N
597.21	—	frag'y	MMS/N

330–340 AD follis
M7 R 547
Gloria Exercitus 1 or 2 standards

598.1	15	1.23	MMS/N

342–347 AD AE3
Head or bust r.
Victory l. with wreath and palm VICT[...]

599.1	13	0.59	MMS/N
599.2	11	0.56	MMS/N

347–348 AD AE3
Head laur.
Victoriae dd Auggq nn

600.1	palm branch btw	18	1.44	MMS
600.2	unc. M/m	16	1.12	Wadi B
600.3	unc. M/m	15	1.88	NoEx
600.4	unc. M/m	15	1.32	MMS
600.5	unc. M/m	13	0.87	MMS/S, H2

348–361 AD AE2
M7 R 556
[..]VSNOBCAES
Fel Temp Reparatio FH3

601.1	22	2.47	MMS

346–361 AD AE2/3
M7 R 556
Fel Temp Reparatio FH3

602.1	18	2.27	F49
602.2	18	1.85	MMS/S
602.3	17	2.00	W Road
602.4	17	1.93	MMS/S
602.5	17	frag'y	Wadi B
602.6	16	2.20	NoEx
602.7	16	1.78	MMS
602.8	16	1.43	Wadi B
602.9	14	1.90	MMS/N
602.10	14	1.41	MMS/N
602.11	14	1.30	MMS/N
602.12	—	frag'y	MMS/N
602.13	—	frag'y	MMS/S, H2

348–361 AD AE3
M7 R 555
As above, but FH4

603.1	15	1.35	MMS/N
603.2	15	1.10	BS-E19

348–361 AD AE2/3
M7 R 557
As above, but uncertain variety

604.1	19	2.48	Wadi B
604.2	19	1.36	MMS
604.3	18	3.04	F55
604.4	18	1.98	MMS
604.5	17	1.79	HoB
604.6	17	1.42	Wadi B
604.7	16	2.29	Wadi B
604.8	16	1.97	F49
604.9	16	1.32	MMS
604.10	15	1.86	MMS/N
604.11	15	1.54	NoEx
604.12	15	1.30	MMS
604.13	14	1.40	MMS/N
604.14	13	1.10	BS-W3
604.15	9	0.91	F55, clipped
604.16	—	frag'y	MMS
604.17	—	frag'y	MMS
604.18	—	frag'y	MMS/N
604.19	—	frag'y	MMS
604.20	—	frag'y	MMS

355–361 AD AE4
M7 R 558
Spes Reipublice

605.1	17	0.66	NoEx
605.2	16	1.80	MMS/N
605.3	15	1.03	MMS/N
605.4	15	0.80	MMS/S
605.5	15	2.20	MMS/N
605.6	15	1.48	MMS
605.7	14	1.51	MMS, clipped
605.8	14	1.10	MMS/N, clipped
605.9	14	1.08	MMS/N, clipped
605.10	13	2.00	MMS/N
605.11	13	1.53	NoEx
605.12	13	1.26	MMS/N
605.13	12	1.10	NoEx
605.14	11	1.12	MMS, clipped?, H5
605.15	11	1.21	MMS
605.16	11	frag'y	MMS
605.17	—	frag'y	MMS/N

324–361 AD AE3
Uncertain rev.

606.1	22	3.12	MMS
606.2	19	1.91	MMS
606.3	17	3.00	CW6
606.4	17	2.47	NoEx
606.5	17	1.64	F55
606.6	17	1.59	MMS
606.7	17	1.50	MMS/N
606.8	17	1.16	Wadi B
606.9	17	frag'y	MMS
606.10	16	2.02	Wadi B
606.11	16	1.90	MMS/S
606.12	16	1.76	MMS
606.13	16	1.73	MD2
606.14	16	1.70	MMS/N
606.15	16	1.50	MMS/N
606.16	16	1.43	HoB
606.17	16	1.20	MMS/S
606.18	16	0.86	Wadi B
606.19	15	2.65	Tomb 07.1
606.20	15	2.16	Wadi B
606.21	15	1.91	NoEx
606.22	15	1.76	NoEx

606.23	15	1.72	Wadi B
606.24	15	1.67	MMS/N
606.25	15	1.60	MMS/S
606.26	15	1.50	MMS/N
606.27	15	1.20	MMS/S
606.28	15	frag'y	MMS/N
606.29	14	1.14	F49
606.30	14	1.11	NoEx
606.31	14	1.08	MMS/S
606.32	13	1.90	F49
606.33	13	1.58	HoB, clipped
606.34	13	1.21	AT-Pac
606.35	13	frag'y	MMS/S
606.36	—	frag'y	MMS/N
606.37	—	frag'y	ByzFort
606.38	—	frag'y	HoB
606.39	—	frag'y	MMS/N
606.40	—	frag'y	MMS/N
606.41	—	frag'y	MMS/N
606.42	—	frag'y	MMS/N
606.43	—	frag'y	MMS/N
606.44	—	frag'y	MMS/S
606.45	—	frag'y	MMS
606.46	—	frag'y	MMS/N
606.47	—	frag'y	MMS/S, H2
606.48	—	frag'y	MMS/N

Jovian

Alexandria

363–364 AD AE3

RIC VIII, p. 546, no. 92

Bust pd. DNIOVIANVSPFAVG

Vot V, ALEA

607.1	15	2.12	NoEx

364–ca. 491 AD

Valentinian I

Heraclea

367–375 AD AE3

RIC IX, p. 194, no. 10a

Bust r. rd. DNVALENTINIANVSPFAVG

Securitas Reipublicae *| wreath

608.1	SMHA	10	1.95	MMS

Constantinople

364–367 AD AE3

RIC IX, p. 215, no. 21a3

As above

609.1	CONSA	18	2.44	NoEx

RIC IX, p. 221, no. 42a8; M7 R 580

As above, but •|

609.2	CONSA	17	1.51	MMS

RIC IX, p. 215, no. 21a4

As above, but *|

609.3	CONSA	17	2.39	MMS/N

364–367 AD AE3

RIC IX, p. 214, no. 16a; M7 R 573, 577

DNVALENTINIANVSPFAVG

Gloria Romanorum 8

610.1	CONSPΔ	21	1.91	MMS/N
610.2	|* CONSΔ	16	2.28	MD2
610.3	CON[..]	17	2.22	Wadi B
610.4	CON[..]	16	1.49	NoEx

Nicomedia

364–367 AD AE3

RIC IX, p. 252, no. 11a; M7 R 581

As above

Restitutor Reip, SMNΓ

611.1	19	3.30	MMS
611.2	15	2.11	MMS/N

364–367 AD AE3

RIC IX, p. 252, no. 12a1

As above

Securitas Reipublicae, SMNA

612.1	16	2.62	MMS/N

364–367 AD AE3

RIC IX, p. 252, no. 9a1

As above

Gloria Romanorum 8, SMNA

613.1	19	2.21	NoEx

Cyzicus

364–367 AD AE3

RIC IX, p. 240, no. 10a; M7 R 582

As above

Restitutor Reip

614.1	SMKA	19	3.27	MMS/N
614.2	SMKA	17	2.55	ByzFort
614.3	SMKA	14	1.63	NoEx, clipped
614.4	SMKB	20	2.13	Wadi B
614.5	SMKB	18	2.83	PW
614.6	SMKΓ	20	3.06	MMS

364–375 AD AE3

RIC IX, p. 241, nos. 11a, 13a; M7 R 584

As above

Securitas Reipublicae

615.1	SMKA	16	2.66	NoEx
615.2	SMKB	18	2.30	NoEx
615.3	SMKB	17	1.96	AT-Pac
615.4	SMKΓ	18	1.42	Wadi B
615.5	SMKΔ	19	2.88	ByzFort

Botched rev. legend: SECVRITAS REIPVBLIAE

615.6	SMK[.]	17	1.58	MMS/N
615.7	SMK[.]	16	2.50	MMS

364–375 AD AE3
RIC IX, p. 240, nos. 8a, 12a; M7 R 583
As above
Gloria Romanorum 8

616.1	SMKB	17	2.13	HoB
616.2	SMKΔ	18	2.32	NoEx
616.3	SMK[.]	17	3.48	ByzFort

Antioch
364–367 AD AE1
RIC IX, p. 274, no. 9a
As above
Restitutor Reipublicae

617.1	ANTΔ	26	7.95	NoEx

364–367 AD AE3
RIC IX, p. 274, no. 11a
As above
Restitutor Reip

618.1	ANT[.]	17	2.42	MMS/N

364–367 AD AE3
RIC IX, p. 275, no. 12a; M7 R 586
As above
Securitas Reipublicae

619.1	ANTA	18	2.19	MD2
619.2	ANTA	13	1.13	MMS/N
619.3	ANT[.]	14	1.20	MMS/N

364–367 AD AE3
RIC IX, p. 274, no. 10a, M7 R 585
As above
Gloria Romanorum 8

620.1	ANTA	16	1.49	MMS/N

Alexandria
364–367 AD AE3
RIC IX, p. 298, nos. 3a, 5a; M7 R 588
As above
Securitas Reipublicae

621.1	ALEA	16	1.97	MMS/N
621.2	ALEB	17	1.10	BS-E1

Uncertain Mint
364–375 AD AE3
M7 R 591
As above

622.1		17	2.00	MMS/N
622.2		17	1.87	MMS
622.3		16	2.49	MMS/N
622.4		16	1.99	ByzFort
622.5		16	1.43	MMS/N
622.6		15	2.89	Tomb 07.1
622.7		15	2.00	MMS
622.8		13	2.46	MMS/N
622.9		—	2.10	NoEx

364–375 AD AE3
As above
Gloria Romanorum 8

623.1		19	1.90	BS-W14
623.2		17	1.93	NoEx
623.3		17	1.84	ByzFort
623.4		17	2.19	MD2
623.5	*|wreath	17	1.60	MMS
623.6		16	1.25	MMS/N
623.7		12	1.39	MMS/N

Valens

Siscia
367–375 AD AE3
RIC IX, p. 147, no. 15b
DNVALENSPFAVG
Securitas Reipublicae, ASISC

624.1	*|• P|M	18	2.08	NoEx

Rome
375–378 AD AE3
RIC IX, p. 123, no. 29
DNVALENSPFAVG (appears unbroken)
Victory l. with wreath and palm, VICTORIA-AVGGG

625.1		14	1.66	MMS/S

Thessalonica
364–367 AD AE3
RIC IX, p. 176, no. 17b; M7 R 603
As above
Securitas Reipublicae

626.1	TESA	18	1.74	NoEx
626.2	*|	16	1.56	HoB

364–367 AD AE3
RIC IX, p. 178, no. 26b; M7 R 602
As above
Gloria Romanorum 8, TESB

627.1		17	2.20	MMS/N

Heraclea
364–367 AD AE3
RIC IX, p. 192, no. 5b; M7 R 609
As above, SMHB
Securitas Reipublicae

628.1		18	3.18	MMS

367–375 AD AE3
RIC IX, p. 193, no. 9b
As above
Gloria Romanorum 8, SMHA

629.1	*|wreath	20	2.25	MMS

Constantinople
364–367 AD AE3
RIC IX, p. 215, no. 20b4; M7 R 612
As above
Restitutor Reip, CONSPΔ

630.1	15	2.78	AT

364–375 AD AE3
RIC IX, p. 216, no. 21b or 21c; M7 R 617–618
As above
Securitas Reipublicae

631.1	CONSB	17	2.20	MMS
631.2	CONSPA	17	2.30	MMS
631.3	CONSPB	18	1.62	MMS
631.4	CONSPΓ	17	2.49	Tomb 07.1
631.5	CONSP[.]	17	2.21	NoEx
631.6	CON[..]	19	1.86	NoEx
631.7	CONS[.]	18	1.98	F55
631.8	CON[..]	6	2.31	NoEx

RIC IX, p. 221, no. 42b7

631.9	•|	CONSA	11	2.45	MMS
631.10	B|	CONSB	15	1.73	MMS/S

367–375 AD AE3
RIC IX, p. 220, no. 41b9; M7 R 625
As above
Gloria Romanorum 8, CONSS

632.1	|•	16	2.23	MMS/S

375–376 AD AE3
RIC IX, p. 221, no. 42b var.
As above
Securitas Reipublicae C|

633.1	CONSB	19	2.06	Wadi B

M/m attested in trade

Nicomedia
364–367 AD AE3
RIC IX, p. 252, no. 12b; M7 R 628
As above
Securitas Reipublicae, SMNB

634.1	17	2.23	MMS/S

364–367 AD AE3
RIC IX, p. 252, no. 9c
As above
Gloria Romanorum 8, SMNA

635.1	16	1.71	MMS/N

Cyzicus
364–367 AD AE3
RIC IX, p. 241, no. 10b; M7 R 633
As above
Restitutor Reip, SMKB

636.1	18	1.65	MMS/N

364–375 AD AE3
RIC IX, p. 241, nos. 11b, 13b; M7 R 635
As above
Securitas Reipublicae

637.1	SMKA	19	2.06	Wadi B
637.2	SMKA	17	2.17	NoEx
637.3	SMKA	17	2.12	NoEx
637.4	SMKB	19	2.39	MMS/N
637.5	SMKA or Δ	19	2.64	HoB

364–367 AD AE3
RIC IX, p. 240, nos. 8b, 12b; M7 R 634
As above
Gloria Romanorum 8, SMK[.]

638.1	18	2.01	MMS/S
638.2	15	1.87	NoEx

Antioch
364–367 AD AE3
RIC IX, p. 275, no. 12b
As above
Securitas Reipublicae, ANTA

639.1	16	2.79	F49

Uncertain Mint
364–367 AD AE3
M7 R 637
As above
Restitutor Reip

640.1	16	2.13	F55

364–375 AD AE3
M7 R 639
As above
Securitas Reipublicae

641.1	17	2.14	NoEx
641.2	16	2.18	MMS/N
641.3	15	2.56	NoEx
641.4	15	2.44	NoEx
641.5	14	2.29	MMS/N
641.6	14	frag'y	MMS/N
641.7	12	1.90	ByzFort

364–375 AD AE3
M7 R 638
As above
Gloria Romanorum 8

642.1		18	2.83	NoEx
642.2		18	2.21	MMS/N
642.3		17	2.17	MMS/N
642.4		17	2.14	MMS/N
642.5		17	2.00	MMS/S
642.6		17	1.92	MMS/N
642.7		15	1.85	MMS/N
642.8		15	1.65	MMS/N
642.9		15	0.73	MMS/N, clipped

364–375 AD AE3
M7 R 640
As above
Illeg. rev.

643.1		16	2.01	NoEx
643.2		16	1.85	NoEx
643.3		12	1.30	MMS/N

Procopius

Constantinople
364–366 AD AE3
RIC IX, p. 215, no. 18
DNPROCOPIVSPFAVG
Reparatio Fel Temp, CON[.]

644.1		17	2.20	Wadi B

Nicomedia
364–366 AD AE3
RIC IX, p. 252, no. 10.1
Bust l. DNPROCOPIVSPFAVG
As above, chi-rho in upper r. field

645.1	SMNB	18	2.87	MMS

Unidentified Eastern Mint
364–366 AD AE3
As above

646.1		22	2.56	MMS/S

Jovian, Valentinian I, or Procopius

Uncertain Eastern Mint
363–366 AD AE1
Standing emperor holding standard, legend unc.

647.1		23	5.28	ByzFort

Gratian

Arelate
367–375 AD AE3
RIC IX, p. 66, no. 15
DNGRATIANVSPFAVGG
Gloria Novi Saeculi, CON

648.1	OF|I or II	13	1.23	NoEx, clipped

Aquileia
378–383 AD AE3
RIC IX, p. 101, no. 32a
As above
Concordia Augg Cp, SMAQP

649.1		18	2.30	PN/E

Thessalonica
367–375 AD AE3
RIC IX, p. 178, no. 26c
As above
Gloria Romanorum 8

650.1	|* / |B	17	2.32	ByzFort

378–383 AD AE3
RIC IX, p. 182, no. 39a4
As above
Concordia Auggg Cp, SMTESA

651.1		18	2.02	Wadi B

383 AD AE4
RIC IX, p. 182, no. 43; M7 R 647
As above
Vot XV Mult XX, TES

652.1		15	1.55	HoB

Heraclea
378–383 AD AE3
RIC IX, p. 195, no. 14a2
As above
Concordia Auggg Roma, SMHB

653.1	I|branch	18	1.62	MD1/S

Nicomedia
378–383 AD AE3
RIC IX, p. 258, no. 30a4
As above, SMNA

654.1	branch|branch	17	1.90	MMS/S
654.2		17	—	MMS/S, halved, H2

378–383 AD AE3
RIC IX, p. 258, no. 33; M7 R 653
As above
Virtus Romanorum, SMNA

655.1		19	1.63	MMS/N
655.2		18	2.91	MMS

383 AD AE4
RIC IX, p. 259, no. 35
As above
Vot XV Mult XX, SMNB

656.1		13	1.44	F49, H8

Cyzicus

364–375 AD AE3
RIC IX, p. 241, nos. 11, 13; M7 R 655
As above
Securitas Reipublicae

657.1	SMKA	16	1.85	MMS/N

378–383 AD AE2
RIC IX, p. 242, no. 14a1; M7 R 658
Bust r. helm., cuir., spear and shield DNGRATIANVSPFAVG
Gloria Romanorum emperor galley wreath|, SMKA

658.1		22	5.38	MMS/N

378–383 AD AE3
RIC IX, p. 243, no. 17a2 var.; M7 R 656
As above
Concordia Auggg Roma (looks l., r. leg bare, globe in r., reversed spear in l.)

659.1	SMKA	19	3.10	NoEx
659.2	|+ SMKB	18	2.31	EH

RIC IX only records Roma 2; variant seen online in A off.

383 AD AE4
RIC IX, p. 244, no. 21a2
As above
Vot X Mult XX, SMKΓ

660.1		14	1.54	ThSt

383 AD AE4
RIC IX, p. 244, no. 22a; M7 R 659
As above
Vot XX Mult XXX

661.1	SMKA	12	1.12	MMS/N
661.2	SMKB	15	1.50	NoEx
661.3	SMKB	14	1.34	F49

Antioch

367–375 AD AE3
RIC IX, p. 281, no. 35c
As above
Gloria Romanorum 8, ANTΓ

662.1		15	frag'y	MMS/S, H2

378–383 AD AE3
RIC IX, p. 289, no. 53
As above
Vot XV Mult XX, ANT

663.1		16	1.69	MMS

Alexandria

367–375 AD AE3
RIC IX, p. 299, no. 5c; M7 R 661
As above
Securitas Reipublicae, ALE[.]

664.1		16	2.33	ByzFort

Uncertain Eastern Mint

383 AD AE4
M7 R 664
As above
Vot XX Mult XXX

665.1		17	1.94	MMS/N
665.2		15	1.25	MMS/S
665.3		15	1.02	MMS
665.4		14	1.02	MMS

Uncertain Mint

367–375 AD AE3
Identification poss.
Gloria Romanorum 8

666.1		18	1.90	NoEx

Valentinian I or Valens

Thessalonica

364–367 AD AE3
RIC IX, p. 176, no. 18; M7 R 987
Securitas Reipublicae, TES[.]

667.1		17	2.56	NoEx

364–367 AD AE3
RIC IX, p. 176, no. 16
Gloria Romanorum 8, TESA

668.1		17	2.68	NoEx

Heraclea

364–367 AD AE3
RIC IX, p. 191, no. 3; M7 R 990
As above, SMHA

669.1		16	2.31	NoEx
669.2		14	1.23	MMS/N, clipped

Constantinople

364–375 AD AE3
RIC IX, p. 215, nos. 21, 42; M7 995
Securitas Reipublicae, CONS[..]

670.1		17	2.69	Wadi B
670.2		16	1.92	MMS/N
670.3	*|	16	1.94	NoEx
670.4	branch?|	19	2.29	Wadi B, mint prob.

364–367 AD AE3
RIC IX, p. 214, no. 16; M7 R 994
Gloria Romanorum 8, CON[..]

671.1		20	1.49	MMS/S

Nicomedia
364–367 AD AE3
RIC IX, p. 252, no. 9; M7 R 1009
Gloria Romanorum 8

672.1	SMNA	17	2.12	MD2
672.2	SMN[.]	14	1.45	HoB, clipped

Cyzicus
364–375 AD AE3
RIC IX, p. 241, nos. 11, 13; M7 R 1019
Securitas Reipublicae

673.1	SMKB	14	1.38	MMS/N
673.2	SMK[.]	17	2.00	NoEx

364–375 AD AE3
RIC IX, p. 241, nos. 8, 12; M7 R 1018
Gloria Romanorum 8, SMKA

674.1	15	1.89	Tomb 07.1
674.2	17	1.81	MMS/N

Rev. reads GLORIA ROMANOVM, off. unc.

Antioch
364–367 AD AE3
RIC IX, p. 274, no. 10; M7 R 1030
Gloria Romanorum 8

675.1	ANTH	14	1.48	HoB
675.2	ANT[.]	14	1.04	PA

364–375 AD AE3
RIC IX, p. 275, no. 12; M7 R 1031
Securitas Reipublicae

676.1	ANTB	14	1.30	MMS/N
676.2	ANTΓ	17	1.70	MMS/N
676.3	ANTΔ	14	1.24	HoB, clipped
676.4	ANT[.]	16	1.85	MMS

Alexandria
364–367 AD AE3
RIC IX, p. 298, no. 3; M7 R 1038
Securitas Reipublicae

677.1	ALEA	12	2.00	MMS/N
677.2	ALEB	15	1.83	NoEx
677.3	ALE[.]	15	1.75	MMS/N

Uncertain Mint
364–367 AD AE3
M7 R 1042
Restitutor Reip

678.1	16	3.00	F55
678.2	16	2.10	NoEx
678.3	16	1.80	MMS/N
678.4	16	1.30	PN/E, i.d. prob.
678.5	14	1.40	MMS/N
678.6	13	1.16	NoEx, clipped
678.7	13	1.78	MMS/S, clipped, i.d. poss.
678.8	10	0.90	MMS/N, clipped, i.d. poss.

364–376 AD AE3
M7 R 1044
Securitas Reipublicae

679.1	18	2.61	MMS/S
679.2	17	2.21	ThSt
679.3	16	1.70	MMS
679.4	15	1.53	HoB
679.5	14	1.54	MMS/N
679.6	13	1.60	MMS/N
679.7	13	1.05	MMS/N

364–375 AD AE3
M7 R 1043
Gloria Romanorum 8

680.1	17	1.80	AT
680.2	17	1.78	MMS
680.3	17	1.71	MMS
680.4	15	2.43	ByzFort
680.5	15	2.19	F55
680.6	15	1.29	HoB
680.7	14	1.20	MMS/N

364–378 AD AE3
M7 R 1072
Illeg. rev.

681.1	16	1.39	Tomb 07.1
681.2	10	0.61	MMS, clipped, H5

Valentinian I, Valens, or Gratian

Constantinople
364–367 AD AE3
RIC IX, p. 214, no. 16; M7 R 994
Gloria Romanorum 8, CONS[..]

682.1	18	2.68	MMS
682.2	17	2.24	F55
682.3	15	1.77	MMS/N

Alexandria
364–367 AD AE3
RIC IX, p. 298, no. 3; M7 R 1039
Securitas Reipublicae, ALEA

683.1	15	1.46	Wadi B

Uncertain Mint
364–378 AD AE3
M7 R 1044
Securitas Reipublicae

684.1	18	2.30	BS-E17
684.2	18	1.98	MMS
684.3	18	1.87	MD2
684.4	18	1.78	MMS/S
684.5	17	3.00	Wadi B
684.6	17	2.74	NoEx
684.7	17	2.46	Wadi B
684.8	17	1.92	MMS/N
684.9	17	1.75	Wadi B
684.10	17	1.72	MMS
684.11	17	1.66	MMS
684.12	17	1.57	F55
684.13	17	1.54	F55
684.14	17	1.41	F49
684.15	17	1.26	NoEx
684.16	17	1.21	MMS/N
684.17	16	1.89	MMS
684.18	16	1.88	Wadi B
684.19	16	1.83	NoEx
684.20	16	1.82	MMS
684.21	16	1.81	NoEx
684.22	16	1.78	MMS
684.23	16	1.76	Wadi B
684.24	16	1.66	Wadi B
684.25	16	1.53	ByzFort
684.26	16	1.45	Wadi B
684.27	16	1.30	ByzFort
684.28	16	1.25	MMS/S
684.29	16	1.14	MMS/N
684.30	15	2.66	NoEx
684.31	15	2.33	MMS
684.32	15	2.30	MMS/N
684.33	15	2.18	F55
684.34	15	2.10	MMS/N
684.35	15	2.06	EH
684.36	15	2.04	MMS/N
684.37	15	1.98	MD2
684.38	15	1.96	MMS/N
684.39	15	1.95	MMS/N
684.40	15	1.94	MMS/S
684.41	15	1.83	Wadi B
684.42	15	1.70	MMS/S
684.43	15	1.67	F55
684.44	15	1.59	MMS
684.45	15	1.50	F55
684.46	15	1.43	ThSt
684.47	15	1.41	MMS/N
684.48	15	1.31	MMS/N
684.49	15	1.20	MMS/N
684.50	15	1.14	HoB
684.51	15	1.11	F55
684.52	15	1.10	Wadi B
684.53	15	1.08	Tomb 07.1
684.54	15	1.00	Wadi B
684.55	14	1.75	MMS
684.56	14	1.68	F49, H8
684.57	14	1.67	Wadi B
684.58	14	1.60	NoEx
684.59	14	1.60	BS-W13
684.60	14	1.50	ByzFort
684.61	14	1.50	MMS/N
684.62	14	1.46	MMS/S
684.63	14	1.40	MMS
684.64	14	1.32	F49
684.65	14	1.29	F55
684.66	14	1.12	MMS/N
684.67	14	1.03	MMS/N
684.68	14	frag'y	MMS/N
684.69	13	2.17	ByzFort
684.70	13	1.79	HoB, clipped
684.71	13	1.64	LAW
684.72	13	1.62	HoB
684.73	13	1.40	MMS/N
684.74	13	1.40	NoEx
684.75	13	1.30	RT
684.76	13	1.22	Wadi B
684.77	13	1.20	MMS/N
684.78	13	1.18	MMS/N
684.79	13	1.08	MMS/N
684.80	13	0.58	MMS/N
684.81	12	1.29	MMS/N, clipped
684.82	12	1.00	MMS/N, clipped
684.83	12	0.99	ByzFort
684.84	12	0.82	MMS
684.85	12	0.78	MMS/S
684.86	11	1.39	MMS/N
684.87	11	0.89	MMS
684.88	11	0.88	MMS
684.89	11	0.83	MMS/N, clipped
684.90	11	0.82	MMS
684.91	11	frag'y	MMS/N
684.92	10	1.44	ByzFort
684.93	10	1.08	MMS/N
684.94	10	0.92	MMS/N, clipped?
684.95	10	0.88	ByzFort, H4
684.96	10	0.87	MMS/N, clipped
684.97	10	0.74	ByzFort
684.98	9	1.00	MMS/N, clipped
684.99	8	0.45	MMS, clipped

684.100	8	0.30	MMS/N, ancient copy?
684.101	7	0.25	EH, clipped
684.102	—	frag'y	MMS/N
684.103	—	frag'y	MMS/N
684.104	—	frag'y	MMS

364–378 AD AE3
M7 R 1043
Gloria Romanorum 8

685.1	19	2.92	Wadi B
685.2	19	1.49	Wadi B
685.3	17	2.66	Wadi B
685.4	17	2.66	NoEx
685.5	17	2.38	MMS
685.6	17	2.32	Tomb 07.1
685.7	17	2.06	PA
685.8	17	1.84	F55
685.9	17	1.75	MMS
685.10	16	2.68	MMS
685.11	16	2.46	Wadi B
685.12	16	2.43	MMS/S
685.13	16	2.29	NoEx, clipped
685.14	16	2.08	MD2
685.15	16	1.53	F49, clipped
685.16	16	1.31	MMS
685.17	16	1.13	Wadi B
685.18	16	1.05	NoEx
685.19	16	1.00	MMS/N
685.20	16	frag'y	MMS/N
685.21	15	2.10	NoEx
685.22	15	2.04	HoB
685.23	15	1.99	NoEx
685.24	15	1.96	MMS
685.25	15	1.87	MMS
685.26	15	1.80	MMS
685.27	15	1.75	MMS
685.28	15	1.72	F49
685.29	15	1.70	MMS/N
685.30	15	1.62	Wadi B
685.31	15	1.51	MD1/S
685.32	15	frag'y	MMS/S
685.33	14	2.76	NoEx
685.34	14	2.03	MMS/S, clipped?
685.35	14	2.01	NoEx
685.36	14	1.96	NoEx
685.37	14	1.82	Wadi B
685.38	14	1.79	MMS/N
685.39	14	1.62	NoEx
685.40	14	1.54	HoB
685.41	14	1.52	NoEx, clipped
685.42	14	1.41	NoEx
685.43	14	1.31	F55, clipped
685.44	14	1.23	MMS/N
685.45	14	1.08	NoEx, clipped?
685.46	14	1.04	NoEx, clipped
685.47	13	1.46	F49, clipped?, H8
685.48	13	1.41	MMS/S
685.49	13	1.36	MMS/N
685.50	13	1.19	MMS, clipped, i.d. poss.
685.51	13	1.00	MMS/N, clipped
685.52	13	0.96	MMS/S, clipped, H2
685.53	13	0.91	MMS, clipped, H6
685.54	13	0.79	MMS/N, clipped
685.55	12	1.44	NoEx, clipped
685.56	12	1.27	MMS, clipped
685.57	11	1.13	Tomb 07.1, clipped

364–375 AD AE3
Gloria Novi Saeculi or Restitutor Reip

686.1	15	1.77	NoEx
686.2	14	0.45	MMS/S, clipped
686.3	12	1.22	MMS/N

364–378 AD AE3
Uncertain rev.

687.1	18	2.12	MD2
687.2	15	0.84	F55
687.3	12	1.49	NoEx, clipped?

Valentinian II

Aquileia
383 AD AE4
RIC IX, p. 104, no. 51a
DNVALENTINIANVSPFAVG
Vot X Mult XX, SMAQP

688.1	13	1.46	F49

383–388 AD AE4
RIC IX, p. 104, no. 47a1; M7 R 667
As above
AQP

689.1	14	1.39	NoEx
689.2	12	0.98	MMS/N

Siscia
375–395 AD AE4
RIC IX, p. 155, no. 39a2
As above
Victoria Auggg, BSIS

690.1		13	1.09	MMS/N

Thessalonica
388–393 AD AE4
RIC IX, p. 188, no. 65a var.; M7 R 671
As above
Salus Reipublicae chi-rho|, TES

691.1		13	0.97	MMS/S, H2

Var. in having no officina letter; clipped?

Heraclea
383 AD AE4
RIC IX, p. 196, no. 19b
As above
Vot X Mult XX, SMHB

692.1		13	1.01	HoB

383–392 AD AE4
RIC IX, p. 198, no. 26a1
As above
Salus Reipublicae, SMHA

693.1		11	0.89	MMS/S, H2

Constantinople
378–383 AD AE2
RIC IX not; LRBC, p. 89, no. 2177; M7 R 679
As above
Virtus Exerciti chi-rho|, CONSΔ

694.1		23	5.05	Wadi B

378–383 AD AE3
RIC IX, p. 227, no. 56b; M7 R 674
As above
Concordia Auggg Roma |O

695.1	CONSΔ	18	2.30	NoEx
695.2	CONS[.]	18	2.01	F49

383 AD AE4
RIC IX, p. 229, no. 63a; M7 R 678
As above
Vot X Mult XX, CONΔ

696.1		14	0.90	MMS/N

Nicomedia
383–388 AD AE2
RIC IX, p. 260, no. 40a1
Bust r. helm., cuir., spear, shield
DNVALENTINIANVSPFAVG
Gloria Romanorum emperor galley, SMNA

697.1	T|	23	4.84	Wadi B

378–383 AD AE3
RIC IX, p. 258, no. 30b3
DNVALENTINIANVSPFAVG
Concordia Auggg Roma, SMNB

698.1	|A	18	2.59	Wadi B

378–383 AD AE3
RIC IX, p. 259, no. 34.2
As above
Urbs Roma branch|*, SMNB

699.1		17	2.15	ThSt

388–392 AD AE4
RIC IX, p. 262, no. 45a1
As above
Salus Reipublicae

700.1	SMNA	15	0.92	MMS/S
700.2	SMNA	13	1.30	PA
700.3	•SMNB	13	1.12	MMS/S, H2

Cyzicus
378–383 AD AE3
RIC IX, p. 243, no. 18b
As above
Concordia Auggg Cp +|, SMKA

701.1		19	2.69	F49

383 AD AE4
RIC IX, p. 244, no. 21b; M7 R 690
As above
Vot X Mult XX

702.1	SMKB	16	1.01	NoEx
702.2	SMKB	14	0.99	ByzFort
702.3	SMKB	13	0.62	MMS
702.4	SMKΓ	15	1.28	NoEx
702.5	SMK[.]	14	1.15	NoEx

388–392 AD AE4
RIC IX, p. 246, no. 26a1; M7 R 692
As above
Salus Reipublicae chi-rho|

703.1	SMKA	14	0.94	MMS/N
703.2	SMKA	13	1.05	HoB
703.3	SMKB	12	0.73	MMS/S, H2

Antioch
383–388 AD AE2
RIC IX, p. 290, no. 59a3
Bust r. helm., cuir., spear, shield,
DNVALENTINIANVSPFAVG
Gloria Romanorum emperor galley, ANTA

704.1	T|†	22	3.90	NoEx

Alexandria
388–392 AD AE4
RIC IX, p. 303, no. 20a; M7 R 696
DNVALENTINIANVSPFAVG
Salus Reipublicae † or chi-rho|_, ALE[.]

705.1		16	1.90	NoEx

Uncertain Eastern Mint
383 AD AE4
M7 R 699
As above
Vot X Mult XX

706.1		14	1.20	MMS/N
706.2		13	1.34	NoEx
706.3		13	1.10	MMS/N
706.4		13	0.74	MMS
706.5		12	1.08	ByzFort
706.6		12	0.65	Tomb 07.1

383 AD AE4
M7 R 701
As above
Vot XX Mult XXX

707.1		15	1.62	NoEx
707.2		15	1.29	Wadi B
707.3		13	0.97	MMS/S, H2

Uncertain Mint
375–392 AD AE4
As above
Victoria Auggg

708.1		12	1.57	Tomb 07.1

383–392 AD AE4
M7 R 702
As above
Salus Reipublicae

709.1		14	1.32	MMS/N
709.2		13	0.95	MMS/S, H2
709.3		13	0.67	EH
709.4		12	1.15	MMS/S, H2
709.5		12	1.08	MMS/S
709.6		12	0.98	HoB
709.7		12	0.87	MMS/N
709.8		11	1.40	Church EA
709.9		11	1.40	NoEx
709.10	chi-rho|_	15	1.80	NoEx
709.11	chi-rho|_	14	1.45	F55
709.12	chi-rho|_	14	0.98	MD2
709.13	chi-rho|_	13	1.09	NoEx
709.14	chi-rho|_	13	0.85	Tomb 07.1
709.15	chi-rho|_	12	1.36	NoEx

Theodosius I

Thessalonica
378–383 AD AE3
RIC IX, p. 182, no. 38
DNTHEODOSIVSPFAVG
Concordia Auggg Cp, but turreted and l. hand in lap

710.1	TES	18	2.15	MMS/N

378–383 AD AE3
RIC IX, p. 182, no. 39c var.
As above
Concordia Auggg Roma, SMTES[.]

711.1	_|A	17	2.26	MMS/N

383–388 AD AE2
RIC IX, p. 183, no. 44b3
Bust r. helm., cuir., spear, shield DNTHEODOSIVSPFAVG
Gloria Romanorum emperor galley, •TESΔ

712.1	wreath|_	22	4.80	Wadi B

383 AD AE4
RIC IX, p. 184, no. 49b1; M7 R 710
DNTHEODOSIVSPFAVG
Vot X Mult XX, TES

713.1		12	0.73	MMS/N

383–388 AD AE4
RIC IX, p. 187, no. 62b1; M7 R 712
As above
Gloria Reipublice camp-gate, TES

714.1		10	frag'y	MMS/S, H2

388–393 AD AE4
RIC IX, p. 188, no. 65b1
As above
Salus Reipublicae, TESA

715.1		12	0.95	Tomb 07.1

Heraclea
378–383 AD AE3
RIC IX, p. 195, no. 15c; M7 R 715
As above
Concordia Auggg Roma *|_, SMHA

716.1		20	2.90	MMS/N

383 AD AE4
RIC IX, p. 196, no. 19c1
As above
Vot X Mult XX, SMHA

717.1		14	0.94	MMS/N

Constantinople

378–383 AD AE2
RIC IX, p. 226, no. 52c; M7 R 728
Bust r. helm., cuir., spear, shield DNTHEODOSIVSPFAVG
Gloria Romanorum emperor galley, CONA

718.1		21	4.97	MMS
718.2	wreath|	21	3.57	MMS

378–383 AD AE3
RIC IX, p. 228, no. 57d3
DNTHEODOSIVSPFAVG
Concordia Auggg Cp, CONSB

719.1	O|	19	1.44	NoEx

383 AD AE4
RIC IX, p. 229, no. 63b; M7 R 730
As above
Vot X Mult XX, CONA

720.1		14	1.11	MMS/N
720.2		14	1.20	NoEx
720.3		13	1.16	MMS

383–388 AD AE2
RIC IX, p. 233, no. 83b2
As above
Virtus Exerciti, CONSA

721.1		21	5.60	NoEx

388–395 AD AE4
RIC IX, p. 234, nos. 86b, 90a; M7 R 734
As above
Salus Reipublicae chi-rho|

722.1	CONSA	16	0.93	MMS/S
722.2	CONSA	13	1.22	Church EA
722.3	CONSA	13	1.00	MMS/N
722.4	CONSB	13	0.98	MMS/N
722.5	CONSB	13	0.82	NoEx
722.6	CONS[.]	17	1.20	NoEx
722.7	CONS[.]	13	1.14	MMS/N
722.8	CONS[.]	13	1.10	PN/E
722.9	CONS[.]	13	0.98	MMS/S, H2

392–395 AD AE2
RIC IX, p. 235, no. 88a; M7 R 735
As above
Gloria Romanorum 18

723.1	CONSA	22	4.86	Wadi B
723.2	CONSA	21	5.10	MMS/N
723.3	CONSA	21	4.95	MMS/N
723.4	CONSA	—	frag'y	MMS/N
723.5	CONSΓ	21	4.64	HoB
723.6	CONSΔ	21	5.17	MD1/S
723.7	CONSΔ	21	3.66	MMS
723.8	CONS[.]	21	4.04	Tomb 07.1

392–395 AD AE2
RIC IX, p. 235, no. 88a1
As above
Gloria Romanorum 18, CONSA

724.1		19	2.07	Wadi B

392–395 AD AE3
RIC IX, p. 236, no. 89a1; M7 R 736
As above
Gloria Romanorum emperor horseback, CONSA

725.1		16	2.02	HoB
725.2		16	1.06	NoEx

Nicomedia

378–383 AD AE3
RIC IX, p. 258, no. 31b
As above
Concordia Auggg Cp, SMNΓ

726.1	A|	28	1.96	MMS/N
726.2	*|	19	1.90	MMS/N

383 AD AE4
RIC IX, p. 259, no. 38b2; M7 R 739
As above
Vot X Mult XX, SMNB

727.1		15	1.80	W Road

383 AD AE4
RIC IX, p. 259, no. 39c; M7 R 738
As above
Vot XX Mult XXX

728.1	SMN[.]	14	1.16	ByzFort

383–388 AD AE2
RIC IX, p. 261, no. 44b1
As above
Virtus Exerciti, SMNA

729.1		24	6.20	NoEx

383–395 AD AE4
RIC IX, p. 262, nos. 45b, 48a
As above
Salus Reipublicae

730.1	SMNA	14	0.75	AT
730.2	SMN[.]	13	1.20	RT
730.3	chi-rho|, SMNA	13	1.50	F49
730.4	chi-rho|, SMN[.]	13	1.12	NoEx
730.5	chi-rho|, SMN[.]	11	1.11	Tomb 07.1
730.6	†|, SMNA	14	0.94	MMS

392–395 AD AE2
RIC IX, p. 263, no. 46a1; M7 R 747
As above
Gloria Romanorum 18, SMNA

731.1		23	4.48	MMS/N
731.2		22	3.86	MMS/N

392–395 AD AE3
RIC IX, p. 263, no. 47a
As above
Gloria Romanorum emperor horseback, SMNA

732.1		16	1.85	NoEx, clipped

Cyzicus
378–383 AD AE2
RIC IX, p. 242, no. 14c2; M7 R 752
Bust r. helm., cuir., spear, shield DHTHEODOSIVSPFAVG
Gloria Romanorum emperor galley

733.1	wreath| SMKB	22	5.83	MMS/N

378–383 AD AE3
RIC IX, p. 243, no. 18c
DNTHEODOSIVSPFAVG
Concordia Auggg Cp, SMKΓ

734.1	†|	17	2.26	MMS

383 AD AE4
RIC IX, p. 244, no. 21c; M7 R 755
As above
Vot X Mult XX

735.1	SMKA	—	frag'y	MMS/S
735.2	SMKB	14	1.00	MMS/N
735.3	SMKB	14	1.12	Syn
735.4	SMKB	14	0.89	MMS/N
735.5	SMKΓ	15	1.40	BS-E18
735.6	SMKΓ	14	1.32	MMS/S
735.7	SMK[.]	14	1.60	NoEx
735.8	SMK[.]	14	1.24	EH
735.9	SMK[.]	13	1.64	ByzFort

383–388 AD AE2
RIC IX, p. 245, no. 23; M7 R 757
Bust r. helm., cuir., spear, shield DHTHEODOSIVSPFAVG
Gloria Romanorum emperor galley, SMK[.]

736.1	T|	23	4.71	Wadi B

383–388 AD AE2
RIC IX, p. 245, no. 25b1
DNTHEODOSIVSPFAVG
Virtus Exerciti, SMKA

737.1		22	5.21	MMS/S
737.2		21	4.65	ByzFort

383–395 AD AE4
RIC IX, p. 246, nos. 26b, 30b; M7 R 759
As above
Salus Reipublicae chi-rho|

738.1	SMKA	14	1.26	Syn
738.2	SMKA	14	0.85	MMS
738.3	SMKA	14	0.73	NoEx
738.4	SMKB	14	0.90	MMS/S
738.5	SMKB	13	1.00	MMS/S
738.6	SMKΓ	13	1.21	NoEx
738.7	SMKΔ	15	1.00	MMS
738.8	SMKΔ	14	0.93	MMS
738.9	SMK[.]	15	1.14	Wadi B
738.10	SMK[.]	13	1.42	MMS
738.11	SMK[.]	13	1.30	NoEx
738.12	SMK[.]	13	1.01	NoEx

392–395 AD AE3
RIC IX, p. 247, no. 29a; M7 R 761
As above
Gloria Romanorum emperor horseback

739.1	SMKA	16	1.99	MD2
739.2	SMKA	16	1.80	PN/E
739.3	SMKA	11	1.70	NoEx
739.4	SMKB	20	1.55	MMS

Antioch
378–383 AD AE2
RIC IX, p. 283, no. 40d3
Bust r. helm., cuir., spear, shield DNTHEODOSIVSPFAVG
Gloria Romanorum emperor galley, ANTB

740.1	wreath|†	23	5.21	MMS

378–383 AD AE3
RIC IX, p. 287, no. 47d1
Bust rd., DNTHEODOSIVSPFAVG
Concordia Auggg Cp, ANTB

741.1	Θ|	18	2.61	NoEx

383–395 AD AE4
RIC IX, p. 293, nos. 67d, 70a; M7 R 765
DNTHEODOSIVSPFAVG
Salus Reipublicae

742.1	chi-rho| ANTA	13	1.20	MMS/N
742.2	chi-rho?| ANTA	12	0.87	NoEx
742.3	†| ANT[.]	12	1.13	MMS

392–395 AD AE3
RIC IX, p. 294, no. 69a; M7 R 770
As above
Gloria Romanorum emperor horseback, ANTΔ

743.1		15	2.15	NoEx

Alexandria

392–395 AD AE2
RIC IX, p. 304, no. 21a
As above
Gloria Romanorum 18, ALEA

744.1		22	4.57	MMS

392–395 AD AE3
RIC IX, p. 304, no. 22a
DNTHEODOSIVSPFAVG
Gloria Romanorum emperor horseback, ALEΓ

745.1		15	1.58	MMS

Uncertain Mint

378–388 AD AE2
M7 R 782
Bust r. helm., cuir., spear, shield DNTHEODOSIVSPFAVG
Gloria Romanorum emperor galley

746.1		22	4.00	MMS/N
746.2		20	3.69	NoEx
746.3	T|	22	3.78	F55

378–383 AD AE3
DNTHEODOSIVSPFAVG
Concordia Auggg Roma

747.1		18	2.61	NoEx

378–383 AD AE3
M7 R 772
As above
Concordia Auggg Cp

748.1		20	3.30	PN/E
748.2		16	2.07	Tomb 79.3

383–388 AD AE2
M7 R 779
As above
Virtus Exerciti

749.1		24	4.44	Wadi B
749.2		22	4.50	BS-E4
749.3		22	3.88	NoEx

383–395 AD AE4
M7 R 780
As above
Salus Reipublicae

750.1		14	1.21	MMS/S, H2
750.2		13	1.46	MMS/N
750.3		13	1.42	F49
750.4		13	1.22	MMS/N
750.5		13	1.18	ByzFort
750.6		13	1.10	HoB
750.7		13	1.06	MMS/N
750.8		12	1.19	MMS, H5
750.9		12	1.13	MMS/N
750.10		12	0.91	MMS/S, H2
750.11		12	0.85	NoEx
750.12		12	0.75	Syn
750.13		11	0.98	MMS/N
750.14		10	0.42	MMS/N
750.15		9	0.43	NoEx, clipped
750.16	chi-rho|	15	1.44	MMS/N
750.17	chi-rho|	14	1.32	MMS/N
750.18	chi-rho|	14	1.06	Tomb 07.1
750.19	chi-rho|	14	1.01	NoEx
750.20	chi-rho|	14	1.04	MMS/S
750.21	chi-rho|	14	0.80	MMS
750.22	chi-rho|	14	0.80	MMS/S
750.23	chi-rho|	13	1.16	MMS/N
750.24	chi-rho|	13	1.08	ThSt
750.25	chi-rho|	13	0.99	CW6
750.26	chi-rho|	13	0.98	HoB
750.27	chi-rho|	13	0.90	HoB
750.28	chi-rho|	13	0.83	MMS
750.29	chi-rho|	12	1.10	NoEx
750.30	chi-rho|	12	1.01	HoB
750.31	chi-rho|	11	0.80	RT
750.32	†|	12	1.13	HoB

383 AD AE4
M7 R 774
As above
Vot X Mult XX

751.1		16	1.45	MD2
751.2		15	1.67	MMS
751.3		15	1.30	MMS/S
751.4		15	0.92	MMS/N
751.5		15	0.86	MMS
751.6		15	0.72	NoEx
751.7		14	1.10	NoEx
751.8		14	1.10	MMS/S, H2
751.9		14	0.87	Wadi B
751.10		13	1.30	MD1/S
751.11		13	0.88	NoEx
751.12		13	0.84	MMS/S, H2
751.13		12	1.76	Tomb 07.1
751.14		12	1.40	MMS
751.15		12	0.84	MMS

392–395 AD AE2
M7 R 781
As above
Gloria Romanorum 18

752.1		22	4.24	NoEx
752.2		20	3.39	MMS

378–395 AD AE3
M7 R 783
As above
Uncertain type
753.1 15 2.00 MMS/N

FLACILLA

Constantinople
383 AD AE4
RIC IX, p. 226, no. 61
AELFLACILLAAVG
Salus Reipublicae Victory seated, CON[.]
754.1 14 1.65 MMS/N

Uncertain Mint
379–386 AD AE4
M7 R 791
AELFLACILLAAVG
Salus Reipublicae Victory shield
755.1 13 1.04 MMS/S, H2

383 AD AE2
M7 R 792
AELFLACILLAAVG
Salus Reipublicae empress
756.1 24 3.83 NoEx

MAGNUS MAXIMUS

Arelate
387–388 AD AE2
RIC IX, p. 69, no. 27b
DNMAGMAXIMVSPFAVG
Victoria Augg emperor, PCON
757.1 18 1.60 MMS/N

Aquileia
387–388 AD AE4
RIC IX, p. 105 no. 55a
As above
Spes Romanorum camp-gate, SMAQ[.]
758.1 13 0.86 MMS/N

Uncertain Western Mint
387–388 AD AE4
RIC IX, p. 180, no. 793
As above
Spes Romanorum camp-gate
759.1 14 1.19 MMS/N

FLAVIUS VICTOR

Aquileia
387–388 AD AE4
RIC IX, p. 105, no. 55b3
DNFLVICTORPFAVG
Spes Romanorum camp-gate
760.1 13 0.80 MMS/S, H2

VALENTINIAN I, VALENS, OR VALENTINIAN II

Uncertain Mint
364–392 AD AE3/4
DNVAL[…]
Illeg.
761.1 15 1.32 MMS
761.2 14 1.44 F49
761.3 13 1.10 MMS/N
761.4 11 0.97 MMS/N

GRATIAN, VALENTINIAN II, OR THEODOSIUS I

Rome
383 AD AE4
Vot XV Mult XX, SMRP
762.1 13 1.13 HoB

Uncertain Mint
378–383 AD AE3
M7 R 1047
Concordia Auggg Cp or Roma
763.1 18 1.70 MMS
763.2 16 1.27 MMS/N (Roma)
763.3 14 2.06 NoEx, clipped
763.4 12 frag'y MMS/N
763.5 11 1.76 MMS/N, clipped
763.6 — frag'y MMS/N
763.7 — frag'y MMS/N
763.8 — frag'y MMS/N

383 AD AE3
Vot XV Mult XX
764.1 15 1.64 NoEx
764.2 12 0.93 NoEx

383 AD AE4
Vot X~V Mult XX
765.1 13 1.19 MD2

ARCADIUS

Thessalonica
383–388 AD AE4
RIC IX, p. 187, no. 62c1
DNARCADIVSPFAVG
Gloria Reipublice camp-gate, TES
766.1 13 0.80 E Road

388–393 AD AE4
RIC IX, p. 188, no. 65c
As above
Salus Reipublicae chi-rho| , TESΓ
767.1 15 1.32 MMS/N

Heraclea

378–383 AD AE2
RIC IX, p. 195, no. 12
Bust pd., cuir., dr., spear, shield, above, hand holding wreath DNARCADIVSPFAVG
Gloria Romanorum 16, SMH[.]

768.1		25	4.00	ByzFort

383 AD AE4
RIC IX, p. 196, no. 18b; M7 R 800
DNARCADIVSPFAVG
Vot V, SMHA

769.1		12	1.05	MMS/N

388–392 AD AE4
RIC IX, p. 198, no. 26c; M7 R 801
As above
Salus Reipublicae, SMHB

770.1		14	1.19	HoB

392–395 AD AE2
RIC IX, p. 199, no. 27b; M7 R 802
As above
Gloria Romanorum 18, SMHA

771.1		20	4.80	MMS/N
771.2	⊥*	22	5.34	Wadi B

395–401 AD AE3
RIC X: 58; M7 R 804
As above
Virtus Exerciti 2 ⊥•, SMHA

772.1		17	2.18	MMS/N
772.2		16	2.01	MMS/S

Constantinople

383 AD AE4
RIC IX, p. 229, no. 62b
As above
Vot V, CON[.]

773.1		13	1.53	NoEx

383–388 AD AE2
RIC IX, p. 233, no. 83c1; M7 R 806
As above
Virtus Exerciti, CONSΓ

774.1	†⊥	23	5.06	MMS

388–392 AD AE4
RIC IX, p. 234, no. 86c; M7 R 808
As above
Salus Reipublicae chi-rho|

775.1	CONSA	12	1.20	MMS
775.2	CONSA	12	1.17	F55
775.3	CONSΓ	13	1.13	Tomb 07.1
775.4	CONSΓ	12	1.33	MMS/S
775.5	CONSΔ	15	1.20	MMS/N
775.6	CONSΔ	13	0.90	MMS/N
775.7	CONS[.]	14	0.97	MMS
775.8	CONS[.]	14	frag'y	HoB
775.9	CONS[.]	13	1.20	Tomb 07.1
775.10	CONS[.]	13	0.80	HoB
775.11	CONS[.]	9	0.90	MMS/S

392–395 AD AE2
RIC IX, p. 235, no. 88b1; M7 R 812
As above
Gloria Romanorum 18, CONSB

776.1		20	4.60	MMS/N

392–395 AD AE3
RIC IX, p. 236, no. 89b var.; M7 R 810
As above
Gloria Romanorum emperor horseback, CONSΓ

777.1		15	1.54	NoEx

Officina Γ is not listed as producing for Arcadius; example found in trade. The style of the coin seems good, but this was a coin turned in to the excavation.

395–401 AD AE3
RIC X: 60; M7 R 813
As above
Virtus Exerciti 2

778.1	CONSA	20	1.99	HoB
778.2	CONSA	19	2.46	MMS/N
778.3	CONSA	18	2.82	Tomb 07.1
778.4	CONSA	18	2.32	MMS/N
778.5	CONSA	18	2.15	MMS/N
778.6	CONSA	17	2.74	MMS/S
778.7	CONSA	17	1.68	MMS
778.8	CONSA	16	2.36	Tomb 07.1
778.9	CONSA	16	1.60	NoEx
778.10	CONSB	18	2.40	MMS/S
778.11	CONSB	18	2.00	MMS/S
778.12	CONSB	17	1.80	MMS/S
778.13	CONSB	17	1.42	HoB
778.14	CONSB	16	2.06	Tomb 07.1
778.15	CONSΓ	18	1.80	BS-W14
778.16	CONSΓ	17	2.03	HoB
778.17	CONSΔ	18	2.06	NoEx
778.18	CONSΔ	18	1.51	MMS
778.19	CONS[.]	18	3.53	MMS/N
778.20	CONS[.]	18	2.74	HoB
778.21	CONS[.]	18	2.71	HoB
778.22	CONS[B?]	18	2.40	MMS/N
778.23	CONS[.]	18	1.91	NoEx
778.24	CONS[.]	18	1.80	BS-W13
778.25	CONS[.]	17	2.03	MMS/S
778.26	CONS[.]	17	2.00	MMS/N
778.27	CONS[.]	17	1.96	MMS/N
778.28	CONS[.]	17	1.53	NoEx

778.29	CONS[.]	17	0.80	PN/E, clipped
778.30	CONS[.]	16	1.98	Tomb. 07.1
778.31	CONS[.]	16	1.80	MMS/N
778.32	CONS[.]	—	frag'y	MMS

401–403 AD AE3
RIC X: 86; M7 R 816
Bust facing, helm., cuir., spear, shield DNARCADIVSPFAVG
Concordia Augg Cp Victoriola, CONSA

779.1		19	2.38	MMS/N
779.2		18	1.92	NoEx
779.3		18	1.76	MMS

404–406 AD AE4
RIC X: 114 var.; M7 R 814
DNARCADIVSPFAVG
Concordia Aug cross

780.1	CONSΓ	10	0.76	MMS/S
780.2	CONS[.]	12	0.73	HoB

Officina Γ listed as poss. but not attested for Arcadius.

Nicomedia
383–388 AD AE4
RIC IX, p. 262, no. 45c3
As above
Salus Reipublicae chi-rho|_, SMNΓ

781.1		13	0.70	MMS/N

392–395 AD AE2
RIC IX, p. 263, no. 46b2; M7 R 825
As above
Gloria Romanorum 18, SMNB

782.1		22	5.53	MMS/S
782.2		22	5.06	HoB
782.3		21	5.55	MMS/S
782.4		20	4.48	MMS/S
782.5		21	3.07	ByzFort

395–401 AD AE3
RIC X: 62, 64; M7 R 827, 828
As above
Virtus Exerciti 2

783.1	SMNA	17	2.76	MMS
783.2	SMNA	17	2.65	Wadi B
783.3	SMNA	17	1.92	MMS/S
783.4	SMNA	17	1.90	MMS
783.5	SMN[.]	17	1.62	MMS/S
783.6	⊥* SMNA	18	3.35	MMS/N
783.7	⊥* SMNA	17	2.48	MD2

401–403 AD
RIC X: 91; M7 R 830
Bust facing, helm., cuir., spear, shield DNARCADIVSPFAVG
Concordia Auggg Cp Victoriola

784.1	SMNA	18	2.72	MMS/S
784.2	SMN[.]	15	1.54	NoEx

Cyzicus
383 AD AE4
RIC IX, p. 244, no. 20d; M7 R 835
DNARCADIVSPFAVG
Vot V

785.1	SMKA	13	1.45	MMS/S
785.2	SMKB	14	0.93	F49
785.3	SMKΔ	15	1.01	NoEx
785.4	SMKΔ	14	0.72	NoEx
785.5	SMK[.]	14	1.01	MMS
785.6	SMK[.]	14	0.76	F55

383–388 AD AE2
RIC IX, p. 245, no. 25c; M7 R 836
As above
Virtus Exerciti, SMKΔ

786.1		24	5.79	MMS/S
786.2		23	4.34	MMS

388–395 AD AE4
RIC IX, p. 246, nos. 26c1, 30b; M7 R 837
As above
Salus Reipublicae chi-rho|_, SMKA

787.1		13	0.97	MMS/N
787.2		13	0.80	MMS
787.3		12	1.00	MMS/N

392–395 AD AE2
RIC IX, p. 247, no. 28c; M7 R 838
As above
Gloria Romanorum 18

788.1	SMKA	21	4.61	MMS/N
788.2	SMKA	19	5.11	NoEx
788.3	SMKB	22	4.70	MMS
788.4	SMKΓ	22	4.64	MMS
788.5	SMKΓ	21	4.08	HoB
788.6	SMKΓ	20	3.30	MMS/N
788.7	SMKΓ	20	2.90	BS-E18

392–395 AD AE3
RIC IX, p. 247, no. 29c2; M7 R 840
As above
Gloria Romanorum emperor horseback, SMKB

789.1		17	1.63	NoEx
789.2		16	1.45	MMS

395–401 AD AE3
RIC X: 66; M7 R 841
As above
Virtus Exerciti 2

790.1	SMKA	20	1.36	MMS
790.2	SMKA	19	2.15	ThSt
790.3	SMKA	18	2.70	MMS/S

790.4	SMKA	18	2.24	HoB
790.5	SMKA	18	1.55	PA
790.6	SMKA	18	1.28	MMS
790.7	SMKA	17	1.87	MMS/S
790.8	SMKA	17	1.77	MMS/S
790.9	SMKB	19	2.03	HoB
790.10	SMKB	18	3.12	ThSt
790.11	SMKB	18	1.48	EH
790.12	SMKB	17	2.71	MMS/S

401–403 AD AE3
RIC X: 94; M7 R 844
Bust facing, helm., cuir., spear, shield DNARCADIVSPFAVG
Concordia Augg Cp Victoriola, SMKA

791.1		18	2.53	MMS/S
791.2		18	1.70	MMS/N
791.3		16	2.12	MMS/S
791.4		18	1.95	MMS/N

406–408 AD AE3
RIC X: 148; M7 R 845
Behind head, * DNARCADIVSPFAVG
Gloria Romanorum three emperors

792.1	SMKA	17	1.57	Wadi B
792.2	SMKA	16	2.21	MMS/S
792.3	SMKA	15	1.39	HoB
792.4	SMKA	15	1.39	HoB
792.5	SMKA	15	1.31	MMS/S
792.6	SMKA	14	1.90	MMS/N
792.7	SMKA	14	1.11	HoB
792.8	SMKB	15	1.26	MMS/N

406–408 AD AE4
RIC X: 132; M7 R 846
DNARCADIVSPFAVG
Concordia Auggg cross, SMKA

793.1		12	0.83	MMS/N

Antioch
383–392 AD AE4
RIC IX, p. 293, no. 67d; M7 R 847
As above
Salus Reipublicae chi-rho|

794.1	ANTA	12	0.90	NoEx
794.2	ANTΓ	12	1.49	HoB
794.3	ANT[.]	13	1.37	NoEx
794.4	ANT[.]	13	1.20	MMS/N

392–395 AD AE3
RIC IX, p. 294, no. 69c
As above
Gloria Romanorum emperor horseback, ANTΔ

795.1		16	1.97	MMS/N

395–401 AD AE3
RIC X: 70; M7 R 852
As above
Virtus Exerciti 2

796.1	ANTA	19	1.90	MMS/S
796.2	ANTA	17	1.92	Tomb 07.1
796.3	ANTA	16	1.50	HoB
796.4	ANTB	18	1.66	MMS
796.5	ANT[.]	18	2.18	NoEx
796.6	ANT[.]	18	1.99	NoEx
796.7	ANT[.]	15	2.04	MMS/N

406–408 AD AE4
RIC X: 136
As above
Concordia Auggg cross

797.1	ANTA	12	0.50	MMS/N

Alexandria
388–392 AD AE4
RIC IX, p. 303, no. 20c1
As above
Salus Reipublicae chi-rho|, ALEΓ

798.1		13	1.20	MMS/N

404–406 AD AE4
RIC X: 111, 120
As above
Concordia Aug cross

799.1	ALEA	11	0.60	MMS/N

Uncertain Eastern Mint
383–395 AD AE4
M7 R 858
As above
Salus Reipublicae chi-rho|

800.1		13	1.24	MMS/N
800.2		13	1.22	MMS/N
800.3		13	1.08	Tomb 07.1
800.4		13	1.05	Tomb 07.1
800.5		13	1.00	MMS/N
800.6		13	0.92	MMS/N
800.7		12	1.20	MMS/N
800.8		12	1.12	Tomb 07.1
800.9		12	1.11	F49, H8
800.10		12	1.01	NoEx
800.11		12	1.00	MMS
800.12		12	0.80	BS-E14
800.13		12	0.70	HoB
800.14		11	1.22	MMS

As above, no chi-rho visible

800.15		14	0.88	MMS
800.16		14	0.80	NoEx
800.17		13	2.13	CW32
800.18		13	1.49	F49

800.19	13	1.26	MMS/N
800.20	13	1.16	MD2
800.21	13	1.14	Tomb 07.1
800.22	13	frag'y	MMS/S
800.23	12	1.50	MMS
800.24	12	1.40	F55
800.25	12	1.15	RT
800.26	12	0.86	MMS/S, H2

392–395 AD AE2
M7 R 860
As above
Gloria Romanorum 18

801.1	23	3.90	MMS/N
801.2 ⊥*	21	4.50	BS-E12
801.3	21	4.19	NoEx

392–395 AD AE3
M7 R 859
As above
Gloria Romanorum emperor horseback

802.1	17	1.85	HoB
802.2	16	1.90	MMS/S
802.3	16	1.62	HoB

395–401 AD AE3
M7 R 861
As above
Virtus Exerciti 2

803.1	20	2.20	Wadi B
803.2	19	3.00	PN/E
803.3	19	2.34	NoEx
803.4	19	1.92	MMS/S
803.5	18	2.38	MMS/S
803.6	18	2.00	MMS/S
803.7	18	1.88	HoB
803.8	18	1.86	MMS
803.9	18	1.58	ByzFort
803.10	18	1.57	MMS
803.11	17	2.71	ByzFort
803.12	17	2.57	F49
803.13	17	2.45	HoB
803.14	17	2.15	MMS
803.15	17	1.93	F55
803.16	17	1.60	Tomb 07.1
803.17	17	1.09	MMS/N
803.18	16	3.04	MMS/N
803.19	16	2.48	MMS/N
803.20	16	2.42	Tomb 07.1
803.21	16	1.95	MMS/N
803.22	16	1.87	MMS
803.23	15	2.36	MMS/S
803.24	15	1.71	NoEx
803.25	15	1.58	NoEx
803.26	15	1.39	MMS
803.27	15	1.26	MMS/N
803.28	14	1.80	MMS/N
803.29	14	1.71	MMS/S, H2
803.30	14	1.35	MD1/S
803.31	14	1.21	MMS/N, clipped
803.32	13	1.55	BS-E19
803.33	12	1.26	MMS/N, clipped

401–403 AD AE3
M7 R 862
Bust facing, helm., cuir., spear, shield
DNARCADIVSPFAVG
Concordia Augg Cp Victoriola

804.1	17	2.34	NoEx
804.2	17	2.30	PN/E
804.3	17	2.14	NoEx
804.4	15	1.70	E Road

404–408 AD AE4
M7 R 864
DNARCADIVSPFAVG
Concordia Aug(gg) cross

805.1	14	0.92	MMS/N
805.2	12	0.65	F55
805.3	11	0.90	MMS/N

406–408 AD AE3
M7 R 863
As above
Gloria Romanorum three emperors

806.1	16	1.58	AT-Pac
806.2	16	1.35	E Road

Uncertain Mint
383–388 AD AE2
As above
Gloria Romanorum emperor galley

807.1	18	2.03	MMS

383 AD AE4
M7 R 855
As above
Vot V

808.1	13	1.00	MMS/N
808.2	13	0.79	MMS/S, H2

383–408 AD AE3 or AE4
M7 R 865
As above
Uncertain type

809.1	18	2.82	MMS/N
809.2	14	1.38	MMS/S, H2

809.3		14	1.33	MMS/N, clipped
809.4		14	1.00	F55
809.5		13	1.33	MMS/N
809.6		13	1.32	HoB
809.7		13	frag'y	MMS/N
809.8		12	1.65	F55
809.9		12	1.26	MMS/S, H2
809.10		12	1.18	MMS/N
809.11		—	frag'y	MMS
809.12		14	frag'y	MMS/N

Eudoxia

Constantinople

395–401 AD AE3

RIC X: 78

AELEVDOXIAAVG

Gloria Romanorum empress, in l. field +

810.1	CONΔ	17	1.97	MMS

401–403 AD AE3

RIC X: 101; M7 R 866

AELEVDOXIAAVG

Salus Reipublicae Victory shield

811.1	CONSA	17	2.37	MMS/N
811.2	CONS[.]	17	1.76	HoB
811.3	CONS[.]	17	1.45	MMS/N

Nicomedia

401–403 AD AE3

RIC X: 102

As above

812.1	SMNA	15	2.10	MMS/S

Cyzicus

401–403 AD AE3

RIC X: 103; M7 R 870

As above

813.1	SMKA	17	2.22	Tomb 07.1
813.2	SMKA	17	1.65	MMS/N
813.3	SMKA	15	2.22	MMS/N
813.4	SMK[.]	16	1.62	NoEx

Uncertain Eastern Mint

395–401 AD AE3

M7 R 874

As above

Gloria Romanorum empress

814.1	17	1.84	NoEx
814.2	17	1.61	NoEx
814.3	13	1.39	MMS/N, clipped

401–403 AD AE3

M7 R 873

As above

Salus Reipublicae Victory shield

815.1	17	2.20	MMS/N
815.2	16	1.93	MMS
815.3	16	1.44	ThSt

Gratian, Valentinian II, Theodosius I, or Arcadius

Rome

383–388 AD AE4

RIC IX, p. 130, no. 57; M7 R 982

Victoriae Auggg 2 Victories, _•_, ex. unc.

816.1	12	1.13	ByzFort, H4
816.2	12	0.79	MMS/N

Thessalonica

383–392 AD AE4

RIC IX, p. 187, no. 63; M7 R 989

Victoria Aug 2 Victories, TES[.]

817.1	14	1.39	MMS/N
817.2	13	1.18	Wadi B

(M/m illeg.) between figures, •

383–388 AD AE4

RIC IX, p. 186, no. 62; M7 R 988

Gloria Reipublice camp-gate, TES

818.1	11	1.12	MMS/S, H2

Constantinople

383 AD AE4

RIC IX, p. 229, no. 62

Vot V, CONΓ

819.1	12	1.32	MMS

383 AD AE4

RIC IX, p. 229, no. 64

Vot XX Mult XXX, CON[.]

820.1	14	1.40	MMS/N

Nicomedia

383 AD AE4

RIC IX, p. 259, no. 38; M7 R 1021

Vot X Mult XX, SMNA

821.1	12	1.22	Tomb 07.1

383–392 AD AE2

RIC IX, p. 261, no. 44a

Virtus Exerciti, SMN[.]

822.1	21	4.87	MMS/N

Cyzicus

383 AD AE4

RIC IX, p. 244, no. 21; M7 R 1021

Vot X Mult XX, SMK[.]

823.1	13	0.76	MMS/S, H2

383 AD AE4
RIC IX, p. 244, no. 22; M7 R 1050
Vot XX Mult XXX, SMK[.]

824.1	14	1.29	NoEx
824.2	12	0.93	NoEx, clipped?

Uncertain Eastern Mint
383 AD AE4
M7 R 1048, 1050
Vot X Mult XX or Vot XX Mult XXX

825.1	15	1.36	MMS/N
825.2	14	1.91	MMS/N
825.3	14	1.18	MMS/N
825.4	14	1.17	MMS/N
825.5	14	0.98	NoEx
825.6	14	0.91	F49
825.7	14	0.54	NoEx
825.8	14	—	F55
825.9	13	1.50	MMS
825.10	13	0.64	MMS
825.11	12	1.09	MMS (Vot X), H6
825.12	12	0.93	HoB
825.13	10	0.97	Tomb 07.1
825.14	10	0.90	MMS/N
825.15	8	frag'y	MMS/S
825.16	11	frag'y	Wadi B

383 AD AE4
M7 R 1054
Vot V

826.1	14	0.85	NoEx
826.2	11	1.03	NoEx
826.3	9	0.42	MMS/N

Uncertain Mint
383–388 AD AE4
M7 R 1051
Victoria Auggg 2 Victories

827.1	13	—	F55
827.2	12	0.53	HoB

383–392 AD AE4
Gloria Reipublicae camp-gate

828.1	11	0.86	MMS/S, H2

Honorius

Rome
394–395 AD AE3
RIC IX, p. 135, no. 67f; M7 R 875
Reduced module on thick flan
DNHONORIVSPFAVG
Urbs Roma Felix

829.1		13	1.88	MMS/N
829.2		12	1.85	MMS/N
829.3	OF|P SMROM	17	1.82	Tomb 07.1

410–423 AD AE3
RIC X: 1357
As above
Victoria Augg, RM

830.1		12	1.22	HoB
830.2		12	1.09	MMS/N
830.3	S|	12	1.15	MMS/N
830.4		12	0.98	MMS/N

402–408 AD AE4
RIC X: 1249
As above
Salus Reipublicae

831.1	12	0.60	MMS/S, H2, Lunate banker's mark on rev.

Heraclea
395–401 AD AE3
RIC X: 57, 59; M7 R 882
As above
Virtus Exerciti 2

832.1	SMHA	16	2.52	MMS/N
832.2	|• SMHA	19	2.45	NoEx
832.3	• SMHA	17	1.89	MMS/N
832.4	SMHB	15	1.27	HoB

408–423 AD AE3
RIC X: 407; M7 R 885
Behind head, * DNHONORIVSPFAVG
Gloria Romanorum 2 emperors globe

833.1	SMHA M/m prob.	14	1.40	MMS/N
833.2	SMH[.]	15	2.22	Wadi B

Constantinople
392–395 AD AE2
RIC IX, p. 236, no. 88c or RIC X: 55; M7 R 887
DNHONORIVSPFAVG
Gloria Romanorum 18, CONS[.]

834.1		22	4.00	MMS
834.2	CONSA or Δ	21	4.88	MMS

392–395 AD AE3
RIC IX, p. 236, no. 89c; M7 R 886
As above
Gloria Romanorum emperor horseback, CONSΔ

835.1	18	1.74	NoEx
835.2	16	2.26	MD2
835.3	15	1.50	NoEx
835.4	14	2.06	MMS/N

395–401 AD AE3
RIC X: 61; M7 R 888
As above
Virtus Exerciti 2

836.1	CONSB	17	1.79	HoB
836.2	CONSΓ	19	2.62	MMS
836.3	CONSΓ	18	2.40	HoB
836.4	CONSΓ	18	2.02	HoB
836.5	CONSΓ	17	2.01	MMS/N
836.6	CONSΓ	17	1.90	F55
836.7	CONSΓ	17	1.89	HoB
836.8	CONSΓ	17	1.34	NoEx
836.9	CONSΘ	17	1.71	MMS/N
836.10	CONS[.]	18	2.52	HoB
836.11	CONS[.]	18	2.00	NoEx
836.12	CONS[.]	17	2.08	ThSt
836.13	CONS[.]	17	1.90	Wadi B
836.14	CONS[.]	15	2.05	PA

401–403 AD AE3
RIC X: 88; M7 R 890
Bust facing, helm., cuir., spear, shield DNHONORIVSFAVG
Concordia Augg Cp Victoriola

837.1	CONSA	16	1.61	NoEx

408–423 AD AE3
RIC X: 399; M7 R 892
Behind bust * DNHONORIVSPFAVG
Gloria Romanorum 2 emperors shield

838.1	CONSA	17	1.61	MMS
838.2	CONS[.]	15	1.58	F49
838.3	CONS[.]	15	1.57	CW6
838.4	CONS[.]	15	0.89	MMS
838.5	CONS[.]	13	1.29	MMS/S, H2

Nicomedia
395–401 AD AE3
RIC X: 63, 65; M7 R 895–896
DNHONORIVSPFAVG
Virtus Exerciti 2

839.1	SMNA	18	2.03	NoEx
839.2	SMNA	18	1.29	MMS/S
839.3	SMNA	16	1.90	NoEx
839.4	SMNA	15	2.02	Tomb 07.1
839.5	SMNA	15	1.90	MMS/N
839.6	SMNB	18	2.15	MMS/S
839.7	SMN[.]	22	2.33	MMS
839.8	SMN[.]	18	2.02	MMS/N
839.9	•| SMNA	18	1.79	HoB, var.

M/m, which Grierson and Mays 1992 notes for nos. 757, 758 that this type "probably" exists, since there is a parallel for Arcadius.

401–403 AD AE3
RIC X: 92
Bust facing, helm., cuir., spear, shield (cross)
DNHONORIVSPFAVG
Concordia Augg Cp Victoriola

840.1	SMNA	17	2.30	NoEx

406–408 AD AE3
RIC X: 146; M7 R 897
Behind bust, * DNHONORIVSPFAVG
Gloria Romanorum three emperors

841.1	SMNA	17	2.02	MMS
841.2	SMNA	16	1.43	MMS/S
841.3	SMNA	13	1.57	MMS/N
841.4	SMN[.]	16	2.23	Wadi B

408–423 AD AE3
RIC X: 401; M7 R 898
As above
Gloria Romanorum two emperors shield

842.1	SMN[.]	15	1.88	Wadi B
842.2	SMN[.]	13	0.78	MMS/S, H2

408–423 AD AE3
RIC X: 412; M7 R 899
As above, but two emperors globe

843.1	SMNB	16	1.60	HoB

Cyzicus
392–395 AD AE2
RIC IX, p. 247, no. 28c; M7 R 900
DNHONORIVSPFAVG
Gloria Romanorum 18

844.1	SMKA	22	4.26	MMS
844.2	SMKB	22	3.00	ByzFort

393–395 AD AE3
RIC IX, p. 247, no. 29c; M7 R 901
As above
Gloria Romanorum emperor horseback

845.1	SMKA	17	1.78	NoEx
845.2	SMKΓ	17	2.43	NoEx

392–395 AD AE4
RIC IX, p. 247, no. 30c; M7 R 902
As above
Salus Reipublicae <u>chi-rho|</u>, SMKA

846.1		14	1.31	AT-Pac

395–401 AD AE3
RIC X: 68; M7 R 903
As above
Virtus Exerciti 2

847.1	SMKA	19	2.30	NoEx
847.2	SMKA	19	1.20	MMS/N

847.3	SMKA	18	2.46	MD2
847.4	SMKA	18	2.33	NoEx
847.5	SMKA	18	2.08	MMS
847.6	SMKA	17	2.76	NoEx
847.7	SMKA	17	2.48	NoEx
847.8	SMKA	17	2.42	NoEx
847.9	SMKA	17	1.99	F49
847.10	SMKB	18	2.20	HoB
847.11	SMKB	18	2.17	MMS/N
847.12	SMKB	17	2.43	CW6
847.13	SMKB	17	1.98	MMS/S
847.14	SMKΓ	20	3.07	MMS/N
847.15	SMKΔ	19	1.82	MMS/N
847.16	SMKΔ	17	2.81	MMS/S
847.17	SMK[.]	20	2.14	NoEx

406–408 AD AE3
RIC X: 149; M7 R 906
Behind bust, * DNHONORIVSPFAVG
Gloria Romanorum three emperors

848.1	SMKA	15	1.52	HoB
848.2	SMKA	15	1.40	NoEx
848.3	SMKA	14	2.00	MMS/N
848.4	SMKB	15	1.90	HoB
848.5	SMK[.]	15	1.66	MD1/S
848.6	SMK[.]	14	1.40	MMS/N

Antioch
392–395 AD AE3
RIC IX, p. 295, no. 69e; M7 R 909
DNHONORIVSPFAVG
Gloria Romanorum emperor horseback

849.1	ANTΓ	16	1.00	MMS/N
849.2	ANT[.]	16	1.61	NoEx

392–395 AD AE4
RIC IX, p. 295, no. 70c1
As above
Salus Reipublicae, chi-rho|_, ANTΔ

850.1		12	1.20	HoB

395–401 AD AE3
RIC X: 72; M7 R 910
As above
Virtus Exerciti 2

851.1	ANTA	16	2.63	MMS/N
851.2	ANTΓ	16	1.91	HoB
851.3	ANTΓ	15	1.49	MMS/S, H2
851.4	ANT[.]	16	1.89	NoEx

406–408 AD AE3
RIC X: 153; M7 R 912
Behind bust, * DNHONORIVSPFAVG
Gloria Romanorum three emperors, ANTA

852.1	14	frag'y	MMS/N

Alexandria
408–423 AD AE3
RIC X: 406
As above
Gloria Romanorum two emperors shield, ALEA

853.1	15	2.07	MMS/S

Uncertain Eastern Mint
392–395 AD AE3
M7 R 916
DNHONORIVSPFAVG
Gloria Romanorum emperor horseback

854.1	15	2.43	NoEx
854.2	—	frag'y	MMS/N

395–401 AD AE3
M7 R 919
As above
Virtus Exerciti 2

855.1	20	2.54	MMS/S
855.2	19	2.88	NoEx
855.3	19	2.40	MMS/N
855.4	19	1.93	MMS/S
855.5	19	1.85	MMS/N
855.6	18	2.59	MMS/N
855.7	18	2.37	F49
855.8	18	2.04	F55
855.9	18	2.02	HoB
855.10	18	1.81	MMS/S
855.11	18	1.77	Tomb 07.1
855.12	17	2.86	F49
855.13	17	2.69	F49
855.14	17	1.87	F49
855.15	17	1.64	MMS/N
855.16	16	2.26	MMS
855.17	16	2.18	MMS/S
855.18	16	1.98	ByzFort
855.19	16	1.84	MMS
855.20	16	1.61	MMS/S, H2
855.21	16	1.59	HoB
855.22	16	1.40	HoB
855.23	15	2.33	NoEx
855.24	15	1.70	F49
855.25	15	1.48	MMS/N
855.26	15	1.16	MMS/N
855.27	15	1.00	MMS/S
855.28	14	1.52	F49, H8
855.29	12	1.21	MMS/S, clipped

401–403 AD AE3
M7 R 922
Bust facing, helm., cuir., spear, shield
DNHONORIVSPFAVG
Concordia Augg Cp Victoriola

856.1		19	1.81	F55
856.2		16	1.48	NoEx
856.3		15	1.54	NoEx
856.4		11	1.04	Tomb 07.1, clipped

404–406 AD AE4
M7 R 924
DNHONORIVSPFAVG
Concordia Auggg cross

857.1		12	0.57	MMS/N
857.2		10	0.77	MMS/S, H2

406–408 AD AE3
M7 R 923
Behind bust, * DNHONORIVSPFAVG
Gloria Romanorum three emperors

858.1		17	frag'y	BS-E12
858.2		16	1.47	MMS
858.3		15	1.70	MMS/N
858.4		15	1.50	RT
858.5		14	1.75	MMS/N
858.6		13	1.61	MMS
858.7		12	0.85	F49, clipped

408–423 AD AE3
M7 R 926
As above, but two emperors shield

859.1		15	1.60	MMS/N
859.2		15	1.57	HoB
859.3		14	1.74	F55
859.4		14	1.49	Tomb 07.1
859.5		14	1.45	HoB
859.6		14	0.70	MMS/N, clipped
859.7		10	frag'y	MMS/S, H2

408–423 AD AE3
M7 R 927
As above, but two emperors globe

860.1		14	1.52	MMS/N
860.2		13	2.04	HoB, clipped

408–423 AD AE3
M7 R 928
As above but two emperors, globe or shield

861.1		15	1.43	MMS/N

Uncertain Mint
392–408 AD AE4
M7 R 918
DNHONORIVSPFAVG
Salus Reipublicae

862.1		13	1.03	MMS/S, H2
862.2		12	1.65	MMS/S, H2, incisions on cheek
862.3		12	1.28	NoEx
862.4		12	1.17	MMS/S, H2
862.5	chi-rho|	13	0.82	MMS/N

392–423 AD AE3/4
M7 R 929
Uncertain type

863.1		16	frag'y	MMS/S
863.2		14	1.29	MMS/S, H2
863.3		13	1.70	NoEx
863.4		13	1.10	MMS/S, clipped
863.5		11	1.48	F49, clipped, H8

Valentinian II, Theodosius I, Arcadius, or Honorius

Thessalonica
383–395 AD AE4
M7 R 987
Salus Reipublicae chi-rho|

864.1	TESA	13	1.10	MMS/N
864.2	TESB	13	1.15	MMS
864.3	TES[.]	13	0.76	F55

Heraclea
383–395 AD AE4
Salus Reipublicae, SMH[.]

865.1		13	2.22	NoEx

395–401 AD AE3
M7 R 992
Virtus Exerciti 2, SMHA

866.1		17	2.51	MMS

408–423 AD AE3
M7 R 993
Behind bust, * uncertain legend
Gloria Romanorum two emperors shield

867.1	SMHA	15	1.55	Tomb 07.1
867.2	SMH[.]	16	1.58	MD1/S
867.3	SMH[.]	14	1.40	MMS/N

383–395 AD AE4
Salus Reipublicae, SMH[.]

868.1		13	1.03	MMS/S, H2

Constantinople
388–395 AD AE4
RIC IX, p. 234, nos. 86, 90; M7 R 998
Salus Reipublicae chi-rho|

869.1	CONSA	13	1.29	NoEx
869.2	CONSA	13	0.84	MMS/N
869.3	CONSB	13	1.14	NoEx
869.4	CONSB	12	0.81	MMS/N

869.5	CONS[.]	13	0.87	HoB
869.6	CONS[.]	12	0.88	MMS

395–401 AD AE3
M7 R 1001
Virtus Exerciti 2

870.1	CONSA	15	2.20	Tomb 07.1
870.2	CONSB	16	1.66	HoB
870.3	CONS[.]	19	2.11	Tomb 07.1
870.4	CONS[.]	17	2.10	F49
870.5	CONS[.]	16	2.30	MMS/N
870.6	CONS[.]	15	2.01	NoEx
870.7	CONS[.]	14	0.94	MMS/N
870.8	CONS[.]	13	1.85	Tomb 07.1
870.9	CONS[.]	11	1.08	MMS
870.10	CONS[.]	—	1.79	CW6

408–423 AD AE3
M7 R 1006
Behind bust, * uncertain legend
Gloria Romanorum, two emperors shield

871.1	CON[.]	14	1.98	Tomb 07.1

408–423 AD? AE4
[…]VSPFAVG
Image effaced SAB(?)LICAE […], CONS

872.1		14	0.93	F49, H8

Nicomedia
395–401 AD AE3
M7 R 1013
Virtus Exerciti 2

873.1	SMNA	19	2.08	NoEx
873.2	SMNA	17	1.86	MMS/S
873.3	SMNA	17	1.69	Wadi B
873.4	SMNA	16	1.88	NoEx
873.5	SMNA	14	1.13	MMS/N
873.6	SMNB	18	1.80	MMS/S
873.7	SMNB	16	2.48	HoB
873.8	SMN[.]	18	2.19	MMS/S
873.9	SMN[.]	18	1.78	MMS

Cyzicus
388–395 AD AE4
RIC IX, p. 246, nos. 26, 30; M7 R 1023
Salus Reipublicae chi-rho|_

874.1	SMKB	12	1.14	MD1/S
874.2	SMK[.]	12	0.90	HoB

392–395 AD AE3
RIC IX, p. 247, no. 29; M7 R 1024
Gloria Romanorum emperor horseback, SMKΓ

875.1		16	1.32	Tomb 07.1

395–401 AD AE3
RIC IX, p. 245, no. 25; M7 R 1026
Virtus Exerciti 2

876.1	SMKA	17	1.70	MMS/S
876.2	SMKA	17	1.33	MMS/S
876.3	SMKA	15	2.42	HoB
876.4	SMKB	17	2.30	MMS/S
876.5	SMKB	17	1.25	HoB

408–423 AD AE3
Behind bust, * uncertain legend
Gloria Romanorum two emperors shield

877.1	SMKB	15	1.25	MMS

Antioch
388–395 AD AE4
RIC IX, pp. 293, 295, nos. 67, 70
Salus Reipublicae, ANTA

878.1		10	1.13	MMS/N

392–395 AD AE2
RIC IX, p. 294, no. 69
Gloria Romanorum emperor horseback

879.1	ANTA	16	1.59	MMS/N
879.2	ANTB	16	1.89	NoEx

395–401 AD AE3
M7 R 1035
Virtus Exerciti 2

880.1	ANTA	15	1.51	MMS
880.2	ANT[.]	16	1.71	MMS/N
880.3	ANT[.]	15	3.22	MMS/N
880.4	ANT[.]	14	2.92	MMS/S
880.5	ANT[.]	13	1.39	F49, clipped

383–395 AD AE4
M7 R 1034
Salus Reipublicae chi-rho|_, ANT[.]

881.1		12	0.80	NoEx

Alexandria
388–395 AD AE4
M7 R 1039
Salus Reipublicae

882.1	missing ALEΓ	14	2.69	MMS
882.2	chi-rho|_, ALE[.]	12	1.20	MMS/S

395–401 AD AE3
M7 R 1040
Virtus Exerciti 2, ALEA

883.1		15	2.01	MMS/N

Uncertain Eastern Mint				
392–395 AD				AE2
M7 R 1058				
Gloria Romanorum 18				
884.1	23	5.69	MD1/S	
884.2	22	4.55	MD1/S	
884.3	20	4.52	NoEx	
884.4	20	3.41	F55	
395–401 AD				AE3
M7 R 1059				
Virtus Exerciti 2				
885.1	18	2.57	MMS/N	
885.2	18	2.41	HoB	
885.3	18	1.96	F55	
885.4	18	1.90	RT	
885.5	18	1.90	MMS	
885.6	18	1.58	MMS/N	
885.7	17	3.21	NoEx	
885.8	17	2.66	MMS	
885.9	17	2.38	MMS/N	
885.10	17	2.34	NoEx	
885.11	17	2.31	MMS/N	
885.12	17	2.29	MMS/N	
885.13	17	2.23	HoB	
885.14	17	2.09	F49	
885.15	17	2.05	MMS	
885.16	17	1.93	MMS/N	
885.17	17	1.83	MMS	
885.18	17	1.80	MMS	
885.19	17	1.72	NoEx	
885.20	17	1.70	BS-E14	
885.21	17	1.67	MMS	
885.22	17	1.35	MMS	
885.23	16	2.41	NoEx	
885.24	16	1.97	MMS	
885.25	16	1.84	PN	
885.26	16	1.81	F55	
885.27	16	1.72	MMS/N	
885.28	16	1.62	F49, H8	
885.29	16	1.60	MMS/N	
885.30	16	1.59	NoEx	
885.31	16	1.53	F55	
885.32	16	1.51	NoEx	
885.33	16	1.50	NoEx	
885.34	16	1.46	NoEx	
885.35	16	1.40	MMS	
885.36	16	1.33	MMS/S	
885.37	16	1.08	F49, H8	
885.38	16	frag'y	NoEx	
885.39	16	frag'y	MMS/N	
885.40	15	2.54	Wadi B	
885.41	15	2.50	MMS/N	
885.42	15	2.35	F49	
885.43	15	2.00	MMS/N	
885.44	15	1.90	MMS	
885.45	15	1.80	MMS/N	
885.46	15	1.73	MMS/N	
885.47	15	1.31	MMS/N	
885.48	15	1.27	HoB	
885.49	15	1.20	MMS/N	
885.50	15	1.15	MMS/N	
885.51	15	1.10	NoEx	
885.52	15	1.10	MMS	
885.53	15	1.01	MMS/S	
885.54	15	0.95	MMS/N	
885.55	15	0.90	PN/E	
885.56	14	2.19	NoEx	
885.57	14	2.16	HoB	
885.58	14	2.15	MMS	
885.59	14	1.83	MMS/S	
885.60	14	1.82	NoEx	
885.61	14	1.52	F49, clipped?	
885.62	14	1.30	MMS	
885.63	14	1.25	NoEx	
885.64	14	1.24	F49, H8	
885.65	14	1.02	MMS, H5	
885.66	14	0.78	NoEx	
885.67	13	2.17	HoB	
885.68	13	2.05	NoEx	
885.69	13	1.82	MMS/N	
885.70	13	1.80	MD1/S	
885.71	13	1.71	MMS/N	
885.72	13	1.56	MMS/N	
885.73	13	1.22	MMS/N, clipped	
885.74	13	1.22	MMS, clipped	
885.75	13	1.11	MMS, clipped, H5	
885.76	13	frag'y	MMS	
885.77	13	frag'y	MMS	
885.78	13	frag'y	F55	
885.79	12	1.60	AT-Pac, clipped	
885.80	12	1.48	MMS/S, clipped	
885.81	12	1.44	HoB, clipped	
885.82	12	0.90	MMS/N, clipped	
885.83	12	0.64	MMS/S, clipped	
885.84	11	1.01	MMS/N, clipped	
885.85	—	frag'y	MMS/N	
885.86	—	frag'y	F55	
885.87	13x16	1.06	MMS	

383–408 AD AE4
M7 R 1056
Salus Reipublicae chi-rho|_

886.1	15	1.67	NoEx
886.2	15	0.87	MMS
886.3	14	1.96	NoEx
886.4	14	1.42	F49, H8
886.5	14	1.23	MMS/N
886.6	14	1.20	MMS/N
886.7	14	1.04	MMS
886.8	14	0.89	MMS, H6
886.9	13	1.57	F49, H8
886.10	13	1.50	ByzFort, H4
886.11	13	1.45	ByzFort
886.12	13	1.40	MMS/N
886.13	13	1.34	MMS/N
886.14	13	1.30	MMS/N
886.15	13	1.17	NoEx
886.16	13	1.04	NoEx
886.17	13	1.03	HoB
886.18	13	1.02	Tomb 07.1
886.19	13	0.91	MMS/S
886.20	13	0.80	MMS
886.21	13	0.63	F49, H8
886.22	12	1.45	ByzFort
886.23	12	1.40	HoB
886.24	12	1.35	NoEx
886.25	12	1.28	MMS/N
886.26	12	1.25	MMS/N
886.27	12	1.21	MMS/N
886.28	12	1.18	F55
886.29	12	1.17	MMS/S, H2
886.30	12	1.16	ByzFort
886.31	12	1.15	MMS
886.32	12	0.97	MMS
886.33	12	0.94	MMS/S, H2
886.34	12	0.91	F49, H8
886.35	12	0.80	RT
886.36	12	0.76	MMS
886.37	12	0.73	MMS/N
886.38	11	1.55	F49, H8
886.39	11	1.35	MMS, H5
886.40	11	1.32	MMS/N
886.41	11	1.22	NoEx
886.42	11	1.03	MMS/S, H2
886.43	11	0.97	MMS/N
886.44	11	0.91	Tomb 07.1
886.45	11	0.65	MMS, H5
886.46	11	0.56	MMS
886.47	11	0.49	NoEx
886.48	11	0.40	MMS/N
886.49	10	1.16	MMS/N
886.50	10	1.13	F49
886.51	10	0.90	NoEx
886.52	10	0.55	F49, H8
886.53	10	0.26	MMS
886.54	15	0.78	HoB
886.55 +|_	11	0.90	NoEx

As above, but no chi-rho visible

886.56	15	1.22	HoB
886.57	—	frag'y	MMS
886.58	14	1.16	F55
886.59	14	1.05	HoB
886.60	13	1.80	MMS/S
886.61	13	1.61	ByzFort
886.62	13	1.53	F55
886.63	13	1.45	MMS/N
886.64	13	1.41	MMS/S, H2
886.65	13	1.36	F55
886.66	13	1.30	MMS/N
886.67	13	1.26	MMS/N
886.68	13	1.26	MMS/N
886.69	13	1.25	Wadi B
886.70	13	1.21	F49
886.71	13	1.16	MMS/N
886.72	13	1.10	MMS/N
886.73	13	1.07	Tomb 07.1
886.74	13	1.07	Tomb 07.1
886.75	13	1.03	NoEx
886.76	13	1.00	Wadi B
886.77	13	1.00	MMS/S
886.78	13	0.89	CW6
886.79	12	1.48	MMS/N
886.80	12	1.46	HoB
886.81	12	1.30	BS-E17
886.82	12	1.39	MMS/N
886.83	12	1.35	F49, H8
886.84	12	1.40	F49, H8
886.85	12	1.30	MMS/S
886.86	12	1.27	MMS/N
886.87	12	1.21	MMS/N
886.88	12	1.20	MMS/S
886.89	12	1.16	NoEx
886.90	12	1.11	MMS/S, H2
886.91	12	1.07	Tomb 07.1
886.92	12	1.07	F55
886.93	12	1.07	F55
886.94	12	1.05	MMS/S, H2
886.95	12	1.00	MMS
886.96	12	0.99	F55
886.97	12	0.96	Wadi B
886.98	12	0.93	MMS
886.99	12	0.91	HoB
886.100	12	0.90	MMS/N
886.101	12	0.89	NoEx
886.102	12	0.85	F49
886.103	12	0.75	MMS
886.104	12	0.73	MMS
886.105	12	0.70	NoEx
886.106	12	0.67	MMS/N

886.107	12	0.64	ThSt
886.108	12	0.64	MMS/S, H2
886.109	12	0.63	Tomb 07.1
886.110	12	0.62	NoEx
886.111	12	0.61	NoEx
886.112	12	0.60	Tomb 07.1
886.113	12	0.56	NoEx
886.114	12	0.50	MMS/N
886.115	11	1.37	MMS/S
886.116	11	1.30	NoEx
886.117	11	1.18	F49, H8
886.118	11	1.17	MMS/S, H2
886.119	11	1.15	MMS, H5
886.120	11	1.10	NoEx
886.121	11	1.09	MMS/N
886.122	11	1.06	NoEx
886.123	11	1.01	NoEx
886.124	11	0.97	MMS/N
886.125	11	0.86	AT
886.126	11	0.82	F55
886.127	11	0.82	MMS
886.128	11	0.79	MMS/N
886.129	11	0.77	NoEx
886.130	11	0.75	MMS/S, H2
886.131	11	0.72	MMS/N
886.132	11	0.69	MMS/S
886.133	11	0.63	MMS
886.134	10	1.25	MMS/N
886.135	10	1.22	MMS/S, H2
886.136	10	1.12	MMS
886.137	10	1.07	MMS
886.138	10	1.05	MMS/S
886.139	10	1.02	MMS/S
886.140	10	0.96	MMS/N
886.141	10	0.80	NoEx
886.142	10	0.74	MMS/N
886.143	10	0.64	NoEx
886.144	10	0.53	MMS/N
886.145	10	frag'y	MMS/N
886.146	9	0.46	MMS/N
886.147	9	frag'y	MMS/N
886.148	8	frag'y	MMS/S
886.149	—	frag'y	F55

364–435 AD AE3 or AE4

Victory l., all else uncertain

887.1	16	2.02	MMS/S
887.2	14	1.63	MMS
887.3	13	1.86	ByzFort
887.4	13	1.66	NoEx
887.5	13	1.54	NoEx
887.6	13	1.19	MMS/N
887.7	13	1.11	HoB, clipped
887.8	13	0.93	F55
887.9	13	0.90	MMS
887.10	13	frag'y	Wadi B
887.11	12	1.57	MMS/N
887.12	12	1.52	ByzFort
887.13	12	1.39	MMS/N
887.14	12	1.27	MMS, H7
887.15	12	1.01	F55
887.16	12	0.92	MMS
887.17	12	0.90	MMS/S
887.18	12	0.83	MMS/N
887.19	12	0.83	MMS
887.20	12	0.79	F49, H8
887.21	12	0.79	Wadi B
887.22	12	0.73	MMS
887.23	12	0.70	MMS
887.24	12	frag'y	MMS
887.25	11	1.50	MMS/N
887.26	11	1.41	NoEx
887.27	11	1.30	MMS/N
887.28	11	1.21	NoEx
887.29	11	1.20	MMS/N
887.30	11	1.26	MMS
887.31	11	1.19	NoEx
887.32	11	1.18	Wadi B
887.33	11	1.08	HoB
887.34	11	1.06	MMS/N
887.35	11	1.01	F49
887.36	11	1.00	MMS
887.37	11	0.97	F55
887.38	11	0.95	MMS
887.39	11	0.90	NoEx
887.40	11	0.86	MMS
887.41	11	0.83	MMS/N
887.42	11	0.74	MMS/N
887.43	11	0.70	MMS
887.44	11	0.65	MMS
887.45	11	frag'y	MMS/N
887.46	10	1.33	NoEx
887.47	10	1.33	MMS/S, clipped?
887.48	10	0.73	MMS
887.49	10	0.71	MMS
887.50	10	0.70	MMS/N
887.51	10	0.66	MMS
887.52	10	0.60	MMS/N
887.53	10	0.60	MMS/N
887.54	10	0.51	MMS/S, H2
887.55	10	0.50	MMS/S
887.56	10	0.48	MMS
887.57	9	1.12	NoEx
887.58	9	0.75	MMS
887.59	9	0.65	MMS/S
887.60	9	0.57	MMS
887.61	9	0.40	MMS
887.62	8	0.40	RT, clipped
887.63	—	frag'y	MMS

887.64 | 10 | 0.93 | MMS/S, bust l., ancient copy

Uncertain Mint
392–395 AD AE3
M7 R 1057
Gloria Romanorum emperor horseback

888.1	17	2.45	NoEx
888.2	16	1.46	Wadi B, clipped

392–408 AD AE4
Obscure type

889.1	15	1.87	NoEx
889.2	14	1.95	Tomb 07.1
889.3	—	frag'y	MMS/N

THEODOSIUS II

Rome
404–408 AD AE3
RIC X: 1276; M7 R 930
DNTHEODOSIVSPFAVG
Urbs Roma Felix, M/m illeg.

890.1	12	frag'y	MMS/N

423–425 AD AE4
RIC X: 1914
As above
Salus Reipublice S|_, RM

891.1	12	1.45	MMS/N

Thessalonica
408–423 AD AE3
RIC X: 396; M7 R 931
DNTHEODOSIVSPFAVG, * behind
Gloria Romanorum two emperors shield

892.1	TESB	15	1.40	HoB
892.2	TES[.]	15	1.18	MMS/N

Heraclea
425–435 AD AE4
RIC X: 442; M7 R 935
DNTHEODOSIVSPFAVG
Cross in wreath, SMHA

893.1	11	1.00	MMS/N
893.2	12	1.03	ByzFort

Constantinople
401–403 AD AE3
RIC X: 89, 90; M7 R 936
Bust facing, helm., cuir., dr., spear, shield
DNTHEODOSIVSPFAVG
Concordia Augg Cp Victoriola

894.1	CONSA	17	1.87	Wadi B
894.2	CONS[.]	15	2.74	Tomb 07.1

404–406 AD AE4
RIC X: 128
DNTHEODOSIVSPFAVG
Concordia Auggg cross, CONS[.]

895.1	12	10.9	Tomb 07.1

423–435 AD AE4
RIC X: 433
As above
Concordia Aug Victory, CONS

896.1	12	1.66	Tomb 07.1
896.2	11	0.90	MMS/N

425–429 AD? AE4
RIC X: 4333
As above
Concordia Aug Victory l.

897.1	10	0.75	MMS/N

425–435 AD AE3/4
RIC X: 445; M7 R 941
As above
Cross in wreath, CON

898.1	12	0.97	Tomb 07.1
898.2	11	1.29	HoB
898.3	11	1.19	MMS, H6
898.4	11	0.53	F49, H8

430 AD AE4
RIC X: 456
As above
Vot XXX

899.1	10	0.95	MMS/N
899.2	8	0.70	MMS/N

435 AD AE4
RIC X: 457; M7 R 943
As above
VT XXX V

900.1	12	0.84	MMS/N

437 AD? AE2
RIC X: 460
As above
Concordia Agv

901.1	15	1.02	MMS/N

Nicomedia
404–406 AD AE4
RIC X: 131
As above
Concordia Auggg cross, SMN[.]

902.1	11	0.98	NoEx

425–435 AD AE4
RIC X: 447–448; M7 R 948
As above
Cross in wreath

903.1	SMNA	11	1.16	HoB
903.2	SMN[.]	12	1.50	MMS/N
903.3	SMN[.]	11	0.60	MMS

425–435 AD AE4
RIC X: 436; M7 R 946
As above
Concordia Aug Victory, SMN[.]

904.1	12	1.34	Tomb 07.1

Cyzicus
401–403 AD AE3
RIC X: 96; M7 R 949
As above
Concordia Augg Cp Victoriola

905.1	SMKA	16	2.26	MMS/S
905.2	SMK[,]	19	2.67	MMS

406–408 AD AE3
RIC X: 150; M7 R 950
DNTHEODOSIVSPFAVG, * behind head
Gloria Romanorum three emperors

906.1	SMKA	15	1.22	F55
906.2	SMKΓ	18	1.46	F55

408–423 AD AE3
RIC X: 404; M7 R 951
As above
Gloria Romanorum two emperors shield

907.1	SMKA	14	1.50	NoEx

408–423 AD AE3
RIC X: 415
As above, but two emperors globe, SMK[.]

908.1	15	1.28	Wadi B

425–435 AD AE4
RIC X: 437; M7 R 952
DNTHEODOSIVSPFAVG
Concordia Aug Victory, SMKA

909.1	13	1.11	MMS/N

425–435 AD AE4
RIC X: 451; M7 R 954
As above
Cross in wreath

910.1	SMKA	13	1.02	ByzFort
910.2	SMKA	12	0.46	MMS, H6
910.3	SMKB	14	0.89	MMS, H6
910.4	SMKB	12	0.73	MMS, H6
910.5	SMKB	11	0.68	MMS
910.6	SMK[.]	12	0.90	PA

445–450 AD AE4
LRBC, RIC not
As above
Monogram RIC X, type 5, SMKB

911.1	11	0.70	MMS/N

Antioch
425–435 AD AE4
RIC X: 453; M7 R 956
As above
Cross in wreath

912.1	ANTA	12	1.17	MMS/N
912.2	ANTA	12	1.07	MMS/N
912.3	ANTA	12	0.92	MMS/S, H2
912.4	ANTΓ	12	0.81	MMS/S, H2
912.5	ANT[.]	11	1.01	MMS/S, H2
912.6	ANT[.]	9	0.70	MMS/S, H2

Uncertain Eastern Mint
401–403 AD AE3
M7 R 959
Bust facing, helm., cuir., spear, shield
DNTHEODOSIVSPFAVG
Concordia Augg Cp Victoriola

913.1	18	2.08	MMS/N
913.2	17	1.92	MMS/N
913.3	16	1.96	NoEx
913.4	15	1.72	NoEx

404–406 AD AE4
M7 R 961
DNTHEODOSIVSPFAVG
Concordia Aug or Auggg cross

914.1	12	0.80	BS-W14
914.2	12	0.75	MMS
914.3	11	0.94	F55
914.4	10	1.00	MMS, H5

406–408 AD AE3
M7 R 960
DNTHEODOSIVSPFAVG, * behind head
Gloria Romanorum three emperors

915.1	17	1.60	E Road
915.2	16	1.55	MMS/N
915.3	14	1.17	MMS/N
915.4	13	1.37	HoB
915.5	13	1.34	MMS/S, H2

408–423 AD AE3
M7 R 964
As above, but two emperors globe

916.1	15	1.07	MMS/N

408–423 AD AE3
M7 R 963
As above, but two emperors shield

917.1	16	1.68	MMS/N
917.2	14	1.26	NoEx

408–423 AD AE3
M7 R 965
As above, but uncertain shield or globe

918.1	14	1.30	MMS/N

919 - vacat -

423–425 AD AE3
M7 R 966
DNTHEODOSIVSPFAVG
Glor orvis terrar

920.1	13	1.78	ByzFort
920.2	10	1.45	MMS, H5
920.3	10	0.58	MMS/S

425–435 AD AE4
M7 R 967
As above
Concordia Aug Victory

921.1	10	1.17	Tomb 07.1
921.2	10	0.91	MMS/S

425–435 AD AE4
M7 R 968
As above
Cross in wreath

922.1	15	0.82	MMS
922.2	14	0.94	HoB
922.3	13	0.83	HoB
922.4	12	1.19	F49, H8
922.5	12	1.12	MMS
922.6	12	0.99	HoB
922.7	12	0.93	MMS
922.8	12	0.84	F49
922.9	12	0.70	MMS/N
922.10	11	1.30	HoB
922.11	11	1.20	MMS/N
922.12	11	1.05	MMS/N
922.13	11	0.94	ByzFort
922.14	11	0.91	HoB
922.15	11	0.90	MMS/N
922.16	11	0.76	HoB
922.17	11	0.76	MMS/S, H2
922.18	11	0.70	HoB
922.19	11	0.56	MMS/S
922.20	11	0.49	MMS/N
922.21	10	1.32	MMS/N
922.22	10	1.04	MMS/N
922.23	10	1.00	MMS, H5
922.24	10	0.97	MMS/S, H2
922.25	10	0.78	MMS, H5
922.26	10	0.65	MMS, H5
922.27	10	0.64	MMS, H6
922.28	10	0.62	MMS/N
922.29	9	0.90	MMS, H5
922.30	8	0.45	MMS, H5
922.31	9	0.26	MMS/N

430 AD AE4
RIC X: 456
As above
Vot XXX

923.1	11	1.03	MMS/S

435 AD AE4
M7 R 969
As above
Vt XXX V

924.1	13	0.48	MMS/N
924.2	11	1.20	HoB
924.3	11	1.00	PN/E
924.4	10	0.95	MMS/S, H2
924.5	10	0.82	MMS/S, H2
924.6	10	0.40	MMS/N
924.7	9	0.72	MMS/N
924.8	9	0.39	MMS/N

430–435 AD AE4
As above
V[ot…]

925.1	11	1.16	MMS

445–450 AD AE4
As above
Monogram of uncertain type

926.1	11	1.10	MMS/N
926.2	9	0.59	MMS/S
926.3	8	0.26	MMS/S
926.4	7	0.32	MMS/S

Theodosius I or Theodosius II

Uncertain Mint
379–450 AD AE4
M7 R 1073
As above
Illeg.

927.1	13	1.45	MMS/N
927.2	13	1.04	ByzFort
927.3	13	1.01	F49, H8
927.4	13	0.95	NoEx
927.5	12	1.00	MMS/N
927.6	12	0.85	MMS/N
927.7	12	0.48	MMS/N
927.8	11	1.31	Tomb 07.1

927.9		11	1.00	NoEx
927.10		10	0.72	MMS

Eudocia?

Constantinople

423–425 AD AE3

RIC X: 428?, M7 R 971?

AELEVDOCIAAVG?

Concordia Aug empress

928.1		16	1.97	MMS/N

Pulcheria, Galla Placidia, or Eudocia

Constantinople

423–425 AD AE3

RIC X: 425–428

Concordia Aug empress enthroned

929.1		13	1.02	MMS
929.2		12	1.57	MMS/S, H2

Arcadius, Honorius, or Theodosius II

Rome

402–408 AD AE3

M7 R 983

Urbs Roma Felix

930.1	OF|Q	13	1.91	MMS
930.2	OF| uncertain	13	1.75	MMS/N

Constantinople

401–403 AD AE3

M7 R 1002

Concordia Augg Cp Victoriola, CONSA

931.1		15	1.33	ByzFort

406–408 AD AE3

M7 R 1003

Behind bust, * uncertain legend

Gloria Romanorum three emperors

932.1	CONSA	14	1.50	MD2
932.2	CONS[.]	15	1.45	NoEx
932.3	CONS[.]	13	1.06	NoEx

Nicomedia

406–408 AD AE3

M7 R 1016

Behind bust, * uncertain legend

Gloria Romanorum three emperors

933.1	SMNA	17	1.77	MMS
933.2	SMNA	13	1.79	HoB
933.3	SMNA	13	1.39	NoEx
933.4	SMN[.]	14	2.12	HoB

408–423 AD AE3

M7 R 1017

As above, but two emperors shield

934.1		14	1.53	MMS/N

Cyzicus

406–408 AD AE3

M7 R 1028

Behind bust, * uncertain legend

Gloria Romanorum three emperors

935.1	SMKB	14	1.70	NoEx
935.2	SMKΔ	14	1.51	NoEx
935.3	SMK[.]	15	1.18	MMS/S

Antioch

402 AD AE3

Bust facing, helm., cuir., spear, shield, uncertain legend

Concordia Augg Cp Victoriola, ANT[.]

936.1		17	1.52	Wadi B
936.2		—	frag'y	MMS

404–406 AD AE4

M7 R 1037

Concordia Aug(gg) cross, ANTA

937.1		11	0.65	MMS/N

406–408 AD AE3

M7 R 1036

Behind bust, * uncertain legend

Gloria Romanorum three emperors

938.1	ANTA	12	0.98	MMS/S, H2
938.2	ANT[.]	13	1.40	MMS/N

Uncertain Mint

401–403 AD AE3

M7 R 1062

Bust facing, helm., cuir., spear, shield, uncertain legend

Concordia Augg Cp Victoriola

939.1		17	1.89	Wadi B
939.2		16	2.57	Wadi B
939.3		15	2.25	MMS/S
939.4		15	2.07	F55
939.5		15	2.04	HoB
939.6		15	1.75	MMS/S
939.7		15	1.60	PN/E
939.8		15	1.30	PA
939.9		15	1.07	NoEx
939.10		14	2.30	MMS
939.11		14	1.95	MMS/S
939.12		14	1.89	HoB
939.13		14	1.33	MMS
939.14		13	1.85	MMS/N
939.15		13	1.44	HoB, clipped
939.16		12	1.50	NoEx, clipped
939.17		12	1.45	MMS/N, clipped
939.18		11	0.97	MMS, clipped
939.19		—	frag'y	MMS/N
939.20		10	frag'y	MMS, ancient copy?

406–408 AD AE3
M7 R 1063
Behind bust, * uncertain legend
Gloria Romanorum three emperors

940.1	18	1.29	HoB
940.2	17	1.51	MMS
940.3	16	1.96	Tomb 07.1
940.4	16	1.58	MMS/N
940.5	16	1.43	MMS
940.6	16	1.39	HoB
940.7	16	1.28	MMS/N
940.8	16	1.26	MMS
940.9	16	1.17	MMS/N
940.10	16	0.92	Wadi B
940.11	15	2.02	F55
940.12	15	1.81	MMS/N
940.13	15	1.76	NoEx
940.14	15	1.70	MMS/N
940.15	15	1.63	MMS/S
940.16	15	1.20	F55
940.17	15	1.20	NoEx
940.18	15	1.11	F55
940.19	15	1.00	MMS
940.20	15	frag'y	F55
940.21	14	2.16	HoB
940.22	14	1.91	MMS/N
940.23	14	1.89	F55
940.24	14	1.89	HoB
940.25	14	1.79	HoB
940.26	14	1.72	EH
940.27	14	1.57	MMS/N
940.28	14	1.22	MMS
940.29	14	1.10	MMS/N
940.30	14	1.07	MMS/S
940.31	14	1.05	MMS/N
940.32	14	1.00	MMS/N
940.33	13	2.31	MMS/N
940.34	13	1.71	MMS/N
940.35	13	1.44	MMS/N
940.36	13	1.35	HoB
940.37	13	1.34	NoEx
940.38	13	1.32	MMS/S, clipped
940.39	13	1.26	NoEx
940.40	13	1.24	NoEx
940.41	13	1.20	MMS/S, H2
940.42	13	1.19	MMS
940.43	13	0.91	MMS/N
940.44	12	1.45	Tomb 07.1
940.45	12	0.96	Tomb 07.1, clipped
940.46	12	0.70	MMS/N, clipped
940.47	11	0.71	MMS, clipped, H6
940.48	11	0.66	ByzFort, clipped

408–423 AD AE3
M7 R 1067
As above, but two emperors shield

941.1	16	1.21	NoEx
941.2	16	1.00	MMS/N
941.3	15	1.60	W Road
941.4	15	1.59	MMS
941.5	15	1.40	MMS/N
941.6	15	1.40	HoB
941.7	15	1.36	F49
941.8	15	1.20	MMS/N
941.9	15	frag'y	MMS/N
941.10	14	1.98	F55
941.11	14	1.64	Tomb 07.1
941.12	14	1.63	HoB
941.13	14	1.51	F49
941.14	14	1.01	MMS
941.15	14	0.68	ByzFort
941.16	13	1.77	MMS/N
941.17	13	1.63	HoB
941.18	13	1.52	NoEx
941.19	13	1.30	RT
941.20	13	1.02	MMS/S, H2
941.21	12	1.19	F55
941.22	11	1.25	MMS/S, H2
941.23	11	0.60	MMS/N, clipped
941.24	10	0.63	MMS, clipped, H5
941.25	10	0.44	Tomb 07.1, clipped
941.26	10	0.40	MMS/S, clipped

408–423 AD AE3
M7 R 1068
As above, but two emperors globe

942.1	17	2.04	Tomb 07.1
942.2	16	frag'y	MD2
942.3	15	2.20	MMS/N
942.4	15	2.01	MMS/N
942.5	15	1.50	MMS/N
942.6	15	1.49	MMS/N
942.7	15	1.48	MMS/N, pierced
942.8	14	1.29	MMS/N
942.9	14	1.18	MMS/S
942.10	13	1.64	MMS/N
942.11	13	1.47	MMS/N
942.12	13	1.41	MMS/S
942.13	13	1.30	MMS/S
942.14	13	1.06	NoEx
942.15	13	0.77	MMS/N, clipped

942.16	12	1.47	MMS/S
942.17	11	1.30	MMS/N, clipped
942.18	11	0.60	MMS/N
942.19	—	frag'y	MMS/N

408–423 AD AE3
M7 R 1065
As above, but uncertain variety

943.1	15	1.30	RT
943.2	14	1.66	NoEx
943.3	13	0.96	MMS/N
943.4	12	1.20	MMS/N, clipped
943.5	12	0.90	MMS/N, clipped
943.6	12	frag'y	MMS/N
943.7	11	1.31	Tomb 07.1, clipped

404–408 AD AE4
M7 R 1064
Concordia Aug(gg) cross

944.1	12	1.50	MMS/N
944.2	12	0.79	ThSt
944.3	11	1.09	MMS/S, H2
944.4	11	0.96	HoB
944.5	11	0.90	MMS/S
944.6	11	0.90	MMS/N
944.7	11	0.71	MMS/N
944.8	11	0.70	MMS/N
944.9	11	0.67	F55
944.10	10	0.94	MMS/S, H2
944.11	10	0.92	MMS/N
944.12	10	0.90	MMS/S, H2
944.13	10	0.67	MMS, H5
944.14	10	0.52	MMS
944.15	10	0.45	MMS/N
944.16	9	0.70	MMS/N
944.17	9	0.53	MMS/N
944.18	—	frag'y	MMS/S
944.19	—	frag'y	MMS/S

Valentinian III

Rome

425–435 AD AE4
RIC X: 2106
Obv. legend missing
Salus Reipublice, M/m missing

945.1	12	1.38	HoB
945.2	11	0.62	MMS/N
945.3	9	1.09	MMS/S, H2

425–435 AD AE4
RIC X: 2118, 2121; M7 R 972
DNVALENTINIANVSPFAVG
Victoria Augg, RM

946.1	S|	11	1.20	MMS/N
946.2	S|	11	1.07	F49, H8
946.3	S|	10	0.92	NoEx
946.4	T|	11	1.05	HoB
946.5	Q|	11	0.80	MMS/N
946.6	Q|	10	1.34	MMS/N
946.7	E|	11	1.36	HoB
946.8	unc.	10	0.59	MMS/N

425–435 AD AE4
RIC X: 2129–2130
As above
Vot XX, M/m uncertain

947.1	13	1.21	MMS/N
947.2	10	0.89	MMS

425–435 AD AE4
RIC X: 2135; M7 R 973
As above
Vot Pvb camp-gate, two towers, star between

948.1	11	1.50	W Road

425–435 AD AE4
RIC X: 2144–2145, M7 R 979
As above
Cross in wreath

949.1	10	0.80	MMS/N

425–435 AD AE4
RIC X: 2147–2148
DNVAL[...]AVG
Victoria Aug emperor standing with globe in r. and spear in l.

950.1	12	1.30	NoEx

425–435 AD AE4
RIC X: 2152–2158
[...]AVG
VICTO[...] Victory l. with wreath

951.1	12	0.67	MMS

Uncertain Mint

425–455 AD AE4
M7 R 980
DNVALENTINIANVSPFAVG
Uncertain rev.

952.1	11	1.03	ByzFort, H4

440–455 AD AE4
As above
Victori Aug(ust) Victory l.

953.1	11	0.79	MMS/S, H2

Galla Placidia

Rome
425–435 AD AE4
RIC X: 2109
DNGALLIA PLACIDIAPFAVG
Salus Reipublicae S|, RM

954.1	11	0.91	MMS/N

Valentinian II or Valentinian III

Uncertain mint
378–455 AD AE4
DNVALENTINIANVSPFAVG
Victory l.

955.1	14	1.16	Syn

Gratian, Valentinian II, Theodosius I, or Valentinian III

Uncertain Mint
383–435 AD AE4
M7 R 1049
Vot Mult, uncertain year

956.1	13	1.00	MMS/S
956.2	12	0.90	ByzFort
956.3	12	0.86	MMS
956.4	12	0.42	MMS/N
956.5	11	0.90	MMS/N
956.6	11	0.87	MMS/N

Arcadius, Honorius, Theodosius II, or Valentinian III

Rome
395–430 AD
Victoria Augg S|, RM

957.1	11	1.19	MMS/S, H2

Uncertain Mint
383–437 AD AE4
Victoria Augg(g) 2 Victories

958.1		12	1.18	MMS/N
958.2		12	0.57	MMS/N
958.3	chi-rho|	11	0.71	MMS/N

395–430 AD AE4
M7 R 1070
Victoria Augg Victory l.

959.1	13	1.08	MMS/N
959.2	11	1.13	MMS/S
959.3	11	1.13	NoEx

Theodosius II or Valentinian III

Trier
425–435 AD AE4
RIC X: 2166
VRTVS ROMANORVM emperor standing facing, holds standard and shield

960.1	11	1.17	MMS/N
960.2	11	0.76	MMS/S, H2

Constantinople
425–435 AD AE4
M7 R 1008
Uncertain legend
Cross in wreath, CON

961.1	13	1.10	MMS
961.2	11	1.13	MMS, H6
961.3	10	0.32	F49, H8

Cyzicus
425–435 AD AE4
M7 R 1029
Uncertain legend
Cross in wreath

962.1	SMKA	11	0.65	MMS/N
962.2	SMKB	11	0.80	ByzFort
962.3	SMKB	10	0.67	MMS
962.4	SMK[.]	13	0.98	EH

Uncertain Mint
425–435 AD AE4
M7 R 1071
(very likely almost all of these are minted for Theodosius II)
Cross in wreath

963.1	18	0.93	MMS
963.2	14	1.39	Tomb 07.1
963.3	14	1.14	MMS/N
963.4	14	0.84	MMS/N
963.5	14	0.52	MMS/N
963.6	13	2.40	MMS/N
963.7	13	2.02	Tomb 07.1
963.8	13	1.40	MMS/N
963.9	13	1.40	MMS/N
963.10	13	1.36	NoEx
963.11	13	1.07	MMS
963.12	13	0.86	MMS, H6
963.13	13	0.66	NoEx
963.14	13	0.61	MMS/N
963.15	13	0.42	MMS/N
963.16	12	1.19	MMS/N
963.17	12	1.15	MMS/N
963.18	12	1.04	MMS/N
963.19	12	0.95	MMS/N
963.20	12	0.86	MMS/N
963.21	12	0.78	MMS/N
963.22	12	0.78	MMS/S, H2
963.23	12	0.75	HoB
963.24	12	0.67	MMS/S, H2
963.25	12	0.66	MMS
963.26	12	0.65	MMS/S, H2
963.27	12	0.63	MMS
963.28	12	0.63	MMS

963.29	12	0.60	MMS/N	963.83	11	0.70	MMS/S, H2
963.30	12	frag'y	MMS/N, i.d. prob.	963.84	11	0.64	MMS, H5
				963.85	11	0.63	MMS/S, H2
963.31	11	1.84	MMS/S	963.86	11	0.60	MMS/N
963.32	11	1.34	NoEx	963.87	11	0.60	MMS/N
963.33	11	1.33	Tomb 07.1	963.88	11	0.50	NoEx
963.34	11	1.29	Tomb 07.1	963.89	11	0.37	MMS/N
963.35	11	1.24	Tomb 07.1	963.90	11	0.34	MMS
963.36	11	1.22	MMS	963.91	11	0.30	MMS/N
963.37	11	1.17	MMS/N	963.92	11	frag'y	MMS/N
963.38	11	1.14	MD1/S	963.93	10	1.90	MMS
963.39	11	1.12	MMS/S, H2	963.94	10	1.58	ByzFort
963.40	11	1.10	MMS/N	963.95	10	1.45	MMS/N
963.41	11	1.10	MMS/N	963.96	10	1.40	Tomb 07.1
963.42	11	1.10	MMS/S, H2	963.97	10	1.34	MMS, H5
963.43	11	1.08	MMS/S, H2	963.98	10	1.32	Tomb 07.1
963.44	11	1.07	MMS	963.99	10	1.27	MMS/N
963.45	11	1.07	F49, H8	963.100	10	1.25	MMS, H5
963.46	11	1.05	MMS/N	963.101	10	1.22	F49
963.47	11	1.04	MMS/N	963.102	10	1.20	MMS/S, H2
963.48	11	1.03	MMS/N	963.103	10	1.13	MMS/N
963.49	11	1.00	MMS/N	963.104	10	1.11	MMS/N
963.50	11	1.00	MMS/S, H2	963.105	10	1.04	MMS/N
963.51	11	0.97	MMS/N	963.106	10	1.01	MMS/S, H2
963.52	11	0.97	EH	963.107	10	1.00	MMS/N
963.53	11	0.97	MMS/S, H2	963.108	10	1.00	Tomb 07.1
963.54	11	0.96	MMS/S, H2	963.109	10	0.96	Tomb 07.1
963.55	11	0.95	MMS/N	963.110	10	0.94	MMS/N
963.56	11	0.94	MMS	963.111	10	0.91	HoB
963.57	11	0.92	MMS/S, H2	963.112	10	0.90	MMS/N
963.58	11	0.92	ByzFort, H4	963.113	10	0.86	MMS
963.59	11	0.90	MMS/N	963.114	10	0.85	MMS/S, H2
963.60	11	0.89	MMS/N	963.115	10	0.82	MMS/N
963.61	11	0.87	MMS/N	963.116	10	0.82	MMS/S
963.62	11	0.87	Tomb 07.1	963.117	10	0.80	MMS/N
963.63	11	0.85	MMS	963.118	10	0.80	MMS/N
963.64	11	0.84	MMS/N	963.119	10	0.78	Wadi B
963.65	11	0.83	HoB	963.120	10	0.75	MMS/N
963.66	11	0.82	F49, H8	963.121	10	0.70	MMS
963.67	11	0.82	MMS/S, H2	963.122	10	0.70	MMS/N
963.68	11	0.80	MMS/N	963.123	10	0.70	ThSt
963.69	11	0.78	Tomb 07.1	963.124	10	0.67	MMS/N
963.70	11	0.77	MMS	963.125	10	0.60	MMS/N
963.71	11	0.76	MMS/N	963.126	10	0.60	MMS/N
963.72	11	0.76	ThSt	963.127	10	0.60	MMS/N
963.73	11	0.76	MMS/N	963.128	10	0.60	MMS/N
963.74	11	0.75	MMS	963.129	10	0.60	ByzFort, poss. Concordia Auggg
963.75	11	0.75	MMS/N				
963.76	11	0.74	ByzFort	963.130	10	0.59	MMS/N
963.77	11	0.74	Tomb 07.1	963.131	10	0.56	MMS
963.78	11	0.73	Tomb 07.1	963.132	10	0.55	NoEx
963.79	11	0.72	Tomb 07.1	963.133	10	0.53	CW6
963.80	11	0.71	Tomb 07.1	963.134	10	0.50	MMS/N
963.81	11	0.70	W Road	963.135	10	0.48	MMS
963.82	11	0.70	MMS/N	963.136	10	0.48	MMS/N

963.137	10	0.47	NoEx
963.138	10	0.42	MMS
963.139	9	1.64	MMS
963.140	9	1.11	CW6
963.141	9	1.05	MMS, H5
963.142	9	1.03	MMS/S, H2
963.143	9	0.98	MMS
963.144	9	0.87	MMS/N
963.145	9	0.87	MMS, H5
963.146	9	0.86	MMS/N
963.147	9	0.85	MMS/N
963.148	9	0.82	Tomb 07.1
963.149	9	0.79	MMS
963.150	9	0.78	MMS/N
963.151	9	0.76	NoEx
963.152	9	0.76	Tomb 07.1
963.153	9	0.74	NoEx
963.154	9	0.74	MMS
963.155	9	0.74	MMS/N
963.156	9	0.72	MMS/N
963.157	9	0.71	F49, H8
963.158	9	0.70	NoEx
963.159	9	0.65	MMS/S
963.160	9	0.64	MMS, H5
963.161	9	0.62	MMS, H5
963.162	9	0.59	MMS/N
963.163	9	0.59	MD2
963.164	9	0.58	BE-B
963.165	9	0.56	HoB
963.166	9	0.53	MMS/N
963.167	9	0.49	ByzFort, H4
963.168	9	0.46	MMS
963.169	9	0.42	MMS
963.170	9	0.40	MMS/N
963.171	9	0.40	MMS/N
963.172	9	0.38	MD2
963.173	9	0.36	MMS/N
963.174	9	0.33	MMS/N
963.175	9	0.29	MMS/N
963.176	9	0.25	ThSt
963.177	8	0.95	E Road
963.178	8	0.77	MMS, H5
963.179	8	0.77	MMS/N
963.180	8	0.76	MMS/N
963.181	8	0.70	NoEx
963.182	8	0.68	MMS
963.183	8	0.46	MMS
963.184	8	0.44	MMS/N
963.185	8	0.41	MMS/S, H2
963.186	8	0.39	MMS
963.187	8	0.38	MMS, H5
963.188	8	0.32	MMS
963.189	8	0.30	MMS
963.190	8	0.26	MMS, H5
963.191	7	0.35	MMS/N
963.192	7	0.23	MMS/N
963.193	7	0.51	MMS
963.194	5	0.90	MMS/N
963.195	—	frag'y	MMS/N
963.196	—	frag'y	MMS
963.197	—	frag'y	MMS

Marcian

Thessalonica
450–457 AD AE4
RIC X: 535–536
DNMARCIANVSPFAVG
Monogram LRBC, type 9 (RIC X not), CHES

964.1	10	0.98	NoEx

As above, type uncertain

964.2	12	0.91	MMS/N

Heraclea
450–457 AD AE4
RIC X: 540
As above
Monogram RIC X, type 2, cross above

965.1	SMHA	10	1.20	MMS
965.2	SMH[.]	11	0.88	MMS/N

Constantinople
450–457 AD AE4
RIC X: 545
As above
Monogram RIC X, type 2, CON, + above

966.1	11	1.28	MMS
966.2	11	1.28	MMS/N
966.3	11	1.22	MMS
966.4	9	1.30	MMS, H5
966.5	9	0.58	ByzFort, H4

As above, but RIC X, type 5 (RIC X: 541–542)

966.6	11	1.06	AT-Pac

Nicomedia
450–457 AD AE4
RIC X: 551; M7 R 1078
As above
Monogram RIC X, type 2, NIC, + above

967.1	9	1.15	MMS/N
967.2	9	0.37	MMS/N

As above, but RIC X, type 3 (RIC X: 557)

967.3	9	0.82	MMS

As above, but RIC X, type 4 (RIC X: 553, 558)

967.4	10	1.22	MMS/N
967.5	10	1.22	MMS/S, H2

As above, but variant of type 2

967.6	* above	10	1.14	MMS/N

Cyzicus
450–457 AD AE4
RIC X: 560
As above
Monogram RIC X, type 7, SMKA

968.1		11	0.76	MMS/N

As above but RIC X, type 1, CVZ (RIC X: 561)

968.2		10	0.69	HoB

As above but RIC X, type 2, CVZ (RIC X: 563); imitation?

968.3		10	1.11	MD1/S
968.4		9	1.32	MMS, H5

Uncertain Eastern Mint
400–457 AD AE 4
As above
Monogram RIC X, type 1

969.1		11	1.17	MMS/S, H2
969.2		10	1.23	Tomb 07.1
969.3		10	0.71	MMS/S
969.4		9	0.78	MMS, H5
969.5		9	0.57	MMS/N

As above but RIC X, type 2; M7 R 1083, 1085, 1087

969.6	+ above	12	1.33	MMS
969.7	* above	12	0.71	MMS/N
969.8	+ above	11	1.32	MMS/N
969.9		11	0.98	MMS, H5
969.10		11	0.96	ByzFort, H4
969.11	+ above	11	0.74	MMS/S, H2
969.12	* above	11	0.60	MMS
969.13		10	1.16	F49, H8
969.14	+ above?	10	1.16	MMS/S, H2
969.15		10	1.04	MMS/N
969.16	+ above	10	1.00	MMS
969.17	+ above?	10	0.91	MMS/S, H2
969.18		10	0.86	MMS/N
969.19	+ above	10	0.69	MMS, H6
969.20	+ or * above	10	0.66	MMS
969.21	+ above	10	0.65	MMS
969.22	+ above	10	0.53	MMS
969.23	+ or * above	9	1.15	MMS/S, H2
969.24	+ above	9	0.97	MMS, H6
969.25	+ or * above	9	0.69	MMS/S, H2
969.26	+ above	9	0.40	MMS/N

As above but RIC X, type 5; M7 R 1080–1081

969.27		10	1.06	MMS/N
969.28		10	1.00	MMS/N
969.29		9	1.16	HoB
969.30		9	0.80	MMS

Monogram of uncertain type, M7 R 1088

969.31		12	1.36	F49, H8
969.32		12	1.30	MMS/S
969.33		12	1.08	ByzFort, H4
969.34		12	0.90	Tomb 07.1
969.35		12	0.85	MMS/N
969.36		12	0.82	MMS
969.37		12	0.60	MMS/N
969.38		11	1.93	MMS
969.39		11	1.20	MMS/N
969.40		11	1.00	F49, H8
969.41		11	0.99	F49, H8
969.42		11	0.96	NoEx
969.43		11	0.77	Tomb 07.1
969.44		11	0.57	ByzFort, H4
969.45		10	1.57	MMS/N
969.46		10	1.50	MMS/N
969.47		10	1.27	F49, H8
969.48		10	1.20	MMS/N
969.49		10	1.20	MMS/N
969.50		10	1.10	MMS/N
969.51		10	1.01	MMS
969.52		10	1.01	MMS/S
969.53		10	1.00	MMS
969.54		10	0.99	MMS/N
969.55		10	0.99	HoB
969.56		10	0.96	MMS
969.57		10	0.77	MMS/N
969.58		10	0.67	MMS/S
969.59		10	0.55	RT
969.60		10	0.40	MMS/N
969.61		9	1.17	MMS
969.62		9	0.99	ByzFort, H4
969.63		9	0.97	MMS
969.64		9	0.88	MMS, H7
969.65		9	0.83	ByzFort
969.66		9	0.78	MMS, H5
969.67		9	0.71	ByzFort, H4
969.68		9	0.65	MMS/N
969.69		9	0.47	MMS/N
969.70		9	0.46	MMS
969.71		9	0.32	HoB
969.72		9	0.27	MMS/N
969.73		8	1.15	MMS/N
969.74		8	1.10	BW-Lat
969.75		8	0.85	MMS/N
969.76		8	0.70	MMS/N
969.77		8	0.63	ByzFort, H4
969.78		8	0.62	MMS/S, H2
969.79		8	0.58	MMS/N
969.80		8	0.55	MMS, H5
969.81		8	0.52	MMS
969.82		8	0.46	MMS/N
969.83		8	0.44	MMS/S, H2
969.84		8	0.41	MMS/N
969.85		8	0.38	HoB
969.86		8	0.36	MMS/N
969.87		7	0.74	MMS, H6
969.88		7	0.69	MMS
969.89		7	0.60	MMS/N
969.90		7	0.43	MMS
969.91		7	0.30	MMS/N
969.92		7	0.30	MMS/N

Uncertain Mint
450 AD and later AE4
Wroth WPBC, p. 31, nos. 107–108
Bust r. pd., dots for legend
Monogram in wreath, imitation

970.1	11	0.41	MMS/N
970.2	8	0.33	MMS/N

Bust r. pd. […]PFAVG
Monogram? KYZ (RIC X not)

971.1	11	1.25	HoB, imit.?

Leo I

Rome
457–474 AD AE4
RIC X: 2628
DNLEOPERPETAVG
Victoria Augg

972.1	10	1.90	MMS
972.2	11	0.79	MMS/N, i.d. poss.

Thessalonica
457–474 AD AE4
RIC X: 695–697; M7 R 1089
Uncertain legend
RIC X, type 4 monogram

973.1	10	0.64	ByzFort, H4
973.2	9	0.40	MMS/N

Constantinople
457–474 AD AE4
RIC X: 667–668; M7 R 1091
DNLEOPFAVG or similar
Lion standing l., looking r. in wreath, CON

974.1	12	1.30	MMS/N
974.2	10	1.62	ByzFort
974.3	10	1.11	MMS/S, H2
974.4	9	1.24	MMS, H5
974.5	9	0.85	MMS
974.6	8	0.41	MMS
974.7	12	1.01	MMS/N, i.d. poss.

457–474 AD AE4
RIC X: 674
DNLEOPFAVG
Lion crouching l., head r. in wreath, CON

975.1	11	1.33	MMS/N
975.2	11	1.29	MMS/N
975.3	11	1.00	BS-W8
975.4	11	0.93	HoB
975.5	11	0.93	MMS/S, H2
975.6	10	1.05	MMS/N
975.7	10	1.04	MMS/S, H2
975.8	10	1.00	MMS
975.9	10	0.95	MMS/S, H2
975.10	10	0.89	MMS/S, H2
975.11	9	1.18	MMS/S, H2

457–474 AD AE4
RIC X: 683–688; M7 R 1092
DNLEOPFAVG or similar
RIC X, type 1, monogram in wreath, CON

976.1	11	1.70	MMS/N
976.2	10	1.23	MMS/S, H2
976.3	10	1.16	MMS/S, H2
976.4	9	0.96	MMS, H5
976.5	8	0.82	MMS/N

As above, but RIC X, type 4, monogram in wreath, CON or KOC

976.6	10	0.92	MMS/S, H2

As above, but monogram of uncertain type, CON

976.7	11	0.85	MMS/N
976.8	9	0.50	HoB
976.9	8	0.30	MMS/N

457–474 AD AE4
RIC X: 700–702; M7 R 1093
Uncertain legend
Emperor and captive, CON

977.1	11	0.66	MMS/N
977.2	10	0.83	MMS/S, H2

On obv., * in l. field
As above, but M/m CN, RIC X: 703

977.3	11	1.10	MMS

473–474 AD AE4
RIC X: 724; M7 R 1095
DNLE[…]
Two enthroned emperors, KOC

978.1	11	0.96	MMS/S, H2
978.2	11	0.85	HoB
978.3	11	1.10	MMS/S, H2 M/m KON

457–474 AD AE4
DNL[…]
Uncertain rev., CON

979.1	10	0.57	MMS/N

Nicomedia
457–474 AD AE4
RIC X: 669
DNΛEONSPFAVG
Lion standing l., head r., NIC

980.1	11	0.74	MMS, H6

457–474 AD AE4
RIC X: 705
DNLEOSPFAVG
Emperor and captive, NIC

981.1	11	1.51	MMS/S
981.2	10	1.25	MMS

Obv. legend DNLEO[PER]PETAVG

981.3	12	1.44	MMS/S, H2
981.4	10	1.39	MMS/S, H2
981.5	11	1.11	MMS/S, H2

457–474 AD AE4
RIC X: 722
DNLEOPERPEAVG
RIC X, type 6 monogram in wreath, NIC

982.1	11	0.83	MMS
982.2	10	1.45	MMS/S
982.3	9	0.78	ByzFort, H4

Cyzicus
457–474 AD AE4
RIC X: 678
DNLEONSPFAVG
Lion crouching l., head r. in wreath, CVZ

983.1	11	0.80	MMS/N

Uncertain Eastern Mint
457–474 AD AE4
M7 R 1098
DNLEOPFAVG or similar
Lion crouching l. in wreath

984.1	11	1.30	MMS/S, H2
984.2	11	1.01	MMS/S, H2
984.3	11	0.95	MMS
984.4	11	0.70	MMS/N
984.5	11	frag'y	MMS/N
984.6	10	1.62	MMS
984.7	10	1.17	MMS/S, H2
984.8	10	1.10	MMS/S, H2
984.9	10	0.53	MMS/S, H2
984.10	9	0.80	MMS/S, H2
984.11	9	0.78	MMS
984.12	9	0.71	MMS/S, H2
984.13	9	0.63	MMS/N

As above, no wreath, M7 R 1097

984.14	10	1.42	MMS, H5
984.15	10	1.32	HoB
984.16	10	1.25	MMS/N

As above, but lion standing l. in wreath

984.17	11	0.86	ByzFort
984.18	10	1.08	F49
984.19	10	0.75	MMS/N
984.20	10	0.75	MMS/N
984.21	9	0.71	MMS
984.22	9	0.50	MMS/N
984.23	8	0.75	HoB
984.24	8	0.49	MMS/N
984.25	8	0.31	MMS
984.26	7	0.46	MMS
984.27 in wreath	9	0.71	MMS/N
984.28 in wreath	7	0.28	MMS/N

As above, lion either standing or crouching

984.29	10	0.51	MMS/N
984.30	10	0.37	MMS
984.31	9	0.41	MMS
984.32	9	0.34	MMS
984.33	8	0.46	NoEx

457–474 AD AE4
M7 R 1099
Uncertain legend
RIC X, type 1, monogram

985.1	11	1.80	MMS/N
985.2	11	1.25	MMS/S, H2
985.3	11	1.24	MMS
985.4	11	0.89	MMS/N
985.5	11	0.33	MMS/N
985.6	10	1.34	MMS/N
985.7	10	1.15	MMS/N
985.8	10	0.95	MMS/N
985.9	10	0.91	MMS/S, H2
985.10	10	0.90	MMS/N
985.11	10	0.88	MMS/N
985.12	10	0.86	MMS/S, H2
985.13	10	0.82	MMS/N
985.14	10	0.75	MMS/N
985.15	10	0.67	NoEx
985.16	10	0.56	MMS/N
985.17	10	0.53	MMS/N
985.18	10	0.49	MMS/S, H2
985.19	10	0.47	MMS, H7
985.20	9	0.82	MMS/S, H2
985.21	9	0.79	F49
985.22	9	0.76	MMS/S, H2
985.23	9	0.68	MMS/S, H2
985.24	9	0.67	MMS, H5
985.25	9	0.66	MMS/S, H2
985.26	9	0.55	MMS/S, H2
985.27	9	0.45	MMS
985.28	9	0.40	MMS/S, H2
985.29	9	0.39	MMS, H5
985.30	8	0.95	MMS, H5
985.31	8	0.89	MMS/N
985.32	8	0.72	MMS/N
985.33	8	0.66	MMS/S, H2
985.34	8	0.62	MMS
985.35	8	0.57	MMS/S, H2
985.36	8	0.55	MMS/N
985.37	8	0.50	MMS/N
985.38	8	0.48	MMS/S, H2

985.39	8	0.39	MMS
As above, but RIC X, type 1 or type 2			
985.40	8	0.46	MMS/N
As above, but RIC X, type 1 or type 4			
985.41	9	0.93	ByzFort, H4
As above, but RIC X, type 5; M7 R 1100			
985.42	10	1.01	MMS, H7
As above, but type uncertain; M7 R 1101			
985.43	11	0.96	ByzFort, H4
985.44	11	0.47	ByzFort, H4
985.45	10	1.34	MMS, H5
985.46	10	frag'y	MMS/N
985.47	9	0.89	MMS/S, H2
985.48	9	0.87	MMS
985.49	9	0.67	MMS, H5
985.50	9	0.62	MMS/S
985.51	9	0.62	MMS/S, H2 i.d. prob.
985.52	8	0.67	MMS, H5
985.53	8	0.62	MMS/N
985.54	8	0.45	MMS
985.55	7	0.31	ByzFort, H4

457–474 AD AE4
M7 R 1102
Uncertain legend
Emperor and captive

986.1	13	0.97	F49
986.2	12	1.07	F49, H8
986.3	12	1.03	F49, H8
986.4	12	1.03	MMS/S, H2
986.5	11	1.13	MMS/S, H2
986.6	11	1.07	MMS
986.7	11	0.92	MMS/N
986.8	11	0.83	MMS
986.9	11	0.60	MMS/S
986.10	11	frag'y	MMS/N
986.11	10	1.10	NoEx
986.12	10	1.00	MMS/S, H2
986.13	10	0.93	MMS/S
986.14	10	0.85	MMS/S
986.15	10	0.80	MMS/N
986.16	10	0.80	MMS/N
986.17	10	0.78	F55
986.18	10	0.59	MMS/S, H2
986.19	10	0.48	MMS
986.20	10	0.44	MMS
986.21	9	1.20	MMS/N
986.22	9	1.13	MMS/S, H2
986.23	9	0.88	MMS/S, H2
986.24	9	0.87	MD2
986.25	9	0.86	MMS/S
986.26	9	0.64	MMS
986.27	9	0.59	MMS
986.28	9	0.52	MMS
986.29	9	0.45	MMS
986.30	9	0.42	MMS/N
986.31	9	0.42	MMS/N
986.32	9	0.33	MMS
986.33	8	0.84	MMS/N
986.34	8	0.60	MMS/N
986.35	7	0.30	MMS

457–474 AD AE4
M7 R 1094
Uncertain legend
Empress b/E

987.1	12	1.64	MMS
987.2	12	0.88	F49, H8
987.3	12	0.63	MMS/N
987.4	11	1.24	MMS/S
987.5	11	1.19	MMS/N
987.6	11	1.17	MMS/S, H2
987.7	11	1.15	MMS/N
987.8	11	1.07	MMS/S, H2
987.9	11	0.99	F49, i.d. prob.
987.10	11	0.93	MMS/S, H2
987.11	11	0.85	MMS/S, H2
987.12	11	0.84	MMS/N
987.13	11	0.82	MMS/S
987.14	11	0.73	MMS/S, H2
987.15	11	0.62	MMS/N
987.16	11	0.56	MMS/N
987.17	11	0.38	MMS/N
987.18	10	1.32	MMS/S
987.19	10	1.32	MMS/S, H2
987.20	10	1.29	MMS/S, H2
987.21	10	1.08	MMS/S, H2
987.22	10	1.07	MMS/S, H2
987.23	10	1.07	MMS/S, H2
987.24	10	1.06	ByzFort, H4
987.25	10	0.96	MMS/S, H2
987.26	10	0.76	MMS/S, H2
987.27	10	0.76	MMS/S, H2
987.28	10	0.74	MMS
987.29	10	0.72	MMS
987.30	10	0.70	ThSt
987.31	10	0.66	MMS/S
987.32	10	0.61	MMS
987.33	10	0.58	MMS/S, H2
987.34	10	0.53	MMS/N
987.35	9	1.10	Tomb 07.1
987.36	9	0.98	ByzFort, H4
987.37	9	0.95	MD2
987.38	9	0.93	MMS/S, H2
987.39	9	0.90	MMS
987.40	9	0.89	MMS/S, H2
987.41	9	0.84	MMS/S, H2
987.42	9	0.72	F49
987.43	9	0.71	ThSt

987.44	9	0.65	MMS/N
987.45	9	0.55	MD2
987.46	9	0.39	MMS/S, H2
987.47	8	0.81	MMS
987.48	8	0.63	MMS/N
987.49	8	0.60	MMS
987.50	8	0.52	MMS
987.51	8	0.39	MMS
987.52	8	0.37	MMS/N
987.53	8	0.30	MMS/S
987.54	8	0.22	MMS
987.55	7	0.42	MMS/S
987.56	7	0.32	MMS/N
987.57	7	0.31	MMS/N

457–474 AD AE4
M7 R 1103
DNLEOSE[...]
Uncertain rev.

988.1	11	0.92	MMS
988.2	10	1.05	MMS
988.3	10	0.78	MMS/S
988.4	10	0.54	MMS/N
988.5	10	0.49	MMS/N
988.6	9	0.80	ByzFort
988.7	9	0.56	ByzFort, H4
988.8	8	0.80	MMS/N

Libius Severus

Rome
461–465 AD AE4
RIC X: 2715–2717
Legend illeg.
Monogram RIC X, type 1

989.1	10	0.84	MMS

Odavacar

Ravenna
477 AD AE4
RIC X: 3502
Obscure legend
Monogram in wreath

990.1	9	0.79	MMS
990.2	9	0.40	MMS/S

Basiliscus

Constantinople
475–476 AD AE4
LRBC, p. 91, no. 2283; RIC X not
DNBASIL[...]
Monogram LRBC, type 1 in wreath

991.1	9	0.44	MMS/S, H2

Zenonis

Constantinople?
475–476 AD AE4
RIC X: 1017
DNZENONIS or similar
Monogram RIC X, type 1

992.1	10	1.24	MMS/S, H2
992.2	10	0.92	MMS/S, H2
992.3	10	0.82	MMS/S, H2
992.4	10	0.65	MMS/S, H2
992.5	9	1.06	MMS/S, H2
992.6	9	0.69	MMS/S, H2
992.7	8	0.72	MMS/S, H2

Zeno

Constantinople
476–491 AD AE4
RIC X: 954 var.
Uncertain legend
Emperor cross and globe, CON

993.1	10	0.68	MMS

Example in RIC has no M/m

Nicomedia
476–491 AD AE4
RIC X: 964
As above
Monogram RIC X, type 1, NIC

994.1	9	frag'y	MMS
994.2	8	0.86	MMS/S, H2
994.3	8	0.61	MMS/N

Cyzicus
476–491 AD AE4
RIC X: 965
As above
Monogram RIC X, type 4, CVZ

995.1	12	0.69	MMS
995.2	10	0.90	MMS/N

As above, monogram type 13; RIC X: 966

995.3	10	0.68	MMS/S, H2
995.4	10	0.43	MMS/N
995.5	9	0.68	F49
995.6	9	0.36	MMS/S, H2
995.7	8	0.37	MMS/S, H2

As above, monogram type 14; RIC X: 967

995.8	11	0.44	ByzFort, H4
995.9	9	0.85	ByzFort
995.10	9	0.39	MMS
995.11	9	0.35	F49, H8
995.12	9	0.33	MMS
995.13	8	0.73	MMS/N
995.14	8	0.62	MMS
995.15	8	0.61	MMS/N
995.16	8	0.52	MMS/S

995.17	8	0.47	MMS/N
995.18	8	0.45	MMS/N
995.19	8	0.43	MMS
995.20	8	0.35	MMS
995.21	8	0.24	MMS

As above, type 13 or 14

995.22	10	1.15	F49, H8
995.23	8	0.37	MMS/N

Antioch
476–491 AD AE4
RIC X: 973
As above
Monogram RIC X, type 10

996.1	10	0.93	MMS
996.2	9	0.26	MMS/N
996.3	8	0.67	ByzFort, H4
996.4	8	0.32	MMS
996.5	7	0.42	MMS/S

Uncertain Eastern Mint
476–491 AD AE4
M7 R 1107
As above
Monogram RIC X, type 1

997.1	10	1.23	MMS/S, H2
997.2	10	0.88	MMS/N
997.3	10	0.70	MMS/S
997.4	10	0.51	ByzFort, H4
997.5	10	0.35	MMS/N
997.6	9	1.28	ByzFort, H4
997.7	9	1.11	MMS/S, H2
997.8	9	1.06	MMS/S, H2
997.9	9	0.97	MMS/S, H2
997.10	9	0.87	ByzFort, H4
997.11	9	0.83	MMS/S, H2
997.12	9	0.82	MMS/S, H2
997.13	9	0.72	ByzFort, H4
997.14	9	0.61	ByzFort, H4
997.15	9	0.61	MMS/N
997.16	9	0.61	MMS
997.17	8	1.09	MMS/N
997.18	8	1.06	MMS/S, H2
997.19	8	1.02	MMS/S, H2
997.20	8	0.96	MMS/S, H2
997.21	8	0.92	ByzFort, H4
997.22	8	0.90	MMS/S, H2
997.23	8	0.83	ByzFort, H4
997.24	8	0.82	MMS/S, H2
997.25	8	0.82	MMS/S, H2
997.26	8	0.80	MMS/S, H2
997.27	8	0.79	ByzFort, H4
997.28	8	0.77	MMS/S, H2
997.29	8	0.77	MMS/S, H2
997.30	8	0.76	MMS/S, H2
997.31	8	0.56	MMS/S, H2
997.32	8	0.54	MMS/S, H2
997.33	8	0.41	ByzFort, H4
997.34	7	0.53	MMS/S, H2

As above, monogram RIC X, type 4; M7 R 1105

997.35	10	1.31	MMS/S, H2
997.36	10	1.12	MMS/S, H2
997.37	10	0.98	MMS/S, H2

DИΣENOP

997.38	10	0.84	MMS/S, H2
997.39	10	0.73	MMS/S, H2
997.40	9	1.22	MMS/S, H2
997.41	9	1.05	MMS/S, H2
997.42	9	0.92	MMS/S, H2

[...]ZENOSPFA

997.43	9	0.80	MMS/S, H2
997.44	9	0.66	MMS/S, H2
997.45	9	0.61	MMS/S, H2
997.46	9	0.61	MMS/S, H2
997.47	8	1.01	MMS/S, H2
997.48	8	0.88	MMS/S, H2
997.49	8	0.84	MMS/S, H2
997.50	8	0.75	MMS/S, H2
997.51	8	0.69	MMS/S, H2
997.52	8	0.52	MMS/S, H2
997.53	8	0.50	MMS/S, H2
997.54	8	0.35	MMS/S, H2

As above, monogram RIC X, type 5

997.55	12	1.12	MMS/N
997.56	9	0.61	MMS/N
997.57	9	0.46	MMS/N
997.58	8	1.13	MMS/N

As above, uncertain type; M7 R 1109

997.59	11	1.39	F49, H8
997.60	10	1.24	NoEx
997.61	10	1.07	ByzFort, H4
997.62	10	0.48	MMS/N
997.63	9	0.68	MMS/N
997.64	9	0.58	MMS/N
997.65	9	0.47	MMS
997.66	8	0.83	MMS
997.67	8	0.70	RT
997.68	8	0.38	MMS
997.69	8	frag'y	MMS/N
997.70	7	0.41	MMS/N

476–491 AD AE4
M7 R 1104
As above
Emperor cross and globe

998.1	11	0.87	MMS/S, H2
998.2	11	0.80	MMS/N
998.3	7	1.05	ByzFort, H4

450–498 AD AE4
M7 R 1112
Monogram of uncertain emperor

999.1	12	2.30	F49
999.2	12	1.07	MMS
999.3	12	0.99	MMS
999.4	12	0.78	ByzFort
999.5	12	0.62	MMS/N
999.6	12	0.51	MMS
999.7	12	0.36	MMS/N
999.8	11	1.48	ByzFort
999.9	11	1.33	MMS
999.10	11	1.05	MMS
999.11	11	1.04	F49, H8
999.12	11	1.03	PA
999.13	11	1.01	MMS/S, H2
999.14	11	0.85	MMS/N
999.15	11	0.85	MMS, H5
999.16	11	0.80	MMS/S
999.17	11	0.80	MMS/S
999.18	11	0.74	MMS/N
999.19	11	0.70	MMS/N
999.20	11	0.65	MMS
999.21	11	0.63	MMS
999.22	11	0.54	MMS
999.23	11	0.50	MMS
999.24	10	1.62	MMS, H5
999.25	10	1.36	MMS/N
999.26	10	1.35	MMS/S
999.27	10	1.31	MMS
999.28	10	1.20	BS-E13
999.29	10	1.17	MMS
999.30	10	1.16	MMS/N
999.31	10	1.15	MMS
999.32	10	1.14	MMS
999.33	10	1.11	MMS/N
999.34	10	1.10	Tomb 07.1
999.35	10	1.08	MMS
999.36	10	1.07	F55
999.37	10	1.05	MMS/N
999.38	10	1.03	MMS/S, H2
999.39	10	1.00	MMS/N
999.40	10	0.99	MMS/S, H2
999.41	10	0.94	MMS
999.42	10	0.90	ByzFort, H4
999.43	10	0.90	MMS
999.44	10	0.90	MMS
999.45	10	0.89	MMS/S, H2
999.46	10	0.88	ByzFort, H4
999.47	10	0.87	MMS
999.48	10	0.86	MMS/S, H2
999.49	10	0.85	MMS/S, H2
999.50	10	0.84	MMS/N
999.51	10	0.83	MMS
999.52	10	0.83	F49, H8
999.53	10	0.81	ByzFort
999.54	10	0.75	MMS/N
999.55	10	0.70	MMS, H5
999.56	10	0.69	MMS
999.57	10	0.69	ByzFort, H4
999.58	10	0.68	MMS/S, H2
999.59	10	0.68	MMS/N
999.60	10	0.67	MMS, H5
999.61	10	0.66	Wadi B
999.62	10	0.65	MMS/N
999.63	10	0.65	MMS
999.64	10	0.64	MMS
999.65	10	0.63	MMS, H5
999.66	10	0.63	F49, H8
999.67	10	0.63	MMS
999.68	10	0.62	MMS/N
999.69	10	0.62	MMS/S, H2
999.70	10	0.61	MMS
999.71	10	0.60	MMS/N
999.72	10	0.60	MMS
999.73	10	0.57	ByzFort, H4
999.74	10	0.57	MMS
999.75	10	0.56	MMS
999.76	10	0.56	MMS
999.77	10	0.54	MMS/S, H2
999.78	10	0.54	MMS
999.79	10	0.53	MMS/S, H2
999.80	10	0.50	MMS/N
999.81	10	0.47	MMS/N
999.82	10	0.47	MMS/S, H2
999.83	10	0.45	MMS/S, H2
999.84	10	0.39	MMS
999.85	10	0.39	MMS/N
999.86	10	0.38	MMS/N
999.87	10	0.38	F49, H8
999.88	10	0.38	MMS/S, H2
999.89	10	0.36	MMS
999.90	10	0.34	MMS/N
999.91	10	0.33	MMS
999.92	10	0.32	MMS/S, H2
999.93	10	0.28	MMS
999.94	10	0.25	NoEx
999.95	10	frag'y	MMS/N
999.96	9	1.13	MMS
999.97	9	1.09	MMS/N
999.98	9	1.08	MMS/S, H2
999.99	9	1.06	MMS
999.100	9	1.04	MMS/N
999.101	9	1.04	MMS/N
999.102	9	1.01	MMS/N
999.103	9	0.99	MMS/S, H2
999.104	9	0.97	HoB
999.105	9	0.96	AT-Pac
999.106	9	0.90	MMS
999.107	9	0.90	F49, H8

999.108	9	0.89	MMS/S, H2
999.109	9	0.89	MMS/S, H2
999.110	9	0.86	MMS
999.111	9	0.85	MMS/S, H2
999.112	9	0.85	MMS/S, H2
999.113	9	0.85	MMS/N
999.114	9	0.83	MMS, H5
999.115	9	0.82	MMS
999.116	9	0.82	MMS/N
999.117	9	0.81	MMS/S
999.118	9	0.80	MMS/N
999.119	9	0.80	MMS/N
999.120	9	0.80	MMS/N
999.121	9	0.79	MMS
999.122	9	0.79	F49, H8
999.123	9	0.78	MMS
999.124	9	0.77	MMS/N
999.125	9	0.75	MMS/N
999.126	9	0.74	MMS/N
999.127	9	0.74	MMS/N
999.128	9	0.73	MMS
999.129	9	0.73	MMS
999.130	9	0.72	MMS/S, H2
999.131	9	0.70	MMS
999.132	9	0.69	MMS
999.133	9	0.68	MMS
999.134	9	0.68	MMS/S
999.135	9	0.67	MMS
999.136	9	0.66	MD1/S
999.137	9	0.65	MMS
999.138	9	0.65	AT
999.139	9	0.64	HoB
999.140	9	0.64	F49, H8
999.141	9	0.62	ByzFort, H4
999.142	9	0.62	HoB
999.143	9	0.59	MMS/S
999.144	9	0.59	MMS
999.145	9	0.59	NoEx
999.146	9	0.56	MMS/N
999.147	9	0.55	MMS/S, H2
999.148	9	0.54	MMS/S
999.149	9	0.53	MMS/N
999.150	9	0.52	MMS
999.151	9	0.52	MMS/N
999.152	9	0.51	MMS/N
999.153	9	0.50	MMS
999.154	9	0.50	MMS
999.155	9	0.50	MMS
999.156	9	0.49	MMS
999.157	9	0.48	MMS/N
999.158	9	0.48	MMS/N
999.159	9	0.47	MMS/S, H2
999.160	9	0.47	MMS/S, H2
999.161	9	0.47	MMS/N
999.162	9	0.45	MMS
999.163	9	0.44	MMS/S, H2
999.164	9	0.44	MMS
999.165	9	0.44	MMS
999.166	9	0.42	MMS
999.167	9	0.41	MMS/N
999.168	9	0.38	MMS
999.169	9	0.37	MMS
999.170	9	0.35	MMS/N
999.171	9	0.35	MMS
999.172	9	0.34	MMS/S
999.173	9	0.34	MMS
999.174	9	0.33	MMS/N
999.175	9	0.33	MMS/N
999.176	9	0.33	MMS
999.177	9	0.33	MMS
999.178	9	0.33	MMS
999.179	9	0.31	MMS
999.180	9	0.29	MMS
999.181	9	0.22	MMS
999.182	9	0.14	MMS/N
999.183	9	frag'y	MMS
999.184	9	frag'y	MMS/S, H2
999.185	9	frag'y	MMS/N
999.186	8	1.10	ByzFort
999.187	8	1.02	MMS/N
999.188	8	1.00	MMS/N
999.189	8	0.92	MMS/N
999.190	8	0.91	MMS/S, H2
999.191	8	0.90	ByzFort
999.192	8	0.86	MMS/S, H2
999.193	8	0.86	MMS/S, H2
999.194	8	0.86	MMS, H5
999.195	8	0.84	MMS/S, H2
999.196	8	0.80	MMS/N
999.197	8	0.78	MMS
999.198	8	0.75	MMS
999.199	8	0.74	MMS
999.200	8	0.73	MMS/S, H2
999.201	8	0.69	MMS, H5
999.202	8	0.67	MMS/S, H2
999.203	8	0.65	MMS/N
999.204	8	0.64	MMS
999.205	8	0.64	MMS/N
999.206	8	0.62	MMS
999.207	8	0.62	ByzFort
999.208	8	0.62	MMS/N
999.209	8	0.61	MMS
999.210	8	0.60	MMS/S, H2
999.211	8	0.60	MMS/N
999.212	8	0.60	MMS/N
999.213	8	0.59	MMS
999.214	8	0.59	MMS, H5
999.215	8	0.58	MMS
999.216	8	0.57	MMS/S, H2
999.217	8	0.56	MMS/N

999.218	8	0.55	MMS, H5
999.219	8	0.54	MMS
999.220	8	0.54	MMS/S
999.221	8	0.53	ByzFort, H4
999.222	8	0.53	MMS
999.223	8	0.51	MMS/S, H2
999.224	8	0.51	MMS/N
999.225	8	0.51	NoEx
999.226	8	0.51	MMS/S
999.227	8	0.50	MMS/S, H2
999.228	8	0.50	ByzFort
999.229	8	0.50	MMS
999.230	8	0.49	MMS
999.231	8	0.48	MMS/N
999.232	8	0.47	MD2
999.233	8	0.45	MMS/S, H2
999.234	8	0.45	MMS/N
999.235	8	0.45	MMS
999.236	8	0.45	MMS
999.237	8	0.45	MMS/N
999.238	8	0.44	ByzFort, H4
999.239	8	0.44	MMS/S
999.240	8	0.43	MMS/S, H2
999.241	8	0.41	MMS/S, H2
999.242	8	0.41	MMS/N
999.243	8	0.41	MMS/N
999.244	8	0.40	F49, H8
999.245	8	0.40	MMS/S
999.246	8	0.40	MMS/S, H2
999.247	8	0.39	MMS/S, H2
999.248	8	0.39	MMS/N
999.249	8	0.36	MMS/N
999.250	8	0.36	MMS
999.251	8	0.35	MMS/N
999.252	8	0.35	MMS
999.253	8	0.33	MMS
999.254	8	0.33	MMS
999.255	8	0.33	MMS/N
999.256	8	0.33	MMS/N
999.257	8	0.32	MMS/N
999.258	8	0.32	ByzFort, H4
999.259	8	0.32	MMS
999.260	8	0.31	MMS/S, H2
999.261	8	0.31	MMS/N
999.262	8	0.31	MMS/N
999.263	8	0.30	MMS/N
999.264	8	0.28	MMS
999.265	8	0.23	MMS
999.266	8	0.15	MMS
999.267	8	frag'y	MMS
999.268	8	frag'y	MMS
999.269	7	0.99	ByzFort, H4
999.270	7	0.84	Tomb 07.1
999.271	7	0.83	MMS
999.272	7	0.75	MMS/N
999.273	7	0.71	MMS/S, H2
999.274	7	0.67	MMS/N
999.275	7	0.66	MMS/S
999.276	7	0.64	MMS/N
999.277	7	0.60	MMS/S, H2
999.278	7	0.57	MMS
999.279	7	0.55	MMS/S, H2
999.280	7	0.54	MMS/N
999.281	7	0.49	MMS/S, H2
999.282	7	0.48	MMS/S, H2
999.283	7	0.47	MMS/S, H2
999.284	7	0.47	MMS/N
999.285	7	0.43	MMS/S, H2
999.286	7	0.42	MMS/S
999.287	7	0.41	MMS/S, H2
999.288	7	0.41	MMS/S, H2
999.289	7	0.40	MMS
999.290	7	0.40	MMS
999.291	7	0.39	MMS/N
999.292	7	0.39	MD2
999.293	7	0.32	MMS/N
999.294	7	0.30	MMS
999.295	7	0.29	MMS/S
999.296	7	0.24	MMS
999.297	7	0.19	MMS
999.298	6	0.48	MMS/S, H2
999.299	6	0.31	MMS
999.300	6	0.30	MMS/N
999.301	6	0.24	MMS/S, H2
999.302	6	0.24	MMS/S, H2
999.303	6	0.22	MMS
999.304	6	0.22	MMS/S
999.305	5	0.31	MMS/S
999.306	4	0.70	MMS
999.307	—	frag'y	MMS/N
999.308	—	frag'y	MMS
999.309	—	frag'y	BE-H

400–498 AD? AE 4 ancient imitation

Bust l. pd., legend illeg.

Emperor standing facing, holds captive in r. and spear in l., illeg. legend

1000.1	10	0.55	MMS/N

Bust l. pd., no legend remains

Emperor standing facing, with (spear) in r., no legend remains

1000.2	10	0.36	HoB

Bust r. pd. dr. in beaded border, legend obscure

Emperor stands with spear in r., captive on l., [...]NOR[...]

1000.3	11	1.15	MMS/S, H2

Legend over three straight lines, BL?

Emperor? with spear standing l.

1000.4	9	0.24	MMS/S, H2

1001. *Uncertain Ruler, Uncertain Mint, illegible fourth century AD*

M7 R 1115: 214 coins
AT: 1 coin
BS: 4 coins
ByzFort: 10 coins
EH: 2 coins
F49: 8 coins, including 3 from H8
F55: 9 coins
HoB: 12 coins
LAW: 1 coin
MD1/S: 1 coin
MD2: 1 coin
MMS: 52 coins, including 2 from H5
MMS/N: 46 coins
MMS/S: 7 coins, including 3 from H2
PN/E: 1 coin
RT: 1 coin
Tomb 07.1: 17 coins
Wadi B: 10 coins
NoEx: 31 coins

1002. *Uncertain Ruler, Uncertain Mint, illegible fourth or fifth century AD*

M7 R 1116: 650 coins
AT: 1 coin
BS: 3 coins
Byz Fort: 21 coins, including 3 from H4
CW6: 1 coin
CW32: 1 coin
E Road: 1 coin
EH: 1 coin
F49: 16 coins, including 13 from H8
F55: 12 coins
HoB: 6 coins
MD1/S: 7 coins
MD2: 4 coins
MMS: 171 coins, including 2 from H5 and 4 from H6
MMS/N: 281 coins
MMS/S: 41 coins, including 20 from H2
PA: 3 coins
PN/E: 3 coins
Syn: 5 coins
ThSt: 1 coin
Tomb 07.1: 29 coins
Wadi B: 17 coins
NoEx: 25 coins

1003. *Uncertain Ruler, Uncertain Mint, illegible fifth century AD*

Prob. M7 R 1117: 1884 coins, of which 18 are pure lead and 13 are thin flans with arrow-shaped casting sprues.
B: 5 coins
BS: 10 coins
ByzFort: 61 coins, including 24 from H4
E Road: 1 coin
EH: 3 coins
F49: 71 coins, including 50 from H8
F55: 17 coins
HoB: 18 coins
LAW: 1 coin
MD1: 1 coin
MD2: 9 coins
MMS: 699 coins, including 26 from H5, 9 from H6, and 6 from H7
MMS/N: 555 coins
MMS/S: 314 coins, including 241 from H2
PA: 2 coins
PN/E: 3 coins
RT: 3 coins
Syn: 27 coins
ThSt: 7 coins
Tomb 07.1: 49 coins
Wadi B: 8 coins
NoEx: 20 coins

Byzantine Coins (491–ca. 1250)

Unless stated, coins are copper alloy. The specific entries list the substitute officina (when relevant), die axis (when relevant), diameter, weight, and sector. H1–H8 designates that the coin belongs to one of the hoards discussed in Section 3.6.

Anastasius I
Constantinople
491–498 AD nummus
Bust r. pd. DNANASTASIVSPPAVC
Monogram
DOC I, p. 11, no. 15; M7 B 1–43

1004.1	12	0.85	MMS/S, H2
1004.2	11	1.21	MMS/S, H2
1004.3	11	1.20	MMS/N
1004.4	11	1.11	F49
1004.5	11	0.60	MMS/S, H2
1004.6	11	0.59	MMS/S, H2
1004.7	11	frag'y	MMS/N
1004.8	11	frag'y	MMS/S, H2
1004.9	10	1.30	MMS/N
1004.10	10	1.20	MMS
1004.11	10	1.11	MMS/S, H2
1004.12	10	1.11	MMS/S, H2
1004.13	10	1.11	MMS/S, H2
1004.14	10	1.10	MMS/S, H2
1004.15	10	1.07	MMS
1004.16	10	1.06	MMS/S, H2
1004.17	10	1.03	MMS/S, H2
1004.18	10	0.97	MMS/S, H2
1004.19	10	0.85	MMS/S, H2
1004.20	10	0.82	MMS/S, H2
1004.21	10	0.82	MMS/S, H2
1004.22	10	0.80	MMS/S, H2
1004.23	10	0.77	F55
1004.24	10	0.76	MMS/S, H2
1004.25	10	0.74	MMS/S, H2
1004.26	10	0.68	MMS/S, H2
1004.27	10	0.66	MMS/S, H2
1004.28	10	0.63	MMS/S, H2
1004.29	10	0.58	MMS/S, H2
1004.30	10	0.58	MMS/S, H2
1004.31	10	0.50	MMS/S, H2
1004.32	10	0.49	MMS/S, H2
1004.33	10	0.47	MMS/S, H2
1004.34	10	frag'y	MMS/S, H2
1004.35	10	frag'y	MMS/S, H2
1004.36	10	frag'y	MMS/S, H2
1004.37	9	1.03	MMS/S, H2
1004.38	9	0.95	MMS/S, H2
1004.39	9	0.94	MMS/S, H2
1004.40	9	0.92	MMS/S, H2
1004.41	9	0.92	MMS/S, H2
1004.42	9	0.91	MMS/N
1004.43	9	0.90	MMS/S, H2
1004.44	9	0.89	MD1/S
1004.45	9	0.87	MMS
1004.46	9	0.84	MMS/S, H2
1004.47	9	0.82	MMS
1004.48	9	0.81	MMS/N
1004.49	9	0.80	BS-E
1004.50	9	0.80	RT
1004.51	9	0.78	MMS/S
1004.52	9	0.77	MMS
1004.53	9	0.77	MMS/S, H2
1004.54	9	0.76	MMS/S, H2
1004.55	9	0.76	MMS/N
1004.56	9	0.76	MMS/S, H2
1004.57	9	0.74	MMS/S, H2
1004.58	9	0.73	MMS/S, H2
1004.59	9	0.71	MMS
1004.60	9	0.70	BE-A
1004.61	9	0.70	MMS/S, H2
1004.62	9	0.66	MMS/S, H2
1004.63	9	0.66	MMS/S, H2
1004.64	9	0.65	MMS/S, H2

1004.65	9	0.64	MMS/N
1004.66	9	0.64	MMS/N
1004.67	9	0.64	MMS/S, H2
1004.68	9	0.63	MMS/S, H2
1004.69	9	0.63	MMS/S, H2
1004.70	9	0.62	MMS/S, H2
1004.71	9	0.61	MMS
1004.72	9	0.61	MMS/S, H2
1004.73	9	0.60	MMS
1004.74	9	0.59	MMS
1004.75	9	0.58	MMS/S, H2
1004.76	9	0.57	MMS/S, H2
1004.77	9	0.57	MMS/S, H2
1004.78	9	0.56	MMS/S, H2
1004.79	9	0.55	MMS/S, H2
1004.80	9	0.55	MMS/S, H2
1004.81	9	0.55	MMS/N
1004.82	9	0.53	MMS/N
1004.83	9	0.52	MMS/S, H2
1004.84	9	0.51	MMS/S, H2
1004.85	9	0.51	MMS/S, H2
1004.86	9	0.50	MMS
1004.87	9	0.47	MMS/S, H2
1004.88	9	0.47	MMS
1004.89	9	0.47	MMS
1004.90	9	0.45	HoB
1004.91	9	0.45	MMS/N
1004.92	9	0.45	MMS/S, H2
1004.93	9	0.42	MMS/S, H2
1004.94	9	0.42	MMS/S, H2
1004.95	9	0.37	MMS/S, H2
1004.96	9	0.35	MMS
1004.97	9	0.33	MMS/S, H2
1004.98	9	0.28	MMS/S, H2
1004.99	9	frag'y	MMS/N
1004.100	9	frag'y	MMS/N
1004.101	9	frag'y	MMS
1004.102	9	frag'y	MMS/S, H2
1004.103	8	1.12	MMS/S, H2
1004.104	8	1.08	MMS/S, H2
1004.105	8	1.08	MMS/S, H2
1004.106	8	1.00	MMS/S, H2
1004.107	8	0.95	MMS/S, H2
1004.108	8	0.89	MMS/S, H2
1004.109	8	0.89	MMS/S, H2
1004.110	8	0.87	MMS/S, H2
1004.111	8	0.87	MMS/S, H2
1004.112	8	0.82	MMS/S, H2
1004.113	8	0.77	MMS/S, H2
1004.114	8	0.77	MMS/S, H2
1004.115	8	0.76	MMS/N
1004.116	8	0.76	MMS/S, H2
1004.117	8	0.75	MMS/S
1004.118	8	0.74	MMS/S, H2
1004.119	8	0.74	MMS/S, H2
1004.120	8	0.74	MMS/S, H2
1004.121	8	0.74	MMS/S, H2
1004.122	8	0.72	MMS/S, H2
1004.123	8	0.71	MMS/S, H2
1004.124	8	0.71	MMS/S, H2
1004.125	8	0.70	MMS/S, H2
1004.126	8	0.67	MMS/S, H2
1004.127	8	0.66	MMS/S, H2
1004.128	8	0.65	MMS/N
1004.129	8	0.65	MMS/S, H2
1004.130	8	0.61	MMS/S, H2
1004.131	8	0.61	MMS/S, H2
1004.132	8	0.60	MMS/N
1004.133	8	0.59	MMS/S, H2
1004.134	8	0.58	MMS/S, H2
1004.135	8	0.56	MMS/N
1004.136	8	0.56	MMS/S, H2
1004.137	8	0.55	MMS
1004.138	8	0.55	MMS/N
1004.139	8	0.55	ThSt
1004.140	8	0.54	MMS
1004.141	8	0.54	MMS/S, H2
1004.142	8	0.52	MMS/S, H2
1004.143	8	0.51	MMS/S, H2
1004.144	8	0.50	MMS/S, H2
1004.145	8	0.50	MMS/N
1004.146	8	0.50	MMS
1004.147	8	0.49	HoB
1004.148	8	0.49	MMS/S
1004.149	8	0.48	MMS/N
1004.150	8	0.48	MMS/S, H2
1004.151	8	0.47	MMS/S, H2
1004.152	8	0.47	MMS/S, H2
1004.153	8	0.47	MMS/S, H2
1004.154	8	0.47	MMS/S, H2
1004.155	8	0.47	MMS/N
1004.156	8	0.46	MMS/S, H2
1004.157	8	0.45	MMS/S, H2
1004.158	8	0.44	MMS/N
1004.159	8	0.44	MMS
1004.160	8	0.43	MMS/S, H2
1004.161	8	0.43	MMS/S, H2
1004.162	8	0.42	MMS/S, H2
1004.163	8	0.42	Syn
1004.164	8	0.41	ByzFort
1004.165	8	0.41	MMS/S, H2
1004.166	8	0.40	MMS/S, H2
1004.167	8	0.40	MMS/S, H2
1004.168	8	0.34	MMS/S, H2
1004.169	8	0.34	MMS/S, H2
1004.170	8	0.33	MMS/S, H2
1004.171	8	0.31	MMS/S, H2
1004.172	8	0.28	MMS/S, H2
1004.173	8	0.21	MMS/S, H2
1004.174	8	0.20	MMS

1004.175		8	0.16	MMS/S, H2
1004.176		8	frag'y	MMS
1004.177		7	0.77	MMS/S, H2
1004.178		7	0.67	MMS
1004.179		7	0.64	MMS/S, H2
1004.180		7	0.62	MMS/S, H2
1004.181		7	0.62	MMS/S, H2
1004.182		7	0.55	MMS/S, H2
1004.183		7	0.47	MMS/S, H2
1004.184		7	0.46	MMS/S, H2
1004.185		7	0.45	MMS/S, H2
1004.186		7	0.44	MMS/S, H2
1004.187		7	0.40	MMS/S, H2
1004.188		7	0.37	MMS/S, H2
1004.189		7	0.28	MMS/S, H2
1004.190		7	0.28	MMS/S, H2
1004.191		7	0.27	MMS/S, H2
1004.192		7	0.25	MMS/S, H2
1004.193		7	frag'y	MMS/N
1004.194		7	frag'y	MMS/S
1004.195		6	0.56	MMS
1004.196		6	0.52	MMS/S, H2
1004.197		6	0.43	MMS/S, H2
1004.198		6	0.39	MMS/S, H2
1004.199		6	0.29	MMS
1004.200		—	frag'y	MMS

MIBE I: 28 suggests that the minute variations in the monograms belong to different mints. Yet note that the variations they list do not occur in Burrell (2007, p. 273), and Burrell lists more that are not discussed in MIBE I. Thus, unless a mintmark is present, I have grouped all the nummi of Anastasius I in the conventional mint of Constantinople.

498–512 AD half-follis, light
As above
†K off. letter, above, below ✶
DOC I, p. 16, no. 21

1005.1	A	—	20	4.60	RT
1005.2	Δ	12	19	4.81	MMS/N

512–518 AD half-follis, heavy
As above
†K off. letter
DOC I, p. 23, no. 24

1006.1	Γ	7	27	9.16	MMS

As above, but star on emperor's shoulder

1006.2	Δ	6	28	8.86	F55

As above, no star

1006.3	Є	7	26	8.81	MMS/N
1006.4	Є	7	26	8.19	NoEx

512–518 AD pentanummium
As above
Є, between arms •, to r. off. letter
DOC I, p. 25, no. 26

1007.1	B	6	14	2.00	MMS/N
1007.2	Γ	1	13	1.70	MMS/N
1007.3	Δ	12	14	1.77	MMS/N
1007.4	Δ	6	13	1.62	MMS/N

Nicomedia
491–498 AD nummus
As above
Monogram, in ex. NI
DOC I, p. 27, no. 28

1008.1		—	7	0.63	MMS

Justin I
Constantinople
518–527 AD follis
Bust r. cuir. pal. DNIVSTINVSPPAVC
✶M †, above †, below A, in ex. CON
DOC I, p. 40, no. 9a

1009.1		6	32	16.30	BS-E13
1009.2		—	30	12.41	NoEx

518–527 AD half-follis
As above
†K off. letter
DOC I, p. 42, no. 15

1010.1	A	6	26	8.75	MMS/N
1010.2	A	7	25	9.30	BE-A
1010.3	A	12	23	7.68	MMS

As above
†K off. letter, above and below, ✶
DOC I, p. 42, no. 14

1010.4	A	12	23	8.29	MMS/S
1010.5	A	6	23	10.33	MMS
1010.6	A	8	23	5.71	NoEx
1010.7	Є	6	23	11.49	Syn

518–527 AD pentanummium
As above
Є, to r. off. letter
DOC I, p. 44, no. 18

1011.1	B	6	12	2.38	MMS
1011.2	A or Δ	7	13	2.04	MMS

518–527 AD pentanummium
As above
Є, • between bars, to r. off. letter
DOC I, p. 44, no. 19

1012.1	(btw bars <, unc.)	1	13	1.80	MMS/N
1012.2	(unc.)	6	14	1.36	NoEx

518–527 AD pentanummium
As above
A chi-rho Є
DOC I, p. 45, no. 21

1013.1		6	13	1.82	NoEx
1013.2		—	12	1.90	MMS/S
1013.3		6	11	1.98	HoB

518–527 AD pentanummium
As above
B chi-rho, between arms • Є
DOC I, p. 46, no. 22

1014.1		—	14	1.50	BS-E11
1014.2		1	13	2.20	MMS
1014.3		—	13	1.60	MMS

Antioch
518–527 AD decanummium
As above
I, to l. and r., pellets, A/C/O/N-C/O/R/D/I, in ex. ANTX
DOC I, p. 54, no. 54a

1015.1		4	22	3.90	NoEx

JUSTINIAN I
Constantinople
527–538 AD follis
Bust r. cuir. pal. DNIVSTINIANVSPPAVC
✶ M ✶, above ✝, below off. letter, in ex. CON
DOC I, p. 78, no. 28

1016.1	A	7	33	16.60	MMS/N
1016.2	A	7	30	16.73	MD2
1016.3	A	6	30	14.10	BE-A

527–538 AD follis
As above
✝M ✝ , above ✝, below Є, in ex. CON
DOC I, p. 79, no. 29a

1017.1		6	29	13.32	NoEx

527–538 AD follis
As above
✶ M ✝on globe, below A, in ex. CON
DOC I, p. 80, no. 31a

1018.1		2	30	16.43	MMS/S
1018.2	unc.	6	31	10.84	MMS

527–538 AD half-follis
As above
✝ K off. letter, above and below ✶
DOC I, p. 81, no. 33

1019.1	A	1	23	6.25	MMS/S
1019.2	Є	6	25	8.41	MMS

538–542 AD pentanummium (large)
As above
E, to r. off. letter
DOC I, p. 103, no. 96d

1020.1	Δ	7	18	2.26	MMS/S
1020.2	unc.	—	17	4.33	ByzFort

539/40 AD follis
Bust facing helm. cuir. holding gl. cr. and shield with horseman device, in r. ✝ DNIVSTINIANVSPPAVC
A/N/N/O M X/III, above ✝, below Δ, in ex. CON
DOC I, p. 85, no. 38d

1021.1		7	39	21.35	MMS/S
1021.2		6	38	22.65	MMS/N

540/1 AD half-follis
As above
A/N/N/O K X II/II, above ✝, below A
DOC I, p. 216, no. 64a

1022.1		7	28	10.04	MMS/N

540/1 AD decanummium
Bust r. cuir. pal. DNIVSTINIANVSPPAVC
A/N/N/O I X/II/II, in ex. CON
DOC I, p. 98, no. 77

1023.1		7	22	5.75	MMS/N

542/3 AD follis
Bust facing helm. cuir. holding gl. cr. and shield with horseman device, in r. ✝ DNIVSTINIANVSPPAVC
A/N/N/O M X/ЧI, above ✝, below B, in ex. CON
DOC I, p. 88, no. 41b

1024.1		7	32	21.39	MMS/N

544/5 AD follis
As above
A/N/N/O M X/Ч/III, in ex. CON
DOC I, p. 90, no. 43

1025.1		7	34	20.3	HoB

n.s., no photo, no info on off.

543–565 AD pentanummium (small)
Bust r. cuir. pal. DNIVSTINIANVSPPAVC
Є, to r. off. symbol
DOC I, p. 103, no. 97

1026.1	A	12	13	1.40	MMS/N
1026.2	A	6	12	1.83	NoEx
1026.3	A	2	12	1.70	MMS/N
1026.4	A	12	12	1.57	ThSt
1026.5	✝	12	16	1.59	NoEx
1026.6	✝	1	15	2.70	MMS/S
1026.7	✝	6	13	2.44	F49
1026.8	✝	6	13	1.93	MMS/N
1026.9	✝	6	13	1.90	BS-E8
1026.10	✝	6	13	1.90	MMS/N

1026.11 †	12	13	1.75	MMS/N
1026.12 †	12	12	1.80	RT
1026.13 †	6	12	1.36	ThSt
1026.14 S	6	12	1.83	MMS/N
1026.15 unc.	3	12	2.18	MMS
1026.16 unc.	—	11	2.22	MMS/N

545/6 AD follis
Bust facing helm. cuir. holding gl. cr. and shield with horseman device, in r. † DNIVSTINIANVSPPAVC
A/N/N/O M X/ЧI/III above†, below Δ, in ex. CON
DOC I, p. 90, no. 44

1027.1	8	36	20.62	MMS

545/6 AD half-follis
As above
A/N/N/O K U/XII/II, above †, unc. off. below
DOC I, p. 97, no. 68 var. in arrangement of numbers

1028.1	6	26	7.44	Syn

546/7 AD follis
As above
A/N/N/O M X/X, above †, below Γ
DOC I, p. 91, no. 45c

1029.1	1	33	19.90	MMS/N

547/8 AD follis
As above
A/N/N/O M X/X/I, above †, below Є
DOC I, p. 91, no. 46e

1030.1	2	35	19.15	MMS

547/8 AD decanummium
Bust r. cuir. pal. DNIVSTINIANVSPPAVC
A/N/N/O I X/X/I, in ex. CON
DOC I, p. 99, no. 82

1031.1	12	17	2.21	NoEx

555/6 AD follis
Bust facing helm. cuir. holding gl. cr. and shield with horseman device, in r. † DNIVSTINIANVSPPAVC
A/N/N/O M X/X/ΓI/II, above †, below Γ, in ex. CON
DOC I, p. 92, no. 52c

1032.1	7	31	14.62	NoEx

556/7 AD decanummium
Bust r. cuir. pal. DNIVSTIANVSPPAVC
A/N/N/O I X/X/X, in ex. CON
DOC I, p. 101, no. 90

1033.1	5	18	3.37	MMS/N
1033.2	7	16	2.54	NoEx

539–557 AD decanummium
As above
A/N/N/O I X/?, above †, in ex. CON

1034.1	2	18	1.97	NoEx

552–563 AD decanummium
As above
A/N/N/O I date obscure, above †, in ex. CON

1035.1	6	15	3.68	MMS

559/60 AD
As above
A/N/N/O I X/XX/III, above †, in ex. CON
DOC I, p. 101, no. 92.2

1036.1	2	16	3.33	ThSt
1036.2	6	15	2.48	MMS/N
1036.3	7	14	2.04	MMS/S

561/2 AD
As above
A/N/N/O I X/XX/II/II, above †, in ex. CON
DOC not; M1 151–152

1037.1	9	17	3.96	MMS/S
1037.2	6	16	3.59	MMS/N

As above, but year recorded as X/XX/Ч
DOC I, p. 101, no. 93

1038.1	10	16	2.99	MMS

561–564
As above
A/N/N/O I X/XX/?, above †, in ex. CON
DOC p. 101, nos. 93–95

1039.1	6	17	3.40	RT

Thessalonica
562–565 AD half-follis
Bust facing helm. cuir. holding gl. cr. and shield with horseman device, in r. † DNIVSTINIANVSPPAVC
A/N/N/O K date illeg., above †, below TЄS

1040.1	6	23	11.40	MMS/N

563/4 AD half-follis
As above
A/N/N/O K XXX/ЧII, above †, below TЄS

1041.1	6	22	4.63	MMS/S

564/5 AD half-follis
As above
A/N/N/O K XXX/ЧIII, above †, below TЄS

1042.1	6	21	5.34	NoEx

Nicomedia

538–561 AD follis

As above

A/N/N/O M date illeg., above ✝, below B, in ex. NIK

1043.1	7	30	11.80	MMS/N

538/9 AD half-follis

As above

A/N/N/O K XII, above ✝, below NI

DOC I, p. 119, no. 140

1044.1	9	28	5.24	MMS

547/8 AD half-follis

As above

A/N/N/O K XX/I, above ✝, below NI

DOC I, p. 121, no. 148

1045.1	7	27	9.67	MMS

555/6 AD follis

As above

A/N/N/O M X/X/Ч/II, above ✝, below A, in ex. NIK

DOC I, p. 118, no. 135a

1046.1	6	31	17.05	MMS

558/9 AD decanummium

Bust r. cuir. pal. DNIVSTINIANVSPPAVC

A/N/N/O I X/X/X/II, in ex. NIK

DOC I, p. 123, no. 157

1047.1	1	13	3.30	MMS

Cyzicus

541/2 AD follis

Bust facing helm. cuir. holding gl. cr. and shield with horseman device, in r. ✝ DNIVSTINIANVSPPAVC

A/N/N/O M X/Ч, above ✝, below B, in ex. KYZ

DOC I, p. 126, no. 167b

1048.1	12	44	20.04	NoEx

Pierced twice for attachment.

556/7 AD decanummium

Bust r. cuir. pal. DNIVSTINIANVSPPAVC

A/N/N/O I X/X/X, above ✝, in ex. KYZ

DOC I, p. 132, no. 194

1049.1	6	16	4.11	Syn
1049.2	6	15	3.84	MMS/N
1049.3	12	15	2.70	PN/E

538–578 AD? pentanummium

Bust r. dr. diad. [...]NVIS[...] (Justinian I or Justin II?)

E, to r. K

DOC, MIBE not

1050.1	12	11	2.48	MMS/N Mule?

Antioch

527 AD follis

Bust facing helm. cuir. holding gl. cr. and shield with horseman device, in r. ✝ DNIVSTINIANVSPPAVC

A/N/N/O M X/X/Ч, above ✝, below Γ, in ex. ЧHЧП/

DOC I, p. 143, no. 217d

1051.1	5	36	18.80	MMS/S

533–537 AD half-follis

As above

✝ surrounded by ΤΗЄЧOP K, to r. A

DOC I, p. 139, no. 211

1052.1	6	24	7.50	MMS/N
1052.2	7	25	7.42	MMS/S
1052.3	12	27	7.05	MMS

556/7 AD half-follis

As above

A/N/N/O K XXX, above ✝, below P with long diagonal tail

DOC I, p. 150, no. 245

1053.1	11	30	12.09	MMS/N

527–565 AD pentanummium

Monogram

E, to r. ✝

DOC I, p. 250, nos. 185–186

1054.1	9	12	1.64	NoEx
1054.2	—	12	1.50	MMS, i.d. poss.

Carthage or Constantinople

527–565 AD nummus

Head r. diad.

A

DOC I, p. 82, no. 36; BMC Vandal, p. 34, nos. 141–148

1055.1	12	9	0.41	MMS/S
1055.2	11	9	0.40	MMS
1055.3	4	8	0.69	MMS/N
1055.4	1	8	0.46	MMS
1055.5	—	8	0.34	MMS/N

Uncertain Mint

527–538 AD follis

Bust r.

1056.1	—	30	10.23	MMS/N
1056.2	—	30	13.90	MMS

538–565 AD half-follis

1057.1	—	21	6.28	MMS/N

556–566 AD decanummium
Bust r.
I rev.

1058.1	1	20	4.66	HoB
1058.2	8	16	3.80	MMS
1058.3	—	16	2.07	HoB
1058.4	12	15	3.72	MMS/N
1058.5	6	14	2.36	Syn

538–565 AD decanummium
Bust facing cuir. pal. DNIVSTINIANVSPPAVC
Cross in wreath, ✝ in upper quadrants only
DOC I, p. 191, no. 366.1 var.

1059.1	9	16	2.10	MMS/N

538–565 AD pentanummium
Bust r. cuir. pal. DNIVSTINIANVSPPAVC
V in wreath, above ✶
DOC I, p. 192, no. 370

1060.1	—	12	1.65	ByzFort

Justinianic? nummus
Bust r. pd. illeg. legend
VOT in crude wreath
M7 B 68, and note p. 221

1061.1	—	10	0.29	HoB

Anastasius I to Justinian I

Constantinople
498–565 AD pentanummium, chi-rho

1062.1	off. chi-rho	6	13	2.43	F55
1062.2	off. Є	—	12	frag'y	MMS

Justin I to Justinian I

Constantinople
518–565 AD pentanummium, chi-rho

1063.1	1	13	2.14	MMS/N
1063.2	—	13	2.10	BS-E1
1063.3	6	13	1.92	Syn

Uncertain Mint
Before Justinianic reform follis

1064.1	—	32	10.60	NoEx

pentanummium, Є

1065.1	6	12	1.99	MMS/S
1065.2	6	13	1.60	MMS/N

Justin II

Constantinople
569/70 AD follis
Enthroned nimbate couple DNIVSTINVSAVC
A/N/N/O M Ч, above ✝, in ex. CON, to r. Є
DOC I, p. 206, no. 26

1066.1	7	31	13.10	MMS/N

571/2 AD follis
As above
A/N/N/O M GII, above ✝, in ex. CON, to r. Є
DOC I, p. 210, no. 34

1067.1	12	31	12.83	NoEx

571/2 AD half-follis
As above
A/N/N/O K GI, above chi-rho, in ex. A
DOC I, p. 216, no. 51

1068.1	7	24	5.89	MMS/N

573/4 AD follis
As above
A/N/N/O M GII, above ✝, below A, in ex. CON
DOC I, p. 210, no. 36

1069.1	2	29	11.85	NoEx
1069.2	6	30	13.64	NoEx

Var. in off. with arrangement of year

1069.3	7	33	13.35	MMS

575/6 AD follis
As above
A/N/N/O M X/I, above ✝, in ex. CON
DOC I, p. 212, no. 40

1070.1 off. A	1	30	12.80	MMS/N

575/6 AD half-follis
As above
A/N/N/O K XI, above ✝, below off. letter
DOC I, p. 217, no. 57

1071.1	A or Δ	12	25	8.65	NoEx
1071.2	Є	6	25	8.60	MMS/N

Rev. has brokage impression of obv., and double-struck obv.

576/7 AD follis
As above
A/N/N/O M X/II, above ✝, below A, in ex. CON
DOC I, p. 213, no. 42

1072.1	7	28	12.68	MMS/N
1072.2	1	31	13.88	NoEx

565–578 AD pentanummium
Monogram
Є off. letter
DOC I, p. 218, no. 60

1073.1	A	7	16	2.00	RT
1073.2	A	3	16	1.50	MMS/N
1073.3	A	1	16	1.50	MMS/N
1073.4	A	12	16	1.15	RT
1073.5	A	7	13	1.82	MMS/S
1073.6	A	1	16	1.67	HoB
1073.7	A	2	16	1.39	NoEx
1073.8	A	7	15	1.83	MMS/N
1073.9	A	7	14	2.30	MMS/N

1073.10	A	6	14	1.42	HoB
1073.11	A	11	15	1.75	MMS/N
1073.12	A	12	15	1.73	NoEx
1073.13	A	4	14	1.89	MMS/N
1073.14	A	12	16	1.75	MMS/N
1073.15	A	6	14	1.62	HoB
1073.16	A	7	14	1.60	MMS/N
1073.17	✝	6	17	frag'y	MMS/N
1073.18	✝	6	16	1.45	HoB
1073.19	✝	12	15	2.64	MMS
1073.20	✝	—	15	1.92	MMS/N
1073.21	✝	11	14	2.44	MMS/N
1073.22	✝	4	14	2.00	MMS/N
1073.23	✝	7	14	1.96	MMS/N
1073.24	✝	7	12	1.65	NoEx
1073.25	unc.	6	14	1.76	MMS/N

Note: Although DOC does not clearly differentiate for off. ✝ between Constantinople and Antioch, MIBE II: 29 does, saying a linear border is typical of Constantinople. All the coins above have a linear border.

Thessalonica

566/7 AD half-follis

Bust facing helm. cuir. holding gl. cr. and shield with horseman device DNIVSTINVSPPAVC

A/N/N/O K II, above ✝, below TЄS

DOC I, p. 220, no. 62

1074.1	6	23	6.45	MMS/N
1074.2	12	20	4.28	MMS/N

567/8 AD half-follis

As above

A/N/N/O K III, above ✝, below TЄS

DOC I, p. 221, no. 63

1075.1	6	23	5.27	NoEx
1075.2	6	21	5.20	MMS

568/9 AD half-follis

As above

A/N/N/O K Δ, above ✝, below TЄS

DOC I, p. 221, no. 64

1076.1	5	20	4.60	MMS/N

568/9 AD half-follis

Enthroned nimbate couple DNIVSTINVSPPAVC

A/N/N/O K Δ, above ✝, below TЄS

DOC I, p. 221, no. 65

1077.1	12	20	7.30	MMS/N
1077.2	12	21	5.23	NoEx
1077.3	6	21	5.63	NoEx
1077.4	6	22	5.67	MMS/S
1077.5	6	22	6.13	MMS/N

569/70 AD half-follis

As above

A/N/N/O K Є, above ✝, below TЄS

DOC I, p. 221, no. 66

1078.1	7	20	5.46	MMS/N

569/70 AD half-follis

As above

A/N/N/O K Ч, above ✝, below TЄS

DOC I, p. 222, no. 68

1079.1	12	20	5.74	MMS/N
1079.2	6	22	5.52	HoB

569/70 AD half-follis

As above

A/N/N/O K S, above ✝, below TЄS

DOC I, p. 222, no. 69

1080.1	6	20	5.37	RT

574/5 AD half-follis

As above

A/N/N/O K X, above ✝, below TЄS

DOC I, p. 223, no. 77

1081.1	6	20	5.94	MMS/S

574/5 AD half-follis

As above

A/N/N/O K X, above ✝/M, below TЄS

DOC I, p. 224, no. 80

1082.1	8	21	4.90	MMS/N

575/6 AD half-follis

As above

A/N/N/O K XI, above ✝, below TЄS

DOC I, p. 225, no. 82

1083.1	6	20	5.40	MMS/S
1083.2	6	22	6.25	MMS/N

Nicomedia

566/7 AD follis

As above

A/N/N/O M II, above ✝, in ex. NIKO

DOC I, p. 226, no. 92, off. A

1084.1	12	30	13.30	MMS/N

569/70 AD follis

As above

A/N/N/O M Ч, above ✝, in ex. NIKO

DOC I, p. 227, no. 95, off. A

1085.1	6	29	13.40	MMS/N

570/1 AD follis

As above

A/N/N/O M G, above ✝, in ex. NIKO

DOC I, p. 228, no. 96, off. A

1086.1	7	28	13.30	MMS/S

571/2 AD follis
As above
A/N/N/O M GI, above †, in ex. NIKO
DOC I, p. 228, no. 97, off. B
1087.1 12 27 10.50 BS-E9

572/3 AD follis
As above
A/N/N/O M G/II, above †, in ex. NIKO
DOC I, p. 229, no. 98, off. A
1088.1 6 31 15.30 F55

573/4 AD follis
As above
A/N/N/O M ЧI/II, above †, in ex. NIKO
DOC I, p. 229, no. 99, off. B
1089.1 12 30 13.24 NoEx

574/5 AD follis
As above
A/N/N/O M X, above †, in ex. NIKO
DOC I, p. 229, no. 100, off. A
1090.1 6 28 13.77 MMS/N

575/6 AD follis
As above
A/N/N/O M XI, above †, in ex. NIKO
DOC I, p. 230, no. 101 n.s.
1091.1 12 31 13.25 HoB

576/7 AD follis
As above
A/N/N/O K X/II, above †, in ex. NI
DOC I, p. 233, no. 114
1092.1 6 18 4.10 BE-A

Cyzicus
567/8 AD follis
As above
A/N/N/O M II/I, above †, in ex. KYZ
DOC I, p. 234, no. 117, off. B
1093.1 12 33 15.09 MMS

567/8 AD half-follis
As above
A/N/N/O K III, above †, in ex. KYZ
DOC I, p. 238, no. 128
1094.1 12 23 7.03 MMS/S

573/4 AD follis
As above (no cross between heads)
A/N/N/O M G/III, above †, in ex. KYZ
DOC I, p. 229, no. 99 b, off. A
1095.1 12 29 14.14 MMS/N

half-follis
As above
A/N/N/O K G/III, above †, in ex. KYZ
DOC I, p. 239, no. 132 var. in form of date
1096.1 12 28 7.20 NoEx

565–578 AD pentanummium
Monogram
Є to r. K
DOC I, p. 240, no. 137; M1 470
1097.1 2 13 1.73 HoB
1097.2 12 13 1.75 MMS/N
1097.3 1 14 1.77 MMS/N
1097.4 6 17 2.27 MMS/N

Antioch
566 AD half-follis
Bust facing helm. cuir. holding globe with Victoriola and shield with horseman device in r. field †
A/N/N/O K II, above †, below P with long diagonal tail
DOC I, p. 242, no. 146
1098.1 7 22 5.40 MMS/N

570/1 AD half-follis
As above
A/N/N/O K ЧI, above †, ex. unc.
DOC I, p. 246, no. 165
1099.1 6 20 5.80 RT

575/6 AD follis
Enthroned nimbate couple DNIVSTINVSPPAVC
A/N/N/O M X/I, above †, below Γ, in ex. THЄUP’
DOC I, p. 245, no. 158a
1100.1 7 32 15.30 MMS

Uncertain Mint
565–578 AD half-follis
1101.1 6 21 6.00 MMS
1101.2 7 22 6.30 NoEx
1101.3 1 24 7.01 NoEx

Anastasius I to Justin II
Uncertain mint
498–578 AD follis
1102.1 11 35 16.20 MMS
1102.2 6 32 18.12 NoEx

half-follis
1103.1 — 24 9.57 MMS/N

pentanummium
1104.1 1 12 1.31 MMS/N
1104.2 7 13 2.08 MMS/N
1104.3 — 14 2.49 MMS

Ostrogothic

Rome, quasi-autonomous
Illeg. obv.
IMVICTA ROMA Wolf and twins XX
BMC Vandals, p. 105, no. 30
1105.1 10 15 2.59 Church EA

Vandalic, Thrasamund

Carthage
496–523 AD nummus
Bust r. pd., DNRGTRSI
Victory l.
BMC Vandals, p. 21, nos. 32–36

1106.1	4	10	0.67	MMS/S, H2
1106.2	4	10	0.52	MMS/S, H2
1106.3	9	9	0.51	MMS/S, H2
1106.4	5	9	0.46	MMS/S, H2
1106.5	1	9	0.36	MMS/S, H2
1106.6	1	8	0.55	MMS/S, H2
1106.7	—	8	0.27	MMS/S, H2
1106.8	5	8	0.35	MMS/S, H2

As above, but Victory r.

Vandalic?

Carthage?
Fourth–sixth century AD nummus
Bust r., rude style
Victory striding l.
1107.1 8 10 1.00 MMS/N
1107.2 — 9 0.60 ByzFort
Vandalic anonymous?, cf. BMC Vandals, Victory type 21–31

Bust r. nummus
Palm, letters? in wreath
1108.1 — 8 0.28 MMS/N

_____, no legend nummus?
^^^^^^
Victory striding l., no legend?
1109.1 — 7 0.20 MMS/N

Illeg. obv. nummus?
Retrograde VOT
1110.1 — 6 0.17 MMS/N

nummus?
“Tyche” bust r., mural crown [...]ETMIO[...]
Emperor charging l. with shield in l. and transverse spear in r. [...]IL[...]
1111.1 12 10 0.30 MMS/N
For obv., cf. BMC Vandals, p. 106, nos. 34–40

Bust r. pd. III nummus
Imitative monogram of Marcian
1112.1 12 9 0.40 ByzFort
cf. BMC Vandals, p. 30, no. 98ff

Bust r. pd. nummus
Garbled monogram?
1113.1 — 8 0.15 MMS/N

As above nummus
Eight-pointed star in wreath
BMC Vandals, p. 38, nos. 165–172
1114.1 — 9 0.70 MMS/S, H2

Bust r. pd., rude style, no legend visible nummus?
Debased lion standing?, no legend
1115.1 — 12 0.80 NoEx

Parallel lines, no legend nummus?
Emperor standing?
1116.1 — 8 0.50 MMS
1116.2 — 9 0.50 MMS/S

BMC Vandals, p. 23, no. 144 Pb nummus
None
A
1117.1 — 11 0.50 F55

No image Pb nummus
†A†
1118.1 — 10 1.00 MMS/N
cf. DOC I, p. 82, no. 36, though not Pb; poss. Vandalic (cf. BMC Vandals, p. 34, nos. 141–148) or ancient imitation.

Bust r. rude style nummus
Cross pattée in beaded border
1119.1 — 9 0.36 MMS/N
cf. BMC Vandals, cross type 201v, pl. IV, 44

Bust r.? [...]IFIVS[...] nummus
TAV/TJVI/• in three lines in beaded border
1120.1 3 10 0.42 MMS/N
Imitative Vot Mult

Bust r. dr. pd., no legend nummus?
Imitative Vot Mult?
1121.1 12 9 0.35 MMS/N

decanummium?
Bust l. helm. with plume, necklace, dr., rude style
IIDCII(sign)-II(branch)II
Debased legend, ++ in wreath
1122.1 — 17 1.97 MMS/N
Imitation INVICTA ROMA, cf. BMC Vandals, p. 67, no. 57

Tiberius II

Constantinople

579 AD follis
Bust facing in consular robes with mappa and scepter
dmTIbCONSTANTPPAVI
A/N/N/O m U, above †, below CONB
DOC I, p. 270, no. 11b

1123.1	7	16.51	35	MMS/N

579–582 AD half-follis
Bust facing helm. cuir. pal. dmTIbCONSTANTPPAV
XX, above †, in ex. CON, to r. B or Γ
DOC I, p. 274, no. 17

1124.1	12	25	5.98	MMS/S

578 AD decanummium
Bust facing in consular robes ONTIbЄRPPAV
✶I✶, above †, in ex. CON
DOC I, p. 274, no. 18

1125.1	12	15	2.60	RT
1125.2	12	18	4.13	Syn

578 AD decanummium
As above
✶I off. letter, above †, in ex. CON
DOC I, p. 274, no. 19, off. B

1126.1	6	22	3.14	MMS/N

579 AD follis
Bust facing in consular robes with mappa and scepter
dmTIbCONSTANTPPAVI
A/N/N/O m Ч, above †, in ex. CONA
DOC I, p. 270, no. 11

1127.1	1	36	16.30	MMS/N

580/1 AD follis
Bust facing in consular robes with mappa and scepter
dmTIbCONSTANTPPAVI
A/N/N/O m GI, above †, below CONA
DOC I, p. 271, no. 13

1128.1	6	30	12.60	BE-A
1128.2	6	31	12.99	MMS/N

581/2 AD follis
As above
A/N/N/O m G/II, above †, below CONA
DOC I, p. 272, no. 14

1129.1	11	31	12.48	MMS

579–582 AD pentanummium
Bust r. cuir. pal. dMTIbPPAVI
Ч
DOC I, p. 276, no. 22

1130.1	6	18	1.95	MMS/S

Bust facing helm. cuir. pal. dmTIbCONTATPP
X, above †
DOC I, p. 275, no. 20

1131.1	8	20	2.47	MMS/S

Thessalonica

579 AD half-follis
Enthroned couple DmTIbCONSTANTPPAV
A/N/N/O K Ч, above †, below TЄS
DOC I, p. 277, no. 23

1132.1	6	20	6.51	ByzFort
1132.2	6	21	7.43	MMS/N

580/1 AD half-follis
As above
A/N/N/O K Ч/II, above †, below TЄS
DOC I, p. 277, no. 25 (sic); picture shows date as on this coin

1133.1	6	21	4.85	MMS/N

Nicomedia

579–582 AD half-follis
Bust facing helm. cuir. with gl. cr. and shield
dmTIbCONSTANTPPAVI
XX, above †, in ex. NIKO (off. letter unc.)
DOC I, p. 280, no. 33

1134.1	1	25	6.30	MMS/N

Antioch

581/2 AD follis
Bust facing in consular robes with mappa and scepter
DNTIbCONSTANTPPAVI
A/N/N/O m GII, above †, below THЄUP'
DOC I, p. 283, no. 44

1135.1	5	30	12.80	MMS/S
1135.2	5	30	12.15	HoB

Regnal year recorded as III/Ч; DOC, MIBE not

Uncertain Mint

579 AD follis
Bust facing DmTIbCONSTANTPPAV
A/N/N/O M Ч, above †, below A

1136.1	1	32	12.23	MMS

578–582 AD half-follis
Illeg.
XX

1137.1	5	25	4.70	MMS/S

o/s on 20 nummia of Justinian I or Justin II, Cyzicus

Maurice

Constantinople

582/3 AD follis
Bust facing cuir. with gl. cr. DNTIbЄRMAVRCPPAVI
A/N/N/O M I, above †, below A
DOC I, p. 301, no. 20

1138.1	6	27	10.73	PA

582/3 AD half-follis
Bust facing cuir. with gl. cr. dNMAVRCPPAV
A/N/N/O K I, above †, below Δ
DOC I, p. 311, no. 46

1139.1	6	25	6.23	MMS

583/4 AD follis
As above DNTIbЄRMAVRCPPAVI
A/N/N/O M II, above †, below off. letter, in ex. CON
DOC I, p. 303, no. 22

1140.1	off. Δ	8	31	12.00	NoEx

Obv. legend: dNMAV-CPPAV, new off.

1140.2	off. Є	12	30	11.08	NoEx
1140.3	off. Є	1	32	11.97	MMS

584/5 follis
As above ONMAVRCPPAV
A/N/N/O M II/I, above †, below A, in ex. CON
DOC I, p. 303, no. 25

1141.1	7	29	11.54	MMS/N

o/s on follis of uncertain date

1141.2	7	30	11.09	MMS/N

584/5 AD half-follis
As above ONMAVRTIbЄR
A/N/N/O K III, above †, below Є
DOC I, p. 311, no. 48, new off.

1142.1	1	21	4.70	MMS/S

585/6 AD follis
As above dNMAVRICTIbЄRPPAV
A/N/N/O M II/II, above †, below Δ, in ex. CON
DOC I, p. 304, no. 27

1143.1	4	33	10.70	MMS/N

585/6 AD half-follis
Bust facing cuir. pal. ONMAVRCPPA
A/N/N/O K IIII, above †, below off. letter
DOC I, p. 312, no. 49

1144.1	B	12	22	5.51	NoEx
1144.2	Є	1	23	5.00	MMS

587/8 AD half-follis
Bust facing cuir. with gl. cr. and shield DNMAVTIbЄRPPA
A/N/N/O K G, above †, below A
DOC I, p. 312, no. 51

1145.1	6	22	4.84	MMS
1145.2	1	22	5.10	MMS/N

588/9 AD half-follis
As above DNMAVTIbЄRPPAV
A/N/N/O K GI, above †, below unc.
DOC I, p. 313, no. 52

1146.1	12	23	5.90	MMS/N

589/90 AD half-follis
Bust facing cuir. pal. with gl. cr. dNMAVRTIbЄRPPAV
A/N/N/O K GII, above †, below A
DOC I, p. 313, no. 53

1147.1	6	22	5.74	MMS/N
1147.2	12	24	5.67	MMS/N

590/1 AD follis
Bust facing cuir. pal. with gl. cr. and shield dNMAVRTIbЄRPPAV
A/N/N/O M GI/II, above †, below Δ, in ex. CON
DOC I, p. 307, no. 32

1148.1	12	31	12.30	MMS/N

591/2 AD follis
Bust facing cuir. with gl. cr. and shield DNTIbЄRMAVRCPPAVI
A/N/N/O M X, above †, below off. letter, in ex. CON
DOC I, p. 307, no. 33

1149.1	unc.	1	32	9.80	BS-E1
1149.2	Є	6	23	5.02	MD1/S

DOC var. in new officina

591/2 AD half-follis
Bust facing cuir. with gl. cr. DNMAVRTIbЄRPPA
A/N/N/O K X, above †, below A
DOC I, p. 314, no. 55

1150.1	12	24	5.70	NoEx

592/3 AD follis
Bust facing cuir. with gl. cr. and shield DNTIbЄRMAVRCPPAVI
A/N/N/O M X/I, above †, below Δ, in ex. CON
DOC I, p. 307, no. 34 var., new off.

1151.1	7	28	9.90	MMS/N

596/7 AD follis
As above
A/N/N/O M X/Ч, above †, below Є, in ex. CON
DOC I, p. 308, no. 38

1152.1	6	30	11.00	MMS/N

597/8 AD half-follis
Bust facing cuir. with gl. cr. and shield
DNmAVRICITIbЄRPP
A/N/N/O K XG, above †, below B
DOC I, p. 315, no. 60

1153.1	8	21	5.39	MMS/S

583–602 AD AU tremissis
Bust r. cuir. pal. DNmVARC-TIbPPAV
Cross potent VICTORTIbЄRIAVIS, in ex. CONOB
DOC I, p. 301, no. 17 var. in obv. and rev. legend

1154.1	6	17	1.39	MMS

582–602 AD decanummium
Bust facing cuir. DNTIbЄRPPAV
✶I Є, above †, in ex. CON
DOC I, p. 316, no. 64

1155.1	2	20	3.91	NoEx

As above, but DNmAVRICPPAV
✶I B, above †, in ex. CON
DOC I, p. 316, no. 65

1156.1	7	18	2.49	MMS/N

As above, but DNmAVTIbЄRPP
✶I Є, above †, in ex. CON
DOC I, p. 318, no. 66

1157.1	10	17	2.73	MMS/N

582–602 AD pentanummium
Bust r. cuir. pal. DNmAVRTIbЄRPP
Є, to r. off. letter

1158.1	A	12	15	1.38	F49

Officina letter not perpendicular to E; DOC not
DOC I, p. 319, no. 68b

1158.2	B	12	16	2.12	MMS/S

Thessalonica
582/3 AD half-follis
Bust facing cuir. with gl. cr. and shield [...]AVRICPPA
A/N/N/O K I, above †, below TES
DOC I, p. 320, no. 72

1159.1	12	19	4.67	MMS/N

584/5 AD half-follis
As above DNmAVRCTIbPPA
A/N/N/O K III, above †, below TES
DOC I, p. 321, no. 74

1160.1	6	23	6.52	MMS/N

586/7 AD half-follis
As above
A/N/N/O K Ч, above †, below TES
DOC I, p. 321, no. 77

1161.1	6	19	5.42	MMS/N
1161.2	6	22	5.45	MMS/S

Nicomedia
582/3 AD follis
As above dNTIbЄRImAVRPPA
A/N/N/O M I, above †, below A, in ex. NIKO
DOC I, p. 323, no. 91

1162.1	8	30	11.97	NoEx

583/4 AD half-follis
As above DNmARPPAV
A/N/N/O K II, above †, below unc. off. letter
DOC I, p. 328, no. 110

1163.1	12	22	4.57	MMS/N

590/1 AD follis
As above dNTIbЄRImAVRCPPA
A/N/N/O M G/III, above †, below B, in ex. NIKO
DOC I, p. 325, no. 99

1164.1	12	29	11.70	MMS/N

591–602 AD follis
As above, legend illeg.
A/N/N/O M, date unc., above †, below A, in ex. CON

1165.1	1	27	10.95	MMS/S

o/s on follis of uncertain date

582–602 AD pentanummium
Bust r. cuir. pal. OmTIbONmAV
Є N
DOC I, p. 330, no. 118

1166.1	—	13	1.10	Syn

Cyzicus
583/4 AD follis
Bust facing cuir. with gl. cr. and shield, legend illeg.
A/N/N/O M II, above †, below A, in ex. KYZ
DOC I, p. 330, no. 119

1167.1	6	29	12.65	F55

584/5 AD follis
As above ONmAVRICTIbЄRPPA
A/N/N/O M III, above †, below A, in KYZ
DOC I, p. 330, no. 120 var. in form of date

1168.1	6	29	10.43	MMS/N

583–593 AD follis
Bust facing cuir. with gl. cr. and shield ONTIbЄR(wreath) mAVRIC
A/N/N/O M ?/II, above †, below B, in ex. KYZ
1169.1 3 30 11.40 NoEx

600/1 AD follis
As above
A/N/N/O M X/GII/I, above †, below B, in ex. KYZ
DOC I, p. 333, no. 132
1170.1 1 31 12.43 MMS/S

Antioch
585/6 AD follis
Bust facing in consular robes with mappa and scepter OΠTIOCΓ~ NITPPΛIV
A/N/N/O m II/II, above †, in ex. THЄUP'
DOC I, p. 339, no. 155
1171.1 12 30 11.30 BS-E1

589/90 AD follis
As above OΠTIOCONS~TANPPAVI
A/N/N/O m II/Ч, above †, in ex. THЄUP'
DOC I, p. 340, no. 159
1172.1 6 29 11.05 MMS/N

593/4 AD follis
As above OΠTIOCΓ~ NITPPΛIV
A/N/N/O M X/II, above †, below Γ, in ex. THЄUP'
DOC I, p. 342, no. 164
1173.1 6 30 12.10 RT

601/2 AD follis
As above ONmAVΓICNPAЧC
A/N/N/- M X/X, above †, below A, in ex. THЄUP'
DOC I, p. 345, no. 172
1174.1 6 28 10.86 NoEx

Ravenna
582–602 AD pentanummium
Bust r.
Є ✶
MIB III: 148, DOC not
1175.1 — 12 1.97 NoEx

Uncertain Mint
582–602 AD follis
Bust facing in consular robes with mappa and scepter, legend missing
A/N/N/O M date illeg., mint illeg.
1176.1 6 30 11.10 MMS/N
o/s on follis of Justin II, Constantinople, off. B, uncertain date

582–602 AD half-follis
Bust facing cuir. with gl. cr.
A/N/N/O K, above †
1177.1 6 24 7.00 Syn

Justin I to Maurice

Uncertain Mint
518–602 AD half-follis

1178.1	—	18	frag'y	MMS/N
1178.2	—	21	5.03	MMS
1178.3	—	22	5.19	Syn

pentanummium, Є

1179.1	12	17	1.48	MMS/S
1179.2	6	14	1.47	MMS/N
1179.3	—	14	1.91	MMS

pentanummium, chi-rho
1180.1 — 14 1.25 MMS/S

Phocas

Constantinople
602/3 AD follis
Two standing figures dMFOCAЄPPAVC
A/N/N/O m I, above †, in ex. CON off. letter
DOC II.1, p. 163, no. 24

1181.1	A	8	32	11.20	PA
1181.2	A	7	33	12.08	MMS/N
1181.3	Є	12	31	11.92	HoB

follis, class 2
Bust facing in consular robes with mappa and †, dNFOCASPЄRPAVC
XXXX Ч, above ANNO, in ex. CON[.]
DOC II.1, p. 164, no. 29
1182.1 7 30 10.60 MMS/N
Pierced for suspension

603–610 AD follis
As above
XXXX (date unc.), above ANNO, in ex. CON
1183.1 1 24 10.05 MMS/S

603–610 AD half-follis
As above
XX, above † or ✶, in ex. CON off. letter
DOC II.1, p. 167, no. 36 or 37

1184.1	†, unc.	7	24	7.69	MMS/S, o/s on follis, clipped
1184.2	unc. sym. A	12	26	5.99	MMS/N
1184.3	unc. sym. B	6	22	6.0	MMS/S
1184.4	unc. sym.	1	23	4.80	MMS/S, o/s on decanummium

1184.5 ✶, unc. 12 28 6.30 MMS, o/s on half-follis of Maurice, ca. 590 AD
1184.6 ✶, A 1 23 6.10 MMS/N
1184.7 ✶, B 12 21 5.90 MMS/N
1184.8 ✶, B 7 25 5.20 MMS/N
1184.9 ✶, B 6 30 5.14 NoEx, o/s on half-follis of Maurice? in consular robes
1184.10 ✶, Δ 2 21 5.82 MMS/N

602–610 AD pentanummium
Bust r. dr. dNFOCPPAV
Ч
DOC II.1, p. 170, no. 40
1185.1 6 15 1.41 MMS/S

Thessalonica
603–610 AD half-follis
Two standing figures OmFOCASPЄRPAVC
XX, above †, in ex. TЄS
DOC II.1, p. 175, no. 51
1186.1 6 20 4.73 MMS/N
o/s on decanummium

Nicomedia
603/4 AD follis
As above dmFOCAINPЄRAV
A/N/N/O m II, above †, in ex. NIKOB
DOC II.1, p. 176, no. 54
1187.1 7 26 6.40 MMS
1187.2 7 32 13.53 MMS/S

606/7 AD follis
Bust facing in consular robes with mappa and †, dNFOCASPЄRPAVC
XXXX Ч, above ANNO, below NIKOB
DOC II.1, p. 178, no. 58
1188.1 7 31 10.67 MMS/S
1188.2 6 31 11.04 MMS

608/9 AD half-follis
As above
✶ XX Ч/II, above †, ex. NIKO, to r. unc. off.
DOC II.1, p. 180, no. 68
1189.1 6 21 5.46 MMS
o/s on decanummia of Maurice? ✶ survives

Cyzicus
602/3 AD half-follis
Two standing figures dmFOCASPERPAVC
XX, above †, ex. KYZB
DOC II.1, p. 184, no. 78
1190.1 6 24 7.90 NoEx

602/3 AD half-follis
Bust facing in consular robes with mappa and †, in l. field †, dNFOCASPЄRPAVC
XX, above †, KYZΓ
DOC II.1, p. 185, no. 79
1191.1 6 25 5.40 BS-E12

603/4 AD follis
As above
XXXX II, above ANNO, in ex. KYZB
DOC II.1, p. 181, no. 70
1192.1 12 32 11.80 BS-W1

605/6 AD follis
As above
XXXX II/II, above ANNO, in ex. KYZB
DOC II.1, p. 182, no. 72
1193.1 12 31 11.45 MMS/N

607/8 AD follis
As above
XXXX G, above ANNO, in ex. KYZA
DOC II.1, p. 192, no. 73
1194.1 12 28 10.90 BS-E12

Uncertain Mint
603–610 AD follis
As above
XXXX II, above ANNO
1195.1 6 34 8.57 NoEx
o/s on earlier follis of Phocas, Constantinople, which was itself o/s on earlier follis (obv. legend ends in SPPAVC of Constantinople, possibly of Justinian I)

Anonymous Issue

Constantinople
330–580 AD ⅓ siliqua
Bust r., plumed helm., dr. no legend
K in beaded border, no legend
1196.1 6 14 0.87 MMS
Proposed to have been struck for games in the city; Bendell 2002.

Anastasius I to Phocas

Uncertain mint
498–607 AD follis
1197.1 — 29 9.80 BS

half-follis
1198.1 — 20 2.40 NoEx

decanummium
1199.1 — 15 4.07 MD2
1199.2 12 16 3.70 MMS/N
1199.3 — 18 2.74 MMS

				pentanummium
1200.1	—	—	frag'y	MMS
1200.2	—	—	frag'y	Syn
1200.3	—	11	1.09	MMS
1200.4	—	11	1.59	MMS
1200.5	—	11	1.80	BS-E3
1200.6	—	12	1.17	MMS
1200.7	—	12	1.40	MMS
1200.8	—	12	2.59	ThSt
1200.9	—	13	1.70	BS-E1
1200.10	—	13	1.85	MMS/S
1200.11	—	13	2.02	MMS
1200.12	—	13	2.07	HoB
1200.13	—	14	1.82	MMS/S
1200.14	—	14	2.19	Syn
1200.15	—	15	1.43	NoEx
1200.16	—	15	2.40	BS-E14
1200.17	—	15	2.58	MMS

Justinian I to Phocas

Antioch

527–606 AD follis

1201.1 12 24 5.01 NoEx

Heraclius

Constantinople

611/2 AD follis

Bust facing cuir. with gl. cr. dNhRACLIЧSPЄRPAVI
A/N/N/O M II, above †, below Γ, in ex. CON
DOC II.1, p. 275, no. 70
1202.1 2 27 12.27 NoEx

As above dNhRACLIPERPAVI
A/N/N/O M II/I, above †, below Є, in ex. CON
DOC II.1, p. 276, no. 71d1
1203.1 2 31 12.52 MMS

613 AD follis

Two standing figures, varying legends
A/N/N/O M II/I, above chi-rho, below off. letter, in ex. CON
DOC II.1, p. 281, nos. 76–78
1204.1 A 1 34 13.00 BE-A
Date is given only as II. o/s on follis of Phocas, 602–610 AD, Constantinople
1204.2 A 12 34 12.46 MMS
o/s on Class 2 follis of Phocas, 604–610 AD
1204.3 Є 6 26 8.40 MMS
o/s on follis, poss. earlier issue of Heraclius, Cyzicus
1204.4 Є — 30 8.30 BS-E4
o/s on follis of uncertain date
1204.5 Є 7 33 10.37 HoB
But † above; o/s on follis of Maurice, 582–602 AD, Nicomedia

610–613 AD follis, class 1

Bust facing cuir. with gl. cr., dNhRAI-LIVSPPAV
A/N/N/O M, date unc., above †, off. unc., in ex. CON
1205.1 7 27 10.70 MMS/N, o/s?

610–613 AD follis, class 2

Two standing figures, varying legends
A/N/N/O M date unc., above unc., below Γ, in ex. CON
1206.1 7 32 12.50 MMS/N
o/s on class 2 follis of Phocas, 605–609 AD, Nicomedia

613/4 AD follis

As above JJNNhERAЄThЄRACON
A/N/N/O M II/II, above chi-rho, below off. letter, in ex. CON
DOC II.1, p. 282, no. 79, off. A
1207.1 7 30 12.43 MMS
o/s on follis of Maurice, 582–602 AD, Antioch
1207.2 2 30 10.84 NoEx
o/s on uncertain

614/5 AD follis

As above, varying legends
A/N/N/O M Ч, above chi-rho, below off. letter, in ex. CON
DOC II.1, p. 284, no. 80, unc. off.
1208.1 7 27 9.53 MMS/S
1208.2 1 31 14.90 RT
o/s on follis of Justin and Sophia (DOC I, p. 206, no. 26c, 569/70 AD, Constantinople)

615/6 AD follis

As above
A/N/N/O M G, above †, below Γ, in ex. CON
DOC II.1, p. 284, no. 81
1209.1 3 16 10.21 MMS

615/6 AD follis

Three standing figures standing, varying legends
A/N/N/O M G, above †, below Δ, in ex. CON
DOC II.1, p. 289, no. 89
1210.1 7 26 7.67 MMS/S

613–616 AD follis

Two standing figures, ..ЄThЄRACON
A/N/N/O M date unc., above †, off. unc., in ex. CON
1211.1 12 28 8.15 NoEx
o/s on follis or ¾ follis of Phocas, 602–610 AD

614–616 AD follis

As above, varying legends
A/N/N/O M date unc., above unc. below Є, in ex. CON
1212.1 6 27 10.58 MD1/S
o/s on follis of Phocas, 602–609 AD, Antioch

610–641 AD decanummium
Bust facing cuir. pal. [...]AVYbA[...]
✶ I Δ, in ex. CON
DOC II.1, p. 278, no. 75
1213.1 7 20 3.10 BS-E3

615–624 AD follis
Three standing figures, unc. legend
M date unc., above †, in ex. CON
1214.1 12 27 8.11 MMS

624–629 AD follis
As above, no legend
hR ligatured M date unc., above †ANNO, in ex. CON
1215.1 1 26 7.27 MMS
o/s on half-follis of unc. date

632–634 AD follis
Two standing figures, illeg. legend
A/N/N/O M X/X..., above †, below A, in ex. CON
1216.1 6 20 3.42 Tomb 07.1

Nicomedia
611/2 AD follis
Bust facing helm. cuir. pal. with gl. cr. dNhRACLIPERPAVC
A/N/N/O K II, above †, below B
DOC II.1, p. 317, no. 156
1217.1 6 24 6.17 MMS/S

612/3 AD follis
Two standing figures, varying legends
A/N/N/O M II/I, above †, below A, in ex. NIKO
DOC II.1, p. 317, no. 158
1218.1 7 30 12.45 MMS/N
o/s on follis of Justinian, 527–565 AD, Constantinople

Cyzicus
610/1 AD half-follis
Bust facing cuir. with gl. cr. and shield
dNhRACLIPЄRPAVC
A/N/N/O K I, above †, unc. off.
DOC II.1, p. 324, no. 171
1219.1 2 23 5.76 MMS/S

612/3 AD follis
Two standing figures, varying legends
A/N/N/O M III, above †, below A, in ex. KYZ
DOC II.1, p. 325, no. 175
1220.1 6 29 10.60 MMS/N
o/s on follis of unc. date, Constantinople

Uncertain Mint
613–616 AD follis, class 2
Two standing figures ...PAC..
A/N/N/O M date missing, above chi-rho, below Є, ex. missing
1221.1 2 23 13.71 MMS
o/s on follis of Maurice, 592 AD and later, Constantinople
1221.2 6 27 10.13 Tomb 07.1
o/s on follis of Constantinople

610–614 AD half-follis
Bust facing with gl. cr. and shield
K, all else illeg.
1222.1 6 27 4.54 MMS/S

615–624 AD follis, class 3
Three standing figures, legend unc.
A/N/N/O M date unc., above †, below unc., in ex. unc.
1223.1 9 31 12.27 MMS/S
o/s on class 1 follis of Phocas, 602–604 AD

Anastasius I to Heraclius

Uncertain mint
498–640 AD follis
1224.1 — 27 5.68 MMS/N
1224.2 — 30 7.02 Tomb 07.1

Maurice to Heraclius

Antioch
582–641 AD decanummium
1225.1 — 13 1.30 Syn

Constans II

Constantinople
647/8 AD follis, class 4
Standing emperor with long cross and gl. cr.
A/N/A m N/Є/O/S, above †, in ex. GIB
DOC II.2, p. 448, no. 66
1226.1 2 21 3.67 NoEx

641–644 AD follis, class 1–4
Standing emperor with long cross and gl. cr.
A/N/A? m, all else illeg.
1227.1 6 18 3.49 Tomb 07.1
1227.2 1 21 2.90 Tomb 07.1

651/2 AD follis, class 5
As above
A/N/A M N/Є/O/S, above †, below off. letter, in ex. IA
DOC II.2, p. 450, no. 69
1228.1 A 1 23 4.93 ByzFort
1228.2 Δ 2 18 2.90 NoEx

652/3 AD follis, class 5
As above
A/N/A M N/Є/O/S, above ✶, in ex. IIX
DOC II.2, p. 450, no. 70 var. (date backwards)
1229.1 1 19 2.50 RT

653/4 AD follis, class 5
As above …ONIKA
A/N/A M N/E/O/S, above ✶, below unc., in ex. XIIII
DOC II.2, p. 451, no. 71

1230.1	6	23	11.60	MMS/N

655–657 AD follis, class 6
As above EN…
M CTAN, in ex. uncertain number or letter

1231.1	12	23x15	3.10	RT

Uncertain Mint, most likely Constantinople
641–650 AD follis
As above …NIKA
A/N/A m legend uncertain

1232.1	12	23x15	4.30	BE-A
1232.2	12	25	4.10	BSH

o/s on uncertain coin

1232.3	—	23	3.90	BE-A

641–668 AD follis
Illeg.

1233.1	—	19x12	2.30	BE-H

Tiberius III

Constantinople
698/9 AD follis, class 1
Bust facing cuir. with spear and shield
A/N/N/O M I, above †, below unc. off. letter, in ex. CON
DOC II.2, p. 629, no. 7

1234.1	—	25	6.51	NoEx

640–700 AD? fals?
Two seated? figures, figure on l. with long cross in r. and in l. cross-topped scepter (still to r. of head); on r. consular robes? and gl. cr.?, no legend
A/N/A? m, obscure date, in ex. [..]O[.]

1235.1	2	22	4.20	Tomb 07.1

fals?
Bust facing, bearded, crown but no cross, holding with long cross-topped scepter in r.
A/N/A M [..]OS, below A, in ex. obscure
Nice style

1236.1	6	18	1.96	NoEx

Nikephoros I

Constantinople
803–811 AD follis, class 2
Busts of emperors facing, each in chlamys and crown topped by cross, between †, no legend
X/X/X/ M N/N/N, above †, below A
DOC III.1, p. 358, no. 5

1237.1	6	24	3.86	NoEx

Theophilus

Constantinople
829–830/1 AD follis, class 1
Bust facing in chlamys and crown with cross; in r. hand patriarchal cross and in l. akakia, in l. field ✶
✶•ΘЄOFILbASIL X/X/X/ M N/N/N, above †, below Θ
DOC III.1, p. 433, no. 13

1238.1	6	32	12.32	MMS

o/s on uncertain

830–842 AD follis, class 3
Half-length bust facing in loros and tufa with labarum with cross and streamers in r. and gl. cr. in l. ΘЄOFILbASIL
+ΘЄO/FILЄAVg/OVSTЄSV/nICAS
DOC III.1, p. 435, no. 15a

1239.1	6	27	8.60	MMS/S

Leo VI

Constantinople
886–912 AD follis, class 2
Enthroned emperors, between them they hold labarum
+LЄONSALЄXAn6ROS
+LЄO/SALЄXAn/6ROSbASIL'/ROmЄOn
DOC III.1, p. 517, no. 6

1240.1	6	26	7.10	NoEx

886–912 AD follis, class 3
Bust facing in chlamys and crown with cross; holds akakia in l. +LЄOnbASILЄVSROm'
+LЄOn/ЄnΘЄObA/SILЄVSR/OmЄON
DOC III.1, p. 519, no. 8

1241.1	6	28	7.80	NoEx
1241.2	6	27	6.70	NoEx

Constantine VII and Romanos I Lekapenos

Constantinople
931–944 AD follis, class 4
Bust facing in chlamys and crown with cross, holds in r. labarum scepter with trefoil and in l. gl. cr.
+RWMAn'bASILЄVSRWM'
+RωmA/n'ЄnΘЄWbA/SILЄVSRW/MAIWn
DOC III.2, p. 562, no. 25

1242.1	6	27	6.53	MMS/N
1242.2	6	26	6.64	NoEx
1242.3	12	25	7.90	NoEx

945–ca. 950 AD follis, class 5
Bust facing in loros and crown with cross, in r. akakia and in l. gl. cr. +CONST'bASIL'ROm'
+COnST'/ЄnΘЄObA/SILЄVSR/OMЄOn
DOC III.2, p. 565, no. 26

1243.1	6	27	5.44	NoEx
1243.2	6	25	6.85	F55
1243.3	12	22	4.99	NoEx

Nikephoros II Phokas
Constantinople
963–969 AD follis, class 1
Bust facing in robe and crown with pendilia, in r. cross-topped scepter, in l. gl. cr. with trefoil
+ՈICIFRbASILЄVRW
+ՈICHF/ЄՈΘЄωbA/SILЄVSRW/ՊAIWՈ
DOC III.2, p. 586, no. 7

1244.1	6	25	6.65	NoEx

Double-struck, so obv. legend is missing

Anonymous Follis, class A1
John I Tzimiskes
Constantinople
972–976 AD
Bust of Christ facing holding book IX XC
+EMMANOVHA
+IhSЧS/XRISTЧS/bASILЄЧ'/bASILЄ'
DOC III.2, p. 648

1245.1	12	31	9.48	NoEx
1245.2	12	29	11.53	NoEx
1245.3	12	28	10.10	NoEx
1245.4	9	25	6.58	NoEx
1245.5	6	25	5.69	MMS/N

Anonymous Follis, class A2
Basil II
Constantinople
976–1028 AD
As above, but with variations in nimbus cross and ornament on book; ornament above and below rev. legend
DOC III.2, pp. 649–75

1246.1	var. 14b	5	26	6.40	NoEx
1246.2	leaf m leaf above	6	28	7.98	NoEx
1246.3	spray beneath	12	27	8.48	NoEx
1246.4	unc. ornament	12	29	9.62	NoEx
1246.5	prob. var.	6	27	10.36	NoEx
1246.6	single dot? Below, poss. var. 24b; large module	6	31	15.99	NoEx

Anonymous Follis, class C
Michael IV?
Constantinople
1042?–ca.1050 AD
Three-quarter figure of Christ facing, holding book IX XC +ЄMMANOVHA
Legend in jeweled cross IC XC NI KA
DOC III.2, p. 681, no. 4

1247.1	6	26	8.21	NoEx
1247.2	6	26	6.50	NoEx

Anonymous Follis, class D
Constantine IX
Constantinople
ca. 1050–1060 AD
Christ enthroned, holds book IC XC
-+-/ISXS/bASILЄ/bASIL, below, -◡-
DOC III.2, p. 685

1248.1	12	30	7.20	NoEx
1248.2	6	29	8.90	NoEx

Constantine X
Constantinople
1059–1067 AD follis, class 1
Christ standing facing on souppedion, in l. hand book IC XC +ЄMMANOVHA
Emperor and empress standing facing, between labarum on stepped platform +KWNTΔK ЄVΔKAVΓO
DOC III.2, p. 774, no. 8; M1 1172

1249.1	12	30	7.90	PN/E
1249.2	12	24	3.75	NoEx

1059–1067 AD follis, class 2
Bust facing of nimbate Christ, holding book IX XC +EMMANOVHA
Bust facing of emperor in loros and crown with cross and pendilia, in r. cross and in l. akakia +KWNRACI ΛЄVCO ΔOVK
DOC III.2, p. 777, no. 9

1250.1	6	27	7.83	NoEx
1250.2	6	27	6.74	ByzFort
1250.3	12	24	4.95	NoEx, i.d. prob.

Anonymous Follis, class G
Romanos IV Diogenes
Constantinople
ca. 1065–1070 AD
Bust of Christ facing with scroll IX XC
Bust of Mary facing, as orans MHP ΘV
DOC III.2, p. 692

1251.1	6	29	6.12	NoEx
1251.2	6	27	10.83	NoEx
1251.3	12	27	9.24	NoEx
1251.4	12	27	8.10	NoEx

Romanos IV Diogenes
Constantinople
1068–1071 AD follis
Bust of Christ facing, holds book IX XC NI KA
Cross, between arms CRPΔ
DOC III.2, p. 796, no. 8

1252.1	6	26	5,45	NoEx
1252.2	6	25	3.00	PN/E
1252.3	6	23	4.10	PN/E

Anonymous Follis, class I
Nikephoros III Botaneiates

Constantinople
ca. 1075–1080 AD
Bust of Christ facing, holds book IX XC
Latin cross overlain by X with pellets between arms, at end of each arm, globule and two pellets; vine scrolls in lower quadrants
DOC III.2, p. 696

1253.1	6	22	2.13	PyT
1253.2	12	26	4.54	NoEx

Alexios I Komnenos

Constantinople
1092–1118 AD Bi. aspron trachy, scyphate
Christ enthroned, holds book in l. IC XC
Standing emperor in stemma, scaramangion, holds jeweled scepter in r., l. hand on hip, legend illeg.
Hendy 1969, p. 86, second coinage

1254.1	—	18	3.07	NoEx

Post-reform

Manuel I Komnenos

Constantinople
1143–1180 AD Bi. aspron trachy, scyphate
Christ facing on backless throne IC XC
Standing emperor in stemma, divitision, loros, with labarum in r. and gl. cr. in l., crowned by Mary MΛNȣHΛ ΔЄCΠOT MHP ΘV
Hendy 1969, p. 118, fourth coinage

1255.1	—	23	3.00	NoEx

Hendy var. A

1255.2	6	30	2.90	F49

Hendy var. A

1255.3	12	24	2.87	NoEx

Variety uncertain

Isaac I Komnenos

Nicosia
1184–1191 AD Bi. aspron trachy, scyphate
Virgin enthroned with infant Christ MHP ΘV
Emperor standing facing in stemma, divitision, chlamys, holds akakia in l., with St. George facing, in military tunic, breastplate and sword in l., holding between them patriarchal cross; legend obscure
Hendy 1969, p. 136, type A

1256.1	6	16	3.33	NoEx

Bi. aspron trachy, scyphate
Bust of youthful Christ, holds scroll in l., legend obscure
Emperor standing facing in stemma, scaramangion and sagion, holds cross-topped scepter in r. and akakia in l. Manus Dei in upper r. legend obscure
Hendy 1969, p. 136, type B

1257.1	—	25	frag'y	NoEx
1257.2	6	19	3.17	NoEx

Isaac II Angelos

1185–1195 AD Bi. aspron trachy, scyphate
Mary enthroned facing with nimbed infant Jesus MHP ΘV
Emperor standing facing with stemma, divitision, loros and sagion, with cross-topped scepter in r. and akakia in l. ICAAKKI DECPOTHC, hand of God above
Hendy 1969, p. 144, var. B

1258.1	12	17	2.29	NoEx

Alexios III Angelos

Constantinople
1195–1203 AD Bi. aspron trachy, scyphate
Bust of youthful Christ, holds scroll IX XC
Emperor standing, crowned by St. Constantine; both in stemma, divitision, each with labarum, gl. cr. between, legend illeg.
Hendy 1969, p. 151, uncertain variation

1259.1	6	27	3.15	MMS

Latin Imitation

Constantinople
1204–1261 AD Bi. trachy, scyphate
Nothing visible
Emperor standing wearing divitision, holding labarum topped with cross potent in r.
Hendy 1969, p. 191, type A

1260.1	12	20	1.46	NoEx

No obv. image
Emperor standing with saint or Virgin
Hendy 1969, p. 192, type F, N

1261.1	—	23	1.60	NoEx

No obv. image
Standing emperor in stemma, divitision, holding patriarchal cross-topped scepter held transversely (other hand on hip) ΘX NIC
Hendy 1969, p. 194, type M?

1262.1	—	26	2.29	NoEx

John III Doukas Vatatzes

Nicaea
1222–1254 AD Bi. trachy, scyphate
Bust of young Christ facing, with scroll in l. IC XC
Half-length bust facing of emperor in stemma, divitision, sagion with scepter in r. and gl. cr. with patriarchal cross in l. [...]TIO[...]?
Hendy 1969, p. 243, type J, although does not mention rev. legend

1263.1	6	25	2.39	MMS/N

Magnesia ad Sipylum AE tetarteron
Bust of St. George in tunic, breastplate, sagion, holds spear in r. hand and shield in l.
Standing emperor in stemma, divitision, sagion with labarum in r. and akakia in l. Iω/ΔEC/ΠO/O/ΔY/K/A/C
Hendy 1969, p. 245, type C

1264.1	6	19	2.42	NoEx

Manuel Doukas

Constantinople
1230–1237 AD Bi. trachy, scyphate
Christ enthroned, star to l. and r.
Emperor crowned by Virgin; he holds akakia in r., gl. cr. in l., wears loros and divitsion. She wears pallium and maphorium, blesses with her l.
Hendy 1969, p. 119

1265.1	5	26	2.99	NoEx

Uncertain Ruler

Uncertain Mint
1100–1350 AD? follis
Bust of Christ facing
Bust of emperor? facing

1266.1	12	24	4.29	NoEx

Constantinople
1092–1350 AD Fragment of Bi. trachy, scyphate

1267.1	—	—	—	NoEx
1267.2	—	24	—	EH

Lead and Other Materials

Bifacial token/tessera

L1 7 11 2.74 F49
Artemis Ephesia/bee with straight wings in linear border. Context in which it was found dates to the early first century AD (Bruce, Final Field Report: F49 12.1, p. 19). A bifacial tessera with this pairing is known from Ephesus; see Gülbay and Kireç, 2008, no. 107.

L2 23 0.53 F55
Victory l. holding long cross in l. hand, linear border/same. Context in which it was found dates to sixth century AD or later; copper alloy (Gallart Marqués, Final Field Report: F55 04.2, p. 7).

Uniface tokens

L3 10 1.20 NoEx
Seated nude figure l. raising hand to drink (satyr)?; in linear border.

L4 10 0.97 ThSt
Anchor, to l. Δ; Hellenistic?
Found in topsoil; see parallel, Gülbay and Kireç 2008, no. 36b.

L5 16 2.40 MMS/N
Cornucopia, to l. Γ; to r. Δ, in beaded border.
From a Late Roman context. cf. Gülbay and Kireç, 2008, no. 257.

L6 18 2.79 MMS/S
Theater mask of a young woman.
From a Byzantine context. Parallels in Gülbay and Kireç 2008, nos. 136–139b, 144 and p. 32. This very likely was made as a theater ticket, but could have been used in later periods as a coin (see countermarked examples in Gülbay and Kireç 2008, p. 32).

L7 12 1.33 NoEx
Herakles standing with club and lionskin, M in l. field.
cf. Gülbay and Kireç 2008, nos. 17, 18, 32.

L8 17 2.66 ByzFort
Inscription in three lines, all in wreath: ?E?/TAN (or M)OI/NOC
Dated 300–400 AD; associated with mosaic subfloor that was dated to fourth century AD by coins, style of mosaic and not contradicted by the pottery associated with the bedding (Ratté, Final Field Report ByzFort 86.12, p. 2).

L9 13 1.85 MMS/S
Illeg.

L10 10 1.23 MD2
Illeg.

L11 19 4.67 NoEx
Seal or token laureate bearded? head r.; uncertain rev., possibly an impression of the object this was placed against. first century BC to second century AD, based on the style of the head. cf. Gülbay and Kireç 2008, nos. 188–189.

Lead Seals

L12 (M64.012) 16 3.52 HoB
Head of mature Herakles r., beaded border
Hellenistic–Roman Imperial (note object no., not previously published); cf. Gülbay and Kireç 2008, nos. 205, 214.

L13 20 × 24 15.99 NoEx
Quadruped walking r.; mg. (see App. 2), pierced for hanging 450–700 AD?

L14 19 1.84 MMS/N
Illeg., pierced twice for attachment.

L15 24 7.00 MMS/N
Illeg.

L16 17 2.92 (broken) NoEx
Bust r., dr., beaded border DN(?)[…]; cross with pendants on each arm: to l. A?, to r. N?, below, W, beaded border, 500–600 AD?

L17 26 9.28 NoEx
Cruciform invocative mg.: ΘΕΟΤΟΚΕ or ΚΥΡΙΕ ΒΟΘΕΙ; in quarters, [TW CW] ΔΟV-ΛW; rev. is inscription in 5? lines: [missing]/CΠΑΘ'[K]/OM[.]'OΨ[I?]/K?[…]I/missing?
Prob. ninth century AD. The name of the imperial spatharios and comes of the Opsikion is not preserved.

L18 25 15.48 NoEx
Obv.: cruciform invocative mg. in linear border, ΘΕΟΤΟΚΕ ΒΟΗΘΕΙ (nothing in quadrants), wreath border; rev.: inscription in three lines, with cross between triangles above, in wreath h(K?)ANCΓ/PATΘA/ATO(?), [uncertain name], strategos (possibly stratelates) of uncertain area, seventh–ninth century AD.

L19 (M66.016) 20 × 17 6.70 PA
Obv.: cruciform invocative mg.: ΘΕΟΤΟΚΕ ΒΟΗΘΕΙ (nothing in quadrants); rev.: cruciform ΘΕΟΠΕΜΠΤΟΥ (Theopemptos)
Note object number, not previously published. cf. Zacos and Veglery 1972, I.3, no. 2830; dated generally by Zacos and Veglery (1972, p. 367) to ca. 550 to the end of the seventh century AD. Seal with the name of a Theopemptos (moderator), in wreath border is dated to the second half of the sixth century AD.

L20 (M88.010) 19 × 17 7.14 MMS
Obv.: +/ΔΙΑΚ/ΟΝ + rev.: +/KOC/MA
Note object number. Found in a mid-sixth century AD wall: Kosmas, deacon. Bilateral seals are dated ca. 500–850 AD by Zacos and Veglery (1972, I, p. 549); published in Greenewalt, Ratté, and Rautman 1994, p. 8, fig. 6, where it is noted that the context of the seal is early evidence for the spread of the office.

Lead Slugs or Blanks

L21 9 0.60 MMS/N
Uniface: E, similar to pentanummium mark, similar to coins of 500–600 AD, but much smaller.

L22 21 5.00 MMS
Illeg.

L23 14 1.80 MMS/N
No types, found folded over. Also see no. 1003.

Clay Token

L24 13 CW6
Uniface: amphora with pointed foot.

Bibliography

Abdy, R. 2012. "Tetrarchy and the House of Constantine." In Metcalf 2012, pp. 584–600.

Adelson, H. L., and G. L. Kustas. 1960. "A Bronze Hoard of the Period of Leo I." *ANSMN* 9: 139–88.

———. 1962. *A Bronze Hoard of the Period of Zeno I.* ANSNNM 148. New York: American Numismatic Society.

Adkins, R., J. Perry, and J. Evans. 1989. ". . . Of Sherds and Soil and Sealing Layers, of Cobbling and Coins . . ." *OJA* 8: 119–29.

Alram, M. 2012. "The Coinage of the Persian Empire." In Metcalf 2012, pp. 61–87.

Amandry, M. 2012. "The Coinage of the Roman Provinces through Hadrian." In Metcalf 2012, pp. 391–404.

Amandry, M., A. Burnett, J. Mairat, W. Metcalf, L. Bricault, and M. Blet-Lemarquand. 2015. *Roman Provincial Coinage III.* London: British Museum.

Ambraseys, N. 2009. *Earthquakes in the Mediterranean and Middle East: A Multidisciplinary Study of Seismicity up to 1900.* Cambridge: Cambridge University Press.

Andrews, B. N. 2006. "Sediment Consolidation and Archaeological Site Formation." *Geoarchaeology* 21: 461–78.

Aperghis, G. G. 2004. *The Seleukid Royal Economy: The Finances and Financial Administration of the Seleukid Empire.* Cambridge: Cambridge University Press.

Archontidou, A. 2004. "The Archaeological Museum of Mytilene." *Museology: International Scientific Electronic Journal* 1: 70–73.

Arslan, E. A. 2003. "Problemi ponderali di V secolo: verso la riforma del Nummus. Il deposito di Cafarnao." *RevNum* 6, 159: 27–39.

Arthur, P. 2012. "Hierapolis of Phrygia: The Drawn-Out Demise of an Anatolian City." In *Vrbes Extinctae: Archaeologies of Abandoned Classical Towns*, edited by N. Christie and A. Augenti, pp. 275–305. Surrey: Ashgate.

Ashton, R. 1998. "The Coins of the Macedonian Kings, Lysimachos and Eupolemos in the Museums of Fethiye and Afyon." In *Coins of Macedonia and Rome: Essays in Honour of Charles Hersh*, edited by A. Burnett, U. Wartenberg, and R. Witschonke, pp. 19–48. London: Spink & Son.

———. 2012. "The Hellenistic World: The Cities of Mainland Greece and Asia Minor." In Metcalf 2012, pp. 191–210.

Atlan, S. 1976. *1947–1967 yılları Side kazıları sırasında elde edilen sikkeler.* Türk Tarih Ankara: Kurumu Basimevi.

Bates, G. E. 1971. *Byzantine Coins.* Archaeological Exploration of Sardis Monograph 1. Cambridge, MA: Harvard University Press.

Beckmann, M. 2012. "Trajan and Hadrian." In Metcalf 2012, pp. 405–22.

Bell, H. W. 1902. "Coins from Assos." In *Expedition of the Archaeological Institute of America Investigations at Assos*, edited by J. T. Clarke, F. H. Bacon, and R. Koldewey, pp. 298–313. Cambridge: Archaeological Institute of America.

———. 1916. *Sardis XI: Coins.* Pt. 1: *1910–1914.* Leiden: Brill.

Bellinger, A. 1965. *Catalogue of the Byzantine Coins in the Dumbarton Oaks Collection and in the Whittemore Collection*. Vol. 1: *Anastasius I to Maurice, 491–602*. Washington, D.C.: Dumbarton Oaks Research Library and Collection.

———. 1968. "Electrum Coins from Gordion." In *Essays in Greek Coinage Presented to Stanley Robinson*, edited by C. Kraay and G. K. Jenkins, pp. 10–15. Oxford: Clarendon.

Bennett, R. 2014. *Local Elites and Local Coinage: Elite Self-Representation on the Provincial Coinage of Asia, 31 BC to AD 275*. Royal Numismatic Society Special Publications 51. London: Royal Numismatic Society.

Berlin, A. 2016. "Not So Fast: Ceramic Conservatism and Change at Sardis in the Early Hellenistic Period." In *Traditions and Innovations: Tracking the development of pottery from the late classical to the early imperial periods: Proceedings of the first conference of IARPotHP, Berlin, November 2013, 7th–10th*, edited by S. Japp and P. Kogler, pp. 351–58. IARPotHP 1. Vienna: Phoibos Verlag.

———. Forthcoming. "The Archaeology of a Changing City." In Berlin and Kosmin Forthcoming.

Berlin, A., and P. Kosmin, eds. Forthcoming. *Spear-Won Land: Sardis, from the King's Peace to the Peace of Apamea*. Madison: University of Wisconsin Press.

Besly, E., and R. Bland. 1983. *The Cunetio Treasure: Roman Coinage of the Third Century AD*. London: British Museum.

Bijovsky, G. I. 2004. "Coins from Ashquelon, Semadar Hotel." *'Atiqot* 48: 111–21.

———. 2011. "Monetary Circulation in Palestine during the Byzantine Period." PhD diss., University of Haifa.

———. 2012. *Gold Coin and Small Change: Monetary Circulation in Fifth–Seventh Century Byzantine Palestine*. Polymnia: Numismatica Antica e Medievale. Studi. Trieste: Edizioni Università de Trieste.

———. 2015. "Coins." In *Samaritan Cemeteries and Tombs in the Central Coastal Plain: Archaeology and History of the Samaritan Settlement outside Samaria (ca. 300–700 CE)*, edited by O. Tal and I. Taxel, pp. 81–98. Ägypten und Altes Testament 82. Münster: Ugarit Verlag.

Bland, R. 1988. "Minster, Sheppey, Kent." In *The Normandy Hoard and other Roman Coin Hoards*, edited by R. Bland and A. Burnett, pp. 74–90. Coin Hoards from Roman Britain VIII. London: British Museum.

———. 2012. "From Gordian III to the Gallic Empire (AD 238–274)." In Metcalf 2012, pp. 514–37.

Boehringer, C. 1984. "Münzen." In *Peristylhäuser westlich der Unteren Agora*, edited by Doris Pinkwart, pp. 163–64. Altertümer von Pergamon 14. Berlin: De Gruyter.

Bonner, C. 1950. "A Reminiscence of Paul on a Coin Amulet." *HTR* 43.2: 165–68.

Brandes, W. 1999. "Byzantine Cities in the Seventh and Eighth Centuries." In Brogiolo and Ward-Perkins 1999, pp. 25–57.

Bransbourg, G. 2011. "Fides et Pecunia Numerata: Chartalism and Metallism in the Roman World. Part 1: The Republic." *AJN* 23: 87–152.

Brogiolo, G., and B. Ward-Perkins. 1999. *The Idea and Ideal of the Town between Late Antiquity and the Early Middle Age*. Leiden: Brill.

Bruce, W. 2015. "Industry, Community and the Sacred: Life Outside the City Walls at Sardis." PhD diss., University of Wisconsin at Madison.

Bruun, P. 1966. *The Roman Imperial Coinage VII: Constantine I to Licinius (313–337)*. London: Spink & Son.

Buchwald, H. 2015. *Churches EA and E at Sardis*. Archaeological Exploration of Sardis Report 6. Cambridge, MA: Harvard University Press.

Buckler, W. H., and D. M. Robinson. 1932. *Sardis VII: Greek and Latin Inscriptions*. Leiden: Brill.

Burnett, A. 1987. *Coinage in the Roman World*. London: Seaby.

———. 1999. "Buildings and Monuments on Roman Coins." In *Roman Coins and Public Life under the Empire: E. Togo Salmon Papers II*, edited by G. M. Paul and M. Ierardi, pp. 137–64. Ann Arbor: University of Michigan Press.

———. 2011. "The Augustan Revolution Seen from the Mints of the Provinces." *JRS* 101: 1–30.

Burnett, A., M. Amandry, and I. Carradice. 1999. *Roman Provincial Coinage II: The Flavians*. London: British Museum.

Burnett, A., M. Amandry, and P. P. Ripollés. 2005. *Roman Provincial Coinage I: Augustus to the Julio-Claudians*. London: British Museum.

Burrell, B. 2004. *Neokoroi: Greek Cities and Roman Emperors*. Leiden: Brill.

———. 2007. "A Hoard of Minimi from Sardis and the Currency of the Fifth Century C.E." *RevNum* 163: 235–82.

———. 2008. "Small Bronze Hoards at Late Fifth Century C. E. Sardis." In *Love for Lydia: A Sardis Anniversary Volume Presented to Crawford H. Greenewalt, Jr.*, edited by N. D. Cahill, pp. 159–228. Archaeological Exploration of Sardis Report 4. Cambridge, MA: Harvard University Press.

Butcher, K. 1988. *Roman Provincial Coins: An Introduction to the Greek Imperials*. London: Seaby.

———. 1995. "The Coins." In *Nicopolis ad Istrum: A Roman, Late Roman and Early Byzantine City: Excavations 1985–1992*, by A. G. Poulter, pp. 269–314. Journal of Roman Studies Monograph 8. London: Society for the Promotion of Roman Studies.

———. 2001/2. *Small Change in Ancient Beirut: Coins from BEY 006 and 045: Persian, Hellenistic, Roman, and Byzantine Periods*. Berytus 45–46. Beirut: American University of Beirut.

———. 2013. "Coins and Hoards." In *Excavations at Zeugma Conducted by Oxford Archaeology*, edited by W. Aylward, pp. 1–92. Los Altos, CA: The Packard Humanities Institute.

———. 2016. "Coin Finds and the Monetary Economy: the Good, the Bad, and the Irrelevant." In *Les Monnaies de Fouille du Monde Grec (VIe–Ier s. a.C.): Apports, approches et méthodes*, edited by F. Duyrat and C. Grandjean, pp. 225–37. Scripta Antiqua 93. Bordeaux: Ausonius.

Butler, H. C. 1922. *Sardis I: The Excavations*. Pt. 1: *1910–1914*. Leiden: Brill.

Buttrey, T. V. 1993. "The President's Address: Calculating Ancient Coin Production: Facts and Fantasies." *NC* 153: 335–51.

Buttrey, T. V., A. Johnston, K. Mackenzie, and M. Bates. 1981. *Greek, Roman, and Islamic Coins from Sardis*. Archaeological Exploration of Sardis Monograph 7. Cambridge: Harvard University Press.

Buttrey, T. V., and I. McPhee. 1998. *The Extramural Sanctuary of Demeter and Persephone at Cyrene, Libya: Final Reports*. Vol. VI: *The Coins and Attic Pottery*. Philadelphia: University of Pennsylvania.

Cahill, N. D. 2010. "Sardis, 2008." *Kazı Sonuçları Toplantısı* 31: 63–78.

———. 2011. "Sardis, 2009." *Kazı Sonuçları Toplantısı* 32: 358–67.

———. 2012. "Sardis, 2010." *Kazı Sonuçları Toplantısı* 33: 209–29.

———. 2013. "Sardis, 2011." *Kazı Sonuçları Toplantısı* 34: 147–60.

———. 2014a. "Sardis, 2012." *Kazı Sonuçları Toplantısı* 35, 3: 119–35.

———. 2014b. "Rituelle Ei-Niederlegung in Sardes." *Antike Welt* 3, 14: 4.

———. 2015. "Sardis, 2013." *Kazı Sonuçları Toplantısı* 36, 2: 413–30.

———. 2016. "Sardis, 2014." *Kazı Sonuçları Toplantısı* 37, 3: 147–64.

Cahill, N. D., and C. H. Greenewalt, Jr. 2016. "The Sanctuary of Artemis at Sardis: Preliminary Report, 2002–2012." *AJA* 120, 3: 473–508.

Cahill, N. D., J. Hari, B. Önay, and E. Dokimacı. Forthcoming. "Depletion Gilding of Lydian Electrum Coins and the Sources of Lydian Gold." In van Alfen et al. Forthcoming.

Cahill, N. D., and J. Kroll. 2005. "New Archaic Coin Finds at Sardis." *AJA* 109, 4: 589–617.

de Callataÿ, F. 1995. "Calculating Ancient Coin Production: Seeking a Balance." *NC* 155: 289–311.

———. 2013. "White Gold: An Enigmatic Start to Greek Coinage." *ANS Magazine* 12, 2: 7–17.

Callu, J. P. 1980. "The Distribution and Role of the Bronze Coinage from AD 348 to 392." In *Imperial Revenue, Expenditure and Monetary Policy in The Fourth Century A.D.*, edited by C. E. King, pp. 95–122. BAR International Series 76. Oxford: BAR.

Canti, M. G. 2003. "Earthworm Activity and Archaeological Stratigraphy: A Review of Products and Processes." *JAS* 30: 135–48.

Carradice, I. 1987. "The 'Regal' Coinage of the Persian Empire." In *Coinage and Administration in the Athenian and Persian Empires, The Ninth Oxford Symposium on Coinage and Monetary History*, edited by I. Carradice, pp. 73–93. BAR International 343. Oxford: BAR.

Carson, R. A. G., P. V. Hill, and J. P. C. Kent. 1965. *Late Roman Bronze Coinage, A.D. 324–498*. London: Spink.

Casey, J. 1974. "The Interpretation of Romano-British Site Finds." In *Coins and the Archaeologist*, edited by J. Casey and R. Reece, pp. 37–51. British Archaeological Reports 4. Oxford: BAR.

Chameroy, J. 2012. "Chronologie und Verbreitung der hellenistischen Bronzeprägungen von Pergamon: der Beitrag der Fundmünzen." *Chiron* 42: 131–81.

Chankowski, V. 2011. "Divine Financiers: Cults as Consumers and Generators of Value." In *The Economies of Hellenistic Societies, Third to First Centuries BC*, edited by Z. H. Archibald, J. K. Davies, and V. Gabrielsen, pp. 142–65. Oxford: Oxford University Press.

Charanis, P. 1972/3. "A Note on the Byzantine Coin Finds in Sardis and their Historical Significance." *Epeteris Hetaireias Byzantinon Spoudon* 39: 175–80.

Christie, N., and S. T. Loseby. 1996. *Towns in Transition: Urban Evolution in Late Antiquity and the Early Middle Ages*. Brookfield, VT: Aldershot.

Çizmeli-Öğün, Z., and M.-C. Marcellesi. 2011. "Reseaux d'échanges régionaux en Asie Mineure occidentale: l'apport des monnaies de fouilles." In *Nomisma: La circulation monétaire dans le monde grec antique: actes du colloque international, Athènes, 14–17 avril 2010*, edited by T. Faucher, M.-C. Marcellesi, and O. Picard, pp. 297–342. Bulletin de correspondance hellénique Supplément 53. Athens: Ecole française d'Athènes.

Clay, C. L. 1989. "The Supply of Bronze Coins to Britain in the Second Century AD." *NC* 149: 209–24.

Cormack, R. 1990. "Byzantine Aphrodisias. Changing the Symbolic Map of a City." *CCJ* 36: 26–41.

Cormack, S. 2004. *The Space of Death in Roman Asia Minor*. Wiener Forschungen zur Archäologie 6. Vienna: Phoibos Verlag.

Cox, D. H. 1950. "The Coins." In *Excavations at Gözlü Kule, Tarsus*. Vol. 1: *The Hellenistic and Roman Periods*, edited by H. Goldman, pp. 38–83. Princeton: Princeton University Press.

Cramme, S. 2001. "Die Bedeutung des Euergetismus für die Finanzierung städtischer Aufgaben in der Provinz Asia." PhD diss., Universität zu Köln.

Crawford, J. S. 1990. *The Byzantine Shops at Sardis*. Archaeological Exploration of Sardis Monograph 9. Cambridge, MA: Harvard University Press.

Crawford, M. 1974. *Roman Republican Coinage*. Cambridge: Cambridge University Press.

———. 2003. "Thesauri, Hoards and Votive Deposits." In *Sanctuaires et sources dans l'antiquité: les sources documentaires et leurs limites dans la description des lieux de culte: actes de la table ronde, organisée par le Collège de France, l'UMR 8585 Centre Gustave-Glotz, l'École Française de Rome, et le Centre Jean Bérard: Naples, Centre Jean Bérard, 30 novembre 2001*, edited by O. de Cazanove and J. Scheid, pp. 69–84. Collection du Centre Jean Bérard 22. Napoli: Centre Jean Bérard.

Delmaire, R. 2003. "Aspects normatifs de la politique monétaire du Bas Empire: une nouvelle lecture de CTh IX, 23, 1." *RevNum* 6: 163–74.

Delrieux, F. 2012. "Séismes et reconnaissance civique dans l'ouest de l'Asie Mineure. La représentation monétaire des empereurs romains restaurateurs de cités." In *Stephanèphoros. De l'économie antique à l'Asie Mineure. Hommages à Raymond Descat*, edited by K. Konuk, pp. 216–74. Mémoires 28. Bordeaux: Ausonius.

Dignas, B. 2005. "Sacred Revenues in Roman Hands: The Economic Dimension of Sanctuaries in Western Asia Minor." In *Patterns in the Economy of Roman Asia Minor*, edited by S. Mitchell and C. Katsari, pp. 207–24. Swansea: Classical Press of Wales.

Dmitriev, S. 2005. *City Government in Hellenistic and Roman Asia Minor*. Oxford: Oxford University Press.

Doyen, J.-M. 2011. "Cliométrie et numismatique contextuelle: compter et quantifier le passé? Petite histoire de la méthode (1960–2011)." *JAN* 1: 9–46.

Drew-Bear, T. 1974. "Representations of Temples on the Greek Imperial Coinage." *ANSMN* 19: 27–63.

Duchemin, J.-P. 2012. "Numismatique et archéologie du rituel: réflexion sur le rite dit de l'"obole à Charon' à partir de l'exemple de la nécropole tardo-antique de Nempont-Saint-Firmin (Pas-de-Calais, France)." *Archaeological Numismatics* 2: 127–98.

Duncan-Jones, R. 1998. *Money and Government in the Roman Empire*. Cambridge: Cambridge University Press.

Dzielska, M. 1986. *Apollonius of Tyana in Legend and History*. Rome: L'Erma di Bretschneider.

Edwards, K. M. 1933. *Corinth VI: Coins, 1896–1929*. Cambridge, MA: American School of Classical Studies at Athens, Harvard University Press.

———. 1937. "Report on the Coins Found in the Excavations at Corinth during the Years 1930–1935." *Hesperia* 6, 2: 241–56.

Ellis, S. J. R. 2017. "Reevaluating Pompeii's Coin-Finds: Monetary Transactions and Urban Waste in the Retail Economy of an Ancient City." In *The Economy of Pompeii*, edited by M. Flohr and W. Wilson, pp. 293–337. Oxford: Oxford University Press.

Elton, H. 2005. "Military Supply and the South Coast of Anatolia in the Third Century AD." In *Patterns in the Economy of Roman Asia Minor*, edited by S. Mitchell and C. Katsari, pp. 289–304. Swansea: Classical Press of Wales.

Evans, J. D. 2007. *Caesarea Maritima: The Coins and the Hellenistic, Roman and Byzantine Economy of Palestine*. American Schools of Oriental Research Archaeological Reports 10. Boston: American Schools of Oriental Research.

———. 2013a. "Coins and the Archaeology of the Roman Republic." In *A Companion to the Archaeology of the Roman Republic*, edited by J. D. Evans, pp. 110–22. Oxford: Wiley-Blackwell.

———. 2013b. "Five Small Bronze Hoards from Sardis and Their Implications for Coin Circulation in the Fifth Century C.E." *BASOR* 369: 137–56.

———. 2015. "The Third Neokorate of Sardis in Light of a New Coin Type Found in Sardis." In *FIDES: Contributions to Numismatics in Honor of Richard B. Witschonke*, edited by P. G. van Alfen, G. Bransbourg, and M. Amandry, pp. 417–25. New York: American Numismatic Society.

———. Forthcoming. "The Mint at Sardis." In Berlin and Kosmin Forthcoming.

Evans, J. D., A. Ferdière, and E. Marot. 2009. "Anderitum: Excavations in a Roman Town in Gallia Aquitania." *AJA* 113, 2: 255–72.

Fisher, J. E. 1984. "Coins: Corinth Excavations, 1977, Forum Southwest." *Hesperia* 53, 2: 217–250.

Foss, C. 1975. "The Fall of Sardis in 616 and the Value of Evidence." *JÖB* 24: 11–22.

———. 1976. *Byzantine and Turkish Sardis*. Archaeological Exploration of Sardis Monograph 4. Cambridge, MA: Harvard University Press.

———. 1979. *Ephesus After Antiquity: A Late Antique, Byzantine, and Turkish City*. Cambridge: Cambridge University Press.

Foss, C., and J. A. Scott. 2002. "Sardis." In *The Economic History of Byzantium from the Seventh through the Fifteenth Century*, edited by A. E. Laiou, Vol. 2, pp. 615–22. Washington, D.C.: Dumbarton Oaks Research Library and Collection.

Frascone, D. 2013. *Zeugma IV: Les monnaies*. Lyon: Jean Pouilloux.

Frey-Kupper, S. 2013. *Die antiken Fundmünzen vom Monte Iato: 1971–1990: ein Beitrag zur Geldgeschichte Westsiziliens*. Studia Ietina 10. Lausanne: Éditions du Zebre.

von Fritze, H. 1910. *Die Münzen von Pergamon*. Berlin: Verlag der Königlichen Akademie der Wissenschaften.

Fulghum, M. M. 2001. "Coins Used as Amulets in Late Antiquity." In *Between Magic and*

Religion: Interdisciplinary Studies in Ancient Mediterranean Religion and Society, edited by S. R. Asirvatham, C. O. Pache, and J. Watrous, pp. 139–48. Lanham, MD: Rowman & Littlefield.

Gallart Marqués, F. 2015. "The Coroplastic Art from Sardis: Emergence and Development of Local Traditions." PhD diss., Cornell University.

Gândilă, A. 2009. "Early Byzantine Coin Circulation in the Eastern Provinces: a Comparative Statistical Approach." *AJN* 21: 151–226.

Gauthier, P. 1989. *Nouvelles Inscriptions de Sardes II.* Hautes Études du Monde Gréco-Romain 15. Geneva: Droz.

Gerrard, R. 1993. "Beyond Crossmends: Stratigraphic Analysis and the Content of Historic Artefact Assemblages on Urban Sites." In *Practices of Archaeological Stratigraphy*, edited by E. C. Harris, M. R. Brown, III, and G. J. Brown, pp. 229–49. San Diego: Academic.

Golenko, V. 1993. "Notes on the Coinage and Currency of the Early Seleucid State I: the Reign of Seleucus I." *Mesopotamia* 28: 71–167.

Greenewalt, Jr., C. H. 1991. "Sardis: Archaeological Research in 1990." *Kazı Sonuçları Toplantısı* 13, 1: 457–70.

———. 2004. "Sardis: Archaeological Research and Conservation Projects in 2002." *Kazı Sonuçları Toplantısı* 25: 481–90.

———. 2006. "Sardis: Archaeological Research and Conservation Projects in 2004." *Kazı Sonuçları Toplantısı* 27: 175–86.

———. 2007. "Sardis: Archaeological Research and Conservation Projects in 2005." *Kazı Sonuçları Toplantısı* 28: 743–56.

———. 2008. "Sardis: Archaeological Research and Conservation Projects in 2006." *Kazı Sonuçları Toplantısı* 29, 3: 371–86.

Greenewalt, Jr., C. H., N. D. Cahill, H. Dedeoğlu, and P. Herrmann. 1990. "The Sardis Campaign of 1986." *BASOR Suppl.* 26: 137–77.

Greenewalt, Jr., C. H., N. D. Cahill, and M. L. Rautman. 1988. "The Sardis Campaign of 1984." *BASOR Suppl.* 25: 13–54.

Greenewalt, Jr., C. H., M. L. Rautman, and N. D. Cahill. 1988. "The Sardis Campaign of 1985." *BASOR Suppl.* 25: 55–92.

Greenewalt, Jr., C. H., A. Johnston, and T. V. Buttrey. 1973. "The Fifteenth Campaign at Sardis (1972)." *BASOR* 211: 14–36.

Greenewalt, Jr., C. H., A. Ramage, D. G. Sullivan, K. Nayir, and A. Tulga. 1983. "The Sardis Campaigns of 1979 and 1980." *BASOR* 249: 1–44.

Greenewalt, Jr., C. H., C. Ratté, and M. L. Rautman. 1994. "The Sardis Campaigns of 1988 and 1989." *AASOR* 51: 1–44.

———. 1995. "The Sardis Campaigns of 1990 and 1991." *AASOR* 52: 1–36.

Greenewalt, Jr., C. H., C. Ratté, D. G. Sullivan, and T. N. Howe. 1985. "The Sardis Campaigns of 1981and 1982." *BASOR Suppl.* 23: 53–92.

Greenewalt, Jr., C. H., and M. L. Rautman. 1998. "The Sardis Campaigns of 1994 and 1995." *AJA* 102, 3: 469–505.

———. 2000. "The Sardis Campaigns of 1996, 1997, and 1998." *AJA* 104, 4: 643–81.

Greenewalt, Jr., C. H., M. L. Rautman, and N. D. Cahill. 1988. "The Sardis Campaign of 1985." *BASOR Suppl.* 25: 55–92.

Greenewalt, Jr., C. H., M. L. Rautman, and R. Meriç. 1986. "The Sardis Campaign of 1983." *BASOR Suppl.* 24: 1–30.

Greenewalt, Jr., C. H., E. L. Sterud, and D. F. Belknap. 1982. "The Sardis Campaign of 1978." *BASOR* 245: 1–34.

Grierson, P. 1965. "The President's Address: Session 1964–1965: The Interpretation of Coin Finds (1)." *NC* 5: i–xvi.

———. 1966. "The President's Address: Session 1965–1966: The Interpretation of Coin Finds (2)." *NC* 6: i–xxi.

———. 1968a. *Catalogue of the Byzantine Coins in the Dumbarton Oaks Collection and in the Whittemore Collection.* Vol. 2.1: *Phocas and Heraclius (602–641).* Washington, D.C.: Dumbarton Oaks Research Library and Collection.

———. 1968b. *Catalogue of the Byzantine Coins in the Dumbarton Oaks Collection and in the Whittemore Collection.* Vol. 2.2: *Heraclius Constantine to Theodosius III (641–717).* Washington, D.C.: Dumbarton Oaks Research Library and Collection.

———. 1973a. *Catalogue of the Byzantine Coins in the Dumbarton Oaks Collection and in the Whittemore Collection.* Vol. 3.1: *Leo III to Michael III (717–867).* Washington, D.C.: Dumbarton Oaks Research Library and Collection.

———. 1973b. *Catalogue of the Byzantine Coins in the Dumbarton Oaks Collection and in the Whittemore Collection.* Vol. 3.2: *Basil I to Nicephorus III (867–1081).* Washington, D.C.: Dumbarton Oaks Research Library and Collection.

———. 1975. *Numismatics.* London: Oxford University Press.

———. 1986. "Iconografia, circolazione monetaria e tesaurizzazione, B: Interpretation de quelques fouilles archeologiques." In *La cultura bizantina, oggetti e messaggio: moneta ed economia*, edited by A. Guillou, pp. 44–53. Università degli Studi di Bari Centro di Studi Bizantini 4. Roma: L'Erma di Bretschneider.

Griffin, M. 2004. "Apollo's Hawk at Aristophanes, 'Birds' 516." *CQ* 54: 610–13.

Guest, P. 2012. "The Production, Supply and Use of Late Roman and Early Byzantine Copper Coinage in the Eastern Empire." *NC* 172: 105–31.

Guest, P., J. Mitchell, E. Nallbani, and G. Shpresa. 2004. "The Small Finds and Coins." In *Byzantine Butrint: Excavations and Surveys 1994–99*, edited by R. Hodges, W. Bowden, and K. Lako, pp. 293–305. Oxford: Oxbow, Oxford.

Gülbay, O., and H. Kireç. 2008. *Efes Kurşun Tesseraeları/Ephesian Lead Tessera.* Selçuk-Efes Kent Belleği 2. Selçuk: Selçuk Belediyesi.

Gysen, P. 1999. "A propos des ateliers de Smyrne et de Cyzique sous Claude II le Gothique." *Cercle d'Études Numismatiques Bulletin* 36: 29–41.

Hahn, W. 1973. *Moneta Imperii Byzantini: Rekonstruktion des Prageaufbaues auf synoptisch-tabellarischer Grundlage.* Vienna: Verlag der Österreichischen Akademie der Wissenschaften.

———. 2000. *Money of the Incipient Byzantine Empire (Anastasius I–Justinian I, 491–565).* Veröffentlichen des Instituts für Numismatik und Geldgeschichte 6. Vienna: Österreichische Forschungsgesellschaft für Numismatik.

Hahn, W., and M.A. Metlich. 2009. *Money of the Incipient Byzantine Empire Continued (Justin II–Revolt of the Heraclii, 565–610).* Vienna: Österreichische Forschungsgesellschaft für Numismatik.

Haldon, J. F. 1997. *Byzantium in the Seventh Century: The Transformation of a Culture.* Cambridge: Cambridge University Press.

———. 2012. "Commerce and Exchange in the Seventh and Eighth Centuries: Regional Trade and the Movement of Goods." In *Trade and Markets in Byzantium*, edited by C. Morrison, pp. 99–122. Washington, D.C.: Dumbarton Oaks Research Library and Collection.

Haldon, J. F., N. Roberts, A. Izdebski, D. Fleitmann, et al. 2014. "The Climate and Environment of Byzantine Anatolia: Integrating Science, History, and Archaeology." *Journal of Interdisciplinary History* 45, 2: 113–61.

Hanfmann, G. M. A. 1962. "The Fourth Campaign at Sardis (1961)." *BASOR* 166: 1–57.

———. 1963. "The Fifth Campaign at Sardis (1962)." *BASOR* 170: 1–65.

———. 1964. "The Sixth Campaign at Sardis (1963)." *BASOR* 174: 3–58.

———. 1965. "The Seventh Campaign at Sardis (1964)." *BASOR* 177: 2–37.

———. 1983. *Sardis from Prehistoric to Roman Times: Results of the Archaeological Exploration of Sardis 1958–1975.* Cambridge, MA: Harvard University Press.

Hanfmann, G. M. A., D. G. Mitten, and A. Ramage. 1968. "The Tenth Campaign at Sardis (1967)." *BASOR* 191: 2–41.

Hanfmann, G. M. A., G. F. Swift, Jr., D. G. Mitten, and J. Whittlesey. 1966. "The Eighth Campaign at Sardis (1965)." *BASOR* 182: 2–54.

Hanfmann, G. M. A., and J. Waldbaum. 1975. *A Survey of Sardis and the Major Monuments Outside the Walls.* Archaeological Exploration of Sardis Report 1. Cambridge, MA: Harvard University Press.

Harl, K. W. 1996. *Coinage in the Roman Economy, 300 B.C. to A.D. 700.* Baltimore: Johns Hopkins University Press.

———. 1997. "Greek Imperial Coins in the Economic Life of the Roman East." In *Internationales Kolloquium zur kaiserzeitlichen Münzprägung Kleinasiens: 27.–30. April 1994 in der Staatlichen Münzsammlung, München*, edited by J. Nollé, B. Overbeck, and P. Weiss, pp. 223–29. Nomismata 1. Milano: Ennerre.

Harris, J. 1941. "Coins Found at Corinth." *Hesperia* 10, 2: 143–62.

Harvey, A. 1989. *Economic Expansion in the Byzantine Empire, 900–1200*. Cambridge: Cambridge University Press.

Head, B. V. 1892a. *A Catalogue of the Greek Coins in the British Museum: Catalogue of the Greek Coins of Ionia*. London: British Museum.

———. 1892b. *A Catalogue of the Greek Coins in the British Museum: Catalogue of the Greek Coins of Lydia*. London: British Museum.

———. 1897. *A Catalogue of the Greek Coins in the British Museum: Caria, Cos, Rhodes, etc.* London: British Museum.

———. 1906. *A Catalogue of the Greek Coins in the British Museum: Phrygia*. London: British Museum.

———. 1908. "Ephesian Tesserae." *NC* 8: 281–86.

Head, B. V., and P. Gardner. 1877. *A Catalogue of the Greek Coins in the British Museum: Catalogue of the Greek Coins of the Tauric Chersonese, Sarmatia, Dacia, Moesia and Thrace, etc.* London: British Museum.

Heinrichs, J. 2007. "Münzverbote in der römischen Kaiserzeit?" In *Herrschen und Verwalten: der Alltag der römischen Administration in der Hohen Kaiserzeit*, edited by R. Haensch and J. Heinrichs, pp. 80–116. Cologne: Böhlau.

Heller, A. 2006. *"Les bêtises des Grecs": conflits et rivalités entre cités d'Asie et de Bithynie à l'époque romaine (129 a.C.–235 p.C.)*. Bordeaux: De Boccard.

Hendy, M. F. 1969. *Coinage and Money in the Byzantine Empire 1081–1261*. Dumbarton Oaks Studies 12. Washington, D.C.: Dumbarton Oaks Research Library and Collection.

———. 1985. *Studies in the Byzantine Monetary Economy c. 300–1450*. Cambridge: Cambridge University Press.

———. 2007. "Coins." In *Kalenderhane in Istanbul: The Excavations*, edited by C. L. Striker and Y. D. Kuban, pp. 175–276. Mainz: von Zabern.

Herrmann, P. 1995. "Sardeis zur Zeit der julisch-claudischen Kaiser." In *Asia Minor Studien 17. Forschungen in Lydien*, edited by E. Schwertheim, pp. 21–36. Bonn: R. Habelt.

Heuchert, V., and C. J. Howgego. 2006–2017. *Roman Provincial Coinage Online*. Vol. IV: *Antoninus Pius to Commodus (AD 138–192)*. Web resource. http://rpc.ashmus.ox.ac.uk/search/advanced/?v=4&search=Search

Hill, G. F. 1897. *A Catalogue of the Greek Coins in the British Museum: Lycia, Pamphylia, and Pisidia*. London: British Museum.

Hohlfelder, R. L. 1973. "A Sixth Century Hoard from Kenchreai." *Hesperia* 42: 89–101.

———. 1978. *Kenchreai, Eastern Port of Corinth III: The Coins*. Leiden: Brill.

Hoover, O. 2004. "Ceci n'est pas l'autonomie. The Coinage of Seleucid Phoenicia as Royal and Civic Power Discourse." *Topoi* Suppl. 6: 485–507.

Hopkins, K. 1980. "Taxes and Trade in the Roman Empire (200 B.C.–A.D. 400)." *JRS* 70: 101–25.

Horden, P. 2005. "Mediterranean Plague in the Age of Justinian." In *The Cambridge Companion to the Age of Justinian*, edited by M. Maas, pp. 134–60. Cambridge: Cambridge University Press.

Houghton, A. 2012. "The Seleucids." In Metcalf 2012, pp. 235–51.

Houghton, A., and C. Lorber. 2002. *Seleucid Coins: A Comprehensive Catalogue*. Part 1: *Seleucus I to Antiochus III*. New York: American Numismatic Society.

Howgego, C. 1985. *Greek Imperial Countermarks*. London: Royal Numismatic Society.

———. 1992. "The Supply and Use of Money in the Roman World 200 B.C. to A.D. 300." *JRS* 82: 1–31.

Hoyer, D. 2013. "Calculating the Use-Wear Rates of Roman Coins Using Regression Analysis: A Case Study of Bronze Sestertii from Imperial Gaul." *AJN* 25: 259–82.

Imhoof-Blumer, F. 1890. *Griechische Münzen; neue Beiträge und Untersuchungen*. Munich: Franz.

———. 1895. "Zur Münzkunde Kleinasiens." *SNR* 5: 193–293.

———. 1901. *Kleinasiatische Münzen*. Vienna: Olms.

———. 1923. "Fluß-und Meergotter auf griechischen und römischen Münzen." *SNR* 23: 173–421.

Ivison, E. A. 2012. "Excavations at the Lower City Enclosure, 1996–2008." In *Amorium Reports 3: The Lower City Enclosure. Finds Reports and Technical Studies*, edited by C. S. Lightfoot and E. A. Ivison, pp. 5–151. Istanbul: MAS Matbaacılık A.Ş.

Jaia, A. M., and M. C. Molinari. 2011. "Two Deposits of Aes Grave from the Sanctuary of Sol Indiges (Torvajanica / Rome): Considerations about Dating and Function of the Roman Libral Series." *NC* 171: 87–97.

Johnston, A. 1982. "Caracalla or Elagabalus? A Case of Unnecessarily Mistaken Identity." *ANSMN* 27: 97–148.

———. 1983. "Die Sharing in Asia Minor: The View from Sardis." *INJ* 6–7: 59–78.

———. 1984. "Greek Imperial Statistics: A Commentary." *RevNum* 26: 240–57.

———. 2007. *Greek Imperial Denominations, ca. 200–275: A Study of the Roman Provincial Bronze Coinages of Asia Minor.* Royal Numismatic Society Special Publications 43. London: Royal Numismatic Society.

———. 2012. "The Provinces after Commodus." In Metcalf 2012, pp. 453–67.

Kaçar, T. 2005. "Church Councils and their Impact on the Economy of the Cities in Asia Minor." In *Patterns in the Economy of Roman Asia Minor*, edited by S. Mitchell and C. Katsari, pp. 305–18. Swansea: Classical Press of Wales.

Kacynski, B., and M. Nüsse. 2009. "Reverse Type Selection in Sanctuaries? A Study of Antoniniani Found in Various Contexts." In *Coins in Context I: New Perspectives for the Interpretation of Coin Finds*, edited by H. von Kaenel and F. Kemmers, pp. 93–107. Studien zu Fundmünzen der Antike 23. Mainz: von Zabern.

Kampmann, U. 1997. "Eine gemeinsame Emission der Städte Pergamon und Ephesos für das Koinon der 13 Ionischen Städte. Beiträge des Münzhandels zur imperialforschung." In *Internationales Kolloquium zur kaiserzeitlichen Münzprägung Kleinasiens: 27.–30. April 1994 in der Staatlichen Münzsammlung, München*, edited by J. Nollé, B. Overbeck, and P. Weiss, pp. 83–91. Nomismata 1. Milano: Ennerre.

Karweise, S. 1986. "Vorausliste der ephesischen Fundmünzen 1983–1985." In *Ephesos: Vorläufiger Grabungsbericht für die Jahre 1984 und 1985*, by H. Vetters and S. Karweise, pp. 110–55. Anzeiger der Österreichischen Akademie der Wissenschaften 123. Vienna: Österreichischen Akademie der Wissenschaften.

Katsari, C. 2003. "The Organisation of Roman Mints during the Third Century CE: The View from the Eastern Provinces." *Classics Ireland* 10: 27–53.

———. 2005. "The Monetization of Roman Asia Minor in the Third Century AD." In *Patterns in the Economy of Roman Asia Minor*, edited by S. Mitchell and C. Katsari, pp. 261–88. Swansea: Classical Press of Wales.

———. 2011. *The Roman Monetary System: The Eastern Provinces from the First to the Third Century AD*. Cambridge: Cambridge University Press.

Katsari, C., C. S. Lightfoot, and A. Özme. 2012. *The Amorium Mint and the Coin Finds*. Amorium Reports 4. Berlin: De Gruyter.

Kent, J. P. C. 1981. *The Roman Imperial Coinage VIII: The Family of Constantine (337–364)*. London: Spink & Son.

———. 1994. *The Roman Imperial Coinage X: The Divided Empire (395–491)*. London: Spink & Son.

Kerschner, M., and K. Konuk. Forthcoming. "The Chronology of the Electrum Coins Found in the Artemision of Ephesos: The Contribution of the Archaeological Find Context." In van Alfen et al. Forthcoming.

Kiernan, P. 2001. "The Ritual Mutilation of Coins on Romano-British Sites." *BNJ* 71: 18–33.

Kindler, A. 2000. "The Tel Malot Hoard." *Judea and Samaria Research Studies* 9: 219–25. [Hebrew with English abstract]

King, A. 2013. *Coins and Samian Ware*. BAR International Series 2573. Oxford: BAR.

Klose, D. O. A. 1987. *Die Münzprägung von Smyrna in der Römischen Kaiserzeit.* Antike Münzen und Geschittene Steine 10. Berlin: De Gruyter.

Knapp, R. C., and J. D. MacIsaac. 2005. *Excavations at Nemea III: The Coins.* Berkeley: University of California Press.

Koder, J. 1996. "Climatic Change in the Fifth and Sixth Centuries?" In *The Sixth Century, End or Beginning?*, edited by P. Allen and E. M. Jeffreys, pp. 270–85. Byzantina Australiensia 10. Brisbane: Australian Association for Byzantine Studies.

Koenig, F. E. 1999. "Les monnaies." In *La Nécropole Gallo-Romaine d'Avenches "En Chaplix": Fouilles 1987–1992.* Vol. 2: *Etude du Mobilier*, edited by D. Castella, C. M. Pruvot, H. Amrein, A. Duvauchelle, and F. E. Koenig, pp. 427–62. Aventicum 9–10. Cahiers d'archeologie romande 77–78. Lausanne: Cahiers d'archeologie romande.

Konuk, K., ed. 2002. *Sylloge Nummorum Graecorum Turkey 1: The Muharrem Kayhan Collection.* Numismatica Anatolia 1. Istanbul: Ausonius Publications.

———. 2005. "The Electrum Coinage of Samos in the Light of a Recent Hoard." *Neue Forschungen zu Ionien: Fahri Işık zum 60. Geburtstag gewidmet*, edited by E. Winter and E. Schwertheim, pp. 43–55. Bonn: R. Habelt.

———. 2012. "Asia Minor to the Ionian Revolt." In Metcalf 2012, pp. 43–60..

Kosmin, P. Forthcoming. "Remaking a Capital." In Berlin and Kosmin Forthcoming.

Kraay, C. 1976. *Archaic and Classical Greek Coinage.* London: Methuen.

Kraft, K. 1972. *Das System der Kaiserzeitlichen Münzprägung in Kleinasien.* Istanbuler Forschungen 29. Berlin: Gebr. Mann.

Kremydi, S., and A. Iakovidou. 2015. "Corinth and Athens: Numismatic Circulation from the Late Republic to the High Empire." In *FIDES: Contributions to Numismatics in Honor of Richard B. Witschonke*, edited by P. G. van Alfen, G. Bransbourg, and M. Amandry, pp. 457–83. New York: American Numismatic Society.

Kroll, J., 1993. *The Greek Coins.* The Athenian Agora 26. Princeton: American School of Classical Studies at Athens.

Lacroix, L. 1949. *Les reproductions de statues sur les monnaies grecques: la statuaire archaïque et classique.* Bibliothèque de la Faculté de Philosophie et Lettres de l'Université de Liège 116. Liege: Faculté de Philosophie et Lettres.

Laiou, A. E., and C. Morrison. 2007. *The Byzantine Economy.* Cambridge Medieval Textbooks. Cambridge: Cambridge University Press.

Lauritsen, F. M. 1984. "A Late Roman Hoard from Aphrodisias, Turkey." In *Ancient Coins of the Graeco-Roman World: The Nickle Numismatic Papers*, edited by W. Heckel and R. Sullivan, p. 295. Waterloo, Ont.: Wilfred Laurier University.

Levick, B. 2004. "The Roman Economy: Trade in Asia Minor and the Niche Market." *Greece & Rome* 51, 2: 180–98.

Lightfoot, C. 2002. "Byzantine Anatolia: Reassessing the Numismatic Evidence." *RevNum* 6: 229–39.

———. 2007. "Trade and Industry in Byzantine Anatolia: The Evidence from Amorium." *DOP* 61: 269–86.

Ma, John. 1999. *Antiochus III and the Cities of Western Asia Minor.* Oxford: Oxford University Press.

MacDonald, D. 1976. *Greek and Roman Coins from Aphrodisias.* BAR International 9. Oxford: BAR.

———. 1992. *The Coinage of Aphrodisias.* RNS Special Publication 23. London: Royal Numismatic Society.

MacIsaac, J. D. 1987. "Corinth: The Coins, 1925–1926. The Theater District and the Roman Villa." *Hesperia* 56, 2: 97–157.

Magie, D. 1950. *Roman Rule in Asia Minor, to the End of the Third Century after Christ.* Princeton: Princeton University Press.

Magness, J. 2005. "The Date of the Sardis Synagogue in Light of the Numismatic Evidence." *AHA* 109, 3: 443–75.

Maguire, H. 1997. "Magic and Money in the Early Middle Ages." *Speculum* 72, 4: 1037–54.

Martin, T. R. 1985. *Sovereignty and Coinage in Classical Greece.* Princeton: Princeton University Press.

Matthew, C. 2009. "For Valour: The 'Shield Coins' of Alexander and the Successors." *Journal of the Numismatic Association of Australia* 20: 15–34.

Mattingly, H., and E. A. Sydenham. 1930. *The Roman Imperial Coinage III: Antoninus Pius to Commodus*. London: Spink & Son.

———. 1936. *The Roman Imperial Coinage IV, 1: Pertinax to Geta*. London: Spink & Son.

———. 1968. *The Roman Imperial Coinage II: Vespasian to Hadrian*. London: Spink & Son.

Mattingly, H., E. A. Sydenham, and C. H. V. Sutherland. 1938. *The Roman Imperial Coinage IV, 2: Macrinus to Pupienus*. London: Spink & Son.

———. 1949. *The Roman Imperial Coinage IV, 3: Gordian III to Uranius Antoninus*. London: Spink & Son.

Meadows, A. 2001. "Money, Freedom, and Empire in the Hellenistic World." In *Money and Its Uses in the Ancient Greek World*, edited by A. Meadows and K. Shipton, pp. 53–63. Oxford: Oxford University Press.

———. 2002. "Stratonikeia in Caria: the Hellenistic City and its Coinage." *NC* 162: 79–134.

———. 2014. "The Spread of Coins in the Hellenistic World." In *Explaining Monetary and Financial Innovation*, edited by P. Bernholz and R. Vaubel, pp. 169–94. Financial and Monetary Policy Studies 39. Lausanne: Springer.

Melfi, M. 2014. "Religion and Society in Early Roman Corinth: A Forgotten Coin Hoard and the Sanctuary of Asklepios." *Hesperia* 83: 747–76.

Melville-Jones, J. 1990. *A Dictionary of Ancient Roman Coins*. London: Seaby.

Metcalf, W. E., ed. 2012. *The Oxford Handbook of Greek and Roman Coinage*. Oxford: Oxford University Press.

Milne, J. G. 1914. "A Hoard of Constantinian Coins from Egypt." *Journal International d'Archéologie Numismatique* 16: 1–27.

———. 1923. "The Autonomous Coinage of Smyrna I." *NC* 5, 3: 1–30.

———. 1928. "The Autonomous Coinage of Smyrna III." *NC* 5, 8: 131–71.

———. 1941. *Kolophon and its Coinage*. ANSNNM 96. New York: American Numismatic Society.

Mionnet, T. E. 1809. *Description de Médailles Antiques, Grecques et Romaines*. Paris: La Bibliothèque du Roi Paris.

Mitchell, S. 1990. "Festivals, Games, and Civic Life in Roman Asia Minor." *JRS* 80: 183–93.

———. 1993. *Anatolia: Land, Men, and Gods in Asia Minor*. Vol.1: *The Celts and the Impact of Roman Rule*. Oxford: Clarendon Press.

Mitchell, S., and C. Katsari. 2005. *Patterns in the Economy of Roman Asia Minor*. Swansea: Classical Press of Wales.

Moorhead, S. 2007. "The Ancient and Early Mediaeval Coins from the Triconch Palace at Butrint, c. 2nd century BC–c. AD 600." *NC* 167: 287–304.

———. 2012. "The Coinage of the Later Roman Empire, 364–498." In Metcalf 2012, pp. 601–32.

Moorhead, S., S. Gjongecaj, and R. Abdy. 2007. "Coins from the Excavations at Butrint, Diaporit and the Vrina Plain." In *Roman Butrint: An Assessment*, edited by I. L. Hansen and R. Hodges, pp. 78–94. Oxford: Oxbow.

Mørkholm, O. 1984. "The Monetary System in the Seleucid Empire after 187 BC." In *Ancient Coins of the Graeco-Roman World: The Nickle Numismatic Papers*, edited by W. Heckel and R. Sullivan, pp. 93–114. Waterloo, Ont.: Wilfred Laurier University.

———. 1991. *Early Hellenistic Coinage from the Accession of Alexander to the Peace of Apamea (336–188 BC)*. Cambridge: Cambridge University Press.

Morrisson, C. 2002. "Byzantine Money: Its Production and Circulation." In *The Economic History of Byzantium from the Seventh through the Fifteenth Century*, edited by A. E. Laiou, Vol. III, pp. 909–66. Washington, D.C.: Dumbarton Oaks Research Library and Collection.

Morrisson, C., and J.-P. Sodini. 2002. "The Sixth-Century Economy." In *The Economic History of Byzantium from the Seventh through the Fifteenth Century*, edited by A. E. Laiou, Vol. I, pp. 171–220. Washington, D.C.: Dumbarton Oaks Research Library and Collection.

Naster, P. 1965. "Remarques charactéroscopiques et technologiques au sujet des Créséides." In *Congresso Internazionale di Numismatica Roma 11–16 settembre 1961.* Vol. II: *Atti*, pp. 25–36. Roma: Istituto Italiano di Numismatica.

———. 1976. "The Weight System of the Coinage of Croesus." In *Actes du 8ème Congrès international de numismatique, New York-Washington, Septembre 1973*, edited by H. Cahn, pp. 125–33. Publications de l'Association internationale des numismates professionnels 4. Paris: Association de Numismates Professionnels.

Newell, E. T. 1941. *Coinage of the Western Seleucid Mints.* Numismatic Studies 4. New York: American Numismatic Society.

Newton, D. P. 2006. "Found Coins as Indicators of Coins in Circulation: Testing Some Assumptions." *European Journal of Archaeology* 9: 211–27.

Nielsen, A. E. 1991. "Trampling the Archaeological Record: An Experimental Study." *AA* 56: 483–503.

Nimchuk, C. 2000. "The Lion-and-Bull Coinage of Croesus." *Journal of the Classical & Medieval Numismatic Society* 1: 5–44.

Noeske, H.-C. 2000. *Münzfunde aus Ägypten I: Die Münzfund des Ägyptischen Pilgerzentrums.* Studien zu Fundmünzen der Antike 12. Berlin: Gebr. Mann.

Nollé, J. 2005. "Boars, Bears and Bugs: Farming in Asia Minor and the Protection of Men, Animals, and Crops." In *Patterns in the Economy of Roman Asia Minor*, edited by S. Mitchell and C. Katsari, pp. 53–82. Swansea: Classical Press of Wales.

Pearce, J. W. E. 1951. *The Roman Imperial Coinage IX: Valentinian I to Theodosius I.* London: Spink & Son.

Penella, R. J. 1975. "An Unpublished Letter of Apollonius of Tyana to the Sardians." *HSCP* 79: 305–11.

Petzl, G. Forthcoming. *Greek and Latin Inscriptions from Sardis.* Part II: *Finds since 1958.* Archaeological Exploration of Sardis Monograph 14. Cambridge, MA: Harvard University Press.

Pharr, C. 1952. *The Theodosian Code and Novels and the Sirmondian Constitutions.* Princeton: Princeton University Press.

Poblome, J. 1995. "Sherds and Coins: a Question of Chronology." In *Sagalassos III: Report on the Fourth Excavation Campaign of 1993*, edited by M. Waelkens and J. Poblome, pp. 185–206. Leuven: Leuven University Press.

———. 2008. "Sherds and Coins from a Place under the Sun: Further Thoughts from Sagalassos." *FACTA: A Journal of Roman Material Studies* 2: 193–213.

Pottier, H. 1983. *Analyse d'un trésor de monnaies en bronze enfoui au VIème siècle en Syrie Byzantine: Contribution à la méthodologie numismatique.* Travaux 10. Bruxelles: Cercle d'études numismatiques.

Preacher, K. J. 2001. "Calculation for the Chi-Square Test: An Interactive Calculation Tool for Chi-Square Tests of Goodness of Fit and Independence." Web resource. http://quantpsy.org/chisq/chisq.htm

Price, M. 1983. "Thoughts on the Beginnings of Coinage." In *Studies in Numismatic Method Presented to Philip Grierson*, edited by C. Brooke, B. Stewart, J. Pollard, and T. Volk, pp. 1–10. Cambridge: Cambridge University Press.

———. 1991. *The Coinage in the Name of Alexander the Great and Philip Arrhidaeus.* Zurich and London: Swiss Numismatic Society and the British Museum.

Raphael, K., and G. Bijovsky. 2014. "The Coin Hoard from Caesarea Maritima and the 363 CE Earthquake." *INR* 9: 173–92.

Ratté, C. 2008. "Reflections on the Urban Development of Hellenistic Sardis." In *Love for Lydia: A Sardis Anniversary Volume Presented to Crawford H. Greenewalt, Jr.*, edited by N. D. Cahill, pp. 125–34. Archaeological Exploration of Sardis Report 4. Cambridge, MA: Harvard University Press.

Ratté, C., T. N. Howe, and C. Foss. 1986. "An Early Imperial Pseudodipteral Temple at Sardis." *AJA* 90: 45–68.

Rautman, M. L. 1995a. "Two Late Roman Wells at Sardis." *AASOR* 53: 37–84.

———. 1995b. "A Late Roman Townhouse at Sardis." *Asia Minor Studien 17. Forschungen in Lydien*, edited by E. Schwertheim, pp. 49–66. Bonn: R. Habelt.

———. 2011. "Sardis in Late Antiquity." In *Archaeology and the Cities of Asia Minor in Late Antiquity*, edited by O. Dally and C. Ratté, pp. 1–26. Kelsey Museum Publication 6. Ann Arbor: University of Michigan Press.

von Reden, S. 2010. *Money in Classical Antiquity. Key Themes in Ancient History*. New York: Cambridge University Press.

Reece, R. 1975. "Roman Currency: New Thoughts and Problems." *World Archaeology* 6: 299–306.

———. 1984a. "Coins." In *Excavations at Carthage: The British Mission*. Vol. I: *The Avenue du President Habib Bourguiba, Salammbo*. Pt. 1: *The Site and Finds Other than Pottery*, edited by H. R. Hurst and S. P. Roskams, pp. 171–81. Sheffield: British Academy.

———. 1984b. "The Use of Roman Coinage." *OJA* 3: 197–210.

———. 1993. "Coins as Minted, and Coins as Found." *Acta Numismatica* 21–23: 57–62.

———. 2003. "Coins and the Late Roman Economy." In *Theory and Practice in Late Antique Archaeology*, edited by L. Lavan and W. Bowden, pp. 139–68. Leiden: Brill.

Regling, K. 1913. "Verzeichnis der beiden Ausgrabungen von Pergamon gefundenen Münzen." In *Stadt und Landschaft, Altertümer von Pergamon*, edited by A. Conze, 355–65. Berlin: G. Reimer.

———. 1927. *Die Münzen von Priene*. Berlin: H. Schoetz.

Rick, J. W. 1976. "Downslope Movement and Archaeological Intrasite Spatial Analysis." *AA* 41: 133–44.

Rife, J. L., M. M. Morison, A. Barbet, et al. 2007. "Life and Death at a Port in Roman Greece: The Kenchreai Cemetery Project, 2002–2006." *Hesperia* 76: 143–81.

Robinson, E. S. G. 1958. "The Beginnings of Achaemenid Coinage." *NC* 18: 187–93.

Rotroff, S., and A. Oliver, Jr. 2003. *The Hellenistic Pottery from Sardis: The Finds through 1994*. Archaeological Exploration of Sardis Monograph 12. Cambridge, MA: Harvard University Press.

Russell, J. 1986. "Transformations in Early Byzantine Life: Contributions and Limitations of Archaeological Evidence." In *The 17th International Byzantine Congress: Major Papers, Dumbarton Oaks/Georgetown University, Washington, D.C., August 3–8, 1986*, pp. 137–54. New Rochelle, NY: A. D. Caratzas.

———. 1995. "The Archaeological Context of Magic in the Early Byzantine Period." In *Byzantine Magic*, edited by H. Maguire, pp. 35–50. Washington, D.C.: Dumbarton Oaks Research Library and Collection.

Safrai, Z. 1998. *The Missing Century: Palestine in the Fifth Century: Growth and Decline*. Amsterdam: Peeters.

von Saldern, A. 1980. *Ancient and Byzantine Glass from Sardis*. Archaeological Exploration of Sardis Monograph 6. Cambridge, MA: Harvard University Press.

Sanders, G. D. R. 2002. "Corinth." In *The Economic History of Byzantium from the Seventh through the Fifteenth Century*, edited by A. E. Laiou, Vol. II, pp. 647–54. Dumbarton Oaks Studies 39. Washington, D.C.: Dumbarton Oaks Research Library and Collection.

Sarris, P. 2011. *Empires of Faith: the Fall of Rome to the Rise of Islam, 500–700*. The Oxford History of Medieval Europe. Oxford: Oxford University Press.

Scheers, S. 1993a. "Catalogue of the Coins found during the Years 1990 and 1991." In *Sagalassos I: First General Report on the Survey and Excavations*, edited by M. Waelkens, pp. 197–206. Acta Archaeologica Lovaniensia Monographiae 5. Leuven: Leuven University Press.

———. 1993b. "Catalogue of Coins Found in 1992." In *Sagalassos II: Report on the Survey and Excavations 1992*, edited by M. Waelkens and J. Poblome, pp. 249–60. Acta Archaeologica Lovaniensia Monographiae 6. Leuven: Leuven University Press.

———. 1995. "Catalogue of Coins Found in 1993." In *Sagalassos III: Report on the Fourth Excavation Campaign of 1993*, edited by M. Waelkens and

J. Poblome, pp. 307–23. Acta Archaeologica Lovaniensia Monographiae 7. Leuven: Leuven University Press.

———. 2000. "Coins Found during 1996 and 1997." In *Sagalassos V: Report on the Survey and Excavation Campaigns of 1996 and 1997*, edited by M. Waelkens and L. Loots, pp. 509–52. Acta Archaeologica Lovaniensia Monographiae 11. Leuven: Leuven University Press.

Scheers, S., H. Vanhaverbeke, and J. Poblome. 1997. "Catalogue of Coins Found in 1994 and 1995." In *Sagalassos IV: Report on the Survey and Excavations 1994 and 1995*, edited by M. Waelkens and J. Poblome, pp. 315–50. Acta Archaeologica Lovaniensia Monographiae 9. Leuven: Leuven University Press.

Schiffer, M. B. 1996. *Formation Processes of the Archaeological Record*. Salt Lake City: University of Utah Press.

Schindel, N. 2009. "Die Fundmünzen von der Kuretenstrasse 2005 und 2006. Numismatische und historische Auswertung." In *Neue Forschungen zur Kuretenstraße von Ephesos. Akten des Symposiums für Hilke Thür vom 13. Dezember 2006 am der Österreichischen Akademie der Wissenschaften*, edited by S. Ladstätter, pp. 171–245. Vienna: Verlag der Österreichischen Akademie der Wissenschaften.

Schultz, H.-D. 1997. "The Coinage of Pergamon until the End of the Attalid Dynasty (133 B.C.)." In *Pergamon: The Telephos Frieze from the Great Altar*, edited by R. Dreyfuss and E. Schraudolph, pp. 11–22. San Francisco: Fine Arts Museums.

Schwartz, H. 1893. "Гермезъ Праксителя на монете Анхiала [Hermes of Praxiteles on a Coin of Anchialus]." Archeologičeskije Izvestija i Zametki ot Imperatorskago Moskovkago Archeologičeskago Obščestva *Moscow Archaeological Society*: 1–23. [in Russian]

Scott, J. A. 1987. "Sardis in the Byzantine and Turkish Eras." In *Sardis: Twenty-Seven Years of Discovery*, edited by E. Guralnick, pp. 74–87. Chicago: Chicago Society of the Archaeological Institute of America.

Seager, A. 1974. "The Synagogue at Sardis." *Qadmoniot* 7: 123–28.

Seyrig, H. 1986. *Scripta Numismatica*. Paris: Libraire Orientaliste Paul Geuthner.

Shear, T. L. 1922. "Sixth Preliminary Report on the American Excavations at Sardes in Asia Minor." *AJA* 26: 389–409.

Sherwin-White, S., and A. Kuhrt. 1993. *From Samarkhand to Sardis*. Berkeley: University of California Press.

Slane, K. W. 2017. *Corinth XXI. Tombs, Burials, and Commemoration in Corinth's Northern Cemetery*. Princeton: American School of Classical Studies at Athens.

Slane, K. W., and M. E. H. Walbank. 2006. "Anointing and Commemorating the Dead: Funerary Rituals of Roman Corinthians." In *Old pottery in a new century: innovating perspectives on Roman pottery studies: Atti del convegno internazionale di studi, Catania, 22–24 aprile 2004*, edited by D. Malfitana, J. Poblome, and J. Lund, pp. 377–87. Monografie dell'Istituto per i beni archeologici e monumentali 1. Roma: L'Erma di Bretschneider.

Spoerri Butcher, M. 2006a. *Roman Provincial Coinage VII, 1: Gordian I to Gordian III*. London: British Museum.

———. 2006b. "L'organisation de la production monétaire au sein de la province d'Asie à l'époque de Gordien III (238–244)." *SNR*: 97–132.

———. 2009. "Dénomination et systèmes monétaires en Asie Mineure à l'époque romaine: A propos de 'Greek Imperial Denominations' et des colonies romaines." *SNR* 88: 217–24.

Stinson, P. Forthcoming. "The City Plan: Looking Forward, Looking Back." In Berlin and Kosmin Forthcoming.

Stroobants, F., and J. Poblome. 2015. "Buying and Selling in Late Roman Pisidia: A Hypothetical Framework of Coin Use in Sagalassos and its Countryside." *RevBelgeNum* 161: 73–104.

Stumpf, G. 1991. *Numismatische Studien zur Chronologie der römischen Statthalter in Kleinasien*. Saarbrücken: Saarbrücker Druckerei und Verlag.

Sutherland, C. H. V. 1967. *The Roman Imperial Coinage VI: From Diocletian's Reform (A.D. 294) to the Death of Maximinus II (A.D. 313)*. London: British Museum.

———. 1984. *The Roman Imperial Coinage I: Augustus to Vitellius (31 BC–AD 69).* 2nd ed. London: British Museum.

Svoronos, J. N. 1904. *Τα Νομισματα του Κρατους των Πτολεμαιων.* Athens: P. D. Sakellarios.

Sylloge Nummorum Graecorum, Deutschland: Munich Staatliche Münzsammlung. 1968. Berlin: Mann.

Sylloge Nummorum Graecorum, Deutschland: Sammlung von Aulock. 1957. Berlin: Mann.

Sylloge Nummorum Graecorum, Deutschland: Tübingen, Münzsammlung der Universität. 1981. Berlin: Mann.

Sylloge Nummorum Graecorum, France: Cabinet des Monnaies, Médailles et Antiques, Bibliothéque Nationale, Paris. 1983. Paris: Bibliothéque Nationale de France.

Sylloge Nummorum Graecorum, Great Britain V: Ashmolean Museum, Oxford. 1951. London: British Academy.

Sylloge Nummorum Graecorum: The Royal Collection of Coins and Medals, Danish Museum. 1942. Copenhagen: Danish National Museum.

Thoen, H. 2003. "Burial Goods." In *Excavations in Pessinus: The So-Called Acropolis: From Hellenistic and Roman Cemetery to Byzantine Castle*, edited by J. Devreker, H. Thoen, and F. Vermeulen, pp. 59–116. Ghent: Academia.

Thompson, M. 1954. *Coins from the Roman through the Venetian Period.* The Athenian Agora 2. Princeton: American School of Classical Studies at Athens.

———. 1968. "The Mints of Lysimachus." In *Essays in Greek Coinage Presented to Stanley Robinson*, edited by C. M. Kraay and G. K. Jenkins, pp. 163–82. Oxford: Clarendon Press.

———. 1983. *Alexander's Drachm Mints I: Sardes and Miletus.* New York: American Numismatic Society.

Thonemann, P. 2013. "The Attalid State, 188–133 BC." In *Attalid Asia Minor: Money, International Relations and the State*, edited by P. Thonemann, pp. 1–48. Oxford: Oxford University Press.

———. 2016. *The Hellenistic World: Using Coins as Sources. Guides to the Coinage of the Ancient World.* Cambridge: Cambridge University Press.

Toynbee, J. M. C. 1971. *Death and Burial in the Roman World.* Aspects of Greek and Roman Life. Ithaca, NY: Cornell University Press.

Travaglini, A., and C. V. Camilleri. 2010. *Hierapolis di Frigia. Le Monete. Campagne di Scavo 1957–2004.* Hierapolis di Frigia IV. Istanbul: Ege Yayınları, Istanbul.

Trombley, F. 1986. "The Decline of the Seventh-Century Town: The Exception of Euchaita." In *Byzantine Studies in Honor of Milton V. Anastos, Byzantina Kai Metabyzantina*, edited by S. Vryonis, Jr., pp. 65–90. Malibu: Undena.

Troxell, H. A. 1982. "The Coinage of the Lycian League." *ANSNNM* 162: ii–255.

van Alfen, P., W. Fischer-Bossert, H. Gitler, K. Konuk, and U. Wartenberg, eds. Forthcoming. *White Gold: Studies in Early Electrum Coinage.* New York and Jerusalem: American Numismatic Society and Israel Museum.

Vann, R. L. 1976. "A Study of Roman Construction in Asia Minor: The Lingering Role of a Hellenistic Tradition in Ashlar Masonry." PhD Diss., Cornell University.

Vetters, H. 1979. *Ephesos: vorläufiger Grabungsbericht 1978.* Verlag der Österreichischen Akademie der Wissenschaften 116. Vienna: Österreichischen Akademie der Wissenschaften.

———. 1980. *Ephesos: vorläufiger Grabungsbericht 1979.* Verlag der Österreichischen Akademie der Wissenschaften 117. Vienna: Österreichischen Akademie der Wissenschaften.

———. 1983. *Ephesos: vorläufiger Grabungsbericht 1982.* Verlag der Österreichischen Akademie der Wissenschaften 120. Vienna: Österreichischen Akademie der Wissenschaften.

Voegtli, H. 1984. "Münzen." In *Das Asklepieion, Altertümer von Pergamon*, edited by G. de Luca, pp. 60–77. Berlin: De Gruyter.

Voegtli, H., S. Bendall, L. Ilisch, and C. Morrisson. 1993. *Die Fundmünzen aus der Stadtgrabung von Pergamon.* Berlin: De Gruyter.

Waddington, W. H., E. Babelon, and T. Reinach. 1910. *Recueil général des monnaies grecques d'Asie Mineure.* Vols. 1.1–1.4. Paris: Leroux.

Walbank, M. E. H., and M. Walbank. 2015. "A Roman Corinthian Family Tomb and its Afterlife." *Hesperia* 84: 149–206.

Walburg, R. 1991. "Lydisch oder persisch?: ein Goldobjekt aus der frühzeit der Münzprägung." *SNR* 70: 5–21.

Wallace, R. 1987. "The Origin of Electrum Coinage." *AJA* 91: 385–97.

———. 2016. "Redating Croesus: Herodotean Chronologies, and the Dates of the Earliest Coinages." *JHS* 136: 168–81.

Webb, P. H. 1927. *The Roman Imperial Coinage II: Marcus Aurelius Probus to Maximiman (276–310).* London: British Museum.

———. 1968. *The Roman Imperial Coinage V, 1: Valerian to Florian (253–276).* London: Spink & Son.

Weidauer, L. 1975. *Probleme der frühen Elektronprägung.* Typos 1. Fribourg: Schweizerische Numismatische Gesellschaft.

Weiss, Z. 2005. *The Sepphoris Synagogue: Deciphering an Ancient Message Through Its Archaeological and Socio-historical Contexts.* Jerusalem: Israel Exploration Society.

Weisser, B., K. Dörtlük, O. Tekin, and R. Boyraz Seyhan. 2014. "Die Fundmünzen aus dem Felsheiligtum Ost in Priene." In *Proceedings of the First International Congress of the Anatolian Monetary History and Numismatics, 25–28 February 2013, Antalya*, edited by B. Weisser et al., pp. 653–68. Antalya: Suna & İnan Kıraç Research Institute on Mediterranean Civilizations.

Westermark, U. 1991. "Bronze Coins of Pergamon." *QuadTic* 20: 147–59.

———. 1995. "On the Pergamene Bronze Coins in the Name of Athena Nikephoros." *Studii și cercetări de numismatică* 11: 29–35.

Whittow, M. 1996. *The Making of Byzantium, 600–1025.* Berkeley: University of California Press.

———. 2003. "Decline and Fall? Studying Long-Term Change in the East." In *Theory and Practice in Late Antique Archaeology*, edited by L. Lavan and W. Bowden, pp. 404–23. Leiden: Brill.

Wigg-Wolf, D. 2005. "Coins and Ritual in Late Iron Age and Early Roman Sanctuaries in the Territory of the Treveri." In *Iron Age Coinage and Ritual Practices*, edited by C. Haselgrove and D. Wigg-Wolf, pp. 361–79. Studien zu Fundmünzen der Antike 20. Mainz: von Zabern.

———. 2009. "Sites as Context." In *Coins in Context I: New perspectives for the interpretation of coin finds: Colloquium Frankfurt a.M., October 25–27, 2007*, edited by H.-M. von Kaenel and F. Kemmers, pp. 109–25. Studien zu Fundmünzen der Antike 23. Mainz am Rhein: Philipp von Zabern.

Williams, C. 1977. "A Byzantine Well-Deposit from Anemurium (Rough Cilicia)." *Anatolian Studies* 27: 175–90.

Wroth, W. 1892. *A Catalogue of the Greek Coins in the British Museum: Catalogue of the Greek Coins of Mysia.* London: British Museum.

———. 1894. *A Catalogue of the Greek Coins in the British Museum: Catalogue of the Greek Coins of Troas, Aeolis, and Lesbos.* London: British Museum.

———. 1889. *A Catalogue of Greek Coins in the British Museum: A Catalogue of the Greek Coins of Pontus, Paphlagonia, Bithynia, and the Kingdom of Bosporus.* London: British Museum.

———. 1899. *A Catalogue of Greek Coins in the British Museum: A Catalogue of the Greek Coins of Galatia, Cappadocia, and Syria.* London: British Museum.

———. 1966. *Western & Provincial Byzantine Coins of the Vandals, Ostrogoths, and Lombards, and of the Empires of Thessalonica, Nicaea, and Trebizond, in the British Museum.* 1st American ed. Chicago: Argonaut.

Yegül, F. K. 1986. *The Bath-Gymnasium Complex at Sardis.* Archaeological Exploration of Sardis Report 3. Cambridge, MA: Harvard University Press.

———. 1987. "Roman Architecture at Sardis." In *Sardis: Twenty-Seven Years of Discovery*, edited by E. Guralnick, pp. 46–61. Chicago: Chicago Society of the Archaeological Institute of America.

Zacos, G., and A. Veglery, A. 1972. *Byzantine Lead Seals*. Basel: J. J. Augustin.

Zavagno, L. 2009. *Cities in Transition: Urbanism in Byzantium between Late Antiquity and the Early Middle Ages (AD 500–900)*. BAR International Series 2030. Oxford: Archaeopress.

Zervos, O. 1986. "Coins Excavated at Corinth, 1978–1980." *Hesperia* 55: 183–205.

Ziegler, R. 1996. "Civic Coins and Imperial Campaigns." In *The Roman Army in the East*, edited by D. Kennedy, pp. 119–34. JRA Suppl. 18. Ann Arbor: Journal of Roman Archaeology.

Zuiderhoek, A. 2009. *The Politics of Munificence in the Roman Empire: Citizens, Elites and Benefactors in Asia Minor*. Cambridge: Cambridge University Press.

Concordance of Field Numbers/M13 Numbers

M13 No.	Sardis Field No.
1.0001	2008.0020
1.0002	2009.0005
2.0001	2002.0002
3.0001	2009.0008
4.0001	2002.0008
5.0001	2004.0026
5.0002	1989.0018
6.0001	2002.0003
7.0001	2007.0199
7.0002	2007.0215
8.0001	1981.C81.0062
8.0002	1978.1455
9.0001	1993.0112
9.0002	2010.0019
9.0003	1978.1595
9.0004	1978.1597
9.0005	1980.C80.0071
9.0006	1984.0193
10.0001	1980.C80.0319
11.0001	1978.1454
11.0002	1998.0011
11.0003	1986.C86.0009
12.0001	1999.0026
13.0001	2012.0050
13.0002	1984.0144
14.0001	1990.0292
15.0001	1978.1601
15.0002	1973.1298
16.0001	2008.0023
17.0001	1986.C86.0010
17.0002	2011.0009
17.0003	1989.0193
18.0001	1986.C86.0002
18.0002	1986.0030
18.0003	1994.0064
19.0001	2012.0058
20.0001	1987.0066
21.0001	2008.0014
21.0002	1983.0061
22.0001	2005.0007
23.0001	2002.0070
23.0002	2007.0245
23.0003	1985.C85.0007
23.0004	2009.0021
23.0005	1994.0225
23.0006	1996.0162
23.0007	1996.0148
23.0008	1984.0007
23.0009	1996.0042
23.0010	2012.0024
23.0011	1996.0150
23.0012	1993.0098
24.0001	1980.C80.0334
24.0002	1984.C84.0011
25.0001	1978.1663
25.0002	1992.NoEx92.0003
25.0003	1981.C81.0027
25.0004	2007.0248
25.0005	1989.NoEx89.0007
25.0006	1973.1309
25.0007	1980.C80.0086
25.0008	1982.C82.0160
25.0009	1980.C80.0424
25.0010	1973.1340
25.0011	1994.0174
26.0001	1998.0058
26.0002	1998.0059
27.0001	2007.0196
27.0002	1977.1425
27.0003	1978.1600
27.0004	2012.0005
27.0005	1986.0022
28.0001	1992.0237
28.0002	1985.C85.0022
28.0003	1991.0070
28.0004	1973.1344
29.0001	1973.1321
30.0001	1986.0038
30.0002	2009.0024
31.0001	1987.NoEx87.0014
32.0001	1993.0095
33.0001	2010.0051
34.0001	1978.1799
34.0002	1984.C84.0046
34.0003	1984.C84.0045
35.0001	1973.1252
36.0001	2011.0026
37.0001	1979.1933
38.0001	1993.0142
39.0001	2012.0029
40.0001	1993.0023
41.0001	1981.C81.0025
42.0001	1980.C80.0174
43.0001	1977.1447
44.0001	1977.1446
45.0001	1985.0247
46.0001	1978.1599
47.0001	1996.0149
48.0001	1984.C84.0012
48.0002	1985.C85.0023
49.0001	1996.0078
49.0002	1987.NoEx87.0012
50.0001	1983.C83.0017
51.0001	2005.0023
51.0002	2008.0004
51.0003	1986.0015
51.0004	1996.0158
51.0005	1983.0037
52.0001	2001.0018
52.0002	2010.0015
52.0003	1973.1282
52.0004	1986.0018
52.0005	2008.0006
52.0006	1973.1264
52.0007	1993.0143
52.0008	1978.1763
52.0009	1992.0113
52.0010	2007.0161
52.0011	1982.C82.0017
52.0012	1978.1592
52.0013	1985.NoEx85.0009
52.0014	2010.0016
52.0015	1993.0094
52.0016	1993.NoEx93.0031
52.0017	2007.0181
52.0018	1980.C80.0152
52.0019	2010.0011
52.0020	1982.C82.0036
52.0021	1983.0028
52.0022	1994.0158
52.0023	1994.0187
52.0024	1996.0043
52.0025	1984.C84.0042
52.0026	1998.0066
52.0027	1994.0027
52.0028	1975.1398
52.0029	1979.1882
52.0030	1973.1272
52.0031	2012.0052
52.0032	2009.0028
52.0033	2009.0031
52.0034	1978.1604
52.0035	1989.0143
52.0036	2005.0081
52.0037	1997.0108
52.0038	1980.C80.0121
52.0039	1985.0010
52.0040	1986.0007
52.0041	1981.C81.0026
52.0042	1993.0134
52.0043	1984.0195
52.0044	1984.0042
52.0045	1981.C81.0040
52.0046	2009.0011
52.0047	1992.0332
52.0048	1984.0194
52.0049	2010.0027
52.0050	2002.0311
52.0051	1983.0014
52.0052	1993.0031
52.0053	2009.0014
52.0054	1985.0203
52.0055	1993.0177
52.0056	1993.NoEx93.0001
52.0057	1991.0083
52.0058	1993.0035
52.0059	1992.0035
52.0060	2003.0003
52.0061	1982.C82.0133
52.0062	1978.1528
52.0063	1983.0145
52.0064	1988.NoEx88.0002
52.0065	1982.0109
52.0066	2004.0056
52.0067	1993.0007
52.0068	1980.0062
52.0069	2012.0048
52.0070	2012.0040
52.0071	1992.0125
52.0072	1977.1441
52.0073	2002.0323
52.0074	2010.0017
52.0075	1983.0003
52.0076	1993.NoEx93.0023
52.0077	1978.1593
52.0078	1992.0122
52.0079	1987.0059
52.0080	1973.1328
52.0081	2002.0325
52.0082	2006.0002
52.0083	1993.0026
52.0084	1994.0035
52.0085	1997.0074
52.0086	2004.0007
52.0087	1994.0110
52.0088	1993.0100
52.0089	2007.0168
52.0090	1983.0192
52.0091	2013.0001
52.0092	1980.C80.0134
52.0093	1994.0083
52.0094	1989.0086
52.0095	1993.NoEx93.0004
52.0096	1996.0051
52.0097	1973.1317
52.0098	1986.0005
52.0099	1993.0186
52.0100	1978.1639
52.0101	1993.NoEx93.0040
52.0102	1996.0161
52.0103	1994.0010
52.0104	1993.0139
52.0105	1992.0334
52.0106	1978.1778
52.0107	1993.0167
52.0108	1993.0156
52.0109	1993.0163
52.0110	1998.0009
52.0111	2009.0017

52.0112	1997.0103
52.0113	2009.0019
52.0114	1994.0223
52.0115	2010.0003
52.0116	1993.0166
52.0117	1989.C89.0018
52.0118	1982.C82.0132
52.0119	1993.0164
52.0120	2005.0021
52.0121	1992.0331
52.0122	2010.0021
52.0123	1996.0160
52.0124	1993.NoEx93.0033
52.0125	1993.0185
52.0126	1997.0005
52.0127	1978.1603
52.0128	2013.0008
52.0129	1993.0176
52.0130	1994.0242
52.0131	1986.0043
53.0001	1996.0145
53.0002	1980.0220
54.0001	1992.0114
55.0001	1986.C86.0008
55.0002	1993.0024
55.0003	1985.0248
55.0004	2000.0012
55.0005	1973.1302
55.0006	1985.NoEx85.0049
55.0007	1992.0173
55.0008	1999.0019
55.0009	1980.C80.0167
55.0010	1994.0062
55.0011	1973.1259
55.0012	1978.1793
55.0013	1984.C84.0029
55.0014	1979.1930
55.0015	1986.0039
55.0016	2004.0011
55.0017	1993.0025
55.0018	1993.0089
55.0019	1977.1440
55.0020	1997.0080
55.0021	1973.1322
55.0022	1978.1594
55.0023	1987.0069
55.0024	1997.0024
55.0025	1980.0216
55.0026	1973.1263
55.0027	1973.1284
55.0028	1979.2137
55.0029	1984.0097

55.0030	1987.NoEx87.0005
55.0031	1973.1271
56.0001	1985.0196
56.0002	1995.0019
56.0003	1993.0136
56.0004	2012.0028
57.0001	1993.NoEx93.0028
57.0002	1999.0025
58.0001	1996.0050
59.0001	1986.0008
59.0002	1990.C90.0016
60.0001	1978.1771
61.0001	1992.0336
62.0001	2004.0046
63.0001	1990.0015
64.0001	1982.C82.0239
65.0001	2012.0030
66.0001	1996.0088
67.0001	1990.C90.0007
68.0001	2012.0045
69.0001	1997.0007
69.0002	1980.0136
70.0001	1993.NoEx93.0022
71.0001	1981.0002
72.0001	1979.1893
72.0002	2010.0052
72.0003	2009.0027
72.0004	2009.0025
72.0005	1978.1596
73.0001	1991.0318
74.0001	1989.0007
75.0001	1985.C85.0019
76.0001	1978.1800
77.0001	1999.0020
78.0001	1992.0308
78.0002	1978.1640
78.0003	2005.0012
78.0004	1993.0130
79.0001	1993.NoEx93.0063
79.0002	1962.C62.0386
80.0001	1999.0022
80.0002	1993.0189
80.0003	1990.0309
80.0004	1995.0003
81.0001	1983.0154
81.0002	2002.0324
81.0003	2009.0023
82.0001	1993.0147
83.0001	1993.NoEx93.0021
84.0001	1992.NoEx92.0014
85.0001	1983.0117
86.0001	1985.0194

86.0002	2005.0008
86.0003	2007.0234
87.0001	2010.0025
87.0002	1993.C93.0010
88.0001	2011.0040
88.0002	2011.0039
88.0003	1982.C82.0035
89.0001	2013.0011
90.0001	1996.0143
90.0002	1994.0226
90.0003	1982.C82.0126
91.0001	1984.C84.0041
91.0002	2013.0007
92.0001	2013.0002
93.0001	1992.0337
93.0002	2012.0047
93.0003	2004.0027
93.0004	1994.0224
93.0005	2013.0017
93.0006	2008.0017
93.0007	2005.0084
93.0008	1993.0162
93.0009	1999.0018
93.0010	1979.1827
93.0011	1994.0222
93.0012	1982.0046
93.0013	2005.0006
93.0014	1998.0005
93.0015	1994.0243
93.0016	2010.0038
93.0017	1993.0184
93.0018	1984.0022
93.0019	2004.0031
93.0020	1994.0244
93.0021	1982.0110
93.0022	1993.0006
93.0023	2005.0059
93.0024	1998.0047
93.0025	1998.0051
93.0026	1993.0169
93.0027	1992.0044
93.0028	2012.0039
93.0029	1988.0112
93.0030	2011.0042
93.0031	1992.0333
93.0032	2004.0016
93.0033	1999.0035
93.0034	2004.0023
93.0035	1996.0147
93.0036	2012.0011
93.0037	2010.0029
93.0038	1993.0150

93.0039	1993.0191
93.0040	1993.0168
93.0041	1982.0083
93.0042	1982.0045
93.0043	1982.0039
94.0001	1982.0604
94.0002	1993.0097
94.0003	1986.0040
94.0004	1999.0017
94.0005	1985.0184
94.0006	1980.C80.0087
94.0007	2011.0043
94.0008	1978.1641
94.0009	1978.1602
94.0010	2009.0030
94.0011	1985.0202
94.0012	2001.0020
94.0013	1986.0012
94.0014	1994.0157
94.0015	1992.0222
94.0016	1993.0033
94.0017	2010.0026
94.0018	1985.0183
94.0019	2010.0032
94.0020	1992.0284
94.0021	1994.0221
94.0022	1992.0330
94.0023	1992.0266
94.0024	1986.0010
94.0025	1998.0065
94.0026	2010.0035
94.0027	2005.0074
94.0028	2005.0053
94.0029	1998.0064
94.0030	1992.0050
94.0031	1995.0020
94.0032	1983.0129
94.0033	1985.0210
94.0034	1992.0160
94.0035	2005.0054
94.0036	1999.0008
94.0037	2011.0019
94.0038	1992.0267
94.0039	1993.0120
94.0040	2005.0022
94.0041	1978.1459
94.0042	1980.0109
94.0043	2013.0004
94.0044	2010.0031
94.0045	1993.0165
94.0046	1986.0044
94.0047	1998.0057

94.0048	1998.0048
94.0049	1986.0037
94.0050	1993.0099
94.0051	1993.0148
94.0052	1986.0058
94.0053	1996.0176
94.0054	2013.0006
94.0055	1988.0093
94.0056	1983.0093
94.0057	1982.C82.0066
94.0058	1988.0111
94.0059	1996.0144
94.0060	1999.0001
94.0061	1983.0086
94.0062	1994.0251
94.0063	1990.0290
94.0064	1993.0034
94.0065	1998.0049
94.0066	1986.0068
94.0067	1999.0028
94.0068	1993.0141
94.0069	1981.C81.0059
94.0070	2009.0032
94.0071	2011.0021
94.0072	2012.0053
94.0073	2001.0001
94.0074	1986.0053
94.0075	1978.1486
94.0076	2012.0056
94.0077	1992.0338
94.0078	1989.0075
94.0079	1998.0010
94.0080	1998.0036
94.0081	1998.0050
94.0082	1983.0006
94.0083	2009.0026
94.0084	2004.0003
94.0085	1992.0063
94.0086	1979.2154
95.0001	1991.0464
95.0002	1992.0339
95.0003	1982.0099
95.0004	1986.0041
95.0005	1989.0192
95.0006	1993.0161
95.0007	1998.0054
95.0008	1993.0144
95.0009	1984.C84.0001
96.0001	1994.0067
97.0001	1995.NoEx95.0002
98.0001	2009.0022
98.0002	1975.1399

98.0003	1993.0002
98.0004	1980.0115
98.0005	1992.0246
98.0006	1986.0009
98.0007	1980.C80.0169
98.0008	2008.0003
98.0009	1999.0029
99.0001	1987.0058
99.0002	1978.1804
100.0001	1981.C81.0081
101.0001	1980.C80.0346
102.0001	2007.0218
102.0002	1992.0124
103.0001	1993.NoEx93.0002
103.0002	1996.0174
103.0003	1979.1820
104.0001	2007.0169
104.0002	1989.C89.0022
105.0001	1992.0034
106.0001	1996.0139
106.0002	1992.C92.0005
107.0001	1989.0126
107.0002	1986.0054
108.0001	1984.0146
109.0001	2008.0001
110.0001	1993.NoEx93.0020
111.0001	1984.C84.0020
112.0001	1978.1638
113.0001	1984.0192
114.0001	2010.0022
115.0001	1979.1940
116.0001	2008.0018
117.0001	1997.0109
118.0001	1981.C81.0060
119.0001	1983.C83.0014
120.0001	1978.1457
121.0001	1989.C89.0001
121.0002	2004.0012
122.0001	1994.0128
123.0001	1983.0045
124.0001	2013.0009
125.0001	1984.0156
126.0001	1981.C81.0080
127.0001	2012.0016
128.0001	1982.0013
129.0001	1983.0087
130.0001	1987.C87.0005
130.0002	1985.NoEx85.0021
131.0001	1982.C82.0165
132.0001	1979.1912
133.0001	1980.C80.0034
134.0001	1979.1936

135.0001	1980.0180
136.0001	1991.0459
137.0001	1992.0021
138.0001	1978.1485
139.0001	1983.0161
140.0001	1989.0121
141.0001	1984.C84.0026
142.0001	1978.1542
143.0001	1979.1872
144.0001	1980.C80.0260
145.0001	1973.1320
145.0002	1979.1944
145.0003	1983.0012
145.0004	1988.C88.0005
145.0005	1989.NoEx89.0001
145.0006	1993.0001
145.0007	1996.0039
145.0008	1973.1292
145.0009	1992.0039
145.0010	1980.C80.0072
146.0001	2005.0082
146.0002	1994.0036
147.0001	1995.0029
147.0002	2009.0004
147.0003	1986.0046
148.0001	1995.0023
149.0001	1973.1332
149.0002	2013.0003
149.0003	1978.1637
150.0001	2007.0233
150.0002	1975.1397
150.0003	1996.0067
150.0004	1980.C80.0074
150.0005	1992.0003
151.0001	1991.0360
151.0002	1998.0014
151.0003	1996.0142
151.0004	1989.0042
151.0005	1981.C81.0001
151.0006	1986.C86.0012
151.0007	1980.C80.0240
152.0001	1997.0042
153.0001	1978.1772
153.0002	1985.C85.0013
153.0003	1983.0030
154.0001	1983.C83.0013
154.0002	1990.0291
154.0003	1982.C82.0060
154.0004	1986.C86.0013
155.0001	1962.C62.1693
156.0001	1996.0049
156.0002	1980.C80.0224

156.0003	1980.C80.0223
157.0001	2013.0013
157.0002	2007.0197
158.0001	1992.0060
158.0002	1998.0032
158.0003	1993.NoEx93.0057
159.0001	1983.0067
160.0001	1993.NoEx93.0008
161.0001	1982.0160
162.0001	1984.C84.0009
163.0001	1983.0060
163.0002	1980.C80.0497
164.0001	2002.0309
165.0001	1973.1316
166.0001	1979.1951
166.0002	2011.0034
167.0001	2005.0004
168.0001	1979.2138
169.0001	2007.0254
169.0002	1983.0038
169.0003	1988.0087
170.0001	1986.0049
170.0002	1984.C84.0006
170.0003	2001.0008
170.0004	1980.C80.0060
171.0001	1985.0164
172.0001	2007.0217
172.0002	1972.1112
172.0003	1992.0062
173.0001	1979.1943
174.0001	1978.1598
174.0002	2012.0020
174.0003	1986.0027
174.0004	1978.1694
175.0001	1983.C83.0033
176.0001	1979.1937
176.0002	1997.0038
177.0001	1982.0222
178.0001	1982.0223
178.0002	1982.C82.0161
178.0003	1982.C82.0163
178.0004	1983.C83.0036
178.0005	1982.C82.0164
178.0006	1980.C80.0385
178.0007	1993.C93.0004
178.0008	1982.C82.0162
179.0001	1984.C84.0043
180.0001	1981.C81.0082
180.0002	2002.0015
180.0003	1973.1269
181.0001	1985.NoEx85.0005
182.0001	1979.1932

182.0002	1978.1453
182.0003	1979.2098
182.0004	1977.1416
182.0005	1984.0143
183.0001	1997.0111
183.0002	1979.1914
184.0001	1979.1847
184.0002	1976.0003
184.0003	1984.C84.0044
184.0004	1980.0145
185.0001	1973.1287
186.0001	2004.0033
187.0001	1973.1136
188.0001	1987.C87.0012
189.0001	1991.0310
190.0001	1984.C84.0002
191.0001	1980.C80.0049
192.0001	1999.0037
192.0002	1996.0058
192.0003	1973.1314
193.0001	1985.C85.0002
194.0001	1997.0087
195.0001	1993.NoEx93.0058
196.0001	1997.0019
197.0001	2012.0027
198.0001	1973.1270
199.0001	1981.C81.0091
200.0001	1989.0043
201.0001	1985.NoEx85.0010
202.0001	2011.0024
202.0002	1985.NoEx85.0012
203.0001	1990.C90.0010
203.0002	1978.1681
204.0001	1978.1683
204.0002	1973.1279
204.0003	1978.1589
205.0001	1995.0044
206.0001	1983.0138
207.0001	1981.C81.0071
208.0001	1993.C93.0003
209.0001	1989.0014
210.0001	1990.C90.0018
211.0001	1982.C82.0029
212.0001	1991.C91.0011
213.0001	2001.0004
214.0001	1992.0059
215.0001	1989.0012
216.0001	1991.0460
216.0002	1992.0002
216.0003	2007.0204
216.0004	1982.0517
216.0005	1980.C80.0237

217.0001	1986.0077
218.0001	1982.0224
218.0002	1978.1654
219.0001	1987.0071
219.0002	1997.0086
219.0003	1996.0062
220.0001	1999.0033
220.0002	1988.0076
220.0003	2002.0001
220.0004	2007.0159
221.0001	1984.0197
222.0001	1982.C82.0088
223.0001	1991.0065
224.0001	2002.0097
225.0001	1977.1430
226.0001	1982.0249
227.0001	1980.C80.0062
228.0001	1997.0117
229.0001	1978.1805
230.0001	2002.0085
230.0002	1999.0032
230.0003	1991.0325
230.0004	2005.0009
230.0005	1982.C82.0107
230.0006	2012.0036
230.0007	1983.0136
230.0008	1984.0191
230.0009	1992.0061
230.0010	1998.0012
230.0011	1979.1870
230.0012	1973.1172
230.0013	1997.0124
230.0014	1978.1770
230.0015	1991.0001
230.0016	2007.0214
230.0017	2011.0001
230.0018	1989.0038
230.0019	1992.0083
230.0019	1989.0039
230.0021	1985.0264
230.0022	1991.0555
230.0023	1980.C80.0067
230.0024	1990.0302
230.0025	1983.0024
230.0026	1989.0040
230.0026	1982.C82.0004
230.0028	1973.1291
230.0029	1978.1458
230.0030	2002.0108
230.0031	2010.0007
230.0032	1978.1456
230.0033	1985.NoEx85.0017

230.0034	2012.0019
230.0035	2012.0017
230.0036	1978.1796
230.0037	1998.0056
230.0038	1996.0173
230.0039	1979.1927
230.0040	1989.0187
230.0041	1979.1837
230.0042	2007.0232
230.0043	2011.0005
230.0044	1993.0151
230.0045	2005.0051
230.0046	1993.0019
230.0047	1983.0146
230.0048	1982.C82.0116
230.0049	1978.1525
230.0050	1999.0024
230.0051	1973.1153
230.0052	1998.0037
230.0053	1997.0126
230.0054	2011.0029
230.0055	2004.0040
230.0056	1989.0033
230.0057	1982.0006
230.0058	1982.0034
230.0059	1982.C82.0050
230.0060	2012.0008
230.0061	2009.0020
230.0062	1982.C82.0010
230.0063	1993.0157
230.0064	1978.1695
230.0065	1998.0053
230.0066	1985.0177
230.0067	2013.0010
230.0068	2007.0241
230.0069	1993.NoEx93.0037
230.0070	1986.0075
230.0071	1985.NoEx85.0043
230.0072	1983.0091
230.0073	1992.0111
230.0074	2002.0010
230.0075	1978.1698
230.0076	1989.0032
230.0077	1977.1439
230.0078	1980.C80.0339
230.0079	1982.0037
230.0080	1993.0010
230.0081	2008.0008
230.0082	1996.0151
230.0083	1986.0076
230.0084	2011.0016
230.0085	1989.0035

230.0086	1995.0013
230.0087	1997.0004
230.0088	2007.0202
230.0089	1996.0090
230.0090	1997.0106
230.0091	1997.0120
230.0092	1986.0051
230.0093	1999.0002
230.0094	1989.0037
230.0095	1982.C82.0101
230.0096	1993.0074
230.0097	1989.0004
230.0098	1981.C81.0083
230.0099	1982.0158
230.0100	1986.0001
230.0101	1998.0052
230.0102	1989.0055
230.0103	1998.0035
230.0104	2011.0012
230.0105	1984.0074
230.0106	1980.0060
230.0107	1983.0109
230.0108	1989.0053
230.0109	1989.0034
230.0110	1992.0064
230.0111	1973.1318
230.0112	1989.0094
230.0113	1989.0056
230.0114	1983.0108
230.0115	1982.0105
230.0116	1993.0064
230.0117	2001.0009
230.0118	1991.0038
231.0001	2007.0067
232.0001	1996.0159
233.0001	1991.C91.0003
234.0001	1984.C84.0048
235.0001	1980.C80.0164
236.0001	1982.C82.0110
237.0001	1994.0065
238.0001	1982.0226
239.0001	1996.0081
240.0001	1983.0043
241.0001	1993.NoEx93.0050
242.0001	1991.0554
243.0001	1981.C81.0063
244.0001	1978.1510
244.0002	1996.0135
244.0003	1978.1476
245.0001	1985.C85.0025
246.0001	1997.0017
247.0001	2012.0034

248.0001	1990.0308
249.0001	1997.0020
249.0002	1996.0063
250.0001	1985.C85.0026
251.0001	1980.0197
252.0001	1985.C85.0027
253.0001	1985.0245
254.0001	1977.1453
255.0001	1978.1477
256.0001	1989.0021
257.0001	1984.0147
258.0001	1997.0035
259.0001	1985.C85.0003
260.0001	1988.NoEx88.0001
261.0001	1984.C84.0021
262.0001	1990.0206
263.0001	1999.0041
264.0001	1985.NoEx85.0030
265.0001	1972.1050
266.0001	1982.C82.0169
267.0001	1988.NoEx88.0012
268.0001	1997.0121
269.0001	1991.0457
270.0001	1992.0019
271.0001	1978.1605
271.0002	1992.0236
271.0003	1978.1606
272.0001	1999.0038
273.0001	1999.0034
273.0002	2012.0006
274.0001	1986.0029
275.0001	1980.C80.0064
276.0001	1997.0012
276.0002	1993.0017
277.0001	1986.0021
278.0001	1973.1137
279.0001	1977.1438
279.0002	1992.0309
280.0001	1992.0234
281.0001	1994.0118
282.0001	1984.C84.0004
282.0002	1979.1939
283.0001	1989.C89.0023
284.0001	1982.C82.0105
285.0001	1992.0146
286.0001	2012.0004
287.0001	1988.0104
288.0001	1992.0031
289.0001	1978.1664
289.0002	1980.C80.0338
289.0003	1989.0002
290.0001	1983.0214

290.0002	1980.C80.0425
291.0001	1982.0225
292.0001	1982.C82.0007
292.0002	2005.0017
292.0003	1978.1460
292.0004	1979.1839
292.0005	1973.1300
292.0006	1973.1146
292.0007	2011.0103
292.0008	1998.0031
292.0009	1991.0358
292.0010	1991.0548
292.0011	1994.0022
292.0012	1994.0111
292.0013	1978.1768
293.0001	1973.1265
294.0001	1993.0158
294.0002	2007.0109
294.0003	1981.C81.0070
294.0004	2007.0071
294.0005	1980.C80.0423
294.0006	1979.1828
294.0007	1982.0875
294.0008	1998.0063
294.0009	1978.1650
294.0010	1985.0302
294.0011	2010.0044
294.0012	1978.1651
295.0001	2011.0050
296.0001	1983.0232
297.0001	1984.0057
297.0002	1983.0089
297.0003	1996.0146
297.0004	1980.0174
297.0005	1992.0018
297.0006	2011.0069
297.0007	1978.1652
297.0008	1994.0032
297.0009	1989.0147
297.0010	2012.0018
297.0011	2007.0054
298.0001	1978.1649
299.0001	1980.C80.0337
300.0001	1992.0025
300.0002	1980.C80.0426
300.0003	2012.0022
300.0004	1980.C80.0397
301.0001	2011.0011
302.0001	2002.0193
303.0001	1993.0082
303.0002	2010.0005
304.0001	1979.2110

305.0001	1993.NoEx93.0007
306.0001	1983.0020
307.0001	1983.0163
308.0001	1988.NoEx88.0013
309.0001	1982.C82.0166
310.0001	1973.1262
311.0001	1986.0036
312.0001	1993.NoEx93.0060
313.0001	2000.0007
313.0002	2007.0001
314.0001	1997.0022
315.0001	1992.0073
315.0002	1985.0301
316.0001	1984.0035
317.0001	1995.0016
318.0001	1992.C92.0006
319.0001	1984.C84.0025
320.0001	1980.C80.0151
321.0001	1994.0178
322.0001	1973.1293
323.0001	1979.1935
324.0001	1982.C82.0009
324.0002	1982.C82.0049
325.0001	2007.0194
326.0001	1999.0039
327.0001	1992.0017
327.0002	1992.C92.0001
327.0003	1993.0160
327.0004	1992.0047
327.0005	2012.0015
327.0006	1990.0295
327.0007	1985.C85.0011
327.0008	1996.NoEx96.0001
328.0001	1980.C80.0075
328.0002	1978.1617
328.0003	1992.0172
329.0065	1992.0032
330.0001	2007.0167
330.0002	1980.C80.0288
331.0001	1991.0334
331.0002	1980.0121
331.0003	1992.0022
331.0004	1991.0552
331.0005	1993.C93.0019
331.0006	1973.1145
331.0007	1991.C91.0001
331.0008	1989.C89.0007
332.0001	2002.0258
333.0001	1985.0170
334.0001	1991.C91.0015
335.0001	1990.C90.0023
335.0002	1973.1260

336.0001	1989.C89.0016
337.0001	1990.C90.0014
338.0001	1982.C82.0104
338.0002	1997.0006
338.0003	1980.C80.0326
339.0001	1992.0048
340.0001	1994.0155
340.0002	1990.C90.0020
341.0001	1991.0463
341.0002	1982.C82.0167
341.0003	1979.1881
341.0004	1992.C92.0007
342.0001	1991.C91.0010
343.0001	1990.C90.0012
344.0001	1992.0243
344.0002	1982.0010
345.0001	1990.C90.0008
346.0001	1983.0075
347.0001	1990.0303
348.0001	1996.0177
349.0001	1990.C90.0021
349.0002	1993.C93.0017
349.0003	1991.C91.0004
350.0001	2002.0310
350.0002	1985.C85.0020
350.0003	1991.C91.0016
351.0001	1992.0279
351.0002	1993.0004
351.0003	1973.NoEx.1973.3
351.0004	1991.0546
351.0005	2008.0021
351.0006	1990.C90.0024
351.0007	1983.C83.0027
351.0008	2007.0041
352.0001	1980.C80.0046
353.0001	1978.1767
353.0002	1973.1108
353.0003	1997.0085
353.0004	1992.0020
353.0005	1990.0293
353.0006	2008.0002
353.0007	1983.C83.0029
353.0008	1982.C82.0168
354.0001	1983.0160
355.0001	1993.0138
356.0001	2001.0007
357.0001	2002.0192
358.0001	1992.0126
359.0001	1977.1415
360.0001	1979.1830
360.0002	1992.0037
360.0003	1996.0178

361.0001	1978.1769
361.0002	1990.C90.0019
362.0001	1980.0192
363.0001	1990.C90.0002
364.0001	1980.C80.0373
365.0001	1992.C92.0004
366.0001	1993.0008
367.0001	2007.0246
368.0001	1990.0306
369.0001	1984.C84.0028
370.0001	1991.0349
370.0002	1980.C80.0454
371.0001	1983.0175
372.0001	1985.0002
373.0001	1992.0038
374.0001	1990.C90.0022
375.0001	1992.0078
376.0001	1980.C80.0024
377.0001	1982.C82.0170
378.0001	2002.0322
378.0002	1980.C80.0063
379.0001	1990.0304
380.0001	1985.0198
381.0001	1994.0056
382.0001	1991.0287
383.0001	1992.0036
384.0001	1993.0159
385.0001	1991.0364
386.0001	1977.1433
387.0001	1987.NoEx87.0011
387.0002	1997.0023
387.0003	1993.0152
387.0004	1980.C80.0429
387.0005	1982.0116
387.0006	1982.0200
387.0007	2002.0012
387.0008	1979.2118
387.0009	1980.0217
387.0010	1982.0004
387.0011	1990.0307
387.0012	1983.0076
387.0013	1988.0004
387.0014	1978.1682
387.0015	1983.0128
387.0016	1994.0161
387.0017	1980.0218
387.0018	1991.0093
387.0019	2012.0043
387.0020	1980.0018
387.0021	1993.0005
387.0022	1990.0001
387.0023	1991.0285

387.0024	2002.0278
388.0001	2011.0006
389.0001	2011.0048
389.0002	1991.C91.0002
390.0001	2002.0279
390.0002	1997.0095
390.0003	1992.NoEx92.0005
390.0004	1980.0074
391.0001	1995.0024
392.0001	1992.0164
393.0001	1979.1919
393.0002	1997.0002
394.0001	1992.C92.0002
394.0002	2007.0103
395.0001	1991.0437
395.0002	1993.NoEx93.0026
396.0001	1999.0007
396.0002	2002.0312
397.0001	1977.1426
397.0002	1985.NoEx85.0027
398.0001	1991.0003
398.0002	1992.0299
398.0003	1991.0550
398.0004	1977.1413
398.0005	1980.C80.0238
398.0006	1992.NoEx92.0006
398.0007	1992.0287
399.0001	1999.0013
399.0002	1983.0011
399.0003	1997.0082
400.0001	1973.1122
401.0001	1990.C90.0015
401.0002	1980.C80.0265
401.0003	1991.C91.0006
401.0004	1983.C83.0030
402.0001	1983.0157
403.0001	1986.C86.0006
404.0001	1973.1179
404.0002	1983.C83.0008
405.0001	1997.0010
406.0001	1993.C93.0018
407.0001	2007.0055
407.0002	1981.C81.0079
408.0001	1979.2117
409.0001	1990.0271
410.0001	1985.0161
411.0001	1983.C83.0010
411.0002	1996.0059
412.0001	1982.0228
413.0001	1980.C80.0472
413.0002	1983.C83.0009
414.0001	2011.0056

414.0002	1992.0076
415.0001	1980.C80.0486
415.0002	1980.C80.0193
415.0003	1973.1183
415.0004	1982.0251
416.0001	1984.C84.0023
417.0001	1980.C80.0450
418.0001	1991.0008
418.0002	1987.NoEx87.0002
418.0003	1984.C84.0031
418.0004	1973.NoEx.1973.6
418.0005	1980.C80.0439
418.0006	1980.C80.0460
418.0007	1979.2114
419.0001	1980.C80.0360
420.0001	2004.0020
421.0001	1991.0356
421.0002	1983.0275
421.0003	1982.C82.0022
421.0004	1991.0281
421.0005	1991.0208
422.0001	1990.0294
422.0002	1991.0426
423.0001	1980.C80.0480
423.0002	2005.0058
423.0003	1980.C80.0112
423.0004	1991.0432
423.0005	1980.C80.0456
423.0006	1973.1308
423.0007	2005.0018
423.0008	1982.0049
423.0009	1979.1926
423.0010	2002.0014
423.0011	2010.0040
423.0012	1980.0173
424.0001	1984.C84.0027
425.0001	1973.1345
426.0001	2011.0178
427.0001	1979.1858
427.0002	1980.C80.0042
428.0001	1996.0113
429.0001	1992.0163
430.0001	1983.C83.0025
431.0001	1990.0297
432.0001	1990.0176
432.0002	1991.C91.0005
433.0001	1982.C82.0067
434.0001	1984.0139
435.0001	1991.C91.0012
436.0001	1985.0294
436.0002	1991.0007
436.0003	1993.0020

436.0004	1984.0127
437.0001	1994.0005
437.0002	1992.0199
438.0001	1980.C80.0030
439.0001	1990.0282
440.0001	1979.1879
440.0002	1992.0153
440.0003	1979.1884
440.0004	1992.0168
441.0001	1982.C82.0190
441.0002	1991.0227
442.0001	1993.C93.0005
442.0002	1998.NoExC98.0002
443.0001	1990.C90.0011
443.0002	1978.1498
443.0003	1982.0488
444.0001	2011.0003
445.0001	2011.0149
445.0002	1982.0250
446.0001	1993.0135
447.0001	1979.2113
448.0001	1990.C90.0017
449.0001	1991.C91.0008
450.0001	1984.C84.0035
450.0002	1991.C91.0007
451.0001	1992.0115
452.0001	1995.0037
452.0002	1992.0188
453.0001	2012.0013
454.0001	1981.C81.0034
454.0002	1992.0079
454.0003	1978.1619
454.0004	1978.1812
454.0005	1983.0088
455.0001	1993.C93.0002
456.0001	1984.C84.0016
457.0001	1978.1499
458.0001	1980.C80.0453
459.0001	1982.C82.0189
460.0001	1978.1535
460.0002	1977.1428
461.0001	1991.0368
462.0001	1973.1206
462.0002	1978.1618
463.0001	1993.0081
464.0001	1973.1167
464.0002	1989.C89.0019
464.0003	2009.0006
465.0001	1992.0290
466.0001	1991.0283
467.0001	1994.0033
468.0001	1978.1630

469.0001	1973.1139
470.0001	1982.C82.0027
471.0001	1980.0211
472.0001	1983.C83.0019
472.0002	1985.NoEx85.0011
473.0001	1989.C89.0020
474.0001	1993.0155
474.0003	1979.1987
474.0004	1988.C88.0001
475.0001	1983.C83.0001
475.0002	1982.0181
475.0003	1980.C80.0467
475.0004	1980.C80.0484
475.0005	1980.C80.0459
476.0001	2011.0027
477.0001	1978.1506
478.0001	1999.0016
478.0002	1987.0078
478.0003	1992.0230
479.0001	1989.0118
479.0002	1980.C80.0446
479.0003	1980.C80.0256
480.0001	1991.0556
480.0002	1973.1225
480.0003	1989.0161
481.0001	2012.0057
482.0001	1996.0003
482.0002	1990.0210
483.0001	2012.0051
483.0002	1991.0433
483.0003	1984.C84.0019
484.0001	1991.0016
484.0002	1991.0540
484.0003	1991.0539
484.0004	1983.0081
484.0005	1980.C80.0466
485.0001	1990.C90.0003
486.0001	1991.0424
486.0002	1984.C84.0036
486.0003	1980.C80.0474
486.0004	1982.C82.0013
486.0005	1988.C88.0004
486.0006	1997.0028
487.0001	1991.0427
487.0002	1996.0152
488.0001	1991.0538
488.0002	1992.0229
488.0003	1983.0002
488.0004	1991.0009
488.0005	1980.C80.0475
488.0006	1989.0104
488.0007	1991.0551

488.0008	1991.0431
488.0009	1980.C80.0275
488.0010	1980.C80.0444
488.0011	1980.C80.0432
488.0012	1985.0013
488.0013	1991.0312
488.0014	1996.0157
488.0015	1984.0148
488.0016	1987.NoEx87.0004
488.0017	1980.0199
488.0018	1982.C82.0147
488.0019	1980.C80.0383
489.0001	1980.0188
490.0001	1982.0191
490.0002	1980.C80.0032
491.0001	1980.C80.0352
491.0002	1980.C80.0433
492.0001	1982.C82.0191
493.0001	1991.0244
494.0001	1973.1134
495.0001	1980.0182
495.0002	1980.C80.0469
495.0003	1980.0209
496.0001	1980.C80.0279
496.0002	2012.0031
497.0001	2007.0117
498.0001	1992.0077
499.0001	1982.C82.0152
500.0001	1980.C80.0441
501.0001	1980.C80.0278
501.0002	1996.0096
502.0001	1981.C81.0049
503.0001	1980.C80.0478
503.0002	1990.0060
503.0003	1980.C80.0487
503.0004	1980.C80.0465
503.0005	1982.C82.0142
504.0001	1989.0194
505.0001	1991.0553
505.0002	2012.0054
505.0003	1991.0088
506.0001	1985.C85.0014
506.0002	1980.C80.0477
507.0001	1980.C80.0457
507.0002	1982.C82.0192
508.0001	2002.0130
509.0001	1981.C81.0038
510.0001	1988.0081
511.0001	1992.0082
511.0002	1980.C80.0463
511.0003	1985.0305
512.0001	1982.C82.0090

513.0001	1981.C81.0044
513.0002	1980.0201
514.0001	1987.0019
515.0001	1978.1484
516.0001	2007.0163
517.0001	1979.1924
518.0001	1983.0021
519.0001	1994.0034
520.0001	1991.0013
521.0001	1980.C80.0291
521.0002	1992.0224
522.0001	1975.1408
523.0001	1988.C88.0003
524.0001	1991.0369
525.0001	1980.C80.0471
525.0002	1992.0108
526.0001	1996.NoEx96.0002
526.0002	1990.0157
527.0001	1978.1629
527.0002	1982.C82.0089
527.0003	1978.1472
527.0004	1979.2092
527.0005	1996.0040
527.0006	1992.0288
527.0007	1982.0174
527.0008	1984.0149
527.0009	1978.1631
528.0001	1993.NoEx93.0018
528.0002	1982.C82.0155
529.0001	1988.0091
530.0001	1991.0428
530.0002	1980.C80.0491
530.0003	1983.0162
531.0001	1981.C81.0046
531.0002	1982.0089
532.0001	1987.NoEx87.0016
532.0002	1973.1113
532.0003	1996.0140
533.0001	1982.C82.0001
533.0002	2007.0037
533.0003	1986.0069
533.0004	1982.C82.0117
533.0005	1982.0092
534.0001	1991.0072
534.0002	1978.1720
535.0001	1973.1119
536.0001	1978.1655
536.0002	2001.0013
537.0001	1980.C80.0461
538.0001	1980.0196
539.0001	2005.0010
539.0002	1997.0008

540.0001	1980.C80.0468
541.0001	1989.0128
542.0001	1991.0019
542.0002	1978.1628
542.0003	1982.0155
542.0004	1997.0118
542.0005	1992.NoEx92.0001
542.0006	1989.C89.0005
542.0007	1981.C81.0075
542.0008	1973.1186
543.0001	2005.0024
544.0001	1989.C89.0004
545.0001	1978.1532
545.0002	1991.0445
545.0003	1987.C87.0009
545.0004	2011.0081
545.0005	1980.C80.0047
545.0006	1980.C80.0473
545.0007	1980.C80.0282
546.0001	1990.0136
546.0002	1996.0064
547.0001	1990.0251
547.0002	2008.0009
548.0001	1994.0007
549.0001	1992.0049
550.0001	1980.C80.0329
551.0001	1982.C82.0153
552.0001	1978.1727
553.0001	1973.1184
554.0001	1983.0083
554.0002	1993.NoEx93.0062
555.0001	1992.0440
556.0001	1980.C80.0485
556.0002	1992.0221
557.0001	1980.C80.0150
557.0002	1991.0421
557.0003	1983.0112
557.0004	2004.0002
557.0005	1973.1203
557.0006	1996.0094
557.0007	1994.0113
557.0008	2002.0280
557.0009	1980.C80.0283
557.0010	1989.0174
557.0011	1973.1281
557.0012	1982.C82.0016
557.0013	1985.NoEx85.0008
557.0014	1980.C80.0421
557.0015	1980.C80.0494
557.0016	1993.C93.0001
557.0017	1982.C82.0052
557.0018	1982.C82.0058

557.0019	2004.0015
557.0020	1991.0216
557.0021	1997.0107
557.0022	1979.1918
557.0023	1983.0216
557.0024	1992.0242
557.0025	1980.C80.0483
557.0026	1984.0172
557.0027	1994.0106
557.0028	1991.0255
557.0029	1989.0186
557.0030	1983.0156
557.0031	1989.0125
557.0032	1997.0011
557.0033	1985.0018
557.0034	1980.C80.0191
557.0035	2004.0024
557.0036	1996.0172
557.0037	1992.0161
558.0001	1980.C80.0266
558.0002	1991.0362
558.0003	1996.0077
558.0004	1984.0152
558.0005	1991.0458
558.0006	1991.0276
558.0007	1985.NoEx85.0041
558.0008	1990.0071
558.0009	1987.0138
558.0010	1985.NoEx85.0035
558.0011	1987.0064
558.0012	1990.0101
558.0013	2007.0253
559.0001	1977.1452
559.0002	1982.C82.0171
559.0003	1978.1648
559.0004	1980.C80.0284
559.0005	1984.0038
559.0006	1985.0009
559.0007	1978.1469
559.0008	1991.0059
559.0009	2002.0195
559.0010	1993.NoEx93.0032
559.0011	1996.0097
559.0012	1982.0183
559.0013	1985.NoEx85.0045
559.0014	1980.C80.0088
559.0015	1997.0129
559.0016	1982.C82.0086
559.0017	1982.0189
559.0018	1991.0203
559.0019	1992.0276
559.0020	1987.0060

559.0021	1973.1248
559.0022	2013.0015
559.0023	1991.0435
559.0024	1980.C80.0495
559.0025	1994.0156
559.0026	2005.0033
559.0027	1977.1443
559.0028	2011.0111
559.0029	1978.1656
559.0030	1983.0033
559.0031	1979.2141
559.0032	2007.0007
559.0033	1992.0067
559.0034	1992.0074
559.0035	1993.0050
559.0036	1991.0363
560.0001	1980.C80.0094
560.0002	1991.0326
560.0003	1982.0175
560.0004	1990.0006
560.0005	1984.0163
560.0006	1982.C82.0129
560.0007	1991.0021
560.0008	1991.0226
560.0009	1992.0226
560.0010	1985.0208
560.0011	1993.NoEx93.0016
560.0012	1980.C80.0249
560.0013	1991.0161
560.0014	1991.0073
560.0015	1979.1925
560.0016	1990.0299
560.0017	1979.1889
560.0018	1985.0251
560.0019	1991.0075
560.0020	1983.C83.0006
560.0021	2010.0014
560.0022	1980.C80.0202
560.0023	2011.0057
560.0024	1991.0231
560.0025	1994.0086
560.0026	2001.0025
560.0027	1990.0070
560.0028	1998.0004
560.0029	2012.0012
560.0030	1989.0110
560.0031	1991.0165
560.0032	1992.0179
560.0033	1996.0009
560.0034	1980.C80.0173
560.0035	1981.C81.0055
560.0036	1978.1511

560.0037	1985.0289
560.0038	1980.C80.0168
560.0039	1982.0253
560.0040	1992.0104
560.0041	1990.0268
560.0042	1991.0311
560.0043	1988.0106
560.0044	2011.0010
560.0045	1991.0197
560.0046	1993.0066
560.0047	1996.0107
560.0048	2011.0157
560.0049	1995.0032
560.0050	1985.NoEx85.0006
560.0051	1993.0065
560.0052	1990.0016
560.0053	1991.0409
560.0054	1980.0152
560.0055	1982.0252
561.0001	1978.1500
561.0002	1985.0019
562.0001	1990.C90.0004
563.0001	1984.C84.0030
564.0001	1980.C80.0343
565.0001	1981.C81.0035
566.0001	1986.0025
566.0002	2010.0012
567.0001	1980.C80.0264
567.0002	1990.0198
568.0001	2003.0002
569.0001	1978.1777
570.0001	1997.0097
570.0002	1992.0075
571.0001	1992.0364
572.0001	2008.0022
572.0002	1980.C80.0447
572.0003	1980.C80.0396
573.0001	1983.0084
574.0001	1978.1657
575.0001	1984.0089
575.0002	1977.1442
575.0003	1992.0436
575.0004	1985.C85.0021
575.0005	1996.0073
575.0006	1990.0063
575.0007	1998.0003
575.0008	1992.0300
575.0009	1987.0054
576.0001	1978.1626
577.0001	1980.C80.0320
578.0001	2005.0044
579.0001	1980.C80.0327

580.0001	1980.C80.0470
580.0002	1982.0084
581.0001	1973.1326
581.0002	1991.0089
582.0001	1980.C80.0362
582.0002	1983.C83.0007
582.0003	1985.NoEx85.0034
583.0001	1980.0204
583.0002	1980.C80.0316
583.0003	1980.C80.0276
583.0004	1992.0157
583.0005	1985.NoEx85.0046
583.0006	2010.0033
583.0007	1981.C81.0088
583.0008	1978.1673
584.0001	1992.0272
584.0002	1988.0089
585.0001	2000.0001
586.0001	1993.0101
586.0002	1980.C80.0350
587.0001	1980.C80.0479
587.0002	2011.0126
587.0003	1980.C80.0271
587.0004	1983.0137
587.0005	1992.0216
587.0006	1980.C80.0298
587.0007	1980.0092
588.0001	2000.0018
588.0002	1983.C83.0034
589.0001	1979.2111
589.0002	2012.0055
589.0003	1980.C80.0476
590.0001	1984.C84.0015
591.0001	1980.C80.0142
592.0001	1992.0142
593.0001	1989.0178
594.0001	1996.0156
595.0001	1980.0131
595.0002	1982.C82.0154
595.0003	1980.0041
595.0004	1991.0394
595.0005	1982.C82.0150
595.0006	1980.C80.0464
595.0007	1991.0224
595.0008	1992.0081
595.0009	1982.0246
595.0010	1983.0243
595.0011	1982.C82.0156
595.0012	1980.0208
595.0013	1996.0120
595.0014	1979.1831
595.0015	1990.0002

595.0016	1980.0212
595.0017	1973.1285
595.0018	1988.NoEx88.14
595.0019	1992.0220
595.0020	1979.1863
595.0021	1984.0044
595.0022	1980.C80.0129
595.0023	1979.1916
595.0024	1980.C80.0449
595.0025	1973.1121
595.0026	1980.C80.0061
595.0027	1989.0135
595.0028	1980.C80.0451
595.0029	1991.0377
595.0030	1992.0201.1
596.0001	1994.0028
596.0002	1980.C80.0393
597.0001	1984.0167
597.0002	1980.C80.0292
597.0003	1978.1753
597.0004	1991.0304
597.0005	2007.0113
597.0006	1992.0169
597.0007	1983.0099
597.0008	1992.0080
597.0009	1980.C80.0058
597.0010	1978.1670
597.0011	2007.0229
597.0012	1980.C80.0242
597.0013	2008.0019
597.0014	1992.0170
597.0015	1989.0117
597.0016	1985.0006
597.0017	1979.2077
597.0018	1988.0075
597.0019	1980.0181
597.0020	1984.C84.0022
597.0021	1992.0372
598.0001	1990.0049
599.0001	1979.1826
599.0002	1980.C80.0057
600.0001	1983.0174
600.0002	1982.0156
600.0003	1981.C81.0047
600.0004	1982.C82.0182
600.0005	1982.0254
601.0001	1989.0129
602.0001	2012.0021
602.0002	1982.0008
602.0003	1973.1204
602.0004	1997.0039
602.0005	1982.0081

602.0006	1993.NoEx93.0059
602.0007	1985.0197
602.0008	1981.C81.0093
602.0009	1994.0126
602.0010	1994.0236
602.0011	1992.0231
602.0012	1994.0095
602.0013	1982.0681
603.0001	1989.0195
603.0002	1973.1224
604.0001	2005.0047
604.0002	1982.0043
604.0003	2005.0055
604.0004	1982.C82.0143
604.0005	1980.C80.0431
604.0006	1982.0082
604.0007	2004.0025
604.0008	2009.0003
604.0009	1982.0227
604.0010	1980.C80.0003
604.0011	1984.0171
604.0012	1991.0352
604.0013	1993.0109
604.0014	1973.1099
604.0015	2002.0092
604.0016	1988.0018
604.0017	1982.0020
604.0018	1978.1582
604.0019	1982.0187
604.0020	1982.0107
605.0001	1981.C81.0053
605.0002	1992.0183
605.0003	1990.0208
605.0004	1992.0265
605.0005	1994.0043
605.0006	1986.0003
605.0007	1991.0354
605.0008	1992.0435
605.0009	1994.0232
605.0010	1992.0296
605.0011	1981.C81.0061
605.0012	1980.C80.0207
605.0013	1973.1305
605.0014	1987.0091
605.0015	1986.0002
605.0016	1984.0079
605.0017	1993.0079
606.0001	1982.0042
606.0002	1990.0288
606.0003	2001.0028
606.0004	1986.0062
606.0005	2005.0027

606.0006	1983.0082	611.0001	1991.C91.0009	631.0001	1982.C82.0141	653.0001	1997.0049	678.0007	1989.0134
606.0007	1992.0269	611.0002	1995.0022	631.0002	1993.0171	654.0001	1995.0002	678.0008	1994.0117
606.0008	1982.C82.0053	612.0001	1990.0275	631.0003	1982.0097	654.0002	1982.0255	679.0001	1979.1829
606.0009	1993.0027	613.0001	1978.1761	631.0004	2007.0021	655.0001	1991.0092	679.0002	2007.0160
606.0010	1982.0186	614.0001	1990.C90.0006	631.0005	1987.NoEx87.0015	655.0002	1982.C82.0180	679.0003	1982.C82.0054
606.0011	1993.0028	614.0002	1984.C84.0017	631.0006	1983.0115	656.0001	2011.0104	679.0004	1980.C80.0318
606.0012	1983.0085	614.0003	1978.1470	631.0007	2004.0001	657.0001	1979.1921	679.0005	1990.0255
606.0013	1996.0137	614.0004	1982.C82.0097	631.0008	1984.0142	658.0001	1978.1732	679.0006	1992.0343
606.0014	1992.0217	614.0005	1981.C81.0073	631.0009	1984.0047	659.0001	1990.NoEx90.1	679.0007	1991.0372
606.0015	1994.0029	614.0006	1985.C85.0006	631.0010	1979.1941	659.0002	2006.0001	680.0001	1973.1180
606.0016	1980.C80.0440	615.0001	1984.0184	632.0001	1996.0141	660.0001	2010.0037	680.0002	1982.0090
606.0017	1992.0144	615.0002	1993.NoEx93.0061	633.0001	1982.C82.0128	661.0001	1990.0224	680.0003	1982.C82.0043
606.0018	1982.C82.0096	615.0003	2007.0237	634.0001	1990.0310	661.0002	1975.1409	680.0004	1991.0024
606.0019	2007.0162	615.0004	1982.C82.0082	635.0001	1984.C84.0013	661.0003	2012.0010	680.0005	2005.0013
606.0020	1982.C82.0093	615.0005	1985.C85.0001	636.0001	1994.0203	662.0001	1982.0571	680.0006	1980.0186
606.0021	1978.1661	615.0006	1994.0131	637.0001	2004.0034	663.0001	1982.C82.0024	680.0007	1991.0289
606.0022	1986.0060	615.0007	1989.0096	637.0002	1977.1414	664.0001	1989.C89.0008	681.0001	2007.0179
606.0023	1982.C82.0057	616.0001	1980.C80.0458	637.0003	1981.C81.0043	665.0001	1991.0158	681.0002	1987.0159
606.0024	1980.C80.0109	616.0002	1984.C84.0037	637.0004	1991.0005	665.0002	1997.0050	682.0001	1989.0026
606.0025	1990.0211	616.0003	1984.C84.0007	637.0005	1980.C80.0452	665.0003	1983.0140	682.0002	2002.0320
606.0026	1984.0128	617.0001	1975.1401	638.0001	1983.0277	665.0004	2002.0288	682.0003	1990.0265
606.0027	1996.0053	618.0001	1990.0276	638.0002	1979.1891	666.0001	1978.1468	683.0001	1982.0143
606.0028	1980.0132	619.0001	1996.0076	639.0001	2011.0041	667.0001	1984.C84.0033	684.0001	1973.1089
606.0029	2010.0030	619.0002	1979.2058	640.0001	2005.0019	668.0001	1984.0162	684.0002	1985.0017
606.0030	1973.1275	619.0003	1994.0105	641.0001	1975.1402	669.0001	1984.0176	684.0003	1996.0093
606.0031	2003.0005	620.0001	1980.C80.0035	641.0002	1980.C80.0253	669.0002	1978.1737	684.0004	1983.0016
606.0032	2013.0018	621.0001	1990.0278	641.0003	1979.1883	670.0001	1982.C82.0146	684.0005	1982.0230
606.0033	1980.C80.0304	621.0002	1973.1232	641.0004	2011.0189	670.0002	1980.C80.0267	684.0006	1984.0158
606.0034	2007.0200	622.0001	1994.0023	641.0005	1979.1968	670.0003	1984.0169	684.0007	1982.0243
606.0035	1989.0171	622.0002	1987.C87.0013	641.0006	1979.1988	670.0004	1982.0102	684.0008	1979.2159
606.0036	1996.0128	622.0003	1980.C80.0059	641.0007	1986.C86.0003	671.0001	1982.0093	684.0009	1982.0179
606.0037	1984.0109	622.0004	1984.0094	642.0001	1979.1890	672.0001	1999.0010	684.0010	1988.0078
606.0038	1980.0162	622.0005	1990.0019	642.0002	1979.1824	672.0002	1980.C80.0248	684.0011	1982.0232
606.0039	1992.0383	622.0006	2007.0108	642.0003	1991.0192	673.0001	1989.0097	684.0012	2002.0103
606.0040	1992.0317	622.0007	1991.0355	642.0004	1994.0119	673.0002	1981.C81.0057	684.0013	2004.0009
606.0041	1991.0305	622.0008	1979.2017	642.0005	1982.C82.0011	674.0001	2007.0190	684.0014	2011.0046
606.0042	1991.0282	622.0009	1993.NoEx93.0047	642.0006	1978.1735	674.0002	1994.0145	684.0015	1977.1419
606.0043	1992.0201.2	623.0001	1973.1105	642.0007	1978.1731	675.0001	1980.C80.0146	684.0016	1978.1724
606.0044	1993.0145	623.0002	1978.1474	642.0008	1978.1741	675.0002	2000.0008	684.0017	1982.C82.0061
606.0045	1980.0103	623.0003	1983.0053	642.0009	1978.1736	676.0001	1992.0024	684.0018	2005.0035
606.0046	1991.0087	623.0004	1996.0092	643.0001	1978.1803	676.0002	1992.0232	684.0019	1984.0174
606.0047	1982.0475	623.0005	1982.C82.0006	643.0002	1977.1420	676.0003	1980.C80.0430	684.0020	1983.0065
606.0048	1979.1990	623.0006	1978.1725	643.0003	1989.0172	676.0004	1988.0086	684.0021	1984.0164
607.0001	1984.0145	623.0007	1978.1726	644.0001	1982.C82.0098	677.0001	1978.1743	684.0022	1982.C82.0173
608.0001	1987.C87.0011	624.0001	1978.1607	645.0001	1980.C80.0290	677.0002	2001.0014	684.0023	1982.C82.0179
609.0001	1986.0059	625.0001	1991.0296	646.0001	1983.0116	677.0003	1991.0042	684.0024	2005.0039
609.0002	1982.C82.0069	626.0001	1977.1424	647.0001	1986.0004	678.0001	2013.0014	684.0025	1986.0035
609.0003	1978.1524	626.0002	1980.C80.0076	648.0001	1983.0158	678.0002	1992.NoEx92.0007	684.0026	1982.C82.0099
610.0001	1991.0374	627.0001	1978.1526	649.0001	1973.1236	678.0003	2001.0002	684.0027	1992.0010
610.0002	1996.0069	628.0001	1984.0046	650.0001	1987.C87.0010	678.0004	1973.1242	684.0028	1997.0036
610.0003	1982.C82.0149	629.0001	1991.0351	651.0001	1982.C82.0044	678.0005	1992.0316	684.0029	1990.0065
610.0004	1978.1624	630.0001	2010.0042	652.0001	1980.0222	678.0006	1981.C81.0065	684.0030	1976.0009

684.0031	1980.C80.0289
684.0032	1992.0046
684.0033	2004.0008
684.0034	1992.0345
684.0035	1979.1957
684.0036	1979.2003
684.0037	1996.0068
684.0038	1980.C80.0008
684.0039	1982.C82.0138
684.0040	1989.0127
684.0041	1982.C82.0095
684.0042	1992.0305
684.0043	2005.0079
684.0044	1988.0103
684.0045	2004.0005
684.0046	2007.0195
684.0047	1989.0170
684.0048	1979.1823
684.0049	1978.1738
684.0050	1980.0150
684.0051	2005.0056
684.0052	1982.C82.0100
684.0053	2007.0079
684.0054	1982.0038
684.0055	1991.0414
684.0056	2011.0125
684.0057	2005.0037
684.0058	1992.NoEx92.0012
684.0059	1973.1216
684.0060	1992.0028
684.0061	1992.0283
684.0062	1996.0048
684.0063	1993.0093
684.0064	2011.0004
684.0065	2002.0281
684.0066	1990.0202
684.0067	1991.0291
684.0068	1992.0143.1
684.0069	1984.0136
684.0070	1980.C80.0299
684.0071	1980.C80.0122
684.0072	1980.C80.0143
684.0073	1991.0284
684.0074	1981.C81.0051
684.0075	1973.1154
684.0076	1981.C81.0002
684.0077	1992.0023
684.0078	1991.0246
684.0079	1991.0279
684.0080	1991.0163
684.0081	1991.0167
684.0082	1990.0118

684.0083	1984.0066
684.0084	1985.0063
684.0085	1990.0256
684.0086	1996.0124
684.0087	1984.0088
684.0088	1983.0240
684.0089	1980.0061
684.0090	2002.0265
684.0091	1980.0100
684.0092	1984.0067
684.0093	1994.0123
684.0094	1991.0149
684.0095	1991.0512
684.0096	1990.0270
684.0097	1989.0045
684.0098	1991.0159
684.0099	1987.0022
684.0100	1992.0313
684.0101	1979.1917
684.0102	1992.0190
684.0103	1994.0139
684.0104	1982.0115
685.0001	1982.C82.0183
685.0002	1982.C82.0174
685.0003	2004.0029
685.0004	1986.0063
685.0005	1987.0082
685.0006	2007.0059
685.0007	2000.0010
685.0008	2002.0283
685.0009	2002.0006
685.0010	1982.0094
685.0011	1982.0142
685.0012	2003.0004
685.0013	1981.C81.0058
685.0014	1998.0061
685.0015	2010.0001
685.0016	1989.0085
685.0017	1982.0176
685.0018	1983.0142
685.0019	1994.0094
685.0020	1992.0403
685.0021	1973.1333
685.0022	1980.0153
685.0023	1978.1665
685.0024	1991.0350
685.0025	1983.0231
685.0026	1983.0050
685.0027	1982.C82.0102
685.0028	2010.0034
685.0029	1984.0043
685.0030	1982.0244

685.0031	1997.0090
685.0032	1997.0099
685.0033	1973.1342
685.0034	1996.0046
685.0035	1978.1677
685.0036	1973.1267
685.0037	1982.0157
685.0038	1984.0051
685.0039	1987.NoEx87.0009
685.0040	1980.C80.0347
685.0041	1973.1273
685.0042	1978.1700
685.0043	2002.0098
685.0044	1979.1931
685.0045	1973.1277
685.0046	1984.0182
685.0047	2011.0094
685.0048	1983.0044
685.0049	1978.1744
685.0050	1983.0062
685.0051	1990.0225
685.0052	1982.0256
685.0053	1983.0255
685.0054	1980.C80.0232
685.0055	1985.NoEx85.0032
685.0056	1982.C82.0108
685.0057	2007.0062
686.0001	1987.NoEx87.0010
686.0002	1996.0008
686.0003	1996.0164
687.0001	1996.0091
687.0002	2005.0072
687.0003	1984.0180
688.0001	2009.0009
689.0001	1982.C82.0139
689.0002	1980.C80.0028
690.0001	1989.C89.0021
691.0001	1982.0876
692.0001	1980.C80.0247
693.0001	1982.0257
694.0001	1982.C82.0151
695.0001	1993.NoEx93.0019
695.0002	2010.0039
696.0001	1993.0053
697.0001	1981.C81.0077
698.0001	1982.C82.0125
699.0001	2010.0004
700.0001	1996.0006
700.0002	2000.0015
700.0003	1982.C82.0193
701.0001	2010.0045
702.0001	1978.1762

702.0002	1984.C84.0010
702.0003	1985.0004
702.0004	1978.1792
702.0005	1978.1475
703.0001	1991.0232
703.0002	1980.C80.0445
703.0003	1982.0258
704.0001	1983.0159
705.0001	1993.NoEx93.0045
706.0001	1994.0014
706.0002	1978.1471
706.0003	1992.0227
706.0004	1987.C87.0002
706.0005	1985.0032
706.0006	2007.0114
707.0001	1985.NoEx85.0024
707.0002	1982.0103
707.0003	1982.C82.0196
708.0001	2007.0060
709.0001	1980.C80.0029
709.0002	1982.C82.0194
709.0003	1979.1896
709.0004	1982.C82.0195
709.0005	1999.0003
709.0006	1980.C80.0145
709.0007	1980.C80.0214
709.0008	1973.1198
709.0009	1992.0145
709.0010	1987.NoEx87.0013
709.0011	2002.0321
709.0012	1996.0080
709.0013	1986.0078
709.0014	2007.0115
709.0015	1985.0003
710.0001	1983.0278
711.0001	1991.0062
712.0001	1982.C82.0127
713.0001	1990.0177
714.0001	1982.0581
715.0001	2007.0164
716.0001	1992.0238
717.0001	1980.C80.0011
718.0001	1987.C87.0006
718.0002	1990.C90.0009
719.0001	1981.C81.0036
720.0001	1990.0244
720.0002	1993.NoEx93.0024
720.0003	1988.0095
721.0001	1979.2108
722.0001	1983.C83.0021
722.0002	1980.C80.0044
722.0003	1993.0039

722.0004	1991.0207
722.0005	1984.0185
722.0006	1993.NoEx93.0036
722.0007	1995.0010
722.0008	1973.1188
722.0009	1982.C82.0197
723.0001	1981.C81.0092
723.0002	1992.C92.0003
723.0003	1991.0201
723.0004	1978.1785
723.0005	1980.C80.0315
723.0006	1997.0113
723.0007	1987.C87.0003
723.0008	2007.0134
724.0001	1982.C82.0092
725.0001	1980.C80.0418
725.0002	1984.0179
726.0001	1978.1742
726.0002	1992.0397
727.0001	1973.1194
728.0001	1991.0327
729.0001	1982.C82.0030
730.0001	1973.1178
730.0002	1973.1202
730.0003	2012.0026
730.0004	1988.NoEx88.0004
730.0005	2007.0175
730.0006	1982.C82.0033
731.0001	1991.0002
731.0002	1990.0277
732.0001	1985.NoEx85.0018
733.0001	1991.0379
734.0001	1985.C85.0004
735.0001	1997.0066
735.0002	1992.0355
735.0003	1973.1346
735.0004	1980.C80.0004
735.0005	1973.1195
735.0006	1979.1929
735.0007	1985.NoEx85.0002
735.0008	1979.1908
735.0009	1984.C84.0003
736.0001	1982.0188
737.0001	1998.0006
737.0002	1986.C86.0004
738.0001	1973.1347
738.0002	1991.0387
738.0003	1973.1301
738.0004	1993.0146
738.0005	1997.0125
738.0006	1978.1463
738.0007	1982.C82.0137

738.0008	2002.0055
738.0009	1982.C82.0158
738.0010	1982.C82.0042
738.0011	1978.1464
738.0012	1987.NoEx87.0003
739.0001	1999.0012
739.0002	1973.1210
739.0003	1993.C93.0012
739.0004	1991.0315
740.0001	1991.C91.0014
741.0001	1986.C86.0007
742.0001	1992.0286
742.0002	1973.NoEx.1973.5
742.0003	1982.C82.0041
743.0001	1984.C84.0032
744.0001	1989.0001
745.0001	1983.C83.0011
746.0001	1978.1722
746.0002	2012.0044
746.0003	2005.0070
747.0001	1984.0165
748.0001	1973.1215
748.0002	1979.1848
749.0001	2005.0046
749.0002	1973.1144
749.0003	1978.1643
750.0001	1982.0271
750.0002	1989.0070
750.0003	2012.0009
750.0004	1994.0165
750.0005	1984.0095
750.0006	1980.C80.0482
750.0007	1989.0150
750.0008	1987.0168
750.0009	1980.C80.0097
750.0010	1982.0270
750.0011	1978.1669
750.0012	1973.1348
750.0013	1994.0200
750.0014	1991.0061
750.0015	1985.NoEx85.0031
750.0016	1979.1905
750.0017	1990.0253
750.0018	2007.0052
750.0019	1973.1315
750.0020	1983.C83.0026
750.0021	1982.C82.0026
750.0022	1992.0154
750.0023	1979.2127
750.0024	2008.0012
750.0025	2001.0022
750.0026	1980.C80.0370
750.0027	1980.C80.0419
750.0028	1987.0065
750.0029	1984.0153
750.0030	1980.C80.0408
750.0031	1973.1117
750.0032	1980.0170
751.0001	1999.0011
751.0002	1988.0055
751.0003	1992.0134
751.0004	1988.0083
751.0004	1979.2124
751.0006	1984.0170
751.0007	1993.NoEx93.0027
751.0008	1982.0268
751.0009	1982.C82.0175
751.0010	1997.0130
751.0011	1973.1343
751.0012	1982.0269
751.0013	2007.0225
751.0014	1992.0090
751.0015	1984.0056
752.0001	1984.0177
752.0002	1987.C87.0008
753.0001	1990.0300
754.0001	1979.2072
755.0001	1982.0272
756.0001	1976.0010
757.0001	1993.0086
758.0001	1991.0300
759.0001	1980.C80.0257
760.0001	1982.0273
761.0001	1989.0019
761.0002	2011.0055
761.0003	1994.0114
761.0004	1979.1992
762.0001	1980.C80.0407
763.0001	1992.0119
763.0002	1979.1991
763.0003	1983.C83.0016
763.0004	1989.0169
763.0005	1990.0089
763.0006	1980.C80.0013
763.0007	1980.0094
763.0008	1992.0410
764.0001	1977.1429
764.0002	1978.1808
765.0001	1996.0089
766.0001	1973.1249
767.0001	1990.0252
768.0001	1983.0151
769.0001	1989.0106
770.0001	1980.C80.0490
771.0001	1992.0351
771.0002	2005.0040
772.0001	1990.0298
772.0002	1995.0001
773.0001	1980.C80.0251
774.0001	1980.C80.0070
775.0001	1985.0149
775.0002	2002.0102
775.0003	2007.0208
775.0004	1996.0052
775.0005	1991.0048
775.0006	1996.0012
775.0007	1982.C82.0112
775.0008	1980.C80.0138
775.0009	2007.0093
775.0010	1980.C80.0372
775.0011	1993.0032
776.0001	1994.0006
777.0001	1977.1427
778.0001	1980.C80.0437
778.0002	1989.C89.0011
778.0003	2007.0135
778.0004	1989.0189
778.0005	1991.0004
778.0006	1997.0021
778.0007	1988.0031
778.0008	2007.0091
778.0009	1993.NoEx93.0042
778.0010	1993.0154
778.0011	1994.0172
778.0012	1994.0166
778.0013	1980.0165
778.0014	2007.0178
778.0015	1973.1106
778.0016	1980.C80.0417
778.0017	1984.C84.0038
778.0018	1983.0122
778.0019	1979.2002
778.0020	1980.0161
778.0021	1980.C80.0077
778.0022	1993.0087
778.0023	1977.1411
778.0024	1973.1104
778.0025	1996.0005
778.0026	1995.0006
778.0027	1979.2116
778.0028	1978.1625
778.0029	1973.1213
778.0030	2007.0130
778.0031	1992.0340
778.0032	1985.0015
779.0001	1991.0307
779.0002	1984.C84.0049
779.0003	1985.C85.0024
780.0001	1995.0004
780.0002	1980.C80.0415
781.0001	1980.C80.0259
782.0001	1996.0060
782.0002	1980.C80.0420
782.0003	1996.0168
782.0004	1996.0054
782.0005	1986.C86.0005
783.0001	1990.0201
783.0002	1981.C81.0084
783.0003	1994.0171
783.0004	1988.0077
783.0005	1997.0031
783.0006	1991.0211
783.0007	1996.0087
784.0001	1996.0001
784.0002	1973.1283
785.0001	1998.0002
785.0002	2012.0035
785.0003	1984.C84.0024
785.0004	1983.C83.0032
785.0005	1983.C83.0022
785.0006	2005.0083
786.0001	1979.1928
786.0002	1989.C89.0013
787.0001	1980.C80.0021
787.0002	1983.0170
787.0003	1993.0182
788.0001	2001.0005
788.0002	1977.1444
788.0003	1983.0183
788.0004	1982.C82.0113
788.0005	1980.0172
788.0006	1979.1876
788.0007	1973.1187
789.0001	1983.C83.0031
789.0002	1983.0078
790.0001	1985.C85.0028
790.0002	2008.0007
790.0003	1992.C92.0008
790.0004	1980.C80.0394
790.0005	1973.1111
790.0006	1984.0138
790.0007	1997.0046
790.0008	1994.0170
790.0009	1980.C80.0409
790.0010	2007.0231
790.0011	2002.0094
790.0012	1997.0037
791.0001	1983.0046
791.0002	1990.0025
791.0003	1997.0009
791.0004	1990.C90.0005
792.0001	2004.0058
792.0002	1994.0168
792.0003	1980.C80.0404
792.0004	1980.C80.0246
792.0005	1979.1938
792.0006	1991.0286
792.0007	1980.C80.0402
792.0008	1996.0155
793.0001	1996.0099
794.0001	1993.NoEx93.0025
794.0002	1980.C80.0297
794.0003	1978.1627
794.0004	1992.0241
795.0001	1979.1880
796.0001	1993.0102
796.0002	2007.0210
796.0003	1980.C80.0406
796.0004	1989.C89.0014
796.0005	1991.NoEx90.0001
796.0006	1985.NoEx85.0004
796.0007	1991.0429
797.0001	1992.0362
798.0001	1989.0071
799.0001	1992.0349
800.0001	1990.0257
800.0002	1980.C80.0103
800.0003	2007.0148
800.0004	2007.0149
800.0005	1993.0122
800.0006	1994.0125
800.0007	1990.0205
800.0008	2007.0081
800.0009	2011.0105
800.0010	1973.1339
800.0011	1991.0353
800.0012	1973.1163
800.0013	1980.C80.0496
800.0014	1989.0084
800.0015	1983.0073
800.0016	1973.NoEx.1973.7
800.0017	1999.0009
800.0018	2012.0001
800.0019	1989.0022
800.0020	1996.0085
800.0021	2007.0087
800.0022	1992.0116
800.0023	1988.0088
800.0024	2004.0041
800.0025	1973.1135

800.0026	1982.0274
801.0001	1992.0244
801.0002	1973.1161
801.0003	1978.1623
802.0001	1980.0164
802.0002	1993.0096
802.0003	1980.0159
803.0001	1982.0025
803.0002	1973.1209
803.0003	1979.1885
803.0004	1990.0050
803.0005	1994.0159
803.0006	1993.0009
803.0007	1980.0167
803.0008	1991.0342
803.0009	1986.0014
803.0010	1988.0097
803.0011	1991.0361
803.0012	2011.0044
803.0013	1980.C80.0443
803.0014	1985.0320
803.0015	2005.0031
803.0016	2007.0145
803.0017	1989.0190
803.0018	1978.1503
803.0019	1996.0004
803.0020	2007.0107
803.0021	1989.0090
803.0022	1985.0304
803.0023	1997.0101
803.0024	1976.0005
803.0025	1989.NoEx89.0009
803.0026	1987.0057
803.0027	1991.0233
803.0028	1992.0166
803.0029	1982.0278
803.0030	1997.0112
803.0031	1991.0306
803.0032	1973.1222
803.0033	1990.0012
804.0001	1979.1892
804.0002	1973.1247
804.0003	1981.C81.0037
804.0004	1973.1245
805.0001	1990.0184
805.0002	2004.0043
805.0003	1994.0237
806.0001	2007.0240
806.0002	1973.1227
807.0001	1989.0080
808.0001	1991.0076
808.0002	1982.0275

809.0001	1979.1997
809.0002	1982.0527
809.0003	1980.C80.0020
809.0004	2004.0022
809.0005	1990.0147
809.0006	1980.0178
809.0007	1991.0040
809.0008	2004.0049
809.0009	1982.0276
809.0010	1996.0165
809.0011	1991.0400
809.0012	1992.0348
810.0001	1985.C85.0005
811.0001	1991.0288
811.0002	1980.C80.0412
811.0003	1990.0034
812.0001	1992.0152
813.0001	2007.0193
813.0002	1990.0011
813.0003	1979.2099
813.0004	1979.1888
814.0001	1983.C83.0035
814.0002	1983.0166-2
814.0003	1980.C80.0197
815.0001	1979.2145
815.0002	1982.C82.0018
815.0003	2007.0152
816.0001	1991.0467
816.0002	1991.0302
817.0001	1978.1539
817.0002	2005.0036
818.0001	1982.0564
819.0001	1982.C82.0077
820.0001	1992.0178
821.0001	2007.0051
822.0001	1994.0185
823.0001	1982.0259
824.0001	1978.1764
824.0002	1973.1311
825.0001	1991.0012
825.0002	1978.1747
825.0003	1994.0120
825.0004	1991.0434
825.0005	1978.1712
825.0006	2011.0047
825.0007	1984.0175
825.0008	2004.0013
825.0009	1982.0161
825.0010	1985.0297
825.0011	1983.0263
825.0012	1980.C80.0378
825.0013	2007.0095

825.0014	1993.0070
825.0015	1996.0056
825.0016	1982.0170
826.0001	1973.1312
826.0002	1994.NoEx94.0004
826.0003	1994.0218
827.0001	2005.0020
827.0002	1980.C80.0324
828.0001	1982.0690
829.0001	1990.0091
829.0002	1990.0090
829.0003	2007.0104
830.0001	1980.C80.0325
830.0002	1991.0174
830.0003	1990.0059
830.0004	1980.C80.0017
831.0001	1982.0282
832.0001	1989.0191
832.0002	1989.NoEx89.0012
832.0003	1991.0280
832.0004	1980.0168
833.0001	1994.0020
833.0002	2005.0030
834.0001	1988.0090
834.0002	1983.C83.0005
835.0001	1978.1466
835.0002	1996.0079
835.0003	1993.NoEx93.0017
835.0004	1978.1733
836.0001	1980.0169
836.0002	1983.0007
836.0003	1980.C80.0401
836.0004	1980.C80.0392
836.0005	1979.1877
836.0006	2005.0026
836.0007	1980.C80.0399
836.0008	1979.1907
836.0009	1991.0430
836.0010	1980.0156
836.0011	1993.NoEx93.0054
836.0012	2006.0003
836.0013	1982.C82.0021
836.0014	2000.0006
837.0001	1981.C81.0033
838.0001	1991.0367
838.0002	2010.0008
838.0003	2001.0019
838.0004	1982.0229
838.0005	1982.0285
839.0001	1983.0133
839.0002	1983.0040
839.0003	1993.NoEx93.0012

839.0004	2007.0132
839.0005	1992.0158
839.0006	1996.0098
839.0007	1983.0005
839.0008	1983.0070
839.0009	1980.C80.0377
840.0001	1993.NoEx93.0041
841.0001	1982.0100
841.0002	1997.0044
841.0003	1989.0137
841.0004	1981.C81.0003
842.0001	2004.0057
842.0002	1982.0283
843.0001	1980.0184
844.0001	1988.C88.0002
844.0002	1991.C91.0013
845.0001	1984.C84.0034
845.0002	1978.1748
846.0001	2007.0249
847.0001	1994.NoEx94.0008
847.0002	1993.0107
847.0003	1996.0086
847.0004	1975.1403
847.0005	1985.0001
847.0006	1978.1810
847.0007	1978.1811
847.0008	2011.0037
847.0009	2012.0037
847.0010	1980.0160
847.0011	1978.1547
847.0012	2001.0024
847.0013	1998.0008
847.0014	1991.0190
847.0015	1990.0281
847.0016	1982.C82.0106
847.0017	1983.0153
848.0001	1980.C80.0405
848.0002	1982.C82.0136
848.0003	1992.0395
848.0004	1980.C80.0391
848.0005	1997.0115
848.0006	1994.0009
849.0001	1994.0144
849.0002	1978.1465
850.0001	1980.0134
851.0001	1991.0425
851.0002	1980.C80.0501
851.0003	1982.0284
851.0004	1975.1404
852.0001	1991.0079
853.0001	1995.0033
854.0001	1979.1845

854.0002	1991.0202
855.0001	1994.0167
855.0002	1973.1341
855.0003	1992.0177
855.0004	1991.0028
855.0005	1978.1773
855.0006	1979.2119
855.0007	2012.0041
855.0008	2004.0019
855.0009	1980.C80.0078
855.0010	1983.0023
855.0011	2007.0102
855.0012	2009.0002
855.0013	2011.0018
855.0014	2012.0023
855.0015	1994.0181
855.0016	2002.0005
855.0017	1997.0096
855.0018	1989.C89.0006
855.0019	1989.C89.0012
855.0020	1982.0286
855.0021	1980.C80.0403
855.0022	1980.C80.0386
855.0023	1978.1608
855.0024	2011.0053
855.0025	1989.0107
855.0026	1991.0213
855.0027	1993.0133
855.0028	2011.0164
855.0029	1997.0040
856.0001	2005.0050
856.0002	1985.NoEx85.0025
856.0003	1985.NoEx85.0028
856.0004	2007.0083
857.0001	1996.0126
857.0002	1982.0471
858.0001	1973.1162
858.0002	1988.0082
858.0003	1994.0050
858.0004	1973.1132
858.0005	1979.2140
858.0006	1987.0062
858.0007	2010.0023
859.0001	1990.0262
859.0002	1980.C80.0442
859.0003	2005.0076
859.0004	2007.0183
859.0005	1980.C80.0411
859.0006	1979.2066
859.0007	1982.0281
860.0001	1991.0219
860.0002	1980.C80.0416

861.0001	1994.0116
862.0001	1982.0279
862.0002	1982.0261
862.0003	1983.0164
862.0004	1982.0280
862.0005	1990.0237
863.0001	1997.0059
863.0002	1982.0526
863.0003	1978.1473
863.0004	1994.0096
863.0005	2011.0177
864.0001	1992.0187
864.0002	1982.C82.0056
864.0003	2002.0104
865.0001	1989.NoEx89.0003
866.0001	1989.0003
867.0001	2007.0184
867.0002	1997.0084
867.0003	1994.0018
868.0001	1982.0263
869.0001	1973.1296
869.0002	1978.1728
869.0003	1981.C81.0045
869.0004	1994.0245
869.0005	1980.C80.0427
869.0006	1984.0085
870.0001	2007.0056
870.0002	1980.C80.0422
870.0003	2007.0106
870.0004	1982.C82.0118
870.0005	1992.0367
870.0006	1984.0173
870.0007	1978.1813
870.0008	2007.0209
870.0009	1985.0096
870.0010	2005.0011
871.0001	2007.0133
872.0001	2011.0092
873.0001	1978.1632
873.0002	1982.C82.0085
873.0003	2005.0057
873.0004	1978.1659
873.0005	1989.0011
873.0006	1996.0055
873.0007	1980.C80.0413
873.0008	2003.0006
873.0009	1983.C83.0003
874.0001	1997.0047
874.0002	1980.0149
875.0001	2007.0110
876.0001	1992.0150
876.0002	1998.0007

876.0002	1980.C80.0492
876.0003	1980.0163
876.0004	1993.0021
877.0001	1984.0045
878.0001	1991.0090
879.0001	1978.1588
879.0002	1985.NoEx85.0007
880.0001	1983.0058
880.0002	1991.0299
880.0003	1979.2081
880.0004	1997.0029
880.0005	2012.0042
881.0001	1992.NoEx92.0004
882.0001	1987.0046
882.0002	1994.0085
883.0001	1991.0046
884.0001	1997.0128
884.0002	1997.0048
884.0003	1978.1467
884.0004	2004.0018
885.0001	1990.0269
885.0002	1980.C80.0349
885.0003	2005.0052
885.0004	1973.1152
885.0005	1990.0287
885.0006	1979.1835
885.0007	1977.1436
885.0008	1989.0015
885.0009	1991.0439
885.0010	1989.NoEx89.0006
885.0011	1991.0251
885.0012	1978.1517
885.0013	1980.C80.0462
885.0014	2009.0010
885.0015	1983.0066
885.0016	1978.1529
885.0017	1982.C82.0008
885.0018	1993.0170
885.0019	1978.1671
885.0020	1973.1176
885.0021	1985.0306
885.0022	2002.0254
885.0023	1978.1478
885.0024	1988.0102
885.0025	1983.0029
885.0026	2005.0064
885.0027	1979.1913
885.0028	2011.0135
885.0029	1992.0310
885.0030	1978.1806
885.0031	2002.0282
885.0032	1983.C83.0015

885.0033	1973.1306
885.0034	1989.NoEx89.0010
885.0035	1992.0128
885.0036	1994.0160
885.0037	2011.0139
885.0038	1978.1678
885.0039	1980.0093
885.0040	1982.C82.0091
885.0041	1980.C80.0001
885.0042	2012.0007
885.0043	1990.0248
885.0044	1980.C80.0069
885.0045	1992.0342
885.0046	1994.0121
885.0047	1991.0436
885.0048	1980.C80.0434
885.0049	1992.0282
885.0050	1990.0077
885.0051	1978.1797
885.0052	1987.0077
885.0053	1989.0140
885.0054	1990.0038
885.0055	1973.1250
885.0056	1985.NoEx85.0016
885.0057	1980.0151
885.0058	1982.C82.0015
885.0059	1989.0141
885.0060	1978.1658
885.0061	2010.0010
885.0062	1982.C82.0076
885.0063	1973.1295
885.0064	2011.0067
885.0065	1987.0142
885.0066	1978.1705
885.0067	1980.0154
885.0068	1985.NoEx85.0039
885.0069	1994.0072
885.0070	1997.0133
885.0071	1991.0247
885.0072	1989.0114
885.0073	1990.0266
885.0074	1988.0051
885.0075	1987.0145
885.0076	1985.0098
885.0077	1987.0086
885.0078	2002.0191
885.0079	2007.0221
885.0080	1994.0169
885.0081	1980.C80.0435
885.0082	1993.0085
885.0083	1997.0025
885.0084	1994.0122

885.0085	1979.2150
885.0086	1979.1981
885.0087	1981.C81.0089
886.0001	1984.0178
886.0002	1991.0444
886.0003	1989.NoEx89.0011
886.0004	2011.0154
886.0005	1991.0006
886.0006	1990.0062
886.0007	1991.0341
886.0008	1983.0247
886.0009	2011.0076
886.0010	1991.0468
886.0011	1989.0057
886.0012	1978.1489
886.0013	1989.0103
886.0014	1993.0080
886.0015	1978.1635
886.0016	1978.1660
886.0017	1980.C80.0364
886.0018	2007.0131
886.0019	1983.0015
886.0020	1991.0316
886.0021	2011.0096
886.0022	1989.0048
886.0023	1980.C80.0481
886.0024	1973.1304
886.0025	1991.0035
886.0026	1991.0229
886.0027	1991.0031
886.0028	2005.0042
886.0029	1982.0265
886.0030	1984.0063
886.0031	1988.0105
886.0032	1985.0039
886.0033	1982.0267
886.0034	2011.0088
886.0035	1973.1182
886.0036	1985.0262
886.0037	1983.0068
886.0038	2011.0095
886.0039	1987.0170
886.0040	1991.0169
886.0041	1978.1642
886.0042	1982.0262
886.0043	1990.0058
886.0044	2007.0066
886.0045	1987.0150
886.0046	1985.0176
886.0047	1986.0079
886.0048	1994.0040
886.0049	1980.C80.0031

886.0050	2011.0058
886.0051	1992.NoEx92.0008
886.0052	2011.0100
886.0053	1982.C82.0070
886.0054	1980.C80.0300
886.0055	1992.0156
886.0056	1980.C80.0140
886.0057	1982.0076
886.0058	2002.0090
886.0059	1980.C80.0341
886.0060	1995.0015
886.0061	1989.0046
886.0062	2005.0048
886.0063	1991.0074
886.0064	1982.0260
886.0065	2002.0106
886.0066	1993.0188
886.0067	1978.1545
886.0068	1979.1867
886.0069	2005.0028
886.0070	2011.0015
886.0071	1983.0069
886.0072	1992.0431
886.0073	2007.0154
886.0074	2007.0068
886.0075	2001.0017
886.0076	1982.C82.0087
886.0077	1993.0131
886.0078	2001.0010
886.0079	1979.2010
886.0080	1980.C80.0301
886.0081	1973.1083
886.0082	1991.0198
886.0083	2011.0124
886.0084	2011.0158
886.0085	1993.0003
886.0086	1991.0249
886.0087	1978.1590
886.0088	1996.0038
886.0089	1984.0157
886.0090	1982.0264
886.0091	2007.0165
886.0092	2004.0010
886.0093	2004.0028
886.0094	1982.0643
886.0095	1989.0017
886.0096	2002.0176
886.0097	2005.0038
886.0098	1988.0029
886.0099	1980.C80.0149
886.0100	1992.0182
886.0101	1981.C81.0048

886.0102	2011.0035
886.0103	1982.0104
886.0104	1982.0144
886.0105	1993.NoEx93.0009
886.0106	1979.1842
886.0107	2010.0006
886.0108	1982.0266
886.0109	2007.0002
886.0110	1984.0159
886.0111	1981.C81.0042
886.0112	2007.0075
886.0113	1985.NoEx85.0048
886.0114	1991.0181
886.0115	1979.1904
886.0116	1984.0161
886.0117	2011.0140
886.0118	1982.0489
886.0119	1987.0155
886.0120	1993.NoEx93.0064
886.0121	1991.0166
886.0122	1984.0168
886.0123	1977.1421
886.0124	1996.0018
886.0125	2010.0018
886.0126	2005.0014
886.0127	1988.0011
886.0128	1980.C80.0092
886.0129	1981.C81.0041
886.0130	1982.0600
886.0131	1991.0164
886.0132	1983.0094
886.0133	1984.0093
886.0134	1980.C80.0025
886.0135	1982.0576
886.0136	1987.0016
886.0137	1985.0051
886.0138	1994.0097
886.0139	1997.0032
886.0140	1991.0257
886.0141	1993.NoEx93.0005
886.0142	1979.1834
886.0143	1988.NoEx88.0005
886.0144	1991.0293
886.0145	1980.0125
886.0146	1991.0147
886.0147	1980.C80.0228
886.0148	1997.0072
886.0149	2002.0087
887.0001	1982.0127
887.0002	1982.C82.0181
887.0003	1989.0059
887.0004	1978.1675

887.0005	1978.1688
887.0006	1979.2075
887.0007	1980.0135
887.0008	2004.0006
887.0009	1989.0013
887.0010	1982.0113
887.0011	1980.C80.0036
887.0012	1984.0121
887.0013	1980.C80.0186
887.0014	1985.0027
887.0015	2004.0054
887.0016	1989.0023
887.0017	1992.0151
887.0018	1989.0109
887.0019	1983.0123
887.0020	2011.0145
887.0021	1982.0173
887.0022	1983.0004
887.0023	1992.0109
887.0024	1982.0134
887.0025	1979.2070
887.0026	1978.1703
887.0027	1991.0188
887.0028	1985.NoEx85.0036
887.0029	1992.0281
887.0030	1985.0285
887.0031	1978.1685
887.0032	1982.0210
887.0033	1980.0215
887.0034	1978.1775
887.0035	2011.0030
887.0036	1985.0066
887.0037	2004.0004
887.0038	1983.0219
887.0039	1978.1684
887.0040	1983.0105
887.0041	1990.0170
887.0042	1989.0136
887.0043	1980.0087
887.0044	1987.0014
887.0045	1980.0005
887.0046	1978.1676
887.0047	1994.0057
887.0048	1982.C82.0177
887.0049	1985.0314
887.0050	1992.0274
887.0051	1983.0188
887.0052	1993.0090
887.0053	1992.0385
887.0054	1982.0567
887.0055	1992.0251
887.0056	1985.0217

887.0057	1978.1679
887.0058	1983.0273
887.0059	1994.0011
887.0060	1987.0040
887.0061	1987.0047
887.0062	1973.1116
887.0063	1992.0070
887.0064	1994.0084
888.0001	1984.0196
888.0002	2005.0029
889.0001	1977.1434
889.0002	2007.0112
889.0003	1991.0218
890.0001	1980.0086
891.0001	1996.0166
892.0001	1980.C80.0235
892.0002	1991.0176
893.0001	1980.C80.0131
893.0002	1986.0080
894.0001	2005.0045
894.0002	2007.0155
895.0001	2007.0078
896.0001	2007.0063
896.0002	1992.0411
897.0001	1994.0017
898.0001	2007.0224
898.0002	1980.C80.0376
898.0003	1983.0256
898.0004	2011.0182
899.0001	1978.1513
899.0002	1978.1516
900.0001	1991.0160
901.0001	1990.0095
902.0001	1975.1405
903.0001	1980.C80.0365
903.0002	1990.0284
903.0003	1992.0068
904.0001	2007.0176
905.0001	1997.0016
905.0002	1983.0010
906.0001	2002.0096
906.0002	2002.0194
907.0001	1993.NoEx93.0048
908.0001	1982.C82.0148
909.0001	1991.0206
910.0001	1983.0180
910.0002	1983.0250
910.0003	1983.0248
910.0004	1983.0251
910.0005	1980.C80.0414
910.0007	2000.0003
911.0001	1992.0456

912.0001	1991.0043
912.0002	1980.C80.0210
912.0003	1982.0553
912.0004	1982.0293
912.0005	1982.0296
912.0006	1982.0301
913.0001	1991.0057
913.0002	1978.1774
913.0003	2000.0011
913.0004	1977.1418
914.0001	1973.1110
914.0002	1988.0028
914.0003	2004.0036
914.0004	1987.0115
915.0001	1973.1151
915.0002	1991.0054
915.0003	1991.0378
915.0004	1980.C80.0438
915.0005	1982.C82.0200
916.0001	1990.0088
917.0001	1991.0228
917.0002	1987.NoEx87.0007
918.0001	1989.0180
920.0001	1984.0101
920.0002	1987.0146
920.0003	1997.0068
921.0001	2007.0121
921.0002	1997.0030
922.0001	1989.0083
922.0002	1980.0166
922.0003	1980.C80.0147
922.0004	2011.0163
922.0005	2000.0017
922.0006	1980.C80.0369
922.0007	1985.0107
922.0008	2011.0188
922.0009	1980.C80.0272
922.0010	1980.C80.0395
922.0011	1994.0019
922.0012	1989.0160
922.0013	1984.0070
922.0014	1980.C80.0387
922.0015	1980.C80.0262
922.0016	1980.C80.0139
922.0017	1982.C82.0199
922.0018	1980.C80.0148
922.0019	1983.0034
922.0020	1980.C80.0026
922.0021	1979.2146
922.0022	1989.0144
922.0023	1987.0100
922.0024	1982.0297

922.0025	1987.0149
922.0026	1987.0163
922.0027	1983.0257
922.0028	1990.0114
922.0029	1987.0124
922.0030	1987.0137
922.0031	1990.0150
923.0001	1998.0018
924.0001	1989.0105
924.0002	1980.C80.0314
924.0003	1973.1212
924.0004	1982.C82.0198
924.0005	1982.0501
924.0006	1980.C80.0037
924.0007	1980.C80.0023
924.0008	1991.0204
925.0001	1981.C81.0087
926.0001	1992.0235
926.0002	1983.0026
926.0003	1996.0025
926.0004	1996.0020
927.0001	1979.2021
927.0002	1989.0029
927.0003	2011.0071
927.0004	1978.1697
927.0005	1994.0025
927.0006	1991.0225
927.0007	1990.0054
927.0008	2007.0188
927.0009	1993.NoEx93.0051
927.0010	1985.0065
928.0001	1979.2016
929.0001	1982.0233
929.0002	1982.C82.0201
930.0001	1989.0091
930.0002	1989.0133
931.0001	1985.0034
932.0001	1996.0044
932.0002	1982.C82.0140
932.0003	1984.0181
933.0001	1988.0096
933.0002	1980.C80.0382
933.0003	1977.1412
933.0004	1980.C80.0398
934.0001	1990.0261
935.0001	1973.1303
935.0002	1994.NoEx94.0009
935.0003	1981.0005
936.0001	1982.C82.0012
936.0002	1982.0019
937.0001	1994.0051
938.0001	1982.0290

938.0002	1994.0046
939.0001	1982.C82.0063
939.0002	2004.0032
939.0003	1994.0098
939.0004	2004.0048
939.0005	1980.C80.0410
939.0006	1997.0018
939.0007	1973.1243
939.0008	1973.1093
939.0009	1973.1313
939.0010	1993.0137
939.0011	1994.0066
939.0012	1980.C80.0448
939.0013	1987.0025
939.0014	1994.0068
939.0015	1980.C80.0400
939.0016	1978.1653
939.0017	1980.C80.0124
939.0018	1982.C82.0114
939.0019	1993.0076
939.0020	1993.0192
940.0001	1984.0141
940.0002	1988.0098
940.0003	2007.0111
940.0004	1978.1541
940.0005	1983.0106
940.0006	1980.C80.0390
940.0007	1994.0195
940.0008	1989.0005
940.0009	1991.0381
940.0010	2004.0047
940.0011	2005.0032
940.0012	1979.2052
940.0013	1983.0155
940.0014	1990.0254
940.0015	1991.0295
940.0016	2004.0021
940.0017	1978.1765
940.0018	2004.0039
940.0019	1983.0080
940.0020	2002.0099
940.0021	1980.C80.0455
940.0022	1978.1819
940.0023	2005.0069
940.0024	1980.C80.0389
940.0025	1980.C80.0428
940.0026	2002.0009
940.0027	1979.1851
940.0028	1988.0045
940.0029	1992.0323
940.0030	1982.0005
940.0031	1980.0016

940.0032	1993.0187
940.0033	1979.2130
940.0034	1984.0050
940.0035	1994.0177
940.0036	1980.C80.0493
940.0037	1978.1666
940.0038	1997.0033
940.0039	1973.1310
940.0040	1978.1701
940.0041	1982.0291
940.0042	2002.0004
940.0043	1994.0078
940.0044	2007.0098
940.0045	2007.0125
940.0046	1993.0181
940.0047	1983.0246
940.0048	1991.0055
941.0001	1980.C80.0081
941.0002	1990.0105
941.0003	1973.1205
941.0004	1983.0059
941.0005	1992.0228
941.0006	1980.C80.0351
941.0007	2012.0002
941.0008	1992.0205
941.0009	1979.1983
941.0010	2005.0075
941.0011	2007.0185
941.0012	1980.C80.0120
941.0013	2010.0013
941.0014	1988.0010
941.0015	1984.0055
941.0016	1989.0138
941.0017	1980.C80.0367
941.0018	1973.1276
941.0019	1973.1138
941.0020	1982.0292
941.0021	2004.0052
941.0022	1982.0877
941.0023	1992.0420
941.0024	1987.0160
941.0025	2007.0180
941.0026	1992.0155
942.0001	2007.0028
942.0002	1998.0020
942.0003	1992.0270
942.0004	2001.0012
942.0005	1991.0064
942.0006	1994.0147
942.0007	1990.0246
942.0008	1978.1754
942.0009	1998.0015

942.0010	1991.0199
942.0011	1980.C80.0243
942.0012	1989.0123
942.0013	1993.0178
942.0014	1978.1668
942.0015	1990.0064
942.0016	1998.0001
942.0017	1989.0146
942.0018	1994.0164
942.0019	1991.0375
943.0001	1973.1141
943.0002	1989.NoEx89.0008
943.0003	1994.0188
943.0004	1994.0082
943.0005	1993.0062
943.0006	1989.0149
943.0007	2007.0013
944.0001	1989.0120
944.0002	2010.0009
944.0003	1982.0277
944.0004	1980.C80.0436
944.0005	1993.0125
944.0006	1992.0185
944.0007	1990.0041
944.0008	1990.0035
944.0009	2005.0065
944.0010	1982.0289
944.0011	1991.0324
944.0012	1982.0288
944.0013	1987.0152
944.0014	1985.0271
944.0015	1980.0080
944.0016	1994.0150
944.0017	1978.1508
944.0018	1980.0028
944.0019	1997.0060
945.0001	1980.C80.0137
945.0002	1991.0047
945.0003	1982.0305
946.0001	1980.C80.0212
946.0002	2011.0097
946.0003	1984.0150
946.0004	1980.C80.0345
946.0005	1992.0171
946.0006	1980.C80.0022
946.0007	1980.0187
946.0008	1990.0100
947.0001	1980.C80.0309
947.0002	1982.C82.0023
948.0001	1973.1237
949.0001	1978.1507
950.0001	1992.NoEx92.0011

951.0001	1982.0192
952.0001	1991.0503
953.0001	1982.0550
954.0001	1991.0242
955.0001	1973.1394
956.0001	1990.0007.1
956.0002	1992.0015
956.0003	1980.0104
956.0004	1980.C80.0192
956.0005	1992.0415
956.0006	1996.0010
957.0001	1982.0601
958.0001	1990.0026
958.0002	1991.0301
958.0003	1996.0125
959.0001	1996.0109
959.0002	1989.0142
959.0003	2000.0020
960.0001	1980.C80.0010
960.0002	1982.0287
961.0001	1988.0099
961.0002	1983.0261
961.0003	2011.0175
962.0001	1979.1849
962.0002	1985.0021
962.0003	1982.C82.0145
962.0004	1979.1897
963.0001	1980.C80.0222
963.0002	2007.0227
963.0003	1991.0058
963.0004	1991.0303
963.0005	1983.0071
963.0006	1993.0105
963.0007	2007.0072
963.0008	1992.0285
963.0009	1990.0258
963.0010	1986.0028
963.0011	1982.C82.0123
963.0012	1983.0244
963.0013	1984.0155
963.0014	1990.0039
963.0015	1989.0184
963.0016	1978.1563
963.0017	1991.0177
963.0018	1980.C80.0157
963.0019	1989.0163
963.0020	1979.2064
963.0021	1980.C80.0048
963.0022	1982.0524
963.0023	1980.C80.0375
963.0024	1982.0295
963.0025	1985.0168

963.0026	1982.0522
963.0027	2002.0061
963.0028	1991.0336
963.0029	1992.0219
963.0030	1994.0044
963.0031	1999.0004
963.0032	1977.1445
963.0033	2007.0127
963.0034	2007.0050
963.0035	2007.0086
963.0036	1982.C82.0083
963.0037	1994.0206
963.0038	1997.0105
963.0039	1982.0566
963.0040	1992.0380
963.0041	1990.0020
963.0042	1982.0302
963.0043	1982.0499
963.0044	1985.0095
963.0045	2011.0122
963.0046	1980.C80.0039
963.0047	1978.1497
963.0048	1980.C80.0230
963.0049	1992.0292
963.0050	1982.0299
963.0051	1990.0263
963.0052	2002.0086
963.0053	1982.0516
963.0054	1982.0300
963.0055	1979.2013
963.0056	1984.0087
963.0057	1982.0294
963.0058	1991.0529
963.0059	1992.0324
963.0060	1991.0200
963.0061	1990.0249
963.0062	2007.0222
963.0063	1988.0035
963.0064	1979.1894
963.0065	1980.C80.0488
963.0066	2011.0106
963.0067	1982.0304
963.0068	1992.0189
963.0069	2007.0137
963.0070	1983.0271
963.0071	1979.1967
963.0072	2007.0211
963.0073	1991.0253
963.0074	1982.0091
963.0075	1991.0259
963.0076	1988.0092
963.0077	2007.0244

963.0078	2007.0120
963.0079	2007.0140
963.0080	2007.0076
963.0081	1973.1235
963.0082	1992.0193
963.0083	1982.0469
963.0084	1987.0151
963.0085	1982.0836
963.0086	1992.0375
963.0087	1992.0373
963.0088	1985.NoEx85.0026
963.0089	1991.0030
963.0090	1985.0265
963.0091	1990.0146
963.0092	1980.0049
963.0093	1985.0284
963.0094	1984.0105
963.0095	1991.0294
963.0096	2007.0147
963.0097	1987.0113
963.0098	2007.0069
963.0099	1979.2054
963.0100	1987.0129
963.0101	2011.0059
963.0102	1982.0298
963.0103	1990.0032
963.0104	1978.1512
963.0105	1980.C80.0009
963.0106	1982.0497
963.0107	1992.0391
963.0108	2007.0182
963.0109	2007.0123
963.0110	1996.0175
963.0111	1980.0175
963.0112	1993.0128
963.0113	1982.C82.0078
963.0114	1982.0303
963.0115	1978.1815
963.0116	1997.0041
963.0117	1992.0386
963.0118	1993.0115
963.0119	1982.C82.0157
963.0120	1989.0009
963.0121	2002.0112
963.0122	1992.0444
963.0123	2007.0158
963.0124	1979.2143
963.0125	1993.0117
963.0126	1989.0157
963.0127	1990.0134
963.0128	1992.0209
963.0129	1992.0009

963.0130	1990.0145
963.0131	1985.0036
963.0132	1984.0154
963.0133	2001.0023
963.0134	1994.0069
963.0135	1984.0080
963.0136	1990.0156
963.0137	1987.NoEx87.0008
963.0138	1985.0242
963.0139	1984.0076
963.0140	2001.0026
963.0141	1987.0147
963.0142	1982.0738
963.0143	1984.0048
963.0144	1978.1502
963.0145	1987.0125
963.0146	1978.1494
963.0147	1994.0140
963.0148	2007.0236
963.0149	1984.0084
963.0150	1979.2045
963.0151	1978.1801
963.0152	2007.0084
963.0153	1988.NoEx88.0011
963.0154	2002.0235
963.0155	1996.0019
963.0156	1996.0127
963.0157	2011.0109
963.0158	1992.NoEx92.0010
963.0159	1994.0099
963.0160	1987.0135
963.0161	1987.0154
963.0162	1990.0081
963.0163	1998.0021
963.0164	1971.C71.0541
963.0165	1980.C80.0135
963.0166	1979.1920
963.0167	1991.0522
963.0168	1985.0275
963.0169	1987.0081
963.0170	1992.0107
963.0171	1980.0027
963.0172	1996.0136
963.0173	1991.0222
963.0174	1990.0207
963.0175	1984.0054
963.0176	2007.0203
963.0177	1973.1190
963.0178	1987.0116
963.0179	1994.0211
963.0180	1979.2102
963.0181	1978.1620

963.0182	1985.0133
963.0183	1984.0082
963.0184	1990.0061
963.0185	1982.0494
963.0186	1985.0187
963.0187	1987.0128
963.0188	1991.0390
963.0189	1991.0389
963.0190	1987.0130
963.0191	1996.0123
963.0192	1996.0103
963.0193	1987.0002
963.0194	1993.0108
963.0195	1992.0393
963.0196	1988.0040
963.0197	1982.0085
964.0001	1978.1634
964.0002	1990.0142
965.0001	1982.C82.0172
965.0002	1990.0148
966.0001	1988.0073
966.0002	1980.C80.0296
966.0003	1990.0191
966.0004	1987.0121
966.0005	1991.0531
966.0006	2007.0239
967.0001	1990.0126
967.0002	1991.0371
967.0003	1991.0461
967.0004	1989.0115
967.0005	1982.C82.0202
967.0006	1980.C80.0104
968.0001	1990.0079
968.0002	1980.C80.0321a
968.0003	1995.0040
968.0004	1987.0141
969.0001	1982.0310
969.0002	2007.0017
969.0003	1998.0030
969.0004	1987.0140
969.0005	1991.0078
969.0006	1982.C82.0109
969.0007	1979.1995
969.0008	1980.C80.0179
969.0009	1987.0095
969.0010	1991.0507
969.0011	1982.0568
969.0012	1980.0155
969.0013	2011.0072
969.0014	1982.C82.0203
969.0015	1979.1942
969.0016	1992.0072

969.0017	1982.0307
969.0018	1990.0069
969.0019	1983.0253
969.0020	1991.0406
969.0021	1983.0270
969.0022	1982.0231
969.0023	1982.0306
969.0024	1983.0262
969.0025	1982.0308
969.0026	1992.0452
969.0027	1980.C80.0244
969.0028	1992.0388
969.0029	1980.C80.0132
969.0030	1992.0138
969.0031	2011.0113
969.0032	1992.0253
969.0033	1991.0485
969.0034	2007.0061
969.0035	1980.C80.0016
969.0036	1982.C82.0115
969.0037	1980.0106
969.0038	1982.0190
969.0039	1980.C80.0208
969.0040	2011.0063
969.0041	2011.0061
969.0042	1981.C81.0056
969.0043	2007.0251
969.0044	1991.0483
969.0045	1978.1548
969.0046	1992.0301
969.0047	2011.0085
969.0048	1978.1566
969.0049	1990.0107
969.0050	1992.0275
969.0051	1982.C82.0144
969.0052	1995.0018
969.0053	1993.0013
969.0054	1996.0122
969.0055	1980.0183
969.0056	1987.0087
969.0057	1990.0066
969.0058	1998.0016
969.0059	1973.1120
969.0060	1980.C80.0258
969.0061	1985.0123
969.0062	1991.0476
969.0063	1982.C82.0135
969.0064	1985.C85.0009
969.0065	1984.0119
969.0066	1987.0131
969.0067	1991.0478
969.0068	1990.0140

969.0069	1990.0222
969.0070	1984.0081
969.0071	1980.0129
969.0072	1990.0173
969.0073	1979.1852
969.0074	1973.1193
969.0075	1980.C80.0263
969.0076	1992.0174
969.0077	1991.0536
969.0078	1982.0534
969.0079	1979.1868
969.0080	1987.0127
969.0081	1985.0086
969.0082	1980.C80.0355
969.0083	1982.0544
969.0084	1980.C80.0189
969.0085	1980.C80.0498
969.0086	1980.0120
969.0087	1983.0264
969.0088	1985.0250
969.0089	1992.0390
969.0090	1985.0118
969.0091	1978.1717
969.0092	1990.0203
970.0001	1980.C80.0053
970.0002	1989.0159
971.0001	1980.C80.0374
972.0001	1990.0195
972.0002	1994.0129
973.0001	1991.0504
973.0002	1991.0376
974.0001	1991.0320
974.0002	1989.0054
974.0003	1982.0543
974.0004	1987.0114
974.0005	1985.0035
974.0006	1985.0199
974.0007	1991.0172
975.0001	1979.1999
975.0002	1978.1492
975.0003	1973.1217
975.0004	1980.C80.0313
975.0005	1982.0314
975.0006	1978.1546
975.0007	1982.0321
975.0008	1985.0283
975.0009	1982.C82.0211
975.0010	1982.0338
975.0011	1982.0322
976.0001	1990.0106
976.0002	1982.C82.0205
976.0003	1982.0315

976.0004	1987.0161
976.0005	1990.0023
976.0006	1982.0577
976.0007	1990.0031
976.0008	1980.C80.0388
976.0009	1992.0404
977.0001	1991.0017
977.0002	1982.0317
977.0003	1985.0057
978.0001	1982.0324
978.0002	1980.C80.0136
978.0003	1982.C82.0210
979.0001	1990.0008
980.0001	1983.0241
981.0001	1997.0014
981.0002	1988.0107
981.0003	1982.0326
981.0004	1982.0323
981.0005	1982.0320
982.0001	1988.0064
982.0002	1997.0098
982.0003	1991.0491
983.0001	1980.C80.0233
984.0001	1982.0318
984.0002	1982.0549
984.0003	1985.C85.0017
984.0004	1993.0057
984.0005	1980.0054
984.0006	1985.0152
984.0007	1982.0487
984.0008	1982.0335
984.0009	1982.0473
984.0010	1982.C82.0248
984.0011	1985.0085
984.0012	1982.0339
984.0013	1991.0215
984.0014	1987.0123
984.0015	1980.C80.0344
984.0016	1980.C80.0241
984.0017	1984.0140
984.0018	2011.0031
984.0019	1978.1752
984.0020	1980.C80.0322
984.0021	1988.0048
984.0022	1992.0347
984.0023	1980.C80.0499
984.0024	1980.C80.0187
984.0025	1985.0225
984.0026	1987.0017
984.0027	1996.0015
984.0028	1994.0088
984.0029	1980.0038

984.0030	1985.0062
984.0031	1983.0211
984.0032	2002.0137
984.0033	1988.NoEx88.0003
985.0001	1990.0236
985.0002	1982.0329
985.0003	1985.0291
985.0004	1991.0263
985.0005	1991.0309
985.0006	1995.0012
985.0007	1990.0133
985.0008	1991.0322
985.0009	1982.0343
985.0010	1992.0400
985.0011	1979.1865
985.0012	1982.0309
985.0013	1989.0151
985.0014	1990.0028
985.0015	1989.NoEx89.0005
985.0016	1980.C80.0038
985.0017	1990.0005
985.0018	1982.0590
985.0019	1985.C85.0010
985.0020	1982.0477
985.0021	2011.0002
985.0022	1982.0332
985.0023	1982.0583
985.0024	1987.0158
985.0025	1982.0559
985.0026	1982.0313
985.0027	1985.0138
985.0028	1982.0603
985.0029	1987.0133
985.0030	1987.0118
985.0031	1980.C80.0101
985.0032	1980.C80.0226
985.0033	1982.0381
985.0034	1985.0151
985.0035	1982.0330
985.0036	1991.0153
985.0037	1991.0082
985.0038	1982.0503
985.0039	1985.0131
985.0040	1995.0030
985.0041	1991.0477
985.0042	1985.C85.0008
985.0043	1991.0501
985.0044	1991.0499
985.0045	1987.0107
985.0046	1980.0051
985.0047	1982.C82.0245
985.0048	1982.0162

985.0049	1987.0136
985.0050	1997.0056
985.0051	1982.0586
985.0052	1987.0120
985.0053	1991.0115
985.0054	1985.0160
985.0055	1991.0524
986.0001	2009.0007
986.0002	2011.0083
986.0003	2011.0089
986.0004	1982.0340
986.0005	1982.0334
986.0006	2002.0117
986.0007	1980.C80.0252
986.0008	1982.C82.0025
986.0009	1996.0033
986.0010	1991.0370
986.0011	1992.NoEx92.0009
986.0012	1982.0342
986.0013	1997.0027
986.0014	1997.0119
986.0015	1993.0063
986.0016	1993.0056
986.0017	2002.0175
986.0018	1982.0510
986.0019	2002.0160
986.0020	1991.0344
986.0021	1994.0235
986.0022	1982.0461
986.0023	1982.C82.0204
986.0024	1996.0041
986.0025	1996.0027
986.0026	2002.0060
986.0027	2002.0202
986.0028	2002.0274
986.0029	2002.0157
986.0030	1980.C80.0203
986.0031	1996.0111
986.0032	2002.0129
986.0033	1980.C80.0219
986.0034	1993.0121
986.0035	2002.0125
987.0001	1980.C80.0302
987.0002	2011.0147
987.0003	1978.1561
987.0004	1996.0171
987.0005	1980.C80.0176
987.0006	1982.0319
987.0007	1980.C80.0182
987.0008	1982.C82.0206
987.0009	2009.0016
987.0010	1982.0337

987.0011	1982.0327
987.0012	1991.0053
987.0013	1997.0034
987.0014	1982.C82.0208
987.0015	1991.0178
987.0016	1980.C80.0183
987.0017	1991.0091
987.0018	1995.0026
987.0019	1982.0633
987.0020	1982.0325
987.0021	1982.0336
987.0022	1982.C82.0207
987.0023	1982.C82.0212
987.0024	1991.0470
987.0025	1982.0341
987.0026	1982.0316
987.0027	1982.0328
987.0028	1989.0067
987.0029	1983.0049
987.0030	2007.0212
987.0031	1983.0013
987.0032	1991.0412
987.0033	1982.0311
987.0034	1980.C80.0015
987.0035	2007.0187
987.0036	1991.0475
987.0037	1996.0083
987.0038	1982.C82.0209
987.0039	1986.0042
987.0040	1982.0312
987.0041	1982.0331
987.0042	2011.0022
987.0043	2008.0010
987.0044	1980.C80.0119
987.0045	1996.0131
987.0046	1982.0557
987.0047	1982.C82.0122
987.0048	1996.0101
987.0049	1993.0140
987.0050	1985.0102
987.0051	1985.0103
987.0052	1980.C80.0317
987.0053	1996.0024
987.0054	1985.0261
987.0055	1996.0034
987.0056	1996.0163
987.0057	1978.1549
988.0001	1985.0119
988.0002	1983.0032
988.0003	1983.0096
988.0004	1978.1490
988.0005	1991.0264

988.0006	1992.0026
988.0007	1991.0533
988.0008	1994.0238
989.0001	1980.C80.0277
990.0001	1998.0026
990.0002	1992.0264
991.0001	1982.0591
992.0001	1982.0531
992.0002	1982.0370
992.0003	1982.0371
992.0004	1982.0369
992.0005	1982.0356
992.0006	1982.0491
992.0007	1982.0482
993.0001	1980.C80.0221
994.0001	1988.0066
994.0002	1982.0358
994.0003	1980.C80.0184
995.0001	1983.0119
995.0002	1989.0179
995.0003	1982.C82.0214
995.0004	1980.C80.0294
995.0005	2010.0047
995.0006	1982.0350
995.0007	1982.0592
995.0008	1991.0494
995.0009	1984.0060
995.0010	1982.0234
995.0011	2011.0150
995.0012	1983.0226
995.0013	1979.1903
995.0014	1985.0125
995.0015	1980.C80.0194
995.0016	1982.C82.0039
995.0017	1978.1760
995.0018	1980.C80.0354
995.0019	1984.0135
995.0020	1983.0144
995.0021	1988.0007
995.0022	2011.0123
995.0023	1978.1540
996.0001	1982.C82.0178
996.0002	1994.0124
996.0003	1991.0514
996.0004	1989.0131
996.0005	1997.0069
997.0001	1982.0366
997.0002	1991.0077
997.0003	1979.1922
997.0004	1991.0525
997.0005	1991.0154
997.0006	1991.0513

997.0007	1982.0348
997.0008	1982.0479
997.0009	1982.C82.0213
997.0010	1991.0532
997.0011	1982.0357
997.0012	1982.0560
997.0013	1991.0515
997.0014	1991.0521
997.0015	1980.C80.0108
997.0016	1983.0205
997.0017	1979.1934
997.0018	1982.0353
997.0019	1982.0483
997.0020	1982.0500
997.0021	1991.0511
997.0022	1982.C82.0215
997.0023	1991.0516
997.0024	1982.0359
997.0025	1982.0344
997.0026	1982.0352
997.0027	1991.0510
997.0028	1982.0476
997.0029	1982.0367
997.0030	1982.C82.0244
997.0031	1982.0364
997.0032	1982.0495
997.0033	1991.0537
997.0034	1982.0580
997.0035	1982.0355
997.0036	1982.0545
997.0037	1982.0345
997.0038	1982.0554
997.0039	1982.0368
997.0040	1982.0587
997.0041	1982.0349
997.0042	1982.0363
997.0043	1982.0468
997.0044	1982.0362
997.0045	1982.0347
997.0046	1982.0538
997.0047	1982.0360
997.0048	1982.0365
997.0049	1982.0481
997.0050	1982.0346
997.0051	1982.0361
997.0052	1982.0533
997.0053	1982.0351
997.0054	1982.0582
997.0055	1978.1759
997.0056	1980.C80.0229
997.0057	1980.C80.0177
997.0058	1980.C80.0162

997.0059	2011.0155
997.0060	2005.0005
997.0061	1991.0482
997.0062	1980.C80.0163
997.0063	1991.0100
997.0064	1980.C80.0115
997.0065	1985.0071
997.0066	1984.0086
997.0067	1973.1142
997.0068	1989.0158
997.0068	1985.0105
997.0069	1980.0075
998.0001	1982.0542
998.0002	1992.0176
998.0003	1991.0530
999.0001	2009.0015
999.0002	2003.0012
999.0003	1985.0012
999.0004	1991.0096
999.0005	1990.0104
999.0006	1982.0165
999.0007	1991.0026
999.0008	1984.0103
999.0009	2002.0132
999.0010	1990.0187
999.0011	2011.0086
999.0012	2000.0004
999.0013	1982.0791
999.0014	1991.0011
999.0015	1987.0126
999.0016	1992.0258
999.0017	1992.0255
999.0018	1980.0076
999.0019	1978.1522
999.0020	2002.0201
999.0021	1985.0023
999.0022	2002.0243
999.0023	2002.0216
999.0024	1987.0108
999.0025	1980.C80.0002
999.0026	1979.1952
999.0027	1988.0050
999.0028	1973.1079
999.0029	1983.0239
999.0030	1978.1496
999.0031	1982.C82.0073
999.0032	1990.0272
999.0033	1994.0248
999.0034	2007.0064
999.0035	1985.0115
999.0036	2004.0017
999.0037	1990.0215

999.0038	1982.0333
999.0039	1992.0099
999.0040	1982.0662
999.0041	1980.0107
999.0042	1991.0498
999.0043	2002.0033
999.0044	1982.0146
999.0045	1982.0854
999.0046	1991.0471
999.0047	1985.0070
999.0048	1982.0872
999.0049	1982.0736
999.0050	1995.0028
999.0051	2002.0238
999.0052	2011.0062
999.0053	1984.0110
999.0054	1990.0029
999.0055	1987.0112
999.0056	1990.0188
999.0057	1991.0495
999.0058	1982.0695
999.0059	1991.0119
999.0060	1987.0106
999.0061	1982.0203
999.0062	1990.0004
999.0063	1991.0466
999.0064	1982.0086
999.0065	1987.0117
999.0066	2011.0161
999.0067	2002.0155
999.0068	1991.0101
999.0069	1982.0717
999.0070	1985.0223
999.0071	1992.0186
999.0072	1992.0406
999.0073	1991.0472
999.0074	1985.0237
999.0075	1982.0096
999.0076	1985.0069
999.0077	1982.0529
999.0078	1984.0025
999.0079	1982.0826
999.0080	1992.0295
999.0081	1995.0005
999.0082	1982.0865
999.0083	1982.0354
999.0084	1985.0236
999.0085	1980.C80.0054
999.0086	1991.0278
999.0087	2011.0167
999.0088	1982.0509
999.0089	2002.0260

999.0090	1980.C80.0199
999.0091	1988.0036
999.0092	1982.0511
999.0093	1985.0130
999.0094	1989.NoEx89.0004
999.0095	1980.0052
999.0096	1985.0296
999.0097	1980.C80.0170
999.0098	1982.0556
999.0099	1983.0186
999.0100	1994.0152
999.0101	1990.0172
999.0102	1991.0223
999.0103	1982.0764
999.0104	1980.C80.0312
999.0105	2007.0238
999.0106	2002.0081
999.0107	2011.0144
999.0108	1982.0372
999.0109	1982.0589
999.0110	2002.0249
999.0111	1982.0539
999.0112	1982.0519
999.0113	1994.0091
999.0114	1987.0099
999.0115	1985.0318
999.0116	1980.C80.0051
999.0117	1999.0005
999.0118	1994.0137
999.0119	1992.0356
999.0120	1992.0327
999.0121	1990.0192
999.0122	2011.0128
999.0123	1985.0058
999.0124	1990.0220
999.0125	1994.0234
999.0126	1979.1841
999.0127	1990.0162
999.0128	1982.C82.0019
999.0129	1982.0150
999.0130	1982.0697
999.0131	1988.0052
999.0132	2002.0153
999.0133	1979.1866
999.0134	2002.0269
999.0135	1985.0310
999.0136	1995.0038
999.0137	1985.0087
999.0138	2010.0043
999.0139	1980.C80.0305
999.0140	2011.0183
999.0141	1991.0500

999.0142	1980.C80.0330
999.0143	1997.0064
999.0144	2002.0236
999.0145	1986.0072
999.0146	1979.1958
999.0147	1982.0719
999.0148	1979.1959
999.0149	1990.0153
999.0150	1982.C82.0028
999.0151	1991.0127
999.0152	1980.C80.0359
999.0153	1991.0441
999.0154	1987.0028
999.0155	1985.0316
999.0156	1985.0277
999.0157	1994.0249
999.0158	1991.0102
999.0159	1982.0653
999.0160	1982.0540
999.0161	1980.C80.0206
999.0162	2002.0300
999.0163	1982.0558
999.0164	2002.0199
999.0165	2002.0045
999.0166	1991.0338
999.0167	1979.1972
999.0168	2002.0226
999.0169	2002.0229
999.0170	1990.0010
999.0171	1987.0041
999.0172	1997.0054
999.0173	2002.0066
999.0174	1990.0218
999.0175	1990.0024
999.0176	1988.0024
999.0177	1988.0008
999.0178	1991.0365
999.0179	1990.0190
999.0180	1991.0340
999.0181	1985.0101
999.0182	1990.0230
999.0183	1988.0023
999.0184	1982.0548
999.0185	1980.0037
999.0186	1984.0096
999.0187	1989.0108
999.0188	1993.0103
999.0189	1990.0130
999.0190	1982.0515
999.0191	1984.0129
999.0192	1982.0579
999.0193	1982.0664

999.0194	1987.0089
999.0195	1982.0742
999.0196	1993.0119
999.0197	1987.0009
999.0198	1983.0225
999.0199	2002.0242
999.0200	1982.0696
999.0201	1987.0139
999.0202	1982.0480
999.0203	1994.0214
999.0204	2002.0032
999.0205	1980.C80.0333
999.0206	2002.0217
999.0207	1984.0058
999.0208	1980.C80.0209
999.0209	2002.0046
999.0210	1982.0720
999.0211	1994.0092
999.0212	1993.0060
999.0213	1991.0413
999.0214	1987.0110
999.0215	1998.0028
999.0216	1982.0562
999.0217	1994.0071
999.0218	1987.0098
999.0219	2002.0187
999.0220	1997.0051
999.0221	1991.0488
999.0222	2002.0208
999.0223	1982.0673
999.0224	1980.C80.0188
999.0225	1985.NoEx85.0023
999.0226	1997.0081
999.0227	1982.0732
999.0228	1992.0013
999.0229	1985.0060
999.0230	1989.0069
999.0231	1996.0017
999.0232	1996.0070
999.0233	1982.0700
999.0234	1980.C80.0040
999.0235	2002.0285
999.0236	2002.0227
999.0237	1994.0093
999.0238	1991.0490
999.0239	1997.0058
999.0240	1982.0710
999.0241	1982.0768
999.0242	1979.1854
999.0243	1990.0040
999.0244	2011.0132
999.0245	1992.0254

999.0246	1982.0688
999.0247	1982.0828
999.0248	1991.0051
999.0249	1991.0099
999.0250	1983.0198
999.0251	1994.0196
999.0252	1982.C82.0040
999.0253	1991.0399
999.0254	2002.0240
999.0255	1980.0064
999.0256	1996.0119
999.0257	1990.0217
999.0258	1991.0502
999.0259	1985.0126
999.0260	1982.0754
999.0261	1980.C80.0161
999.0262	1980.0098
999.0263	1992.0360
999.0264	2002.0188
999.0265	1982.0220
999.0266	2002.0069
999.0267	2002.0073
999.0268	1982.0074
999.0269	1991.0484
999.0270	2007.0053
999.0271	1985.0188
999.0272	1980.C80.0204
999.0273	1982.0595
999.0274	1996.0002
999.0275	1997.0043
999.0276	1980.C80.0196
999.0277	1982.0507
999.0278	2002.0063
999.0279	1982.0621
999.0280	1990.0149
999.0281	1982.0508
999.0282	1982.0676
999.0283	1982.0486
999.0284	1989.0166
999.0285	1982.0569
999.0286	1989.0139
999.0287	1982.0693
999.0288	1982.0561
999.0289	1992.0089
999.0290	1993.0029
999.0291	1991.0230
999.0292	1996.0071
999.0293	1980.0073
999.0294	2002.0263
999.0295	1996.0057
999.0296	1987.0001
999.0297	1983.0272

999.0298	1982.0594
999.0299	1989.0078
999.0300	1994.0021
999.0301	1982.0761
999.0302	1982.0760
999.0303	1983.0102
999.0304	1996.0032
999.0305	1997.0065
999.0306	1983.0042
999.0307	1992.0387
999.0308	1980.0101
999.0309	1975.C75.0001
1000.0001	1996.0016
1000.0002	1980.C80.0144
1000.0003	1982.0565
1000.0004	1982.0726
1001.0001	1976.0001
1001.0002	1993.NoEx93.0053
1001.0003	1993.NoEx93.0065
1001.0004	1994.NoEx94.0002
1001.0005	1994.NoEx94.0007
1001.0006	1977.1422
1001.0007	1977.1431
1001.0008	1977.1432
1001.0009	1977.1437
1001.0010	1973.1085
1001.0011	1986.0019
1001.0012	1986.0047
1001.0013	1986.0048
1001.0014	1986.0050
1001.0015	1986.0052
1001.0016	1986.0056
1001.0017	1986.0057
1001.0018	1986.0064
1001.0019	1986.0067
1001.0020	1986.0074
1001.0021	1984.0151
1001.0022	1984.0166
1001.0023	1981.C81.0064
1001.0024	1998.0022
1001.0025	2002.0089
1001.0026	2007.0247
1001.0027	1988.NoEx88.0006
1001.0028	1984.0122
1001.0029	2011.0186
1001.0030	1982.0095
1001.0031	1982.0131
1001.0032	1980.0035
1001.0033	1979.2076
1001.0034	2011.0052
1001.0035	2002.0095
1001.0036	2004.0037

1001.0037	2004.0038
1001.0038	2004.0042
1001.0039	2004.0044
1001.0040	2004.0051
1001.0041	2004.0053
1001.0042	2005.0078
1001.0043	1980.C80.0079
1001.0044	1980.C80.0323
1001.0045	1980.0177
1001.0046	1980.0185
1001.0047	1980.0189
1001.0048	1980.0190
1001.0049	1980.0198
1001.0050	1980.0200
1001.0051	1980.0205
1001.0052	1980.0213
1001.0053	1980.0171
1001.0054	1980.C80.0500
1001.0055	1980.0063
1001.0056	1997.0134
1001.0057	1980.C80.0303
1001.0058	1982.0003
1001.0059	1982.0016
1001.0060	1982.0017
1001.0061	1982.0022
1001.0062	1982.0023
1001.0063	1982.C82.0068
1001.0064	1982.C82.0074
1001.0065	1982.C82.0075
1001.0066	1983.0190
1001.0067	1983.0200
1001.0068	1983.0228
1001.0069	1983.0171
1001.0070	1983.0172
1001.0071	1985.0008
1001.0072	1985.0048
1001.0073	1985.0134
1001.0074	1985.0145
1001.0075	1985.0286
1001.0076	1988.0108
1001.0077	1991.0420
1001.0078	1980.0102
1001.0079	1980.0108
1001.0080	1980.C80.0287
1001.0081	1982.0024
1001.0082	1982.0035
1001.0083	1985.0159
1001.0084	1985.0166
1001.0085	1985.0290
1001.0086	1985.0317
1001.0087	1987.0006
1001.0088	1988.0013

1001.0089	1988.0027
1001.0090	1991.0348
1001.0091	1992.0086
1001.0092	2002.0021
1001.0093	1984.0009
1001.0094	1984.0010
1001.0095	1984.0016
1001.0096	1984.0034
1001.0097	1984.0077
1001.0098	1984.0090
1001.0099	1985.0255
1001.0100	1985.0269
1001.0101	1987.0144
1001.0102	1987.0162
1001.0103	1989.0073
1001.0104	1989.0095
1001.0105	1978.1515
1001.0106	1978.1521
1001.0107	1978.1572
1001.0108	1979.1899
1001.0109	1979.1906
1001.0110	1979.1956
1001.0111	1980.0003
1001.0112	1980.0007
1001.0113	1980.0113
1001.0114	1980.0119
1001.0115	1980.C80.0306
1001.0116	1980.C80.0321b
1001.0117	1982.C82.0176
1001.0118	1989.0116
1001.0119	1989.0148
1001.0120	1990.0033
1001.0121	1990.0047
1001.0122	1990.0072
1001.0123	1990.0073
1001.0124	1990.0078
1001.0125	1990.0085
1001.0126	1990.0086
1001.0127	1990.0096
1001.0128	1990.0097
1001.0129	1990.0116
1001.0130	1990.0159
1001.0131	1990.0279
1001.0132	1990.0301
1001.0133	1991.0134
1001.0134	1991.0142
1001.0135	1991.0148
1001.0136	1991.0175
1001.0137	1991.0029
1001.0138	1991.0060
1001.0139	1991.0071
1001.0140	1991.0422

1001.0141	1992.0352
1001.0142	1992.0399
1001.0143	1993.0049
1001.0144	1993.0051
1001.0145	1993.0052
1001.0146	1992.0201.3
1001.0147	1994.0073
1001.0148	1994.0107
1001.0149	1996.0154
1001.0150	1982.0128
1001.0151	1982.0518
1001.0152	1982.0523
1001.0153	1982.0466
1001.0154	1990.0087
1001.0155	1994.0016
1001.0156	1994.0220
1001.0157	1983.0100
1001.0158	1983.0177
1001.0159	1989.0024
1001.0160	1973.1189
1001.0161	2007.0057
1001.0162	2007.0004
1001.0163	2007.0011
1001.0164	2007.0012
1001.0165	2007.0014
1001.0166	2007.0018
1001.0167	2007.0019
1001.0168	2007.0029
1001.0169	2007.0030
1001.0170	2007.0034
1001.0171	2007.0036
1001.0172	2007.0046
1001.0173	2007.0047
1001.0174	2007.0088
1001.0175	2007.0090
1001.0176	2007.0189
1001.0177	2007.0207
1001.0178	2007.0220
1001.0179	2005.0034
1001.0180	2005.0041
1001.0181	1982.0182
1001.0182	1982.0248
1001.0183	1982.0185
1001.0184	1982.0026
1001.0185	1982.0036
1001.0186	1982.0159
1001.0187	1982.C82.0094
1001.0188	1982.0171
1001.0189	1981.0004
1001.0190	2011.0023
1001.0191	2011.0136
1001.0192	2011.0108

1001.0193	2011.0068
1001.0194	1979.1898
1001.0195	1992.0007
1001.0196	1988.0110
1001.0197	1984.0061
1001.0198	1984.0133
1001.0199	1984.0039
1001.0200	1984.0104
1001.0201	1984.0131
1001.0202	1984.0130
1001.0203	1983.0035
1001.0204	1973.1173
1001.0205	1973.1086
1001.0206	1973.1219
1001.0207	1976.0008
1001.0208	1976.0006
1001.0209	1985.NoEx85.0022
1001.0210	1978.1706
1001.0211	1978.1696
1001.0212	1978.1687
1001.0213	1978.1672
1001.0214	1978.1461
1002.0001	1986.0055
1002.0002	1986.0061
1002.0003	1986.0065
1002.0004	1986.0066
1002.0005	1984.0183
1002.0006	1983.0165
1002.0007	1983.0194
1002.0008	1978.1462
1002.0009	1978.1662
1002.0010	1978.1674
1002.0011	1978.1680
1002.0012	1978.1689
1002.0013	1978.1690
1002.0014	1978.1691
1002.0015	1978.1692
1002.0016	1978.1709
1002.0017	1978.1710
1002.0018	1973.1274
1002.0019	1987.NoEx87.0006
1002.0020	1985.NoEx85.0037
1002.0021	1985.NoEx85.0042
1002.0022	1978.1462a
1002.0023	1973.NoEx.1973.4
1002.0024	2010.0050
1002.0025	1973.1174
1002.0026	1973.1211
1002.0027	1973.1107
1002.0028	1984.0115
1002.0029	1988.0101
1002.0030	1989.0016

1002.0031	1989.0028
1002.0032	1989.0031
1002.0033	1989.0036
1002.0034	1989.0041
1002.0035	1989.0044
1002.0036	1989.0047
1002.0037	1989.0051
1002.0038	1989.0052
1002.0039	1989.0060
1002.0040	1991.0023
1002.0041	1991.0056
1002.0042	1991.0456
1002.0043	1991.0469
1002.0044	1991.0508
1002.0045	1991.0523
1002.0046	1992.0006
1002.0047	1992.0027
1002.0048	1992.0045
1002.0049	1999.0036
1002.0050	2001.0027
1002.0051	1979.1860
1002.0052	2011.0060
1002.0053	2011.0073
1002.0054	2011.0077
1002.0055	2011.0079
1002.0056	2011.0112
1002.0057	2011.0116
1002.0058	2011.0119
1002.0059	2011.0120
1002.0060	2011.0133
1002.0061	2011.0156
1002.0062	2011.0160
1002.0063	2011.0172
1002.0064	2011.0174
1002.0065	2011.0181
1002.0066	2011.0038
1002.0067	2002.0013
1002.0068	2002.0071
1002.0069	2002.0101
1002.0070	2002.0107
1002.0071	2002.0177
1002.0072	2004.0050
1002.0073	2005.0062
1002.0074	2005.0063
1002.0075	2005.0066
1002.0076	2005.0067
1002.0077	2005.0077
1002.0078	2005.0080
1002.0079	1980.0088
1002.0080	1980.C80.0255
1002.0081	1980.0193
1002.0082	1980.C80.0342

1002.0083	1980.C80.0380
1002.0084	1980.0031
1002.0085	1997.0104
1002.0086	1997.0110
1002.0087	1997.0114
1002.0088	1997.0116
1002.0089	1997.0131
1002.0090	1997.0132
1002.0091	1997.0135
1002.0092	1996.0132
1002.0093	1996.0133
1002.0094	1998.0060
1002.0095	1998.0062
1002.0096	2003.0014
1002.0097	2009.0001
1002.0098	1980.0116
1002.0099	1980.0117
1002.0100	1982.0002
1002.0101	1982.0033
1002.0102	1982.0064
1002.0103	1982.0068
1002.0104	1982.0106
1002.0105	1982.0117
1002.0106	1982.0125
1002.0107	1982.0126
1002.0108	1982.0129
1002.0109	1982.0136
1002.0110	1982.0139
1002.0111	1982.0151
1002.0112	1982.0154
1002.0113	1982.0166
1002.0114	1982.0167
1002.0115	1983.0018
1002.0116	1983.0019
1002.0117	1983.0181
1002.0118	1983.0182
1002.0119	1983.0199
1002.0120	1983.0220
1002.0121	1983.0224
1002.0122	1983.0242
1002.0123	1983.0245
1002.0124	1983.0258
1002.0125	1983.0269
1002.0126	1983.0041
1002.0127	1983.0055
1002.0128	1983.0132
1002.0129	1983.0173
1002.0130	1983.0233
1002.0131	1985.0045
1002.0132	1985.0046
1002.0133	1985.0049
1002.0134	1985.0052

1002.0135	1985.0053
1002.0136	1985.0067
1002.0137	1985.0072
1002.0138	1985.0078
1002.0139	1985.0080
1002.0140	1985.0081
1002.0141	1985.0082
1002.0142	1985.0084
1002.0143	1985.0088
1002.0144	1985.0089
1002.0145	1985.0099
1002.0146	1985.0109
1002.0147	1985.0111
1002.0148	1985.0120
1002.0149	1985.0142
1002.0150	1985.0153
1002.0151	1985.0282
1002.0152	1985.0288
1002.0153	1985.0293
1002.0154	1985.0295
1002.0155	1987.0061
1002.0156	1987.0067
1002.0157	1987.0068
1002.0158	1987.0073
1002.0159	1990.0171
1002.0160	1990.0183
1002.0161	1990.0231
1002.0162	1990.0264
1002.0163	1990.0289
1002.0164	1991.0418
1002.0165	1991.0440
1002.0166	1991.0443
1002.0167	1992.0102
1002.0168	1997.0091
1002.0169	1997.0094
1002.0170	1998.0033
1002.0171	1980.C80.0285
1002.0172	1982.0088
1002.0173	1982.0196
1002.0174	1982.0197
1002.0175	1982.0211
1002.0176	1982.0219
1002.0177	1982.0221
1002.0178	1982.C82.0014
1002.0179	1983.0054
1002.0180	1983.0134
1002.0181	1985.0155
1002.0182	1985.0157
1002.0183	1985.0163
1002.0184	1985.0298
1002.0185	1985.0308
1002.0186	1985.0321

1002.0187	1987.0008
1002.0188	1987.0032
1002.0189	1987.0035
1002.0190	1987.0039
1002.0191	1988.0001
1002.0192	1988.0006
1002.0193	1988.0009
1002.0194	1988.0012
1002.0195	1988.0014
1002.0196	1988.0015
1002.0197	1988.0016
1002.0198	1988.0020
1002.0199	1988.0022
1002.0200	1988.0039
1002.0201	1988.0041
1002.0202	1988.0044
1002.0203	1988.0047
1002.0204	1988.0054
1002.0205	1988.0057
1002.0206	1988.0060
1002.0207	1988.0079
1002.0208	1989.0182
1002.0209	1989.0183
1002.0210	1991.0317
1002.0211	1991.0343
1002.0212	1991.0345
1002.0213	1991.0347
1002.0214	1991.0366
1002.0215	1991.0382
1002.0216	1991.0451
1002.0217	1991.0453
1002.0218	1991.0462
1002.0219	1991.0543
1002.0220	1992.0016
1002.0221	1992.0043
1002.0222	1992.0065
1002.0223	1992.0097
1002.0224	2002.0007
1002.0225	2002.0018
1002.0226	2002.0049
1002.0227	2002.0050
1002.0228	2002.0064
1002.0229	2002.0169
1002.0230	2002.0234
1002.0231	2002.0259
1002.0232	2002.0297
1002.0233	1984.0017
1002.0234	1984.0134
1002.0235	1985.0212
1002.0236	1985.0213
1002.0237	1985.0219
1002.0238	1985.0224
1002.0239	1985.0227
1002.0240	1985.0230
1002.0241	1985.0231
1002.0242	1985.0235
1002.0243	1985.0252
1002.0244	1985.0256
1002.0245	1985.0258
1002.0246	1985.0259
1002.0247	1985.0266
1002.0248	1985.0267
1002.0249	1985.0273
1002.0250	1987.0092
1002.0251	1987.0119
1002.0252	1986.0045
1002.0253	1989.0065
1002.0254	1989.0074
1002.0255	1989.0076
1002.0256	1992.0110
1002.0257	1992.0127
1002.0258	1992.0214
1002.0259	1993.0014
1002.0260	1993.0022
1002.0261	1993.0030
1002.0262	1988.0071
1002.0263	1988.0072
1002.0264	1988.0080
1002.0265	1978.1487
1002.0266	1978.1493
1002.0267	1978.1501
1002.0268	1978.1504
1002.0269	1978.1505
1002.0270	1978.1519
1002.0271	1978.1536
1002.0272	1978.1552
1002.0273	1978.1553
1002.0274	1978.1564
1002.0275	1978.1565
1002.0276	1978.1577
1002.0277	1978.1585
1002.0278	1978.1591
1002.0279	1978.1716
1002.0280	1978.1721
1002.0281	1978.1734
1002.0282	1978.1740
1002.0283	1978.1782
1002.0284	1979.1836
1002.0285	1979.1843
1002.0286	1979.1874
1002.0287	1979.1946
1002.0288	1979.2006
1002.0289	1979.2008
1002.0290	1979.2012
1002.0291	1979.2022
1002.0292	1979.2031
1002.0293	1979.2032
1002.0294	1979.2033
1002.0295	1979.2034
1002.0296	1979.2035
1002.0297	1979.2036
1002.0298	1979.2037
1002.0299	1979.2038
1002.0300	1979.2039
1002.0301	1979.2042
1002.0302	1979.2043
1002.0303	1979.2044
1002.0304	1979.2046
1002.0305	1979.2047
1002.0306	1979.2049
1002.0307	1979.2050
1002.0308	1979.2055
1002.0309	1979.2059
1002.0310	1979.2060
1002.0311	1979.2061
1002.0312	1979.2062
1002.0313	1979.2078
1002.0314	1979.2079
1002.0315	1979.2080
1002.0316	1979.2084
1002.0317	1979.2086
1002.0318	1979.2090
1002.0319	1979.2103
1002.0320	1979.2106
1002.0321	1979.2134
1002.0322	1979.2135
1002.0323	1979.2139
1002.0324	1979.2142
1002.0325	1979.2148
1002.0326	1979.2153
1002.0327	1980.0002
1002.0328	1980.0006
1002.0329	1980.0023
1002.0330	1980.0043
1002.0331	1980.0056
1002.0332	1980.0058
1002.0333	1980.0079
1002.0334	1980.0140
1002.0335	1980.0142
1002.0336	1980.C80.0156
1002.0337	1980.C80.0159
1002.0338	1980.C80.0201
1002.0339	1980.C80.0245
1002.0340	1982.0101
1002.0341	1989.0092
1002.0342	1989.0093
1002.0343	1989.0099
1002.0344	1989.0101
1002.0345	1989.0102
1002.0346	1989.0113
1002.0347	1989.0119
1002.0348	1989.0145
1002.0349	1989.0153
1002.0350	1989.0154
1002.0351	1989.0155
1002.0352	1989.0156
1002.0353	1989.0176
1002.0354	1989.0185
1002.0355	1990.0003
1002.0356	1990.0007.2
1002.0357	1990.0030
1002.0358	1990.0036
1002.0359	1990.0037
1002.0360	1990.0042
1002.0361	1990.0044
1002.0362	1990.0045
1002.0363	1990.0056
1002.0364	1990.0057
1002.0365	1990.0075
1002.0366	1990.0080
1002.0367	1990.0109
1002.0368	1990.0110
1002.0369	1990.0113
1002.0370	1990.0117
1002.0371	1990.0132
1002.0372	1990.0139
1002.0373	1990.0143
1002.0374	1990.0151
1002.0375	1990.0152
1002.0376	1990.0155
1002.0377	1990.0163
1002.0378	1990.0164
1002.0379	1990.0165
1002.0380	1990.0167
1002.0381	1990.0174
1002.0382	1990.0175
1002.0383	1990.0180
1002.0384	1990.0234
1002.0385	1990.0238
1002.0386	1990.0239
1002.0387	1990.0245
1002.0388	1990.0259
1002.0389	1990.0260
1002.0390	1990.0267
1002.0391	1990.0273
1002.0392	1990.0274
1002.0393	1990.0280
1002.0394	1990.0285
1002.0395	1990.0286
1002.0396	1990.0296
1002.0397	1990.0305
1002.0398	1991.0117
1002.0399	1991.0121
1002.0400	1991.0129
1002.0401	1991.0130
1002.0402	1991.0136
1002.0403	1991.0144
1002.0404	1991.0146
1002.0405	1991.0150
1002.0406	1991.0151
1002.0407	1991.0155
1002.0408	1991.0157
1002.0409	1991.0162
1002.0410	1991.0170
1002.0411	1991.0184
1002.0412	1991.0186
1002.0413	1991.0187
1002.0414	1991.0189
1002.0415	1991.0191
1002.0416	1991.0194
1002.0417	1991.0205
1002.0418	1991.0209
1002.0419	1991.0214
1002.0420	1991.0217
1002.0421	1991.0220
1002.0422	1991.0237
1002.0423	1991.0239
1002.0424	1991.0241
1002.0425	1991.0243
1002.0426	1991.0245
1002.0427	1991.0248
1002.0428	1991.0254
1002.0429	1991.0266
1002.0430	1991.0268
1002.0431	1991.0269
1002.0432	1991.0272
1002.0433	1991.0290
1002.0434	1991.0292
1002.0435	1992.0200
1002.0436	1992.0143.2
1002.0437	1991.0032
1002.0438	1991.0034
1002.0439	1991.0036
1002.0440	1991.0044
1002.0441	1991.0045
1002.0442	1991.0050
1002.0443	1991.0080
1002.0444	1991.0081
1002.0445	1991.0085
1002.0446	1991.0297

1002.0447	1991.0298
1002.0448	1991.0308
1002.0449	1991.0328
1002.0450	1991.0335
1002.0451	1991.0423
1002.0452	1991.0547
1002.0453	1991.0549
1002.0454	1992.0098
1002.0455	1992.0100
1002.0456	1992.0105
1002.0457	1992.0175
1002.0458	1992.0184
1002.0459	1992.0195
1002.0460	1992.0207
1002.0461	1992.0213
1002.0462	1992.0233
1002.0463	1992.0268
1002.0464	1992.0273
1002.0465	1992.0289
1002.0466	1992.0298
1002.0467	1992.0320
1002.0468	1992.0350
1002.0469	1992.0353
1002.0470	1992.0358
1002.0471	1992.0363
1002.0472	1992.0365
1002.0473	1992.0366
1002.0474	1992.0376
1002.0475	1992.0378
1002.0476	1992.0379
1002.0477	1992.0384
1002.0478	1992.0389
1002.0479	1992.0396
1002.0480	1992.0402
1002.0481	1992.0409
1002.0482	1992.0413
1002.0483	1992.0418
1002.0484	1992.0419
1002.0485	1992.0423
1002.0486	1992.0426
1002.0487	1992.0427
1002.0488	1992.0429
1002.0489	1992.0432
1002.0490	1992.0433
1002.0491	1992.0434
1002.0492	1992.0438
1002.0493	1992.0439
1002.0494	1992.0441
1002.0495	1992.0443
1002.0496	1992.0455
1002.0497	1993.0036
1002.0498	1993.0041
1002.0499	1993.0043
1002.0500	1993.0045
1002.0501	1993.0054.2
1002.0502	1993.0054.3
1002.0503	1993.0055
1002.0504	1993.0059
1002.0505	1993.0067
1002.0506	1993.0071
1002.0507	1993.0072
1002.0508	1993.0077
1002.0509	1993.0078
1002.0510	1993.0083
1002.0511	1993.0084
1002.0512	1993.0091
1002.0513	1992.0315.2
1002.0514	1992.0162
1002.0515	1992.0167
1002.0516	1993.0104
1002.0517	1993.0110
1002.0518	1993.0116
1002.0519	1993.0118
1002.0520	1993.0179
1002.0521	1994.0001
1002.0522	1994.0042
1002.0523	1994.0070
1002.0524	1994.0090
1002.0525	1994.0132
1002.0526	1994.0133
1002.0527	1994.0135
1002.0528	1994.0136
1002.0529	1994.0141
1002.0530	1994.0142
1002.0531	1994.0149
1002.0532	1994.0151
1002.0533	1994.0153
1002.0534	1994.0154
1002.0535	1994.0179
1002.0536	1994.0180
1002.0537	1994.0190
1002.0538	1994.0199
1002.0539	1994.0212
1002.0540	1994.0215
1002.0541	1994.0216
1002.0542	1994.0227
1002.0543	1994.0246
1002.0544	1994.0030
1002.0545	1996.0114
1002.0546	1979.1960
1002.0547	1982.C82.0037
1002.0548	1982.0573
1002.0549	1982.0832
1002.0550	1982.0694
1002.0551	1982.0563
1002.0552	1982.0498
1002.0553	1982.0747
1002.0554	1982.0464
1002.0555	1982.0521
1002.0556	1982.0467
1002.0557	1982.0470
1002.0558	1982.0646
1002.0559	1982.0843
1002.0560	1982.0512
1002.0561	1982.0861
1002.0562	1982.0645
1002.0563	1982.0766
1002.0564	1982.0773
1002.0565	1982.0842
1002.0566	1982.0678
1002.0567	1982.0805
1002.0568	1983.0017
1002.0569	1983.0095
1002.0570	1989.0124
1002.0571	1992.0101
1002.0572	1992.0141
1002.0573	1992.0223
1002.0574	1992.0257
1002.0575	1993.0153
1002.0576	1993.0173
1002.0577	1993.0175
1002.0578	1994.0101
1002.0579	1994.0013
1002.0580	1994.0015
1002.0581	1994.0100
1002.0582	1996.0170
1002.0583	1997.0026
1002.0584	1997.0073
1002.0585	1998.0038
1002.0586	1998.0045
1002.0587	1989.0087
1002.0588	1989.0089
1002.0589	1999.0014
1002.0590	1999.0031
1002.0591	1973.1228
1002.0592	1973.1240
1002.0593	1973.1255
1002.0594	1973.1386
1002.0595	1973.1387
1002.0596	1973.1388
1002.0597	1973.1391
1002.0598	1973.1392
1002.0599	1973.1191
1002.0600	2009.0029
1002.0601	2007.0003
1002.0602	2007.0023
1002.0603	2007.0027
1002.0604	2007.0031
1002.0605	2007.0039
1002.0606	2007.0070
1002.0607	2007.0077
1002.0608	2007.0089
1002.0609	2007.0094
1002.0610	2007.0096
1002.0611	2007.0097
1002.0612	2007.0099
1002.0613	2007.0100
1002.0614	2007.0101
1002.0615	2007.0116
1002.0616	2007.0118
1002.0617	2007.0122
1002.0618	2007.0126
1002.0619	2007.0129
1002.0620	2007.0138
1002.0621	2007.0141
1002.0622	2007.0172
1002.0623	2007.0177
1002.0624	2007.0186
1002.0625	2007.0191
1002.0626	2007.0192
1002.0627	2007.0223
1002.0628	2007.0226
1002.0629	2007.0228
1002.0630	2004.0045
1002.0631	2005.0049
1002.0632	1981.C81.0076
1002.0633	1982.0247
1002.0634	1982.0012
1002.0635	1982.0011
1002.0636	1982.0080
1002.0637	1982.0172
1002.0638	1982.0212
1002.0639	1982.C82.0159
1002.0640	1982.0177
1002.0641	1982.0180
1002.0642	1982.0184
1002.0643	1982.0204
1002.0644	1982.0206
1002.0645	1982.0208
1002.0646	1982.0209
1002.0647	1978.1766
1002.0648	2011.0187
1002.0649	1978.1667
1002.0650	2000.0009
1003.0001	1992.0135
1003.0002	1993.NoEx93.0046
1003.0003	1977.1435
1003.0004	1986.0016
1003.0005	1986.0026
1003.0006	1984.0160
1003.0007	1981.C81.0050
1003.0008	1981.C81.0068
1003.0009	1978.1686
1003.0010	1978.1693
1003.0011	1978.1699
1003.0012	1978.1702
1003.0013	1978.1707
1003.0014	1978.1708
1003.0015	1978.1711
1003.0016	1978.1798
1003.0017	1978.1802
1003.0018	1988.NoEx88.0010
1003.0019	1987.NoEx87.0001
1003.0020	1985.NoEx85.0044
1003.0021	1973.1156
1003.0022	1973.1157
1003.0023	1973.1169
1003.0024	1973.1171
1003.0025	1973.1103
1003.0026	1973.1090
1003.0027	1973.1220
1003.0028	1973.1221
1003.0029	1973.1100
1003.0030	1973.1148
1003.0031	1973.1101
1003.0032	1973.1095
1003.0033	1973.1096
1003.0034	1973.1097
1003.0035	1973.1098
1003.0036	1973.1115
1003.0037	1973.1147
1003.0038	1973.1087
1003.0039	1984.0098
1003.0040	1984.0100
1003.0041	1984.0102
1003.0042	1984.0107
1003.0043	1984.0108
1003.0044	1984.0111
1003.0045	1984.0112
1003.0046	1984.0113
1003.0047	1984.0114
1003.0048	1984.0116
1003.0049	1984.0123
1003.0050	1984.0124
1003.0051	1984.0049
1003.0052	1984.0118
1003.0053	1984.0120
1003.0054	1984.0062
1003.0055	1984.0065
1003.0056	1984.0068

1003.0057	1984.0069
1003.0058	1985.0022
1003.0059	1986.0013
1003.0060	1989.0030
1003.0061	1989.0049
1003.0062	1989.0050
1003.0063	1991.0022
1003.0064	1991.0025
1003.0065	1991.0438
1003.0066	1991.0455
1003.0067	1991.0473
1003.0068	1991.0474
1003.0069	1991.0479
1003.0070	1991.0480
1003.0071	1991.0481
1003.0072	1991.0486
1003.0073	1991.0487
1003.0074	1991.0489
1003.0075	1991.0492
1003.0076	1991.0493
1003.0077	1991.0496
1003.0078	1991.0497
1003.0079	1991.0505
1003.0080	1991.0506
1003.0081	1991.0509
1003.0082	1991.0517
1003.0083	1991.0518
1003.0084	1991.0519
1003.0085	1991.0520
1003.0086	1991.0526
1003.0087	1991.0527
1003.0088	1991.0528
1003.0089	1991.0534
1003.0090	1991.0535
1003.0091	1992.0004
1003.0092	1992.0005
1003.0093	1992.0011
1003.0094	1992.0012
1003.0095	1992.0014
1003.0096	1992.0029
1003.0097	1992.0030
1003.0098	1992.0033
1003.0099	2002.0011
1003.0100	1979.1859
1003.0101	1979.1895
1003.0102	2009.0013
1003.0103	2011.0032
1003.0104	2011.0064
1003.0105	2011.0065
1003.0106	2011.0066
1003.0107	2011.0070
1003.0108	2011.0074

1003.0109	2011.0075
1003.0110	2011.0078
1003.0111	2011.0080
1003.0112	2011.0082
1003.0113	2011.0084
1003.0114	2011.0087
1003.0115	2011.0090
1003.0116	2011.0091
1003.0117	2011.0093
1003.0118	2011.0098
1003.0119	2011.0099
1003.0120	2011.0101
1003.0121	2011.0102
1003.0122	2011.0107
1003.0123	2011.0110
1003.0124	2011.0114
1003.0125	2011.0115
1003.0126	2011.0117
1003.0127	2011.0118
1003.0128	2011.0121
1003.0129	2011.0127
1003.0130	2011.0129
1003.0131	2011.0130
1003.0132	2011.0131
1003.0133	2011.0134
1003.0134	2011.0138
1003.0135	2011.0141
1003.0136	2011.0143
1003.0137	2011.0146
1003.0138	2011.0148
1003.0139	2011.0151
1003.0140	2011.0152
1003.0141	2011.0153
1003.0142	2011.0159
1003.0143	2011.0162
1003.0144	2011.0165
1003.0145	2011.0166
1003.0146	2011.0168
1003.0147	2011.0169
1003.0148	2011.0170
1003.0149	2011.0171
1003.0150	2011.0173
1003.0151	2011.0176
1003.0152	2011.0179
1003.0153	2011.0180
1003.0154	2011.0184
1003.0155	2011.0185
1003.0156	2011.0007
1003.0157	2011.0008
1003.0158	2011.0014
1003.0159	2011.0017
1003.0160	2011.0020

1003.0161	2011.0025
1003.0162	2011.0028
1003.0163	2011.0033
1003.0164	2011.0036
1003.0165	2011.0045
1003.0166	2011.0049
1003.0167	2011.0051
1003.0168	2011.0054
1003.0169	2012.0014
1003.0170	2012.0032
1003.0171	2012.0033
1003.0172	2012.0049
1003.0173	2002.0016
1003.0174	2002.0028
1003.0175	2002.0308
1003.0176	2002.0029
1003.0177	2002.0091
1003.0178	2002.0093
1003.0179	2002.0105
1003.0180	2004.0030
1003.0181	2004.0035
1003.0182	2004.0055
1003.0183	2005.0016
1003.0184	2005.0043
1003.0185	2005.0060
1003.0186	2005.0061
1003.0187	2005.0068
1003.0188	2005.0071
1003.0189	2005.0073
1003.0190	1980.0122
1003.0191	1980.0123
1003.0192	1980.0176
1003.0193	1980.0179
1003.0194	1980.0195
1003.0195	1980.0210
1003.0196	1980.0214
1003.0197	1980.0221
1003.0198	1980.C80.0489
1003.0199	1980.C80.0331
1003.0200	1980.C80.0336
1003.0201	1980.C80.0340
1003.0202	1980.0144
1003.0203	1980.0158
1003.0204	1980.C80.0381
1003.0205	1980.0030
1003.0206	1984.0091
1003.0207	1984.0092
1003.0208	1980.C80.0073
1003.0209	1995.0041
1003.0210	1996.0066
1003.0211	1996.0074
1003.0212	1996.0075

1003.0213	1996.0084
1003.0214	1996.0129
1003.0215	1996.0130
1003.0216	1996.0134
1003.0217	1996.0138
1003.0218	1998.0013
1003.0219	2003.0008
1003.0220	2003.0009
1003.0221	2003.0010
1003.0222	2003.0011
1003.0223	2003.0013
1003.0224	2003.0015
1003.0225	1980.0118
1003.0226	1981.0003
1003.0227	1984.0071
1003.0228	1982.0001
1003.0229	1982.0007
1003.0230	1982.0014
1003.0231	1982.0021
1003.0232	1982.0027
1003.0233	1982.0028
1003.0234	1982.0029
1003.0235	1982.0030
1003.0236	1982.0031
1003.0237	1982.0032
1003.0238	1982.0040
1003.0239	1982.0047
1003.0240	1982.0048
1003.0241	1982.0050
1003.0242	1982.0052
1003.0243	1982.0053
1003.0244	1982.0054
1003.0245	1982.0055
1003.0246	1982.0056
1003.0247	1982.0057
1003.0248	1982.0058
1003.0249	1982.0059
1003.0250	1982.0060
1003.0251	1982.0061
1003.0252	1982.0062
1003.0253	1982.0063
1003.0254	1982.0066
1003.0255	1982.0067
1003.0256	1982.0069
1003.0257	1982.0070
1003.0258	1982.0071
1003.0259	1982.0072
1003.0260	1982.0073
1003.0261	1982.0075
1003.0262	1982.0077
1003.0263	1982.0098
1003.0264	1982.0108

1003.0265	1982.0114
1003.0266	1982.0118
1003.0267	1982.0119
1003.0268	1982.0120
1003.0269	1982.0121
1003.0270	1982.0122
1003.0271	1982.0123
1003.0272	1982.0124
1003.0273	1982.0130
1003.0274	1982.0132
1003.0275	1982.0133
1003.0276	1982.0135
1003.0277	1982.0137
1003.0278	1982.0138
1003.0279	1982.0140
1003.0280	1982.0141
1003.0281	1982.0145
1003.0282	1982.0147
1003.0283	1982.0148
1003.0284	1982.0149
1003.0285	1982.0152
1003.0286	1982.0153
1003.0287	1982.0163
1003.0288	1982.0164
1003.0289	1982.0168
1003.0290	1982.0169
1003.0291	1982.0199
1003.0292	1982.0214
1003.0293	1982.0217
1003.0294	1982.0218
1003.0295	1982.0235
1003.0296	1982.0241
1003.0297	1982.0242
1003.0298	1982.C82.0034
1003.0299	1982.C82.0045
1003.0300	1982.C82.0059
1003.0301	1982.C82.0064
1003.0302	1982.C82.0072
1003.0303	1982.C82.0079
1003.0304	1982.C82.0080
1003.0305	1982.C82.0081
1003.0306	1982.C82.0103
1003.0307	1982.C82.0119
1003.0308	1982.C82.0120
1003.0309	1982.C82.0121
1003.0310	1982.C82.0124
1003.0311	1982.C82.0131
1003.0312	1982.C82.0134
1003.0313	1983.0008
1003.0314	1983.0009
1003.0315	1983.0110
1003.0316	1983.0169

1003.0317	1983.0184
1003.0318	1983.0185
1003.0319	1983.0187
1003.0320	1983.0189
1003.0321	1983.0191
1003.0322	1983.0195
1003.0323	1983.0196
1003.0324	1983.0197
1003.0325	1983.0201
1003.0326	1983.0202
1003.0327	1983.0203
1003.0328	1983.0204
1003.0329	1983.0206
1003.0330	1983.0207
1003.0331	1983.0208
1003.0332	1983.0209
1003.0333	1983.0210
1003.0334	1983.0212
1003.0335	1983.0213
1003.0336	1983.0215
1003.0337	1983.0217
1003.0338	1983.0218
1003.0339	1983.0221
1003.0340	1983.0222
1003.0341	1983.0223
1003.0342	1983.0227
1003.0343	1983.0229
1003.0344	1983.0235
1003.0345	1983.0236
1003.0346	1983.0237
1003.0347	1983.0238
1003.0348	1983.0249
1003.0349	1983.0252
1003.0350	1983.0254
1003.0351	1983.0259
1003.0352	1983.0260
1003.0353	1983.0265
1003.0354	1983.0266
1003.0355	1983.0267
1003.0356	1983.0268
1003.0357	1983.0274
1003.0358	1983.0276
1003.0359	1983.0039
1003.0360	1983.0056
1003.0361	1983.0063
1003.0362	1983.0064
1003.0363	1983.0103
1003.0364	1983.0104
1003.0365	1983.0111
1003.0366	1983.0113
1003.0367	1983.0126
1003.0368	1983.0127

1003.0369	1983.0230
1003.0370	1983.0234
1003.0371	1985.0007
1003.0372	1985.0014
1003.0373	1985.0020
1003.0374	1985.0024
1003.0375	1985.0025
1003.0376	1985.0026
1003.0377	1985.0028
1003.0378	1985.0029
1003.0379	1985.0030
1003.0380	1985.0037
1003.0381	1985.0038
1003.0382	1985.0040
1003.0383	1985.0041
1003.0384	1985.0042
1003.0385	1985.0043
1003.0386	1985.0044
1003.0387	1985.0047
1003.0388	1985.0050
1003.0389	1985.0055
1003.0390	1985.0056
1003.0391	1985.0059
1003.0392	1985.0061
1003.0393	1985.0064
1003.0394	1985.0068
1003.0395	1985.0073
1003.0396	1985.0074
1003.0397	1985.0075
1003.0398	1985.0076
1003.0399	1985.0077
1003.0400	1985.0079
1003.0401	1985.0083
1003.0402	1985.0090
1003.0403	1985.0091
1003.0404	1985.0092
1003.0405	1985.0093
1003.0406	1985.0094
1003.0407	1985.0097
1003.0408	1985.0100
1003.0409	1985.0104
1003.0410	1985.0106
1003.0411	1985.0108
1003.0412	1985.0110
1003.0413	1985.0112
1003.0414	1985.0113
1003.0415	1985.0116
1003.0416	1985.0117
1003.0417	1985.0121
1003.0418	1985.0122
1003.0419	1985.0127
1003.0420	1985.0128

1003.0421	1985.0129
1003.0422	1985.0132
1003.0423	1985.0135
1003.0424	1985.0136
1003.0425	1985.0137
1003.0426	1985.0139
1003.0427	1985.0140
1003.0428	1985.0141
1003.0429	1985.0143
1003.0430	1985.0144
1003.0431	1985.0146
1003.0432	1985.0148
1003.0433	1985.0150
1003.0434	1985.0154
1003.0435	1985.0165
1003.0436	1985.0185
1003.0437	1985.0249
1003.0438	1985.0287
1003.0439	1985.0292
1003.0440	1985.0124
1003.0441	1987.0070
1003.0442	1987.0076
1003.0443	1987.0079
1003.0444	1987.0080
1003.0445	1987.0083
1003.0446	1987.0084
1003.0447	1987.0085
1003.0448	1990.0186
1003.0449	1990.0193
1003.0450	1990.0194
1003.0451	1990.0196
1003.0452	1990.0197
1003.0453	1990.0199
1003.0454	1990.0200
1003.0455	1990.0209
1003.0456	1991.0415
1003.0457	1991.0416
1003.0458	1991.0417
1003.0459	1991.0419
1003.0460	1998.0024
1003.0461	1998.0025
1003.0462	1998.0027
1003.0463	1998.0029
1003.0464	1980.0071
1003.0465	1980.0072
1003.0466	1980.0096
1003.0467	1980.0097
1003.0468	1980.0105
1003.0469	1980.0219
1003.0470	1980.C80.0234
1003.0471	1980.C80.0286
1003.0472	1981.C81.0086

1003.0473	1982.0041
1003.0474	1982.0087
1003.0475	1982.0111
1003.0476	1982.0193
1003.0477	1982.0194
1003.0478	1982.0195
1003.0479	1982.0198
1003.0480	1982.0201
1003.0481	1982.C82.0062
1003.0482	1980.0032
1003.0483	1983.0031
1003.0484	1983.0079
1003.0485	1983.0097
1003.0486	1983.0107
1003.0487	1983.0118
1003.0488	1983.0139
1003.0489	1983.0141
1003.0490	1983.0143
1003.0491	1985.0156
1003.0492	1985.0158
1003.0493	1985.0178
1003.0494	1985.0180
1003.0495	1985.0182
1003.0496	1985.0186
1003.0497	1985.0189
1003.0498	1985.0200
1003.0499	1985.0201
1003.0500	1985.0204
1003.0501	1985.0205
1003.0502	1985.0206
1003.0503	1985.0207
1003.0504	1985.0299
1003.0505	1985.0300
1003.0506	1985.0303
1003.0507	1985.0307
1003.0508	1985.0311
1003.0509	1985.0313
1003.0510	1985.0315
1003.0511	1985.0319
1003.0512	1987.0003
1003.0513	1987.0004
1003.0514	1987.0007
1003.0515	1987.0010
1003.0516	1987.0013
1003.0517	1987.0015
1003.0518	1987.0020
1003.0519	1987.0021
1003.0520	1987.0026
1003.0521	1987.0027
1003.0522	1987.0033
1003.0523	1987.0034
1003.0524	1987.0036

1003.0525	1987.0037
1003.0526	1987.0042
1003.0527	1987.0043
1003.0528	1987.0044
1003.0529	1987.0045
1003.0530	1987.0048
1003.0531	1987.0049
1003.0532	1987.0050
1003.0533	1987.0051
1003.0534	1987.0052
1003.0535	1987.0053
1003.0536	1987.0055
1003.0537	1987.0056
1003.0538	1988.0002
1003.0539	1988.0003
1003.0540	1988.0005
1003.0541	1988.0017
1003.0542	1988.0019
1003.0543	1988.0021
1003.0544	1988.0025
1003.0545	1988.0026
1003.0546	1988.0030
1003.0547	1988.0032
1003.0548	1988.0033
1003.0549	1988.0034
1003.0550	1988.0037
1003.0551	1988.0038
1003.0552	1988.0042
1003.0553	1988.0043
1003.0554	1988.0046
1003.0555	1988.0049
1003.0556	1988.0053
1003.0557	1988.0056
1003.0558	1988.0058
1003.0559	1988.0059
1003.0560	1988.0061
1003.0561	1988.0062
1003.0562	1988.0063
1003.0563	1988.0065
1003.0564	1988.0067
1003.0565	1988.0068
1003.0566	1988.0069
1003.0567	1988.0070
1003.0568	1988.0094
1003.0569	1989.0130
1003.0570	1989.0132
1003.0571	1989.0164
1003.0572	1989.0181
1003.0573	1991.0329
1003.0574	1991.0330
1003.0575	1991.0331
1003.0576	1991.0332

1003.0577	1991.0333
1003.0578	1991.0337
1003.0579	1991.0346
1003.0580	1991.0357
1003.0581	1991.0359
1003.0582	1991.0383
1003.0583	1991.0384
1003.0584	1991.0385
1003.0585	1991.0388
1003.0586	1991.0392
1003.0587	1991.0393
1003.0588	1991.0398
1003.0589	1991.0401
1003.0590	1991.0402
1003.0591	1991.0403
1003.0592	1991.0404
1003.0593	1991.0405
1003.0594	1991.0407
1003.0595	1991.0408
1003.0596	1991.0410
1003.0597	1991.0411
1003.0598	1991.0447
1003.0599	1991.0448
1003.0600	1991.0449
1003.0601	1991.0450
1003.0602	1991.0452
1003.0603	1991.0454
1003.0604	1991.0465
1003.0605	1991.0541
1003.0606	1991.0542
1003.0607	1991.0544
1003.0608	1991.0545
1003.0609	1992.0040
1003.0610	1992.0041
1003.0611	1992.0042
1003.0612	1992.0051
1003.0613	1992.0052
1003.0614	1992.0053
1003.0615	1992.0054
1003.0616	1992.0055
1003.0617	1992.0056
1003.0618	1992.0057
1003.0619	1992.0058
1003.0620	1992.0066
1003.0621	1992.0069
1003.0622	1992.0085
1003.0623	1992.0088
1003.0624	1992.0092
1003.0625	1992.0093
1003.0626	1992.0094
1003.0627	1992.0095
1003.0628	1992.0096

1003.0629	2002.0017
1003.0630	2002.0019
1003.0631	2002.0022
1003.0632	2002.0023
1003.0633	2002.0024
1003.0634	2002.0025
1003.0635	2002.0026
1003.0636	2002.0027
1003.0637	2002.0031
1003.0638	2002.0034
1003.0639	2002.0036
1003.0640	2002.0037
1003.0641	2002.0038
1003.0642	2002.0039
1003.0643	2002.0040
1003.0644	2002.0041
1003.0645	2002.0042
1003.0646	2002.0043
1003.0647	2002.0044
1003.0648	2002.0048
1003.0649	2002.0051
1003.0650	2002.0052
1003.0651	2002.0053
1003.0652	2002.0054
1003.0653	2002.0056
1003.0654	2002.0058
1003.0655	2002.0059
1003.0656	2002.0062
1003.0657	2002.0065
1003.0658	2002.0067
1003.0659	2002.0068
1003.0660	2002.0072
1003.0661	2002.0075
1003.0662	2002.0076
1003.0663	2002.0077
1003.0664	2002.0078
1003.0665	2002.0079
1003.0666	2002.0080
1003.0667	2002.0082
1003.0668	2002.0083
1003.0669	2002.0084
1003.0670	2002.0109
1003.0671	2002.0110
1003.0672	2002.0113
1003.0673	2002.0114
1003.0674	2002.0115
1003.0675	2002.0116
1003.0676	2002.0118
1003.0677	2002.0119
1003.0678	2002.0120
1003.0679	2002.0121
1003.0680	2002.0122

1003.0681	2002.0123
1003.0682	2002.0124
1003.0683	2002.0126
1003.0684	2002.0127
1003.0685	2002.0128
1003.0686	2002.0131
1003.0687	2002.0133
1003.0688	2002.0134
1003.0689	2002.0135
1003.0690	2002.0138
1003.0691	2002.0139
1003.0692	2002.0140
1003.0693	2002.0141
1003.0694	2002.0142
1003.0695	2002.0144
1003.0696	2002.0145
1003.0697	2002.0146
1003.0698	2002.0147
1003.0699	2002.0148
1003.0700	2002.0149
1003.0701	2002.0150
1003.0702	2002.0151
1003.0703	2002.0152
1003.0704	2002.0154
1003.0705	2002.0156
1003.0706	2002.0158
1003.0707	2002.0159
1003.0708	2002.0161
1003.0709	2002.0162
1003.0710	2002.0163
1003.0711	2002.0164
1003.0712	2002.0165
1003.0713	2002.0166
1003.0714	2002.0167
1003.0715	2002.0168
1003.0716	2002.0170
1003.0717	2002.0171
1003.0718	2002.0172
1003.0719	2002.0173
1003.0720	2002.0174
1003.0721	2002.0179
1003.0722	2002.0180
1003.0723	2002.0182
1003.0724	2002.0183
1003.0725	2002.0184
1003.0726	2002.0185
1003.0727	2002.0186
1003.0728	2002.0189
1003.0729	2002.0190
1003.0730	2002.0197
1003.0731	2002.0198
1003.0732	2002.0200

1003.0733	2002.0203
1003.0734	2002.0204
1003.0735	2002.0205
1003.0736	2002.0206
1003.0737	2002.0207
1003.0738	2002.0209
1003.0739	2002.0210
1003.0740	2002.0211
1003.0741	2002.0212
1003.0742	2002.0213
1003.0743	2002.0214
1003.0744	2002.0215
1003.0745	2002.0218
1003.0746	2002.0220
1003.0747	2002.0221
1003.0748	2002.0222
1003.0749	2002.0223
1003.0750	2002.0224
1003.0751	2002.0225
1003.0752	2002.0228
1003.0753	2002.0230
1003.0754	2002.0231
1003.0755	2002.0232
1003.0756	2002.0233
1003.0757	2002.0237
1003.0758	2002.0239
1003.0759	2002.0241
1003.0760	2002.0244
1003.0761	2002.0245
1003.0762	2002.0246
1003.0763	2002.0248
1003.0764	2002.0250
1003.0765	2002.0251
1003.0766	2002.0252
1003.0767	2002.0253
1003.0768	2002.0255
1003.0769	2002.0256
1003.0770	2002.0261
1003.0771	2002.0262
1003.0772	2002.0264
1003.0773	2002.0266
1003.0774	2002.0267
1003.0775	2002.0268
1003.0776	2002.0270
1003.0777	2002.0271
1003.0778	2002.0272
1003.0779	2002.0273
1003.0780	2002.0275
1003.0781	2002.0284
1003.0782	2002.0286
1003.0783	2002.0287
1003.0784	2002.0289

1003.0785	2002.0290
1003.0786	2002.0291
1003.0787	2002.0292
1003.0788	2002.0293
1003.0789	2002.0294
1003.0790	2002.0295
1003.0791	2002.0296
1003.0792	2002.0298
1003.0793	2002.0299
1003.0794	2002.0302
1003.0795	2002.0303
1003.0796	2002.0304
1003.0797	2002.0305
1003.0798	2002.0306
1003.0799	2002.0307
1003.0800	2002.0313
1003.0801	2002.0314
1003.0802	2002.0315
1003.0803	2002.0316
1003.0804	2002.0317
1003.0805	2002.0318
1003.0806	2002.0319
1003.0807	2002.0276
1003.0808	2002.0277
1003.0809	1984.0001
1003.0810	1984.0004
1003.0811	1984.0005
1003.0812	1984.0008
1003.0813	1984.0011
1003.0814	1984.0014
1003.0815	1984.0015
1003.0816	1984.0019
1003.0817	1984.0020
1003.0818	1984.0023
1003.0819	1984.0024
1003.0820	1984.0026
1003.0821	1984.0027
1003.0822	1984.0028
1003.0823	1984.0029
1003.0824	1984.0030
1003.0825	1984.0033
1003.0826	1984.0036
1003.0827	1984.0040
1003.0828	1984.0075
1003.0829	1984.0078
1003.0830	1984.0083
1003.0831	1984.0117
1003.0832	1985.0162
1003.0833	1985.0167
1003.0834	1985.0169
1003.0835	1985.0190
1003.0836	1985.0191

1003.0837	1985.0193
1003.0838	1985.0211
1003.0839	1985.0214
1003.0840	1985.0215
1003.0841	1985.0216
1003.0842	1985.0218
1003.0843	1985.0220
1003.0844	1985.0222
1003.0845	1985.0226
1003.0846	1985.0228
1003.0847	1985.0238
1003.0848	1985.0241
1003.0849	1985.0244
1003.0850	1985.0253
1003.0851	1985.0254
1003.0852	1985.0260
1003.0853	1985.0263
1003.0854	1985.0268
1003.0855	1985.0270
1003.0856	1985.0272
1003.0857	1985.0274
1003.0858	1985.0276
1003.0859	1985.0278
1003.0860	1985.0279
1003.0861	1985.0280
1003.0862	1985.0281
1003.0863	1987.0090
1003.0864	1987.0093
1003.0865	1987.0094
1003.0866	1987.0096
1003.0867	1987.0097
1003.0868	1987.0101
1003.0869	1987.0102
1003.0870	1987.0103
1003.0871	1987.0104
1003.0872	1987.0105
1003.0873	1987.0109
1003.0874	1987.0111
1003.0875	1987.0122
1003.0876	1987.0132
1003.0877	1987.0134
1003.0878	1987.0143
1003.0879	1987.0148
1003.0880	1987.0153
1003.0881	1987.0156
1003.0882	1987.0157
1003.0883	1987.0164
1003.0884	1987.0165
1003.0885	1987.0166
1003.0886	1987.0167
1003.0887	1987.0169
1003.0888	1987.0171

1003.0889	1989.0027
1003.0890	1989.0063
1003.0891	1989.0064
1003.0892	1989.0066
1003.0893	1989.0098
1003.0894	1992.0117
1003.0895	1992.0121
1003.0896	1992.0123
1003.0897	1992.0129
1003.0898	1992.0130
1003.0899	1992.0132
1003.0900	1992.0137
1003.0901	1992.0139
1003.0902	1992.0140
1003.0903	1993.0015
1003.0904	1988.0074
1003.0905	1978.1488
1003.0906	1978.1491
1003.0907	1978.1495
1003.0908	1978.1514
1003.0909	1978.1518
1003.0910	1978.1520
1003.0911	1978.1523
1003.0912	1978.1533
1003.0913	1978.1534
1003.0914	1978.1537
1003.0915	1978.1543
1003.0916	1978.1550
1003.0917	1978.1554
1003.0918	1978.1555
1003.0919	1978.1556
1003.0920	1978.1557
1003.0921	1978.1558
1003.0922	1978.1560
1003.0923	1978.1567
1003.0924	1978.1568
1003.0925	1978.1569
1003.0926	1978.1570
1003.0927	1978.1571
1003.0928	1978.1575
1003.0929	1978.1576
1003.0930	1978.1579
1003.0931	1978.1580
1003.0932	1978.1581
1003.0933	1978.1583
1003.0934	1978.1586
1003.0935	1978.1587
1003.0936	1978.1713
1003.0937	1978.1719
1003.0938	1978.1723
1003.0939	1978.1729
1003.0940	1978.1730

1003.0941	1978.1739
1003.0942	1978.1755
1003.0943	1978.1757
1003.0944	1978.1776
1003.0945	1978.1781
1003.0946	1978.1783
1003.0947	1978.1787
1003.0948	1978.1789
1003.0949	1978.1790
1003.0950	1978.1791
1003.0951	1978.1814
1003.0952	1978.1817
1003.0953	1978.1818
1003.0954	1979.1832
1003.0955	1979.1844
1003.0956	1979.1850
1003.0957	1979.1853
1003.0958	1979.1855
1003.0959	1979.1856
1003.0960	1979.1861
1003.0961	1979.1864
1003.0962	1979.1901
1003.0963	1979.1902
1003.0964	1979.1947
1003.0965	1979.1948
1003.0966	1979.1961
1003.0967	1979.1964
1003.0968	1979.1965
1003.0969	1979.1966
1003.0970	1979.1969
1003.0971	1979.1970
1003.0972	1979.1973
1003.0973	1979.1974
1003.0974	1979.1975
1003.0975	1979.1976
1003.0976	1979.1977
1003.0977	1979.1978
1003.0978	1979.1979
1003.0979	1979.1980
1003.0980	1979.1982
1003.0981	1979.1984
1003.0982	1979.1986
1003.0983	1979.1989
1003.0984	1979.1993
1003.0985	1979.1994
1003.0986	1979.1996
1003.0987	1979.1998
1003.0988	1979.2001
1003.0989	1979.2000
1003.0990	1979.2004
1003.0991	1979.2005
1003.0992	1979.2007

1003.0993	1979.2009
1003.0994	1979.2014
1003.0995	1979.2015
1003.0996	1979.2018
1003.0997	1979.2019
1003.0998	1979.2020
1003.0999	1979.2023
1003.1000	1979.2024
1003.1001	1979.2025
1003.1002	1979.2026
1003.1003	1979.2027
1003.1004	1979.2028
1003.1005	1979.2029
1003.1006	1979.2040
1003.1007	1979.2041
1003.1008	1979.2048
1003.1009	1979.2051
1003.1010	1979.2053
1003.1011	1979.2056
1003.1012	1979.2065
1003.1013	1979.2067
1003.1014	1979.2068
1003.1015	1979.2069
1003.1016	1979.2071
1003.1017	1979.2073
1003.1018	1979.2074
1003.1019	1979.2082
1003.1020	1979.2083
1003.1021	1979.2085
1003.1022	1979.2088
1003.1023	1979.2089
1003.1024	1979.2091
1003.1025	1979.2093
1003.1026	1979.2094
1003.1027	1979.2095
1003.1028	1979.2096
1003.1029	1979.2101
1003.1030	1979.2104
1003.1031	1979.2105
1003.1032	1979.2107
1003.1033	1979.2112
1003.1034	1979.2115
1003.1035	1979.2121
1003.1036	1979.2123
1003.1037	1979.2126
1003.1038	1979.2132
1003.1039	1979.2136
1003.1040	1979.2144
1003.1041	1979.2155
1003.1042	1979.2156
1003.1043	1979.2157
1003.1044	1979.2158

1003.1045	1979.1996a
1003.1046	1980.0004
1003.1047	1980.0009
1003.1048	1980.0011
1003.1049	1980.0012
1003.1050	1980.0013
1003.1051	1980.0015
1003.1052	1980.0017
1003.1053	1980.0020
1003.1054	1980.0024
1003.1055	1980.0025
1003.1056	1980.0026
1003.1057	1980.0029
1003.1058	1980.0044
1003.1059	1980.0045
1003.1060	1980.0046
1003.1061	1980.0053
1003.1062	1980.0055
1003.1063	1980.0057
1003.1064	1980.0059
1003.1065	1980.0065
1003.1066	1980.0066
1003.1067	1980.0068
1003.1068	1980.0070
1003.1069	1980.0077
1003.1070	1980.0078
1003.1071	1980.0081
1003.1072	1980.0084
1003.1073	1980.0085
1003.1074	1980.0089
1003.1075	1980.0090
1003.1076	1980.0091
1003.1077	1980.0099
1003.1078	1980.0110
1003.1079	1980.0111
1003.1080	1980.0112
1003.1081	1980.0124
1003.1082	1980.0130
1003.1083	1980.0138
1003.1084	1980.0143
1003.1085	1980.C80.0005
1003.1086	1980.C80.0006
1003.1087	1980.C80.0007
1003.1088	1980.C80.0012
1003.1089	1980.C80.0014
1003.1090	1980.C80.0019
1003.1091	1980.C80.0027
1003.1092	1980.C80.0041
1003.1093	1980.C80.0043
1003.1094	1980.C80.0052
1003.1095	1980.C80.0055
1003.1096	1980.C80.0056

1003.1097	1980.C80.0065
1003.1098	1980.C80.0066
1003.1099	1980.C80.0068
1003.1100	1980.C80.0082
1003.1101	1980.C80.0083
1003.1102	1980.C80.0084
1003.1103	1980.C80.0085
1003.1104	1980.C80.0089
1003.1105	1980.C80.0090
1003.1106	1980.C80.0093
1003.1107	1980.C80.0098
1003.1108	1980.C80.0099
1003.1109	1980.C80.0100
1003.1110	1980.C80.0102
1003.1111	1980.C80.0105
1003.1112	1980.C80.0111
1003.1113	1980.C80.0114
1003.1114	1980.C80.0116
1003.1115	1980.C80.0118
1003.1116	1980.C80.0126
1003.1117	1980.C80.0127
1003.1118	1980.C80.0130
1003.1119	1980.C80.0158
1003.1120	1980.C80.0171
1003.1121	1980.C80.0172
1003.1122	1980.C80.0175
1003.1123	1980.C80.0178
1003.1124	1980.C80.0180
1003.1125	1980.C80.0181
1003.1126	1980.C80.0185
1003.1127	1980.C80.0190
1003.1128	1980.C80.0195
1003.1129	1980.C80.0198
1003.1130	1980.C80.0200
1003.1131	1980.C80.0205
1003.1132	1980.C80.0211
1003.1133	1980.C80.0213
1003.1134	1980.C80.0216
1003.1135	1980.C80.0218
1003.1136	1980.C80.0227
1003.1137	1980.C80.0231
1003.1138	1980.C80.0261
1003.1139	1980.C80.0269
1003.1140	1980.C80.0270
1003.1141	1980.C80.0280
1003.1142	1980.C80.0281
1003.1143	1980.C80.0295
1003.1144	1980.C80.0307
1003.1145	1980.C80.0308
1003.1146	1980.C80.0356
1003.1147	1980.C80.0357
1003.1148	1980.0034

1003.1149	1980.0039
1003.1150	1980.0040
1003.1151	1983.0072
1003.1152	1984.0052
1003.1153	1984.0053
1003.1154	1984.0072
1003.1155	1989.0010
1003.1156	1989.0072
1003.1157	1989.0100
1003.1158	1989.0111
1003.1159	1989.0112
1003.1160	1989.0152
1003.1161	1989.0162
1003.1162	1989.0168
1003.1163	1989.0173
1003.1164	1989.0177
1003.1165	1990.0009
1003.1166	1990.0013
1003.1167	1990.0014
1003.1168	1990.0018
1003.1169	1990.0022
1003.1170	1990.0027
1003.1171	1990.0046
1003.1172	1990.0048
1003.1173	1990.0051
1003.1174	1990.0052
1003.1175	1990.0053
1003.1176	1990.0055
1003.1177	1990.0068
1003.1178	1990.0074
1003.1179	1990.0076
1003.1180	1990.0083
1003.1181	1990.0084
1003.1182	1990.0092
1003.1183	1990.0093
1003.1184	1990.0094
1003.1185	1990.0098
1003.1186	1990.0099
1003.1187	1990.0102
1003.1188	1990.0103
1003.1189	1990.0108
1003.1190	1990.0112
1003.1191	1990.0115
1003.1192	1990.0119
1003.1193	1990.0120
1003.1194	1990.0121
1003.1195	1990.0122
1003.1196	1990.0123
1003.1197	1990.0124
1003.1198	1990.0125
1003.1199	1990.0127
1003.1200	1990.0128

1003.1201	1990.0129
1003.1202	1990.0131
1003.1203	1990.0135
1003.1204	1990.0137
1003.1205	1990.0138
1003.1206	1990.0141
1003.1207	1990.0144
1003.1208	1990.0154
1003.1209	1990.0158
1003.1210	1990.0161
1003.1211	1990.0166
1003.1212	1990.0168
1003.1213	1990.0169
1003.1214	1990.0178
1003.1215	1990.0181
1003.1216	1990.0182
1003.1217	1990.0204
1003.1218	1990.0213
1003.1219	1990.0216
1003.1220	1990.0219
1003.1221	1990.0221
1003.1222	1990.0223
1003.1223	1990.0226
1003.1224	1990.0229
1003.1225	1990.0232
1003.1226	1990.0247
1003.1227	1991.0097
1003.1228	1991.0103
1003.1229	1991.0105
1003.1230	1991.0106
1003.1231	1991.0107
1003.1232	1991.0108
1003.1233	1991.0109
1003.1234	1991.0110
1003.1235	1991.0111
1003.1236	1991.0112
1003.1237	1991.0113
1003.1238	1991.0114
1003.1239	1991.0116
1003.1240	1991.0118
1003.1241	1991.0120
1003.1242	1991.0122
1003.1243	1991.0123
1003.1244	1991.0124
1003.1245	1991.0125
1003.1246	1991.0126
1003.1247	1991.0128
1003.1248	1991.0131
1003.1249	1991.0132
1003.1250	1991.0133
1003.1251	1991.0135
1003.1252	1991.0137

1003.1253	1991.0138
1003.1254	1991.0139
1003.1255	1991.0141
1003.1256	1991.0143
1003.1257	1991.0145
1003.1258	1991.0152
1003.1259	1991.0156
1003.1260	1991.0168
1003.1261	1991.0171
1003.1262	1991.0173
1003.1263	1991.0179
1003.1264	1991.0180
1003.1265	1991.0182
1003.1266	1991.0183
1003.1267	1991.0185
1003.1268	1991.0193
1003.1269	1991.0196
1003.1270	1991.0212
1003.1271	1991.0221
1003.1272	1991.0234
1003.1273	1991.0235
1003.1274	1991.0236
1003.1275	1991.0240
1003.1276	1991.0250
1003.1277	1991.0252
1003.1278	1991.0258
1003.1279	1991.0260
1003.1280	1991.0261
1003.1281	1991.0262
1003.1282	1991.0265
1003.1283	1991.0267
1003.1284	1991.0270
1003.1285	1991.0271
1003.1286	1991.0273
1003.1287	1991.0274
1003.1288	1991.0275
1003.1289	1991.0277
1003.1290	1991.0014
1003.1291	1991.0015
1003.1292	1991.0018
1003.1293	1991.0020
1003.1294	1991.0033
1003.1295	1991.0041
1003.1296	1991.0049
1003.1297	1991.0052
1003.1298	1991.0084
1003.1299	1991.0094
1003.1300	1991.0313
1003.1301	1991.0314
1003.1302	1991.0319
1003.1303	1991.0321
1003.1304	1991.0323

1003.1305	1991.0373
1003.1306	2004.0059
1003.1307	1992.0106
1003.1308	1992.0148
1003.1309	1992.0181
1003.1310	1992.0191
1003.1311	1992.0192
1003.1312	1992.0194
1003.1313	1992.0204
1003.1314	1992.0206
1003.1315	1992.0208
1003.1316	1992.0210
1003.1317	1992.0212
1003.1318	1992.0218
1003.1319	1992.0239
1003.1320	1992.0278
1003.1321	1992.0280
1003.1322	1992.0306
1003.1323	1992.0307
1003.1324	1992.0311
1003.1325	1992.0312
1003.1326	1992.0314
1003.1327	1992.0315.1
1003.1328	1992.0319
1003.1329	1992.0321
1003.1330	1992.0322
1003.1331	1992.0325
1003.1332	1992.0326
1003.1333	1992.0341
1003.1334	1992.0361
1003.1335	1992.0368
1003.1336	1992.0369
1003.1337	1992.0370
1003.1338	1992.0371
1003.1339	1992.0377
1003.1340	1992.0381
1003.1341	1992.0382
1003.1342	1992.0392
1003.1343	1992.0394
1003.1344	1992.0398
1003.1345	1992.0401
1003.1346	1992.0405
1003.1347	1992.0408
1003.1348	1992.0412
1003.1349	1992.0414
1003.1350	1992.0416
1003.1351	1992.0421
1003.1352	1992.0425
1003.1353	1992.0428
1003.1354	1992.0430
1003.1355	1992.0437
1003.1356	1992.0445

1003.1357	1992.0447	1003.1409	1994.0201	1003.1461	1982.0525	1003.1513	1982.0665	1003.1565	1982.0786
1003.1358	1992.0450	1003.1410	1994.0202	1003.1462	1982.0460	1003.1514	1982.0812	1003.1566	1982.0619
1003.1359	1992.0451	1003.1411	1994.0204	1003.1463	1982.0570	1003.1515	1982.0806	1003.1567	1982.0749
1003.1360	1992.0454	1003.1412	1994.0205	1003.1464	1982.0641	1003.1516	1982.0599	1003.1568	1982.0637
1003.1361	1992.0457	1003.1413	1994.0207	1003.1465	1982.0551	1003.1517	1982.0674	1003.1569	1982.0751
1003.1362	1992.0458	1003.1414	1994.0208	1003.1466	1982.0680	1003.1518	1982.0863	1003.1570	1982.0722
1003.1363	1993.0037	1003.1415	1994.0209	1003.1467	1982.0493	1003.1519	1982.0572	1003.1571	1982.0620
1003.1364	1993.0040	1003.1416	1994.0210	1003.1468	1982.0602	1003.1520	1982.0689	1003.1572	1982.0853
1003.1365	1993.0042	1003.1417	1994.0217	1003.1469	1982.0639	1003.1521	1982.0632	1003.1573	1982.0847
1003.1366	1993.0046	1003.1418	1994.0219	1003.1470	1982.0634	1003.1522	1982.0741	1003.1574	1982.0734
1003.1367	1993.0047	1003.1419	1994.0228	1003.1471	1982.0793	1003.1523	1982.0648	1003.1575	1982.0834
1003.1368	1993.0048	1003.1420	1994.0229	1003.1472	1982.0779	1003.1524	1982.0769	1003.1576	1982.0683
1003.1369	1993.0054.1	1003.1421	1994.0230	1003.1473	1982.0788	1003.1525	1982.0685	1003.1577	1982.0867
1003.1370	1993.0058	1003.1422	1994.0231	1003.1474	1982.0535	1003.1526	1982.0837	1003.1578	1982.0727
1003.1371	1993.0061	1003.1423	1994.0239	1003.1475	1982.0465	1003.1527	1982.0838	1003.1579	1982.0775
1003.1372	1993.0068	1003.1424	1994.0240	1003.1476	1982.0463	1003.1528	1982.0807	1003.1580	1982.0814
1003.1373	1993.0069	1003.1425	1994.0247	1003.1477	1982.0541	1003.1529	1982.0651	1003.1581	1982.0796
1003.1374	1993.0075	1003.1426	1994.0250	1003.1478	1982.0574	1003.1530	1982.0513	1003.1582	1982.0746
1003.1375	1993.0088	1003.1427	1995.0007	1003.1479	1982.0660	1003.1531	1982.0782	1003.1583	1982.0789
1003.1376	1992.0165	1003.1428	1995.0009	1003.1480	1982.0474	1003.1532	1982.0813	1003.1584	1982.0757
1003.1377	1993.0106	1003.1429	1995.0011	1003.1481	1982.0743	1003.1533	1982.0839	1003.1585	1982.0790
1003.1378	1993.0111	1003.1430	1995.0021	1003.1482	1982.0659	1003.1534	1982.0862	1003.1586	1982.0860
1003.1379	1993.0114	1003.1431	1995.0027	1003.1483	1982.0578	1003.1535	1982.0723	1003.1587	1982.0759
1003.1380	1993.0123	1003.1432	1995.0036	1003.1484	1982.0584	1003.1536	1982.0866	1003.1588	1982.0644
1003.1381	1993.0124	1003.1433	1996.0011	1003.1485	1982.0575	1003.1537	1982.0730	1003.1589	1982.0816
1003.1382	1993.0129	1003.1434	1996.0013	1003.1486	1982.0794	1003.1538	1982.0666	1003.1590	1982.0655
1003.1383	1993.0180	1003.1435	1996.0014	1003.1487	1982.0520	1003.1539	1982.0625	1003.1591	1982.0883
1003.1384	1993.0183	1003.1436	1996.0100	1003.1488	1982.0657	1003.1540	1982.0810	1003.1592	1982.0763
1003.1385	1993.0190	1003.1437	1996.0102	1003.1489	1982.0650	1003.1541	1982.0705	1003.1593	1982.0744
1003.1386	1994.0024	1003.1438	1996.0104	1003.1490	1982.0532	1003.1542	1982.0733	1003.1594	1982.0672
1003.1387	1994.0026	1003.1439	1996.0105	1003.1491	1982.0530	1003.1543	1982.0724	1003.1595	1982.0642
1003.1388	1994.0039	1003.1440	1996.0106	1003.1492	1982.0725	1003.1544	1982.0708	1003.1596	1982.0640
1003.1389	1994.0047	1003.1441	1996.0108	1003.1493	1982.0649	1003.1545	1982.0822	1003.1597	1982.0735
1003.1390	1994.0048	1003.1442	1996.0110	1003.1494	1982.0654	1003.1546	1982.0825	1003.1598	1982.0728
1003.1391	1994.0049	1003.1443	1996.0112	1003.1495	1982.0840	1003.1547	1982.0612	1003.1599	1982.0869
1003.1392	1994.0052	1003.1444	1996.0115	1003.1496	1982.0547	1003.1548	1982.0614	1003.1600	1982.0739
1003.1393	1994.0054	1003.1445	1996.0116	1003.1497	1982.0762	1003.1549	1982.0809	1003.1601	1982.0858
1003.1394	1994.0074	1003.1446	1996.0117	1003.1498	1982.0658	1003.1550	1982.0691	1003.1602	1982.0635
1003.1395	1994.0079	1003.1447	1996.0153	1003.1499	1982.0712	1003.1551	1982.0845	1003.1603	1982.0864
1003.1396	1994.0080	1003.1448	1996.0167	1003.1500	1982.0792	1003.1552	1982.0824	1003.1604	1982.0851
1003.1397	1994.0081	1003.1449	1979.1857	1003.1501	1982.0801	1003.1553	1982.0617	1003.1605	1982.0849
1003.1398	1994.0104	1003.1450	1983.0101	1003.1502	1982.0711	1003.1554	1982.0820	1003.1606	1982.0745
1003.1399	1994.0130	1003.1451	1979.1846	1003.1503	1982.0656	1003.1555	1982.0802	1003.1607	1982.0800
1003.1400	1994.0134	1003.1452	1979.1871	1003.1504	1982.0716	1003.1556	1982.0784	1003.1608	1982.0704
1003.1401	1994.0138	1003.1453	1979.1953	1003.1505	1982.0661	1003.1557	1982.0821	1003.1609	1982.0679
1003.1402	1994.0146	1003.1454	1981.0006	1003.1506	1982.0652	1003.1558	1982.0615	1003.1610	1982.0514
1003.1403	1994.0162	1003.1455	1982.0078	1003.1507	1982.0713	1003.1559	1982.0616	1003.1611	1982.0631
1003.1404	1994.0163	1003.1456	1982.0112	1003.1508	1982.0667	1003.1560	1982.0729	1003.1612	1982.0830
1003.1405	1994.0183	1003.1457	1982.0213	1003.1509	1982.0714	1003.1561	1982.0647	1003.1613	1982.0636
1003.1406	1994.0186	1003.1458	1982.0216	1003.1510	1982.0740	1003.1562	1982.0752	1003.1614	1982.0682
1003.1407	1994.0197	1003.1459	1982.0598	1003.1511	1982.0628	1003.1563	1982.0607	1003.1615	1982.0756
1003.1408	1994.0198	1003.1460	1982.0881	1003.1512	1982.0709	1003.1564	1982.0610	1003.1616	1982.0795

1003.1617	1982.0776
1003.1618	1982.0835
1003.1619	1982.0799
1003.1620	1982.0772
1003.1621	1982.0857
1003.1622	1982.0765
1003.1623	1982.0831
1003.1624	1982.0846
1003.1625	1982.0856
1003.1626	1982.0780
1003.1627	1982.0841
1003.1628	1982.0815
1003.1629	1982.0855
1003.1630	1982.0874
1003.1631	1982.0798
1003.1632	1982.0882
1003.1633	1982.0605
1003.1634	1982.0748
1003.1635	1982.0737
1003.1636	1982.0778
1003.1637	1982.0850
1003.1638	1982.0833
1003.1639	1982.0777
1003.1640	1982.0848
1003.1641	1982.0663
1003.1642	1982.0715
1003.1643	1982.0699
1003.1644	1982.0668
1003.1645	1982.0703
1003.1646	1982.0844
1003.1647	1982.0706
1003.1648	1982.0797
1003.1649	1982.0755
1003.1650	1982.0870
1003.1651	1982.0701
1003.1652	1982.0684
1003.1653	1982.0787
1003.1654	1982.0669
1003.1655	1982.0677
1003.1656	1982.0827
1003.1657	1982.0852
1003.1658	1982.0758
1003.1659	1982.0670
1003.1660	1982.0698
1003.1661	1982.0622
1003.1662	1982.0718
1003.1663	1982.0783
1003.1664	1982.0770
1003.1665	1982.0803
1003.1666	1982.0818
1003.1667	1982.0630
1003.1668	1982.0626

1003.1669	1982.0707
1003.1670	1982.0871
1003.1671	1982.0721
1003.1672	1982.0771
1003.1673	1982.0627
1003.1674	1982.0623
1003.1675	1982.0817
1003.1676	1982.0819
1003.1677	1982.0781
1003.1678	1982.0731
1003.1679	1982.0829
1003.1680	1982.0767
1003.1681	1982.0811
1003.1682	1982.0624
1003.1683	1982.0785
1003.1684	1982.0808
1003.1685	1982.0629
1003.1686	1982.0859
1003.1687	1982.0804
1003.1688	1982.0687
1003.1689	1982.0868
1003.1690	1982.0750
1003.1691	1982.0613
1003.1692	1982.0618
1003.1693	1982.0675
1003.1694	1982.0638
1003.1695	1982.0753
1003.1696	1982.0611
1003.1697	1982.0606
1003.1698	1982.0608
1003.1699	1982.0609
1003.1700	1983.0022
1003.1701	1983.0025
1003.1702	1983.0047
1003.1703	1983.0052
1003.1704	1983.0057
1003.1705	1983.0114
1003.1706	1983.0120
1003.1707	1983.0121
1003.1708	1983.0124
1003.1709	1983.0125
1003.1710	1983.0130
1003.1711	1983.0131
1003.1712	1983.0135
1003.1713	1983.0168
1003.1714	1991.0066
1003.1715	1992.0149
1003.1716	1992.0247
1003.1717	1992.0248
1003.1718	1992.0249
1003.1719	1992.0250
1003.1720	1992.0252

1003.1721	1992.0256
1003.1722	1992.0260
1003.1723	1992.0262
1003.1724	1992.0318
1003.1725	1993.0016
1003.1726	1993.0018
1003.1727	1994.0037
1003.1728	1994.0038
1003.1729	1994.0055
1003.1730	1994.0063
1003.1731	1995.0043
1003.1732	1995.0014
1003.1733	1996.0007
1003.1734	1996.0022
1003.1735	1996.0023
1003.1736	1996.0028
1003.1737	1996.0029
1003.1738	1996.0031
1003.1739	1996.0035
1003.1740	1996.0037
1003.1741	1997.0045
1003.1742	1997.0092
1003.1743	1997.0102
1003.1744	1997.0013
1003.1745	1997.0052
1003.1746	1997.0053
1003.1747	1997.0055
1003.1748	1997.0057
1003.1749	1997.0061
1003.1750	1997.0062
1003.1751	1997.0063
1003.1752	1997.0067
1003.1753	1997.0071
1003.1754	1997.0075
1003.1755	1997.0077
1003.1756	1997.0078
1003.1757	1998.0023
1003.1758	1998.0040
1003.1759	1998.0041
1003.1760	1998.0042
1003.1761	1998.0043
1003.1762	1998.0046
1003.1763	1999.0006
1003.1764	1983.0090
1003.1765	1983.0178
1003.1766	1983.0148
1003.1767	1983.0150
1003.1768	1983.0176
1003.1769	1983.0179
1003.1770	1989.0061
1003.1771	1989.0077
1003.1772	2000.0002

1003.1773	1999.0030
1003.1774	1973.1254
1003.1775	1973.1207
1003.1776	1973.1226
1003.1777	1973.1354
1003.1778	1973.1355
1003.1779	1973.1356
1003.1780	1973.1357
1003.1781	1973.1358
1003.1782	1973.1359
1003.1783	1973.1360
1003.1784	1973.1361
1003.1785	1973.1362
1003.1786	1973.1363
1003.1787	1973.1364
1003.1788	1973.1365
1003.1789	1973.1366
1003.1790	1973.1367
1003.1791	1973.1369
1003.1792	1973.1370
1003.1793	1973.1372
1003.1794	1973.1373
1003.1795	1973.1374
1003.1796	1973.1375
1003.1797	1973.1376
1003.1798	1973.1377
1003.1799	1973.1378
1003.1800	1973.1379
1003.1801	1973.1385
1003.1802	1973.1389
1003.1803	1973.1390
1003.1804	1973.1192
1003.1805	2007.0198
1003.1806	2008.0005
1003.1807	2008.0011
1003.1808	2008.0013
1003.1809	2010.0020
1003.1810	2010.0024
1003.1811	2010.0028
1003.1812	2007.0005
1003.1813	2007.0006
1003.1814	2007.0008
1003.1815	2007.0009
1003.1816	2007.0010
1003.1817	2007.0015
1003.1818	2007.0016
1003.1819	2007.0020
1003.1820	2007.0022
1003.1821	2007.0024
1003.1822	2007.0025
1003.1823	2007.0026
1003.1824	2007.0032

1003.1825	2007.0033
1003.1826	2007.0035
1003.1827	2007.0038
1003.1828	2007.0040
1003.1829	2007.0042
1003.1830	2007.0043
1003.1831	2007.0044
1003.1832	2007.0045
1003.1833	2007.0048
1003.1834	2007.0049
1003.1835	2007.0058
1003.1836	2007.0065
1003.1837	2007.0073
1003.1838	2007.0074
1003.1839	2007.0082
1003.1840	2007.0085
1003.1841	2007.0119
1003.1842	2007.0124
1003.1843	2007.0139
1003.1844	2007.0142
1003.1845	2007.0146
1003.1846	2007.0151
1003.1847	2007.0153
1003.1848	2007.0157
1003.1849	2007.0170
1003.1850	2007.0171
1003.1851	2007.0173
1003.1852	2007.0174
1003.1853	2007.0201
1003.1854	2007.0206
1003.1855	2007.0219
1003.1856	2007.0242
1003.1857	2007.0243
1003.1858	2007.0250
1003.1859	2005.0015
1003.1860	1981.C81.0078
1003.1861	1982.0079
1003.1862	1982.0202
1003.1863	1982.0205
1003.1864	1982.0207
1003.1865	1982.0245
1003.1866	1982.C82.0184
1003.1867	1982.C82.0130
1003.1868	1982.C82.0055
1003.1869	1985.0312
1003.1870	1992.0277
1003.1871	1987.0012
1003.1872	1979.1838
1003.1873	1994.0089
1003.1874	1994.0233
1003.1875	1995.0008
1003.1876	2007.0136

1003.1877	1980.C80.0128
1003.1878	1980.C80.0154
1003.1879	1980.C80.0155
1003.1880	1980.C80.0160
1003.1881	1980.C80.0225
1003.1882	1980.C80.0268
1003.1883	1985.0309
1003.1884	1984.0059
1004.0001	1982.0374
1004.0002	1982.0432
1004.0003	1990.0228
1004.0004	2010.0048
1004.0005	1982.0453
1004.0006	1982.0413
1004.0007	1980.C80.0107
1004.0008	1982.0504
1004.0009	1992.0417
1004.0010	1987.0011
1004.0011	1982.0437
1004.0012	1982.0433
1004.0013	1982.C82.0228
1004.0014	1982.C82.0229
1004.0015	1984.0031
1004.0016	1982.0410
1004.0017	1982.C82.0246
1004.0018	1982.C82.0238
1004.0019	1982.C82.0222
1004.0020	1982.0414
1004.0021	1982.0442
1004.0022	1982.0415
1004.0023	2002.0030
1004.0024	1982.0383
1004.0025	1982.0490
1004.0026	1982.0404
1004.0027	1982.0395
1004.0028	1982.0457
1004.0029	1982.C82.0220
1004.0030	1982.0452
1004.0031	1982.0411
1004.0032	1982.0405
1004.0033	1982.0406
1004.0034	1982.0546
1004.0035	1982.0528
1004.0036	1982.0445
1004.0037	1982.0441
1004.0038	1982.0438
1004.0039	1982.0774
1004.0040	1982.C82.0247
1004.0041	1982.C82.0216
1004.0042	1990.0160
1004.0043	1982.0459
1004.0044	1995.0042

1004.0045	2002.0247
1004.0046	1982.0436
1004.0047	1991.0391
1004.0048	1980.C80.0117
1004.0049	1973.1238
1004.0050	1973.1170
1004.0051	1982.0596
1004.0052	1987.0023
1004.0053	1982.0873
1004.0054	1982.0412
1004.0055	1980.0083
1004.0056	1982.C82.0231
1004.0057	1982.C82.0217
1004.0058	1982.0375
1004.0059	1985.0005
1004.0060	1973.1158
1004.0061	1982.0597
1004.0062	1982.0878
1004.0063	1982.0397
1004.0064	1982.C82.0227
1004.0065	1979.1862
1004.0066	1980.C80.0215
1004.0067	1982.0431
1004.0068	1982.0448
1004.0069	1982.0428
1004.0070	1982.0585
1004.0071	1987.0024
1004.0072	1982.0388
1004.0073	1992.0136
1004.0074	2002.0143
1004.0075	1982.C82.0237
1004.0076	1982.0536
1004.0077	1982.0418
1004.0078	1982.0391
1004.0079	1982.0379
1004.0080	1982.0686
1004.0081	1979.2152
1004.0082	1980.C80.0096
1004.0083	1982.0426
1004.0084	1982.0398
1004.0085	1982.0393
1004.0086	1990.0189
1004.0087	1982.0427
1004.0088	1984.0013
1004.0089	1991.0339
1004.0090	1980.C80.0141
1004.0091	1991.0098
1004.0092	1982.0472
1004.0093	1982.0408
1004.0094	1982.0382
1004.0095	1982.0505
1004.0096	2002.0111

1004.0097	1982.0451
1004.0098	1982.0425
1004.0099	1979.2011
1004.0100	1980.0047
1004.0101	1987.0030
1004.0102	1982.0462
1004.0103	1982.C82.0230
1004.0104	1982.C82.0219
1004.0105	1982.0555
1004.0106	1982.0447
1004.0107	1982.0435
1004.0108	1982.0409
1004.0109	1982.0376
1004.0110	1982.0588
1004.0111	1982.0440
1004.0112	1982.0422
1004.0113	1982.0403
1004.0114	1982.0385
1004.0115	1990.0227
1004.0116	1982.0377
1004.0117	1997.0070
1004.0118	1982.0400
1004.0119	1982.C82.0233
1004.0120	1982.0434
1004.0121	1982.0502
1004.0122	1982.0458
1004.0123	1982.C82.0226
1004.0124	1982.C82.0221
1004.0125	1982.0396
1004.0126	1982.0444
1004.0127	1982.0443
1004.0128	1994.0076
1004.0129	1982.0380
1004.0130	1982.0402
1004.0131	1982.0449
1004.0132	1979.1949
1004.0133	1982.C82.0236
1004.0134	1982.0702
1004.0135	1980.C80.0358
1004.0136	1982.0537
1004.0137	1984.0037
1004.0138	1979.1962
1004.0139	2007.0213
1004.0140	1987.0038
1004.0141	1982.0439
1004.0142	1982.C82.0224
1004.0143	1982.0454
1004.0144	1982.0401
1004.0145	1990.0179
1004.0146	1993.0012
1004.0147	1984.0137
1004.0148	1998.0044

1004.0149	1995.0039
1004.0150	1982.C82.0232
1004.0151	1982.0424
1004.0152	1982.0417
1004.0153	1982.0387
1004.0154	1982.0416
1004.0155	1979.2131
1004.0156	1982.0384
1004.0157	1982.0420
1004.0158	1978.1551
1004.0159	1985.0240
1004.0160	1982.0456
1004.0161	1982.0879
1004.0162	1982.C82.0218
1004.0163	1973.1368
1004.0164	1984.0064
1004.0165	1982.0390
1004.0166	1982.0399
1004.0167	1982.0455
1004.0168	1982.0423
1004.0169	1982.0419
1004.0170	1982.0430
1004.0171	1982.0429
1004.0172	1982.0407
1004.0173	1982.0373
1004.0174	1987.0029
1004.0175	1982.0394
1004.0176	1982.0044
1004.0177	1982.0446
1004.0178	1983.0077
1004.0179	1982.0496
1004.0180	1982.0378
1004.0181	1982.0478
1004.0182	1982.0389
1004.0183	1982.0880
1004.0184	1982.C82.0225
1004.0185	1982.0421
1004.0186	1982.0485
1004.0187	1982.C82.0223
1004.0188	1982.0484
1004.0189	1982.0823
1004.0190	1982.0450
1004.0191	1982.0386
1004.0192	1982.0392
1004.0193	1980.0048
1004.0194	1997.0076
1004.0195	2000.0013
1004.0196	1982.C82.0235
1004.0197	1982.C82.0234
1004.0198	1982.0692
1004.0199	1984.0012
1004.0200	1992.0215

1005.0001	1973.1123
1005.0002	1990.0240
1006.0001	1987.C87.0001
1006.0002	2005.0025
1006.0003	1989.C89.0009
1006.0004	2005.0002
1007.0001	1990.C90.0013
1007.0002	1990.0241
1007.0003	1990.0242
1007.0004	1990.0243
1008.0001	1987.0088
1009.0001	1973.1177
1009.0002	1978.1794
1010.0001	1990.0233
1010.0002	1973.1130
1010.0003	1985.C85.0016
1010.0004	1990.0283
1010.0005	1989.0088
1010.0006	1984.0189
1010.0007	1973.1349
1011.0001	2002.0047
1011.0002	1985.0232
1012.0001	1992.0180
1012.0002	1985.NoEx85.0033
1013.0001	1978.1636
1013.0002	1995.0034
1013.0003	1980.C80.0254
1014.0001	1973.1166
1014.0002	1992.0112
1014.0003	1985.0246
1015.0001	1993.NoEx93.0013
1016.0001	1994.0002
1016.0002	1996.0065
1016.0003	1973.1129
1017.0001	1994.NoEx94.0006
1018.0001	1979.1869
1018.0002	1985.0172
1019.0001	1996.0095
1019.0002	1983.0036
1020.0001	1983.0027
1020.0002	1984.0125
1021.0001	1996.0030
1021.0002	1994.0075
1022.0001	1989.0196
1023.0001	1982.C82.0065
1024.0001	1989.0068
1025.0001	1980.C80.0361
1026.0001	1992.0211
1026.0002	1981.C81.0032
1026.0003	1980.C80.0220
1026.0004	2008.0016
1026.0005	1978.1633

1026.0006	2003.0001
1026.0007	2011.0013
1026.0008	1979.2133
1026.0009	1973.1125
1026.0010	1992.0329
1026.0011	1980.C80.0110
1026.0012	1973.1131
1026.0013	2010.0002
1026.0014	1980.C80.0125
1026.0015	2002.0074
1026.0016	2001.0003
1027.0001	2000.0021
1028.0001	1973.1380
1029.0001	1992.0302
1030.0001	1991.0442
1031.0001	1973.1286
1032.0001	1994.NoEx94.0010
1033.0001	1989.0175
1033.0002	1978.1622
1034.0001	1973.1338
1035.0001	1989.0025
1036.0001	2007.0230
1036.0002	1979.2100
1036.0003	1996.0047
1037.0001	1981.C81.0074
1037.0002	1979.2128
1038.0001	1982.0237
1039.0001	1973.1155
1040.0001	1992.0328
1041.0001	1979.1821
1042.0001	1984.0186
1043.0001	1994.0103
1044.0001	1983.0074
1045.0001	1982.C82.0084
1046.0001	1989.C89.0002
1047.0001	1992.0087
1048.0001	1978.1480
1049.0001	1973.1352
1049.0002	1979.1825
1049.0003	1973.1234
1050.0001	1990.0212
1051.0001	1993.0174
1052.0001	1994.0061
1052.0002	1982.C82.0038
1052.0003	1988.0084
1053.0001	1978.1745
1054.0001	1986.0017
1054.0002	1982.C82.0002
1055.0001	1983.0098
1055.0002	1985.C85.0029
1055.0003	1980.C80.0091
1055.0004	1989.0081
1055.0005	1991.0140
1056.0001	1978.1509
1056.0002	1993.0127
1057.0001	1989.0197
1058.0001	1980.C80.0379
1058.0002	1992.0118
1058.0003	1980.C80.0293
1058.0004	1994.0031
1058.0005	1973.1384
1059.0001	1994.0192
1060.0001	1986.0011
1061.0001	1980.0127
1062.0001	2002.0088
1062.0002	1985.0257
1063.0001	1990.0214
1063.0002	1973.1241
1063.0003	1973.1350
1064.0001	1993.NoEx93.0052
1065.0001	1995.0017
1065.0002	1994.0087
1066.0001	1994.0060
1067.0001	1973.1278
1068.0001	1989.C89.0017
1069.0001	1991.NoEx91.0001
1069.0002	1985.NoEx85.0038
1069.0003	1989.0188
1070.0001	1992.0291
1071.0001	1994.NoEx94.0005
1071.0002	1992.0271
1072.0001	1989.0008
1072.0002	1986.C86.0001
1073.0001	1973.1091
1073.0002	1992.0304
1073.0003	1994.0213
1073.0004	1973.1092
1073.0005	1995.0025
1073.0006	1980.C80.0310
1073.0007	1978.1621
1073.0008	1980.C80.0217
1073.0009	1980.C80.0274
1073.0010	1980.C80.0328
1073.0011	1991.0027
1073.0012	1973.1330
1073.0013	1994.0176
1073.0014	1990.0250
1073.0015	1980.C80.0371
1073.0016	1992.0293
1073.0017	1979.1971
1073.0018	1980.C80.0363
1073.0019	1989.0020
1073.0020	1978.1788
1073.0021	1979.1963
1073.0022	1994.0008
1073.0023	1994.0193
1073.0024	1986.0020
1073.0025	1978.1786
1074.0001	1979.2129
1074.0002	1978.1527
1075.0001	1984.0188
1075.0002	1989.C89.0015
1076.0001	1993.0132
1077.0001	1992.0303
1077.0002	1973.1323
1077.0003	1982.C82.0186
1077.0004	1982.C82.0048
1077.0005	1979.1822
1078.0001	1979.2125
1079.0001	1978.1531
1079.0002	1980.C80.0348
1080.0001	2007.0252
1081.0001	1982.C82.0047
1082.0001	1992.0240
1083.0001	1995.0035
1083.0002	1978.1530
1084.0001	1992.0461
1085.0001	1994.0077
1086.0001	1996.0026
1087.0001	1973.1165
1088.0001	2012.0003
1089.0001	1982.C82.0187
1090.0001	1980.C80.0273
1091.0001	1980.C80.0335
1092.0001	1973.1197
1093.0001	1983.C83.0023
1094.0001	1979.1950
1095.0001	1979.1873
1096.0001	1983.C83.0028
1097.0001	1984.C84.0018
1097.0002	1979.2149
1097.0003	1979.1878
1097.0004	1978.1758
1098.0001	1992.0159
1099.0001	1973.1127
1100.0001	1982.C82.0005
1101.0001	1989.0122
1101.0002	1993.NoEx93.0010
1101.0003	1989.NoEx89.0002
1102.0001	1992.0131
1102.0002	1987.NoEx87.0017
1103.0001	1991.0210
1104.0001	1994.0194
1104.0002	1990.0235
1104.0003	1989.0079
1105.0001	1980.C80.0045
1106.0001	1982.C82.0240
1106.0002	1982.0492
1106.0003	1982.0671
1106.0004	1982.C82.0242
1106.0005	1982.0552
1106.0006	1982.C82.0241
1106.0007	1982.0506
1106.0008	1982.0593
1107.0001	1992.0453
1107.0002	1992.0008
1108.0001	1990.0082
1109.0001	1993.0044
1110.0001	1980.C80.0113
1111.0001	1992.0459
1112.0001	1984.0099
1113.0001	1990.0043
1114.0001	1982.C82.0243
1115.0001	1993.NoEx93.0035
1116.0001	1993.0011
1116.0002	1992.0225
1117.0001	2002.0196
1118.0001	1992.0202
1119.0001	1980.0133a
1120.0001	1980.C80.0033
1121.0001	1990.0017
1122.0001	1994.0184
1123.0001	1994.0143
1124.0001	1979.1955
1125.0001	1973.1150
1125.0002	1973.1353
1126.0001	1979.2057
1127.0001	1992.0147
1128.0001	1973.1126
1128.0002	1997.0015
1129.0001	1991.0395
1130.0001	1979.1909
1131.0001	1983.0051
1132.0001	1984.C84.0005
1132.0002	1994.0191
1133.0001	1979.2097
1134.0001	1992.0297
1135.0001	1997.0123
1135.0002	1980.C80.0353
1136.0001	1982.0051
1137.0001	1979.1954
1138.0001	2000.0019
1139.0001	1989.0062
1140.0001	1999.0042
1140.0002	1973.1289
1140.0003	1991.0396
1141.0001	1989.C89.0010
1141.0002	1994.0109
1142.0001	1994.0012
1143.0001	1992.0335
1144.0001	1975.1407
1144.0002	1982.C82.0185
1145.0001	1982.C82.0003
1145.0002	1993.0073
1146.0001	1992.0424
1147.0001	1979.2147
1147.0002	1979.2120
1148.0001	1992.0203
1149.0001	1973.1231
1149.0002	1997.0083
1150.0001	1983.0152
1151.0001	1994.0182
1152.0001	1992.0344
1153.0001	1997.0127
1154.0001	1998.0034
1155.0001	1978.1479
1156.0001	1980.C80.0018
1157.0001	1978.1779
1158.0001	2012.0046
1158.0002	1982.C82.0051
1159.0001	1978.1751
1160.0001	1979.2122
1161.0001	1980.C80.0153
1161.0002	1979.1945
1162.0001	2000.0022
1163.0001	1978.1756
1164.0001	1992.0354
1165.0001	1994.0127
1166.0001	1973.1371
1167.0001	2013.0012
1168.0001	1994.0175
1169.0001	1993.NoEx93.0039
1170.0001	1983.0048
1171.0001	1973.1230
1172.0001	1994.0115
1173.0001	1973.1124
1174.0001	2001.0016
1175.0001	1978.1807
1176.0001	1992.0374
1177.0001	1973.1351
1178.0001	1992.0407
1178.0002	1983.0147
1178.0003	1973.1381
1179.0001	1982.C82.0046
1179.0002	1980.C80.0050
1179.0003	1982.C82.0071
1180.0001	1983.0092
1181.0001	2000.0005
1181.0002	1978.1780
1181.0003	1980.C80.0332

1182.0001	1994.0112
1183.0001	1991.0067
1184.0001	1997.0079
1184.0002	1978.1749
1184.0003	1995.0031
1184.0004	1991.0037
1184.0005	1992.0084
1184.0006	1990.C90.0001
1184.0007	1989.0165
1184.0008	1993.0038
1184.0009	1983.0166
1184.0010	1978.1750
1185.0001	1991.0095
1186.0001	1989.0167
1187.0001	2003.0007
1187.0002	1979.1911
1188.0001	1979.1910
1188.0002	1983.C83.0004
1189.0001	1987.0075
1190.0001	1994.NoEx94.0001
1191.0001	1973.1164
1192.0001	1973.1114
1193.0001	1994.0102
1194.0001	1973.1080
1195.0001	1984.0187
1196.0001	1988.0109
1197.0001	1973.1143
1198.0001	1993.NoEx93.0006
1199.0001	1998.0019
1199.0002	1994.0003
1199.0003	1985.0174
1200.0001	1982.0240
1200.0002	1973.1382
1200.0003	1987.0005
1200.0004	1987.0018
1200.0005	1973.1233

1200.0006	1985.0173
1200.0007	1985.0243
1200.0008	2008.0015
1200.0009	1973.1239
1200.0010	1982.0236
1200.0011	1985.0209
1200.0012	1980.0148
1200.0013	1997.0100
1200.0014	1973.1393
1200.0015	1985.NoEx85.0040
1200.0016	1973.1175
1200.0017	1982.0238
1201.0001	1998.NoEx98.0001
1202.0001	1985.NoEx85.0019
1203.0001	1987.0074
1204.0001	1973.1160
1204.0002	1983.C83.0018
1204.0003	1988.0085
1204.0004	1973.1149
1204.0005	1980.C80.0311
1205.0001	1994.0053
1206.0001	1994.0059
1207.0001	1987.C87.0004
1207.0002	1985.NoEx85.0020
1208.0001	1996.0180
1208.0002	1973.1118
1209.0001	1988.0100
1210.0001	1996.0169
1211.0001	1994.NoEx94.0003
1212.0001	1997.0088
1213.0001	1973.1229
1214.0001	1982.0239
1215.0001	1983.0149
1216.0001	2007.0205
1217.0001	1997.0003
1218.0001	1994.0041

1219.0001	1978.1784
1220.0001	1994.0045
1221.0001	1987.C87.0007
1221.0002	2007.0080
1222.0001	1991.0068
1223.0001	2003.0016
1224.0001	1991.0256
1224.0002	2007.0092
1225.0001	1973.1383
1226.0001	1973.1327
1227.0001	2007.0105
1227.0002	2007.0143
1228.0001	1991.0039
1228.0002	1973.1280
1229.0001	1973.1181
1230.0001	1989.C89.0003
1231.0001	1973.1140
1232.0001	1973.1128
1232.0002	1973.1088
1232.0003	1973.1159
1233.0001	1973.1109
1234.0001	1976.0004
1235.0001	2007.0156
1236.0001	2000.0014
1237.0001	2005.0001
1238.0001	1982.C82.0111
1239.0001	1990.0185
1240.0001	1973.1261
1241.0001	1985.C85.0018
1241.0002	1982.C82.0032
1242.0001	1979.1840
1242.0002	1979.1886
1242.0003	1986.C86.0011
1243.0001	1984.C84.0040
1243.0002	2013.0005
1243.0003	1973.1307

1244.0001	1985.NoEx85.0001
1245.0001	1973.1290
1245.0002	1981.C81.0031
1245.0003	1992.NoEx92.0013
1245.0004	1981.C81.0030
1245.0005	1979.1923
1246.0001	1993.NoEx93.0049
1246.0002	1983.0001
1246.0003	1977.1448
1246.0004	1978.1481
1246.0005	1983.C83.0012
1246.0006	1993.NoEx93.0066
1247.0001	1984.C84.0039
1247.0002	1993.NoEx93.0011
1248.0001	1992.NoEx92.0002
1248.0002	2013.0016
1249.0001	1973.1244
1249.0002	1978.1646
1250.0001	1984.0190
1250.0002	1984.C84.0014
1250.0003	1973.1324
1251.0001	1985.NoEx85.0003
1251.0002	1982.C82.0031
1251.0003	1979.1887
1251.0004	1976.0012
1252.0001	1973.1288
1252.0002	1973.1253
1252.0003	1973.1258
1253.0001	2009.0018
1253.0002	1976.0011
1254.0001	1977.1450
1255.0001	1977.1451
1255.0002	2009.0012
1255.0003	1978.1482
1256.0001	1977.1417
1257.0001	1978.1647

1257.0002	1985.NoEx85.0014
1258.0001	1978.1645
1259.0001	1989.0006
1260.0001	2002.0219
1261.0001	1978.1483
1262.0001	1975.1406
1263.0001	1979.2109
1264.0001	1985.C85.0015
1265.0001	1981.C81.0024
1266.0001	1976.0007
1267.0001	1978.1644
1267.0002	1979.1875
L01	2012.0038
L02	2004.0014
L03	1985.NoEx85.0015
L04	2007.0144
L05	1994.0004
L06	1996.0061
L07	1980.C80.0123
L08	1986.0031
L09	1997.0001
L10	1996.0082
L11	1981.C81.0028
L13	1976.0002
L14	1978.1746
L15	1992.0245
L16	1989.NoEx89.0013
L17	1978.1809
L18	1973.1268
L21	1994.0241
L22	1992.0103
L23	1994.0148
L24	2001.0006

Index of Names and Geographical Places

General Index

PLATES

Lydian Royal Coinage

1.1 1.2 2.1 3.1 4.1 5.1 6.1

Hellenistic Coins

19.1 24.1 26.1 39.1 42.1 48.1 51.2

52.2 52.10 52.15 52.17 52.18 52.19 52.28 52.32

52.46 53.1 55.2 55.7 55.14 57.1 65.1

Seleucid Coinage

69.1 70.1 73.1 75.1 79.1 79.2

85.1 87.1 91.2

Roman Provincial Coinage

97.1 98.2 100.1 109.1 111.1

123.1 124.1 127.1 138.1 139.1 143.1 145.7

147.1

148.1

150.2

151.1

153.2

157.1

157.2

163.2

165.1

167.1

169.1

170.2

172.2

176.2

178.1

184.1

184.3

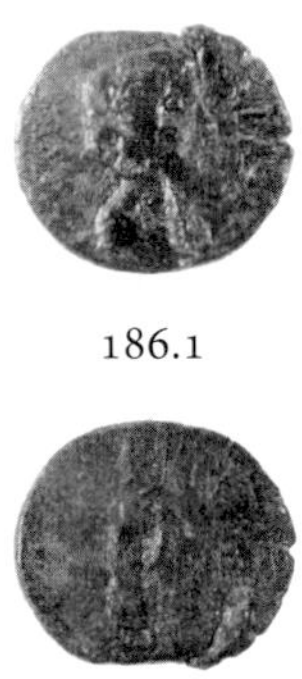
186.1

191.1

192.1

195.1

197.1 208.1 210.1 219.2 220.1 229.1

Roman Imperial Coinage

236.1 237.1 244.2 258.1 259.1 282.2

284.1 286.1 311.1 320.1 384.1

Late Roman Coinage

414.1 540.1 633.1 659.2 694.1 710.1

711.1 777.1 780.1 839.9 911.1

Byzantine Coinage

1021.2 1047.1 1158.1 1255.2 1263.1

Plate 6

Lead and Other Materials

L1

L2

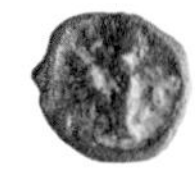
L3

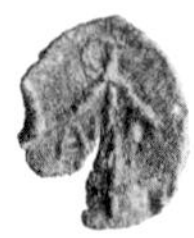
L4

L5

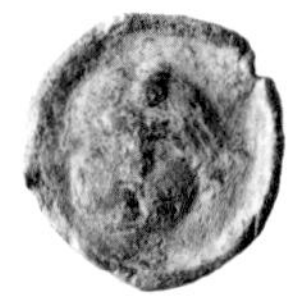
L6

L7

L13

L16

L17

L18

L19

L20

L24

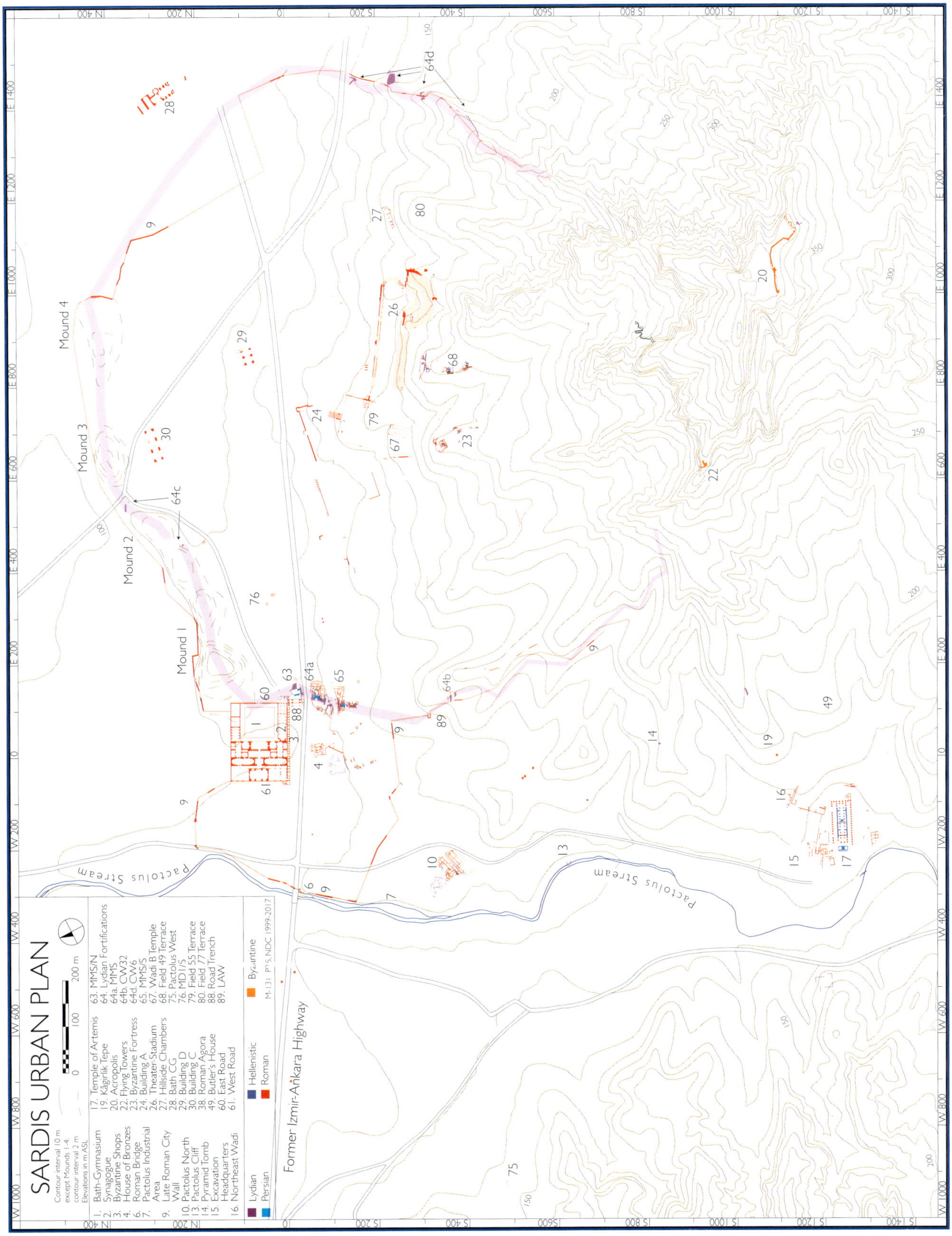

Figure 1.1 Map of Sardis. See p. xxi for full list of sector abbreviations.

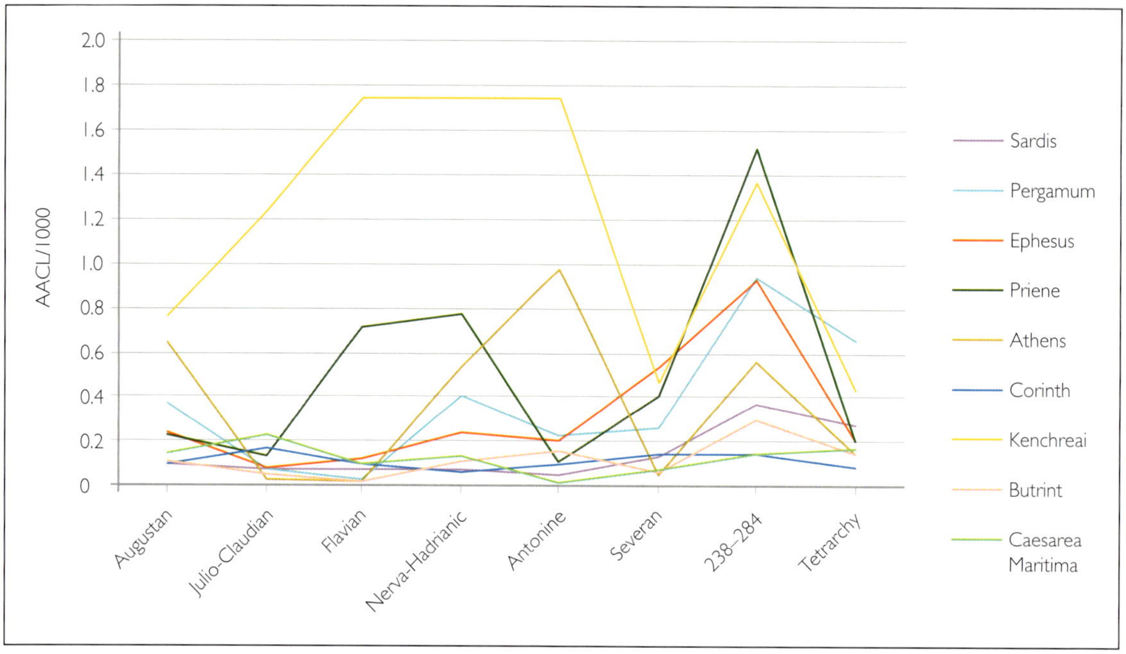

Figure 2.1 Average Annual Coin Loss/1000 for cities in the Roman East, Augustus through the Tetrarchy, all cities tested with Chi-Square Goodness of Fit test.

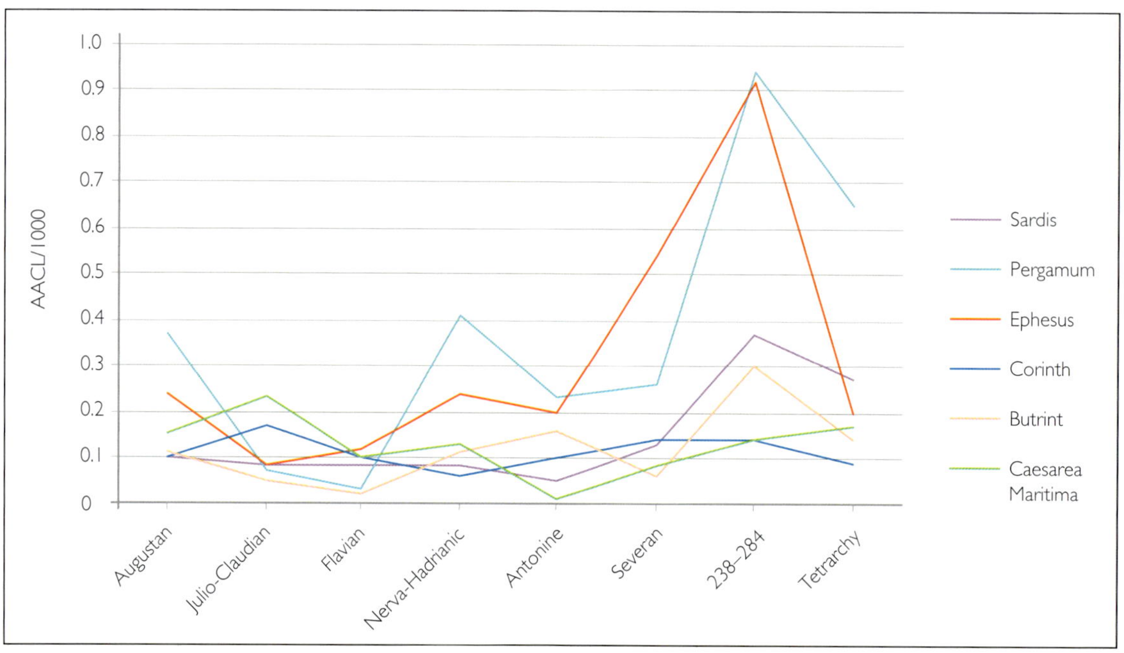

Figure 2.2 Average Annual Coin Loss/1000 for cities in the Roman East, Augustus through the Tetrarchy, cities with "normal" profile.

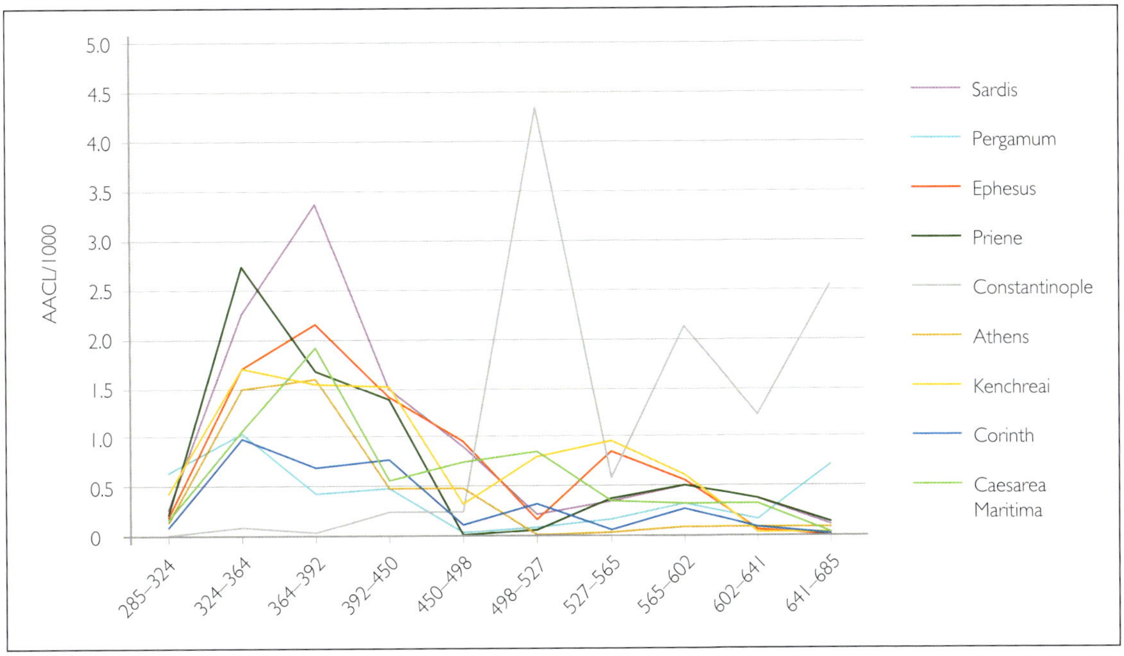

Figure 2.3 Average Annual Coin Loss/1000 for cities in the Roman East, Late Roman to Early Byzantine periods, all cities tested with Chi-Square Goodness of Fit test.

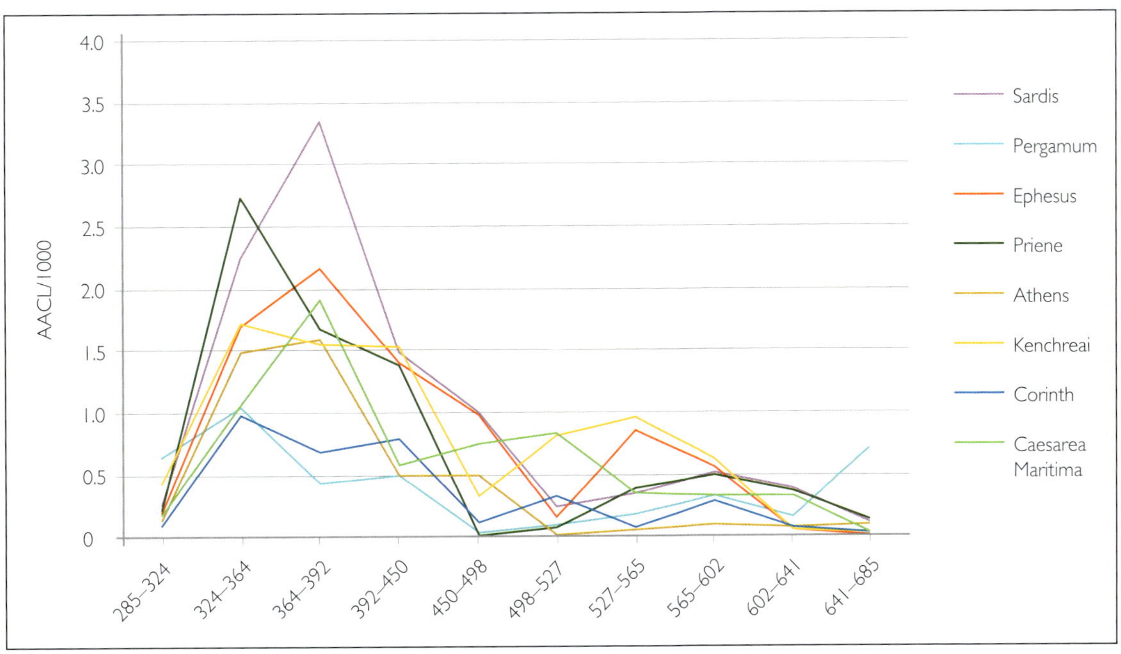

Figure 2.4 Average Annual Coin Loss/1000 for cities in the Roman East, Late Roman through Early Byzantine periods, cities with "normal" profile.

Figure 2.5 Comparative cities for Average Annual Coin Loss/1000 calculations.

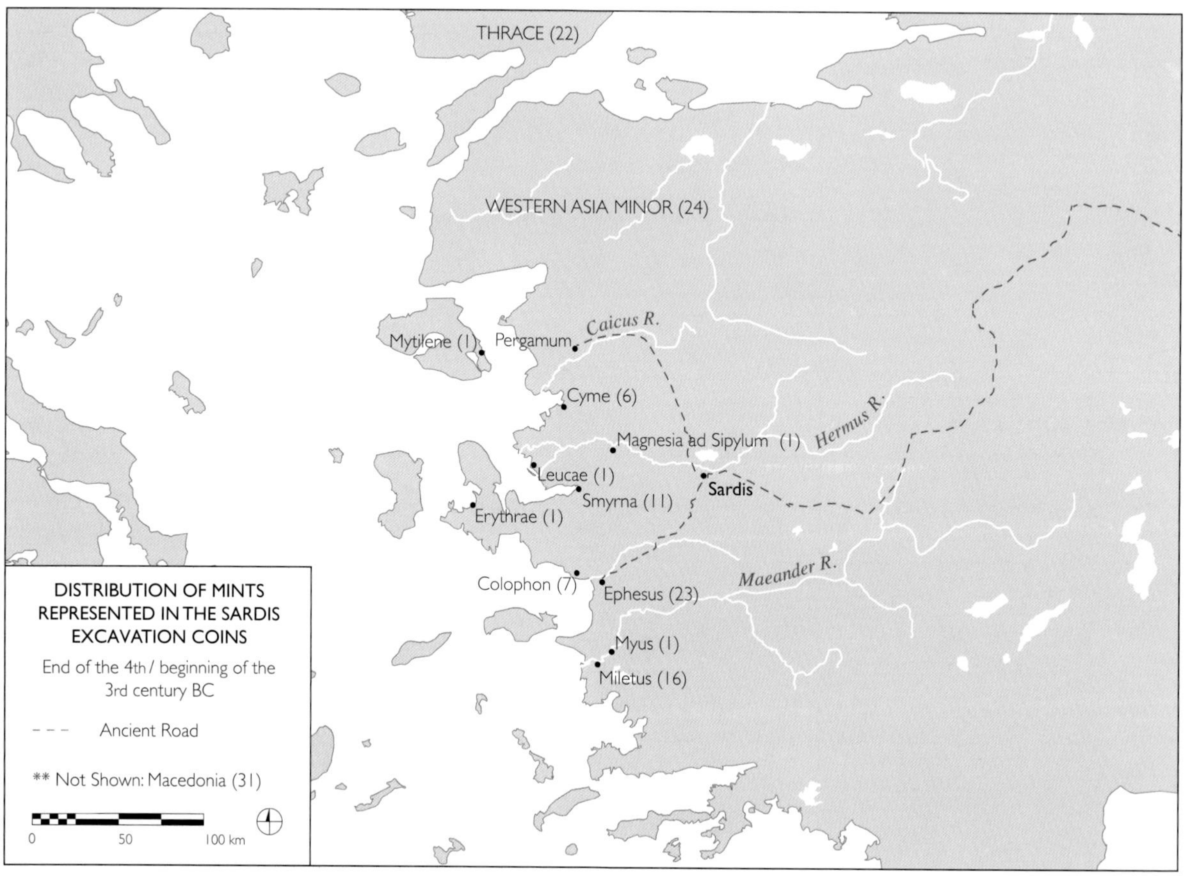

Figure 2.6 Distribution of mints represented in the Sardis excavation coins, end of the fourth to beginning of the third century BC, with major roads (all maps inclusive of years 1958–2013).

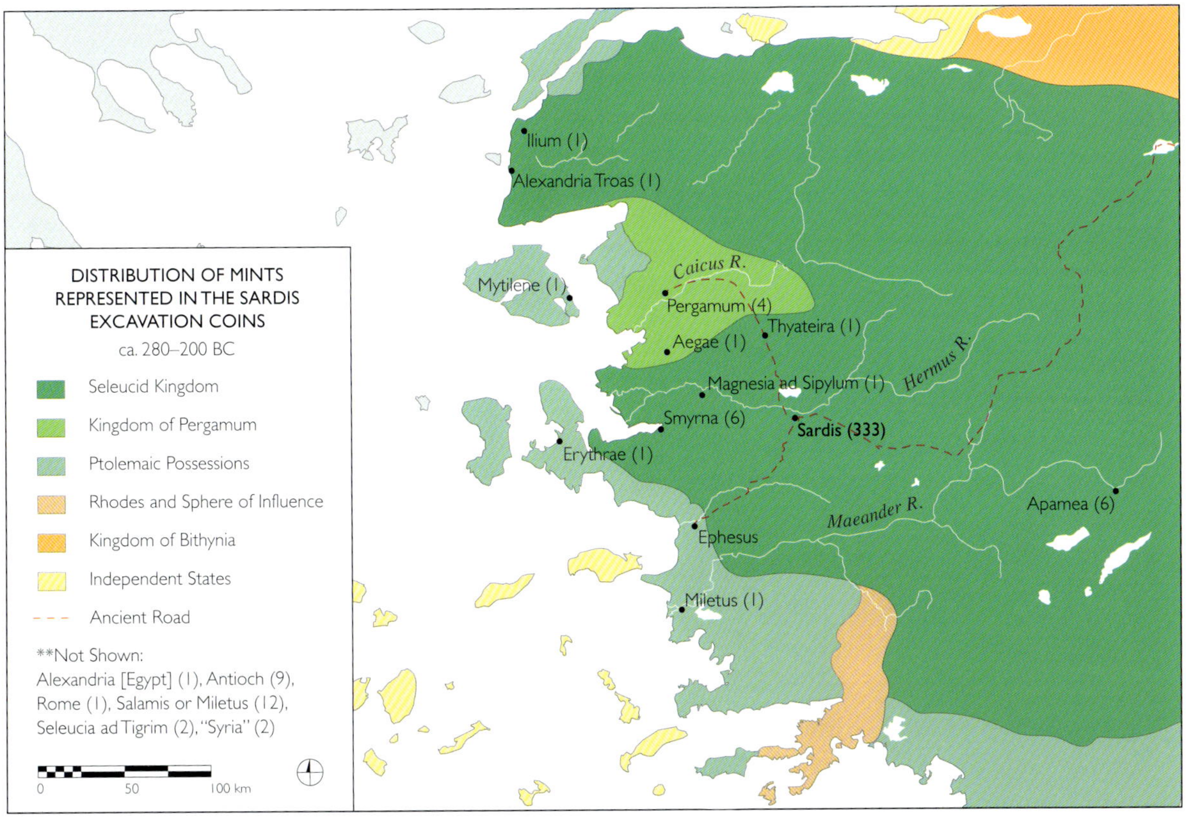

Figure 2.7 Distribution of mints represented in the Sardis excavation coins, ca. 280–200 BC.

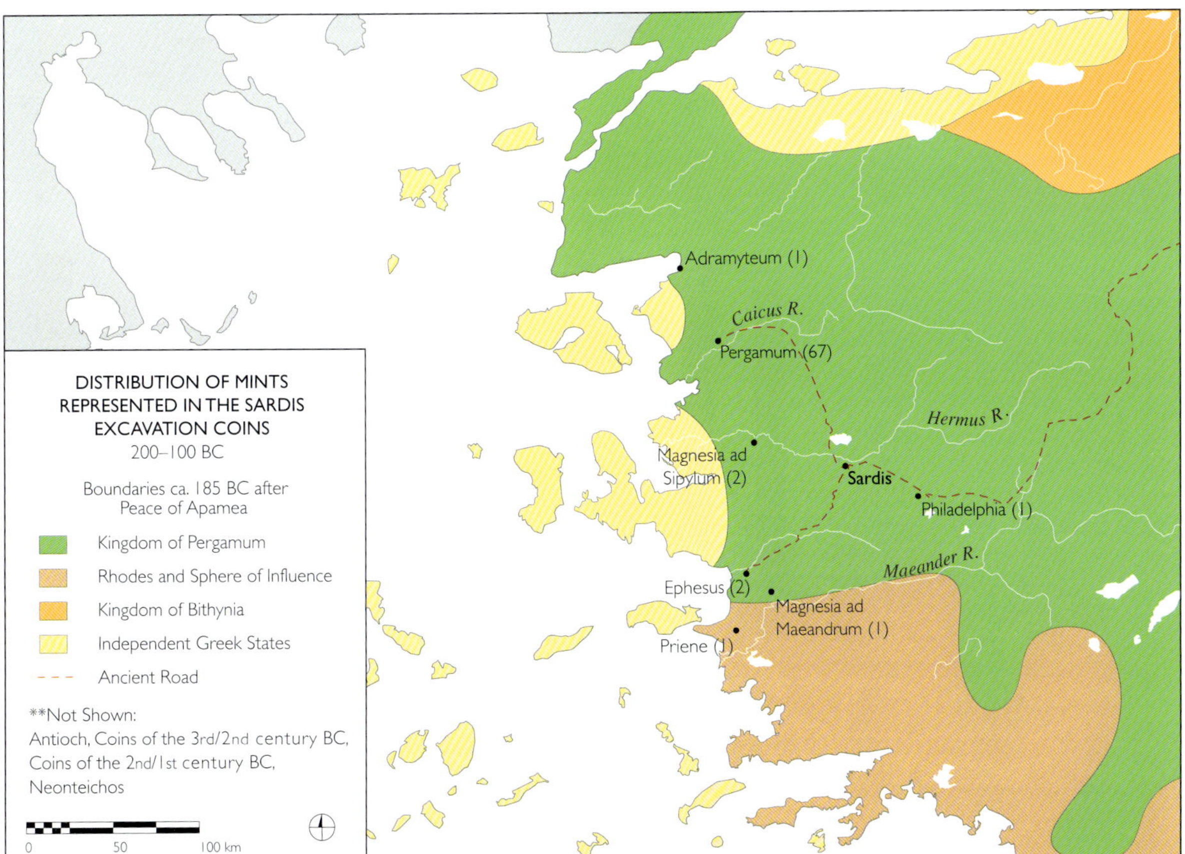

Figure 2.8 Distribution of mints represented in the Sardis excavation coins, 200–100 BC.

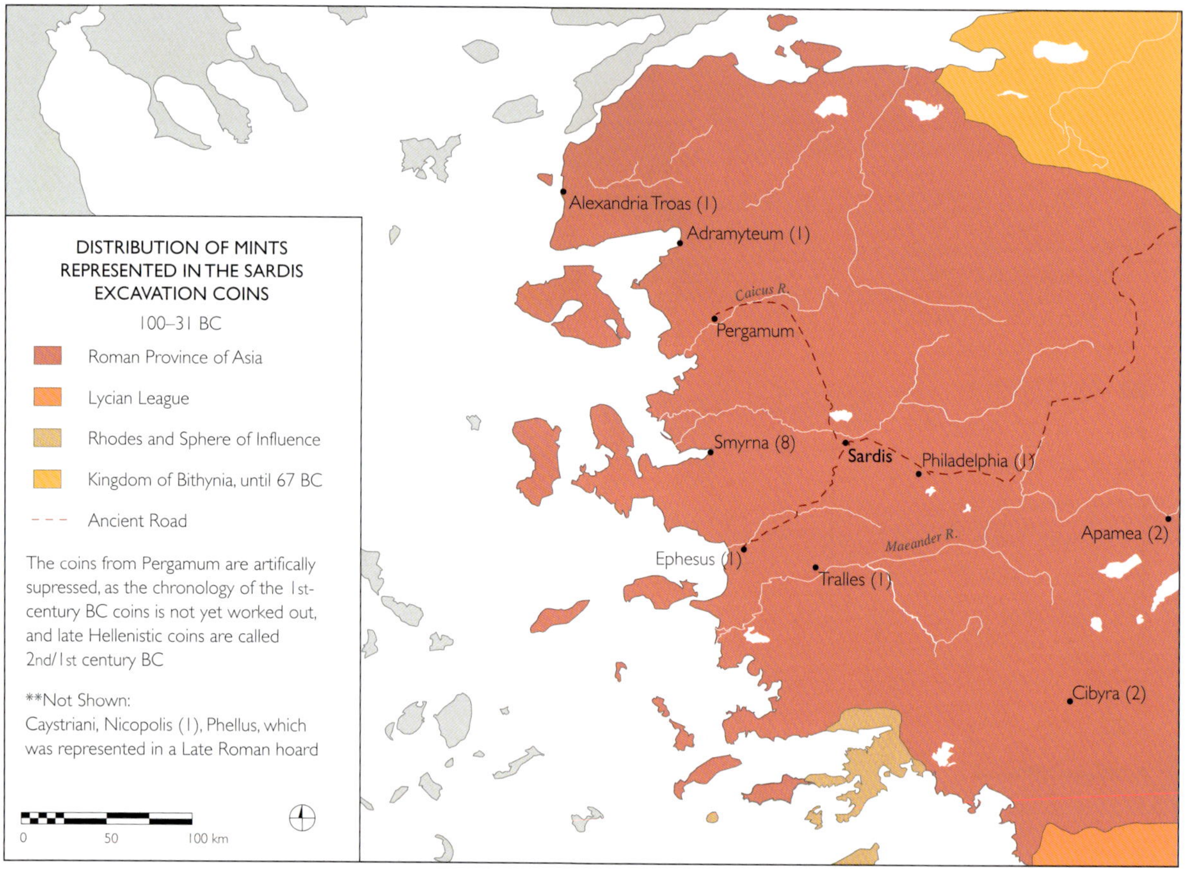

Figure 2.9 Distribution of mints represented in the Sardis excavation coins, 100–31 BC.

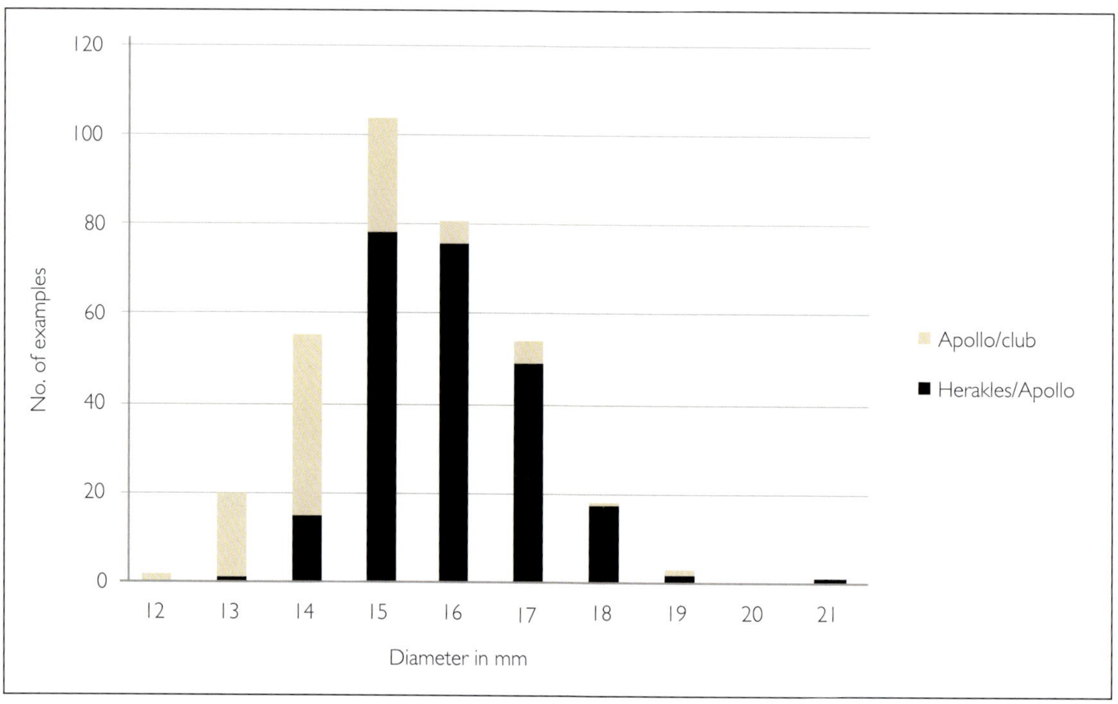

Figure 2.10 Diameters of Herakles/Apollo and Apollo/club coins in millimeters (includes M7 and M13 coins).

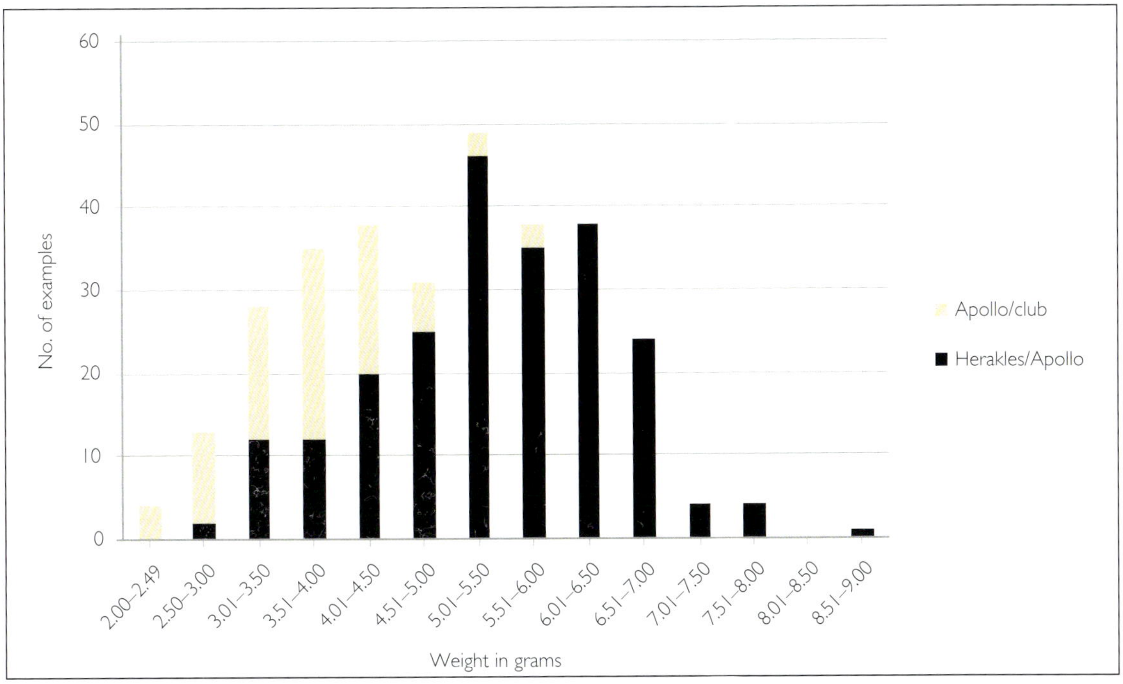

Figure 2.11 Weight of Herakles/Apollo and Apollo/club coins in grams (includes M7 and M13 coins).

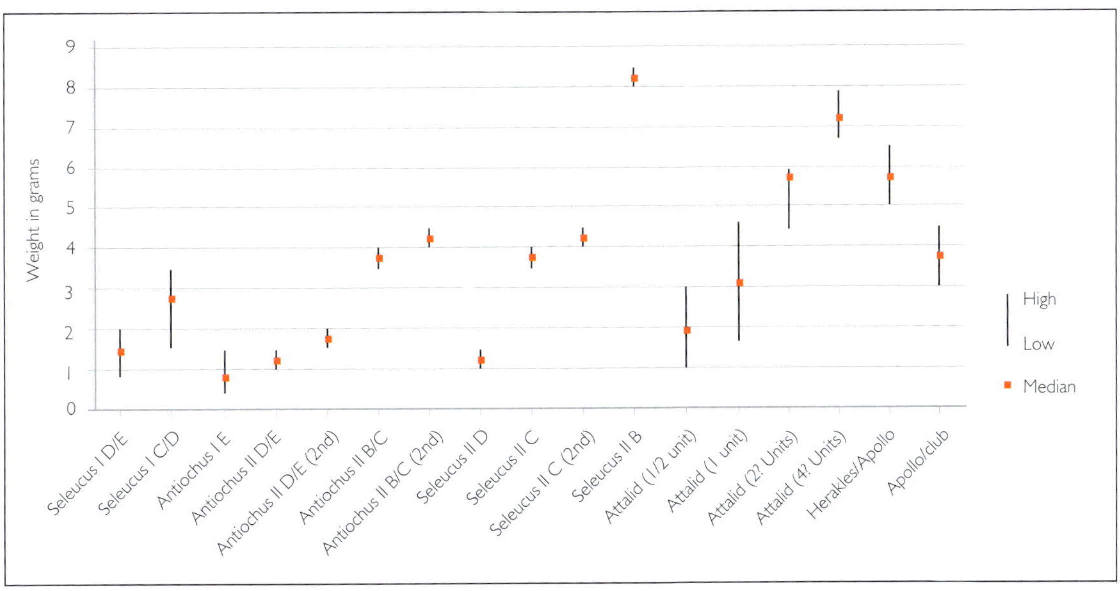

Figure 2.12 Weights of Seleucid bronze issues from Sardis and Pergamum, compared to Herakles/Apollo and Apollo/club bronzes (after Kritt in Houghton and Lorber 2002, II: 7–9; Hoover suggested the denomination titles).

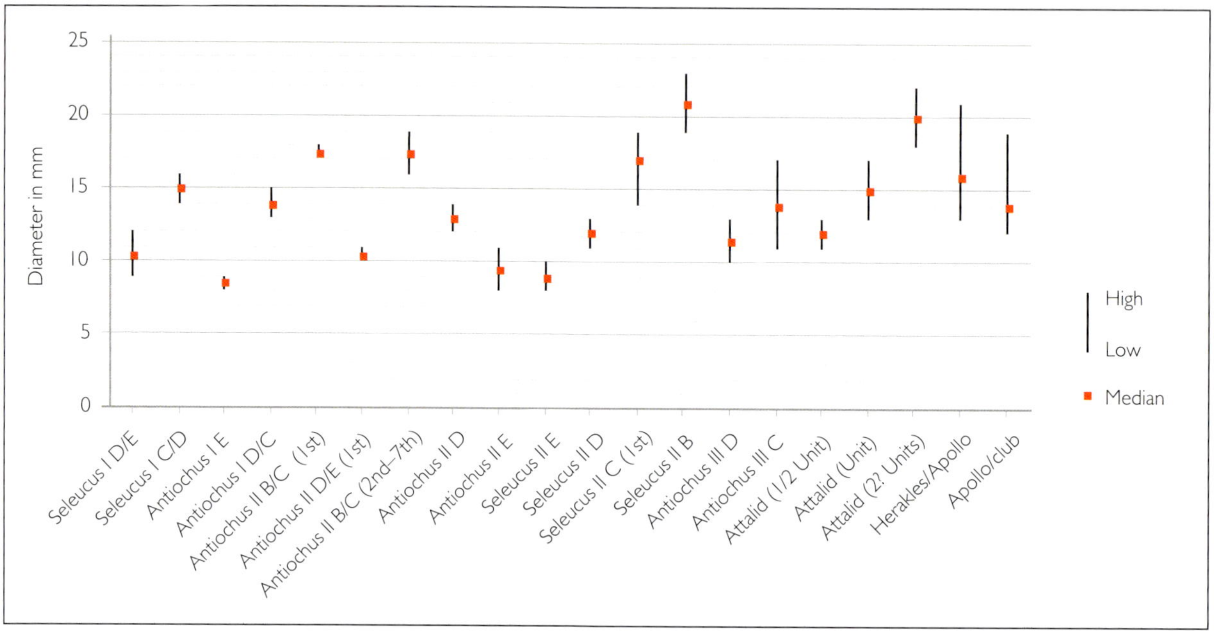

Figure 2.13 Comparison of diameters of Seleucid and Attalid coins, with Herakles/Apollo and Apollo/club bronzes (the high and low of the Seleucid coins are averages given in Houghton and Lorber 2002; diameters for Attalid coins are taken from the M13 catalog).

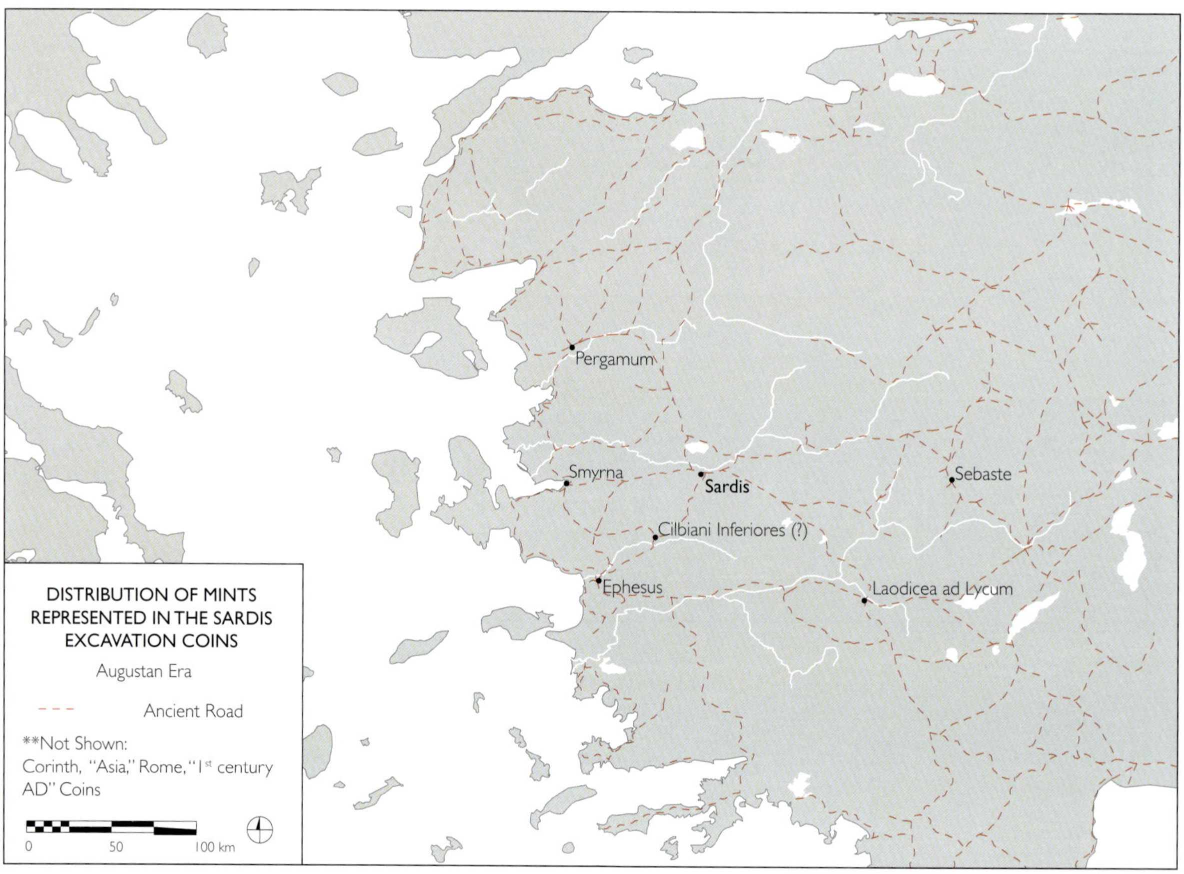

Figure 2.14 Distribution of mints represented in the Sardis excavation coins, Augustan era.

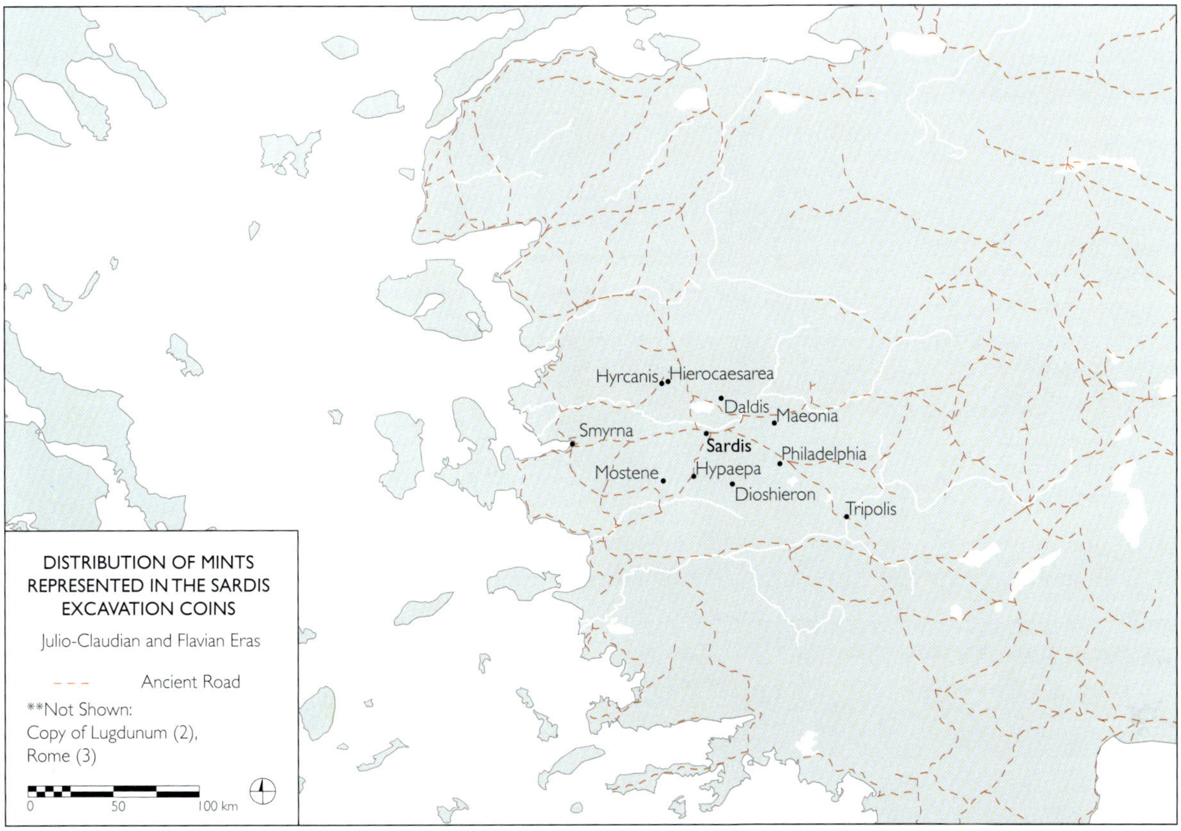

Figure 2.15 Distribution of mints represented in the Sardis excavation coins, Julio-Claudian and Flavian eras.

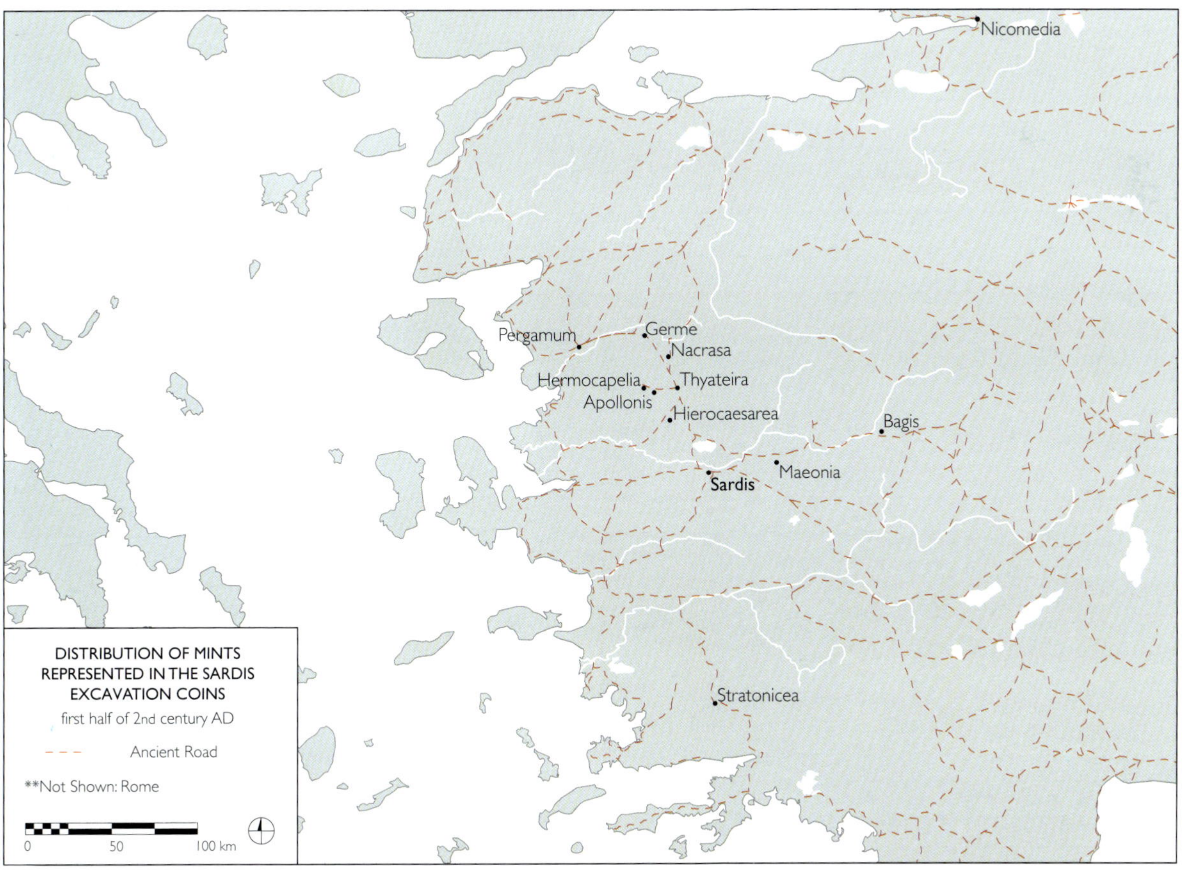

Figure 2.16 Distribution of mints represented in the Sardis excavation coins, first half of the second century AD.

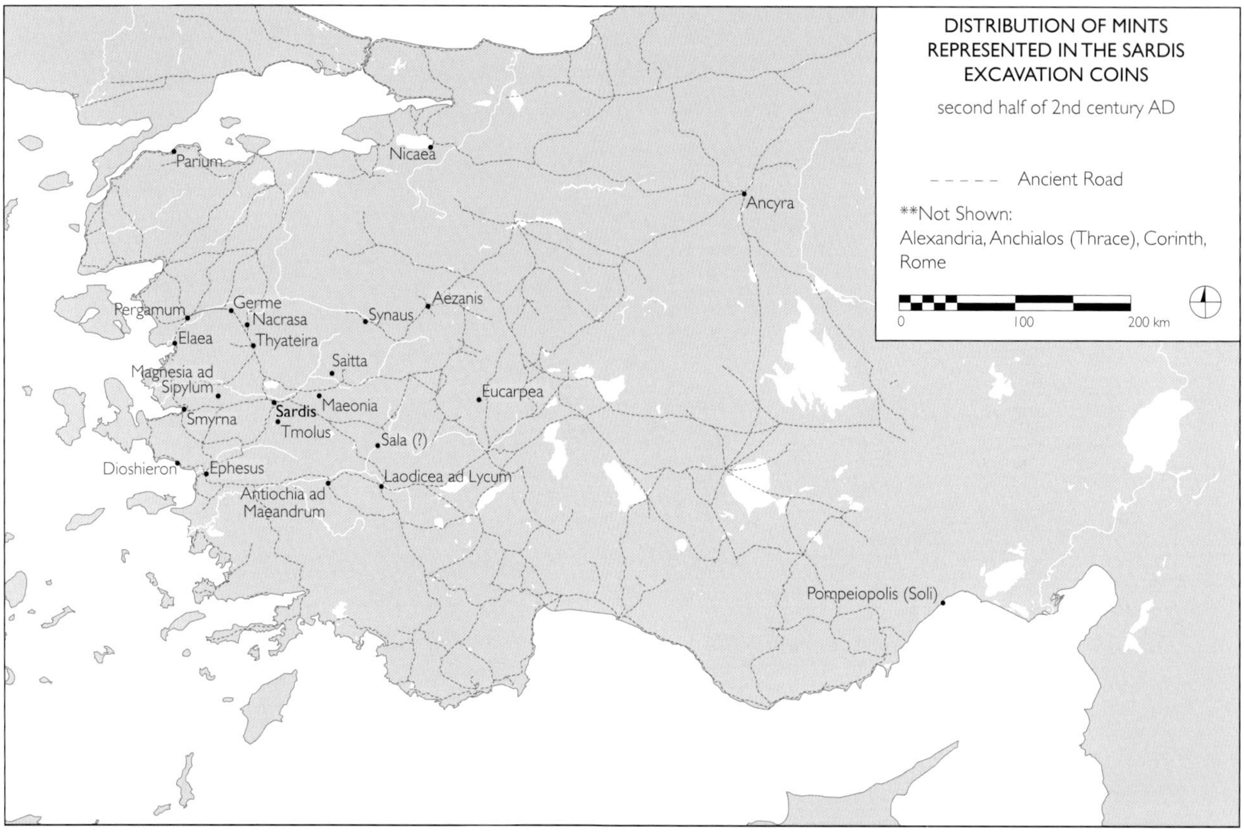

Figure 2.17 Distribution of mints represented in the Sardis excavation coins, second half of the second century AD.

Figure 2.18 Distribution of mints represented in the Sardis excavation coins, 200–270 AD.

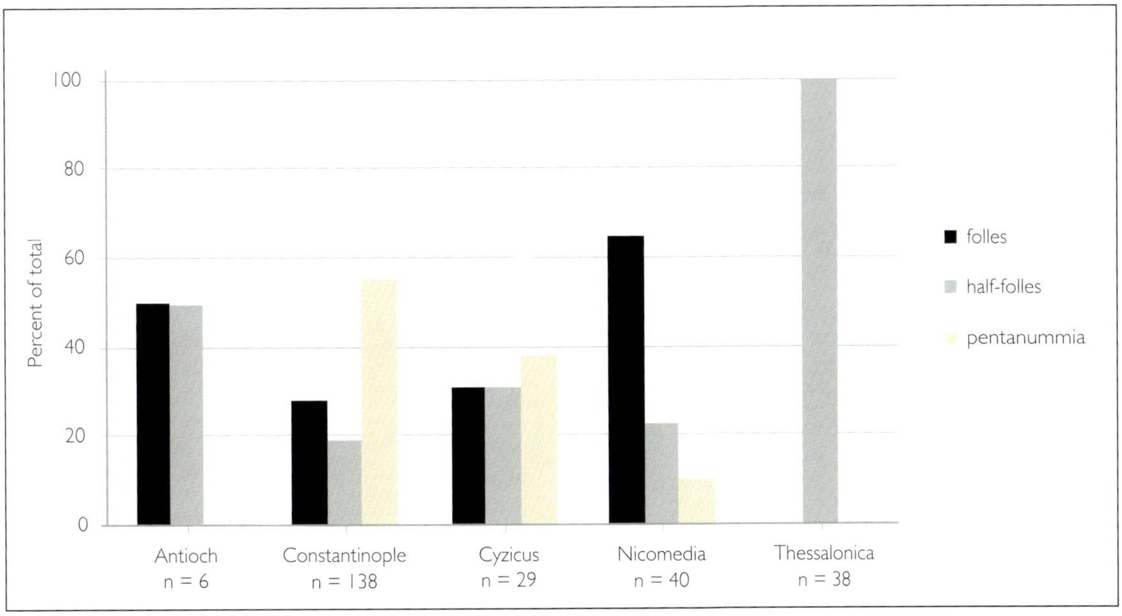

Figure 2.19 Percentages of coins from mints of Justin II from the Sardis excavation coins (M1, M7, and M13).

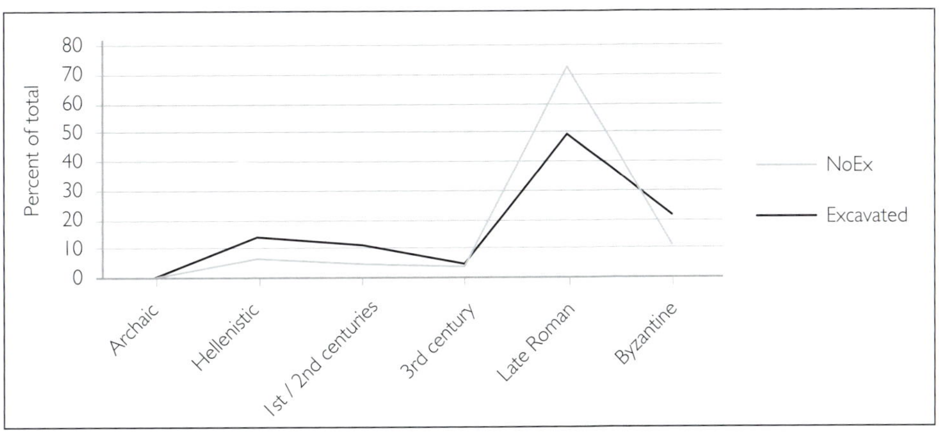

Figure 3.1 Percentage of coins from unstratified (NoEx) and stratified contexts in Sardis (1958–2013).

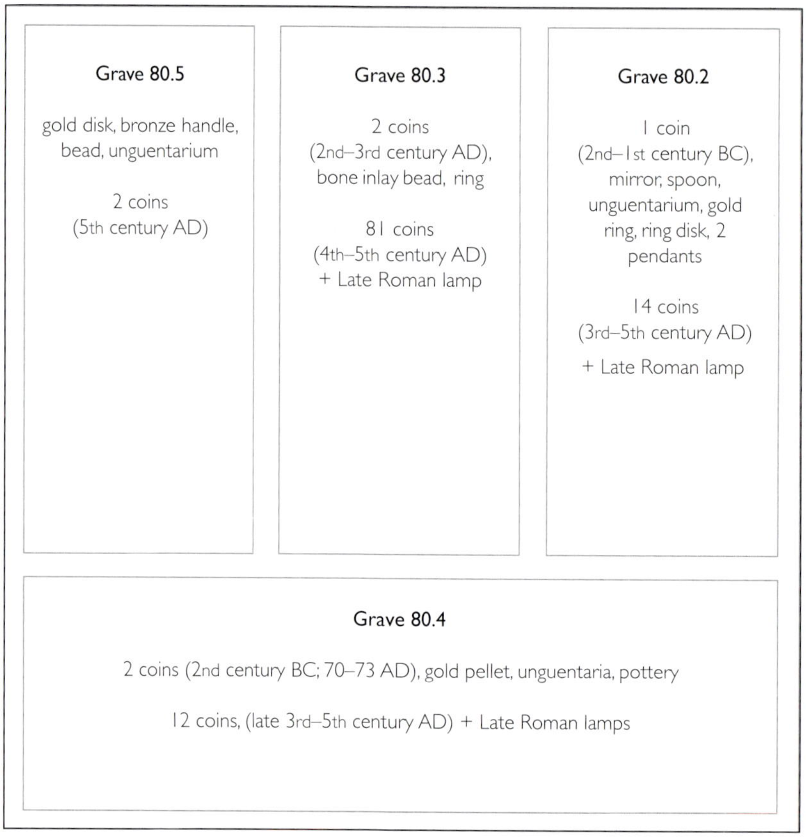

Figure 3.2 Schematic layout of graves in HoB Mausoleum, with grave gifts and coins.

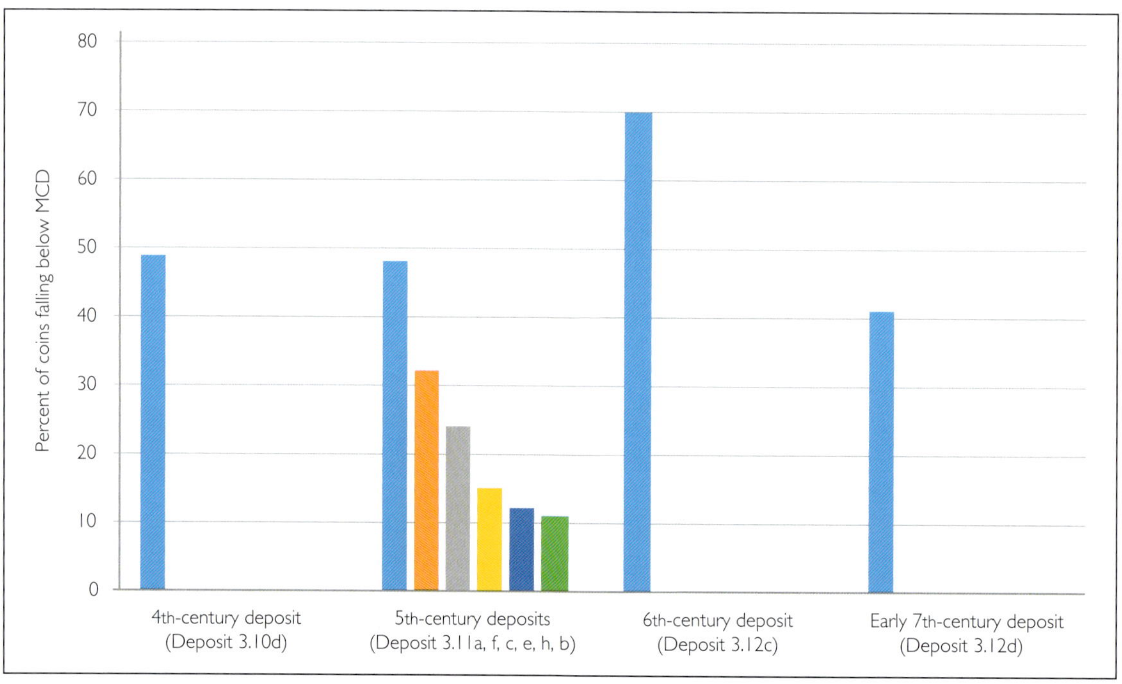

Figure 3.3 Mean Coin Date of fourth- to early seventh-century deposits: percentage of coins in deposit falling below the MCD (fifth-century deposits in chronological order, from early to end of the century).

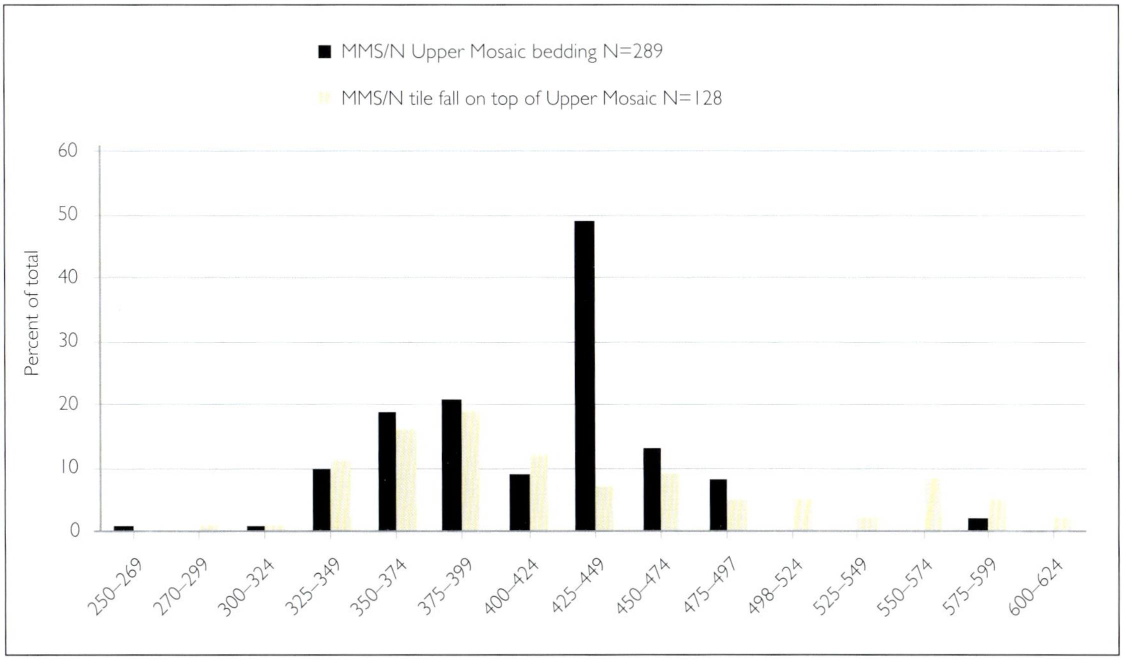

Figure 3.4 Percentages of coins by minting date from contexts in MMS/N (eliminating Hellenistic, Roman Provincial, Provincial, and uncertain coins, or those for dates stretching more than one period). For the latest coins and possible intrusions in the deposits, see above, Chapter 3 n. 163.

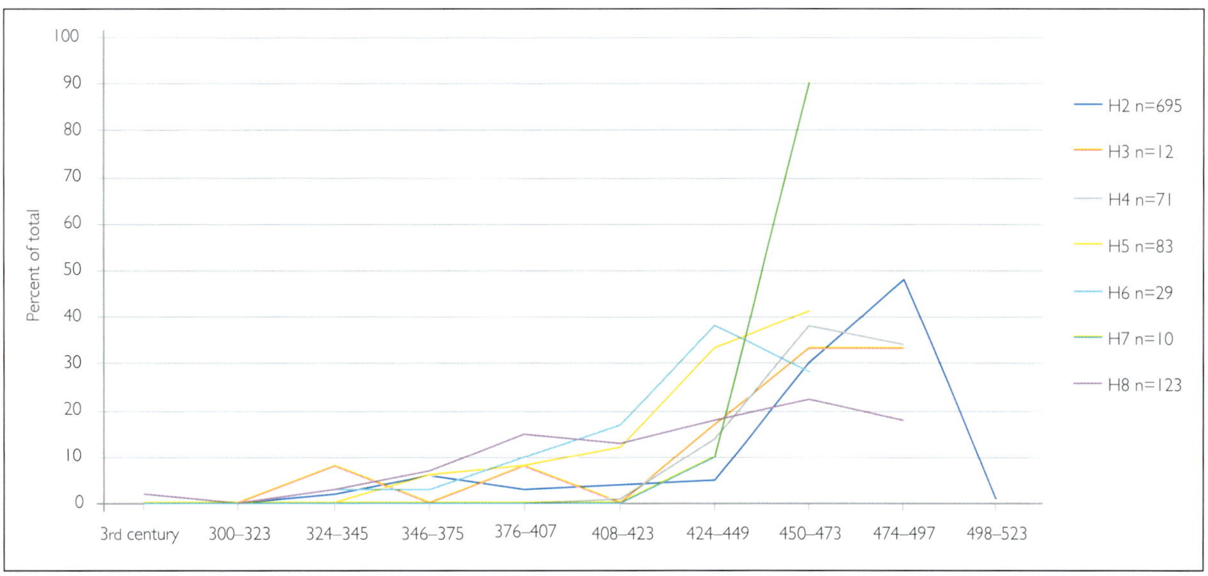

Figure 3.5 Percentages of coins by minting dates from fifth-century hoards at Sardis (for Hoard 2, coins of the first century BC and first century AD have been eliminated from the figure).